Scott Foresman

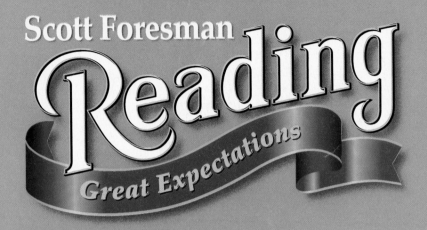

Great Expectations

Discovering Ourselves

The Living Earth

Goals Great and Small

The Way We Were—The Way We Are

Into the Unknown

I've Got It!

PEARSON

Scott Foresman

About the Cover Artist

John Patrick has always had a strong interest in nature. His first major in college was marine biology. Soon, however, he discovered his talent for design and illustration. Patrick especially enjoys projects that combine his interest in art and nature.

John Patrick: cover

ISBN 0-328-03939-X

3 4 5 6 7 8 9 10 V057 10 09 08 07 06 05 04 03

Scott Foresman Reading
Great Expectations

Program Authors

Peter Afflerbach

James Beers

Camille Blachowicz

Candy Dawson Boyd

Wendy Cheyney

Deborah Diffily

Dolores Gaunty-Porter

Connie Juel

Donald Leu

Jeanne Paratore

Sam Sebesta

Karen Kring Wixson

PEARSON

Scott Foresman

Editorial Offices: Glenview, Illinois • Parsippany, New Jersey • New York, New York
Sales Offices: Parsippany, New Jersey • Duluth, Georgia • Glenview, Illinois
Coppell, Texas • Ontario, California • Mesa, Arizona

Unit 1 • Contents

Discovering Ourselves

5

Unit 2 • Contents

The Living Earth

6

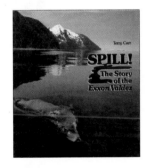

Unit 3 • Contents

Goals Great and Small

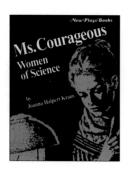

Unit 4 • Contents

The Way We Were– The Way We Are

Unit 5 • Contents

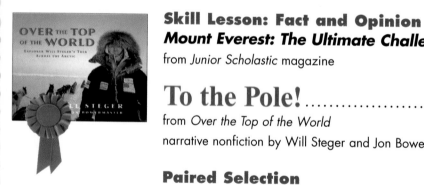

Into the Unknown

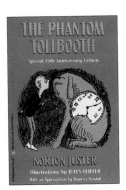

Unit 6 · Contents

I've Got It!

Dear Reader,

Imagine that you have a magic ticket in your hands. That ticket can take you just anywhere on earth. It can even transport you back in time, into the future, or to worlds that exist only in the imagination. You might think that no such tickets exist. But they do. They are called books, and all you need to use them is to be a reader.

By the time I was in sixth grade I was reading just about everything I could get my hands on. Not just books written for kids. And I know that was due, at least in part, to my grandparents. My grandfather Jesse was almost illiterate. His reading was pretty much limited to the local newspaper—*The Saratogian.* But he always encouraged me to read and considered the ability to read well to be of great value—even though, as he put it, "when it come to more'n a word at a time, reading pretty much passed me by."

Grampa Jesse's own experiences with school had been brief and unpleasant. He'd been treated badly because of being poor and darker-skinned. Leaving school in the fourth grade had been a roadblock on his way to a personal love of book learning. But he was pleased when others were educated. Grampa was proud of the way, when I was barely able to walk, that I could pick up anything and just read it right off. He was always asking me to read things to him. When I started writing my own little stories and poems in the second grade, he and my grandmother were always my first and most attentive audience.

Perhaps Grampa's respect for reading and books explained why he and my grandmother hit it off so well, different as they were. Gramma was a reader, a READER. My grandmother had both a college education and an absolute and abiding love for books. There were bookshelves in every room of their old house. In fact, if anything had print on it, she couldn't bear to part with it. We had stacks and stacks of magazines and newspapers going back for years.

We had leather-bound sets of hundreds of old issues of *National Geographic* magazine. I would pull one out and sit reading it from cover to cover, paying special attention to the stories about animals.

I remember reading about the West African rain forest for the first time. "Someday," I said to myself, "I'll go there!" Many years later, after graduating from college, I finally *did* go to Ghana. I went as a volunteer to teach reading and writing to students in an African secondary school. It was in Ghana that I saw even more clearly how being able to read and write could change a person's life forever. Not everyone there could afford to go to secondary school. Whole families would pool their money to support just one child's education. And when that boy or girl was educated and had a good job, he or she would help the poorer relations. At that time in Ghana, a person who could read and write well was thought of as a kind of hero.

It was in Ghana that I walked through a real rain forest for the first time. It was strange and new, and yet it was familiar. The huge-trunked baobab trees, the nests of weaver birds, the call of a Colobus monkey—I knew what they were because I'd read about them when I was young.

Once one of the other American volunteer teachers saw some oranges hanging in a tree above our reach.

"I'm going to shake one down," he said.

"Wait," I said, but it was too late. He shook that tree, bringing down not just an orange, but also a shower of hissing, biting red ants that fell all over him. They missed me, though. Having read about such ants in a long-ago article, I'd been on the lookout for them and had seen the long trail of them winding up that tree! I had jumped back out of the way just in time.

To this day I make it a point to read everything I can find about any new place I am going to visit. The more you know, the more you will see, in more ways than one. And writing will help you to see and remember and share that world with others, just as I've shared with you a little of my own childhood and taken you to the rain forest of West Africa—just by writing these few words.

Discovering Ourselves

How do our relationships with others help us learn about ourselves?

Skill Lesson

Sequence

- **Sequence** is the order in which things happen or characters perform actions.

- Clue words such as *when, first, then,* and *next* will help you follow the order of things happening. Dates and times of day are other clues to the sequence of events.

- Steps in a process occur in a sequence. Events in fiction and in nonfiction may also occur in a sequence.

Read "Jerry Takes Off" from *The Winning Stroke* by Matt Christopher.

Talk About It

1. Name at least three things that Jerry does. Put them in order.

2. What are some clue words from the story that help you follow the sequence of events?

Jerry Takes Off
by Matt Christopher

Jerry is new to the Bolton Blues swim team. Here he practices his flip turns with teammates Lars and Tony.

When Tony arrived at the shallow end, Coach Fulton described the way he wanted Jerry to practice his turns.

"You two guys start out with Jerry about ten feet away. Swim toward the edge, and then all three of you do your turns at the same time. I want you to develop a rhythm to it that's solid and dependable, Jerry. And when you have it down, you can practice on your own. Tanya, you're not doing anything right now," he called to her. "Come on over and keep an eye on their turns. I'll be back in fifteen minutes."

The next quarter hour went like a breeze. Jerry could hardly believe how natural the turn had become after he got it right. How could he even have thought of racing until he knew stuff like this?

During the next week, Jerry managed to work in some extra coaching from Mr. Fulton, Tony, or Tanya—and even from some of the other members of the team once in a while.

After he perfected his flip turn, he learned how to dive properly.

"A long, shallow dive can cut seconds from your time," Tanya explained. "The farther out you go, the less distance you have to swim. And if you don't have to come up from below, you can start swimming sooner. The same is true for the backstroke takeoff. Push yourself as far as possible from the wall."

And with each session, he got more and more comfortable. By the end of the week, he couldn't resist showing Tanya how well he had mastered one of his big problems.

"Just watch this takeoff!" he shouted. Then he demonstrated how well he had learned to start off in a backstroke race. As he pushed off from the side of the pool, Tanya jumped in on one side and Tony, who appeared out of nowhere, jumped in on the other. The two of them started backstroking furiously next to him, churning up a tidal wave of water in their combined wake.

But Jerry wasn't ruffled. He kept his head and continued to do exactly what he had learned. When he touched the opposite edge of the pool, Wayne Cabot shouted down to the three of them.

"The winner by a good palm and a half, Jerry Grayson!"

The winner—Jerry Grayson! It sounded great. Deep down, he knew that he would love to hear those words in a real race.

LOOK AHEAD

In "Tony and the Snark," one event leads to another. As you read this story about adventures on the water, notice the sequence of events.

Vocabulary

Words to Know

cove	disaster	jolt
peninsula	submerged	

When you read, you may come across a word that you don't know. To figure out the meaning of an unfamiliar word, look for clues in the words and sentences around it. A clue might be found in a description given near the unknown word.

Read the paragraph below. Notice how the description of *submerged* helps you understand what it means.

A Stormy Night at Sea

The crew struggled to sail in the angry wind and waves. Through the rain, they saw a glimmer of light. It was a lighthouse perched on what appeared to be a peninsula of the mainland. Land was in sight! However, its glow warned them of a rocky coast. Sailing too near it would mean disaster. Other dangers, like sandbars and submerged rocks, lurked just below the surface of the shallow water. They sailed on anyway, feeling a jolt as each wave crashed against the ship. With luck, they'd be able to sail around the peninsula's tip and reach the safety of a sheltered harbor or cove.

Talk About It

Use some of your vocabulary words to tell a shipwreck story to a classmate.

Sachem Head

Foskett Island

Joshua Cove

Joshua Point

Swallows Bay Harbor

Haycock Point

Tony and the Snark

Horse Island

from *Windcatcher*
by Avi

"Dad," Tony Souza said, "what's money *for* if you can't spend it?" It was a Saturday, the first day of summer vacation, but to Tony his vacation already felt like a disaster.

"Keep your money in the bank," his father said. He was unloading the dish rack.

"Dad," Tony pressed, "if *you* had gotten up every morning at six for a *year,* delivered newspapers, got wet, got cold, fought off dogs, and made collections from people who didn't want to pay, you'd want to use the money *you* earned the way *you* wanted, wouldn't you?"

"Tony, people are not allowed on roads with a motor vehicle until they are fifteen. A motor scooter is a motor vehicle. You are eleven."

"Then what am I going to do with the three hundred dollars I made?"

"I gave you a suggestion."

Tony sat on the front steps. In one week, according to his parents' plan, he would go for a twenty-one-day stay at his grandma's house on the Connecticut shore. When he had been younger, it was fun to learn to swim and to sit on a beach all day. And Grandma Souza—though her English was sort of embarrassing—was all right. But *now,* Tony didn't know any kids where she lived. And he hated doing things alone. It would be a bore.

Back from Connecticut, he would go with his parents on their annual camping trip with Uncle Umberto and his family. Tony grimaced. The only thing worse than being with no kids was being with babies.

That would leave only two weeks before school began. *Some* vacation.

Tony stuck his head inside the house. "I'm going over to Jamal's!" he shouted.

When Tony slumped up Jamal's driveway, Rick, Jamal's older brother, was working on the red motorbike. Jamal was there too.

"They going to let you buy it?" Jamal called.

Tony shook his head.

"Too bad," Rick said. "This baby isn't going to last long. Got two calls this morning from my newspaper ad."

Tony wandered back down to the street.

Jamal ran after him. "What are you going to do with that money?"

"I'll think of something."

"What happens if your parents change their minds?"

"They won't."

"Want to watch TV?" Jamal suggested. "Play ball? Should be some guys at the park."

Tony hesitated. The thought of being with friends was tempting. But spending his money was urgent. "Later," he said. Shoving his hands in his pockets, he set off.

First he went into a bicycle shop. Then a sports shop. After that it was a toy store that carried computer games. Then there was the Mart. As Tony wandered up and down the long aisles, everything seemed like junk.

Then he saw it. It was a sailboat—no more than twelve feet in length—hanging from the ceiling. Made of some plasticlike stuff, its outside was blue, its inside white. A wooden rudder was at the back. The mast was metal. The sail bore red letters which proclaimed the boat's name: *Snark*. A large price tag dangled from the hull.

The moment Tony saw the boat, he knew, sure as he knew anything, what he wanted, what he needed, was a Snark.

He ran home and poured out the news of his discovery, telling his parents all the ways the sailboat would make his summer exciting.

When Tony saw them give each other a look, he knew it was not out of the question. He pressed harder, insisting they go to the store right away.

At the Mart, his mother gazed up at the boat and said, "It's like a polystyrene cup with a sail."

"Ma, it's a *sailboat!* Can I get it?"

"There are some things to check first," his mother returned. "Come on. I have a friend who sails."

"Ma . . . !" Tony wailed again.

"Tony, it's not sailing anywhere."

Once home, Tony's mother called her friend and asked for a reaction to a Snark.

"You can't cross oceans with it," said the friend, "or handle bad weather, but in protected areas it'll do fine. In fact, it's just about perfect for a kid who wants to learn to sail. And you can't beat the price."

When Tony heard the report he did a cartwheel in the dining room, narrowly missing a lamp.

"Cool it!" his father cautioned. "Your mom and I need some privacy to discuss this."

Told to leave the room while they talked, Tony tried to listen through the door to what they were saying. He did hear his father make a call. Speak to someone. Hang up. Then Tony was called back into the room.

"The answer," his mother said, "is yes. . . ."

"*If* . . . ," his father put in quickly, cutting off Tony's cheer, "*if* certain conditions are met."

"I agree to everything," Tony said.

"We called your grandma for her approval."

"And . . . ?"

His parents exchanged looks. "She said yes," his father said.

"All right!" Tony called.

"Second condition!" his mother said hastily. "We'll pay, but you *must* have sailing lessons."

"No problem."

"Finally," his father added, "you have to promise—really promise—that whenever you sail, you'll wear a life jacket."

"Dad," Tony pleaded, "I just said, I agree to *everything*."

Monday morning Tony and his mother went to the bank, withdrew his newspaper money, and headed for the Mart. Heart thumping, Tony counted out fifteen crisp, new twenty-dollar bills onto the counter.

"Plus eighteen dollars tax," the salesperson said.

Tony's heart sank. He looked up at his mother. She looked at him.

"I'll clean the car," Tony said. "And wax it. Three times."

"I would have paid anyway," she said with a laugh. "But that's a deal." She also purchased a life jacket.

Store people loaded the box with the *Snark* atop the car. Once home, Tony spent the day—as he had promised—trying not to open the box. But by eight o'clock that night, with his parents' help, the *Snark* was assembled. She looked cool, if crowded, in the middle of their living room, with her white and blue sail hoisted on the seven-foot mast.

"Wait a minute," Tony said, "what's a Snark?"

"Look it up," his mother suggested.

In the dictionary he read:

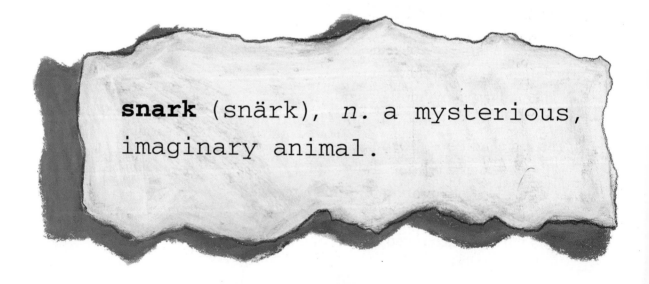

snark (snärk), *n.* a mysterious, imaginary animal.

"Can I go sailing soon as we get there?" Tony wanted to know.

His father laughed. "You have to learn first."

It was Saturday morning. The *Snark* was tied to the top of the car. Tony and his father were speeding west along the interstate. Traffic was heavy under a sky that was turning darker by the moment. From his seat, Tony could see the bow extending over the windshield. In his lap lay a history of sailing ships that his mother had given him as a going-away present. But for most of the trip Tony searched for water. Now and again he caught glimpses of Long Island Sound.

As they got off the interstate it started to rain, a cloudburst. They moved slowly now as they went past the town of Guilford. Then they swung back west on Route 146 before going over the Chaffinch River.

As suddenly as the rain had come, it stopped. It poured sunlight now. Tree leaves seemed to drip emerald green. The black asphalt road steamed. A heavy smell of sea filled the air.

Swallows Bay was on a peninsula with two points spread in fishtail fashion. The western side was called Joshua Point. The east side was Haycock Point. Between the two lay Swallows Bay Harbor.

Down both points ran two rows of houses. None were new. All were white or gray with shingle roofs. Most had porches with trellises through which flowers curled.

As always—a Souza ritual—they drove past Grandma's house, down to the tip of Haycock Point. There they stopped.

At the end was a gravel circle for turning around. In the middle of the circle stood a statue of Captain Ezra Littlejohn, the portly founder of the town. He seemed to be staring out into the sound and sky as if waiting for something to appear. The Souza family joke was that—considering the captain's belly— he was waiting for his dinner.

To the right of the road was Carluci's Fish Store and a wooden dock which extended fifty yards into the harbor. A good number of boats were tied to it. More boats were in the harbor. There was also a public access ramp for people to run their boat trailers directly into the water.

To Tony, the sound always seemed as big as an ocean. On clear days you could see twelve miles, across to Long Island. As he gazed across, he saw the rainstorm scudding across the water. It was like a curtain being pulled away.

When Mr. Souza swung the car around, Tony read the inscription on the statue's base.

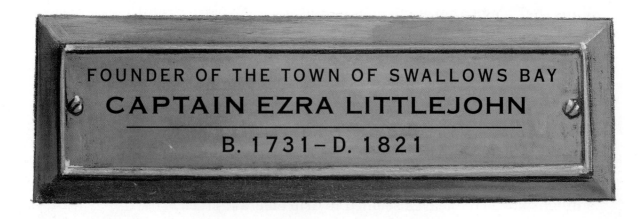

FOUNDER OF THE TOWN OF SWALLOWS BAY
CAPTAIN EZRA LITTLEJOHN
B. 1731 – D. 1821

"1731," Tony said. "Wasn't that before America?"

"Before the United States of America," his father replied as they drove up the road.

Grandma Souza was a short, wide woman. Her broad face and bright, dark eyes were framed by jet black hair. Though she wore nothing but somber dresses, it was rare for Tony to see her without a smile. That moment was no exception. "Here he is!" she cried when she saw him. "Bravo! The new sailor!"

Hardly did Tony leap from the car than she wrapped her arms around him and gave him an engulfing hug.

Tony grinned with delight.

Grandma's house was a small, two-story frame building, both cheerful and bright. The furniture was all white wicker and wood. Pink curtains graced the windows. On a wall over an old upright piano, a map of the area had been placed. Multicolored silk flowers nodded among ceramic shepherds. The air was sweet with lemon, a sure promise of *suspiros,* the meringue cookies Grandma made.

Tony lugged his suitcase up the steps to the second floor. By tradition his room was off to the left. When he entered, the first thing he saw was a ship model on the dresser.

Mounted on a small stand, the ship had three square sails on each of three masts. The sails were yellow with age, the rigging complicated. Eight miniature cannons, four to each side, poked through gunports. On her stern hung a British flag.

Tony tore down the steps. "Grandma! Where did that ship model come from?"

"Something your grandfather got."

"Must have cost a fortune."

She shrugged. "It was stored. But now, I think you like her."

As they sat down for lunch Tony asked, "When can I start sailing lessons?"

"Everything's fixed," Grandma announced. "Chris, from the Carluci family—the fish store people—will do it."

"How much?"

"Tony!" his father cried.

"I said to them," Grandma went on, " 'Mr. Carluci, Tony is a good swimmer.' Right?"

"Got my junior Red Cross swimming card at the Y," Tony said.

"Came in second in the fifty-meter freestyle for his age class," his father added proudly.

"Won five bucks," Tony bragged.

"And he'll always wear his life jacket."

"Can I start soon?" Tony wanted to know.

"If you like, this afternoon."

As soon as lunch was over, Tony rushed outside. Standing in front of his grandma's house, he could look down the two hundred yards of low hill road to the harbor. Boats, most of them brilliant white, rode easily upon glistening blue-green water.

With a burst of excitement, Tony ran all the way to Carluci's Fish Store. There was sawdust on the floor. A fat orange cat slept in a nest of nets. Behind the glass-faced counter were trays of fish, clams, and mussels embedded in crushed ice. A young man stood behind the counter. Another man—looking like an older brother—was sitting on a stool.

"Can I help you?" the one behind the counter asked.

Tony asked, "Is Chris here?"

"Sure is," said the older one. "Out back. You the Souza boy?"

Tony nodded yes.

"Hi. Go on out around the store, onto the dock. Pumping gas. Can't miss."

At the end of the dock, working the gas pump, was a teenage girl dressed in faded jeans, rubber boots, and a T-shirt that read, "Fish Is Brain Food."

Tony, suddenly shy, glanced into the motorboat that was getting gas. A young man and woman were in there. They had digging equipment—shovels, picks, some buckets.

The girl on the dock finished pumping, then collected the money. As the people in the boat pushed off, she watched them go before turning to Tony. "Hi. Help you with something?"

"I'm looking for Chris."

"That's me, Christina," said the girl with a big smile and a welcome hand. "You Tony Souza?"

Tony nodded. He couldn't take his eyes off the speedboat that was roaring out of the harbor.

"Ready to learn sailing?" Chris asked.

"I'd like to."

"Not as fast as those folks," she said with a nod toward the now-disappearing speedboat. "But a lot more fun."

"Where they going so fast?"

"Those folks?" Chris shrugged. "They're looking for the treasure."

"What treasure?"

"The Swallows Bay treasure."

Tony looked at Chris with surprise.

She laughed. "Forget it. It's only a legend. What I want to know is, when are we going to have your first lesson?"

Tony and his father lifted the *Snark* off the car roof and lowered it into the water. The mast was quickly put up. The sail was hoisted. The little boat, rocking gently, sat neat as a duck. Tony glowed with pleasure.

Chris, wearing her own life jacket, came up. She introduced herself to Tony's father.

"Now Tony," Grandma said. "*Boa viagem*—have a good trip!" She and Tony's father drove off.

Tony, suddenly anxious, watched them go. He turned to Chris. "Guess I'm ready."

"Don't worry," Chris said as if reading his mind. "You'll do fine."

Chris began with the basics. She explained the words sailors used, everything from "port," the left side of the boat when facing toward the bow, to "tack," the way you move against the wind.

There were terms like "dagger board"—the blade-like piece of plywood which would allow the boat to sail against the wind; "tiller" (the stick attached to the rudder); "reach"—sailing across the wind; and "luff"—to turn into the wind. With each word, Chris explained something about sailing.

Tony was starting to get dizzy when Chris said, "Enough talk. Time to do it."

First she told Tony to sit forward next to the dagger board. Then she waded into the water, gave them a push, and jumped into the stern. Immediately, one of her hands went to the tiller. The other hand grabbed the sheet, the rope tied to the boom. The boom kept the sail stiff at the bottom.

"Drop the dagger board!" she called.

Tony shoved the dagger board down through the centerboard case.

With what looked to Tony like effortless ease, Chris cut through Swallows Bay Harbor and the maze of moored boats. Then she tacked back around Joshua Point into the place known as Joshua Cove.

There she showed Tony a variety of maneuvers: turning, ways to go faster and slower, even how to come to a relatively quick stop if necessary by turning into the wind.

"Okay," Chris said. "Time to trade places."

"Now?" Tony replied with surprise.

"Hey, it's your boat."

Staying low, Tony moved toward the stern of the boat on the starboard side. Chris, on the port side, moved toward the bow. As they shifted, the boat rocked, making Tony uneasy.

Seated in the stern, Tony placed one hand on the tiller. He put the other on the sheet just as he had seen Chris do.

"Now," Chris said, "we don't want to get out of the cove, okay? You've got a way to go before that. Stay clear of that tidal flat there. Now, see that little island?" she said, pointing to what looked like a pile of rocks.

Tony nodded. "What about it?"

"It's called Horse Island. There are lots of submerged rocks in front of it. So make sure you keep away. Lots of rocks around here. You've got to learn all the danger places."

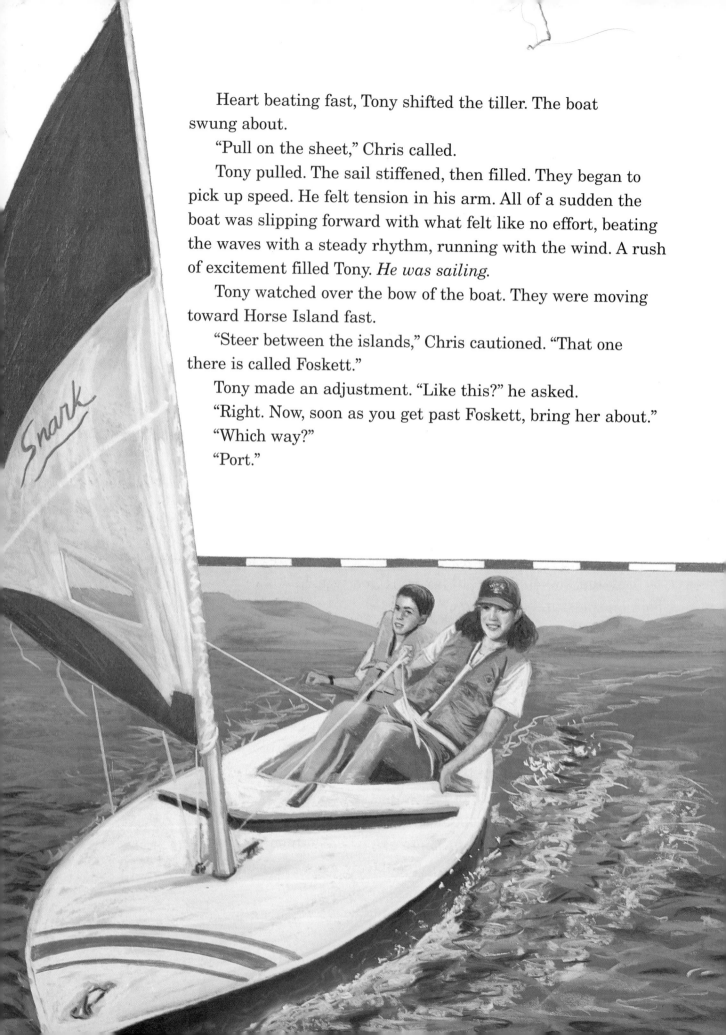

Heart beating fast, Tony shifted the tiller. The boat swung about.

"Pull on the sheet," Chris called.

Tony pulled. The sail stiffened, then filled. They began to pick up speed. He felt tension in his arm. All of a sudden the boat was slipping forward with what felt like no effort, beating the waves with a steady rhythm, running with the wind. A rush of excitement filled Tony. *He was sailing.*

Tony watched over the bow of the boat. They were moving toward Horse Island fast.

"Steer between the islands," Chris cautioned. "That one there is called Foskett."

Tony made an adjustment. "Like this?" he asked.

"Right. Now, soon as you get past Foskett, bring her about."

"Which way?"

"Port."

Excited, Tony pulled the tiller hard. The *Snark* veered sharply, straight for Foskett Island. The next moment there was a wrenching jolt.

"Rocks!" Chris cried. "Turn to starboard!"

Tony, trying to remember which way Chris meant, gave the tiller a yank. The boat slipped from the rocks. As they sailed between the islands, the *Snark* began rapidly picking up speed. Now they were heading right for the shore, getting closer every moment.

"Bring her about!" Chris shouted suddenly.

Nervous from his last mistake, Tony pushed the tiller.

"The other way!" Chris cried.

Tony did. Too much. The boom swung wildly. Trying to adjust, Tony jerked the tiller back. The *Snark* swung sharply, heeling hard. The mast careened. Tony, frightened, let go of everything. The next second the boat capsized.

As Tony hit the water he lost his breath. Struggling, he began to sink. Even as he did he felt the upward pull of his life jacket. Spitting, flailing arms and legs, he broke through to the water's surface.

"Let your jacket hold you!" he heard Chris shout. "Don't fight! Get your breath!"

Tony stopped thrashing. And when he realized the jacket would hold him, he relaxed. With circular motions of his arms he turned himself about in search of Chris.

"Over here!" she called.

Tony turned again. Chris was standing up, waist deep, laughing. "Think I'd try you out in deep water?" Chris asked. "It's only four feet deep."

Cautiously, Tony let his legs down. To his surprise, he touched bottom. Realizing how funny he must look, he stood up. He felt his face get hot.

"Seriously," Chris said, "good sailing is as much safety as it's anything. Don't ever let anyone tease you from thinking

otherwise. Besides, capsizing like that is good. Now it doesn't scare you. Believe me, it's going to happen."

Tony waded over to where the *Snark* lay, mast and sail flat on the water.

Chris got Tony to reach over and grasp the boat's side while putting his foot onto the dagger board. As he pressed the dagger board down, the boat, still full of water, righted herself. She sat like a full bathtub in the middle of a lake.

"See," Chris said, "this kind of boat can't sink."

Tony, following instructions, lowered the sail. Then he began to splash water out. Chris worked, too. An hour later, with Tony at the tiller, the boat crunched softly onto the landing ramp.

Chris showed Tony how to get the mast down, roll the sail, and tie everything up. They put the boat underneath the dock, tying it securely.

"Won't anyone take it?" Tony worried out loud.

"You're in Swallows Bay Harbor," Chris said. "People don't steal."

They walked up the landing ramp. "Tony," she assured him, "you're going to be terrific."

About the Author
Avi

As a young boy, Avi did not have an easy time in school. "In a school environment," he remembers, "I was perceived as being sloppy and erratic, and not paying attention." In reality, Avi apparently had a learning disability that caused him to reverse letters in his writing and misspell words. But he loved to read, and this love of reading helped him decide that—even though he had difficulty writing without errors—he wanted to be a professional writer.

Now that he is a successful writer, Avi feels it is important to have regular contact with his young readers. He often visits schools and asks especially to speak to kids with learning disabilities. While speaking to them, he lays out copies of his edited manuscripts. The manuscripts are filled with red marks—corrections noted by editors at publishing offices. Avi counts on these editors to help him catch and correct his errors. It takes an average of one year for him to write each book, because he rewrites sections over and over until they are just right.

Several of Avi's stories are historical fiction. *The True Confessions of Charlotte Doyle*, for example, tells the tale of a young girl who is a lonely passenger on a ship traveling across the Atlantic in 1832. Readers often respond strongly to her story.

Reader Response

Open for Discussion

In your opinion, does Tony spend his money wisely? Why or why not?

Comprehension Check

1. Why is Tony reluctant to visit his Grandma Souza? Use evidence from the story to explain.

2. Tony's parents agree to let him buy the sailboat only if certain conditions are met. What are the conditions?

3. Losing control of the *Snark* frightens Tony. Soon after the accident, though, he is only embarrassed. Why? Use details from the story to explain.

4. Near the beginning of the story, Tony maps out the events of the coming summer. "*Some* vacation," he thinks to himself. What **sequence** of events does he expect to take place? (Sequence)

5. List five major events from the story in their correct **sequence**. (Sequence)

Test Prep

Look Back and Write

Look back at pages 34–38. How does Chris help Tony to become more confident about his ability to sail the *Snark*? Use details from the story to explain your answer.

Test Prep

How to Read a Magazine Article

1. Preview

- Read the title and the subheads to get an idea of what the article is about.

- Look over the diagrams and captions. Which ones will help you understand difficult terms in the article?

2. Read and Take Notes

- As you read the main text, jot down each new heading. Then read the section and write the main idea below it.

Heading	Swimming a Drag?
Main Idea	Overcome water resistance to go fast.

- Add a main idea for each diagram.

3. Think and Connect

Think about "Tony and the Snark." Then read your notes about "Swimming for the Gold."

What obstacles do both swimmers and sailboats face?

Swimming for the GOLD

by Nicole Dyer

You may swim for summer fun, but Olmpic champ Amy Van Dyken is swimming for her fifth Olympic gold medal!

It's 5:30 A.M. on a summer morning. You're probably sound asleep, but Amy Van Dyken is already underwater. The 27-year-old swimming star tears across a 52×25-meter Olympic-size pool in Colorado Springs, Colorado, as part of a grueling five-hour daily workout. And despite her *asthma*, a breathing disease, Amy makes her laps look like no sweat. After all, she's out to prove she's the

Amy Van Dyken basks in Olympic glory after winning her fourth gold medal at the 1996 Atlanta Games.

Swimming a Drag?

Amy wasn't born an Olympic champ. "I always had asthma, but it didn't really bother me till I was six," she says. "To help me control it, my doctor told me to start swimming—a good exercise for the lungs." In high school Amy tried out for the swim team. "Even though I was always the worst swimmer, I still had dreams. I kept swimming, losing, and trying again."

"Reducing drag in the water is a key to faster speeds," says swim scientist Scott Riewald, biomechanics director at USA Swimming in Colorado Springs. "An important way to reduce drag on a swimmer is to focus on body position." When Amy does the *crawl*, the fastest and most efficient swimming stroke, she maintains her body in a perfectly horizontal position, moving only her arms and legs. Her head remains in the water at all times, even when she turns to breathe. This keeps Amy's body close to the water surface—the best place to be if you want to swim fast.

world's fastest female swimmer at the 2000 Olympic games. What'll it take? "A lot of very hard work!" Amy says.

She ought to know. At the Atlanta Summer Games in '96, Van Dyken became the first American woman ever to take home four gold medals in a single Olympic Games. What are her secrets for success? Dedication, desire, and *science!*

Make a Splash!

To perfect your own stroke, follow these tips for the crawl:

To breathe in, turn your head toward the arm leaving the water. Keep your face in the water to reduce drag.

Keep your body horizontal. Pushing your chest toward the pool bottom helps keep your hips from sinking.

Propelled to Victory

One factor that propelled Amy towards victory is *propulsion* (the act of moving forward). *Newton's third law of motion* states that every action has an equal and opposite reaction. As Amy pushes on the water with her arms and legs, the water pushes back with equal force, thrusting her forward.

Interestingly, the same force that lifts planes also helps propel swimmers. It's called *lift force*, or the force that moves an object perpendicular to the force that causes resistance (see *figure, right*). Think of an airplane wing: it's curved on top and flat underneath. As air speeds across the wing's curved surface, air speeds up. Fast-moving air creates an area of relatively low pressure above the wings. The higher pressure beneath the wings exerts an upward force called lift, which launches the plane into the air.

Likewise for swimmers, as water passes faster over the knuckle side (the longer side) of the hand, the water creates a difference in pressure.

What else drives Amy forward? Goals. "You have to aim for the stars.

Even if you fall short, you'll still land on the moon—and that's a pretty cool place to be!"

Amy Van Dyken won two gold medals at the 2000 Summer Olympics, giving her a grand total of six.

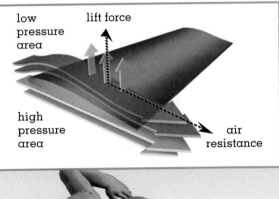

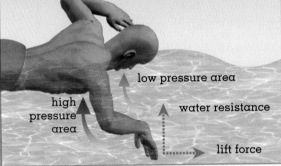

Lift Force

Lift force acts on planes and swimmers. Fast air (red) flowing over a plane's wing creates high pressure beneath the wing. Air flows from high pressure to low pressure, creating an upward lift force perpendicular to the force, causing resistance (air). For the swimmer, fast water (red) flows over the hand, creating a pressure difference. The resulting lift force propels the swimmer forward.

Angle your hand so it encounters the least amount of resistance entering water (usually between 32 degrees and 49 degrees).

Kicking helps with balance and speed. It also helps keep your body horizontal and close to the surface.

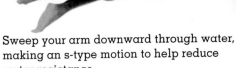

During strokes, stay streamlined by keeping your arms close to your body.

Sweep your arm downward through water, making an s-type motion to help reduce water resistance.

Skill Lesson

Author's Viewpoint

- **Author's viewpoint** is the way an author thinks about the subject of his or her writing.

- An author's viewpoint may be one of fear, admiration, pity, amusement, or some other feeling.

- You can identify an author's viewpoint by thinking about the words an author uses to describe a subject.

Read "Play Ball!" from *Batboy* **by Joan Anderson.**

Write About It

1. List some words and phrases the author uses to describe Kenny. What do they tell you about the author's view of Kenny?

2. What do you think is the author's viewpoint about the game of baseball? How can you tell?

Play Ball!

by Joan Anderson

Kenny works as a batboy for the San Francisco Giants baseball team during spring training.

With eyes blackened to prevent glare from the harsh Arizona sun, the players take their seats in the dugout. A thirty-gallon container of Gatorade is in place along with the first-aid kit. The team's three doctors are also in the dugout, watching how the players' bodies are working during the game.

And then that sacred moment that occurs before every game: "Ladies and gentlemen, would you please rise for the national anthem." Kenny hops up, off the seat he has tucked neatly in the corner beside the bat box, hat over heart, and stands beside the team.

He then dashes to put the rosin bag, pine tar, and towels needed by each batter for warm-up at

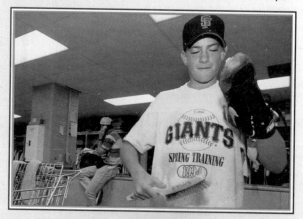

44

the on-deck circle, and runs back into the dugout as the umpire yells: "Play ball!"

Kenny is all concentration. He must stay with the action. Sitting beside the manager, Dusty Baker, he can take in the players' comments amid the grunts a pitcher makes as he winds up and throws the ball.

The peace of just sitting and watching doesn't last long. Suddenly infielder Robby Thompson wants more rosin to get a better grip on his bat. Barry Bonds tosses Kenny a trinket that Bonds wants him to put in his locker. The umpire signals that he needs more balls. The home plate gets muddy after a brief sprinkle, and he needs to mop it off. Kirt Manwaring throws off his face mask as he runs to catch a foul ball, and Kenny must retrieve it. After striking out, a tense batter throws his helmet and bat, which Kenny must pick up between plays.

During all this he remains inconspicuous, and yet his swift darting in and out keeps the rhythm of the game flowing.

LOOK AHEAD

In *Teammates,* the author has a viewpoint about Jackie Robinson and Pee Wee Reese and the time in which they played baseball. As you read, look for statements that show the author's viewpoint.

Vocabulary

Jackie Robinson

Pee Wee Reese

Words to Know

abuse	dedication	hateful
hostility	prejudice	racial
tremendous		

Words with opposite meanings are called **antonyms**. You can often figure out the meaning of an unknown word by finding a clue in the words around it. Sometimes this clue is an antonym.

Read the paragraph below. Notice how *loving* helps you understand what *hateful* means.

A Man of Courage

African Americans have struggled for generations to earn many of the rights denied to them because of <u>racial</u> <u>prejudice</u>. During the 1950s and 1960s, Dr. Martin Luther King, Jr., led the struggle for racial equality. Dr. King was a courageous leader who showed <u>tremendous</u> strength and great <u>dedication</u> to his cause. In the beginning, Dr. King's ideas were met with <u>hostility</u> and <u>abuse</u>. But he refused to give up. Dr. King dreamed of a day when these kinds of <u>hateful</u> attitudes would be replaced with loving ones. His dream lives on to this day.

Talk About It

What do you know about the civil rights movement? Talk to a classmate about it. Use as many vocabulary words as you can.

Teammates

by Peter Golenbock • illustrated by Paul Bacon

"Jackie Robinson was more than just my teammate. He had a tremendous amount of talent, ability, and dedication. Jackie set a standard for future generations of ballplayers. He was a winner. Jackie Robinson was also a man."

—Pee Wee Reese
October 31, 1989

O nce upon a time in America, when automobiles were black and looked like tanks and laundry was white and hung on clotheslines to dry, there were two wonderful baseball leagues that no longer exist. They were called the Negro Leagues.

The Negro Leagues had extraordinary players, and adoring fans came to see them wherever they played. They were heroes, but players in the Negro Leagues didn't make much money and their lives on the road were hard.

Satchel Paige, one of the best-known Negro League ballplayers

Laws against segregation didn't exist in the 1940s. In many places in this country, black people were not allowed to go to the same schools and churches as white people. They couldn't sit in the front of a bus or trolley car. They couldn't drink from the same drinking fountains that white people drank from.

Back then, many hotels didn't rent rooms to black people, so the Negro League players slept in their cars. Many towns had no restaurants that would serve them, so they often had to eat meals that they could buy and carry with them.

Life was very different for the players in the Major Leagues. They were the leagues for white players. Compared to the Negro League players, white players were very well paid. They stayed in good hotels and ate in fine restaurants. Their pictures were put on baseball cards, and the best players became famous all over the world.

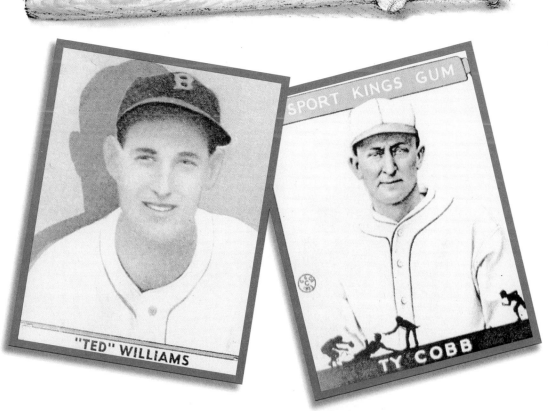

Branch Rickey

Many Americans knew that racial prejudice was wrong, but few dared to challenge openly the way things were. And many people were apathetic about racial problems. Some feared that it could be dangerous to object. Vigilante groups, like the Ku Klux Klan, reacted violently against those who tried to change the way blacks were treated.

The general manager of the Brooklyn Dodgers baseball team was a man by the name of Branch Rickey. He was not afraid of change. He wanted to treat the Dodger fans to the best players he could find, regardless of the color of their skin. He thought segregation was unfair

and wanted to give everyone, regardless of race or creed, an opportunity to compete equally on ball fields across America.

To do this, the Dodgers needed one special man.

Branch Rickey launched a search for him. He was looking for a star player in the Negro Leagues who would be able to compete successfully despite threats on his life or attempts to injure him. He would have to possess the self-control not to fight back when opposing players tried to intimidate or hurt him. If this man disgraced himself on the field, Rickey knew, his opponents would use it as an excuse to keep blacks out of Major League baseball for many more years.

Rickey thought Jackie Robinson might be just the man.

Jackie Robinson meeting with Branch Rickey

Jackie rode the train to Brooklyn to meet Mr. Rickey. When Mr. Rickey told him, "I want a man with the courage not to fight back," Jackie Robinson replied, "If you take this gamble, I will do my best to perform." They shook hands. Branch Rickey and Jackie Robinson were starting on what would be known in history as "the great experiment."

At spring training with the Dodgers, Jackie was mobbed by blacks, young and old, as if he were a savior. He was the first black player to try out for a Major League team. If he succeeded, they knew, others would follow.

Initially, life with the Dodgers was for Jackie a series of humiliations. The players on his team who came from the South, men who had been taught to avoid black people since childhood, moved to another table whenever he sat down next to them. Many opposing players were cruel to him, calling him nasty names from their dugouts. A few tried to hurt him with their spiked shoes. Pitchers aimed at his head. And he received threats on his life, both from individuals and from organizations like the Ku Klux Klan.

Despite all the difficulties, Jackie Robinson didn't give up. He made the Brooklyn Dodgers team.

The 1947 Brooklyn Dodgers team photo

But making the Dodgers was only the beginning. Jackie had to face abuse and hostility throughout the season, from April through September. His worst pain was inside. Often he felt very alone. On the road he had to live by himself, because only the white players were allowed in the hotels in towns where the team played.

The whole time Pee Wee Reese, the Dodger shortstop, was growing up in Louisville, Kentucky, he had rarely even seen a black person, unless it was in the back of a bus. Most of his friends and relatives hated the idea of his playing on the same field as a black man. In addition, Pee Wee Reese had more to lose than the other players when Jackie joined the team.

Jackie had been a shortstop, and everyone thought that Jackie would take Pee Wee's job. Lesser men might have felt anger toward Jackie, but Pee Wee was different. He told himself, "If he's good enough to take my job, he deserves it."

When his Southern teammates circulated a petition to throw Jackie off the team and asked him to sign it, Pee Wee responded, "I don't care if this man is black, blue, or striped"—and refused to sign. "He can play and he can help us win," he told the others. "That's what counts."

Very early in the season, the Dodgers traveled west to Ohio to play the Cincinnati Reds. Cincinnati is near Pee Wee's hometown of Louisville.

The Reds played in a small ballpark where the fans sat close to the field. The players could almost feel the breath of the fans on the backs of their necks. Many who came that day screamed terrible, hateful things at Jackie when the Dodgers were on the field.

More than anything else, Pee Wee Reese believed in doing what was right. When he heard the fans yelling at Jackie, Pee Wee decided to take a stand.

With his head high, Pee Wee walked directly from his shortstop position to where Jackie was playing first base. The taunts and shouting of the fans were ringing in Pee Wee's ears. It saddened him, because he knew it could have been his friends and neighbors. Pee Wee's legs felt heavy, but he knew what he had to do.

As he walked toward Jackie wearing the gray Dodger uniform, he looked into his teammate's bold, pained eyes. The first baseman had done nothing to provoke the hostility except that he sought to be treated as an equal. Jackie was grim with anger. Pee Wee smiled broadly as he reached Jackie. Jackie smiled back.

Stopping beside Jackie, Pee Wee put his arm around Jackie's shoulders. An audible gasp rose up from the crowd when they saw what Pee Wee had done. Then there was silence.

Outlined on a sea of green grass stood these two great athletes, one black, one white, both wearing the same team uniform.

"I am standing by him," Pee Wee Reese said to the world. "This man is my teammate."

GOLENBOCK

About the Author

Peter Golenbock

Peter Golenbock loves sports. He started his career as a sports columnist in Stamford, Connecticut. Since then, he has written many books about sports, especially baseball and auto racing. Several of his books were best sellers. These include *Dynasty: The New York Yankees, 1949–1964; The Bronx Zoo;* and *Number 1.* Sports have become an "integral part of American society," says Mr. Golenbock. "With the public interest in *Dynasty, The Bronx Zoo,* and *Number 1,* I would hope that publishers would begin to take books on sports more seriously than in the past."

Quite a few people have read about their favorite teams in books by Mr. Golenbock. For example, in *Wrigleyville: A Magical History Tour of the Chicago Cubs,* he tells about the history of the team and includes interviews and anecdotes. If football is your sport, you may enjoy *Cowboys Have Always Been My Heroes* about the Dallas Cowboys, a National Football League team.

Mr. Golenbock's book *Teammates,* about Jackie Robinson and Pee Wee Reese, was a 1990 Notable Children's Trade Book.

Reader Response

Open for Discussion

Who are the winners in *Teammates*?
Who are the losers? Why?

Comprehension Check

1. How can you tell that this is a biography? Be sure to look at both the text and the illustrations for clues.

2. Why was making the Dodgers team "only the beginning" for Jackie Robinson? Find evidence to support your answer.

3. How did Branch Rickey and Pee Wee Reese help Jackie Robinson overcome racial prejudice and succeed in baseball?

4. List three words that the author uses to describe Jackie Robinson. How do they reflect the **author's viewpoint?** (Author's Viewpoint)

5. What do you think is the **author's viewpoint** on racial prejudice and segregation? Find evidence to support your answer. (Author's Viewpoint)

 **Test Prep**

Look Back and Write

Jackie Robinson and Pee Wee Reese show their courage in different ways. What does each man do that shows courage? Look back at pages 54–59. Present evidence from the selection to explain your answer.

Baseball Legends

by James Kelley

While African American players could not play in the Major Leagues, nothing was going to stop them from playing the game. As early as the 1870s, all-black amateur teams were competing in the Northeast. By the turn of the century, African American pro teams began to be formed, and leagues followed soon after. The "Negro Leagues," as they were known, included some of the greatest players of the century—players whose skills, most observers felt, would have made them Major League legends.

THE "BLACK BABE RUTH"

Of all the many outstanding players from the Negro Leagues, catcher Josh Gibson was perhaps the greatest player and a batter of enormous strength. Unofficial records give him more than 900 home runs for his career. In 1931 he was credited with 75 home runs, while his career batting average was above .350.

THE 42-YEAR-OLD ROOKIE

Leroy "Satchel" Paige was by far the most famous and successful player from the Negro Leagues. While his outstanding control as a pitcher first got him noticed, it was his infectious, cocky, and enthusiastic personality that made him a star.

Before helmets, catchers wore their hats backward.

Gibson autographed baseball

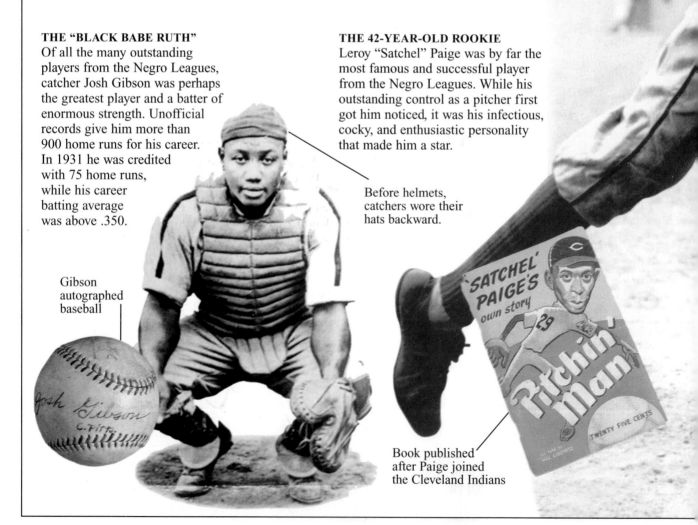

Book published after Paige joined the Cleveland Indians

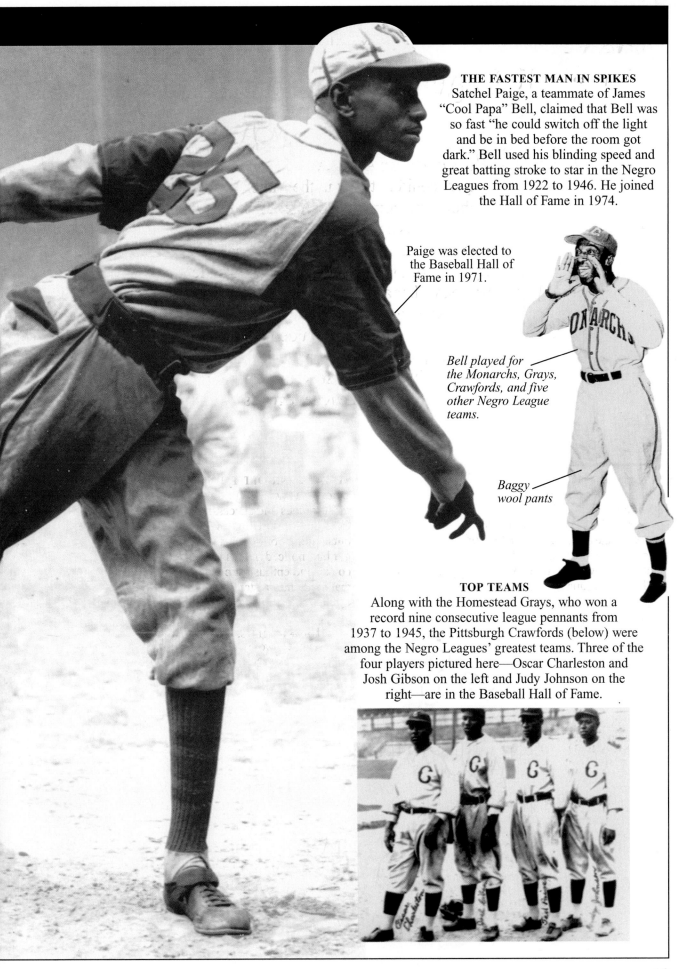

THE FASTEST MAN IN SPIKES

Satchel Paige, a teammate of James "Cool Papa" Bell, claimed that Bell was so fast "he could switch off the light and be in bed before the room got dark." Bell used his blinding speed and great batting stroke to star in the Negro Leagues from 1922 to 1946. He joined the Hall of Fame in 1974.

Paige was elected to the Baseball Hall of Fame in 1971.

Bell played for the Monarchs, Grays, Crawfords, and five other Negro League teams.

Baggy wool pants

TOP TEAMS

Along with the Homestead Grays, who won a record nine consecutive league pennants from 1937 to 1945, the Pittsburgh Crawfords (below) were among the Negro Leagues' greatest teams. Three of the four players pictured here—Oscar Charleston and Josh Gibson on the left and Judy Johnson on the right—are in the Baseball Hall of Fame.

Cause and Effect

- An **effect** is something that happens. A **cause** is why something happens.

- To find an effect, ask yourself "What happened?" To find a cause, ask yourself "Why did this happen?"

- An effect may have more than one cause, and a cause may have more than one effect.

- Sometimes an author does not state a cause, and you need to draw your own conclusions about why something happens.

Read **"Leaving Home"** from **"A Packet of Seeds"** by Deborah Hopkinson from *Cricket* magazine.

Talk About It

1. What is Pa's news? What effect does it have on Mama?

2. Aunt Nancy and Mama are very serious and sad at the end. What might be the cause or causes?

Leaving Home

by Deborah Hopkinson

My pa was a man who wanted to stand alone in an open field, where the only shadow he could see was his own.

One day he came home with news about land to be had out West. I could tell he'd already made up his mind.

"It's too crowded here," he told Mama.

"But this is our home, James," said Mama. "My sister is here, and our friends."

All Pa could see was the new land in front of him. All Mama could feel was the sorrow of leaving everything behind.

After that, Mama never said a word about it. No matter what she felt inside,

she cooked and cleaned and packed
to ready us for the long journey.

We left so early one morning,
I didn't think anyone would come to
say farewell. Then through the
darkness I heard the soft rustling of
skirts. Mama's friends gathered in a
circle. Each one kissed her, then
pressed a small packet into her hand.
Aunt Nancy was last.

"Dear sister," she said, holding
Mama tight. "I wish the sun were up
so I could see your face once more."

My little brother, Dan, was already
perched high on the wagon seat.
The oxen shifted in their traces.

Pa called out, "Mary, it's time."

Aunt Nancy hugged me. "Take care
of your mama, Jane."

Mama was crying so hard she
couldn't even say good-bye.

LOOK AHEAD

In "April's Mud"
you'll read
about April,
a girl who is embarrassed
about her family. As you read,
look for the causes of April's
embarrassment. Watch for other
cause-and-effect relationships.

Vocabulary

Words to Know

adobe	authentic	concrete
converted	heritage	normal

Many words have more than one meaning. To decide which meaning of a word is being used, look for clues in the surrounding sentences or the paragraph.

Read the paragraph below. Decide whether *concrete* means "actually existing" or "a mixture of stone, sand, cement, and water."

All About Adobe

Traditions are handed down from one generation to the next. Some are lost over the years, but others remain. One aspect of American heritage that has survived the passage of time is adobe, a building material commonly used in Mexico and the southwestern United States. If you travel through the Southwest, you might visit museums and restaurants that are located in authentic adobe buildings, such as converted Spanish missions and schools. Newer adobe homes, built upon modern foundations of steel and concrete, are popular too. These homes are often built entirely by family members— a normal practice in this region. Children work alongside adults, thus ensuring that the art of adobe will live on.

Write About It

Write about a house that you admire. Use as many vocabulary words as you can.

April's
Mud
by Carolyn Meyer

April Ellis thought the best thing about going to a new school was nobody knew—*yet!*—that she lived in a converted school bus painted lavender, orange, and green and parked in a weed-grown lot near the Rio Grande.

April had figured that once her grandparents had gone home to Philadelphia after their yearly visit over Labor Day, her family would get back to their "normal" life again. The last thing Nana said to April's parents as she climbed aboard the Amtrak train headed east was, "For the sake of the children, if not for yourselves, *please* give up this . . . this hippie life!" They had made it plain for seven days that what April's family considered normal wasn't "normal" at all. Not to Nana and Poppy. "Normal," April now realized, was a matter of opinion.

Nana and Poppy weren't the only ones who thought her parents were hippies. April had heard people talking about them at her old school. Most people born in the 1950s, as her parents had been, had "gotten it all out of their system" (Poppy's phrase) and gone back to whatever they had dropped out of, cut their hair, shaved their beards, and put on suits and ties and all the rest.

But not Susan and Tom Ellis. (April called them Susan and Tom, not Mom and Dad.) Tom still had a scraggly beard, and his idea of getting dressed up was to put on clean overalls and tie his long, wheat-colored hair back in a ponytail.

Susan was truly beautiful, in April's opinion. Her thick, wiry hair had turned gray early and framed her thin face in a silvery halo. Her pale eyes were silvery too, and she loved to wear bright clothes that fluttered when she walked and silver jewelry that flashed from her ears and jangled on her wrists.

Tom, who was very good with his hands, had bought the school bus a few years earlier when they decided to leave California and move to the Southwest. He pulled out the seats and fitted the inside of the bus with hand-built wooden furnishings, cleverly designed so that everything could be turned into something else: the table they ate their meals on and she and her older brother, Gus, did their homework on became the base for the futon her parents rolled out each night. She and Gus slept in berths—hers was on the bottom—and Susan had sewed bedspreads into curtains that could be drawn for privacy. Each of them had a handsome wooden trunk for personal belongings. The trunks had pillows on top so they could be used as seats.

The bus kitchen was like a playhouse, with its tiny sink, stove, and refrigerator. Somebody had to shop for groceries every day since there was no space to store much food, except sacks of pinto beans stowed on top of the bus and *ristras* of red chiles that hung along the side, drying in the sun. One thing they did have space for was books. April's father studied philosophy and astronomy as well as all kinds of crafts.

Susan waited tables at a natural foods restaurant, and Tom worked for a landscape company. They grew a lot of their own food. It had taken them a while to get used to New Mexico's dry climate, but the property where they parked their bus had water rights. On certain days each month, when it was their turn, Tom opened the sluice gate from the *acequias*, the irrigation ditches that crisscrossed the river valley, and let the water run into the small ditch that ran through their property. Their garden thrived. Now they had rows of corn, a chile patch, and all the fresh tomatoes and zucchini and beans they could eat. Good thing they were vegetarians.

Last winter Tom had decided it was time to build them a house. He brought home piles of books from the library and pored over them every night while April and her brother did homework.

"It's going to be adobe," her father said. "Basically, dried mud. We'll make the adobes ourselves, just like the early settlers did and lots of folks still do today in some parts of New Mexico."

Her mother glanced up from the turquoise beads she was stringing. "Sounds like a lot of hard work," she said.

"Yes, but it's simple," Tom insisted. "This book tells you exactly how to do it. And since we've got the clay right here on our land, why go out and buy materials?"

On the first warm spring day, Tom built wooden forms like a series of shallow boxes to make the large, flat, adobe bricks, which would be several times bigger than ordinary fired bricks. Gus began spading up the dirt in one corner of the lot. Then April and Susan opened the gate of the *acequia*. They all helped mix the dirt and the ditchwater to make a thick, gooey mud, tromping around in it in their bare feet. After lunch that first day it turned into a mud fight when Gus tossed the first handful. All four of them got completely covered and had to run down to the main channel to rinse themselves off. Then they got back to work seriously again.

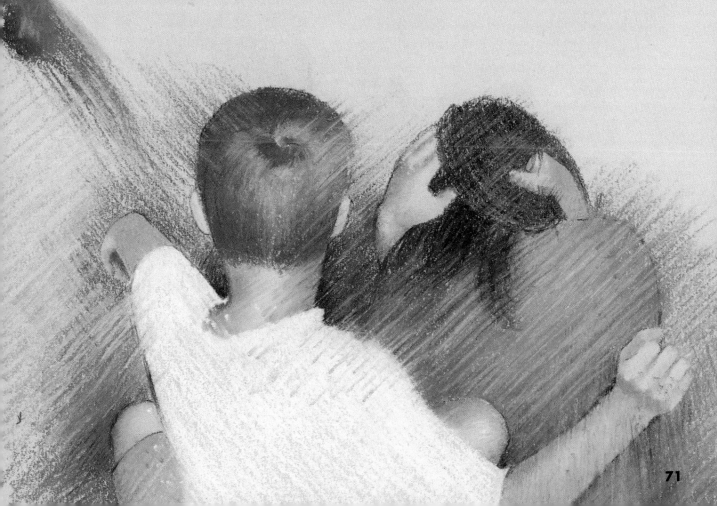

Tom shoveled the mud into the wooden forms, which were laid flat on the ground, open on the bottom to allow the excess water to drain away. The Ellises could make a dozen adobes at a time, letting one batch set while they shoveled mud into another form. "More mud!" Tom would yell, and Gus would rush up with another wheelbarrowful. April tried to run the wheelbarrow, but she had no idea mud could be so heavy. When the adobe bricks had dried out enough to handle, Susan and April stood them on edge, lined up like dominoes to finish drying.

At the end of the day they were all so sore and tired they could hardly move. But they forgot to cover the finished adobes, and when a rainstorm came up suddenly during the night, the adobes melted right back to mud again. Then, because the clay was so dense and Tom hadn't mixed in enough straw, their next batch cracked.

If it hadn't been for one of their neighbors, old Mr. Flores, they might not have gotten anywhere. Tom read his books faithfully, but Mr. Flores had actually built his own adobe house when he was a young man. He came over when he saw them out working and stood around smoking his pipe and offering bits of advice. "Good to wet your forms before you shovel in the mud," he said. "Adobes come out easier." He also showed Tom how to tell if the adobes were ready to use: he broke one in half so they could see that it was still dark in the center, not quite dry enough yet.

April noticed, though, that Mr. Flores himself lived in an ordinary house with fake stone decorating the front and aluminum windows and a concrete patio painted brick color. He sure wasn't living in any adobe house now. And once she heard him say to another neighbor who had stopped by to watch, "You'd think he'd buy his adobes, no? The kind with stabilizer mixed in, so his house won't melt around him!"

Every evening and all day Saturday and Sunday April's family mixed mud and made adobes. By the end of July there were several stacks of bricks protected by sheets of tar paper, enough to start building the house.

Tom insisted on making their home authentic. The traditional flat roof would be supported by *vigas*, beams made of peeled pine logs, which April was afraid, knowing her dad, he'd want to chop down himself in the forest. She was relieved when he mentioned that he had ordered the *vigas* from a man in Española, as well as the *latillas*, thin cottonwood saplings to be laid across the beams.

In the old days, Tom told them, adobe walls were laid right on the ground, but Mr. Flores convinced him the building inspector wouldn't allow it. Better to set them on concrete that would keep the adobes from soaking up groundwater. But Tom clung stubbornly to the idea of an earthen floor—somewhere he'd read about mixing the dirt with animal blood to make it hard and shiny. The idea made April sick.

She knew that some of her friends had rooms of their own where they could keep stuffed animals on the bed and put up posters all over the walls, if they wanted to, and could invite friends to sleep over. But as long as she lived in an old bus with her parents sleeping on the table on the other side of the curtain and her brother in his berth only inches above her head, there was no way she'd invite a friend to spend the night.

When the house was finished, she thought, then she could have someone visit. But when April took a good look at the floor plan Tom had been fussing over, her dream evaporated. The house seemed to be just one big room. "Where's my room?" she asked.

"That's it," he said. "The main room is your room and everybody's room, just like in the old days. Everybody cooked and ate and bathed and slept in that one room. For the first couple of years, that's how we'll do it. See the fireplace over here in the corner? That's probably all we'll need for heat. Adobe is much more energy-efficient than some people believe," he continued, explaining why they'd have just small windows and whitewash on the walls and so on. He seemed to have forgotten about April's wish for a room of her own. "You're going to love it, April! Maybe in a couple of years when we've saved up some more money and made some more adobes, we can build extra rooms onto it."

A couple of years! She'd be grown-up and gone by the time her father got around to adding a room for her!

The first part of the house was still far from finished, no more than an outline of the big room and part of two walls when Nana and Poppy came out from Philadelphia to visit over Labor Day weekend,

driving over from the motel in their rental car to stare disapprovingly at the piles of mud-colored bricks.

"How can you live like this, Thomas?" Poppy had asked sadly, and April felt sorry for her father. Actually the yard looked kind of like the ancient Indian ruins they had gone to visit. Wild purple asters bloomed in the field, and strings of bright red chiles were turning dark on the side of the bus.

Later Mr. Flores began to tease her. "And are you going to be the *enjarradora*, April?" he asked.

She didn't understand what he meant. Susan studied with Spanish language tapes, and April was supposed to be learning too, but she could say no more than a couple of polite phrases. She couldn't even pronounce the word he had just used. "What?"

"In our tradition, it's the women who plaster the adobe," he explained. "*Enjarrar* means 'to plaster.' *La enjarradora* is 'the woman who plasters.' She puts it on with her hands, like this," and he pretended to pat mud on her head.

"Not me," she said, ducking away and hoping her father hadn't heard about that authentic custom.

So far nobody at Rio Grande School knew about the bus or the adobe house or about her hippie parents, and April was completely thrown the fourth week of school by Mr. Wilder's announcement to the Heritage Project. "April's father has volunteered to come next week and help us build an *horno*," he said. "Anybody know what that is?"

Tomás Jaramillo raised his hand. "It's an outdoor oven."

"That's right. You see a lot of them around here."

Pauline Romero spoke up. "We have them at the pueblo," she said. "We bake bread in them. And also dry corn."

"And that's what we'll do with ours, once we get it built," Mr. Wilder said. "Be sure to bring old clothes because we're going to be covered with mud before it's over. I understand Mr. Ellis is building his own adobe house—is that correct, April?"

She was barely able to nod. Her tongue seemed to be cemented to the roof of her mouth. Tom had not said a word about this offer. Was it his idea of a joke? What made him *do* such a thing and without even discussing it with her first! She was so angry she was close to tears.

That evening at supper, while they ate their usual squash and chile and pinto beans, April burst out, "Why didn't you tell me you were going to volunteer? At least ask me! I was so embarrassed!"

Her father looked at her with innocent blue eyes. "I thought it would be a nice surprise, that's all," he said mildly. "I'm sorry if it upset you, but I'm not sure why you're embarrassed that I offered to come in to share a skill with your class."

"Your skill!" April yelped. "Tom, you don't even know how to build an *horno*. You've never built one before in your whole entire life!"

He seemed utterly amazed. "Just because I've never actually built one doesn't mean I can't learn. I'll be learning right along with your class. That's what education's all about, isn't it?"

All week April kept hoping it wouldn't happen. After all, her father was notorious in the family for not getting around to doing things he had promised to do. But on Friday morning he offered to drive her to school. The old wheelbarrow and some lumber and a couple of shovels were in the back of the truck. Climbing into the passenger seat, April could not see how she'd survive this day.

April walked into the school pretending that the tall, thin man in mud-spattered overalls, his long hair flowing out from beneath a red bandanna, was a complete stranger. Her strategy didn't work. Everyone stared. But then Mr. Wilder introduced him—just as "Mr. Ellis" and not as "April's father"—and Tom began to talk about the history of adobe making. After the first few minutes the kids seemed to accept Tom for what he was—an interesting man.

"Did you know that the *horno* originated in the Middle East maybe a thousand years ago? The Moors introduced it to Spain in the Middle Ages, and the Spanish brought it to the New World."

After the history lesson they went outside, and Mrs. Salazar, the principal, came along to help pick the place they were going to build the *horno*. The custodian brought out two more shovels, and everybody took turns spading up the earth. Since the school wasn't on an *acequia*, they ran a couple of lengths of hose out from the outdoor faucet, and everybody waded around in the gooey mud. April, who had done it lots of times at home, showed them how.

Several kids built the forms, sawing and nailing the lumber under Tom's guidance. They took turns with the wheelbarrow, dumping mud into the forms. Soon they had a long line of adobes drying in the sun.

"That's all for today," Tom announced, squinting at the sky. "They'll dry over the weekend. Monday we build the *horno*."

It hadn't been as bad as April expected. She didn't hesitate when her father offered her a ride to school on Monday.

The Heritage Project kids were eager to get on with the next step. Tom directed them to lay out a circular bed of flat stones about three and a half feet across and to arrange a layer of adobes on top of the stones. Manuel Medina put himself in charge of hauling the mud that would go around and between and over this base. Next they set a circle of adobes on edge, cementing them together with mud, then added another row on top of that one. "More mud!" somebody would yell, and Manuel would stagger over with the loaded wheelbarrow.

Tom helped them form the arched opening to the oven and showed them where to put the smoke hole on the north side. They began to tilt the rows inward, gradually forming the beehive shape. They chinked the spaces between the adobes with mud.

It looked great, everyone agreed. "One more step," Mr. Ellis announced, taking off his bandanna and wiping mud out of his beard.

"*Enjarrar,*" April said, surprised that she could remember Mr. Flores's word. "That means 'to plaster.' It's the women's job, putting on the smooth finish." She looked around at the girls in the class. "We're the *enjarradoras,*" she explained. "It's very messy work—the same adobe mud, only more runny. It's up to us to make it look good. Will you guys stand back, *por favor?*"

The girls looked at each other. "All *right!*" said Jacquelyn Cox. "Let's get going."

"More mud!" April called out, and Manuel ran toward their mixing hole with the wheelbarrow.

When they had finished, they had mud everywhere—on their clothes, their shoes, their arms, their faces. The Heritage Project kids clustered around Tom, asking when they could build a fire in their *horno* and bake some bread or roast some chiles. They could fire it up anytime, he told them.

"Pretty soon," April said when they were cleaning up their tools, "you can all come up and see the house we're building. It's an authentic adobe. Actually," she added, "the bus we're living in is really neat too."

About the Author

Carolyn Meyer

Carolyn Meyer became a writer before she even knew how to talk. When she was six months old, her father began a diary for her. In it he wrote what time she woke up, what she ate, and what her parents were doing each day. She still treasures the diary.

As a child, Ms. Meyer was very shy and not athletic. "I couldn't do ANYTHING, like catching a ball or hitting it, or running enough to beat anybody anywhere," she remembers. "Most of the time I managed to bring an excuse from my mother so I wouldn't have to go out at recess." She would play softball occasionally, but only if she were allowed six strikes. Ms. Meyer had a vivid imagination and often used writing to escape to her own world.

As a professional writer, Ms. Meyer writes both fiction and nonfiction. She has spent much time in New Mexico, and the influence of the Southwest comes through in much of her writing. Not only does *Rio Grande Stories*—the book of short stories in which "April's Mud" appears—take place in New Mexico, but her other young adult novels, *The Luck of Texas McCoy, Elliott & Win,* and *Wild Rover,* are also set in the Southwest.

Reader Response

Open for Discussion

April longs for a "normal" life—with a regular house and a room of her own. Put yourself in April's place. Would you like to live as April does? Why or why not?

Comprehension Check

1. What do April and her family learn from Mr. Flores? Point out passages from the story where he is especially helpful.

2. April is sure she knows what her classmates will think about her home and her family. Is April right? Explain, using details from the story.

3. Why do you think April's classmates enjoy working on the Heritage Project? Find examples from the story to support your answer.

4. What is the **cause** of April's embarrassment? Look back at the story for evidence. (Cause and Effect)

5. April's father helps build the *horno*. What **effect** does his involvement with the project have on April and her classmates? Find details in the story to support your answer. (Cause and Effect)

Test Prep

Look Back and Write

April's father, Tom, insists on making their home "authentic." Explain what he means by *authentic*. Include details from page 73 to support your answer.

81

Social Studies Connection

How to Read a How-To Article

1. Preview

- A how-to article shows you how to make or do something. Read the title and the first paragraph to see what the final product will be.

- Look over the pictures and diagrams. They usually show the final product and how it will look at different steps in the process.

2. Read and Make a List

- Read the main text and jot down notes telling what the final product is and what it's used for.

- Read the steps and make a list. For each step on your list, tell what happens.

  Step 1 Make bricks, collect rocks

  Step 2 Lay rocks and bricks

- Use the diagrams to help you visualize the process.

3. Think and Connect

Think about "April's Mud." Then look over your notes on "El Horno."

Both "April's Mud" and "El Horno" tell how to make adobe bricks and how to build an horno. But the authors had different purposes for writing these selections. What were their different purposes?

El Horno

by Michael Miller

The dome-shaped outdoor oven used by Pueblo and Hispanic communities in the southwestern states of Arizona, New Mexico, Texas, and Colorado is called *el horno* in Spanish. It is based on a European design and can be seen today in France and Spain and throughout South and Central America. It is used by people in the Southwest for outdoor cooking.

It is not difficult to build an horno. There are many different types of hornos throughout the Southwest. The one described here has its origins in the Taos area. Many schoolchildren in the Southwest build hornos in their schoolyards.

Figure A

1 Make 30 adobe bricks (see Figure A) and collect a pile of river rocks.

2 Lay the river rocks in a circle 40 inches in diameter. Lay about 10 bricks on top of the rocks. (See Figure B.) Fill in between the bricks with a mixture of mud and mud plaster.

Figure B

3 Place a layer of mud on top of the bricks. Use a *paleta,* a trowel, to smooth the mud over the bricks. The diameter of the circle of bricks should be about 38 inches. The center of this circle will be the floor of the oven.

4 Place a ring of mud about 6 inches thick around the outer edge of the circle. Set 6 adobe bricks on end lengthwise in the mud, leaving a gap for the hearth. The bricks should lean slightly inward. Fill in between the bricks with mud and plaster. The mud should be tight against the bottom. Let the mud set for about 1 hour.

Figure C

5 The next course of bricks should be set on end widthwise on the 2 bricks on either side of the hearth opening. Place a key (a small chunk of adobe) at the top of the unplastered horno and place mud in the gaps between the bricks. This step forms the doorway. (See Figure C.) Plaster with mud to stabilize and secure the adobe course.

6 Place 2 bricks, on end widthwise, on the back side. Use a key to stabilize the bricks. Lean a third brick on top of the other two. A smoke hole should be left toward the top. (See Figure D.) Let the mud set for about 1 hour.

Figure D

7 Using your bare hands, plaster the entire horno on the outside with a thick layer of mud. Shape the horno as if it were a clay sculpture. Lay a rock and the last adobe brick in front of the hearth and plaster it smooth. Let the horno dry for about a week in the hot sun. (See the photograph on page 82.)

8 When you are ready to bake in your horno, start a fire early in the morning and let it burn down to hot ashes. To bake bread, sweep away the ashes until the floor is clean. Place your pans on the floor of the horno; then cover the door opening with a smooth, flat stone and the smoke hole with a rock. To seal the horno, stuff a damp cloth in the cracks around the door and smoke hole. This will keep the heat inside for even baking.

Skill Lesson

Generalizing

- A broad statement about what several people or things have in common is a **generalization.** For example, using what you know and have observed, you could generalize by saying: *Most people in the United States greet each other with a handshake.*

- Clue words, such as *most, many, all, sometimes, generally, always,* and *never,* can help you identify generalizations in what you read.

Read "The Key" from *Even a Little Is Something: Stories of Nong* by Tom Glass.

Write About It

1. Write the generalization the narrator makes about Aunt Ray's neighbors. Circle the clue word.

2. Think about the story. Then decide which of the following generalizations better applies to the story:

a. Many people like to collect things.

b. All people in Thailand eat *somtam.*

The Key

by Tom Glass

Nong and Lek are close friends. They live across the lane from one another in rural Thailand.

Lek was a collector. She saved used stamps and matches and red rubber bands and kept them in old plastic bags. She collected the plastic bags too.

If it was free, Lek kept it.

Collecting made sense to Nong. It seemed to her that Lek was doing something useful with her life.

Nong decided to become a collector.

The problem was deciding what to collect. Lek was already saving most of the good stuff—and Nong didn't want to imitate Lek. She went to her mother for advice.

"We don't have much worth collecting," said her mother. "You could collect old chili seeds or caps off the bottles of fish sauce." She looked around for ideas. "There are all kinds of tree leaves out back."

Nong tried picking up leaves for a minute. Then she grew bored.

"Of course, some people aren't cut out for collecting," said her mother.

Another time Nong went down to Aunt Ray, who was not really her aunt, just as Lek was not really her sister. Nong had often seen Aunt Ray as she sat on her table making *somtam* [papaya salad]. Aunt Ray always sat cross-legged. She seemed to know something about life.

"I've always been partial to garlic," said Aunt Ray. "But I guess that's not the kind of thing people collect." The pestle thump-thump-thumped against the mortar as her arms kept pounding the fresh papaya and sauce.

"I've known people who collected triangular pillows," said a woman who was waiting for *somtam*.

"And lottery tickets that ended in 9," said another.

"And anything shaped like a heart."

Neighbors were always coming around to Aunt Ray's. They shared their opinions while they waited for *somtam*. Then they went home to eat.

Aunt Ray herself took a taste of the fresh batch of *somtam*. "I would love to collect mortars and pestles," she said, "except that my old set might get jealous." She patted the mortar on the table in front of her, then leaned down and whispered to Nong. "I'm kind to my mortar. That's one of the secrets to making good *somtam*."

Aunt Ray sat back up and said, "Well, that doesn't help you much with your collection, does it?" She scooped the *somtam* into a plastic bag and tied it shut with a rubber band, which happened to be red.

Nong kept hunting for things to collect. One day she rode her bike down by the canal. It was hard work. The lane that ran alongside the canal was full of potholes and dogs. Nong had to ride along carefully.

Near the bridge where the boys sat fishing, Nong saw something metal in the dust of the road. It was a key. It was scratchy and dull. But Nong knew immediately that it was the start of her new collection. She put the key in her pocket.

In the autobiography that follows, "Hot Dogs and Bamboo Shoots," a Japanese American girl describes her experiences in America and Japan. As you read, look for generalizations she makes about life in these countries.

Vocabulary

Words to Know

anguish	uprooted	exotic
foreigner	gratitude	homeland
traditional	correspondence	

When you read, you may come across a word that you don't know. To figure out the meaning of an unfamiliar word, look for clues in the words and sentences around it.

Read the paragraph below. Notice how the sentences around *correspondence* help you understand what it means.

To My Pen Pal . . .

Dear Miguel,
Thanks for the letter. It's so nice to begin our correspondence. How are you adjusting to life in the United States? You wrote that you still feel like a foreigner at times. I know how you feel. Every uprooted family feels some anguish. When my family first arrived from Mexico, we were miserable too. Everything was so scary and exotic. To ease our sorrow, we brought a little bit of the homeland with us—our traditional foods, music, holidays, and other customs. Now we're happy here and feel gratitude that we can be together in our adopted country. In time, maybe you will too.
Your new friend,
Maria

Write About It

Write to a pen pal—real or imaginary.
Use as many vocabulary words as you can.

Hot Dogs and Bamboo Shoots

from *The Invisible Thread* by Yoshiko Uchida
illustrated by Dom Lee

Yoshiko Uchida (standing) with her mother, father, Grandmother Uchida, and sister Keiko.

Obah San and My Cousins

Sometimes Papa drove on down to Los Angeles to visit Grandma. (We called her Obah San.) But usually we took the Southern Pacific overnight sleeper on New Year's Eve, arriving just in time to celebrate New Year's with Obah San, my aunt and uncle, and six cousins.

My father's railroad pass enabled us to travel in a cozy compartment, and I loved lying in the snug upper bunk listening to the click of the wheels and the ding-ding-ding of the signal lights rushing by.

In the morning we went to the dining car, sparkling with fresh linens, china, and flowers, where gracious white-coated waiters treated me with the same courtesy they accorded the adults.

As the train neared Union Station, our porter came to brush us off with his little whisk broom, and I knew I would soon see my uncle and cousins smiling and waving to us from the station platform.

Long before I got that far, however, I often came down with a fever. I was not a healthy child. I got carsick and seasick. I had knee aches (Mama called them "growing pains"), and often went to bed with a hot water bottle puffed up like a football because I'd forgotten to let the air out after pouring in the hot water. I also had nosebleeds that seemed to last for hours and a variety of unexplained fevers.

Mama could sometimes relieve my knee aches with the warmth of her "healing hands," but otherwise she resorted to medicine from Japan. Her best cure-alls were the tiny seedlike pills we called Kinbon San, but they didn't always rid me of my pre-New Year's fevers.

Although I really wanted to go to Los Angeles, I was also a bit anxious about being there. It was bad enough being intimidated by an older sister at home, but in Los Angeles I was the youngest of all thirteen of us gathered there. Most of the time I felt inadequate, and sometimes didn't dare open my mouth.

The two youngest girls were only a year or two older than I was, but they were prettier, and I thought more sophisticated, and I was often in awe of them.

They taught us how to sing such songs as "Walking My Baby Back Home," and they knew how to dance when I was still perfecting my roller-skating techniques. They also did such daring things as taking us downtown to see two movies, one right after the other.

To me movies were a special treat to be indulged in only occasionally. To walk out of one theater and march right into another was a thrilling feat Keiko and I never would have attempted back home.

I always looked forward to New Year's Day, for it was a festive occasion that began with a traditional Japanese New Year's feast. We all gathered around the extended dining room table, with a bright red broiled lobster, symbol of long life, dominating its center.

Surrounding it were tiered lacquer boxes and large platters full of such delicacies as sesame daikon salad, herring roe, knotted seaweed, teriyaki chicken, bamboo shoots, taro, burdock and lotus root, sweet black beans, and hard-boiled eggs cut into fancy shapes.

I sampled everything except the herring roe, which I always passed up, for each dish was symbolic of long life, prosperity, or good health, and I wanted to have all those things.

I knew Obah San and my cousins had labored hard for several days preparing the feast. The family had also cleaned house, paid all the bills, and tied up loose ends, for New Year's Day was considered a time for new beginnings unsullied by the old year's debts and obligations.

"Happy New Year, Obah San! Happy New Year everybody!"

The room was filled with happy chatter as we began with traditional toasted rice cakes floating in kelp broth and then progressed to all the other delicacies.

When at last we had eaten our fill, we children drifted away from the table to go outside or to play cards or otherwise entertain ourselves.

One year one of my older cousins taught us new words to the Toreador Song from the opera *Carmen*. "Dorie, oh Dora," he sang in his sweet tenor voice, "don't spit on the floor-ah. Spit in the spit bowl, that's what it's for-ah . . ." After that, I could never listen to *Carmen* without hearing those words.

Keiko and I loved being part of that big lively family of six children who obligingly doubled up to accommodate us.

Because my aunt was not well, Obah San was the central figure of the household. Every morning she was the first one up, and I would find her sitting beside the stove, toasting a dozen pieces of bread at a time in the broiler. She liked to eat her toast with a thick layer of peanut butter on it, and I always believed that was what kept her healthy and well for over ninety years.

Whenever Obah San had a few spare minutes, I would see her reading her Japanese Bible, sounding out the words silently, just as she did when she prayed. God was her best friend, and each night she talked to Him for a half hour. Sitting on her bed, her legs folded beneath her, she rocked back and forth, her eyes shut tight, pouring out her gratitude as well as her hopes and requests.

I wondered if God had time to listen to her nightly outpourings, but supposed He would take good care of anyone who prayed as hard and long as she did.

We all went to the Japanese Union Church on Sundays, and Obah San was always the first one ready. Dressed in her best clothes, wearing her hat and gloves, she would sit on the sofa, patiently waiting for the rest of us to get ready.

She did the same thing if we invited her to go with us to see a movie. Obah San loved going out, and was always ready to have a good time with her grandchildren.

Because she'd never had much in life, she was always frugal and careful. She never let any food go to waste, and any fruit that was beginning to spoil had to be eaten before we could touch the good fruit. Sometimes if we were asked whether we'd like a banana or a peach, we would automatically respond, "Which one's spoiling?" and eat that one first.

Obah San had only a few clothes hanging in her closet, and toward the end of her life, she pinned a note on her best black dress that read, "This one is for my trip to Heaven."

When she had a big party at church on her eighty-eighth birthday, I asked her if she'd be able to blow out all the candles on her cake. "Don't worry," she said, smiling, and when the time came, she calmly took a fan from her purse and extinguished the candles with one grand gesture. I thought she was just great.

Not many of my Nisei friends had grandparents living in the United States, since most of them had remained behind in Japan. I was lucky to have at least one grandmother I could see once in a while, and in 1934 I was lucky enough to visit my other grandmother who lived in Japan.

Foreigner in Japan

I was twelve when we sailed on the *Chichibu Maru* to visit my
Grandmother Umegaki in Japan. My parents had taken me once before
when I was two, but since I didn't remember that visit, I felt it didn't
count. This time we were taking along our Los Angeles grandmother
for her first visit to Japan since her departure so many years before.

I considered this my first ocean voyage, although I had gone often
with my parents to see friends off at the drafty San Francisco piers. We
would be among dozens of well-wishers crowding on board the ship to
visit friends in staterooms bursting with luggage, flowers, and baskets
of fruit. Caught up in the festive excitement, I used to wish I were the
one sailing off to Japan.

When one of the cabin boys traveled through the corridors beating
the brass gong, however, I always felt a cold chill run down my spine.

"Come on, Papa," I would urge. "That's the 'all ashore that's going
ashore' gong. Let's go."

But Papa continued talking with his friends, totally ignoring the
urgent banging of the gong. By the time the passengers moved to the

deck to throw rolls of colored tape to their friends below, the rest of us hurried down the narrow gangplank.

Papa, however, was still on board, smiling and waving from the upper deck. He would throw a roll of blue tape to my sister and a pink one to me.

"Come on, Papa!" we would shriek. "Hurry up!"

Finally, minutes before the gangplank was pulled up, he would saunter down, calmly saying, "Don't worry, they would never sail with me still on board."

Papa had a permanent dock pass to board the ships, and he came so often to meet friends or to see people off that he seemed to know everybody. For him the ships were familiar territory, but to me they were exotic, majestic, and slightly mysterious.

But this time, at last, I didn't have to worry about Papa getting caught on board a departing ship. This time we were passengers. *We* were the ones sailing to Japan. *We* were the ones everybody had come to see off. The baskets of fruits and flowers in the stateroom from Papa's business friends were for *us*. So were the gardenia corsages and the bouquets of flowers.

Now *I* was the one throwing rolls of tape down to our friends on the pier and waving and calling good-bye.

As the ship slowly eased out into San Francisco Bay, the wind tugged at the streamers I held in my hand. But I wouldn't let go. I hung on until the ship snatched them from the hands of the friends we'd left behind, and I watched as they fluttered off into the sky looking like a flying rainbow.

"Hey, we're really going!" I said to Keiko. "We're really going to Japan!"

But ten minutes after we had sailed through the Golden Gate, the ship began to pitch and roll, and my happy grin soon disappeared. The ever-present smell of bouillon I'd found so inviting earlier now made me turn green. All of us except Papa took to our bunks and stayed there for the next four days.

When we were finally able to join Papa in the dining salon, our waiters were so pleased to have a full table to serve, they broke into applause as we appeared.

By this time all shipboard activities were in full swing, and Keiko and I worked hard to catch up. We played shuffleboard and deck tennis. We had hot bouillon served by white-coated boys who rolled the soup cart up and down the decks each morning at ten o'clock. We went to every afternoon tea, stuffing ourselves with little cakes and fancy sandwiches, and amazingly had room for a big dinner in the evening.

One night there was a sukiyaki party on the lantern-festooned deck. For once I didn't have to set the table and neither Mama nor Papa had to cook. *We* were the company, and I was delighted that the ship's waiters did all the work. The Deans of Women of Mills College and the University of California in Berkeley happened to sit at our table, and we showed them how to use chopsticks and eat Japanese food.

"You'll have to send one of your daughters to each of us," they teased Mama and Papa. And that is exactly what happened. Keiko went to Mills College and I went to UC Berkeley.

The day a costume party was scheduled, Keiko and I worked all day to prepare for it. She wore a pair of Papa's pants and suspenders, drew a mustache on her face, and squashed one of his hats on her head.

I dressed up like a doll, painting round circles of rouge on my cheeks. We tied strings to my wrists and ankles, attached them to two sticks, and went to the costume party as Tony the puppeteer and his doll puppet. We were beside ourselves when we won first prize.

By the time we neared Yokohama, I was so charmed with the good life on board the *Chichibu Maru*, I didn't want to get off.

Mama, on the other hand, could hardly wait. The morning we docked, she was up early. As our ship slid noiselessly alongside the pier, she impulsively pushed open one of the cabin's portholes to scan the faces on the pier.

Suddenly I heard her shout, "Oka San! Mother!"

It was a voice I had never heard before—filled with the longing and anguish of years of separation and a joy mingled with tears.

This was a Mama I'd never known before. For the first time in my life, I saw her not just as Mama who cooked and washed and sewed for us, but as someone's daughter. She was a person with a life and feelings of her own quite apart from mine.

For a fleeting moment I thought I understood the turmoil of her uprooted soul. But in the excitement of landing, the feeling passed, and she became once more the Mama I had always known.

None of us ever dreamed then of the terrible war* that would separate her from her family and homeland forever.

It was a wonder to me how Mama could have left behind such a nice family and so many good friends. We met them all while we were in Japan.

Grandmother Umegaki was a plump, friendly woman with a quiet manner that belied her strength. It was that hidden strength that gave her the courage to send her oldest daughter to America, and I believe my mother had a good measure of it in herself as well.

Mama's brother, Yukio, was a silversmith who made all sorts of beautiful gifts for us—a copper hanging engraved with my mother's favorite wildflower, a silver pin of my dog for me, and an engraved silver buckle for Keiko.

Another brother, Minoru, was a college professor who was writing several scholarly books and also painted quite well. I wasn't sure how to behave in front of Seizo, the brother who had become a priest, but he turned out to be the most fun of all and a skilled artist as well.

All three uncles wrote wonderful illustrated letters to my sister and me until the war ended their correspondence, and the life of one uncle as well.

Mama's only sister, Kiyo, was a widow who had lost a baby son and lived with her only daughter. They both seemed permanently saddened by their losses and had none of the easy laughter that dwelled in Mama and her brothers.

We were surrounded by family in Japan, since two of Papa's sisters had returned to live there as well. One lived in Osaka and the other in Tokyo. Wherever we went, we seemed to have a place to stay. Our relatives simply spread out some quilts for us on the *tatami* mat, enclosed us in great billowing mosquito netting, and we were set for the night.

* World War II. The United States declared war on Japan on December 8, 1941.

One of the happiest times for my parents and Grandma Uchida was our stay in Kyoto, with its temples and hills and their beloved Doshisha University. The first friends Obah San wanted to visit were Dr. and Mrs. Learned, for whom she had worked so long ago.

They seemed so old and frail to me, like pale white shadows in a sea of Japanese faces. They showered us with love and affection, and gave Keiko and me the American names we had long wanted to have. Keiko was named Grace, and I was given the name Ruth. But somehow it didn't make me as happy as I thought it would. I just didn't feel like a Ruth, and I never used the name.

Keiko and I tolerated innumerable long dinners and lunches with our parents' many friends, but when things got too boring, we would count the number of times people bowed to each other. In Japan no one hugged or shook hands. They just bowed. And bowed. And bowed some more. My mother set the record, with thirteen bows exchanged in one encounter.

What I liked best was going to temples and shrines on festival days, when the celebration, with costumed dancers and booming drums, was like a holiday parade and carnival rolled into one.

Yoshiko Uchida (bending) with her Uncle Minoru, sister Keiko and a cousin in Japan

But I liked the celebration of Obon (All Souls' Day), too. That was when the spirits of the dead were believed to return home, and some families lit tiny bonfires at their front gate to welcome them at dusk. Inside, there were tables laden with all sorts of delicious dishes, prepared especially for the returning spirits.

In Japan the dead seemed to blend in with the living, as though there were no great black separation by death. And I found that a comforting thought.

Sometimes we climbed wooded hills that rose behind ancient temples to visit graveyards filled with moss-covered tombstones. And one day we went to pay our respects to our samurai grandfathers whom we had never known. Using small wooden scoops, we poured cold water on their tombstones to refresh their spirits, and left them handfuls of summer lilies.

I wondered what they thought of us—their grandchildren from far-off America, dressed in strange clothing and babbling in a foreign tongue. I hoped they liked us.

Once we stayed with an uncle and some cousins at a rural inn, where at the end of the day, we all went to the communal tub to have a pleasant soak together.

Then, wearing cool cotton kimonos provided by the inn, we gathered around the low table, where the maids brought us miso soup, broiled eel, and slivered cucumber on individual black lacquer trays.

After dinner we sat on the veranda and had sweet bean paste cakes and tea, watching a full moon rise over the mountains. The talk was gentle, and whenever it stopped, we could hear the swarms of cicadas in the pine trees buzzing in unison like some demented chorus.

As I sat watching the fireflies darting about in the darkness, I thought maybe I could get quite used to living in Japan. Here, at least, I looked like everyone else. Here, I blended in and wasn't always the one who was different.

And yet, I knew I was really a foreigner in Japan. I had felt like a complete idiot when an old woman asked me to read a bus sign for her, and I had to admit I couldn't read Japanese.

Deep down inside, where I really dwelled, I was thoroughly American. I missed my own language and the casual banter with friends. I longed for hot dogs and chocolate sodas and bathrooms with plumbing.

But the sad truth was, in America, too, I was perceived as a foreigner.

So what was I anyway, I wondered. I wasn't really totally American, and I wasn't totally Japanese. I was a mixture of the two, and I could never be anything else.

About the Author
Yoshiko Uchida

"Hot Dogs and Bamboo Shoots" is a true account of author Yoshiko Uchida's young life. Ms. Uchida grew up as a daughter of Japanese immigrants in California. Although she had a very loving family, she comments, "I lived in a society that in general made me feel different and not as good as my white peers."

During World War II, Ms. Uchida was sent to a Japanese internment camp, where she and other Japanese Americans were forced to live as prisoners. Because Japan was an enemy of the United States during the war, some people feared that Americans of Japanese descent might help Japan in the war. Many years later, our government apologized for its actions. Ms. Uchida wrote about these and other experiences in her books *Journey to Topaz* and *Journey Home*.

About the Illustrator
Dom Lee

Dom Lee always knew that he would be an artist. "When I was a kid," he says, "I always liked to draw, and everybody told me I was good. But I never drew kid's pictures. No stick figures or big suns in the sky. My drawings were always adult pictures."

Born and raised in Korea, Mr. Lee taught art for a while after finishing college, but he decided that he wanted to illustrate books, so he moved to the United States.

Mr. Lee developed a new painting technique—which he used for the illustrations in "Hot Dogs and Bamboo Shoots"—in which he applies beeswax to paper and then scratches out and paints the illustrations. He has won several awards for his work.

Reader Response

Open for Discussion

Some people find a message in what they read. What message—if any—did you get from "Hot Dogs and Bamboo Shoots"?

Comprehension Check

1. The author is both excited and uneasy about her family's trip to Obah San's home in Los Angeles. Why? Look back at the story for details.

2. How do Japanese Americans celebrate the New Year? Include details from the story to support your answer.

3. What does the author realize about her mother upon their arrival in Japan? Look back at the story for details.

4. Find examples from "Hot Dogs and Bamboo Shoots" to support this **generalization:** Some Japanese Americans aren't "totally American" or "totally Japanese," but "a mixture of the two." (Generalizing)

5. How is life in Japan different from life in America? Form a **generalization** about some of the differences between the two cultures, using details from the story. (Generalizing)

 **Test Prep**

Look Back and Write

Look back at pages 90–91. The author likes and admires Obah San. What does Obah San say and do that causes the author to like and admire her? Use details from the story to support your answer.

People buy and sell goods in this market in Ecuador.

Society and Culture

LOOKING AHEAD

As you read, look for—

Key words, people, and **places:**

culture	Lapland
custom	**norm**
Japan	**society**

Answers to these questions about **main ideas:**

1. How does a society and its culture help people meet their needs?

2. What are some important characteristics of culture?

Society and Culture

All people need food, shelter, and safety. Since earliest times people have joined together in groups to help one another meet these and other needs and wants. For example, a group of people who have common goals—helping one another make a living—is called a **society.**

The way of life a society develops to reach its common goals is called a **culture.** Culture is the total way of life, including ways of thinking and behaving, that people in a society share. All people have a culture. It includes all parts of people's lives.

Today the world has many different cultures. Our culture, for example, uses modern technology for most daily activities. Also, most people in our society earn a living from manufacturing jobs or by providing services. Other cultures, such as that of the Laplanders who live in the northern regions of Europe, follow a way of life that is very different. The people of Lapland use traditional technology, earning a living by nomadic herding. In this book you are going to read about many people with cultures different from your own.

The Characteristics of Culture

All cultures have a number of common characteristics. Some important characteristics are listed below. As you read about these characteristics, think about how they apply to the way you lead your life.

Work and Rewards. All cultures have a system of work and rewards through which needs and wants can be met. That is, members of a society have jobs to do, and, in return, they receive a share of the goods and services produced. The way that goods and services are produced, distributed, and used in a culture is called its *economic system*.

Organized Groups. All cultures have organized groups that are part of the culture. These organized groups include governments and groups for work and play. Families are one of a culture's most important organized groups. Families prepare children for life in the society and give support for both parents and children.

Norms. All cultures have standards of behavior, or rules by which members of the society are supposed to live. These standards of behavior are called **norms.** People accept some of these norms simply as the normal way to behave. For example, people in the United States consider eating with a knife and a fork normal behavior. The common way of doing something in a society is called a **custom.**

—from *Our World: Yesterday and Today*

Nomadic herders, such as this Laplander of northern Europe, follow a traditional way of life.

The traditional culture of Japan has been influenced by other cultures. What evidence of this influence do you see?

Character

- **Characters** are the people or animals in stories.

- You can learn about characters by noticing what they think, say, and do.

- You can also learn about characters by paying attention to how other characters in the story treat them and what others say about them.

Read "Granny's Chair" from "Apple Butter Time" by Joann Mazzio from *Cricket* magazine.

Talk About It

1. How do you think Rachel feels about sitting in Granny's chair? What does she do that shows you how she feels?

2. What do you learn about Rachel's character from what she thinks and does?

3. What do you learn about Rachel's character from the way the grownups treat her? Explain.

Granny's Chair

by Joann Mazzio

Rachel heard her cousin Beth's excited scream. "Run, sheepie, run," she yelled. The others, the younger children, shrieked as they ran to hide. Their voices cut through the mellow end-of-summer dusk.

Inside the screened-in porch, a bare light bulb hung from the ceiling. Rachel's father and Uncle Ed had already brought in several empty buckets and a large tub of water. Rachel's mother and Aunt Ann came from the kitchen with baskets of peeled apples.

The grownups, each with a paring knife, settled onto the straight-backed kitchen chairs. Rachel stood awkwardly, holding her knife away from her. She looked at the one empty chair in the circle, a rocking chair with cushions on the caned seat.

"It's OK, Rachel. Sit in Granny's chair," her father said.

Rachel sat gingerly on the edge of the seat and reached for an apple. She cut it into fourths, tossed the pieces into the tub, and dropped the core into a bucket. The grownups settled into a rhythm that Rachel couldn't match. As their hands cut the apples and carved out the cores, they talked and laughed quietly.

Kids outside playing, grownups inside working up the apples. Every year at apple butter time it was thus, Rachel thought. Only this year, Rachel was inside with the grownups, sitting in the chair Granny had always sat in.

"Aha, young lady," Uncle Ed said, "you threw the core into the tub instead of your bucket. If we find stems in the apple butter, we'll know who to blame."

There were heavy shadows on his face, but Rachel could tell he was teasing her. She looked up briefly and returned his smile.

Apple juice dripped through her fingers, the acid stinging the cuts the knife had made in her skin. She remembered Granny's hands, cutting and coring, the juice dripping over her silver ring with the clasped hands on it. Even with her fingers knotted from arthritis, the knife had moved as though alive.

Again the voices called Rachel's attention outside. "You don't dare get her out," Dirk called to the other kids. Cathy, Rachel's little sister, giggled wildly, and Rachel realized that she was a prisoner in the sheep pen. Cathy was always the first one captured. If Rachel were outside, she'd know how to swoop down on the prisoners and free them. She caught herself thinking this, then sighed and tried to imitate the rhythm of the grownups.

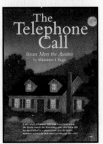

In "The Telephone Call," the Austins cope with a family crisis. As you read, you'll get to know the characters by noticing what they think, say, and do.

Vocabulary

Words to Know

bewilderment	**cope**	**objective**
orphan	**tactful**	

Words with similar meanings are called **synonyms.** You can often figure out the meaning of an unknown word by finding a clue in the words around it. Sometimes this clue is a synonym.

Read the paragraph below. Notice how *confusion* helps you understand what *bewilderment* means.

A Memorable Walk

This morning, I nearly stumbled over a fawn nestled on a local hiking path. We just stared at each other in bewilderment. Where was its mother? Was it an orphan? I didn't know what to do, and I think it sensed my confusion. It stood up and approached me. At first I wanted to hold it, but I remembered that my scent on its fur might drive its mother away. It was so cute, but this was no time to let my emotions get the best of me. I had to stay objective. I've always handled difficult situations pretty well. My mom says that I'm very tactful for my age. Still, this was tough. I didn't want to leave it to cope with the dangers of the woods on its own. Yet, I knew that was exactly what I had to do. As I walked away, its mother returned. She was only waiting for me to leave.

Write About It

Use some of the vocabulary words in a story about how you handled a difficult situation.

The Telephone Call

from *Meet the Austins*

by Madeleine L'Engle

A late-night telephone call from Aunt Elena brings the Austin family the distressing news that Uncle Hal has been killed in a plane crash. Now the family members must help each other get through this crisis.

Sometime during the night the phone rang again; I woke up just enough to realize it. And it rang again in the morning—the house phone both times, not the office ring; but once I had finally gone to sleep I was so sleepy that the sound of the phone hardly got through to me, and it was only as I was waking up, with the sun shining full across my bed, and heard the office phone ringing that I remembered the phone had rung during the night.

We have lots more time on Sundays than we do on schooldays, but there always seems to be more of a rush to get to Sunday school on time than there is to catch the school bus, so we don't make our beds till we get home from Sunday school and church. As soon as we got home from church Mother told us to get out of our good clothes and into play clothes (I don't know why we'd never do it if she didn't tell us, but there's always so much to do that we just don't think about it) and then she told me to strip my bed and make it up with clean sheets. "And check the guest room, Vicky," she said. "Make sure there are clean sheets on the guest-room beds."

"Why?" I asked.

"Because I tell you to," she said, as though I were Rob, and that was all.

I was almost through when she came up and said, "Vicky, would you mind sleeping in Rob's room for a while?"

"Me? Why?" I asked in surprise.

"You must have realized that Aunt Elena called several times last night. I talked with her again this morning, and Uncle Douglas is driving her up here with Maggy."

"Maggy?"

"Margaret Hamilton, the little girl whose father was Uncle Hal's copilot."

I hadn't quite finished making the bed, but I sat down on the edge of it. "When are they coming?"

"They're on their way now," Mother said. "They ought to be here this afternoon. I thought that since Maggy and Suzy are so close in age, I'd put Maggy in your bed."

"What about John?"

"He'll sleep in the study tonight while Aunt Elena's here. When she goes, he can have the guest room. I know you have a lot of homework this year, Vicky, but John has even more, and I think he must be the one to have the room to himself. It won't be all gravy, you know; he'll have to move out whenever we have company."

I thought this over for a moment. Then I said, "How long is the little girl . . . Maggy . . . staying?"

"I don't know," Mother said. "We'll just have to see."

"And Mother . . . why is she coming to us?"

"It's too complicated to go into now," Mother said briskly. "Come along, Vic, let's get the beds done."

Mother usually gives us nice, full explanations for things, but on the rare occasions when she doesn't (I think being cryptic is what I mean), there's no point asking any more questions, so we just finished up with the beds.

After lunch John had to work on his science project, so he went off to the barn, with Daddy warning him to do his project and not his spacesuit. I biked over to the center of Thornhill to check my math homework with Nanny Jenkins, my best friend. Nanny's parents run the store in the village and Mr. Jenkins plays the cello too. Math is not my best subject and I find that if I don't check my problems I'm apt to make silly mistakes in adding or subtracting that make the whole problem wrong even if I've been doing it the right way. We finished about five o'clock and it was time for me to get along home, anyhow. Mother doesn't like us to ride our bikes after dark unless there's a very good reason. It's a nice ride home from the village, up the one real street in Thornhill, a nice wide street with white houses set back on sloping lawns and lots of elms and maples (it's just a typical New England village—at least, that's what Uncle Douglas says), and then off onto the back road. The back road is a dirt road, and it's windy and hilly and roundabout and so bumpy that cars don't drive on it very often. Our house is at the

other end of it, just about a mile and a half. In the autumn it's especially beautiful, with the leaves turned and the ground slowly being carpeted with them. Where the trees are the heaviest and the road cuts through a little wood, the leaves are the last to turn, so that as I pedaled along, the evening sun was shining through green, and up ahead of me, where the trees thinned out, everything was red and orange and yellow.

A little green snake wiggled across the road in front of me, and I thought how thrilled Rob would be if he were along. Almost every day all summer he would go up the lane hunting for a turtle to bring home as a pet. We never found a turtle, but we've seen lots of deer, and a woodchuck that lives in the old stone wall by the brook, and any number of rabbits; and once we saw a red fox.

When I got home, Uncle Douglas's red car was parked outside the garage behind our station wagon, so I knew they were there.

And suddenly I felt very funny about going in, and took twice as long as I needed to put my bike in the shed. I hung my jacket up in the back-hall closet and picked up Suzy's and Rob's jackets, which they'd evidently hung on the floor, and put them on hangers—anything to put off opening the back door and going into the kitchen.

Why was I so shy about seeing Aunt Elena and meeting Maggy, or even saying hello to Uncle Douglas again when I'd been talking with him only the night before?

Finally, there was nothing to do except open the door and go in, so I did. And instead of finding the kitchen full of everybody as it usually is at that time of day, I saw Aunt Elena standing in front of the stove alone. She turned to greet me and she said immediately and briskly, "Ah, Vicky, you've saved me. I am not ten feet tall like your mother and I cannot reach the coffee."

So I didn't have to say anything. I didn't even have to kiss her, which would have been the easiest thing in the world to do up to the time the telephone rang the day before and which now seemed to take more courage than I possessed. I pulled a stool over to the stove and climbed up on it and got the can of coffee.

"No, the other one," Aunt Elena said. "I promised your mother I'd make some café espresso for after dinner."

And all I could say was, "Oh." I stood there, watching her. She didn't look any different; she looked just the same way she had a few weeks before, when she and Uncle Hal were up for the weekend; and yet she wasn't the same person at all. She stood there in her black dress measuring coffee, wearing black not because of Uncle Hal but because she is a city person and she looks beautiful in black and wears it a great deal. Her hair is black, too, and in one portrait Uncle Douglas painted of her, he used great enormous globs of blue and green in the hair, and, funnily enough, when it was done it was exactly right. We have a lovely portrait of Mother Uncle Douglas painted, and he's painted quite a few others of her, too, and one is in a museum. Uncle Douglas says he paints only beautiful women. But, he says, beautiful is not pretty. I don't really know whether Mother is beautiful or not. To me she looks exactly the way a mother should look, but only in the portrait where she's holding Rob just a few weeks after he was born does Uncle Douglas see her the way I do.

Aunt Elena doesn't look like a mother at all—and, of course, she isn't. Her black hair falls loose to her shoulders and she always looks to us as though she were dressed to go to a party. When she plays with us we always have a wonderful time, but it's as though we were brand new to her each time, not as though she were used to being around children at all. Uncle Hal, with his big booming laugh and the way he could roughhouse with us all, was quite different. I thought of Uncle Hal and remembered that I would never see him again, and I looked at Aunt Elena, and it was as though it were terribly cold and my sorrow was freezing inside me so that I couldn't speak.

John came in just then, bursting in through the kitchen door with his jacket still on and his face so pink from the cold that the lenses of his glasses began to steam up from the warmth of the kitchen.

John and I fight a lot, but I have to admit that John is the nicest one of us all. He seems to know what to do and say to people without having to think about it, and whenever there are elections and things John always gets elected president. So now he was able to do what I wanted to do and knew I ought to do and simply couldn't do. He went right up to Aunt Elena and put his arms around her and hugged her hard and kissed her. He didn't say anything about Uncle Hal, but it was perfectly obvious exactly what

he was saying. For a moment Aunt Elena sort of clung to him, and then, just as I thought maybe she was going to start to cry, John took his arms away and said, "Aunt Elena, you're the only person around here who can untie knots, and my shoelace is all fouled up. Could you untie it for me?" And he yanked off his shoe and handed it to her.

Now, I am very good at untying knots and I always untie John's knots for him and I started to say so, indignantly, but then I realized what John was doing and I shut my mouth, just in time. Aunt Elena bent over John's shoe, and the tears that had been starting in her eyes went back, and when she handed John the shoe she smiled and looked like herself.

"Where's everybody?" John demanded.

"Your mother's out picking carrots," Aunt Elena said.

"Oh, no, not carrots again," John groaned. "I wish Rob had never planted those carrots. Where're the kids?"

"Your Uncle Douglas took them for a walk."

"What's for dinner—other than carrots? Carrot sticks this time, I hope. We had 'em cooked last night." He went over to the stove, lifted the lid off a big saucepan, and sniffed. "Um, spaghetti. Garlic bread?"

"But of course," Aunt Elena said as Mother came in, her arms full of carrots.

I was helping Mother scrape the carrots when there came the sounds of shouting and talking and then in they came, seeming like a whole horde of children instead of just three and Uncle Douglas.

And a dark-haired little girl came dancing in, screaming shrilly, "You can't catch me! You can't catch me!" and went dancing around the table, Suzy and Rob after her, and, of course, Rochester came dashing in to see what was going on and knocked over a chair, and the little girl knocked over another chair, not because she was clumsy, like Rochester and me, but because she wanted to hear the crash.

"All right," Mother said, far more pleasantly than she would have if it had been just us or one of our friends from around here, "this furniture has to last us for quite a long while. Let's keep the rougher kind of roughhousing for outdoors, shall we?"

And the little girl paid absolutely no attention. "C'mon, Suzy, chase me!" she shrieked, and knocked over another chair.

Mother's voice was still pleasant but considerably firmer. "Maggy, I said not in here, please. Suzy and Rob, pick up the chairs. Maggy, you haven't met John and Vicky yet. John and Vic, this is Margaret Hamilton."

John shook hands with her and said, "We're glad you've come to stay with us for a while, Maggy."

Maggy looked him up and down and said, "Well, I don't know if I'll like living way out in the country," in a sort of a disapproving way.

I shook hands with her and she looked me up and down in the same way she had John and said, "You're not as pretty as Suzy."

Now, this is true, but it wasn't very tactful. Suzy is pretty and fluffy and she has curly blond hair, and I'm tall and skinny and my hair is sort of mousy and doesn't have any curl at all and I cut off my braids when I went back to school this autumn and I wish I hadn't. I know all of this about myself, but I still got kind of red and unhappy when Maggy said that about Suzy and me.

Uncle Douglas said quickly, "Remember the story of the ugly duckling, Maggy? Vicky's going to be the swan of you all. Someday I'm going to paint her."

I could see that Maggy didn't like that very much, because she flounced over to Suzy, saying, "C'mon, let's go up to our room and play." Even when she flounced she was graceful, sort of like a butterfly, and if you hadn't known she wasn't Aunt Elena's daughter or any relation at all you would have thought Aunt Elena was her mother, because Maggy has the same shiny soft black hair and enormous dark eyes. Well, I guess that's really all that's alike, because under the flesh the bones are shaped differently. Aunt Elena's features are strong and definite, and her nose has a high bridge. And Maggy's face is soft and wistful, and her eyes are just a tiny bit almond-shaped.

She and Suzy started to dash upstairs and Mother called Suzy back down and told her to set the table first, and that from now on Maggy could help her.

"I don't know how," Maggy said flatly.

"Suzy will show you."

"Sure," Suzy said. "Come on, Maggy. How many tonight?"

"Count," Mother said automatically.

"Six of us," Suzy said, "and Maggy and Aunt Elena and Uncle Douglas is . . . is . . . "

"Seventeen," Rob said.

"Nine," Suzy said. "So we'll have to put the leaves in the table."

John went to get the leaves, because they're quite heavy and there was a frantic scratching and a shrill barking, and Rochester bounded to the door, and we realized that Colette had been left out.

"I'll let her in," I said. "I'll be back in just a minute." Usually, just before dinner is the nicest time of day, but this evening I suddenly wanted to be alone for a few minutes. Was it just because Maggy had reminded me that I am plain? Mother says that I'm getting very broody, and part of it is my age, and most of it is just me.

I walked slowly around the house, with Colette prancing about me. It was nearly dark and lights were on in almost all the windows of the house and rectangles of light poured out onto the lawn. There were still a few leftover summer noises—a frog or an insect—and the air was clear and cold, and finally I had to run to keep warm and Colette began yipping and nipping at my heels in excitement, thinking I was playing a game just especially for her.

Then there came the sound of the piano, coming clear and beautiful out into the night, and I knew that Aunt Elena must be in the living room, playing. When she's with us she often sits at the piano and plays and plays and plays, but somehow I hadn't expected her to this time, and it made me feel more the crying kind of unhappy than I'd felt since the phone call. It wasn't that she was playing anything sad or anything—mostly it was Bach, I think— but just having her sit there at the piano, playing, and knowing that Uncle Hal would never hear her again made me want to go find Mother and put my head against her and howl.

I stayed out, listening for a moment, and when I went back in the house things had calmed down considerably. Aunt Elena was still at the piano; Suzy and Maggy must have gone upstairs; Rob and Uncle Douglas were watching television in the study; and John and Mother were talking while Mother made the salad.

"Vicky," Mother said, "tell Rob he hasn't put the napkins on the table yet and to come do it as soon as there's an ad on." Putting on the napkins and the table mats, when we don't use a tablecloth, is Rob's part of setting the table. Suzy does the silver and I do the china and glasses.

I went in to tell Rob, and when he'd gone into the kitchen to do his job I sat down on the arm of Uncle Douglas's chair.

"Turn that thing down, Vicky," he said. "It's blasting my ears off."

I turned down the volume and then went and sat by Uncle Douglas again. "What's on your mind, young lady?" he asked me.

I did have something on my mind; I did want to talk to him; how did he always know? "Uncle Douglas," I said, "why is it that John can show Aunt Elena he's sorry about Uncle Hal and I can't, and I'm so terribly, terribly sorry?"

Uncle Douglas put his arm around me and his beard rubbed gently against my cheek. "Aunt Elena knows you're sorry, dear."

"But why does John know what to say, and how to say it, and all I can do is act stupid, as though it didn't matter?"

"Just because it matters too much. Have you ever heard of empathy?"

I shook my head.

"John can show Aunt Elena how sorry he is because he has a scientific mind and he can see what has happened from the outside. All good scientists have to know how to be observers. He can be deeply upset about Uncle Hal and deeply sorry for Aunt Elena, but he can be objective about it. You can't."

"Why?"

"Because you have an artistic temperament, Vicky, and I've never seen you be objective about anything yet. When you think about Aunt Elena and how she must be feeling right now, it is for

the moment as though you *were* Aunt Elena; you get right inside her suffering, and it becomes your suffering too. That's empathy, and it's something all artists are afflicted with."

"Are you?"

"Sure. But I'm older than you are and I can cope with it better."

"But, Uncle Douglas, I'm not artistic. I haven't any talent for anything."

Uncle Douglas patted me again. "Don't worry, duckling. That will come too."

Uncle Douglas can always make me feel more than I am, as though I were really somebody. It's one of the very nicest things about him.

Rob came in just then and turned the volume up on the TV again, so I kissed Uncle Douglas and went back out to the kitchen because I didn't feel like watching cartoons.

After a while Daddy came home and Mother told me to go up and tell Suzy and Maggy to wash their hands and get ready for dinner. I went into the bathroom with them to wash my hands too. Suzy and Maggy were kind of giggling together while they washed up, as though they were sharing a secret they weren't going to let me in on, but after she'd dried her hands Maggy turned to me and her eyes seemed to grow very dark and big and she said, "My father's plane exploded yesterday."

"Yes," I said. I thought I ought to say something else, but I didn't know what else to say. You can't just politely say "I'm sorry," as though it were one of Rob's toy airplanes.

"If he hadn't died he was going to take me to the ocean for two weeks and I did want to go."

Now I could say, "I'm sorry."

"People ought to be sorry for me," Maggy said. "I'm an orphan."

"I'm sorry for you," Suzy said earnestly. "I'm terribly sorry for you, Maggy."

"So you'll be nice to me, won't you?" Maggy asked.

"Of course!"

I *was* sorry for her; with my mind I was sorry for her, but I wasn't feeling any empathy. And that was peculiar: here was Maggy, almost my age, only a couple of years younger, and her mother and father were both dead, and I couldn't think of anything more horrible in the world; and Aunt Elena was a grownup, so of course I couldn't feel about her the way I could about another girl. But it was Aunt Elena I ached over, and for Maggy I could feel only a strange bewilderment.

Mother called us down for dinner then, and after dinner Aunt Elena and Uncle Douglas left. The funeral was to be the next day, and Mother and Daddy were going down in the morning.

Bedtime was even stranger than it had been the night before. Mother read to us in Suzy's and my room, only now it wasn't Suzy's and my room, it was Suzy and Maggy's room. Suzy and Maggy giggled together while Mother read, and when I told them to be quiet so the rest of us could hear, Maggy said, "My, but she's bossy."

Suzy said, "I should think you'd be ashamed of yourself, Victoria Austin."

Rob said, "What for?"

And John said, "For crying out loud, all of you kids shut up."

Mother didn't say anything. She looked around at us with sort of a quizzical look on her face and went on reading.

Rob went to sleep right away; he always does. I was allowed to read till nine, but even after I turned out the light I couldn't sleep—partly, of course, because I'm older, but also, I wasn't used to being in John's bed. John has a big double bed, and Rob's, which is across the foot of it, is much, much smaller.

Rob has allergies and he often snores in the autumn, and he snored that night and it was a cold night again and he burrowed down under the covers and only a tuft of light brown hair showed and his snores sounded contented and comfortable. I could see him because we always have a night light on in the bathroom all night, and it makes just enough light come into our bedrooms so you can see a little.

I was just about to settle myself and try to go to sleep when John tiptoed in. He had on blue jeans and his heavy red jacket, and he came over to the bed and whispered, "Get dressed in something warm—you know, jeans or slacks—and come on down," and disappeared.

I got up and dressed and went down the back stairs into the kitchen and Mother was standing there in her polo coat and she said, "Get your jacket, Vicky. I thought maybe you and John and I might take some blankets and just go sit outside and watch the sky."

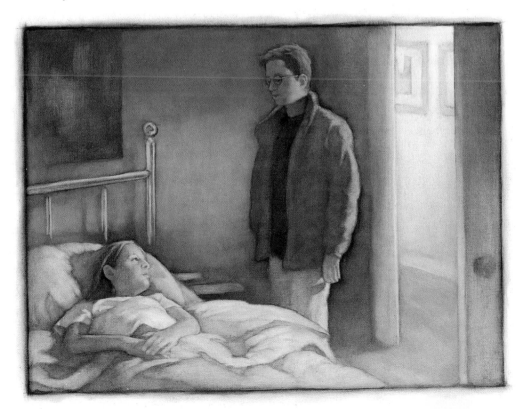

"Can we go up Hawk?" John asked, "and watch from the top of the ski trails?"

Mother hesitated. "Let me check with Daddy."

Daddy was in the study reading an article in a medical magazine, and he said to go on, he wasn't expecting any calls, but we'd better not stay more than half an hour; it was too cold, anyhow.

So we got in the station wagon, with Colette in my lap and Mr. Rochester in back sitting on the three army blankets we'd brought, and drove to Hawk. Hawk is a beautiful mountain with ski trails and picnic places, and from the fire lookout you can see five states, and we love to go there. When we got out of the car Colette dashed out and barked madly and rushed around in circles the way she always does, and Mr. Rochester bounded around, and Mother and John spread one of the blankets out on the grass and we sat down on it and put one of the other blankets about our shoulders and the other one over our laps. Mother sat in the middle and both of us sat as close to her as we possibly could. The sky would probably have been just as beautiful if we'd sat on the north lawn at home, but we could have seen the lights of the village, and up on the mountain it seemed as though we were miles and miles from everywhere. The sky was enormous and terribly high. It's a funny thing: the colder it gets, the farther away the sky seems and the farther off the stars look. The sky was so thick with them it was almost as though it had been snowing stars, and down below us there was a white fog, so it seemed as though we were looking out over a great lake. The Milky Way was a river of light, and John began pointing out the constellations, and I found the Big Dipper and the North Star and Cassiopeia's Chair and Scorpio and Sagittarius. Sagittarius is my favorite because it's my sign of the zodiac and I like the idea of aiming for the stars.

Mother said, "I know you're both very upset about Uncle Hal and Maggy's father. We all are. I thought maybe if we came and looked at the stars it would help us to talk about it a little."

Just then a shooting star flashed across the sky, and John said, "There's a shooting star and I don't know what to wish. I want to wish it back to before yesterday and that none of this would have happened, but I know it wouldn't work."

I said, "Mother, I don't understand it," and I began to shiver.

Mother said, "Sometimes it's very hard to see the hand of God instead of the blind finger of Chance. That's why I wanted to come out where we could see the stars."

"I talked to Aunt Elena for a while," John said, in a strained sort of voice, "when everybody else was busy. We took Mr. Rochester and Colette for a walk." Mr. Rochester came up to us then and lay down beside me with a thud, putting his heavy head across my knees. Colette was already cuddled up in Mother's lap. I looked toward John, and the lenses of his glasses glimmered in the starlight. "She said that she and Uncle Hal knew that they were living on borrowed time," John said. "They'd always hoped it would be longer than it was, but the way their lives were, they only lived together in snatches, anyhow. And she said she was grateful for every moment she'd ever had with him, and, even if it was all over, she wouldn't trade places with anybody in the world."

"She said that to you, John?" Mother asked.

"Yes," John said, and then another star shot across the sky, this time with a shower of sparks. We sat there, close, close, and it was as though we could feel the love we had for one another moving through our bodies, moving from me through Mother, from Mother to John, and back again. I could feel the love filling me, love for Mother and John, and for Daddy and Suzy and Rob too. And I prayed, "Oh, God, keep us together, please keep us together, please keep us safe and well and together."

It was as though our thoughts were traveling to one another, too, because John said, "Oh, Mother, why do things have to change and be different!" He sounded quite violent. "I like us exactly the way we are, our family. Why do people have to die, and people grow up and get married, and everybody grow away from each other? I wish we could just go on being exactly the way we are!"

"But we can't," Mother said. "We can't stop on the road of Time. We have to keep on going. And growing up is all part of it, the exciting and wonderful business of being alive. We can't understand it, any of us, any more than we can understand why Uncle Hal and Maggy's father had to die. But being alive is a gift, the most wonderful and exciting gift in the world. And there'll undoubtedly be many other moments when you'll feel this same way, John, when you're grown up and have children of your own."

"I don't understand about anything," John said. "I don't understand about people dying, and I don't understand about families, about people being as close as we are, and then everybody growing up, and not having Rob a baby anymore, and having to go off and live completely different lives."

"But look how close Grandfather and I still are," Mother said.

John shook his head. "I know. But it isn't the same thing. It's not like when you were little."

"No," Mother said. "But if I'd never grown up and met Daddy and married him you wouldn't be here, or Vicky or Suzy or Rob, and we wouldn't be sitting up here on Hawk Mountain shivering and looking at the stars. And we must have been here at least half an hour. Time to go home."

We went home and then we just stood outside for a while. The moon was sailing high now, and the sky was clear above the black pines at the horizon, with Northern Lights, which we hadn't seen up on Hawk at all, sending occasional rays darting high up into the sky. Daddy had heard us drive up, and he came out and stood with us, his arm about Mother. I'd never seen such a startlingly brilliant night, the fields and mountains washed in a flood of light. The shadows of trees and sunflowers were sharply black and stretched long and thin across the lawn. It was so beautiful that for the moment the beauty was all that mattered; it wasn't important that there were things we would never understand.

About the Author
Madeleine L'Engle

Madeleine L'Engle has some advice for people of any age who want to write. "There are three things that are important: First, if you want to write, you need to keep an honest, unpublishable journal

that nobody reads, nobody but you. Where you just put down what you think about life, what you think about things, what you think is fair, and what you think is unfair. And second, you need to read. You can't be a writer if you're not a reader. It's the writers who teach us how to write. The third thing is to write. Just write a little bit every day. Even if it's for only half an hour—write, write, write."

School was sometimes difficult for Ms. L'Engle. A weakness in her leg caused others to think she had physical problems; some thought this meant she was also not intelligent. When she was declared the winner in a poetry contest, her homeroom teacher stated, "Madeleine isn't bright. She couldn't have written that poem; she must have copied it." Ms. L'Engle remembers how "my mother had to go to school with the mass of poems, novels, and stories I'd written, and they finally had to allow that I probably had written the winning poem."

Perhaps Ms. L'Engle's best-known book is *A Wrinkle in Time*. Turned down by over forty publishers before it was finally accepted, *A Wrinkle in Time* won the Newbery Medal and the Lewis Carroll Shelf Award, and it was a runner-up for the Hans Christian Andersen Award. Her Austin family books have also been very popular. *Meet the Austins* and *A Ring of Endless Light* were both named Notable Books by the American Library Association.

Reader Response

Open for Discussion

Vicky is confused by the crisis that has gripped the Austin household. Imagine that you are her best friend. What would you say to comfort her?

Comprehension Check

1. Vicky remembers a telephone call from the night before. Who was calling? What was the call about? Use evidence from the story to support your answer.

2. At what point in the story does Vicky feel like crying? Why? Use details from the story in your answer.

3. When Uncle Douglas says that Vicky has an "artistic temperament," what does he mean? Support your answer with information from the story.

4. How do the **characters** John and Vicky differ from each other? Use details from the story in your answer. (Character)

5. Who is Margaret Hamilton? How does Vicky react to this **character?** Support your answer with story details. (Character)

Test Prep

Look Back and Write

The story ends with the words "there were things we would never understand." What are those things? Look back at pages 120–124. Use evidence from these pages to support your answer.

Going Through
Phases

by Niki Walker

The Moon may be bright in our night sky, but it does not make its own light. Moonlight is simply sunlight that has been **reflected**, or bounced, off the Moon's surface. The Moon does not make light or heat the way a star does because it is mainly made of rock. Stars, such as the Sun, are made up of burning gases.

From far out in space, the Moon always looks the same, as shown by this inner circle of Moons.

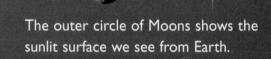

The outer circle of Moons shows the sunlit surface we see from Earth.

Changing Shapes

During each month, the Moon seems to change shape several times. The Moon does not actually change, however. As it revolves, our view of it changes, and we can see different parts of its sunlit surface. The amount of Moon that we see is called a **phase**.

2. A small **crescent** moon is seen next. As the Moon grows larger, it is described as **waxing.**

3. We see a half-moon at the **first-quarter** phase. The Moon has traveled one-quarter of its orbit.

1. The lunar cycle starts with the dark **new moon.** Its sunlit side is facing away from Earth.

4. After the first-quarter phase, the Moon is called **gibbous,** which means "humpbacked." Can you guess why?

The Lunar Month

In ancient times, people watched the phases of the Moon to keep track of time. They made a **lunar calendar** based on the changes of the Moon. It took one lunar month for the Moon to move through its phases and begin the cycle again. The word "month" comes from the word "moon."

8. The Moon is now a **waning crescent.** It is only a few days away from becoming a new moon again.

5. There is a full moon 14 days after the new moon. People say odd things happen at this time.

7. The Moon has traveled three-quarters of its orbit at the **third-quarter** phase.

6. The lit surface **wanes,** or grows smaller. The Moon is described as **waning gibbous.**

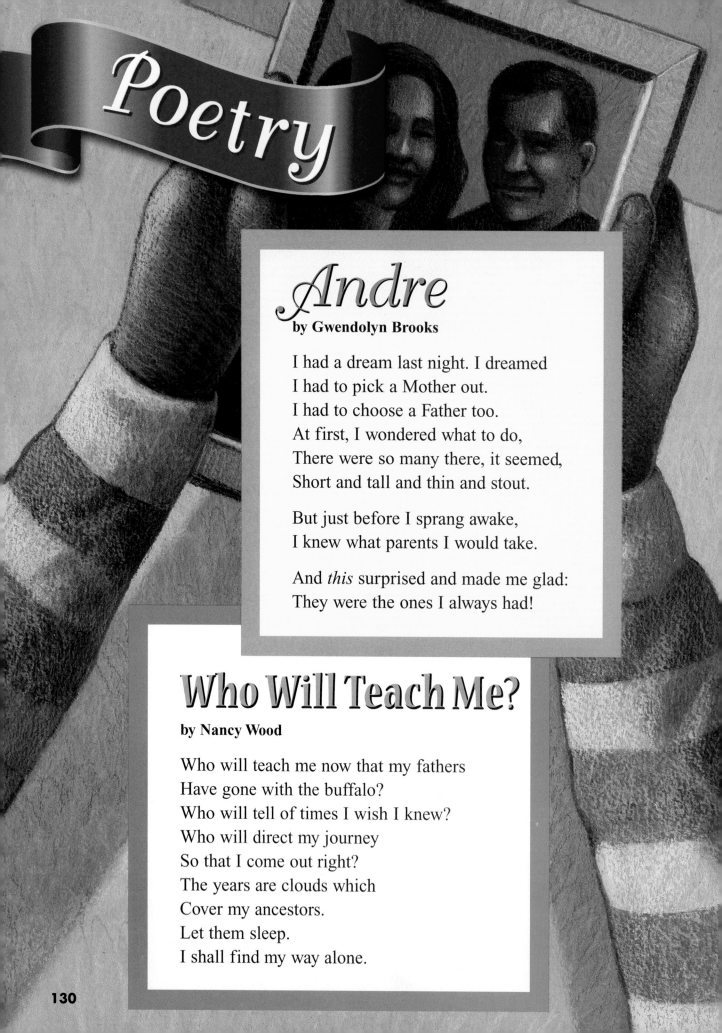

Poetry

Andre
by Gwendolyn Brooks

I had a dream last night. I dreamed
I had to pick a Mother out.
I had to choose a Father too.
At first, I wondered what to do,
There were so many there, it seemed,
Short and tall and thin and stout.

But just before I sprang awake,
I knew what parents I would take.

And *this* surprised and made me glad:
They were the ones I always had!

Who Will Teach Me?
by Nancy Wood

Who will teach me now that my fathers
Have gone with the buffalo?
Who will tell of times I wish I knew?
Who will direct my journey
So that I come out right?
The years are clouds which
Cover my ancestors.
Let them sleep.
I shall find my way alone.

Goodness

by Benny Andersen
translated by Alexander Taylor

I've always tried to be good
it's very demanding
I'm a real hound for
      doing something for someone
hold coats
   doors
      seats
get someone a job
   or something
open up my arms
let someone have his cry on my shirt
but when I get my chance
I freeze completely
some kind of shyness maybe
I urge myself—do it
fling your arms wide
but it's difficult to sacrifice yourself
      when somebody's watching
so hard to be good
      for more than a few minutes
like holding your breath
however with daily practice
I have worked up to a whole hour
if nobody disturbs me
I sit all alone
with my watch in front of me
spreading my arms
   again and again
no trouble at all
I am certainly best
when I'm all alone.

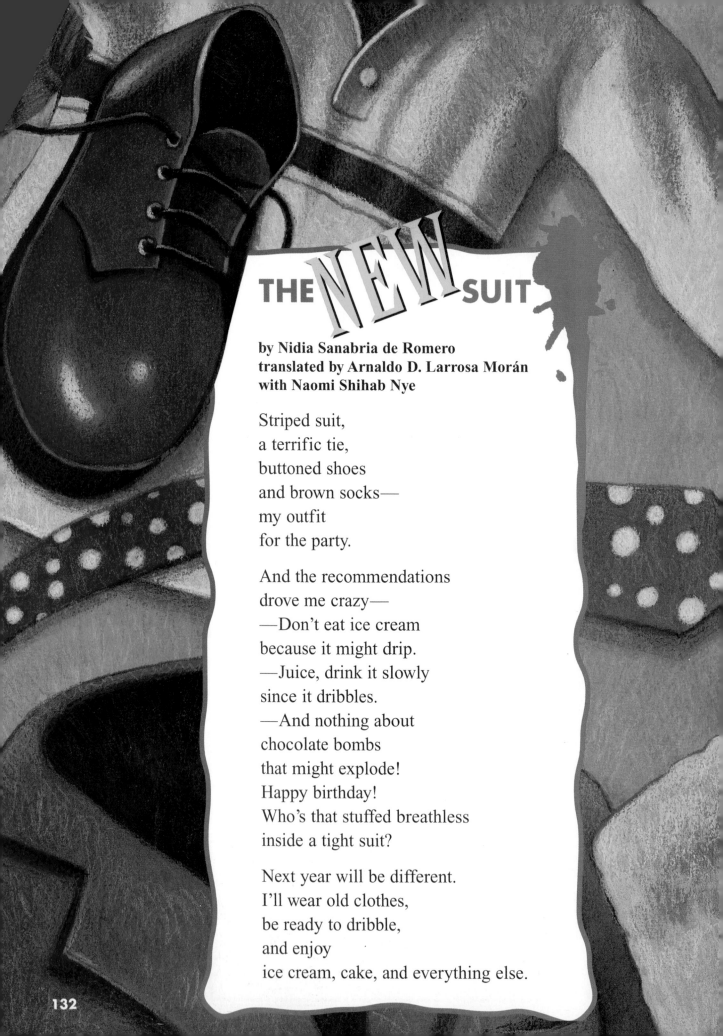

THE NEW SUIT

by Nidia Sanabria de Romero
translated by Arnaldo D. Larrosa Morán
with Naomi Shihab Nye

Striped suit,
a terrific tie,
buttoned shoes
and brown socks—
my outfit
for the party.

And the recommendations
drove me crazy—
—Don't eat ice cream
because it might drip.
—Juice, drink it slowly
since it dribbles.
—And nothing about
chocolate bombs
that might explode!
Happy birthday!
Who's that stuffed breathless
inside a tight suit?

Next year will be different.
I'll wear old clothes,
be ready to dribble,
and enjoy
ice cream, cake, and everything else.

Almost
Ready:

by Arnold Adoff

I
am
going
to
her
birth-
day
party

as	as	as	as	as
this	soon	soon	soon	soon
cool	as	as	as	as
and	I	I	I	I
in-	find	find	find	find
control	my	my	my	my
young	new	hip	deep	right
dude:	shirt,	shoes,	voice,	mask.

Wrap-Up

How do our relationships with others help us learn about ourselves?

Become a Character

Discuss Changes

"Become" a main character from a selection to learn about yourself.

1. **Choose** a main character from a selection in the unit.

2. **Describe** to a partner how your character's attitudes toward people change during the story. "Become" the character as you speak. Then listen to your partner talk about a character.

3. **Decide** if the events that caused your character to change would have changed you in a similar way. Tell your opinion to your partner.

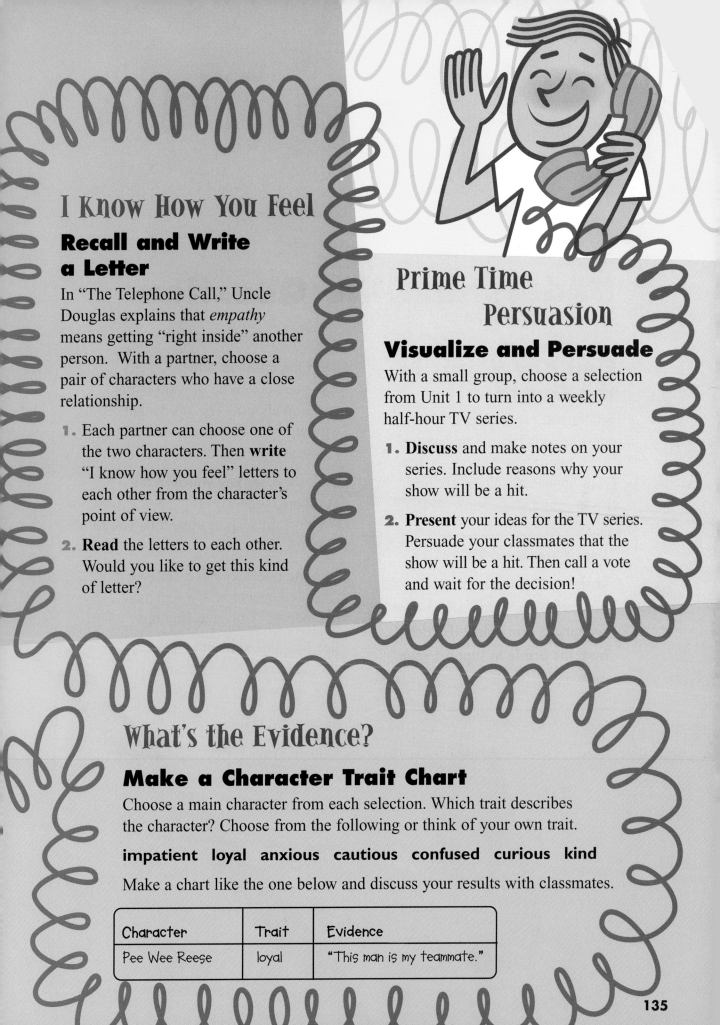

I Know How You Feel

Recall and Write a Letter

In "The Telephone Call," Uncle Douglas explains that *empathy* means getting "right inside" another person. With a partner, choose a pair of characters who have a close relationship.

1. Each partner can choose one of the two characters. Then **write** "I know how you feel" letters to each other from the character's point of view.

2. **Read** the letters to each other. Would you like to get this kind of letter?

Prime Time Persuasion

Visualize and Persuade

With a small group, choose a selection from Unit 1 to turn into a weekly half-hour TV series.

1. **Discuss** and make notes on your series. Include reasons why your show will be a hit.

2. **Present** your ideas for the TV series. Persuade your classmates that the show will be a hit. Then call a vote and wait for the decision!

What's the Evidence?

Make a Character Trait Chart

Choose a main character from each selection. Which trait describes the character? Choose from the following or think of your own trait.

impatient loyal anxious cautious confused curious kind

Make a chart like the one below and discuss your results with classmates.

Character	Trait	Evidence
Pee Wee Reese	loyal	"This man is my teammate."

Test Talk

Understand the Question

Find Key Words in the Question

Before you can answer a test question, you have to understand it. A test about "Swimming for the Gold," pages 41–43, might have this question.

Test Question 1

Based on the diagram on page 43, how are an airplane wing and a swimmer's arm alike? Use details from the article to support your answer.

Read the question slowly.
Ask yourself "Who or what is this question about?" The words that tell *who* or *what* the question is about are key words.

Look for other key words in the question.
A key word such as *alike* tells you to look for similarities.

Turn the question into a statement.
Use the key words in a sentence that begins "I need to find out . . ."

See how one student makes sure she understands the question.

I've read the question. What is it about? Well, it's talking about a swimmer's arm and an airplane wing. **Swimmer's arm** and **airplane wing**—those must be key words.

Okay, I'm going to read the question again. There's the key word **how,** and there's the key word **alike.** I need to find out how an airplane wing is like a swimmer's arm.

Try it!

Now use what you learned to understand these test questions about "Swimming for the Gold," pages 41–43.

Test Question 2

How can you use your face, hands, and arms to reduce drag when you swim the crawl?

Test Question 3

Why do competitive swimmers streamline their bodies?

Ⓐ to increase the amount of drag

Ⓑ to improve their appearance

Ⓒ to reduce the resistance of the water

Ⓓ to maintain a horizontal body position

The Living Earth

What can we learn from observing the world around us?

Skill Lesson

Making Judgments

- **Making a judgment** means forming an opinion about someone or something.

- When you make a judgment, you think about information the author provides as well as your own experiences and beliefs.

- As you read, look for evidence to support your judgments. You may need to change your judgment based on new information.

- When an author expresses a judgment about someone or something, test the author's judgment by looking for evidence to support it.

Read "The Truth About Wolves" from *Wolves* by Seymour Simon.

Write About It

1. In your own words, state the author's judgment about wolves. List facts the author provides to support his judgment.

2. Explain whether or not you agree with the author's judgment. Consider your own experiences and the accuracy and completeness of the author's information.

THE TRUTH ABOUT WOLVES
by Seymour Simon

Imagine snow falling silently in the great woodlands of North America. The only sounds are from the trees creaking and tossing in the wind. Suddenly the quiet is broken by the eerie howling of a wolf. And all the frightening stories and legends that you've heard about the treacherous and sly wolf and the evil werewolf begin to race through your mind.

But what is this animal of our imaginations truly like? Are wolves savage and destructive hunters of people and livestock? Or are they one of nature's most misunderstood creatures? It is possible that people don't like wolves because they don't know very much about them. For example, there is no record of a healthy wolf ever trying to kill a human in North America. Perhaps by learning about the wolf and how it lives in the natural world, we can begin to tell the difference between the real animal and the fables we've created.

In many ways, wolves are like dogs and lions; yet wolves have a bad reputation, unlike dogs and lions. Dogs are our "best friends," but all the dogs in the world are descended from wolves that were domesticated more than ten thousand years ago. And most of the things people like about dogs are also true about wolves.

Like dogs, wolves are very loyal to other wolves in their family. Wolves raised by people become loyal to those people as well. Dogs are friendly and intelligent, and these traits too come from wolves. Wolves in a pack are playful with each other. They are among the most intelligent animals in nature.

Like lions, wolves are marvelous hunters that work together in groups to catch their prey. Yet lions are called the "kings of the jungle," while wolves are described in many nursery tales as "sly and cowardly." It seems strange that people love dogs and admire lions but dislike wolves.

LOOK AHEAD

In the autobiography that follows, "A Trouble-Making Crow," Jean Craighead George expresses a judgment about crows. Do you agree with her, based on the evidence she presents?

Vocabulary

Words to Know

aggressive	**attributes**	**outwit**
persisted	**secretive**	**tolerated**
vengeance		

When you read, you may come across a word that you don't know. To figure out the meaning of an unfamiliar word, look for clues in the words and sentences around it. A clue might be found in an explanation given before or after the unknown word.

Read the paragraph below. Notice how an explanation of *attributes* helps you understand what it means.

The Scarecrow

At first Mr. Hill <u>tolerated</u> the crows in his garden, thinking they would eventually move on. But no, the <u>aggressive</u> birds had no intention of leaving. And with all the tasty vegetables around, who could blame them? Mr. Hill didn't want revenge or <u>vengeance</u>. He simply wanted the birds to leave. Shouting didn't work, nor did waving his arms. Nothing seemed to work, but Mr. Hill <u>persisted</u>. He simply wouldn't give up, for determination was one of his best <u>attributes</u>, or characteristics. He decided he would <u>outwit</u> those crows with the help of something just as clever and <u>secretive</u>. Soon a cat was prowling Mr. Hill's garden.

Talk About It

Tell a classmate a story about a crow. Include some vocabulary words.

A Trouble-Making Crow

from *The Tarantula in My Purse* • by Jean Craighead George

Jean Craighead George lives in rural
New York State. Her three children are
Craig, Twig, and Luke. The George
family often takes in wild animals
in need of aid. Some of the animals
the family has helped are a robin
named Pete and four crows
named Bituminous, Light Foot,
New York, and Crowbar.

he year Luke was one year old, we moved to Chappaqua, New York, and bought our first house. The house sits on a wooded hillside. Through the leafless trees in winter we see the neighbors. In summer we seem to be alone. Uphill from the house there is a spring where salamanders and frogs dwell. The hill is steep and makes for wild sledding in winter. Downhill is a swamp and a shallow lake with a deer woods beyond.

With us on our arrival in our new home came New York and three salamanders. New York walked in the front door and out the back and flew off to explore the neighborhood. Late in the afternoon he settled himself in hemlocks in the backyard. The next day, the first day of school, he followed us down the hill to the bus stop and sat on the rail fence.

At the bus stop were Sis Melvin and Tom and Merry, among others. This was the first day of school for Tom as well as for Craig. Merry Melvin was in her stroller, and Luke was in my backpack. Seven-year-old Twig sat on the fence with New York. Sis glanced from her to the crow. She tapped my shoulder.

"See that big black bird?" she whispered. "It just sits there on the fence. Do you suppose something's wrong with it?"

"That's New York, our pet crow," I said. "He likes people."

"I see," she answered, and the conversation stopped for several minutes.

That was the beginning of a friendship that has lasted to this day.

I went home and unpacked my typewriter and put it in the winterized sunporch at the rear of the house. It was the perfect place for me to work. The windows and glass door looked out on the backyard and woods. It was also a place where the kids could almost always find me.

Craig came running into the porch one day in late autumn.

"Mom," he said, his voice filled with horror, "New York dives at little Hilde Black's eyes. She has to hit him."

I had read just enough about crows to know what that meant. Crows are vindictive. If a person hurts a crow, it will sometimes return the pain with vengeance. Hilde must have hurt him. "Eyes," I thought—he was diving at Hilde's eyes. A chill ran down my spine.

"New York has to go," I said urgently. "Help me catch him."

"Are you going to kill him?" Craig cried.

"I may have to."

"No, Mom, no. He's a bird. He doesn't know he's bad."

"People come first," I said. "How would you feel if Hilde was blinded by our crow?"

His eyes widened as he understood the seriousness of New York's vengeance.

"I don't want to kill him," I said. "I want to take him far away and let him go—far from Hilde."

"Will he dive at anyone else's eyes?"

"No. Hilde must have kicked him or hurt him somehow, and he's taking it out on her. He won't forget. Crows are like that."

Craig ran into the yard to find New York, and I went to the cellar for an animal carrying case.

"I've got him," I heard Craig call as I came out the door.

I walked slowly toward them, trying to act as if I had nothing more serious in mind than weeding the garden.

New York saw right through us. He gave out a frantic cry and took off for the top of the ash tree. We followed below, calling him lovingly and cheerfully. "Haw," he called, and flew into the woods to slink off along the tree limbs. We knew we would never get him by pretending to be dear old friends, so we went inside to make supper.

"Mom," Craig called, "New York's back." I knew better than to let the bird see me, but was so worried about Hilde, I ran outside anyway. With a raucous caw, New York flew from the picnic table to the sunporch roof. He rasped out short caws of distress and pumped his head up and down. He was telling all crowdom that he knew what was going on.

That night three silent and unhappy children went to bed. "New York has to go," I said. "We can't let him hurt Hilde." "We know."

In the darkness of night I approached New York on his roost in the ash tree. He could not see to fly. I threw a beach towel over him and put him in the carrying case, a feat I don't care to repeat.

The next day Twig and Craig said their heartbreaking farewells to New York and then went out the door to catch the school bus. Craig paused and looked back at me.

"It's okay, Mom," he said.

"Thank you" was all I could answer.

I wiped a tear, put Luke in his car seat, and drove north on the Taconic Parkway to James Baird Park.

I opened the door of the carrier and a wild bird, not our friendly New York, took off into the woods. His eyes were hard and glistening and his feathers were pressed to his body. He would never forgive me for catching him in a towel, any more than he would forgive little Hilde for whatever she had done.

We did not feel bad about removing New York to distant woods. Dr. Kalmbach, the U.S. Department of Agriculture's crow expert, wrote in a scientific paper, "Crows are vindictive." I was shocked to read that. My father, a scientist, had taught my brothers and me not to anthropomorphize—that is, not to read human emotions and attributes into animals. They did not hate, love, envy, or even feel happy. So what was this vindictiveness, a very complex human emotion that Dr. Kalmbach was seeing in a crow?

It was this: Dr. Kalmbach kept a pet crow, the better to understand the bird that farmers were at war with for stealing corn and other crops. Next door to him lived a man who raised cabbages and showed them at the state fair. Every day he would proudly tend them with his yappy dog following at his heels.

One day amidst crow caws and dog yaps, the neighbor stormed into Dr. Kalmbach's office.

"Your crow is tearing the leaves off my prize cabbages," he said angrily. "Stop him or I'll shoot him."

To avoid trouble, Dr. Kalmbach called his crow down from the maple tree between the two yards and spanked him with a cabbage leaf.

"No cabbages, no cabbages," he snapped. He did not go so far as to think the bird knew English, but he did know that crows discipline crows and know when they have been punished. I knew what he was talking about. Once, Luke and I saw a group of crows come through the woods chasing a fellow crow. They dove at him, yelled at him, and hit him with their wings. He tumbled, fell, and escaped into the underbrush. When he didn't come out, they flew off.

Dr. Kalmbach's crow seemed to understand that he had been disciplined. He flew to a limb in the maple tree between the two yards and drooped his wings and head. For two days he sulked, but he did not tear the cabbage leaves.

On the third day Dr. Kalmbach heard the neighbor's dog yapping, and the unmistakable sound of cabbage leaves being torn asunder. He ran outside. His crow was holding a piece of meat in his feet and flying just above the nose of the little dog, who ran down one cabbage row and up the next tearing the cabbages asunder.

147

A Talking Crow

Several years after Light Foot, Bituminous, and then New York came and went, Crowbar came into our lives.

Craig found him on the ground in a spruce grove. A violent windstorm had knocked bird and nest out of a tree. Craig looked around for his parents, saw none, and tucked the almost-naked nestling into his shirt and carried him home.

"His name's Crowbar," he said as he put him on the kitchen table. The little crow was somewhat younger than New York had been when we brought him home, and so we knew this bird was going to be more deeply imprinted on us. He would indeed be a member of the family.

The scrappy little crow looked at us, rolled to his back, and clawed the air as if to tear us to pieces. He screamed like an attacking warrior.

I went to the refrigerator, took out a cold cheeseburger, and stuffed a bite in his mouth, pressing it with my finger to make sure he swallowed. He did, and instantly changed his tune. He blinked his pale-blue eyes and got to his feet. Taking a wide stance to keep from falling over, he fluttered his stubby wings. In bird talk this means, "I am a helpless baby bird—feed me." We fed him until he couldn't open his beak.

At the end of the day we had a pet crow. Crows are smart. They know a good thing when they see it.

But it was not just the food. He was young and craved our attention. He cuddled against Luke, begged until Craig petted his head and chin, and dropped spoons and forks off the kitchen table until someone talked to him. He was ours, and he let us know just what that meant.

He did concede one thing to his heredity, however: He slept in the apple tree outside the kitchen window. This greatly pleased me. Although a red fox named Fulva; two mink, Vison and Mustelid; and three skunks had trained themselves to use a litter box while in the house, Crowbar, New York, and our other crows had no inclination to do so. Fortunately they spent most of their time outside, and when they did come in, they treated the house like their nest and kept it clean.

By autumn Crowbar was Crowbar George to Twig, Craig, and Luke. He would wake them at dawn by rapping on their windows with his beak. The three would come downstairs and set the table, including a plate for Crowbar. They would scramble the eggs, serve them up, and open the window. Crowbar would fly to his plate and gulp his food like the young gluttonous crow that he was.

Then he would fly out the window to the apple tree and wait until Twig, Craig, and now Luke came out the door and down the front steps on their way to school. He would drop to the ground and walk beside them all the way down the hill to the school bus stop. Like New York he would sit on the rail fence. When the bus came, he would fly back to the kitchen window, and I would know my children were safely on their way to school. Other mothers had to go down to the bus stop and wait. I sent a crow.

Meanwhile I was reading every scientific paper about crows that I could get my hands on. I read that crows are hard to study because they're so smart. They easily elude and outwit the observer. They hide. They sneak through tree limbs. They count. A farmer learned that if he went crow hunting in the woods, he would not see a crow. They knew about guns. To foil them, the farmer took a friend into the woods with him. The farmer hid and the friend walked out across the fields and away. The crows did not make an appearance until the farmer left.

Crows, I also read, have a language. They communicate with each other. Three caws are an identification—"I'm so-and-so crow." Five desperately given caws mean there is an enemy around—a hawk, an owl, a man with a gun. Many caws given with passion and fury say, "Come—mob the owl." The crow fact that amazed me most, however, was that they can detect poisoned food and warn each other not to eat it.

They can recognize death in any form it takes. In an experiment by Dr. Kalmbach, two farmers who shot some crows in their cornfield found they could never again get close enough to the crows to shoot. Their wives could, however. When they came to the fields, the crows went right on eating within ten feet of them. The farmers decided that the crows recognized them because they wore pants. They put on skirts and aprons and went out to shoot the crows. They still could not get within gunshot range. Putting their heads together once more, they figured the crows must see the guns and know they meant death. They disguised the guns in brooms and went out to the cornfields to kill the crows. Before they got within range the crows were gone.

It must be, wrote Dr. Kalmbach, that when a man picks up a gun, he takes on an aggressive attitude that the crows read. They flee.

Appended to one report on crows was this: "Crows can learn to talk as do parrots or myna birds."

With that we began Crowbar's English lessons.

"Hello, hello, hello," we said slowly and distinctly many times over. "Hello, hello, hello." This went on for days and weeks.

He did not speak. He looked at us intently, his throat feathers rising and falling. Then he would wipe his beak, a reaction to frustration.

"I give up," I said to Twig, and had no more than gotten the words out of my mouth than John Priori, who delivered the milk, came in the back door.

"Oh, good," he said. "You're in the kitchen. I thought I heard you up in the apple tree saying 'hello.'"

"It's Crowbar," we shouted. "Crowbar is talking." Twig and I ran outside to listen.

"Hello," said the clever bird. "Hello, hello, hello."

"Crowbar," Twig said slowly and thoughtfully, "is really the smartest person on the block."

Crowbar did not rest on his laurels. He soon figured out how to make use of that word.

The neighbors on our wooded hillside come outside in summer to picnic and cook on their grill. Most have moved to the suburbs from New York City and know little about the country, much less its wild membership. Crowbar discovered that if he alit on a food-laden table and said, "Hello," he terrified these people. A large black bird might be tolerated, but one that spoke English was too much. They ran into their houses and closed their doors. Crowbar then helped himself to the hamburgers, strawberry shortcake, cheese, and nuts. When he was stuffed, he flew back to his apple tree.

Twig and I were walking under his tree one day as he was returning from one of these picnics. He alit, cocked his eye, and said, "Hiya, Babe."

Because Crowbar was completely free, our new neighbors had no idea he was a pet. Soon the police began to get complaints about a bird that took the clothespins out of their laundry and dumped clean shirts and towels on the ground.

The officers would arrive and, finding only an ordinary crow sitting on a fence or flying off through the trees, they would peg the complainers as cranks and depart. The complaints persisted, however, and one policeman, a hunter and wise to the ways of crows, brought a BB gun to the scene.

As the officer rounded the house, gun in hand, Crowbar gave five frantic caws. Birds stopped singing; crows disappeared. The policeman stood in a silent world where nothing moved but a breeze-touched shirt that Crowbar had not yet released to the ground.

"That bird won't be back," he said to the complainer. "Crows see a gun and they're off—for good."

He left, smiling at his own cleverness. When the patrol car was out of sight, Crowbar dropped down to the wash line and dropped the breeze-touched shirt to the ground.

So much for knowing it all.

Crowbar Goes to the Bank

The sandbox was Crowbar's favorite spot. When Twig and Craig played in the sandbox with Luke, they dumped into the sand a bucket of glittering spoons, bottle caps, toy soldiers, coffee cans and lids. At the sight of the sparkle, Crowbar would materialize from the trees and join them. He walked around forts and castles, picking up bright treasures and carrying them to the apple tree.

One day as I was working at my desk, Twig came to the door of the sunporch, her hands on her hips.

"I'm not going to play with that crow anymore," she said. "He takes all my toys."

I smiled. Here was my Twig. She was seeing the human in Crowbar. But she did have a point, after all. It must be maddening when you are counting on shaping a castle turret with a spoon and a crow steals it.

"Why don't you slide down the slide?" I suggested. "Crows can't slide down slides. Their feet have pads that hold them fast to perches."

She went back to her brothers, and the next time I looked up the three were sliding down the slide.

Then down from the roof sailed Crowbar. He swept his black wings upward, then down, and alit on the top of the slide. We all stared. Would he slide? He stepped on the steeply slanted board—and was stuck.

Twig waved to me; I waved back to her. We had outwitted a crow, which we both knew was a very hard thing to do.

No sooner had we gone on with our businesses than Crowbar flew to the sandbox. He picked up a coffee-can lid, carried it to the top of the slide, stepped on it, and—zoom—we had a sliding crow.

Crowbar was indeed a character. In the morning when the children were in school, he would sit beside my foot when I was working at my typewriter and brood over it. He would lift his feathers and lean against my ankle as if it were some cherished object. Sometimes he would go into a trance and fall over.

Unaware that I was being used, I would pick him up and pet him. He would make soft noises, then hop to my desk and fly off with a paper clip. I would laugh, knowing I had been had—but I never learned. He repeated this game many times, and I always fell for it.

When school reopened after spring vacation, Crowbar began to disappear every day at noon. He would walk to the open door, fly to the ash tree, and sneak uphill into the woods.

For hours I would neither see nor hear him. I assumed he was resting quietly in some leafy tree, which birds do for longer periods than most people realize.

One day a little neighbor girl, Sally, came to my door.

"Mrs. George," she said, "I think Crowbar has enough money to buy a sports car."

"What do you mean?" I asked.

"He comes down to the middle school every day for lunch," she said. "We feed him sandwiches and throw him our milk money. He picks up the money and flies off with it. He must be very rich."

"The middle school," I said, and remembered the crow's-eye view of the ecosystem. Of course: while soaring above the trees, he had spotted the kids and their food and shiny money. I wondered what else Crowbar knew about our town. He probably knew about the baseball games and picnics, the people getting on and off the trains, and the town Dumpsters. But apparently most fascinating to him were the kids at the middle school eating sandwiches and flipping shiny coins into the air, and so it was to them he went at noon.

"We can't find where he hides his money," Sally went on. "Could you help us?"

"I'll try," I answered dubiously, "but crows are clever. He may be investing it in Wall Street."

She didn't laugh, so I answered more seriously. "I'll meet you on the playground tomorrow at noon, and we'll see what he's up to."

Crowbar was walking among the children when I arrived. Sally saw me and came running. Crowbar, who undoubtedly knew I was there, ignored me. A boy waved a coin and spun it in the air. When it sparkled to the ground, Crowbar hopped upon it and took it in his beak.

When he had a beakful of money, he skimmed low over the grass and laboriously climbed into a sugar maple tree that edged the playground. He looked as if he had stolen the crown jewels.

"See?" Sally said. "He hides his money, but we don't know where. He won't hide it while we're watching."

"He sure won't," I said. "Crows are very secretive. Other birds' nests are easy to find by following the parents when they are carrying food home to the young. But not crows.

"They won't go near their nests while you're watching. Those bright coins are kind of like Crowbar's nest. He doesn't want you to find them."

"Seems so," said Sally. "He waits till the bell rings and we have to go inside; then he flies away and we can't see where he goes."

The bell rang, Sally dashed off, and I sat down to see if I could outwait my friend. I could not. After half an hour I gave up and went home.

About a week later I came out of the bank, which is next to the middle school, and saw Crowbar flying low over the recreation field, laboriously carrying his load of quarters and dimes. I stepped back into the doorway. He flew over the fence and the parked cars, then swept up to the rainspout of the bank. He looked around and then deposited his money in the bank's rainspout.

There is something uncanny about crows.

New York gave me my first experience with this otherworldly attribute.

One afternoon the director of the Bronx Zoo and his wife, who were friends of my aunt and uncle, came to visit. Mrs. Tee Van was a very accomplished nature artist, and I

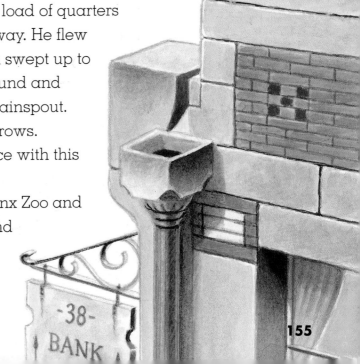

-38-
BANK

was flattered that she would come calling. The day before, I had
returned from a speaking engagement and had brought home
to Twig the hotel shampoo, soap, and shoe-shine rag. She had
put the shoe-shine rag in the dollhouse that stood on the porch.

We adults sat down in the living room to get acquainted.
The children and New York played on the porch in view of us.
At one point in the conversation Mrs. Tee Van looked out the
window and saw New York walking on the porch railing. She
smiled when she saw him.

"I had a pet crow when I was young," she said, and walked
to the window. "I adored him. He was so clever." She paused.
"Your crow's legs are so shiny. How do you manage that?"

Hardly had she spoken than New York flew to the dollhouse,
picked up the shoe-shine cloth, and walked with it in his beak
slowly along the porch railing.

Dr. Tee Van and I chuckled, but Mrs. Tee Van did not. She
turned to me, visibly upset by what seemed to be a crow
answering her question.

"We must go," she said. "That's just too uncanny."

"A funny coincidence," I said, forcing myself to laugh.

"No," she answered. "Crows are eerie. We have a lot
to learn."

A Crow Kidnapping

Crowbar stayed. Two and a half years had passed since he had joined the family. After Pete left, he strutted down to the bus stop on school days, kept me company, and flew to the middle school at noon to call on his moneyed friends.

One morning as the sun was coming up, I heard crows yelling from my trees and yard. I ran to the window. Thirty or forty of the big black birds, who were on migration, were gathered on limbs, lawn, and picnic table. They were directing their caws at Crowbar.

"You're a crow. You're a crow. Come with us," I was certain they were saying. Crows do not like to see their kind become pet crows.

I tried to pick out Crowbar from the mob, but could not. They all looked alike. This was embarrassing, since Crowbar would fly right to my shoulder when I got off the train. He could find me in a mass of humans, but I could not find him in a crowd of crows.

The kids awoke, and we hung out the windows watching the drama below.

"He's going to go away with them," said Luke when the chorus rose to a frantic pitch.

"Get the hamburger," Twig said, and she and Craig dashed downstairs. Before they returned, the sun had flooded the hillside with light and the crows had taken off. Sitting alone was Crowbar. We ran outside and fed him until he could eat no more.

"Crows do know a good thing when they see it," said Luke, glad the family crow had stayed.

The next morning the birds returned. Crows are very sensible migrants. None of this flying fifteen thousand miles from the Arctic to the tip of South America and then back again, as some birds do, or for that matter even from New York to Florida. Crows migrate only as far as their favorite winter roosting sites, which can be no more than twenty miles away.

The telephone rang the third morning of the crow visitation.

"What are all the crows doing here?" asked Art Buckley, who lived at the bottom of the hill. "I've never, in all the twenty years I've lived here, seen so many crows." Then he added, "They wake me up at five. What can we do about it?"

"Wait," I said. "They'll go away."

I was not sure about that. I had never had a massive gang of crows come to abduct a pet. What would happen if they all came to recognize a good thing when they saw it and stayed on too?

On the fifth day we heard a new note in the communal voice of the crows. It was an unmistakable jubilation. Excitement infused their cacophony. Craig sped down to the refrigerator for food.

He got back in time to see the crows take off. They beat their black taffeta wings and flew up over our trees and down the valley—and there was no more Crowbar.

Despite our tears, it was a beautiful ending to a wild-pet story.

About the Author
Jean Craighead George

Jean Craighead George grew up with two brothers (twins) who were also interested in animals and writing. While they were still in high school, her brothers wrote articles about falconry—the raising and training of certain kinds of hawks for hunting—for national magazines. Her brothers were largely responsible for bringing the sport of falconry to the United States.

Ms. George had her own special talent for writing. Her first books were written with her husband, John, but she later started writing on her own. Although biographies usually are about people, the Georges wrote a series of biographies about animals, mostly wild creatures that became family pets. The first animal biography they wrote was called *Vulpes, the Red Fox*. They learned firsthand what foxes were like when they adopted one as a young pup.

Ms. George also writes fiction. Her first novel, *My Side of the Mountain*, was a very successful story about a boy who lives off the land for a year. A hollowed-out tree becomes his house, and he has a falcon and a weasel for friends. *My Side of the Mountain* was named a Newbery Honor Book, an ALA Notable Book, and a Hans Christian Andersen Award Honor Book.

Reader Response

Open for Discussion

What surprises you most about the things that the crows do in the story? Why?

Comprehension Check

1. How does the story about Dr. Kalmbach's crow show that some crows are "vindictive"?

2. Where does Crowbar hide all of the coins? How does the author finally find out?

3. Why does the family have mixed feelings when Crowbar returns to the wild? Use details from the story to support your answer.

4. Do you agree with the author's **judgment** that outwitting a crow is a "very hard thing to do"? Why or why not? (Making Judgments)

5. Make a **judgment** about humans treating wild animals like pets. Defend your position with examples from the story. (Making Judgments)

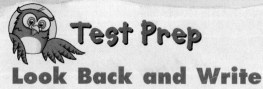

Test Prep
Look Back and Write

Explain why the author would agree with the following statement: *Crows are good at spotting danger.* Use information from pages 149–150 to support your answer.

Literature Connection

How to Read a Fable

1. Preview

- A fable is a story that teaches a lesson. The characters in a fable are often animals that think, talk, and act like human beings.

- Look over the illustration and the sentence in dark type. What lesson do you predict the crow might be showing us and why?

2. Read and Evaluate

- As you read, think about the lesson the fable is teaching. Decide on how the crow's actions help teach that lesson.

3. Think and Connect

Think about "A Trouble-Making Crow." Then think over your ideas on "The Crow and the Pitcher."

How do the birds in "A Trouble-Making Crow" and "The Crow and the Pitcher" help teach the lesson that "Necessity is the mother of invention"?

The Crow and the Pitcher

by Aesop

A crow, so thirsty that he could not even caw, came upon a pitcher which once had been full of water. But when he put his beak into the pitcher's mouth, he found that only a little water was left in it. Strain and strive as he might, he was not able to reach far enough down to get at it. He tried to break the pitcher, then to overturn it, but his strength was not equal to the task.

Just as he was about to give up in despair, a thought came to him. He picked up a pebble and dropped it into the pitcher. Then he took another pebble and dropped that into the pitcher. One by one he kept dropping pebbles into the pitcher until the water mounted to the brim. Then, perching himself upon the handle, he drank and drank until his thirst was quenched.

Necessity is the mother of invention.

Skill Lesson

Predicting

- To **predict** means to state what might happen next in a story or article.

- To make a prediction, think about what you already know and what has already happened. Look for clues in the photographs or illustrations.

- After you make a prediction, continue reading to check its accuracy. Revise your prediction if it does not agree with new information.

Read "At the Water's Edge" from *The Black Stallion* by Walter Farley.

Write About It

1. List the details in the story that helped you predict what would happen.

2. Describe any personal knowledge or experience that helped you make your prediction.

3. How close was your prediction to what actually happened? Could it have been better? Explain.

At the Water's Edge
by Walter Farley

Alec is shipwrecked on a deserted island.

One morning Alec made his way weakly toward the rocky side of the island. He came to the huge rocks and climbed on top of one of them. It was more barren than any other part of the island. It was low tide and Alec's eyes wandered over the stony shore, looking for any kind of shellfish he might be able to eat. He noticed the mosslike substance on all the rocks at the water's edge, and on those that extended out. What was that stuff the biology teacher had made them eat last term in one of their experiments? Hadn't he called it *carragheen* (kar′ə gēn′)? Yes, that was it. A sort of seaweed, he had said, that grew abundantly along the rocky parts of the Atlantic coast of Europe and North America. When washed and dried,

it was edible for humans and livestock. Could the moss on the rocks below be it? Alec scarcely dared to hope.

Predict what Alec will do.

Slowly Alec made the dangerous descent. He reached the water level and scrambled across the rocks. He took a handful of the soft greenish-yellow moss which covered them and raised it to his lips. It smelled the same. He tasted it. The moss was terribly salty from the sea, but it was the same as he had eaten that day in the classroom!

Eagerly he filled his pockets with it, then removed his shirt and filled it full. He climbed up again and hurried back to camp. There he emptied the moss onto the ground beside the spring. The next quarter of an hour he spent washing it, and then placed it out in the sun to dry. Hungrily he tasted it again. It was better—and it was food!

LOOK AHEAD

From a Spark

from *Hatchet* by Gary Paulsen

Brian is on his way to visit his father in northern Canada, when the pilot of the small, single-engine plane in which he is flying suffers a fatal heart attack. Forced to crash-land the plane, Brian suddenly finds himself alone in the Canadian wilderness, with only a hatchet to help him survive.

In "From a Spark," thirteen-year-old Brian struggles to survive in the wilderness. As you read, use information from the story and your own knowledge and experience to predict what will happen.

Vocabulary

Words to Know

hatchet	painstaking	ignite
smoldered	survival	

Words with opposite meanings are called **antonyms.** You can often figure out the meaning of an unknown word by finding a clue in the words around it. Sometimes this clue is an antonym.

Read the paragraph below. Notice how *careless* helps you understand what *painstaking* means.

Preventing Forest Fires

Always pour water on your campfire before leaving the site—even if it appears to be out. Abandoned campfires that have <u>smoldered</u> for days can still burn hot enough to <u>ignite</u> dry grass or leaves. All it takes is one spark. If you don't have water to spare, use a camping tool, like a shovel or <u>hatchet</u>, to loosen enough soil to cover the ashes. Remember, one careless moment can lead to weeks of <u>painstaking</u> work for firefighters. More importantly, it can threaten the <u>survival</u> of wildlife and even humans. Be a careful camper. Do your part to prevent forest fires.

Write About It

Write a short newspaper article about a fire. Be sure to tell how it started and how it could have been prevented. Use as many vocabulary words as you can.

From a Spark

from *Hatchet* by Gary Paulsen

Brian is on his way to visit his father in northern Canada, when the pilot of the small, single-engine plane in which he is flying suffers a fatal heart attack. Forced to crash-land the plane, Brian suddenly finds himself alone in the Canadian wilderness, with only a hatchet to help him survive.

t first he thought it was a growl. In the still darkness of the shelter in the middle of the night his eyes came open, and he was awake, and he thought there was a growl. But it was the wind, a medium wind in the pines had made some sound that brought him up, brought him awake. He sat up and was hit with the smell.

It terrified him. The smell was one of rot, some musty rot that made him think only of graves with cobwebs and dust and old death. His nostrils widened, and he opened his eyes wider, but he could see nothing. It was too dark, too hard dark with clouds covering even the small light from the stars, and he could not see. But the smell was alive, alive and full and in the shelter. He thought of the bear, thought of Bigfoot and every monster he had ever seen in every fright movie he had ever watched, and his heart hammered in his throat.

Then he heard the slithering. A brushing sound, a slithering brushing sound near his feet—and he kicked out as hard as he could, kicked out and threw the hatchet at the sound, a noise coming from his throat. But the hatchet missed, sailed into the wall where it hit the rocks with a shower of sparks, and his leg was instantly torn with pain, as if a hundred needles had been driven into it. "Unnnngh!"

Now he screamed, with the pain and fear, and skittered on his backside up into the corner of the shelter, breathing through his mouth, straining to see, to hear.

The slithering moved again, he thought toward him at first, and terror took him, stopping his breath. He felt he could see a low dark form, a bulk in the darkness, a shadow that lived, but now it moved away, slithering and scraping it moved away, and he saw or thought he saw it go out of the door opening.

He lay on his side for a moment, then pulled a rasping breath in and held it, listening for the attacker to return. When it was apparent that the shadow wasn't coming back he felt the calf of his leg, where the pain was centered and spreading to fill the whole leg.

His fingers gingerly touched a group of needles that had been driven through his pants and into the fleshy part of his calf. They were stiff and very sharp on the ends that stuck out, and he knew

then what the attacker had been. A porcupine had stumbled into his shelter and when he had kicked it the thing had slapped him with its tail of quills.

He touched each quill carefully. The pain made it seem as if dozens of them had been slammed into his leg, but there were only eight, pinning the cloth against his skin. He leaned back against the wall for a minute. He couldn't leave them in, they had to come out, but just touching them made the pain more intense.

So fast, he thought. So fast things change. When he'd gone to sleep he had satisfaction and in just a moment it was all different. He grasped one of the quills, held his breath, and jerked. It sent pain signals to his brain in tight waves, but he grabbed another, pulled it, then another quill. When he had pulled four of them he stopped for a moment. The pain had gone from being a pointed injury pain to spreading in a hot smear up his leg and it made him catch his breath.

Some of the quills were driven in deeper than others and they tore when they came out. He breathed deeply twice, let half of the breath out, and went back to work. Jerk, pause, jerk—and three more times before he lay back in the darkness, done. The pain filled his leg now, and with it came new waves of self-pity. Sitting alone in the dark, his leg aching, some mosquitoes finding him again, he started crying. It was all too much, and he couldn't take it. Not the way it was.

I can't take it this way, alone with no fire and in the dark, and next time it might be something worse, maybe a bear, and it wouldn't be just quills in the leg, it would be worse. I can't do this, he thought, again and again. I can't. Brian pulled himself up until he was sitting upright back in the corner of the cave. He put his head down on his arms across his knees, with stiffness taking his left leg, and cried until he was cried out.

He did not know how long it took, but later he looked back on this time of crying in the corner of the dark cave and thought of it as when he learned the most important rule of survival, which was that feeling sorry for yourself didn't work. It wasn't just that it was wrong to do, or that it was considered incorrect. It was more than that—it didn't work. When he sat alone in the darkness and cried and was done, was all done with it, nothing had changed. His leg still hurt, it was still dark, he was still alone, and the self-pity had accomplished nothing.

At last he slept again, but already his patterns were changing and the sleep was light, a resting doze more than a deep sleep, with small sounds awakening him twice in the rest of the night. In the last doze period before daylight, before he awakened finally with the morning light and the clouds of new mosquitoes, he dreamed. This time it was not of his mother, but of his father at first and then of his friend Terry.

In the initial segment of the dream, his father was standing at the side of a living room looking at him, and it was clear from his expression that he was trying to tell Brian something. His lips moved but there was no sound, not a whisper. He waved his hands at Brian, made gestures in front of his face as if he were scratching something, and he worked to make a word with his mouth but at first Brian could not see it. Then the lips made an *mmmmm* shape but no sound came. *Mmmmm—maaaa.* Brian could not hear it, could not understand it and he wanted to so badly; it was so important to understand his father, to know what he was saying. He was trying to help, trying so hard, and when Brian couldn't understand he looked cross, the way he did when Brian asked questions more than once, and he faded. Brian's father faded into a fog place Brian could not see and the dream was almost over, or seemed to be, when Terry came.

He was not gesturing to Brian but was sitting in the park at a bench looking at a barbecue pit, and for a time nothing happened. Then he got up and poured some charcoal from a bag into the cooker, then some starter fluid, and he took a flick type of lighter and lit the fluid. When it was burning and the charcoal was at last getting hot he turned, noticing Brian for the first time in the dream. He turned and smiled and pointed to the fire as if to say, see, a fire.

But it meant nothing to Brian, except that he wished he had a fire. He saw a grocery sack on the table next to Terry. Brian thought it must contain hot dogs and chips and mustard and he could think only of the food. But Terry shook his head and pointed again to the fire, and twice more he pointed to the fire, made Brian see the flames, and Brian felt his frustration and anger rise, and he thought all right, all right, I see the fire but so what? I don't have a fire. I know about fire; I know I need a fire.

I know that.

His eyes opened and there was light in the cave, a gray dim light of morning. He wiped his mouth and tried to move his leg, which had stiffened like wood. There was thirst, and hunger, and he ate some raspberries from the jacket. They had spoiled a bit, seemed softer and mushier, but still had a rich sweetness. He crushed the berries against the roof of his mouth with his tongue and drank the sweet juice as it ran down his throat. A flash of metal caught his eye and he saw his hatchet in the sand where he had thrown it at the porcupine in the dark.

He scootched up, wincing a bit when he bent his stiff leg, and crawled to where the hatchet lay. He picked it up and examined it and saw a chip in the top of the head.

The nick wasn't large, but the hatchet was important to him, was his only tool, and he should not have thrown it. He should keep it in his hand, and make a tool of some kind to help push an animal away. Make a staff, he thought, or a lance, and save the hatchet. Something came then, a thought as he held the hatchet, something about the dream and his father and Terry, but he couldn't pin it down.

"Ahhh . . ." He scrambled out and stood in the morning sun and stretched his back muscles and his sore leg. The hatchet was still in his hand, and as he stretched and raised it over his head it caught

the first rays of the morning sun. The first faint light hit the silver of the hatchet and it flashed a brilliant gold in the light. Like fire. That is it, he thought. What they were trying to tell me.

Fire. The hatchet was the key to it all. When he threw the hatchet at the porcupine in the cave and missed and hit the stone wall it had showered sparks, a golden shower of sparks in the dark, as golden with fire as the sun was now.

The hatchet was the answer. That's what his father and Terry had been trying to tell him. Somehow he could get fire from the hatchet. The sparks would make fire.

Brian went back into the shelter and studied the wall. It was some form of chalky granite, or a sandstone, but imbedded in it were large pieces of a darker stone, a harder and darker stone. It only took him a moment to find where the hatchet had struck. The steel had nicked into the edge of one of the darker stone pieces. Brian turned the head backward so he would strike with the flat rear of the hatchet and hit the black rock gently. Too gently, and nothing happened. He struck harder, a glancing blow, and two or three weak sparks skipped off the rock and died immediately.

He swung harder, held the hatchet so it would hit a longer, sliding blow, and the black rock exploded in fire. Sparks flew so heavily that several of them skittered and jumped on the sand beneath the rock, and he smiled and struck again and again.

There could be fire here, he thought. I will have a fire here, he thought, and struck again—I will have fire from the hatchet.

Brian found it was a long way from sparks to fire.

Clearly there had to be something for the sparks to ignite, some kind of tinder or kindling—but what? He brought some dried grass in, tapped sparks into it, and watched them die. He tried small twigs, breaking them into little pieces, but that was worse than the grass. Then he tried a combination of the two, grass and twigs.

Nothing. He had no trouble getting sparks, but the tiny bits of hot stone or metal—he couldn't tell which they were—just sputtered and died.

He settled back on his haunches in exasperation, looking at the pitiful clump of grass and twigs.

He needed something finer, something soft and fine and fluffy to catch the bits of fire.

Shredded paper would be nice, but he had no paper.

"So close," he said aloud, "so close . . ."

He put the hatchet back in his belt and went out of the shelter, limping on his sore leg. There had to be something, had to be. Man had made fire. There had been fire for thousands, millions of years. There had to be a way. He dug in his pockets and found the twenty-dollar bill in his wallet. Paper. Worthless paper out here. But if he could get a fire going . . .

He ripped the twenty into tiny pieces, made a pile of pieces, and hit sparks into them. Nothing happened. They just wouldn't take the sparks. But there had to be a way—some way to do it.

Not twenty feet to his right, leaning out over the water were birches and he stood looking at them for a full half-minute before they registered on his mind. They were a beautiful white with bark like clean, slightly speckled paper.

Paper.

He moved to the trees. Where the bark was peeling from the trunks it lifted in tiny tendrils, almost fluffs. Brian plucked some of them loose, rolled them in his fingers. They seemed flammable, dry and nearly powdery. He pulled and twisted bits off the trees, packing them in one hand while he picked them with the other, picking and gathering until he had a wad close to the size of a baseball.

Then he went back into the shelter and arranged the ball of birchbark peelings at the base of the black rock. As an afterthought he threw in the remains of the twenty-dollar bill. He struck and a stream of sparks fell into the bark and quickly died. But this time one spark fell on one small hair of dry bark—almost a thread of bark—and seemed to glow a bit brighter before it died.

The material had to be finer. There had to be a soft and incredibly fine nest for the sparks.

I must make a home for the sparks, he thought. A perfect home or they won't stay, they won't make fire.

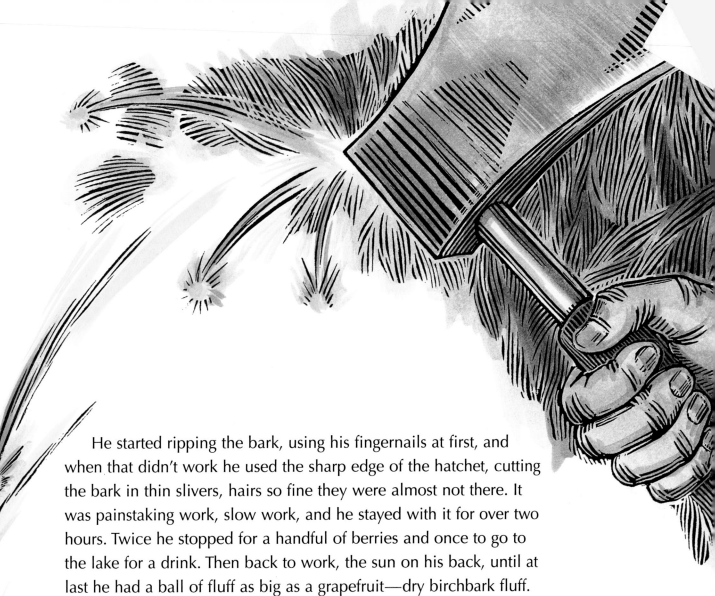

He started ripping the bark, using his fingernails at first, and when that didn't work he used the sharp edge of the hatchet, cutting the bark in thin slivers, hairs so fine they were almost not there. It was painstaking work, slow work, and he stayed with it for over two hours. Twice he stopped for a handful of berries and once to go to the lake for a drink. Then back to work, the sun on his back, until at last he had a ball of fluff as big as a grapefruit—dry birchbark fluff.

He positioned his spark nest—as he thought of it—at the base of the rock, used his thumb to make a small depression in the middle, and slammed the back of the hatchet down across the black rock. A cloud of sparks rained down, most of them missing the nest, but some, perhaps thirty or so, hit in the depression, and of those six or seven found fuel and grew, smoldered, and caused the bark to take on the red glow.

Then they went out.

Close—he was close. He repositioned the nest, made a new and smaller dent with his thumb, and struck again.

More sparks, a slight glow, then nothing.

It's me, he thought. I'm doing something wrong. I do not know this—a cave dweller would have had a fire by now, a Cro-Magnon* man would have a fire by now—but I don't know this. I don't know how to make a fire.

*Cro-Magnon refers to a prehistoric people who lived in southwestern Europe.

Maybe not enough sparks. He settled the nest in place once more and hit the rock with a series of blows, as fast as he could. The sparks poured like a golden waterfall. At first they seemed to take, there were several, many sparks that found life and took briefly, but they all died.

Starved.

He leaned back. They are like me. They are starving. It wasn't quantity, there were plenty of sparks, but they needed more.

I would kill, he thought suddenly, for a book of matches. Just one book. Just one match. I would kill.

What makes fire? He thought back to school. To all those science classes. Had he ever learned what made a fire? Did a teacher ever stand up there and say, "This is what makes a fire . . ."

He shook his head, tried to focus his thoughts. What did it take? You have to have fuel, he thought—and he had that. The bark was fuel. Oxygen—there had to be air.

He needed to add air. He had to fan on it, blow on it.

He made the nest ready again, held the hatchet backward, tensed, and struck four quick blows. Sparks came down and he leaned forward as fast as he could and blew.

Too hard. There was a bright, almost intense glow, then it was gone. He had blown it out.

Another set of strikes, more sparks. He leaned and blew, but gently this time, holding back and aiming the stream of air from his mouth to hit the brightest spot. Five or six sparks had fallen in a tight mass of bark hair and Brian centered his efforts there.

The sparks grew with his gentle breath. The red glow moved from the sparks themselves into the bark, moved and grew and became worms, glowing red worms that crawled up the bark hairs and caught other threads of bark and grew until there was a pocket of red as big as a quarter, a glowing red coal of heat.

And when he ran out of breath and paused to inhale, the red ball suddenly burst into flame.

"Fire!" He yelled. "I've got fire! I've got it, I've got it, I've got it . . ."

But the flames were thick and oily and burning fast, consuming the ball of bark as fast as if it were gasoline. He had to feed the flames, keep them going. Working as fast as he could he carefully placed the dried grass and wood pieces he had tried at first on top of the bark and was gratified to see them take.

But they would go fast. He needed more, and more. He could not let the flames go out.

He ran from the shelter to the pines and started breaking off the low, dead small limbs. These he threw in the shelter, went back for more, threw those in, and squatted to break and feed the hungry flames. When the small wood was going well he went out and found larger wood and did not relax until that was going. Then he leaned back against the wood brace of his door opening and smiled.

I have a friend, he thought—I have a friend now. A hungry friend, but a good one. I have a friend named fire.

"Hello, fire . . ."

The curve of the rock back made an almost perfect drawing flue that carried the smoke up through the cracks of the roof but held the heat. If he kept the fire small it would be perfect and would keep anything like the porcupine from coming through the door again.

A friend and a guard, he thought.

So much from a little spark. A friend and a guard from a tiny spark.

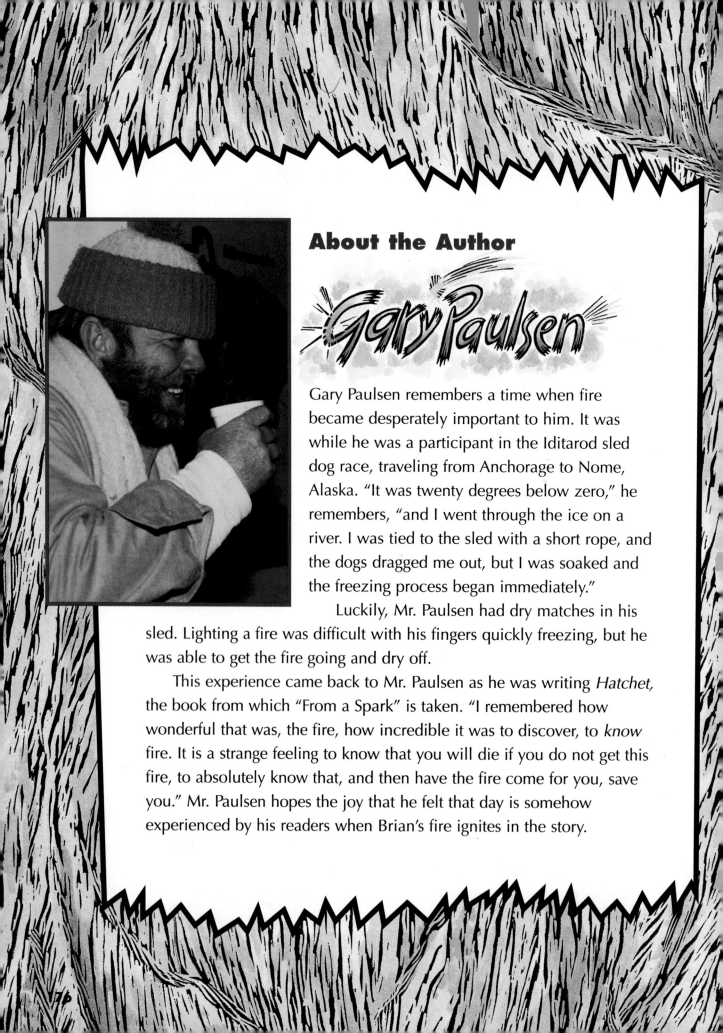

About the Author

Gary Paulsen

Gary Paulsen remembers a time when fire became desperately important to him. It was while he was a participant in the Iditarod sled dog race, traveling from Anchorage to Nome, Alaska. "It was twenty degrees below zero," he remembers, "and I went through the ice on a river. I was tied to the sled with a short rope, and the dogs dragged me out, but I was soaked and the freezing process began immediately."

Luckily, Mr. Paulsen had dry matches in his sled. Lighting a fire was difficult with his fingers quickly freezing, but he was able to get the fire going and dry off.

This experience came back to Mr. Paulsen as he was writing *Hatchet,* the book from which "From a Spark" is taken. "I remembered how wonderful that was, the fire, how incredible it was to discover, to *know* fire. It is a strange feeling to know that you will die if you do not get this fire, to absolutely know that, and then have the fire come for you, save you." Mr. Paulsen hopes the joy that he felt that day is somehow experienced by his readers when Brian's fire ignites in the story.

Reader Response

Open for Discussion

Which moment in the story would you say is the most memorable?
In a few words, describe your impression of the scene.

Comprehension Check

1. What are some lessons that Brian learns? Which do you think is most important for his survival? Explain, using details from the story.

2. The author tries to make you feel as if you are sharing Brian's experiences. Look back in the story to find places where you felt you were a part of the action. Discuss how the author made you feel that way.

3. Living in the wilderness seems very different from living in a city or town. Explain some of the differences. What similarities can you think of?

4. Think about the **predictions** you made before and during the story. Did events happen as you thought they would? Find clues in the story that helped you make your predictions. (Predicting)

5. "From a Spark" is a part of the novel *Hatchet*. Based on what Brian does in this excerpt, **predict** what you think he does on the following day and the day after that. (Predicting)

 Test Prep

Look Back and Write

How does the author create suspense at the beginning of "From a Spark"? Use details from pages 166–167 in your answer.

Wilderness Challenge

by Suzanne Wilson

"It was tough going," says Harrison Moskowitz, 15. Harrison, Meghan McClure, and five other kids owe their adventure to Outward Bound, a program designed for rugged experiences. Participants learn about the environment and how to communicate with other people. They discover, too, how to push themselves to new heights.

The kids spent fifteen days hiking, camping, and climbing in the Beartooth Wilderness, in Montana. Instructors taught them how to find their way over mountain passes and survive in the wilderness. Eventually the kids had to do all the work and make the decisions by themselves. Strangers at the start, they soon became friends, helping each other as they hiked over slippery snow and waded across cold creeks.

It wasn't easy. The kids were exhausted before their bodies adjusted to the mountains' high altitude, which can cause weakness and dizziness. Most kids felt like quitting. After a while though, says Harrison, "we realized we could do it."

After days of strenuous hiking, rock climbing looked like a pleasant break. Some kids could relax while others were climbing. They all needed a break because ahead of them was the ultimate outdoor adventure: the solo.

Each kid hiked to an isolated spot near a lake and stayed there alone for two days and two nights. Each took a tarp and sleeping bag. The instructors delivered food. It rained. It snowed. But for Chris Jaffray, 16, "It was the coolest thing." It was different for Harrison, who says, "I was bored out of my mind. I learned that I rely on other people for company and entertainment." All the kids will remember their days struggling through the mountains together. Meghan McClure sums it up well: "It was such an achievement!"

Lights Out

Warm sleeping bags help protect the campers from low nighttime temperatures. From the left are Chris Jaffray, 16, of Deephaven, Minnesota; Josh Koltowicz, 17, of Livonia, Michigan; and Harrison Moskowitz, 15, of Gastonia, North Carolina.

On the Trail

Carrying a pack weighing more than 50 pounds, Meghan McClure, 16, of Shiremanstown, Pennsylvania, leads the way across rocky high country.

Downside

High above the scenery, Josh rappels down the rock face. Above him an instructor holds the rope to prevent Josh from falling.

Pathfinder

Consulting a topographical map, Meghan McClure, on the left, gauges the steepness of the next hike. Instructor Colin Wann, on the right, gives her helpful advice. The kids take turns navigating for the group.

Skill Lesson

Setting

- The **setting** of a story is the place and time in which the story occurs.

- In some stories, the author describes exactly where and when the story takes place. In other stories, the author reveals the setting through details.

- The setting of a story can influence what happens to a character and how a character behaves. The setting can also contribute to an overall feeling, or mood.

Read "The Glittering Cloud" from *On the Banks of Plum Creek* by Laura Ingalls Wilder.

Talk About It

1. Describe where the story takes place.

2. This story is set in the 1800s. Point out some of the details the author uses to reveal this setting in time.

3. Discuss how the setting influences what happens to Laura and her family.

The Glittering Cloud

by Laura Ingalls Wilder

The weather was very hot. The thin, high sky was too hot to look at. Air rose up in waves from the whole prairie, as it does from a hot stove. In the schoolhouse the children panted like lizards, and the sticky pine-juice dripped down the board walls.

Saturday morning Laura went walking with Pa to look at the wheat. It was almost as tall as Pa. He lifted her onto his shoulder so that she could see over the heavy, bending tops. The field was greeny gold.

At the dinner table Pa told Ma about it. He had never seen such a crop. There were forty bushels to the acre, and wheat was a dollar a bushel. They were rich now. This was a wonderful country. Now they could have anything they wanted. Laura listened and thought, now Pa would get his new boots.

She sat facing the open door and the sunshine streaming through it. Something seemed to dim the sunshine. Laura rubbed her eyes and looked again. The sunshine really was dim. It grew dimmer until there was no sunshine.

"I do believe a storm is coming up," said Ma. "There must be a cloud over the sun."

Pa got up quickly and went to the door. A storm might hurt the wheat. He looked out, then he went out.

The light was strange. It was not like the changed light before a storm. The air did not press down as it did before a storm. Laura was frightened; she did not know why.

She ran outdoors, where Pa stood looking up at the sky. Ma and Mary came out, too, and Pa asked, "What do you make of that, Caroline?"

A cloud was over the sun. It was not like any cloud they had ever seen before. It was a cloud of something like snowflakes, but they were larger than snowflakes, and thin and glittering. Light shone through each flickering particle.

There was no wind. The grasses were still and the hot air did not stir, but the edge of the cloud came on across the sky faster than wind. The hair stood up on the dog's neck. All at once he made a frightful sound up at that cloud, a growl and a whine.

Plunk! Something hit Laura's head and fell to the ground. She looked down and saw the largest grasshopper she had ever seen. Then huge brown grasshoppers were hitting the ground all around her, hitting her head and her face and her arms. They came thudding down like hail.

The cloud was hailing grasshoppers. The cloud *was* grasshoppers. Their bodies hid the sun and made darkness. Their thin, large wings gleamed and glittered. The rasping whirring of their wings filled the whole air and they hit the ground and the house with the noise of a hailstorm.

LOOK AHEAD

In the next story, "Storm-a-Dust," a Midwestern farm family survives a terrible storm. As you read, notice how the setting of the story affects the family.

181

Vocabulary

Words to Know

| grasslands | eerie | gritty |
| hazy | peculiar | spindly |

Words with similar meanings are called **synonyms.** You can often figure out the meaning of an unknown word by finding a clue in the words around it. Sometimes this clue is a synonym.

Read the paragraph below. Notice how *strange* helps you understand what *peculiar* means.

Tornado!

At first there is an eerie silence. The air appears hazy and the sky quickly becomes dark. A peculiar shade of green or purple often settles on the land, covering city streets and country grasslands alike. Everything looks very strange. Warning sirens wail in the distance. Then the wind picks up and rain begins to fall. Leaves begin to swirl along the ground. The sky becomes filled with a dust that makes your skin feel gritty. Small, spindly trees bend and appear ready to snap. The wind now sounds like an oncoming train. Take cover, if you haven't done so already.

Talk About It

Use some of the vocabulary words to describe a storm that you witnessed.

Storm-a-Dust

from Drylongso

by Virginia Hamilton • illustrated by Jerry Pinkney

Lindy skipped along, leaving a trail of dust behind her. She had her wiper rag. She must wipe each plant and flower clean. For red dust covered everything. Dust spotted her cheeks reddish brown. It covered her hands in red dust mittens. She took a last swipe at a stunted sunflower. "How are you this morning, yellow fella?" she asked the sunflower.

"Oh, but I need some water," Lindy answered in a sunflower-high voice.

"I'll water you at sundown, yellow fella," she told the flower.

She tied her wiper around her waist. Her tank top and jeans were dusty. Lindy climbed up on the old wood fence and shook her head at their pie-shaped field. "Don't think the corn will make it," she called over to her dad.

"Lindy, stop your dawdling and come on here," he said back.

"Coming!"

She skipped, barefooted, to the side yard, where her dad worked at his garden-a-chance. "Shielded part way by the house," he'd once told her, "it is chance a garden will grow."

"I'll dig the hole, Lindy," he said now. "You put the baby plant in. Keep it straight and steady while I pour on the *gravy*."

"Gravy! Funny," laughed Lindy.

Her dad worked with the watering can. He poured a skinny stream of water—gravy—down over the young tomato plant, careful not to spill a drop. Lindy held it up with the tips of her fingers. She watched as the gravy dribbled down in the dust. Then, bracing the plant with one hand, she shoved the soil into the hole around it. The dirt was as fine as powder. She smoothed it around until the little plant stood by itself. Already it wilted over at the top.

"*Ka-choo!*" Lindy sneezed. Dust rose around them, reddening the light. "I don't know . . . ," she said.

"Well . . . and if it rains . . . ," her dad said, wistfully. Hope hung there between them.

"*And if it rains,*" Lindy sang, "*I get me some shoes and a dress-up all blue and pink and yellow, with flowers.*"

She leaned way back and smiled at the blue sky.

All was still. Lindy watched Mamalou come out to sweep the tumbledown porch. Mamalou was the name she'd given her mother, who was Louise Esther. Lindy looked off as far as she could see beyond Mamalou, down the road, until the road dipped out of sight and the hard-time town of Osfield started. She frowned. "Feel a north breeze just so cool," Lindy told her dad. "Which way is north again?"

"Over my shoulder is north," he said. "But Lindy, there's no kind of breeze. Haven't ever known such blue sky."

Mamalou worked her way down the steps, sweeping the dust into neat piles.

"So little rain all the time now," Lindy's dad said.

"I never have seen more than a little rain," Lindy told him.

"When it comes down like a cloudburst, it's a lot," said her dad.

"Cloudburst!" said Lindy. "What would that be like?"

"Like the sky is opening up," he said.

"Like a river pouring down from above," said Mamalou, hearing them, all was so still. "Like buckets and buckets of just the longest rain-fella you ever saw in your life!"

"Is that true? It can rain like that?" asked Lindy, gazing at Mamalou, then back to her dad. She imagined a rain-fella, long and dark across the blue sky.

"It sure can," her dad answered. "But it hasn't rained like that in three years."

"I don't 'member three years," she said.

Her dad laughed. "You were so little then. There's just enough rain now to keep a minute of it down in the well."

"A minute of rain," she murmured, thinking about it. She imagined she heard a minute ticking raindrops, as she and her dad labored down the row.

Mamalou busied her broom over. She watched as they finished one short row. "Swept the porch," she told them, "and I swept the yard."

"Humm," Lindy's dad said.

Mamalou gazed at the yard where small clumps of grass struggled to grow. Most of the yard was dry, packed ground.

"Looking like pancakes, is the yard," said Lindy to her. "See, it cracks around into little cakes?"

"I see," said Mamalou. "I would give you pancakes to eat if I could. But I am all out of corn meal."

Lindy pictured syrup spilling over pancakes. Her mouth watered; then the corners turned down a moment. But she never asked for what they didn't have. As was her way, she broke into a grin. "I don't mind my beans and gravy," she told Mamalou.

"Wish there was better," said her dad.

"Well, if it rains . . . ," Mamalou began. She let that fresh, watery thought go. "Think we are whistling in the wind," she said.

"What is that, whistling?" asked Lindy.

"Planting dry is useless work, what it means," said Mamalou. "I traded my corn meal for tomato plants at market; had a taste for big tomatoes."

"But if it rains . . . ," said Lindy.

"These bitty plants will be ready for it," her dad finished.

Mamalou shook her head. She locked her broom like a flagstaff against her shoulder, rolled her hands in her apron, and went off into the house.

Lindy and her dad bent to their work, Lindy on one side of the row and her dad on the other. All at once, granules from the hard ground seemed to rise and jump along. Larger pieces of grit bounced up and rolled.

Lindy laughed. "Funny!" she said.

"What's funny?" asked her dad.

"Jumping dirt," said Lindy. "It's dancing."

"Huh," her dad said, only half listening. He lifted his head, looked toward the back of the land where there used to be a stream. Most rain came from there, from the south. The day was clear there beyond the streambed. Blue sky and no wind.

"Pretty sky," Lindy said. She had turned around, following his gaze.

Her dad said, "huh" again and, "Wouldn't mind to see a cloud come up."

"Is there always rain in a cloud?" she asked.

By way of an answer, her dad pointed to their work. She held the baby plant and covered its roots. But she was watching the grit dancing along.

"Funny-funny," Lindy said. And made a singsong. *"Gritty-funny, funny-gritty, sunny day!"*

"You like turning things 'round," her dad told her.

She grinned and turned herself all the way around. "I do!"

Lindy closed her eyes, leaning her head on her dad's shoulder a moment. She could feel the sun all over her. "I'm a baked potato," she told him.

Her dad laughed at that. She opened her eyes and sat up. That quickly, the day had changed. Maybe change had been creeping up on them. There were a whole lot of birds going by up in the air. Going by so fast, squawking. Just a big flock of them. And then, more change was coming. "Well, for—Dad?"

"Huh?" he said. "Lindy, hold the plant for me."

"But Dad, it's a wall." She looked over his shoulder, behind him.

"What is a wall, Lindy?" he asked.

"Dad, it's all brown and high! Dad, it's . . . it's coming!"

Her dad spun around. For a moment he simply stared northward. His mouth fell open. He took her hand, then, and started toward the house. "Come," he said, almost calmly.

All had grown quiet. There was a wall moving toward them from the north. It was not believable, but on it came. Great numbers of birds had got out of the way of it. Around Lindy and her dad, grit and soil bounced and rolled toward it.

"Dad, it's like a great big wall-a-cloud. Is it if-it-rains?" asked Lindy. And then, "Dad! There's a stick running against the wall."

"What?" her dad said. He squinted hard to see. "Well, I'll be . . . " He saw. It did look like a stick figure was pressed to the wall and trying to run. But it was no stick. And that was no wall, although it looked like one.

"Never have seen a stick running. Never have seen a wall so high moving," said Lindy.

"No, child," her dad said. "It's a storm-a-dust. It's—Come on, Lindy, get in the house!"

Her dad pulled her fast. She flew off her feet. "Dad!" she said, and he eased up on her arm. But the grit was stinging her legs. The sky looked different now. No longer blue, it had turned gray. The air became harder to breathe. Bits of dusty ground went up Lindy's nose. "*Ka-choo! Ka-choo!*" she sneezed.

She and her dad clambered up the porch. Mamalou stood in the door, looking out to the north. "Goodness. Goodness," she said. "There's somebody . . . ," Mamalou began.

They watched what was coming against the wall. "It's bigger than a stick now," said Lindy.

"Looks like some fella," said Mamalou.

As the wall came closer, they could hear it swoosh with air and wind. The stick-fella ran about half a quarter-mile before the wall of dust. His shadowy, stick arms moved like pinwheels. His long legs scissored, in a hurry to cut out of there.

"Inside!" Lindy's dad urged her and Mamalou. They all went in. Quickly, Mamalou wet tatter cloths at the washstand and wrung them out. She handed a wet rag to Lindy and one to Lindy's dad. He stood with the door open just far enough for him to see out as the storm came on.

The air was hot and still outside. It was boiling inside. Lindy saw the sweat drip from her dad's face. Saw his eyes seem to run, even though he stood unmoving.

Mamalou closed all the windows. With her wet tatter cloth over her shoulder, she stuffed more tatters along the windowsills.

"Mamalou, what are you doing? Why are you in a hurry?" Lindy asked. "What must I do with this, my rag-a-wet?"

Mamalou stopped a moment. "You hold the tatter to your mouth. You'll see," Mamalou explained. "Stay close, Lindy! And we must keep the storm outside with these cloths at the windowsills."

Lindy heard a deep, loud sound. She looked out the window. "The wall! It's bigger than big!" she cried. It loomed, scary, at the far end of the field. Now the world around them was misty-dusty.

Somebody came tripping onto the porch. Her dad held the door open as a spindly somebody came through. Somebody full of dust. Quickly her dad shut the door.

"Stick-fella!" Lindy said. She stared. A stranger. He was covered rusty. He stumbled and fell on the floor, coughing.

There was so much going on. Lindy saw their field get wiped away in a red mist. Now the house inside was hazy with a rusty fog. The dust filled the front room. It fell on the linoleum and spread over the white lace tablecloth that had been sewn many times by Lindy and Mamalou, washed and starched, too, so it looked new.

Now Lindy watched the tablecloth get covered with brown. She began coughing, just like the stick-fella on the floor. She held the moist rag to her mouth and sat down at the table.

Only a few minutes had passed. But outside, it was dark as night. The wall never hit them. It was like it went right through them. Dust came in, sifting right through the wallboards. There was wind sound, and grit sound slapping the house. It felt as if the house lifted, then held itself tight.

Lindy couldn't think of anything funny to say. Couldn't smile. She felt gritty. She couldn't get her breath. She made fists. Her chest heaved. A sob rose from her throat.

Her dad was there beside her. "Breathe through the tatter," he told her. "That's it; put it over your nose. Breathe, child." And she did, easier now.

The stick-fella sprawled on the floor. He tried to get up. Mamalou and Lindy's dad took hold of him. They set him upright in a chair. Mamalou had an old dish towel wetted, and she helped him wipe his eyes and face. The stick-fella was a boy. Long and thin as a skinny rail. Spindly, too, and the color of pale wood under the grime of dust.

"You are a long, dusty somebody," Lindy said. "Dad, see? It's a tall boy!" She forgot about crying now. She coughed a few times, but breathing through the tatter made it better.

"Reckon he is older than you, too," her dad said. "What do they call you, son?" he asked the tall boy.

"Tall Boy!" Lindy whispered. And he heard her.

"That's not . . . ," he sputtered, spit, and coughed. He struggled to breathe. " . . . *my name,*" he finished. His voice was a cooling breeze, after he had cleared his throat of dust.

He took some swallows of water from a cup Mamalou gave him. Outside was a hard wind sound. He put the cup down and held the dish towel to his nose. Then, he wiped his arms and neck with it; wiped his head and ears and hands. He wiped his shirt and dungarees, and made mud streaks clear down his front. His movement made a cloud of dust rise around him. He tried to take a deep breath, but it got caught in a cough. Sweat broke out on his cleaned forehead and made it glisten. He took another sip of water and breathed hard. His hands were shaking. Lindy saw them.

Mamalou took another damp tatter and held it by its end. She let it hang down into the small cloud of dust the stick-fella had raised. Slowly she swung the rag and lifted it up and down.

Right before their eyes, Mamalou wiped up the cloud on the rag. All around the room, she wiped rusty dust off the air. She finished when she had done all she could to help them breathe.

"Where do you come from? Where are your people?" Mamalou asked the stick-fella.

The tall boy breathed hard and did not answer at once.

"You ran a long way?" asked her dad.

"Must've wore you out," Mamalou said.

"Did your people get lost in the wall?" Lindy asked. She was the first one of them the boy looked at.

Mamalou and Lindy's dad stared at the boy as though he were an odd-fella. Lindy didn't think so. "Why is it so bad out?" Lindy asked him.

The tall boy looked around. He saw the dust seeping in.

"The floor is covered, look," she told them.

"It gets in everything," Mamalou said.

"You will eat dust for a while," her dad said.

But Lindy was watching the long, tall young'un. "Talk! Why don't you say more?" she asked him.

"I will," he said. "Was afraid I'd start a coughing fit." And then, "Are you the only child?"

Lindy nodded. She thought he sounded fresh, the way her dad said once the stream had sounded. She said, "Someday Mamalou will have me a little brother. How old are you, tall boy?"

They all stared at him. "He can talk," Lindy told.

"Course he can," Mamalou said.

"And your name?" her dad said to the stick-fella.

"It's Tall Boy!" Lindy said, then covered her mouth, ashamed of herself.

"No," the boy said. "It's Drylongso."

"What?" asked Lindy's dad and Mamalou,

"Drylongso," he said again. The name echoed in Lindy's thoughts. *'longso. Drylongso.* "Funny *name!*" Lindy said.

Drylongso looked away. And she was sorry she'd spoken out.

He looked back at them. "Ma says there was drought like this before," he said. "It lasted so long, folks thought it was just ordinary. Dry so long, it was common, like everyday. See, drought came to be Dry-long-so."

"And you, Drylongso . . . ," Mamalou began.

He said, "Ma says she dreamed a hard dust time was coming. Another Dry-long-so. Then, I was born. Ma said, 'He comes into the world, and a time of no clouds will come after him. Where he goes,' she said, 'life will grow better.'"

"Is that right? Well, I'll be," said Lindy's dad.

"And the drought came," said the tall boy, "and long been here, just as ordinary as everyday."

"Drylongso," said Lindy's dad.

"It's a drought for sure," said Mamalou. "And you came here running before the dust wall, Drylongso."

"Drylongso," murmured Lindy.

The house braced itself as a fresh wave of dust hit. Grit scraped and scrabbled at the windows. No matter that Mamalou had covered cracks where she could, dust got in everyplace.

Lindy laughed at her dad. His face was a reddish mask with eyeholes, nose and mouth holes. She brushed away a dusting from the cabinet mirror and saw her own face. She, too, had a mask on. She made its eyes cross. She made it grin, showing teeth.

Drylongso said, "Dust goes where it pleases when it pleases."

"I wish it would go *away!*" Lindy said.

"Pa says that if folks would stop plowing where they shouldn't, the dust would settle down," said Drylongso.

"That so?" said Lindy's dad. "We've no tractors here. Now we use an old push plow. We turn the ground by hand. It's been like turning dust over."

Drylongso said, "We saw the wall coming from far away; me and my family started running. A big dust swirl caught us. I heard them calling me, but I was choking. See, the driver of us field folks couldn't see. Panic got him, and he let us out."

"And you got separated?" Lindy's dad asked.

"I got apart from them," said the boy.

"I'd be afraid without my dad," said Lindy. But they were listening to Drylongso.

"Thistles," the boy said, all at once. "Sunflowers. Plant some, let them spread. They hold down the soil until the grasses grow here again, my pa says. That great wall that came upon all us—don't you see what it was?"

"It was like the earth reared up," said Lindy's dad.

Drylongso's eyes lit up. He nodded, eagerly. "Earth's not made to heave up so, but to lie down. The ground stands up to teach folks not to plow the grasslands."

"Seems so," said Lindy's dad. "There was a dust storm once, started in New Mexico and traveled whole as far as Washington, D.C. Folks had overused the land. Made it rise up."

"Wasn't that the 1930s?" asked Mamalou. "This is 1975; we know more."

Drylongso said, politely, "Pa says we can make plenty, and we think there will always be plenty. He says droughts come about every twenty years. And this here is another one."

Lindy's dad nodded, said, "From the 1890s, and the 1910s, 1930s, 1950s . . . "

"And now, the 1970s," said Drylongso. "Drought will come again in the 1990s, my pa says."

"Aren't you afraid, all by yourself?" asked Lindy. Her eyes were tearing. She coughed. Mamalou gave her some water to drink and put her arm around Lindy's shoulder. Made Lindy feel better.

Drylongso told a joke then, looking right at Lindy, too. "A pilot's plane got stuck in a black blizzard-a-dust, thousands of feet up. He bailed out. Had to shovel his way clear to the ground. When he got down, he carved a car for himself, blizzard black of dust, and drove away."

Her dad laughed at that.

"Is that true?" asked Lindy.

"No, but it's funny," said Mamalou.

They stayed in the house with Drylongso. All day, wind blew. Darkness came and went. Cast over the air was a peculiar bluish color caused by the filtering dust. They all stared out at an eerie blue world. Then they got used to it. Mamalou began making soup for them. They would have bread she had baked. They needn't go to town unless they ran out of water. Unless the well ran dry. Long rattle-car ride to there.

The storm let up, but it didn't stop. "We'd better go out," said Lindy's dad to Drylongso. "Run clothesline to the shed and from there to the field. So Mamalou and Lindy can walk about safely in case bad goes to worst."

"Okay," said Drylongso. Then he asked, "Is there a stream nearby?"

"There was a stream, long dry now," said Lindy's dad. "Nothing left to it but the bed of it."

"You will stay with us, of course," Mamalou told Drylongso.

"I forgot to ask if I could," said Drylongso.

"No need in asking. Course you can stay," Mamalou said.

"You are bigger than me," Lindy said to Drylongso. "I'll let you be my brother anyhow." They all laughed at that.

"Tell me your name," said Drylongso.

"Lindy!" Lindy said.

"It's Linn Dahlia," said Mamalou. "But Lindy is quicker." She smiled.

"And just as pretty," said Lindy's dad.

"And easy for me," said Lindy.

"Okay, Lindy, my sister," said Drylongso. "See? I'm not by myself."

Lindy smiled to everyone.

Through the night, she heard wind and grit strike the windows. Once, she woke to a dead calm outside. In the morning, she awakened to dull sunlight. The windowsill was covered in dust, as was the straight chair and the bedcovers. Lindy sat up. The only clean place was on her pillow where her head had lain.

"Mamalou!" she wailed. Mamalou came quickly to help and comfort her.

"Dust is in everything," Lindy said later as she ate her bread and molasses with a cup of milk. "Storm gone?" she asked.

"Long gone to bother somewheres else," said Drylongso. He sat down at the morning table.

"Didn't think about you!" Lindy said. She'd forgotten all about him.

"Thanks a lot!" he said, smiling. "Want to go and see outside?"

Lindy jumped up from the table. "Yes."

Outside, at the edge of the porch, Lindy saw a whole new world of dust.

"Now these would be white drifts if it'd been a snowstorm," said Drylongso.

Dust had drifted up over half of the porch. It had drifted over the steps. Drifted across the shed, covering the door latch, slanting upward.

Every window had little drifts in the corners. Their pie-shaped field had been swept clean of soil. What was showing was bare, hardpan, hard scrabble. What had been young corn lay flattened, dead or dying, drowning in dust. Dust shifted as high as the fenceposts around the field. It drifted in waves across the road into town.

"A lot of somebody's topsoil," Drylongso said. "A whole bunch of farms without any ground to plant."

"All our baby 'matoes is covered!" Lindy whimpered.

"Well, don't cry," he said. "Let me tell you about this man. Well, he came along on his horse after a dust storm. He saw a ten-gallon hat sitting atop a dust drift by a fencepost. Man went over there on his horse, reached over, picked up the hat. Only to find there was a head under it. It was another fellow, see, dust drift clear to his shoulders, just his head free there under the hat. Man on the horse says to the fellow, says, 'Well, do you want me to help you out of that dirt?' Man under the hat says, 'No, I'll just be a minute, catchin' my breath. Just restin' awhile, sittin' here on my mule.'"

It took a second, but then Lindy smiled and laughed.

"See, the other fellow has a mule under him buried in
the dust," Drylongso explained.

"I got it the first time," said Lindy.

"Well, okay, you're real smart, too!" said Drylongso.

The storm had ended. But there was wind, and the dust
floated around as high as the trees. The town's power had shorted
out from blowing dust, and there was no electricity. Other places,
phone lines were down. They all walked around in a haze, with
blue sky sometimes showing. The sunlight got through a little bit.
They felt hot and gritty all the time. Lindy helped Mamalou wash
and clean everything inside. They swept the dust outside.

About the Author
Virginia Hamilton

"Most of my books have some element of fantasy," says Virginia Hamilton. This is true in the story *Drylongso,* from which "Storm-a-Dust" is taken. The mythical character Drylongso is taken from an African American folk tale told in the Georgia Sea Islands. As Ms. Hamilton says in her story, where Drylongso goes, "life will grow better."

Storytelling runs in Ms. Hamilton's family. "I grew up within the warmth of loving aunts and uncles," she says, "all reluctant farmers but great storytellers." As she grew and started telling stories of her own, she found she had a gift for being able to fill in the "lapses between true memories, which had grown large with the passage of time."

Ms. Hamilton's story *M. C. Higgins, the Great* was the first book to win both the National Book Award and the Newbery Medal.

About the Illustrator
Jerry Pinkney

Book illustrations are only one way Jerry Pinkney expresses his creativity. He has worked on many other projects, including a set of stamps for the U.S. Postal Service. He feels it is important to show that African Americans can be successful in the graphic arts. "I wanted to show my children the possibilities that lay ahead for them," he says. "That was very important. I wanted to be a strong role model for my family and for other African Americans."

Mr. Pinkney is the only artist to have won three Coretta Scott King Awards for Illustration. *The Talking Eggs* by Robert D. San Souci and *Mirandy and Brother Wind* by Pat McKissack, both illustrated by Mr. Pinkney, were named Caldecott Honor Books.

Reader Response

Open for Discussion

In your opinion, what is the worst thing that happens during the dust storm? Why?

Comprehension Check

1. Based on how Lindy and her family treat Drylongso, how do you think they usually treat people in need?

2. What does Drylongso suggest is the cause of the dust storm? How does he suggest it might have been prevented?

3. Are the two stories Drylongso tells true? Why does he tell them? Use details from the story in your answer.

4. Describe the **setting.** Explain how *where* the story happens influences the actions of the characters. Support your answer with examples from the story. (Setting)

5. The story takes place in and around Lindy's house. How does the **setting** change from the beginning of the story to the end? Use examples from the story. (Setting)

Test Prep

Look Back and Write

What do Lindy and her father do and say that show that they are hopeful that it will rain? Look back at pages 184–185 for details to support your answer.

What Is a Drought?

from *Drought*
by Christopher Lampton

A drought is a period when it rains less often than usual. It doesn't usually stop raining completely during a drought. It just doesn't rain enough to replace the water that is used or that disappears through evaporation.

All living things, from plants to human beings, need water to survive. Usually, water is available in abundance. After all, it is one of the most plentiful substances on the surface of the earth. But sometimes water doesn't get to the places where it's needed at the times when it's needed—or in the form in which it's needed. Without rainfall to bring new supplies of fresh water from time to time, life on this planet might well cease to exist.

There will always be water on the planet Earth, but there will always be droughts too. In fact, there are small droughts somewhere on this planet every year. You've probably been through a few of them yourself. Maybe the grass on your lawn or in parks in your neighborhood began to turn brown. Or the local authorities announced that water would be rationed and asked you not to wash your car or water your garden.

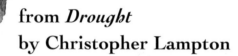

1930	1931	1932	1933	1934
	Severe droughts strike the Great Plains. Dust storms begin.	Number of yearly dust storms increases from 14 to 38.		The drought has spread to 27 states, with 127 million acres of farmland losing topsoil.

Usually, such small droughts are short and not terribly harmful. They tend to happen in the summer, when the weather is hot and dry. But sometimes droughts get out of hand. They can go on for months or even years. In a few cases they can last for as long as a decade. (Sometimes they can go on for thousands of years, but then we don't call them droughts. Rather, we say that the area that doesn't get rain has a naturally dry *climate.* Climate is a weather pattern that lasts for long periods of time.)

The worst drought in American history took place in the twentieth century. Many people still living today remember it. It swept across the Great Plains states in a series of wind and dust storms that, all together, became known as the Dust Bowl.

The drought lasted for almost the entire decade of the 1930s. It changed the lives of millions of people.

1935   1936   1937   1938   1939

1935 Congress begins developing soil conservation programs.

1938 Soil conservation measures reduce topsoil loss, but the drought continues.

1939 Rain comes at last, bringing an end to the drought.

Skill Lesson

Visualizing

- To **visualize** is to create a mental image as you read.

- One way an author helps you visualize is by using imagery, words that produce strong images. *The sun's glare lighted the dew on the leaves* is an example of imagery.

- Another way an author helps you visualize is by using words that describe how something looks, sounds, smells, tastes, or feels. These words are sensory details. *Jagged* and *velvet-smooth* are examples of sensory details.

Read "The Wexford Doe" from *Hold Fast to Dreams* by Andrea Davis Pinkney.

Talk About It

1. Visualize a scene from the story. Describe it to a partner.

2. Point out some words from the story that helped you visualize the scene you described.

3. Look back at the story to find more examples of sensory details.

The Wexford Doe

by Andrea Davis Pinkney

Deirdre lives on Scarlet Oak Lane. One morning she leaves home early to take pictures of the sunrise.

At the end of Scarlet Oak, a low stone wall separated the street from the woods. I leaned against the wall and listened to the sound of no sound—no cars, no kids, no neighbors sending me a "How you do?" The damp air hung silent. To me, it was too much quiet for a morning at rush hour.

There was lots to see, though. Lots to make good pictures. I slid my camera from its case and rested the case on the stone wall. The sun's glare lighted the dew on the leaves, making the trees in the distance twinkle like a forest of crystal-drop chandeliers.

Ch-click . . . ch-click . . . ch-click.

Tiny spiderwebs decorated the wall's jagged stones. One of the webs cradled a sleeping spider. Another shimmered like silk lace in the light.

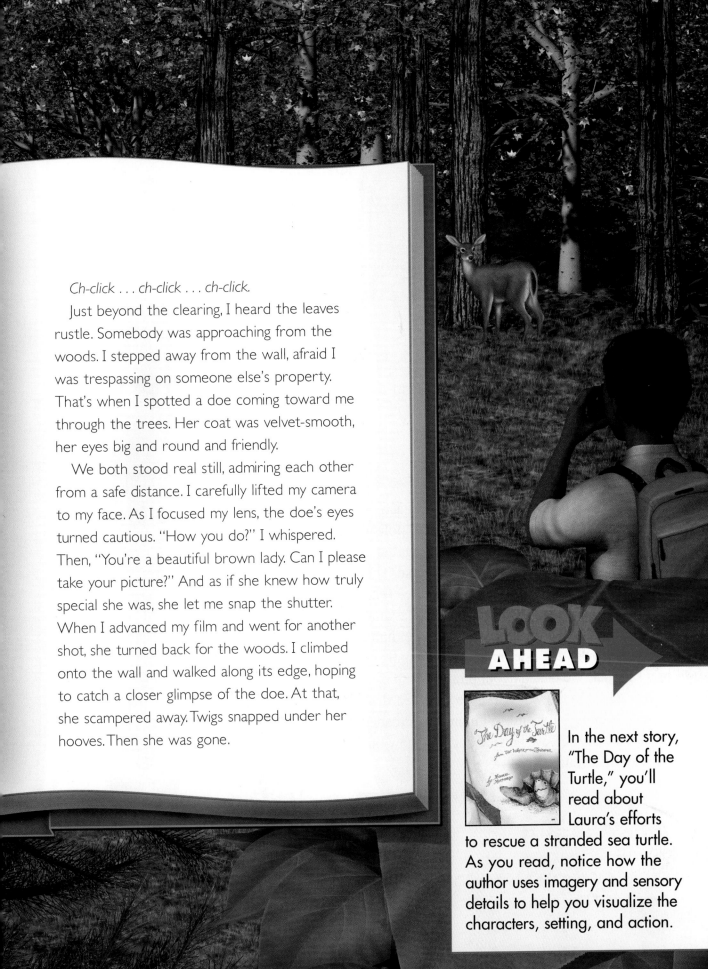

Ch-click . . . ch-click . . . ch-click.

Just beyond the clearing, I heard the leaves rustle. Somebody was approaching from the woods. I stepped away from the wall, afraid I was trespassing on someone else's property. That's when I spotted a doe coming toward me through the trees. Her coat was velvet-smooth, her eyes big and round and friendly.

We both stood real still, admiring each other from a safe distance. I carefully lifted my camera to my face. As I focused my lens, the doe's eyes turned cautious. "How you do?" I whispered. Then, "You're a beautiful brown lady. Can I please take your picture?" And as if she knew how truly special she was, she let me snap the shutter. When I advanced my film and went for another shot, she turned back for the woods. I climbed onto the wall and walked along its edge, hoping to catch a closer glimpse of the doe. At that, she scampered away. Twigs snapped under her hooves. Then she was gone.

LOOK AHEAD

In the next story, "The Day of the Turtle," you'll read about Laura's efforts to rescue a stranded sea turtle. As you read, notice how the author uses imagery and sensory details to help you visualize the characters, setting, and action.

Vocabulary

Words to Know

| driftwood | jellyfish | spar |
| tentacle | wary | |

When you read, you may come across a word that you don't know. To figure out the meaning of an unfamiliar word, look for clues in the words and sentences around it.

Read the paragraph below. To understand what *wary* means, notice how it is used in the sentence.

Beach Dreamers

My sister and I went for a walk on the beach. We collected shells and stones that had been polished smooth by the waves. We threw bread to the seagulls, but they were wary of us and wouldn't come close. They flew over our heads and refused to pick up the crumbs until we had passed. Later, we found a tentacle of a jellyfish that had washed up on shore. Luckily, we didn't touch it! On the horizon, my sister noticed a tall spar, or mast, of a sailboat. We talked about pirates and mermaids and shipwrecks. On the way back, we gathered driftwood for that evening's bonfire. With our arms loaded with the day's treasures, we hurried back to show our parents what we had found.

Talk About It

Use some of your vocabulary words to describe a day at the beach. What made it so special?

The Day of the Turtle

from THE WRECK OF THE ZANZIBAR

by Michael Morpurgo

Fourteen-year-old Laura Perryman lives on an island far off the coast of England in 1907. In her diary she writes about her brother Billy, who left home in search of adventure; about the storms that have left her family with very little food and destroyed the roof on Granny May's house; and about—a new friend.

September 8th

Today I found a turtle. I think it's called a leatherback turtle. I found one once before, but it was dead. This one has been washed up alive.

Father had sent me down to collect driftwood on Rushy Bay. He said there'd be plenty about after a storm like that. He was right.

I'd been there for half an hour or so heaping up the wood, before I noticed the turtle in the tide line of piled seaweed. I thought at first he was just a washed-up tree stump covered in seaweed.

He was upside down on the sand. I pulled the seaweed off him. His eyes were open, unblinking. He was more dead than alive, I thought. His flippers were quite still and held out to the clouds above as if he was worshiping them. He was massive, as long as this bed, and wider. He had a face like a two-hundred-year-old man, wizened and wrinkled and wise, and a gently smiling mouth.

I looked around, and there were more gulls gathering. They were silent, watching, waiting; and I knew well enough what they were waiting for. I pulled away more of the seaweed and saw that the gulls had been at him already. There was blood under his neck where the skin had been pecked. I had got there just in time. I bombarded the gulls with pebbles and they flew off, protesting noisily, leaving me alone with my turtle.

I knew it would be impossible to roll him over, but I tried anyway. I could rock him back and forth on his shell, but I could not turn him over, no matter how hard I tried. After a while I gave up and sat down beside him on the sand. His eyes kept closing slowly as if he was dropping off to sleep, or maybe he was dying—I couldn't be sure. I stroked him under his chin, where I thought he would like it, keeping my hand well away from his mouth.

A great curling storm wave broke and came tumbling toward us. When it went hissing back over the sand, it left behind a broken spar. It was as if the sea was telling me what to do. I dragged the spar up the beach. Then I saw the turtle's head go back, and his eyes closed. I've often seen sea birds like that. Once their heads go back there's nothing you can do. But I couldn't just let him die. I couldn't. I shouted at him, I shook him. I told him that he wasn't going to die, that I'd turn him over somehow, that it wouldn't be long.

I dug a deep hole in the sand beside him. I would lever him up and topple him in. I drove the spar into the sand underneath his shell. I drove it in again and again, until it was as deep as I could get it. I hauled back on it and felt him shift. I threw all my weight on it and at last he tumbled over into the hole, and the right way up too. But when I scrambled over to him, his head lay limp in the sand, his eyes closed to the world. There wasn't a flicker of life about him. He was dead.

I was quite sure of it. It's silly, I know—I had only known him for a few minutes—but I felt like I had lost a friend.

I made a pillow of soft sea lettuce for his head and knelt beside him. I cried till there were no more tears to cry. And then I saw the gulls were back. They knew too. I screamed at them, but they just glared at me and moved in closer.

"No!" I cried. "No!"

I would never let them have him, never. I piled a mountain of seaweed on top of him, and my driftwood on top of that. The next tide would take him away. I left him and went home.

I went back to Rushy Bay this evening at high tide, just before nightfall, to see if my turtle was gone. He was still there. The tide had not come high enough. The gulls were gone though, all of them. I really don't know why, but I wanted to see his face once more. I pulled the wood and seaweed away until I could see the top of his head. As I looked it moved and lifted. He was blinking up at me. He was alive again! I could have kissed him, really I could. But I didn't quite dare.

He's still there now, all covered up against the gulls, I hope. In the morning—I had to stop writing because Father just came in. He hardly ever comes into my room, so I knew at once that something was wrong.

"You all right?" he said, standing in the doorway. "What've you been up to?"

"Nothing," I said. "Why?"

"Old man Jenkins. He said he saw you down on Rushy Bay."

"I was collecting wood," I told him, as calmly as I could. "Like you said I should." Lying is so difficult for me. I'm just not good at it.

"He thought you were crying—crying your eyes out, he says."

"I was not," I said, but I didn't dare look at him. I pretended to go on writing in my diary.

"You are telling me the truth, Laura?" He knew I wasn't; he knew it.

"Of course," I said. I just wished he would go.

"What do you find to write in that diary of yours?" he asked.

"Things," I said. "Just things." And he went out and shut the door behind him. He knows there's something, but he doesn't know what. I'm going to have to be very careful. If Father finds out about the turtle, I'm in trouble. He's only got to go down to Rushy Bay and look. That turtle would just be food to him, and to anyone else who finds him. We're all hungry. Everyone is getting hungrier every day. I should tell Father. I know I should. But I can't do it. I just can't let them eat him.

In the early morning, I'll have to get him back into the sea. I don't know how I'm going to do it, but somehow I will. I must. Now it's not only the gulls I have to save him from.

September 9th

I shall remember today as long as I live. This morning I slipped away as soon as I could. No one saw me go and no one followed me, I made quite sure of that. I'd lain awake most of the night wondering how I was going to get my turtle back into the water. But as I made my way down to Rushy Bay while the morning fog was lifting off the sea, I had no idea at all how I would do it. Even as I uncovered him, I still didn't know. I only knew it had to be done. So I talked to him. I was trying to explain it all to him, how he mustn't worry, how I'd find a way, but that I didn't yet know what. He's got eyes that make you think he understands. Maybe he doesn't, but you never know. Somehow, once I'd started talking, I felt it was rude not to go on.

I fetched some seawater in my hat and poured it over him. He seemed to like it—he lifted his head into it as I poured. So I did it again and again. I told him all about the storm, about Granny May's roof, about the battered boats, and he looked at me. He was listening.

He was so weak, though. He kept trying to move, trying to dig his flippers into the sand, but he didn't have the strength to do it. His mouth kept opening and shutting as if he was gasping for breath.

Then I had an idea. I scooped out a long, deep channel all the way down to the sea. I would wait for the tide to come in as far as it could, and when the time came I would ease him down into the channel and he could wade out to sea. As I dug I told him my plan. When I'd finished I lay down beside him, exhausted, and waited for the tide.

The gulls never left us alone for a minute. They stood eyeing us from the rocks and from the shallows. When I threw stones at them, they didn't fly off anymore. They just hopped a little farther away, and they always came back. I didn't go home for lunch—I just hoped Father wouldn't come looking for me. I couldn't leave my turtle, not with the gulls all around us just waiting for their chance. Besides, the tide was coming in now, closer all the time. Then there were barely five yards of sand left between the sea and my turtle, and the water was washing up the channel just as I'd planned it. It was now or never.

I told him what he had to do. "You've got to walk the rest," I said. "If you want to get back in the sea, you've got to walk, you hear me?"

He tried. He honestly tried. Time and again he dug the edge of his flippers into the sand, but he just couldn't move himself.

The flippers dug in again and again, but he stayed where he was. I tried pushing him from behind. That didn't work. I tried moving his flippers for him one by one. That didn't work. I slapped his shell. I shouted at him. All he did was swallow once or twice and blink at me. In the end I tried threatening him. I crouched down in front of him.

"All right," I said. "All right. You stay here if you like. See if I care. You see those gulls? You know what they're waiting for? If they don't get you, then someone else'll find you and you'll be turtle stew." I was shouting at him now. I was really shouting at him. "Turtle stew, you hear me?" All the while his eyes never left my face, not for a moment. Bullying hadn't worked either. So now I tried begging.

"Please," I said. "Please." But his eyes gave me the answer I already knew. He could not move. He hadn't the strength. There was nothing else left to try. From the look in his eyes I think he knew it too.

I wandered some way away from him and sat down on a rock to think. I was still thinking fruitlessly, when I saw the gig coming around Droppy Nose Point and heading out to sea. Father was there—I recognized his cap. Old man Jenkins

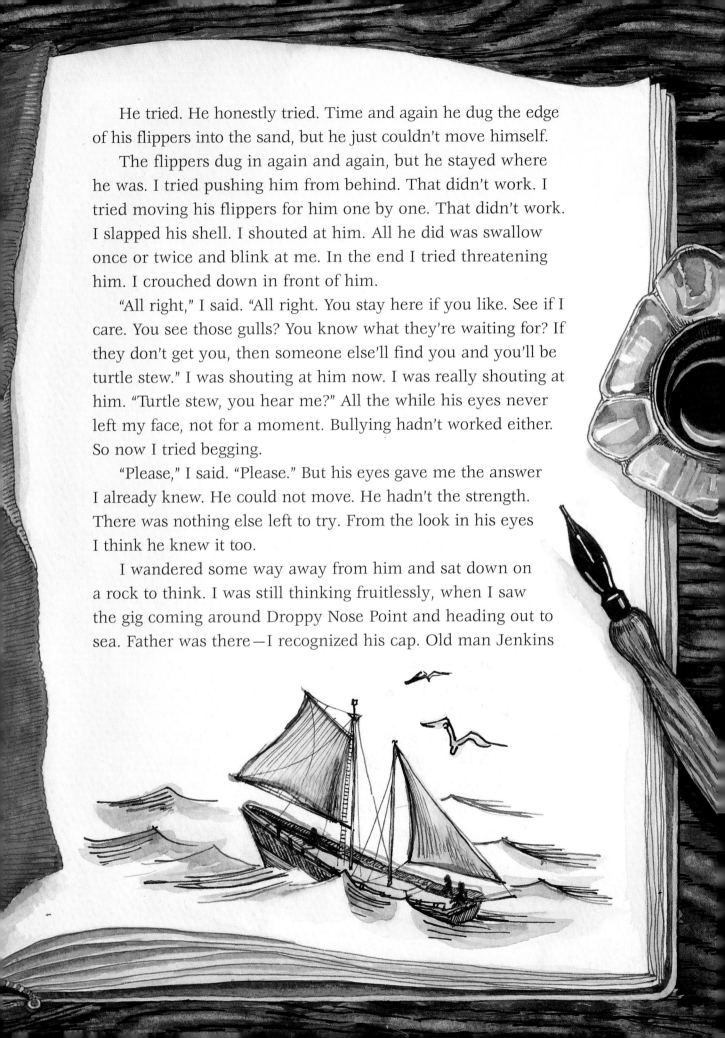

was in Billy's place, and the Chief was setting the jibsail. They were far too far away to see my turtle. I came back to him and sat down.

"See that gig?" I told him. "One day I'm going to row in that gig, just like Billy did. One day."

And I told him all about the gig and the big ships that come into Scilly needing a pilot to bring them in safely, and how the gigs race each other out to get there first. I told him about the wrecks too, and how the gigs will put to sea in any weather if there are sailors to rescue or cargo to salvage. The strange thing is, I didn't feel at all silly talking to my turtle. I mean, I know it *is* silly, but it just seemed the natural thing to do. I honestly think I told the turtle more about me than I've ever told anyone before.

I looked down at him. He was nudging at the sand with his chin; his mouth was open. He was hungry! I don't know why I hadn't thought of it before. I had no idea at all what turtles eat. So I tried what was nearest first—seaweed of all sorts, sea lettuce, bladder wrack, whatever I could find. I dangled it in front of his mouth, brushing his nose with it so he could smell it. He looked as if he was going to eat it. He opened his mouth slowly and snapped at it. But then he turned his head away and let it fall to the ground.

"What, then?" I asked.

A sudden shadow fell across me. Granny May was standing above me in her hat.

"How long have you been there?" I asked.

"Long enough," she said, and she walked around me to get a better look at the turtle.

"Let's try shrimps," she said. "Maybe he'll eat shrimps. We'd better hurry. We don't want anyone else finding him, do we?"

And she sent me off home to fetch the shrimping net. I ran all the way there and all the way back, wondering if Granny May knew about her roof yet.

Granny May is the best shrimper on the island. She knows every likely cluster of seaweed on Rushy Bay—and everywhere else, in fact. One sweep through the shallows and she was back, her net jumping with shrimps. She smiled down at my turtle.

"Useful, isn't it?" she said, tapping him with her stick.

"What?" I replied.

"Carrying your house around with you. Can't hardly have your roof blowed off, can you?" So she did know. "It'll mend," she said. "Roofs you can mend easily enough. Hope is a little harder."

She told me to dig out a bowl in the sand right under the turtle's chin, and then she shook out her net. He looked mildly interested for a moment and then looked away. It was no good. Granny May was looking out to sea, shielding her eyes against the glare of the sun.

"I wonder," she murmured. "I wonder. I won't be long." And she was gone down to the sea. She was wading out up to her ankles, then up to her knees, with her shrimping net scooping through the water around her. I stayed behind with the turtle and threw more stones at the gulls. When she came back, her net was bulging with jellyfish, blue jellyfish. She emptied them into the turtle's sandy bowl. At once he was at them like a vulture, snapping, crunching, swallowing, until there wasn't a tentacle left.

"He's smiling," she said. "I think he likes them. I think perhaps he'd like some more."

"I'll do it," I said.

I picked up the net and rushed down into the sea. They were not difficult to find. I've never liked jellyfish since I was stung on my neck when I was little and came out in a burning welt that lasted for months. So I kept a wary eye around me. I scooped up twelve big ones in as many minutes. He ate those and then lifted his head asking for more. We took turns after that, Granny May and me, until at last he seemed to have had enough and left a half-chewed jellyfish lying there, with the shrimps still hopping all around it. I crouched down and looked my turtle in the eye.

"Feel better now?" I asked, and I wondered if turtles burp when they've eaten too fast. He didn't burp, but he did move. The flippers dug deeper. He shifted—just a little at first. And then he was scooping himself slowly forward, inching his way through the sand. I went crazy. I was cavorting up and down like a wild thing, and Granny May was just the same. The two of us whistled and whooped to keep him moving, but we knew soon enough that we didn't need to. Every step he took was stronger and his neck reached forward purposefully. Nothing would stop him now. When he got near the sea where the sand was tide-rippled and wet, he moved, faster and faster, past the rock pools and across the muddy sand where the lugworms leave their curly cases. His flippers were under the water now. He was half walking, half swimming. Then he dipped his snout into the sea and let the water run over his head and down his neck. He was going, and suddenly I didn't want him to. I was alongside him, bending over him.

"You don't have to go," I said.

"He wants to," said Granny May. "He has to."

He was in deeper water now, and with a few powerful strokes he was gone, cruising out through the turquoise water of the shallows to the deep blue beyond. The last I saw of him he was a dark shadow under the sea making out toward Samson.

I suddenly felt alone. Granny May knew it I think, because she put her arm around me and kissed the top of my head.

Back at home we never said a word about our turtle. It wasn't an arranged secret—nothing like that. We just didn't tell anyone because we didn't want to. It was private somehow.

About the Author

Michael Morpurgo

Michael Morpurgo likes to write historical fiction for children. He lives in England, but the action in his novels takes place in other countries as well as in his homeland. In his book *Twist of Gold,* for example, the characters Sean and Annie O'Brien leave Ireland in the 1840s to look for their father in the United States. The story takes place during the Irish Potato Famine, a terrible disaster in which crops failed and almost one million people died from disease or starvation.

Another award-winning story, *Waiting for Anya,* takes place in France during World War II. This exciting book tells the story of the residents of a village in the Pyrenees mountains who smuggle Jewish children across the border into Spain. *Waiting for Anya* was named a Best Book by the School Library Journal and was a runner-up for England's Guardian Award. A theme of this book—the triumph of good over evil—is one that runs through many of Mr. Morpurgo's books.

Mr. Morpurgo also writes stories that feature animals. Many readers enjoy these animal stories because they are realistic. If you enjoyed the animal rescue in "The Day of the Turtle," look for Mr. Morpurgo's novel *Why the Whales Came.* In this novel, set in England during World War I, two children and a hermit try to convince villagers to help them save some beached whales. The book was adapted for a movie.

Reader Response

Open for Discussion

What appeals to you about living on an island? Would you want to live on Laura's island? Why or why not?

Comprehension Check

1. Why is the turtle in danger? Support your answer with details from the story.

2. Laura confides in her diary that she "must" save the turtle's life. Why do you think she feels this way? Use information from the story to support your answer.

3. Why doesn't Laura ask her father or any of the other villagers to help her save the turtle? Who does help her?

4. **Visualize** Laura's island and the beach where she finds the turtle. List as many details of the landscape and the plant and animal life as you can. Check your list against the story. (Visualizing)

5. **Visualize** the way in which Laura turns the turtle rightside up. Draw a diagram that shows how she uses a wooden spar as a lever. (Visualizing)

Test Prep
Look Back and Write

What do Laura and Granny May do together to help save the turtle? Tell what they do in order, from first to last. Use details from pages 216–219 in your answer.

Tortoises and Turtles

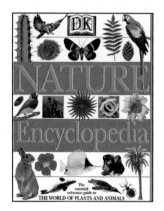

THESE HARD-SHELLED REPTILES belong to a group called chelonians, which includes tortoises, turtles, and terrapins. All reproduce by laying eggs on land, usually in sand, leaf litter, or other animals' burrows. Tortoises can live for more than 100 years.

Starred tortoise *(Geochelone elegans)* has starlike patterns on its knobbly carapace, or covering.

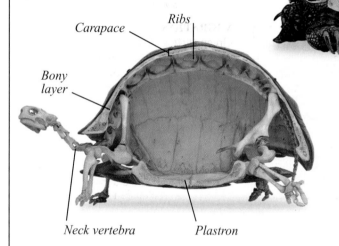

Carapace *Ribs*

Bony layer

Neck vertebra *Plastron*

SHELL ARMOR

The strong shell of a chelonian consists of two parts—a domed carapace covering the back, and a flat plastron under the belly. The shell is made from bony plates that are fused to the ribs and vertebrae to form a solid box of armor.

Spiny soft-shell turtle *(Apalone spinifera)*

The flat shell of this red-eared slider *(Trachemys scripta elegans)* is a typical feature of most aquatic turtles.

SOFT SHELLS

Soft-shelled turtles have shells with a leathery texture and no horny plates. The bony part of the shell contains large air spaces, which makes the turtle lighter, helping it float and swim with ease.

SHELLS AND LEGS

Land-living tortoises have either high-domed or bumpy shells to protect them from predators. They need strong, thick legs, like pillars, to support their weight. Turtles tend to have flatter, lighter shells, which are streamlined for easy movement. Their long front legs are wing-shaped to enable them to "fly" through the water.

FEEDING

Most chelonians are too slow to catch prey, so they feed on plants or small animals such as worms and insect larvae. The camouflaged alligator snapping turtle lures fish into its mouth with a wormlike "bait" on its tongue.

Wormlike appendage attracts prey.

Alligator snapping turtle *(Macroclemys temmincki)*

Once hatched, baby green turtles dash for the open sea to escape predators.

HATCHING OUT

Baby chelonians hatch out of their eggs using a peg, or egg tooth, on the front of their snouts.

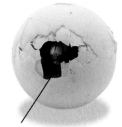

Egg tooth drops off soon after hatching.

EGGS AND YOUNG

Chelonians lay eggs on land so that the developing embryos can breathe oxygen from the air. In a nesting season, most species lay two or more clutches of eggs, and there may be between four and more than a hundred eggs in each clutch. Some species, such as the Florida redbelly *(Pseudemys nelsoni)*, use the nests of other animals.

MIGRATION

Green turtles *(Chelonia mydas)* migrate some 1,400 miles (2,250 km) from their feeding grounds off the coast of Brazil to nesting grounds on Ascension Island in the middle of the South Atlantic.

→ Turtle route to feeding grounds off Brazilian coast

→ Turtle route to nesting grounds on Ascension Island

Streamlined shell allows turtle to swim easily through water.

Turtles come to the surface to breathe through their nostrils.

Front legs are flipper-shaped so the turtle can glide through water.

Back feet are used as rudders for steering.

Green turtle *(Chelonia mydas)*

Sea turtles, such as the green turtle, swim gracefully in the sea, but are clumsy on land.

SEA TURTLES

The seven species of sea turtle all have flat, lightweight, streamlined shells and large front flippers. The largest is the leatherback turtle *(Dermochelys coriacea)*, which is found in warmer oceans.

Persuasive Devices

- **Persuasive devices** are the special techniques an author uses to influence the way you think or feel.

- One type of persuasive device is the use of *loaded words*. Authors use loaded words to bring out an emotional response in readers and to convince readers of their ideas and views.

- As you read persuasive writing, think about whether the author is appealing to your reason through facts and ideas, or to your emotions through loaded words.

Read "Why Care?" from *Our Endangered Planet: Life on Land* by Mary Hoff and Mary M. Rodgers.

Write About It

1. Look back at the first paragraph to find loaded words that describe human behavior. How do they make you feel?

2. What are the authors of this article trying to persuade you to think or feel?

Why Care?

by Mary Hoff and Mary M. Rodgers

Humankind dominates the global environment. We actively—and often negatively—influence the ability of plants and animals to survive and flourish. Because we share this planet with other forms of life, we need to rethink our behavior. We ought not to push our way through existence, bullying the rest of the creatures on the earth.

It may be hard for us to see the value of any one species. But what if we had lost the rosy periwinkle? We would also have lost the anti-cancer drug in its leaves, and many cancer victims would have died. The trees on our planet in rain forests, in national

parks, in backyards, and in countless other spots—help to absorb some of the air pollution we create.

In addition to their usefulness, plants and animals are important sources of beauty and fun. The next time you walk in a wooded park or hear a bird sing or watch the playful antics of your pet, remember that these species enrich our lives just by existing.

We need our partners in the web of life, and they need us. But even if we do not benefit directly from other species, many people believe these living things have as much right to be here as we do. By taking actions that force them toward extinction, we are violating that right.

LOOK AHEAD

In the nonfiction selection that follows, "Saving the Sound," notice how the author uses loaded words and other persuasive devices to influence your thinking about the environment.

225

Vocabulary

Words to Know

cleanup	fragile	muck
contaminated	toll	environment
widespread		

Words that are spelled and pronounced the same but have different origins and meanings—such as *bark* (on a tree) and *bark* (like a dog)—are called **homonyms.** To understand the correct meaning of a homonym, look for clues in the surrounding words and sentences.

Read the paragraph below. Decide whether *toll* means "the sound of a bell" or "something suffered."

Getting Involved

Are you concerned about our fragile environment? Many students are. Polluted air, littered streets, and rivers contaminated with muck are just a few of the widespread environmental problems that kids are helping to clean up. Pollution has taken a terrible toll on our planet, but you can do something about it. Recycle newspapers, bottles, and cans. Organize a cleanup of a local park. Write your mayor or state senators and tell them about environmental issues in your community. Be polite and offer thoughtful suggestions; finding a solution is just as important as pointing out the problem.

Talk About It

Use some of your vocabulary words to explain how you can help the environment.

226

SAVING THE Sound

from *Spill! The Story of the Exxon Valdez*
by Terry Carr

On a spring night in 1989, an oil tanker hit a reef off the coast of Alaska. About 11 million gallons of crude oil spilled into the water. The wreck of the *Exxon Valdez* resulted in the worst oil spill in the history of the United States.

The Sound is home to 5,000 of Alaska's bald eagles.

Prince William Sound, a body of water that connects part of Alaska's southern coast with the Gulf of Alaska, is one of the state's most beautiful regions. At 15,000 square miles (38,850 square km), the Sound is twice the size of the state of New Jersey. Mountains surround the Sound, holding it in a sort of deep cup. Thick forests of spruce grace the mountain slopes. These trees remain green all year, giving the Sound a sharp contrast in winter between the green trees and the white snow.

Dozens of islands—some big, some small—are scattered across the water. In the sunlight the water resembles the brilliant blue of a jewel. The shorelines are not the white sand of Florida or California beaches. They are mostly rugged rocks, gravel, or gray sand. Some shorelines have no beach at all, just steep rock faces that plunge into the water.

Besides Valdez, the towns of Cordova and Whittier are on the Sound. Many tiny villages also dot the shorelines, and others have been built on the islands. These villages depend heavily on fishing for their survival.

Only one road goes to the Sound, the two-lane highway that ends in Valdez. The Alaska Railroad goes to Whittier, but all other places in the Sound can be reached only by boat or airplane.

The Sound is one of the most environmentally sensitive regions in the world. A huge range of animals and plant life thrive there.

Humpback and killer whales roam the water, looking for a meal of shrimp or fish. And, indeed, the Sound is home to many fish, including halibut, pollock, herring, and salmon. Each spring and summer, about 15 million salmon return to the Sound and the rivers that flow into it. They are returning, after two to six years at sea, to the places where they were bred to lay their eggs. These fish are the main source of income for the surrounding towns and villages. Commercial fishermen await their arrival with excitement. Sport fishermen, too, count the days until the salmon will arrive. During the fishing season, canneries open to prepare the commercial fishermen's catch for sale to other states and countries.

Sea lions populate several of the Sound's islands. Sea lions can weigh up to one ton. They come to the Sound in the spring and remain through much of the summer, looking for mates or rearing their young.

Top: The commercial fishing industry brings in yearly revenues of over $100 million to the Sound. *Bottom:* Whales and many other animals live in the Sound.

The playful otter is a popular sight on the Sound.

Seals, too, arrive in the spring. Much smaller than sea lions, they usually weigh less than 250 pounds (113 kg). They come to the Sound to give birth to their pups.

The Sound's most appealing sea creature is the playful sea otter. Otters live in the region year-round. Once they were hunted for their fur, but now they are protected by law. They are an attraction for tourists as well as for the people who live on the Sound. They are superb swimmers and appear to spend as much time playing as they do looking for food. Watching them float on their backs while cracking open a clam or crab or grooming their babies is one of the most popular sights on the Sound.

On land, animals big and small live off the Sound's natural treasures. Bears wander the forests and mountains, searching for food. Deer munch leaves and berries. Marmots, short-legged animals somewhat resembling large squirrels, scurry about feeding on grass, roots, and berries.

Majestic bald eagles dominate the skies. With a wingspan of up to 7 feet (2.1 m), they soar above the water and forests with spectacular grace. They feed on fish and small land animals.

Gulls, sea ducks, and Canada geese spend part or all of the year in the Sound. Murres (a sea bird that returns to the Sound in the spring) and loons (which breed in large colonies in the Sound) populate the area in huge numbers during spring and summer.

In the springtime the Sound is waking from winter. Ice and snow are melting. Bears emerge from their hibernation dens. Fish and birds that winter elsewhere begin to return. Prince William Sound is coming to life.

The wreck of the *Exxon Valdez*, however, changed all that. The oil spill turned a time of awakening and beauty into a time of nightmare and death. The Sound awoke on March 24, 1989, to find itself the victim of a disaster unlike anything that had occurred before in the United States.

One of the worst parts of the first few hours of the spill is that no one was prepared for it. The oil-spill response plan calls for spill-fighting equipment to be on hand five hours after a spill occurs. In fact, ten hours passed before the Alyeska Pipeline Service Company got people and equipment onto the water and to the oil. Alyeska is the company formed by the oil companies that own the trans-Alaska pipeline to operate the line. The company also runs the pipeline terminal and is responsible for responding first to any spill.

During those critical first hours of the spill, Alyeska crews worked frantically to get oil-containment equipment out on the water. But little of the equipment was ready to go. A barge that should have had much of the equipment on it sat nearly empty. Oil-containment booms (floating, flexible tubes of plastic used to corral oil) and other supplies had to be found in Alyeska warehouses, dug out, and loaded on boats. Snow buried other equipment. It took hours to get all this material ready.

By daylight Friday morning, the oil slick from the disabled ship had spread out for miles. Oil had swept over Prince William Sound like an unstoppable ocean wave, only this wave was thick, black, and deadly.

Top: Workers were hoisted aboard a cleanup boat off Eleanor Island. *Bottom:* The Alaska state ferry *Aurora* served as a floating hotel for workers fighting the spill.

Tides and wind pushed the oil southwest, toward the heart of the Sound. This movement spared Valdez itself and the Sound's east coast. Still, it wouldn't take long before the oil reached the islands and the west coast, coating their shores with a thick, gooey slime.

Beautiful weather settled over the Sound during the spill's first few days. Steady, brilliant sunlight warmed the air. The water was mostly calm. The fine weather, however, worked against early attempts to control the advancing oil.

Chemicals, called "dispersants," that might have been used to break up the oil require rough seas. Like dishwater soap, these chemicals need turbulence to work best. They need wind and waves for them to spread, foam, and do their job. The chemicals were tested, but the tests failed. The water was too calm.

By the third day, the oil slick covered 100 square miles (26,000 hectares). Its size grew with remarkable speed. Fishermen took to the

Top: Containment booms formed a necklace around the *Exxon Valdez* to contain its leaking oil. *Bottom:* Alaska's brilliant sunlight reflects off the oil spill's swirling patterns.

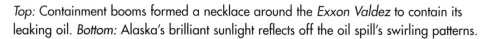

The cleanup effort was a dirty task, staining humans and boats alike.

water in boats. They began using buckets to scoop the oil off the water and take it to shore. These efforts had only a tiny effect.

Then, on the fourth day, the weather worsened. While calm waters had prevented dispersant use earlier, this time the weather was too stormy. Planes could not fly to spread the chemicals. Winds of up to 50 miles (80 km) per hour pushed the oil around the Sound. The poor weather lasted two days. By the time planes could get in the air again, it was too late. The oil covered an area far too large for dispersants to work.

Attempts to corral the oil with containment booms, which are designed to prevent the oil from spreading, weren't working either. There was too much oil and too little boom.

Sea lions aboard a navigational buoy seek refuge from the oily waters.

The Exxon Corporation had taken control of the cleanup after the first hours. Fishermen grew angry at the giant company. They said Exxon wasn't doing enough to stop the oil or to clean it up.

Some fishermen took matters into their own hands. They organized attack forces. They gathered as much equipment as they could and set up barriers of containment booms to protect fishing grounds and hatcheries, where millions of fish are raised in pens. Containment booms float on the water, much like a string of logs would. In some cases, the booms worked. In other cases, there was too much oil. It simply washed over the booms.

Exxon hired dozens of boats. Just about anything that could float went out to try to stop the oil. Some of the boats took workers out to set up camps on islands and shores. Others carried workers out at dawn and returned to Valdez or Cordova at night. It was hard, dirty work. Oil fumes made some workers sick. Oil quickly dirtied any boat or person that got near it.

By the seventh day of the spill, oil had moved out of the mouth of the Sound into the Pacific Ocean. Currents pushed it west, along the state's southern coast. Within a few days, oil threatened the coast of Seward and Kodiak Island, two other major fishing areas.

As days passed, workers built more and more camps. Some were built on shore, but others were built on barges, which floated on the water. Ships and large boats were also used to house workers. These floating living quarters became known as "floatels." In some places, so many people, boats, and equipment moved in that instant towns were created.

All this time, the oil continued to spread. It reached into every corner of some islands. It washed up on hundreds of miles of shoreline. It turned beaches black with slippery slime. Each high tide laid on a new layer of the muck.

The tides also washed up a more terrible toll: dead birds and sea otters. Within a week after the spill, thousands of dead murres, loons, and other birds littered the beaches. One island had 500 dead birds on a 4-mile (6.4-km) stretch of shore. Oil had turned the dead birds into a stiff, black mass.

Some of the birds had drowned. Once the heavy oil got onto their feathers, they could not float. Other birds died from the cold, because feathers contaminated with oil lose their shape and thus their

The black tide left its mark on Treasure Cove.

ability to insulate. This left the birds vulnerable to the deadly cold of the Sound's waters. Yet more birds were poisoned when they ate plants that had oil on them. The toxic chemicals in the oil destroys the birds' internal organs or poisons their blood, causing them to weaken and die.

Bald eagles found the birds on the beaches an easy meal. Some of the eagles, though, would themselves die from eating prey contaminated with oil.

The saddest victims to see on the beaches were the murres and loons covered with oil but not yet dead. Many of them were completely black. They struggled to fly, but could not because they were too heavy with oil. Rescue workers captured many of them and took them to bird-care centers for cleaning.

As much as the birds suffered, the Sound's otters may have suffered more. About 10,000 of the playful creatures live in the Sound. Scientists counted almost 500 dead otters in the spill's first days. Many more otters probably died and sank in the water.

The eye of the storm: 42 million gallons (159 million liters) of the grounded tanker's unspilled oil were pumped into smaller vessels. Twelve days after the accident, the *Exxon Valdez* was towed to safe anchorage.

Oil ruined the otters' ability to stay warm. Matted with oil, their fur could no longer insulate their bodies from the cold water. Others died from damage to internal organs caused by the oil's poisons. Rescue workers were able to capture about 100 oiled otters that were still alive in the first few days. They took them to shore for care and cleaning.

While birds and sea otters were obvious victims of the spill, the effect of oil on the fish and other wildlife was less certain. Whales, for example, seemed to avoid the oil. And even if they got into the slick, they had a thick layer of blubber that would protect them against the cold. Seals and sea lions had the same protection. Still, oil on their food might make them sick or kill them. It would take years of study before scientists would learn the full effects of the oil on these animals.

The effects of oil on salmon, salmon fry (baby salmon), herring, shrimp, and bottomfish would also require study. One thing was certain: Fishermen could not fish in areas contaminated by oil. Therefore, state officials immediately closed all herring fishing in the Sound. They closed many areas to shrimp, crab, and to bottomfish fishing.

Officials closed areas in the Sound and along the state's southern coast to salmon fishing. They even closed some areas reaching up into Cook Inlet, far from the original spill. These closings hit fishermen hard. Many depend on the fishing season to make the money they live on for the rest of the year.

Fishermen feared the oil could affect salmon fishing for years because salmon fry are particularly sensitive to oil. Normally, the hatchery-raised fry are released in April and spend up to three months feeding near the shore before swimming out to sea. During these months, even small amounts of oil can kill them and reduce the numbers returning in later years.

The Sound's food chain was threatened down to the smallest creatures and plants. Zooplankton and phytoplankton are the tiny animals and plants upon which almost everything else in the Sound depends. Salmon fry and other sea life feed on them, bigger creatures feed on the fry, and so on up to the whales, the biggest animals in the Sound. The oil spill struck at just the time when the plankton were beginning to bloom. Widespread destruction of them could affect sources of food all the way up the chain.

The *Exxon Valdez* left behind more than 1,000 miles (1,610 km) of oil-slimed shoreline in Prince William Sound. If the oiled areas of the Sound were laid against the eastern coast of the United States, they would reach from Massachusetts to North Carolina. The tanker left

Wind and current drove the oil slick beyond Kodiak Island, 300 miles (483 km) from the accident. *Inset:* Had the spill occurred on the East Coast, it would have spanned an area from Massachusetts to North Carolina.

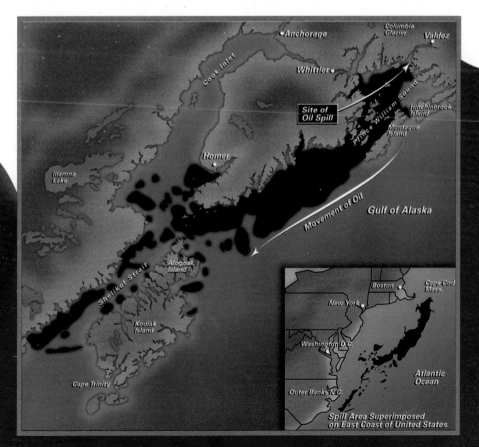

Top: A scientist collects fish from the Sound in an effort to study the spill's long-term effects. *Bottom:* In cold waters, residue from the spill may take years to decompose. The oil could be absorbed into the food chain through plankton and other tiny organisms over time.

behind a trail littered with thousands of dead birds and sea animals. It left a ruined fishing season for fishermen. And it left many questions about whether the Sound would recover from the spill.

By the end of the first summer after the spill, rescue workers had counted about 30,000 dead birds. Wildlife biologists estimated, though, that this number is only 10 to 30 percent of the toll, meaning that between 90,000 and 270,000 birds have probably died and disappeared in the waters of the Sound. They also counted 1,016 dead sea otters. The toll in both otters and birds could increase as the years pass. Nobody can say for sure how high the numbers will go or how long the oil will continue to harm wildlife.

Since the accident, scientists from all over the world have gone to Alaska to study the effects of the spill. In a way, Prince William Sound became a huge laboratory for these scientists. They hope to learn more about what oil can do to land, water, and wildlife. They hope to learn which cleanup methods work best. The amount of our knowledge about the ecological effects of oil spills is small. Scientists say the Prince William Sound spill can add much to this knowledge. The information will be useful in dealing with future spills.

It is a sad fact that accidents happen. But as long as oil has to be moved by ships, oil spills will occur. In fact, other major spills have already occurred in the United States since the Prince William Sound disaster. They were not anywhere as big as the Alaska spill, but they still point to the dangers of transporting oil by sea. That danger will exist as long as Americans need gas for their cars, airplanes, and factories.

Meanwhile, people who live on Prince William Sound and others who care about it can only wait and watch. They wait to see if the playful otters will recover from the oil's deadly effects. They wait to see if the birds will keep coming back to an area that killed so many of their kind. They wait to see if the black stains on the Sound's beaches

About the Author
Terry Carr

Terry Carr knows firsthand how disastrous the *Exxon Valdez* oil spill was. At the time of the spill, he was a writer for the Anchorage Daily News in Anchorage, Alaska. He witnessed the cleanup effort and spoke with many of the people working on the spill. He saw the destructive effects of the spreading oil on the beaches and on wildlife. Mr. Carr considered it important that this topic be brought to the attention of young readers.

Spill! The Story of the Exxon Valdez is Mr. Carr's first book. An essay he wrote about the oil spill appeared in *Newsweek* magazine shortly after the accident occurred.

Reader Response

Open for Discussion

The author states that "as long as oil has to be moved by ships, oil spills will occur." Do you agree?

Comprehension Check

1. Why did it take so long for the cleanup effort to begin? What problems did the cleanup crews face? Use details from the selection in your answer.

2. Oil affects different animals in different ways. Find at least two ways the oil hurt the animals in Prince William Sound.

3. Why was the *Exxon Valdez* spill so terrible? Give specific examples about people and animals.

4. One type of **persuasive device** is *loaded words*. Find and list at least three examples of loaded words in the text. (Persuasive Devices)

5. Reread the last paragraph of "Saving the Sound." Does the author **persuade** you that "it is our responsibility as caretakers of the Earth to guard our environment from such disasters"? Why or why not? (Persuasive Devices)

Test Prep

Look Back and Write

At the bottom of page 230 the author writes, "Prince William Sound is coming to life." What does he mean by this? Use details from pages 229–230 in your answer.

Test Prep

How to Read a Textbook Lesson

1. Preview

- A lesson in a textbook presents information as clearly and efficiently as possible.

- Look over the title, the text in boxes, and the pictures and diagram. Pay particular attention to words in dark or colored type. What large-scale problem do you think this lesson deals with?

2. Read and Make Webs

- As you read the lesson, focus on the two vocabulary words in the box. Use a web to note what you learn about each of these words.

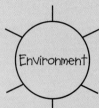

Environment

3. Think and Connect

Think about "Saving the Sound." Then look over your notes on "How Do People Help Provide a Clean Environment?"

Think about the author's purpose in writing each of these selections. What purpose do both authors share? What other purposes does the author of "Saving the Sound" have?

How Do People Help Provide a Clean Environment?

Look around you. Notice everything you see, indoors and outdoors. Listen closely for any sounds. Do you detect any odors? All of the sights, sounds, and odors are part of your **environment.** Your environment is all of the living and nonliving things that surround and affect you. The water you drink, the air you breathe, the sounds you hear, and the ground you walk on are all part of your environment.

The actions of people often cause harmful or undesirable changes in the environment. Any such change is **pollution.** Most pollution comes from wastes that people add to the environment. Sewage, engine exhaust, and garbage are some wastes that pollute the water, air, and land. Many people in your community work to reduce the problems of pollution. They try to provide a clean, healthy environment for everyone.

environment

(en vi′rən mənt), all the living and nonliving surroundings that affect living things.

pollution

(pə lü′shən), a change in the environment that is harmful or undesirable to living things.

242

What Is Sewage?

Sewage, or waste water, from factories, houses, and other buildings threatens the safety of the drinking water supply. Sewage from your home might include human wastes, bits of food that go down the kitchen drain, and water you use to wash your hands. Factory sewage, like that shown in the river at the left, often includes oil, grease, and poisonous chemicals. All sewage usually contains bacteria and viruses, which can cause disease. Sewage also contains sticks, rags, and other large objects that drain into sewers from city streets.

How Do Treatment Plants Improve a Community's Water?

To reduce the amount of water pollution, most communities in the United States pipe their sewage to waste water treatment plants, commonly called sewage treatment plants. Many factories have their own sewage treatment plants. The diagram shows how some harmful substances are removed from sewage at such a plant, although not all plants use all these processes. First, sewage is piped through screens that remove sticks and other large objects. Next, the sewage moves into settling tanks where small, solid materials settle out. The remaining sewage then might go to aeration tanks. Bacteria in the tanks feed on the sewage. Air is pumped into the aeration tanks to keep the bacteria alive. In another settling tank, the bacteria clump together and settle out. Next, chlorine gas is added to kill harmful bacteria and some viruses. Finally, the treated sewage is pumped to a nearby river, lake, or other body of water.

Notice the difference between the sewage that enters the treatment plant and the sewage that leaves it. The treated waste water is clean enough to send to a river or lake, but, of course, the water is still not safe to drink. Many harmful substances remain, even if you cannot see them. Also, the water might have an unpleasant color, taste, and smell.

To make water safe and pleasant for drinking, communities use water treatment plants. These plants help to clean water from rivers or lakes. The water passes through a series of screens, settling tanks, and filters. Chlorine is added to kill harmful bacteria. In some communities, the water is then sprayed into the air. This process adds oxygen to the water to make it taste better. The clean water then is piped to homes and other places in the community.
—from *Health for Life*

Sewage after and before treatment

Sewage is cleaned at a sewage treatment plant.

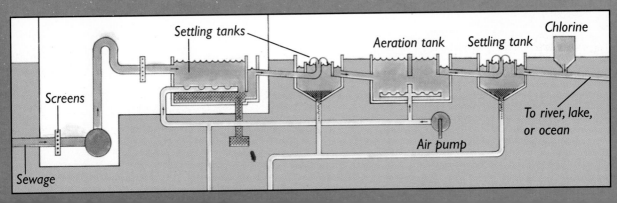

Settling tanks

Aeration tank   Settling tank   Chlorine

Screens

To river, lake, or ocean

Air pump

Sewage

243

Earth Song

by David McCord

Let me dry you, says the desert;
Let me wet you, says the sea.
If that's the way they talk, why don't
They talk that way to me?

Let me fan you, says the wind;
Oh, let me cool you, says the rain.
Let me bury you, the snow says;
Let me dye you with the stain

Of sunset, says the evening;
Let me float you, says the lake;
Let me drift you, says the river.
Says the temblor, let me shake

You. *Freeze* you, says the glacier;
Let me burn you, says the sun.
I don't know what the moon says,
Or that star—the green pale one.

THE BIRTH OF A
STONE

by Kwang-Kyu Kim
translated by Brother Anthony

In those deep mountain ravines
I wonder if there are stones
that no one has ever visited?
I went up the mountain
in quest of a stone no one had ever seen
from the remotest of times

Under ancient pines
on steep pathless slopes
there was a stone
I wonder
how long
this stone all thick with moss
has been
here?

Two thousand years? Two million? Two billion?
No
Not at all
If really till now no one
has ever seen this stone
it is only
here
from now on
This stone
was only born
the moment I first saw it

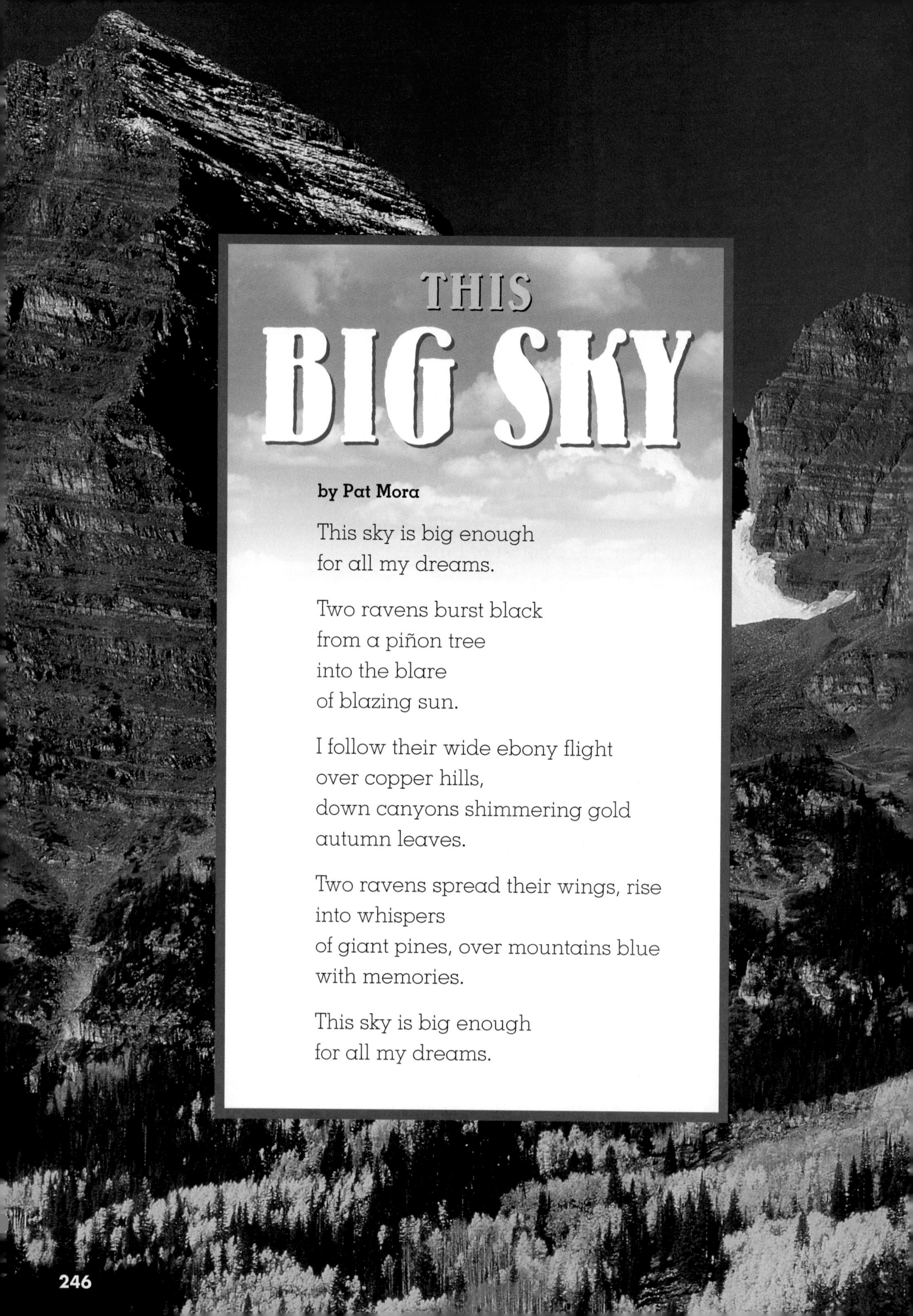

THIS BIG SKY

by Pat Mora

This sky is big enough
for all my dreams.

Two ravens burst black
from a piñon tree
into the blare
of blazing sun.

I follow their wide ebony flight
over copper hills,
down canyons shimmering gold
autumn leaves.

Two ravens spread their wings, rise
into whispers
of giant pines, over mountains blue
with memories.

This sky is big enough
for all my dreams.

This Land Is Your Land

song lyric by Woody Guthrie

This land is your land, this land is my land
From California to the New York island
From the redwood forest to the Gulf Stream waters
This land was made for you and me

As I went walking that ribbon of highway
I saw above me that endless skyway
And saw below me that golden valley
This land was made for you and me

I've roamed and rambled, and I followed my footsteps
To the sparkling sands of her diamond deserts
And all around me, a voice was sounding
This land was made for you and me

When the sun came shining, and I was strolling
And the wheat fields waving, and the dust clouds rolling
As the fog was lifting, a voice was chanting:
This land was made for you and me

This land is your land, this land is my land
From California to the New York island
From the redwood forest to the Gulf Stream waters
This land was made for you and me

Wrap-Up

What can we learn from observing the world around us?

Disaster Reporter

Make an On-the-Scene Report

"Storm-a-Dust" and "Saving the Sound" deal with disasters. Choose one and imagine yourself on the scene. What do you observe around you?

1. **Prepare** an on-the-scene report for radio news.

2. **Tape-record** your report and play it for classmates. Did it hold their attention? Did it seem believable? Ask for comments.

Animal Profiles

Research and Create

With a partner, choose an animal from Unit 2 and make a profile of its habitat.

1. **Research** your animal habitat. Consult the Internet or a library.

2. **Organize** your research notes into categories, for example:

   Location   **Dwelling**
   Plants   **Other Animals**
   Food Sources   **Climate**

3. **Create** a poster profile. Draw the animal and write your profile alongside it, category by category.

Survival Exhibit

Brainstorm and Assemble

The last four selections are about people and animals surviving. How do they manage to survive?

1. With a small group, **brainstorm** things that people and animals use for survival, such as the tatter in "Storm-a-Dust" and the seaweed in "Day of the Turtle."

2. **Write** an explanation of how these things aid survival.

3. **Assemble** the things, or pictures of them. Add information on note cards to make a survival exhibit.

Learning from Experience

Write a Journal Entry

In "A Trouble-Making Crow," "The Day of the Turtle," and "From a Spark," the characters learned new things about animals and themselves. Imagine that you are Jean, Lindy, or Brian. What did you learn?

1. **Make notes.** Use a chart like this one.

What _____ Learned	How _____ Learned It

2. **Write** a journal entry as if you are one of the characters. Tell about what you learned.

Test Talk

Understand the Question

Find Key Words in the Text

Before you can answer a test question, you have to know where to look for the answer. A test about "Wilderness Challenge," pages 178–179, might have this question.

Test Question 1

What rugged experiences are part of the program in the Beartooth Wilderness? Use details from the article to support your answer.

Make sure that you understand the question.

Find the key words. Finish the statement "I need to find out . . ."

Decide where you will look for the answer.

- Some test questions tell you to look in one place in the text. The answer is *right there* in the text.

- Other test questions tell you to look for information that is in different parts of the text. You have to *think and search*.

- Still other test questions tell you to combine what *you* know with what the *author* tells you. The answer comes from the *author and you*.

See how one student figures out where to look for the answer.

Rugged experiences . . .
I think they mean activities you do outside—like camping or rock climbing. Most of the article talks about that. So, this must be one of those questions where I'll have to think and search for the answer.

Here's **program** and **rugged experiences** in the first paragraph, but there's nothing about an outside activity. There's **Beartooth Wilderness** in the next paragraph—"The kids spent fifteen days hiking, camping, and climbing . . ." Those are outdoor activities. I'll write those down. Then I'll skim the rest of the article for more activities.

Try it!

Now figure out where to look for the answer to these test questions about "Wilderness Challenge," pages 178–179.

Test Question 2

What would the kids say they learned on their Outward Bound adventure? Use details from the article to support your answer.

Test Question 3

What is the purpose of the topographical map shown in the photograph on page 179?

Ⓐ to show the surface features of the land

Ⓑ to show the highest mountain range

Ⓒ to show the depth of lakes and rivers

Ⓓ to show the hiking trails and campgrounds

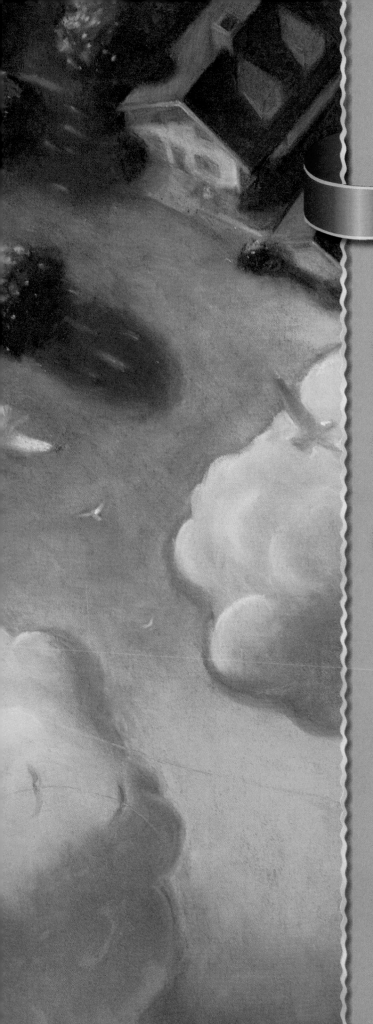

Goals
Great
and Small

How do people
accomplish their
ambitions?

Skill Lesson

Drawing Conclusions

- To **draw** a **conclusion** means to make a decision or form an opinion about what you read.

- A conclusion should be sensible. It should make good sense based on the facts and details in the piece of writing.

- Thinking about your own experience can also help you draw sensible conclusions.

- To test a conclusion, first ask yourself whether the facts are accurate and whether you are taking anything for granted. Then ask yourself whether there are other possible conclusions you could base on the same information.

Read "To the Rescue" from "Clara Barton: Angel of the Battlefield" by Mike Weinstein from *Cobblestone* magazine.

COBBLESTONE
The Battle of
Antietam
September 17, 1862

Talk About It

1. Clara Barton worked in dangerous conditions. What facts and details in the article support this conclusion?

2. If you were to describe Clara Barton, what would you say about her? Base your conclusions on information from the article.

To the Rescue

by Mike Weinstein

During the Civil War, Clara Barton served as a volunteer for the Union troops. On one assignment, she brought medical supplies to the Antietam battlefield near Sharpsburg, Maryland.

By the time Clara Barton's mule-drawn wagon turned down a farm lane near the pretty village of Sharpsburg, Maryland, the roar of battle was deafening. Cannon thundered and bullets whizzed through the air as Barton arrived, wearing a bonnet and a red bow around her neck. She saw a house peeking out above a tall cornfield. She followed a path through the corn and stopped when she saw the scene on the porch of the house.

Four tables were set up. On each table was a wounded soldier. Standing over each soldier was a doctor, who had a wooden box of medical tools and some green corn leaves. The doctors were

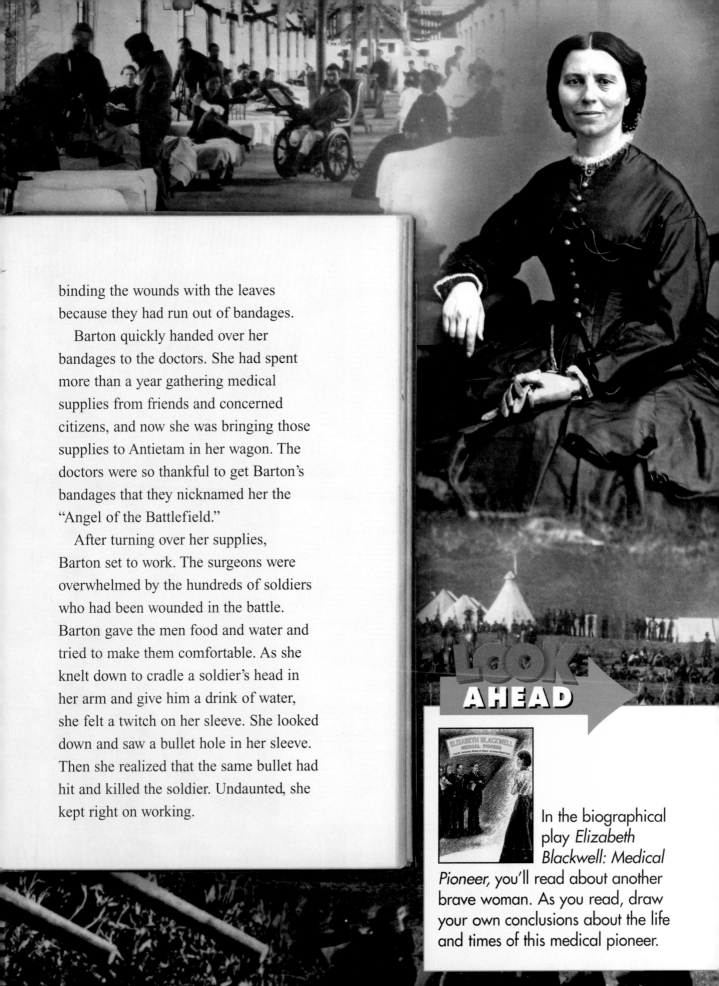

binding the wounds with the leaves because they had run out of bandages.

Barton quickly handed over her bandages to the doctors. She had spent more than a year gathering medical supplies from friends and concerned citizens, and now she was bringing those supplies to Antietam in her wagon. The doctors were so thankful to get Barton's bandages that they nicknamed her the "Angel of the Battlefield."

After turning over her supplies, Barton set to work. The surgeons were overwhelmed by the hundreds of soldiers who had been wounded in the battle. Barton gave the men food and water and tried to make them comfortable. As she knelt down to cradle a soldier's head in her arm and give him a drink of water, she felt a twitch on her sleeve. She looked down and saw a bullet hole in her sleeve. Then she realized that the same bullet had hit and killed the soldier. Undaunted, she kept right on working.

LOOK AHEAD

In the biographical play *Elizabeth Blackwell: Medical Pioneer,* you'll read about another brave woman. As you read, draw your own conclusions about the life and times of this medical pioneer.

Vocabulary

Words to Know

diploma	qualified	clinic
infection	rejection	surgeon
application	independent	

When you read, you may come across a word that you don't know. To figure out the meaning of an unfamiliar word, look for clues in the words and sentences around it.

Read the paragraph below. Notice how an explanation of *qualified* helps you understand what it means.

Big Plans

My dream is to become a doctor, just like my mother. Maybe we'll even work together at the same clinic. I'll be a surgeon, and she'll treat people who have an infection or other illness. I want to be independent, but I also think it would be great to see my mom every day. Of course, becoming a doctor isn't easy, but I think that I will be qualified. My grades are good, especially in science, and I love to help people. First, I'll earn my high school diploma. After that, it's off to college. Once I graduate, I'll send my application to medical schools and hope that one will accept me. Even if I'm turned down, I plan to keep trying until I can make my dream come true. Rejection will only make me work harder.

Write About It

Write about your career plans. Use as many vocabulary words as you can.

ELIZABETH BLACKWELL
MEDICAL PIONEER

from Ms. Courageous: Women of Science • by Joanna Halpert Kraus

CAST OF CHARACTERS

Narrators

Percussion Players or Other Musicians

Elizabeth Blackwell, a medical student

Dr. Barnes, her teacher

Dean Reynolds, Dean of Admissions

Dean Snyder, Dean of Admissions

James, his colleague

Dean Richards, Geneva Medical College Dean

Raymond, first Geneva colleague

Herbert, second Geneva colleague

John, Student Council President

Elmer, a student

Phillip, another student

Betsy, a young servant

Lily Barnes, Dr. Barnes's wife

Mrs. Trotter, a landlady

Mrs. Giles, another landlady

Dr. Benjamin Hale, Geneva College President

Lulu, a new student nurse

Anna, Elizabeth's older sister

Dr. Claude Blot, an intern at La Maternité hospital

Anthony, a recent immigrant

Helga, Anthony's sister

Zac, a physician and Elizabeth's colleague

Sean, an Irish longshoreman

(Setting: A bare stage with varying performance levels and an easel for signs. Costume pieces and properties are available.)

(At Rise: Three NARRATORS stand in different areas of the stage. The two PERCUSSION PLAYERS are on stage and remain there throughout the play.)

(SOUND: Percussion instruments. A soft chant begins.)

ALL NARRATORS *(chanting):* Your own song . . . your own song . . . your own song.

NARRATOR ONE *(moving forward):* DARE!

NARRATORS TWO & THREE *(still chanting):* Your own song . . . your own song.

ALL NARRATORS: DARE!

NARRATOR THREE: Do you dare?

NARRATOR TWO: To sing your own song?

NARRATOR ONE: They did.

NARRATOR TWO *(asks others):* Who did?

NARRATORS ONE & THREE: Women!

NARRATOR ONE: Women in science!

NARRATOR THREE: Warriors all.

NARRATOR ONE: Struggling to be

NARRATOR TWO: All they could be.

NARRATOR THREE: Laughed at.

NARRATOR ONE: Scorned.

NARRATOR TWO: Often unpaid.

NARRATOR THREE: Often ignored.

NARRATOR ONE: They fought for—

NARRATOR TWO: Sought for—

NARRATOR THREE: Hunted for—

NARRATOR TWO *(asks others):* For what?

(They invite audience.)

NARRATOR ONE: Come!

NARRATOR THREE: Investigate.

NARRATOR TWO: Celebrate.

(They swirl. When they merge, each carries a segment of a set piece or property, which has the name of the scene written on it: "Elizabeth Blackwell: Medical Pioneer.")

NARRATOR ONE: Meet—

NARRATOR TWO: Elizabeth Blackwell.

NARRATOR THREE: Medical pioneer.

(PERCUSSION PLAYER flips sign on easel to read "Philadelphia." ELIZABETH BLACKWELL appears, attired in a modest gown and bonnet, carrying a small traveling case. She is in her mid-20s, stubborn, determined, restless, and independent. She mimes walking in place.)

(The NARRATORS take poses, backs to us in separate parts of the stage.)

(ELIZABETH flings her arms wide to the world, as she sets her case down.)

ELIZABETH: I want to be—

NARRATOR ONE *(turns):* Want to be—

NARRATOR TWO *(turns):* Want to be—

ELIZABETH: The first lady surgeon in the United States. No. I want to be the first—in the entire world!

NARRATOR ONE: The first—

NARRATOR TWO: In the world.

NARRATOR THREE *(turns):* CRAZY! *(NARRATORS confer.)*

NARRATOR ONE: Not practical.

NARRATOR TWO *(authoritatively):* A well brought up lady cannot be a doctor.

NARRATOR ONE *(reading from a large period magazine):* "A woman's sphere is in the home." *(Closes magazine decisively.)*

NARRATOR THREE *(reading from a book):* *The Young Lady's Book* says she must be "obedient, submissive, and humble."

(NARRATORS look at one another, then back at ELIZABETH, glaring at her.)

NARRATOR ONE: Shocking!

NARRATOR TWO: Shameful!

NARRATOR THREE: Sinful!

ALL NARRATORS (*pointing at* ELIZABETH): SCANDALOUS!

(NARRATORS *exit.* DR. BARNES *enters. 40s. Wise, pragmatic.*)

DR. BARNES: My dear Miss Blackwell, woman was designed to be the helpmate of man. Man must be the physician; woman the nurse.

ELIZABETH: Doctor, I've paid for three years of pre-medical study with you. I've attended your lectures, used your library, been with you to visit patients. Please! You've got to help me get admitted to medical school.

DR. BARNES: No woman has ever gone to medical school!

ELIZABETH: You told me I had the ability.

DR. BARNES: You do! But it's 1847, Miss Blackwell. There isn't a college in the country that will accept you.

ELIZABETH: Times won't change unless we make them change!

DR. BARNES (*slowly*): There is one way.

ELIZABETH: What? What?

DR. BARNES: Disguise yourself as a man, and go study in Paris.

ELIZABETH (*shocked*): How can I help other women, if I'm in disguise? There must be some school, one school, in this huge nation brave enough to accept a woman. Won't you please write a letter on my behalf?

DR. BARNES: I'll do better than that! I'll send you to a friend, who's Dean of Admissions here in Philadelphia. But don't expect miracles.

ELIZABETH: Miracles are something you make happen!

(DR. BARNES *exits.* ELIZABETH *crosses to a new level, and* DEAN REYNOLDS *enters. He is in his 40s, imperious and patronizing.*)

DEAN REYNOLDS: I've agreed to see you as a courtesy to my colleague, Miss Blackwell. What is it you want?

ELIZABETH: I want to go to medical school.

DEAN REYNOLDS: You can't be serious.

ELIZABETH: I've never been more serious in my life.

DEAN REYNOLDS: Then you're a lunatic.

ELIZABETH: Why won't you consider my request?

DEAN REYNOLDS: Miss Blackwell, it's not seemly or suitable for a lady. *(Peers over his glasses.)* I presume you are one, to pursue such a calling. Why, you'd faint at the first dissection, you'd flinch at the first sign of blood. You'd disrupt the entire class.

ELIZABETH: I've done dissections as part of my pre-medical studies.

DEAN REYNOLDS: An unfortunate mistake on my colleague's part.

(DEAN REYNOLDS *exits.* SOUND: *Door slams shut.*)

ELIZABETH *(to closed door):* And I never flinched or fainted. *(To herself.)* Well, just the first time. He wouldn't even listen to me!

(ELIZABETH *marches back to her room and takes out a writing box and begins a letter.*)

Dear Sir, I wish to apply to your medical college.

(*As she writes,* DEAN SNYDER *and* JAMES *enter a different area.* DEAN SNYDER *is 40s, hard-nosed.* JAMES *is his colleague, 30s. A "yes" person.*)

DEAN SNYDER *(waving* ELIZABETH*'s letter):* If we admit a woman, our enrollment will decline. Therefore, I urge us all to reject the application, despite a fine recommendation.

JAMES *(applauding):* Hear! Hear!

DEAN SNYDER: She can hardly expect us to give her a stick with which to break our own heads! *(To* JAMES.*)* Do you know what will happen if women patients start going to women doctors?

JAMES: What?

DEAN SNYDER: We'll lose our jobs! This is the most absurd application I've ever had. Suddenly there are all these quacks trying to get into medical college. With water cures, electrical cures. We might as well let in all the charlatans as let in a woman!

(They exit. ELIZABETH *opens her letter, reading.)*

ELIZABETH: Rejection from Philadelphia. *(Throws it down. Opens another letter.* NARRATORS *have entered.)* Rejection from New York.

*(*ELIZABETH *crosses to* DR. BARNES*'s parlor. He enters as the rejections increase.)*

NARRATOR ONE: Three.

NARRATOR TWO: Six

NARRATOR THREE: Twelve.

DR. BARNES: Elizabeth, don't give up yet. If the big fish won't let you swim, try the little fish.

ELIZABETH: Do you think it'll make any difference?

DR. BARNES: It might. All you can do is try.

(ELIZABETH *returns to her room, and* DR. BARNES *remains sitting and reading his medical journal, as* NARRATORS *continue.*)

NARRATOR ONE: But the results were—

NARRATOR TWO: Fifteen rejects.

NARRATOR THREE: Twenty-five rejections.

ELIZABETH *(thinks aloud):* All these years I've tried to earn enough to pay for medical school. Teaching music to children who are tone deaf. Trying to pound an education into students who don't care. All these years trying to prepare for medical school, learning Greek, learning anatomy. But it doesn't matter how hard I've worked. As soon as they see my name, Elizabeth, the answer is "No!" Because I'm a female. That's the only reason.

(ELIZABETH *turns away from audience as staff of Geneva Medical College enters:* DEAN RICHARDS, *smooth administrator;* RAYMOND, *his first colleague, action-oriented;* HERBERT, *his second colleague, who follows the rules. All are men in their 30s.*)

(PERCUSSION PLAYER *flips sign to read "Geneva, New York."*)

DEAN RICHARDS: We have a very awkward situation, gentlemen. I need your advice.

RAYMOND AND HERBERT *(turn):* Y-e-e-s.

DEAN RICHARDS *(with a sheaf of papers):* A well-qualified applicant. With an excellent recommendation from Dr. Barnes.

RAYMOND: Philadelphia's best! Find a scholarship for him. Any candidate he recommends, I say we take.

DEAN RICHARDS: I'm afraid it's a graver matter than mere scholarship.

RAYMOND: More serious than money?

HERBERT: An incurable disease?

DEAN RICHARDS: You might say so. The fact is, gentlemen—*(Pauses.)* The he is a she.

HERBERT: A she!

(SOUND: Percussion.)

RAYMOND: Out of the question!

HERBERT: Impossible.

DEAN RICHARDS: I agree. Of course. But what do we write Dr. Barnes?

HERBERT: We don't want to insult him.

DEAN RICHARDS: We want to keep his goodwill. *(They pace.)*

RAYMOND: The request is highly unusual, and it concerns the students. Let them decide!

DEAN RICHARDS: Brilliant! And if any of the students object to admitting a woman, we'll reject the application.

HERBERT: The students have never agreed on anything!

DEAN RICHARDS *(smoothly):* Then we can tell Dr. Barnes it was the students' decision—not ours!

(They exit, as students enter a different area. JOHN, *Student Council President, is 18; bright, fair-minded but not above pranks.* ELMER, *17, is bored. Anything for a laugh.* PHILLIP, *17, is a reactionary.)*

JOHN *(bangs gavel):* I call this meeting of the Student Council to order.

(SOUND: Hoots, whistles, catcalls.)

ELMER: Hurry it up.

PHILLIP: All members present.

JOHN: Good! The Dean has asked the Student Council to make a momentous decision. One that could change this institution.

ELMER: Anything for a change.

JOHN: A lady has applied to Geneva Medical College.

PHILLIP: Can't be a lady if she applied here.

(SOUND: Raucous laughter.)

JOHN: The dean wants our decision this afternoon. May we have some discussion?

ELMER: Heck, just for argument's sake, I say let her come. She'd liven up the place.

PHILLIP: Liven up the place! She'd ruin our reputation!

JOHN: She could put Geneva Medical College on the map.

PHILLIP: If we let her in, she'll slow the whole class down.

ELMER (*to* PHILLIP): Then someone else besides you would be at the bottom!

(SOUND: Laughter.)

JOHN: It's my belief scientific education should be open to all.

PHILLIP: I agree. As long as "all" ain't women!

(SOUND: More laughter.)

ELMER: Call the vote! Call the vote!

JOHN: All those in favor?

PHILLIP: Aye!

(SOUND: Simultaneous chorus of "Ayes.")

JOHN: All those opposed?

PHILLIP: NAY!

(ELMER *rushes to* PHILLIP.)

ELMER: Toss him out the window! Throw him down the stairs!

PHILLIP (*hastily*): Aye! Aye! I vote Aye!

JOHN: Then it's unanimous! *(Grinning.)* This is more fun than Halloween!

(SOUND: "Yeas," whistles, catcalls as students exit.)

(PERCUSSION PLAYER *flips sign to read "Philadelphia."*)

(SOUND: Knock. BETSY, *an eight- to ten-year-old servant, active, curious, mimes running up the stairs.)*

BETSY *(rushes in to* ELIZABETH's *room):* Miss Blackwell. Miss Blackwell. A letter for you.

ELIZABETH: Thank you.

BETSY: Ain't ya gonna open it? I ran up two flights. I never saw anyone get so many letters as you do, Miss Blackwell. More than the Doctor himself. You get more than anyone in the whole city of Philadelphia, I warrant.

ELIZABETH: But they all say the same. They all say "No."

BETSY: The Doctor and the Missus say you're to come down for tea. Hot mince pies, Miss Blackwell.

ELIZABETH: In a minute. I will in a minute.

*(*BETSY *exits.* LILY BARNES, *the doctor's wife, brings tea into the parlor.* LILY *is in her 30s, supportive. Unobtrusively she puts the tea out, as* ELIZABETH *opens her letter halfheartedly.* ELIZABETH *rises, more and more astonished by the letter's content. She races out of her room, delirious with joy.)*

Everybody! Listen! Everybody!

*(*ELIZABETH *flies into the parlor and whirls around the room.)*

I've been accepted.

LILY BARNES *(hugs* ELIZABETH*):* Congratulations.

DR. BARNES: I knew one of those schools would have common sense.

ELIZABETH: They've approved me. Gentlemen—(*Curtsies to an imaginary group.*) I accept.

LILY BARNES: When will you leave?

ELIZABETH: Immediately! Before they change their minds!

(DR. BARNES *brings* ELIZABETH *her travel case and exits as* ELIZABETH *crosses to a new area and* LILY BARNES *exits with tea tray.* NARRATOR ONE *enters.*)

(PERCUSSION PLAYER *flips sign to read "Geneva, New York."*)

NARRATOR ONE: But her troubles were just beginning.

(*SOUND: Door knocker.* ELIZABETH *knocks and waits.* MRS. TROTTER, *50s, landlady, tight-lipped respectability, opens the door.*)

ELIZABETH: I'd like to rent a room.

MRS. TROTTER (*suspiciously*)*:* Traveling by yourself?

ELIZABETH: No. I've come to study at Geneva Medical College.

MRS. TROTTER: A woman doctor? I should say not! I run a respectable boardinghouse!

(*SOUND: Door slams. Wearily,* ELIZABETH *goes to next house as* MRS. GILES, *40s, landlady, open-minded, kind, enters.* ELIZABETH *knocks. SOUND: A different kind of knocker or bell.* MRS. GILES *opens the door.*)

ELIZABETH: Please don't say no! This is the last boardinghouse on my list. I've got to rent a room. Classes have already started.

MRS. GILES (*fascinated*)*:* You're going to medical college?

ELIZABETH: Yes.

MRS. GILES (*dubious*)*:* Never heard of no woman doctor before. Can you cure headaches? I get powerful headaches.

ELIZABETH: I'll try. (MRS. GILES *appraises her.*)

MRS. GILES (*slowly*)*:* Maybe I could let you have the room up in the attic. (*Warns.*) Not much heat!

ELIZABETH: I'll take it.

MRS. GILES: You look like a proper young lady. Not in any trouble are you?

(ELIZABETH *puts her bag in the doorway.*)

ELIZABETH *(offers money):* I'll pay six weeks in advance.

(MRS. GILES *hesitates, then accepts it.*)

MRS. GILES: Now mind, don't expect other folks to talk to you at dinner. Never heard of no lady doctor!

(MRS. GILES *ushers* ELIZABETH *off.*)

(SOUND: Graduation processional march.)

(DR. BENJAMIN HALE, *Geneva Medical College president, enters. 40s. Dignified. He wears a black velvet mortarboard to suggest academic regalia.*)

DR. HALE *(addresses audience):* No one at the college expected her to show up. And when she did no one thought she'd stay. And certainly no one ever thought she'd graduate with top honors!

(SOUND: Applause. Processional march as ELIZABETH *comes forward.)*

Dr. Blackwell! Congratulations! *(Hands her diploma.)*

ELIZABETH: Dr. Benjamin Hale, faculty, family, friends, ladies, and gentlemen, I will do everything in my power to bring honor to this diploma. I promise you!

(SOUND: More wild applause. Shouts of "Hurrah for Elizabeth." DR. BENJAMIN HALE *exits as* NARRATORS *enter and* ELIZABETH *crosses to a new area.)*

NARRATOR ONE: Elizabeth tried to keep her promise.

NARRATOR TWO: She went to Paris to fulfill her dream.

NARRATOR THREE: But no hospital would admit her.

ELIZABETH: What good is my diploma!

NARRATOR TWO: Only the maternity hospital would take her. As a—

ELIZABETH *(reading the letter, shocked):* Student nurse. A STUDENT NURSE! I have a medical degree! *(Squares her shoulders, determined.)* If that's how I have to start, then I will! *(Reflects.)* Besides, I'll learn more in three months there than in three years of reading books.

*(*ELIZABETH *picks up her traveling bag and marches over to don a hospital apron of heavy toweling with huge pockets.)*

(SOUND: PERCUSSION PLAYERS *beat a fast rhythm under chanted work poem.* ELIZABETH *mimes portions of the work poem.)*

NARRATOR THREE: Work.

NARRATOR ONE: Up at five.

NARRATOR TWO: Scrub the floors.

NARRATOR THREE: Dust the corners. Fill the pans.

NARRATOR ONE: Feed the patients.

NARRATOR TWO: Class at seven.

NARRATOR THREE: Follow doctors.

NARRATOR ONE: Visit wards.

NARRATOR TWO: Rushing, rushing.

NARRATOR THREE: Bolt it down.

NARRATOR ONE: A bit of bread.

NARRATOR TWO: A chunk of cheese.

NARRATOR THREE: On the run. On the run.

NARRATOR ONE: Babies born. Night and day.

NARRATOR TWO: Day and night.

NARRATOR THREE: Complications.

NARRATOR ONE: Operations.

NARRATOR TWO: Emergencies. Emergencies.

NARRATOR THREE: Middle of the night.

NARRATOR ONE: Middle of the day.

NARRATOR TWO: No sleep.

NARRATOR THREE: No time.

NARRATOR ONE: No sleep.

NARRATOR TWO: Night after night.

NARRATOR THREE: Day after day.

NARRATOR ONE: Day and night.

NARRATOR TWO: Night and day.

NARRATOR THREE: Work!

(ELIZABETH collapses in a chair and falls asleep. NARRATORS exit.)

(SOUND: Church bells chime three.)

(LULU runs on and shakes ELIZABETH. LULU is a new student nurse. 20s. Anxious.)

LULU: Mademoiselle! Mademoiselle Blackwell!

ELIZABETH *(groggy):* So tired. Go away, please. So tired.

LULU: The baby's worse.

ELIZABETH *(jumps up):* I'll be right there.

(ELIZABETH runs down the hall to the ward. She picks up the swaddled baby. LULU hovers in the background.)

(SOUND: Baby crying.)

ELIZABETH *(soothing):* Sh-h. Of course, it hurts. You can't see. Not with that infection in your eyes. (ELIZABETH *puts baby back in the crib.*) Sh-h. There now. Lie still. I have to use the syringe. Lie still. If only the light were better.

(SOUND: Sharp, discordant.)

ELIZABETH *(screams):* OH-H-H-H! OW-W-W-W-W-! OH-H-H-H.

(LULU *runs off.*)

(SOUND: *More discordant sounds to indicate a passage of time.*)

(DR. CLAUDE BLOT *enters a different area. Mid-20s. He is an intern at* La Maternité. *Knowledgeable.*)

(ELIZABETH *covers her left eye with her hand and crosses to* DR. BLOT.)

DR. BLOT *(very concerned):* How did it happen, Mademoiselle?

ELIZABETH: I was syringing the fluid from the baby's eye. I was very tired; the light was bad. Somehow when I leaned over the crib, some of the fluid squirted into my eye. *(Attempting to make light of it.)* You know the way a lemon squirts.

DR. BLOT *(examining):* More serious than a lemon, Mademoiselle. Why didn't you come to me as soon as it happened?

ELIZABETH: I had so much to do. I washed the eye out immediately. But this morning I couldn't open it at all.

DR. BLOT *(still examining):* The left eye is very inflamed and swollen. I pray to God it doesn't spread.

ELIZABETH: How am I going to do my work in the wards today?

DR. BLOT: You're not! Not for quite some time, Mademoiselle.

ELIZABETH *(shocked):* Not work!

DR. BLOT *(gently but firmly):* That's an order.

ELIZABETH: But I have to!

DR. BLOT: What you have to do, Mademoiselle, is get well. Unfortunately, you have the same disease as the baby you were treating.

ELIZABETH: The same? Are you sure?

DR. BLOT: It's a classic case of purulent ophthalmia. I'm sure you know the dangers already.

ELIZABETH *(slowly):* With a baby, it can mean permanent blindness. That's why I was trying so hard to save his sight.

DR. BLOT: You're a doctor, so I'll be frank. There's no guarantee—

ELIZABETH: *(distraught):* Doctor, can you save my eye? Can you?

DR. BLOT: I will do everything I can. But I'm a doctor, not a magician.

(SOUND: To indicate the passage of time.)

(NARRATORS help ELIZABETH remove hospital apron.
DR. BLOT bends over ELIZABETH with a pincer.)

DR. BLOT: Are you ready? I'm going to remove
the film from the pupil of your eye.

(He performs the delicate procedure.)

DR. BLOT: Sit up very slowly. You've been in bed for three
weeks. (ELIZABETH *does.*) Now tell me what you can see.

ELIZABETH *(as she looks):* Pull the curtains and I will.

DR. BLOT *(stunned):* Mademoiselle . . . there are no curtains.

ELIZABETH *(grabbing and holding DR. BLOT's hand):* Doctor,
tell me I'll get better! Please, tell me I'll get better. A surgeon
cannot be blind!

DR. BLOT: Mademoiselle, you mustn't excite yourself. Your sister's
here. She's come to take you home.

ELIZABETH: Doctor, tell me the truth, please! Am I blind?

DR. BLOT *(upset):* We used the latest medical procedures. And I was
there. Every day. Every night.

ELIZABETH *(quietly):* Will I see again?

DR. BLOT: You might regain the sight in your right eye. But only
if you have absolute rest. That's why I've sent for your sister.

ELIZABETH: And the left eye?

DR. BLOT *(shakes his head):* I did all I could. I wish to God I could
have done more.

(ANNA rushes in. 30. She is ELIZABETH's older sister. Protective.
DR. BLOT exits.)

ANNA: Elizabeth!

ELIZABETH: Anna! Anna! (ELIZABETH *starts to cry.*)

ANNA: Don't, Elizabeth. Don't.

ELIZABETH: Anna, I can't give up. For years I've planned. For years!

(ANNA holds her as ELIZABETH sobs silently.)

ANNA: We can't always do what we planned. Now, you must get your
strength back.

ELIZABETH: What's the point in getting well, Anna, unless I can follow my dream?

ANNA: Sh-h. Put this shawl around you. It's cold outside.

(ANNA *helps* ELIZABETH *cross to a chair in a different area.*)

(*SOUND: To indicate the passage of time.*)

ELIZABETH *(calls):* Anna! Anna!

ANNA *(rushes in):* What is it? What's wrong, Elizabeth?

ELIZABETH: I can see the lamp. On the table. It's like through a mist. But I can see it. I can see it!

(ANNA *hugs her.*)

ANNA: I've waited six months to hear you say that! Oh, Elizabeth. Finally. Your eyes are beginning to heal! *(Producing a letter.)* A letter came this afternoon from St. Bartholomew's Hospital in London.

ELIZABETH: Read it! Don't keep me in suspense. Quick! Is it yes or no?

(ANNA *quickly hopes before she opens the letter to read it.*)

ANNA: It's . . . YES! For next fall. You've been accepted to study surgery. Or to study practical medicine.

ELIZABETH: SURGERY! They accepted me! Anna, cover my eyes. Quickly! One at a time. First the left.

(ANNA *covers the left eye.*)

ANNA: What do you see?

ELIZABETH: You. Better than before. You're wearing a yellow dress. (ANNA *smiles.* ELIZABETH *looks hungrily.*) And the brass lamp. The mist is lifting. And the flowered wallpaper. And tomorrow I'll see even more. The right eye is healing. It's healing! I'm sure of it! *(Tensely.)* Now cover it.

(ANNA *covers the right eye.*)

ANNA *(anxiously):* Can you see anything?

(There is a horrible pause.)

ELIZABETH: Darkness. A wall. *(With a sob.)* Anna, Anna, how do you give up a dream?

ANNA *(gently):* By dreaming another.

(ANNA *holds her distraught sister in her arms. Abruptly* ELIZABETH *holds her head up. She's made a decision.*)

ELIZABETH: Write St. Bartholomew's Hospital. I'm coming.

ANNA: Coming?

ELIZABETH: Not surgery. That door is closed. Forever. But dear sister, Anna, didn't you just say "dream another."

ANNA: But I meant—

ELIZABETH: Practical medicine! Tell them I'll study that. If I can't be a surgeon, Anna, I will be a doctor!

(ELIZABETH *crosses to new area, as* ANNA *exits and* NARRATORS *enter.*)

(PERCUSSION PLAYER *flips sign to read "New York City."*)

(As NARRATORS *speak, two crowd members,* ANTHONY *and* HELGA, *enter.* ANTHONY, *20s, is a recent immigrant, angry.* HELGA, *also 20s and a recent immigrant, is curious.*)

NARRATOR ONE: After St. Bartholomew's Elizabeth returned to America ready to be a doctor.

NARRATOR TWO: But it was a constant struggle.

NARRATOR THREE: No hospital wanted to hire her.

NARRATOR ONE: No landlord wanted to rent space to her.

NARRATOR TWO: Finally she opened a clinic in the immigrant slums of New York City.

NARRATOR THREE: Her medical ideas were shocking!

(ELIZABETH *stands on a platform addressing a crowd.*)

ELIZABETH: Fresh air, exercise, a balanced diet. Children are born to live, not die!

ANTHONY: We need a doctor who can cure the cholera! Not a preacher!

HELGA: What's fresh air got to do with tuberculosis?

ELIZABETH: Everything! Everything! If the body can't breathe, if the body isn't clean, if the body is malnourished, it cannot get well!

(SOUND: Applause and "Boos.")

NARRATOR ONE: She worked round the clock seeing patients, sometimes the only figure on a darkened street hurrying through the night to save someone.

(ZAC *enters, crosses to clinic area.* ZAC, *20s, a physician, is* ELIZABETH'S *colleague.*)

NARRATOR TWO: But one tragic night, a few months later, a patient died.

(SOUND: Angry voices, threatening mob.)

(PERCUSSION PLAYERS *add to the noise of the crowd. If possible, they become crowd members.*)

(ANTHONY *runs across stage, yelling toward the hospital area.*)

ANTHONY: Call yourself a doctor, do you? You killed her. My sister. The lady doctor killed her. And I've got a good mind to do the same to you. Murderer!

(SOUND: Approaching footsteps, voices screaming.)

(From the hospital area, ELIZABETH *and* ZAC *peer nervously out a hospital window.)*

ELIZABETH: I'd better stop that mob before they break in.

(ZAC *holds* ELIZABETH *back.*)

ZAC: Elizabeth, they've got pickaxes and shovels. And rocks. If you walk out there, you'll start a riot!

(SOUND: Window glass shattering.)

ELIZABETH *(shakes loose):* The riot's already started! Someone has to stop it.

(SEAN, *late 20s, a burly Irish longshoreman, races on and bounds up a higher platform area carrying a huge stick.*)

ZAC *(looks out):* There's a man bounding up the stairs. *(They peer out.)*

(SOUND: Crowd noises.)

SEAN: Quiet! Quiet down, all of you. One more rock, and I'll get the entire New York police force here. *(Grins.)* And five of them are my own brothers.

(SOUND: Laughter. SEAN *holds out his stick.)*

Anybody who tries to hurt the good doctors will have to get past me first! Now, listen!

(SOUND: Noise subsides.)

Dr. Blackwell saved my wife, when she nearly died of pneumonia. How many of you out there have husbands, wives, and children she's tended?

(SOUND: Crowd mumbles.)

I thought so. And did she come to your home, when you were too sick to go out?

(SOUND: Crowd mumbles in agreement. "Aye." "Yes, she did," etc.)

Did you get the same care, whether you paid or not?

(SOUND: Crowd louder in agreement. "Yes." "We did." "That's true," etc.)

Some of you couldn't stand here and screech your lungs out, if she hadn't given you the strength!

(SOUND: Crowd ad-libs. "She saved my boy." "You're right," etc.)

Are you forgetting that even a doctor can't keep a patient from dying, when it's the Lord's will? Sure tonight is a heartache. Sure we're all grieving. But I'll tell you this, I'd grieve more if we lost the hospital!

(SOUND: Crowd reaction.)

Do you want to know what kind of medical care the likes of us would get without her? I'll tell you. NOTHING! So, put your rocks down, and go home. We'll never have a better doctor. Don't be making her go away!

(SOUND: Mumbling crowd disperses and exits.)

ZAC: They're going! They're going.

(ELIZABETH dashes to catch SEAN.)

ELIZABETH: Wait! WAIT!

(ZAC exits, as ELIZABETH catches up with SEAN on the street.)

SEAN: Why, it's the little doctor herself. Sorry about that ruckus.

ELIZABETH: Thank you! Thank you for stopping that mob! You saved the Infirmary.

SEAN: Now don't be letting them scare you away.

ELIZABETH: It takes more than a shovel and a stone to scare a Blackwell!

SEAN *(trying to explain):* They just never saw a lady doctor before.

ELIZABETH *(firm):* They're going to see more of us! More and more. Just like me.

SEAN: Begging your pardon, Dr. Blackwell. Not like you. There's only one like you! *(Tips his cap.)* Evening, Doctor.

*(*SEAN *exits, as* NARRATORS *enter.)*

NARRATOR ONE: It wasn't the first time Dr. Blackwell was threatened.

NARRATOR TWO: And it wasn't the last.

ELIZABETH: Because the real sickness is prejudice! And until I conquer that, I can never stop!

ELIZABETH BLACKWELL
FIRST WOMAN DOCTOR
1821–1910

About the Author

Joanna Halpert Kraus was part of an acting company from an early age. "When I was thirteen," she says, "my life was changed by a marvelous director of children's theater, Margaret Dutton. We toured towns in Maine, where no live theater for young audiences had ever appeared. The children were spellbound, but no more so than we, the players. I vowed then to pass on that touch of magic."

Ms. Kraus has been true to her vow. Almost her entire career has centered around young people and the theater. "Children should have stories to grow on and should never have anything less than the best," she says. "Young people are a wonderful audience, for they listen with their hearts as well as their minds." Plays she has written include *Mean to Be Free*, about Harriet Tubman and the Underground Railroad, and *The Ice Wolf*, about an Eskimo village. In her plays, Ms. Kraus entertains and educates adults as well as children.

A different kind of writing is evident in the children's book Ms. Kraus dedicated to her adopted son. *Tall Boy's Journey* is about a Korean orphan who travels to New York to join his new family. The book is based on true accounts of several international adoptions.

Reader Response

Open for Discussion

Do you think Elizabeth Blackwell's struggle to become a doctor was worth the effort and sacrifice? Why or why not?

Comprehension Check

1. Why were the faculties of medical schools in 1847 opposed to admitting women? Support your answer with details from the play.

2. Think about how Elizabeth Blackwell responded to the many medical school rejections. What do her words and actions reveal about her character?

3. Even though Elizabeth Blackwell was a doctor, she accepted a position as a student nurse in a Paris maternity hospital. Explain how this experience changed her life, using details from the play.

4. If you were a nurse or doctor working alongside Elizabeth Blackwell in the New York City clinic, what would you say about the way she practices medicine? Use details from the play to **draw a conclusion** about Elizabeth Blackwell's skill as a doctor. (Drawing Conclusions)

5. Use evidence from the entire play to **draw a conclusion** about what was expected of women in the United States in the 1840s. (Drawing Conclusions)

 Test Prep

Look Back and Write

For what purpose did the author write the play? How do the narrators help the author achieve this purpose? Use information from pages 259–261 in your answer.

Test Prep

How to Read a Magazine Article

1. Preview

- Some magazine articles deal with extraordinary people. The illustrations help show how this person is extraordinary.

- Read the title and the subtitle. Look over the pictures and the sidebar. What is this woman the boss of? What is she first at doing?

2. Read and Focus

- As you read the article, focus on McGrath's accomplishments, large and small.

- Which of her accomplishments are extraordinary? Which are shared by other women in America? Make notes on your ideas.

3. Think and Connect

Think about "Elizabeth Blackwell: Medical Pioneer." Then look over your notes on "She's the Boss!"

Elizabeth Blackwell and Kathleen McGrath lived during different periods of American history. Based on the two selections, how would you say life has changed for women in America since Elizabeth Blackwell's time?

SHE'S ★ THE ★ BOSS!

by Mark Thompson

THE NAVY'S FIRST FEMALE WARSHIP COMMANDER SETS SAIL

"Put the bridge right there where the orange sign is!" the Navy skipper barks at a rookie officer. The warship U.S.S. *Jarrett* has pulled into port in San Diego, California, after a training voyage. The crew's attempt

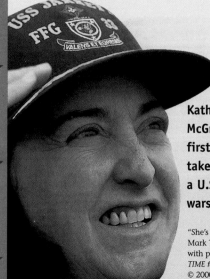

Kathleen McGrath is the first woman to take charge of a U.S. Navy warship.

"She's The Boss!" by Mark Thompson. Used with permission from *TIME for Kids* magazine, © 2000, 2001.

to put a 453-foot vessel alongside a 1,335-foot pier—backward—is not exactly smooth sailing.

A sailor dawdles while writing the commander's orders on a blackboard. "Hey!" the commander snaps. "Pay attention." When a second seaman radios a command, the skipper coolly reminds the crew who gives the orders around here. After careful maneuvering, *Jarrett*'s hull gently kisses the pier bumpers. Home free!

The crew gathers around the commander. "We got to stress all areas today—navigation, communication, and ship handling—and you did it well," the commander says proudly.

The huddle melts away, and sailors stream onto the pier. Two little kids and their dad are headed the other way, up the gangplank toward the commander's cabin. "Did you see Mommy's ship come in? Did you see me wave?" Commander Kathleen McGrath asks as she hugs Nick, 3, and Clare, 2, for the first time in 10 days. Their mom is the big boss.

YOU GO, COMMANDER!

March is Women's History Month, a fitting time for McGrath, 47, to make history herself. On March 31, 2000, she became the first woman commander to lead a U.S. warship to sea. *Jarrett* and a crew of 259 men and four women are headed for the Persian Gulf. Their

Commander McGrath gives orders on the *Jarrett*.

mission: to hunt down ships smuggling oil out of Iraq.

Women served as Navy nurses as early as 1812, but could not serve on board most support ships until 1978. Only in 1994 did they get to serve on warships like the missile-packing, torpedo-shooting *Jarrett*.

Some critics say female sailors still shouldn't command warships—that fighting wars is a man's job. "These are not female jobs," says Dudley Carlson, a retired three-star admiral. "Women simply do not measure up." He says most women sailors are weaker than men, so they might endanger the lives of other sailors in a war.

Even on her ship, not everyone is wild about McGrath's taking charge. "Most of us would prefer to take orders from a male officer," admits Personnelman First Class Arnell Ramos. Others are worried that she lacks experience on a warship.

THE BEST PERSON FOR THE JOB

But no one doubts that McGrath is a first-rate officer with the same qualities that make a man a good commander: she's smart, focused, experienced, and she loves her country. "I don't try to do what a guy would do," she says. "I have to be myself."

Her fellow sailors say she's a bit less formal than most male commanders. The ship's cook, Brian Russell, was surprised when McGrath invited him and some

other senior sailors to her home for a barbecue. Past commanders had invited him to parties as a cook "but never as a person," he says. "I thought it was great."

McGrath's biggest worry is not her popularity. She wants her six-month mission to go smoothly. Sailors will go aboard suspicious ships in international waters and inspect them for smuggled oil. If a ship's crew doesn't appreciate the invasion, it might spark trouble.

McGrath simply dreads the long separation from her kids. "It's real hard being away," she says. Like other Navy dads and moms, she will make videos of herself reading stories to send to Nick and Clare. She and her husband, retired Navy officer Greg Brandon, adopted the children from Russia last year.

Family Time: Greg Brandon holds Nick, and McGrath has Clare.

Brandon left the Navy in 1996, and now works taking care of the kids. He is proud of his wife, whom he met at a Navy school in 1987. "She doesn't like to toot her own horn, so I have to sort of reach over and do it for her," he says.

McGrath won't be the last woman warship commander. Women are moving up the Navy's ranks fast. By 2004, an average crew will be 12% female. Some people snipe that McGrath was made

McGrath, left, often lets her sailors drive the ship.

commander just to show that the Navy is changing its ways. She ignores the talk and sails on.

"She's not in command because she's a woman," says *Jarrett's* Lieutenant Commander Joseph Chiaravallotti. "She's in command because she's better than everyone who's not in command."

WOMEN IN THE U.S. MILITARY

1775–1781
American Revolution: Mary Hays McCauly, nicknamed "Molly Pitcher," brought water to her weary husband in battle and took his place at the cannon.

Molly Pitcher

1861–1865 Civil War: Women played unofficial roles as nurses, aides, and spies.

1914–1918 World War I: The Navy and Marine Corps recruited women for non-nursing positions. The Army hired 200 women as telephone operators.

WACs served in World War II.

1939–1945 World War II: More than 400,000 women performed non-combat services. The Women's Army Corps (WAC) and Navy WAVES were created for them.

1948 Women became eligible for permanent peacetime service in the active forces.

1964–1973 7,500 women served during the Vietnam War, most as nurses.

1991 Gulf War: A record 41,000 women served.

Gulf War soldiers

1992–1993
90% of military jobs were open to women, but not roles in direct ground combat.

Skill Lesson

Compare and Contrast

- To **compare** means to tell how two or more things are alike. To **contrast** means to tell how two or more things are different.

- Sometimes authors use clue words to help you notice likenesses and differences.

- Some common clue words for likenesses are *like, similarly, as, in addition, likewise,* and *in the same way.* Some common clue words for differences are *but, however, different, although, in spite of,* and *on the other hand.*

- When you compare and contrast what you read with your own knowledge and experience, you will better understand the text.

Read "One for All" from *Class President* by Johanna Hurwitz.

Write About It

1. Compare the way Cricket and Lucas behave in Mr. Herbertson's office. Then contrast their behavior with Julio's behavior.

2. To whom does Julio compare Mr. Herbertson? Write the sentence that describes this comparison. Circle the clue word.

One for All
by Johanna Hurwitz

Cricket is running for class president. She and classmates Julio and Lucas meet with their principal, Mr. Herbertson, to discuss a new rule that prohibits soccer playing at recess.

Mr. Herbertson gestured for them to sit in the chairs facing his desk. Cricket looked as pale as Lucas. Maybe she, too, was coming down with the flu.

Julio waited for the future first woman President of the United States to say something, but Cricket didn't say a word. Neither did Lucas. Julio didn't know what to do. They couldn't just sit here and say nothing.

Julio took a deep breath. If Cricket or Lucas wasn't going to talk, he would have to do it. Julio started right in.

"We came to tell you that it isn't fair that no one can play soccer at recess just because Arthur Lewis broke his eyeglasses. Anybody can have an accident. He could have tripped and broken them getting on the school bus." Julio was amazed that so many words had managed to get out of his mouth. No one else said anything, so he went on. "Besides, a girl could fall jumping rope," said Julio. "But you didn't say that they had to stop jumping rope."

"I hadn't thought of that," said Mr. Herbertson.

Cricket looked alarmed. "Can't we jump rope anymore?" she asked.

"I didn't mean that you should make the girls stop jumping rope," Julio went on quickly. He stopped to think of a better example. "Your chair could break while you're sitting on it, Mr. Herbertson," he said.

Mr. Herbertson adjusted himself in his chair. "I certainly hope not," he said, smiling. "What is your name, young man?"

"Julio. Julio Sanchez." He pronounced it in the Spanish way with the *J* having an *H* sound.

"You have a couple of brothers who also attended this school, Julio, don't you?" asked the principal. "Nice fellows. I remember them both."

Julio smiled. He didn't know why he had always been afraid of the principal. He was just like any other person.

"Julio," Mr. Herbertson went on, "you've got a good head on your shoulders, just like your brothers. You made some very good points this afternoon. I think I can arrange things so that there will be more teachers supervising the yard during recess. Then you fellows can play soccer again tomorrow." He turned to Cricket. "You can jump rope if you'd rather do that," he said.

Cricket smiled. She didn't look so pale anymore.

LOOK AHEAD

In the next story, "Born Worker," you'll get to know José and Arnie, cousins who become business partners. As you read, notice how they're alike and different. Then compare them to people you know.

Vocabulary

Words to Know

solution	attitude	grime
laborer	collapsed	supervise
accompanied		

Many words have more than one meaning. To decide which meaning of a word is being used, look for clues in the surrounding sentences or the paragraph.

Read the paragraph below. Decide whether *solution* means "an answer to a problem" or "a liquid mixture."

My Summer Job

Last summer I was a baby-sitter for three children, but there wasn't much sitting involved. In some ways I felt more like a laborer than a "sitter," but I kept a positive attitude. I had to supervise the children as they played, fix them lunch, and clean up after them. One day they forgot to take off their muddy shoes before coming inside for lunch. I scrubbed for twenty minutes with a solution of soap and warm water to clean up the grime they left on the floor. Yet I have to admit we did have fun too. We played baseball, drew pictures, built block towers, and picked up the blocks when the towers collapsed. Once a week I accompanied them to the swimming pool, where we met lots of new friends. By summer's end I realized that sitting around is boring, but baby-sitting isn't!

Write About It

Write about a summer job. Use as many vocabulary words as you can.

BORN WORKER

by Gary Soto

They said that José was born with a ring of dirt around his neck, with grime under his fingernails, and skin calloused from the grainy twist of a shovel. They said his palms were already rough by the time he was three, and soon after he learned his primary colors, his squint was the squint of an aged laborer. They said he was a born worker. By seven he was drinking coffee slowly, his mouth pursed the way his mother sipped. He wore jeans, a shirt with sleeves rolled to his elbows. His eye could measure a length of board, and his knees genuflected over flower beds and leafy gutters.

They said lots of things about José, but almost nothing of his parents. His mother stitched at a machine all day, and his father, with a steady job at the telephone company, climbed splintered, sun-sucked poles, fixed wires, and looked around the city at tree level.

"What do you see up there?" José once asked his father.

"Work," he answered. "I see years of work, mi'jo."*

José took this as a truth, and though he did well in school, he felt destined to labor. His arms would pump, his legs would bend, his arms would carry a world of earth. He believed in hard work, believed that his strength was as ancient as a rock's.

"Life is hard," his father repeated from the time José could first make out the meaning of words until he was stroking his fingers against the grain of his sandpaper beard.

His mother was an example to José. She would raise her hands, showing her fingers pierced from the sewing machines. She bled on her machine, bled because there was money to make, a child to raise, and a roof to stay under.

One day when José returned home from junior high, his cousin Arnie was sitting on the lawn sucking on a stalk of grass. José knew that grass didn't come from his lawn. His was cut and pampered, clean.

"José!" Arnie shouted as he took off the earphones of his CD Walkman.

"Hi, Arnie," José said without much enthusiasm. He didn't like his cousin. He thought he was lazy and, worse, spoiled by the trappings of being middle class. His parents had good jobs in offices and showered him with clothes, shoes, CDs, vacations, almost anything he wanted. Arnie's family had never climbed a telephone pole to size up the future.

Arnie rose to his feet, and José saw that his cousin was wearing a new pair of high-tops. He didn't say anything.

"Got an idea," Arnie said cheerfully. "Something that'll make us money."

* (mē′hō′) Spanish for "my son"

José looked at his cousin, not a muscle of curiosity twitching in his face.

Still, Arnie explained that since he himself was so clever with words, and his best cousin in the whole world was good at working with his hands, that maybe they might start a company.

"What would you do?" José asked.

"Me?" he said brightly. "Shoot, I'll round up all kinds of jobs for you. You won't have to do anything." He stopped, then started again. "Except—you know—do the work."

"Get out of here," José said.

"Don't be that way," Arnie begged. "Let me tell you how it works."

The boys went inside the house, and while José stripped off his school clothes and put on his jeans and a T-shirt, Arnie told him that they could be rich.

"You ever hear of this guy named Bechtel?" Arnie asked.

José shook his head.

"Man, he started just like us," Arnie said. "He started digging ditches and stuff, and the next thing you knew, he was sitting by his own swimming pool. You want to sit by your own pool, don't you?" Arnie smiled, waiting for José to speak up.

"Never heard of this guy Bechtel," José said after he rolled on two huge socks, worn at the heels. He opened up his chest of drawers and brought out a packet of Kleenex.

Arnie looked at the Kleenex.

"How come you don't use your sleeve?" Arnie joked.

José thought for a moment and said, "I'm not like you." He smiled at his retort.

"Listen, I'll find the work, and then we can split it fifty-fifty."

José knew fifty-fifty was a bad deal.

"How about sixty-forty?" Arnie suggested when he could see that José wasn't going for it. "I know a lot of people from my dad's job. They're waiting for us."

José sat on the edge of his bed and started to lace up his boots. He knew that there were agencies that would find you work, agencies that took a portion of your pay. They're cheats, he thought, people who sit in air-conditioned offices while others work.

"You really know a lot of people?" José asked.

"Boatloads," Arnie said. "My dad works with this millionaire—honest—who cooks a steak for his dog every day."

He's a liar, José thought. No matter how he tried, he couldn't picture a dog grubbing on steak. The world was too poor for that kind of silliness.

"Listen, I'll go eighty-twenty," José said.

"Aw, man," Arnie whined. "That ain't fair."

José laughed.

"I mean, half the work is finding the jobs," Arnie explained, his palms up as he begged José to be reasonable.

José knew this was true. He had had to go door-to-door, and he disliked asking for work. He assumed that it should automatically be his since he was a good worker, honest, and always on time.

"Where did you get this idea, anyhow?" José asked.

"I got a business mind," Arnie said proudly.

"Just like that Bechtel guy," José retorted.

"That's right."

José agreed to a seventy-thirty split, with the condition that Arnie had to help out. Arnie hollered, arguing that some people were meant to work and others to come up with brilliant ideas. He was one of the latter. Still, he agreed after José said it was that or nothing.

In the next two weeks, Arnie found an array of jobs. José peeled off shingles from a rickety garage roof, carried rocks down a path to where a pond would go, and spray-painted lawn furniture. And while Arnie accompanied him, most of the time he did nothing. He did help occasionally. He did shake the cans of spray paint and kick aside debris so that José didn't trip while going down the path carrying the rocks. He did stack the piles of shingles, but almost cried when a nail bit his thumb. But mostly he told José what he had missed or where the work could be improved. José was bothered because he and his work had never been criticized before.

But soon José learned to ignore his cousin, ignore his comments about his spray-painting, or about the way he lugged rocks, two in each arm. He didn't say anything, either, when they got paid and Arnie rubbed his hands like a fly, muttering, "It's payday."

Then Arnie found a job scrubbing a drained swimming pool. The two boys met early at José's house. Arnie brought his bike. José's own bike had a flat that grinned like a clown's face.

"I'll pedal," José suggested when Arnie said that he didn't have much leg strength.

With Arnie on the handlebars, José tore off, his pedaling so strong that tears of fear formed in Arnie's eyes.

"Slow down!" Arnie cried.

José ignored him and within minutes they were riding the bike up a gravel driveway. Arnie hopped off at first chance.

"You're scary," Arnie said, picking a gnat from his eye.

José chuckled.

When Arnie knocked on the door, an old man still in pajamas appeared in the window. He motioned for the boys to come around to the back.

"Let me do the talking," Arnie suggested to his cousin. "He knows my dad real good. They're like this." He pressed two fingers together.

José didn't bother to say OK. He walked the bike into the backyard, which was lush with plants—roses in their last bloom, geraniums, hydrangeas, pansies with their skirts of bright colors. José could make out the splash of a fountain. Then he heard the hysterical yapping of a poodle. From all his noise, a person might have thought the dog was on fire.

"Hi, Mr. Clemens," Arnie said, extending his hand. "I'm Arnie Sanchez. It's nice to see you again."

José had never seen a kid actually greet someone like this. Mr. Clemens said, hiking up his pajama bottoms, "I only wanted one kid to work."

"Oh," Arnie stuttered. "Actually, my cousin José really does the work and I kind of, you know, supervise."

Mr. Clemens pinched up his wrinkled face. He seemed not to understand. He took out a pea-sized hearing aid, fiddled with its tiny dial, and fit it into his ear, which was surrounded with wiry gray hair.

"I'm only paying for one boy," Mr. Clemens shouted. His poodle click-clicked and stood behind his legs. The dog bared its small crooked teeth.

"That's right," Arnie said, smiling a strained smile. "We know that you're going to compensate only one of us."

Mr. Clemens muttered under his breath. He combed his hair with his fingers. He showed José the pool, which was shaped as round as an elephant. It was filthy with grime. Near the bottom some grayish water shimmered and leaves floated as limp as cornflakes.

"It's got to be real clean," Mr. Clemens said, "or it's not worth it."

"Oh, José's a great worker," Arnie said. He patted his cousin's shoulders and said that he could lift a mule.

Mr. Clemens sized up José and squeezed his shoulders too.

"How do I know you, anyhow?" Mr. Clemens asked Arnie, who was aiming a smile at the poodle.

"You know my dad," Arnie answered, raising his smile to the old man. "He works at Interstate Insurance. You and he had some business deals."

Mr. Clemens thought for a moment, a hand on his mouth, head shaking. He could have been thinking about the meaning of life, his face was so dark.

"Mexican fella?" he inquired.

"That's him," Arnie said happily.

José felt like hitting his cousin for his cheerful attitude. Instead, he walked over and picked up the white plastic bottle of bleach. Next to it were a wire brush, a pumice stone, and some rags. He set down the bottle and, like a surgeon, put on a pair of plastic gloves.

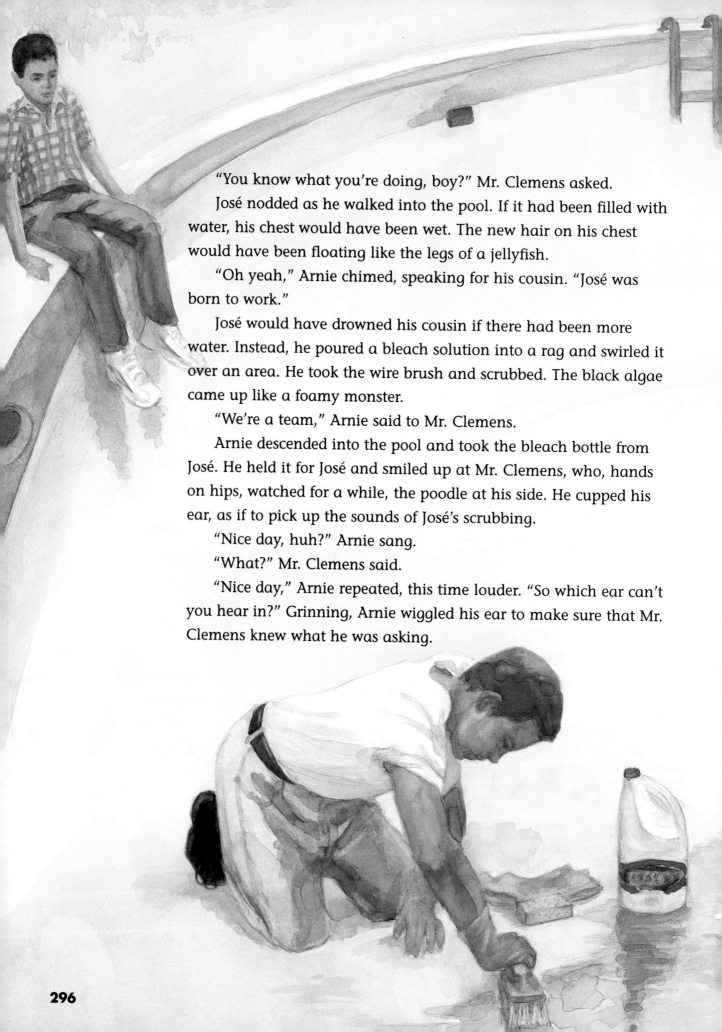

"You know what you're doing, boy?" Mr. Clemens asked.

José nodded as he walked into the pool. If it had been filled with water, his chest would have been wet. The new hair on his chest would have been floating like the legs of a jellyfish.

"Oh yeah," Arnie chimed, speaking for his cousin. "José was born to work."

José would have drowned his cousin if there had been more water. Instead, he poured a bleach solution into a rag and swirled it over an area. He took the wire brush and scrubbed. The black algae came up like a foamy monster.

"We're a team," Arnie said to Mr. Clemens.

Arnie descended into the pool and took the bleach bottle from José. He held it for José and smiled up at Mr. Clemens, who, hands on hips, watched for a while, the poodle at his side. He cupped his ear, as if to pick up the sounds of José's scrubbing.

"Nice day, huh?" Arnie sang.

"What?" Mr. Clemens said.

"Nice day," Arnie repeated, this time louder. "So which ear can't you hear in?" Grinning, Arnie wiggled his ear to make sure that Mr. Clemens knew what he was asking.

Mr. Clemens ignored Arnie. He watched José, whose arms worked back and forth like he was sawing logs.

"We're not only a team," Arnie shouted, "but we're also cousins."

Mr. Clemens shook his head at Arnie. When he left, the poodle leading the way, Arnie immediately climbed out of the pool and sat on the edge, legs dangling.

"It's going to be blazing," Arnie complained. He shaded his eyes with his hand and looked east, where the sun was rising over a sycamore, its leaves hanging like bats.

José scrubbed. He worked the wire brush over the black and green stains, the grime dripping like tears. He finished a large area. He hopped out of the pool and returned hauling a garden hose with an attached nozzle. He gave the cleaned area a blast. When the spray got too close, his cousin screamed, got up, and, searching for something to do, picked a loquat from a tree.

"What's your favorite fruit?" Arnie asked.

José ignored him.

Arnie stuffed a bunch of loquats into his mouth, then cursed himself for splattering juice on his new high-tops. He returned to the pool, his cheeks fat with the seeds, and once again sat at the edge. He started to tell José how he had first learned to swim. "We were on vacation in Mazatlán. You been there, ain't you?"

José shook his head. He dabbed the bleach solution onto the sides of the pool with a rag and scrubbed a new area.

"Anyhow, my dad was on the beach and saw this drowned dead guy," Arnie continued. "And right there, my dad got scared and realized I couldn't swim."

Arnie rattled on about how his father had taught him in the hotel pool and later showed him where the drowned man's body had been.

"Be quiet," José said.

"What?"

"I can't concentrate," José said, stepping back to look at the cleaned area.

Arnie shut his mouth but opened it to lick loquat juice from his fingers. He kicked his legs against the swimming pool, bored. He looked around the backyard and spotted a lounge chair. He got up, dusting off the back of his pants, and threw himself into the cushions. He raised and lowered the back of the lounge. Sighing, he snuggled in. He stayed quiet for three minutes, during which time José scrubbed. His arms hurt but he kept working with long strokes. José knew that in an hour the sun would drench the pool with light. He hurried to get the job done.

Arnie then asked, "You ever peel before?"

José looked at his cousin. His nose burned from the bleach. He scrunched up his face.

"You know, like when you get sunburned."

"I'm too dark to peel," José said, his words echoing because he had advanced to the deep end. "Why don't you be quiet and let me work?"

Arnie babbled on that he had peeled when on vacation in Hawaii. He explained that he was really more French than Mexican, and that's why his skin was sensitive. He said that when he lived in France, people thought that he could be Portuguese or maybe Armenian, never Mexican.

José felt like soaking his rag with bleach and pressing it over Arnie's mouth to make him be quiet.

Then Mr. Clemens appeared. He was dressed in white pants and a flowery shirt. His thin hair was combed so that his scalp, as pink as a crab, showed.

"I'm just taking a little rest," Arnie said.

Arnie leaped back into the pool. He took the bleach bottle and held it. He smiled at Mr. Clemens, who came to inspect their progress.

"José's doing a good job," Arnie said, then whistled a song.

Mr. Clemens peered into the pool, hands on knees, admiring the progress.

"Pretty good, huh?" Arnie asked.

Mr. Clemens nodded. Then his hearing aid fell out, and José turned in time to see it roll like a bottle cap toward the bottom of the pool. It leaped into the stagnant water with a plop. A single bubble went up, and it was gone.

"Dang," Mr. Clemens swore. He took shuffling steps toward the deep end. He steadied his gaze on where the hearing aid had sunk. He leaned over and suddenly, arms waving, one leg kicking out, he tumbled into the pool. He landed standing up, then his legs buckled, and he crumbled, his head striking against the bottom. He rolled once, and half of his body settled in the water.

"Did you see that!" Arnie shouted, big-eyed.

José had already dropped his brushes on the side of the pool and hurried to the old man, who moaned, eyes closed, his false teeth jutting from his mouth. A ribbon of blood immediately began to flow from his scalp.

"We better get out of here!" Arnie suggested. "They're going to blame us!"

José knelt on both knees at the old man's side. He took the man's teeth from his mouth and placed them in his shirt pocket. The old man groaned and opened his eyes, which were shiny wet. He appeared startled, like a newborn.

"Sir, you'll be all right," José cooed, then snapped at his cousin. "Arnie, get over here and help me!"

"I'm going home," Arnie whined.

"You punk!" José yelled. "Go inside and call 911."

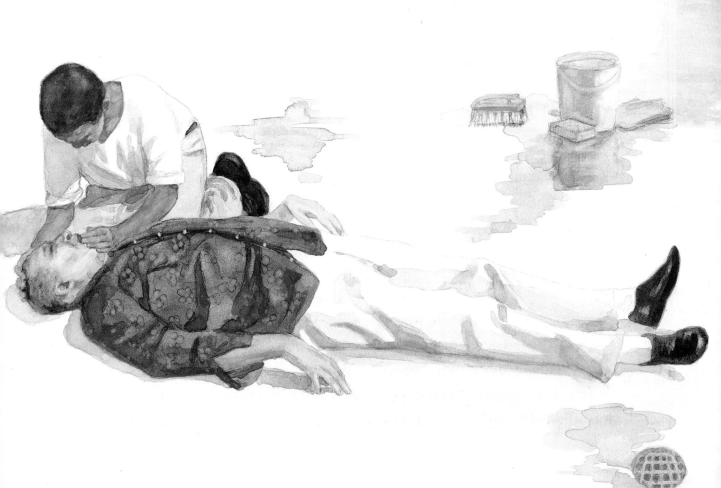

Arnie said that they should leave him there.

"Why should we get involved?" he cried as he started for his bike. "It's his own fault."

José laid the man's head down and with giant steps leaped out of the pool, shoving his cousin as he passed. He went into the kitchen and punched in 911 on a telephone. He explained to the operator what had happened. When asked the address, José dropped the phone and went onto the front porch to look for it.

"It's 940 East Brown," José breathed. He hung up and looked wildly about the kitchen. He opened up the refrigerator and brought out a plastic tray of ice, which he twisted so that a few of the cubes popped out and slid across the floor. He wrapped some cubes in a dishtowel. When he raced outside, Arnie was gone, the yapping poodle was doing laps around the edge of the pool, and Mr. Clemens was trying to stand up.

"No, sir," José said as he jumped into the pool, his own knees almost buckling. "Please, sit down."

Mr. Clemens staggered and collapsed. José caught him before he hit his head again. The towel of ice cubes dropped from his hands. With his legs spread to absorb the weight, José raised the man up in his arms, this fragile man. He picked him up and carefully stepped toward the shallow end, one slow elephant step at a time.

"You'll be all right," José said, more to himself than to Mr. Clemens, who moaned and struggled to be let free.

The sirens wailed in the distance. The poodle yapped, which started a dog barking in the neighbor's yard.

"You'll be OK," José repeated, and in the shallow end of the pool, he edged up the steps. He laid the old man in the lounge chair and raced back inside for more ice and another towel. He returned outside and placed the bundle of cubes on the man's head, where the blood flowed. Mr. Clemens was awake, looking about. When the old man felt his mouth, José reached into his shirt pocket and pulled out his false teeth. He fit the teeth into Mr. Clemens's mouth and a smile appeared, something bright at a difficult time.

"I hit my head," Mr. Clemens said after smacking his teeth so that the fit was right.

José looked up and his gaze floated to a telephone pole, one his father might have climbed. If he had been there, his father would have seen that José was more than just a good worker. He would have seen a good man. He held the towel to the old man's head. The poodle, now quiet, joined them on the lounge chair.

A fire truck pulled into the driveway and soon they were surrounded by firemen, one of whom brought out a first-aid kit. A fireman led José away and asked what had happened. He was starting to explain when his cousin reappeared, yapping like a poodle.

"I was scrubbing the pool," Arnie shouted, "and I said, 'Mr. Clemens, you shouldn't stand so close to the edge.' But did he listen? No, he leaned over and . . . Well, you can just imagine my horror."

José walked away from Arnie's jabbering. He walked away, and realized that there were people like his cousin, the liar, and people like himself, someone he was getting to know. He walked away and in the midmorning heat boosted himself up a telephone pole. He climbed up and saw for himself what his father saw—miles and miles of trees and houses, and a future lost in the layers of yellowish haze.

About the Author

GARY SOTO

Like José, the main character in "Born Worker," Gary Soto worked hard when he was young. He had many chores and earned money by mowing lawns and picking grapes. Despite his family's constant struggles with poverty, Mr. Soto has many happy memories of growing up in the *barrio*—a Mexican American neighborhood—in Fresno, California. He uses these happy memories of a tightly knit community and its ethnic traditions in his stories.

No one encouraged him to read, however, and he didn't develop an interest in writing until he was in college. While in the library one day, Mr. Soto found a collection of poems. The poems made such an impression on him that he decided to try writing some of his own. He later took poetry classes. By the time Mr. Soto finished college and became a professor in California, his first book of poetry was published. The award-winning book was called *The Elements of San Joaquin,* and it was followed by several other books of poetry.

Later Mr. Soto changed his main focus to writing for and about young people. His book *Baseball in April and Other Stories* was named a Best Book for Young Adults by the American Library Association, and his Christmas story *Too Many Tamales* was named a *Booklist* Books for Youth Editors' Choice.

Reader Response

Open for Discussion

What would you like to say to José about the way he conducts himself? to Arnie?

Comprehension Check

1. People call José a "born worker." What do they mean by this? Support your answer with details from the story.

2. Describe the business agreement between José and Arnie. Does it turn out to be a fair deal? Explain, using information from the story.

3. Now that you know José through his actions and thoughts, do you think he will continue his partnership with Arnie? Why or why not?

4. **Compare and contrast** José and Arnie. Use a Venn diagram to show how they are alike and how they are different. First, draw two circles that overlap. Then in one circle, write José's character traits; in the other circle, write Arnie's. In the overlapping space, write the character traits they share. Be sure you have details from the story to back up each trait. (Compare and Contrast)

5. **Contrast** the actions of José and Arnie after Mr. Clemens falls into the swimming pool. Look back at the story for details. (Compare and Contrast)

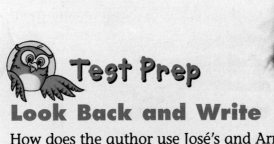

Test Prep

Look Back and Write

How does the author use José's and Arnie's parents to help show that the two boys are different from each other? Use details from pages 290–291 in your answer.

Literature Connection

 **Test Prep**

How to Read a Poem

1. Preview

- Some poems focus on a speaker's reactions to something.

- Read the title and skim through the poem. Do you think the poem is actually about what the title says?

2. Read and Understand

- Read the poem. How does the speaker feel about doing dishes? What details tell you so?

- How long does the speaker say this job takes to do? How long do you think it actually takes?

3. Think and Connect

Think about "Born to Work." Think about your answers to the questions under Read and Understand for "Doing Dishes."

The narrator in "Doing Dishes" and José and Arnie in "Born to Work" all have different attitudes about work. How are these characters' attitudes similar to—or different from—each other?

Doing Dishes

by Gary Soto

Last night
We had one pot
And three dishes.
Tonight, when it's my turn
To throw my hands
Into suds
We have a stack
Of plates
The color of chickens,
White and red.
That's what we
Had tonight—chicken *mole,*
A messy meal
That leaves stains
On your mouth
And greedy fingers.

We have plates.
We have six pots,
A jangle of
Forks and knives,
And a wooden spoon
That paddled
Through sauce
And docked on my lips
When Mom wasn't looking.
We have a rolling pin
Sticky with dough.
We have a potato peeler
And a pie pan
Where the flan
Set in its sweetness.
We have drinking glasses.
I pump the suds
And scrub,
My sponge raking
The *mole* sauce,
The *frijoles,*
The *arroz,*
The *papas.*
The dishwater
Turns orange,
And suds flatten.
I drain the water
And start again,
A curl of steam
Licking my eyebrows.
I wipe my eyebrow.

I pump my sponge.
I sweat over the suds
And wail inside
Because it's boring.
I could be doing
Nothing right now,
Or reading a magazine,
Which is almost
Like doing nothing.
But I scrub and rinse,
And am here
Leaning on my belly
Against the sink
For hours, days, years. . . .
When I finally
Pull my hands
From the water,
They're puckered and old
—that's how long!

Skill Lesson

Cause and Effect

- An **effect** is something that happens. A **cause** is why something happens.

- To find an effect, ask yourself "What happened?" To find a cause, ask yourself "Why did this happen?"

- Clue words such as *cause, because,* and *reason* can help you find a cause. Clue words such as *so, consequently, therefore,* and *thus* can help you find an effect.

- If there are no clue words, try drawing a diagram of a cause and its effect. In one box write the cause, and in another box write its effect. Then draw an arrow from the cause to its effect.

Read "Sunday Visitors" from *Small Steps: The Year I Got Polio* by Peg Kehret.

Write About It

1. Write the sentence from the story that explains why Alice doesn't ask for a special treat. Underline the clue word.

2. Peg's brother, Art, makes a surprise visit. Describe the effect of his visit on Dorothy.

3. Look back at the story. Draw a diagram that shows another cause and its effect.

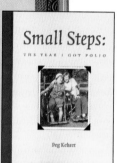

Sunday Visitors

by Peg Kehret

In 1949, twelve-year-old Peg was diagnosed with polio. She received treatment at the Sheltering Arms, where she shared a hospital room with four other girls. On their visits, Peg's parents talked to all the girls.

"There must be something you'd like us to bring you," Dad said. "Something you can't get here at the Sheltering Arms."

Alice shook her head. At first I thought she was being ornery; then I realized Alice had been at the Sheltering Arms for so long she didn't remember things like comic books and marshmallows. Licorice and potato chips were beyond her realm of experience. She didn't know what to ask for because she did not know what she was missing.

A window of understanding opened in my mind, and the breeze of compassion blew in. From that moment on, I was glad to share my visiting family with my roommates.

"If you don't know what you want," Mother told Alice, "we'll surprise you."

The next Sunday, the other girls were as excited about visiting day as I was. Alice combed her hair, though she quit when she saw me watching her.

Once again, Mother and Dad came in right at twelve o'clock. They hugged and kissed me and greeted all the other girls.

"Did you remember our treats?" Renée asked.

"Of course," Mother said. She handed Renée a *Little Lulu* comic book. Dad opened Shirley's bag of marshmallows and put one in her mouth.

"Yum," Shirley said. "That's the first marshmallow I've had for seven months."

"Here is your gift, Alice," Mother said as she gave Alice a pink lipstick.

"Why are you being so nice to me?" Alice asked.

"We like you," Mother said.

Alice didn't say thank you, but she put the lipstick carefully away in her drawer.

"Dorothy's next," Renée said. "Where's her tall, dark, and handsome young man?"

Dad went to the doorway and motioned to someone in the hall.

In walked my brother, Art. Art was eighteen and six feet, two inches tall, with thick, dark hair. He was once voted Campus Dreamboat by a sorority group.

After Art hugged me, he said, "I didn't come to visit you. I came to see Dorothy. Which one is Dorothy?"

Dorothy blushed red as a wagon while the rest of us squealed our delight.

"This is for you," Art said, and he gave Dorothy a bag of licorice.

Every Sunday after that, all of us chattered happily as we waited for my parents to arrive.

LOOK AHEAD

In the biography that follows, *Wilma Unlimited*, you'll read about an athlete who overcame a physical disability. As you read, think about the causes of her success.

307

Vocabulary

Words to Know

memorable	competition	intense
paralyzed	unlimited	athletic

Words with opposite meanings are called **antonyms.** You can often figure out the meaning of an unknown word by finding a clue in the words around it. Sometimes this clue is an antonym.

Read the paragraph below. Notice how *ordinary* helps you understand what *memorable* means.

The Paralympics

The Paralympic Games are an international competition for people with physical disabilities. Paralympic athletes, many of whom are paralyzed from the waist down, compete in track-and-field, archery, basketball, and other athletic events. Some athletes compete in wheelchairs; others use artificial limbs. All of them test their physical limitations to unlock their seemingly unlimited potential. Paralympic competitors do intense training to prepare for the games. Their desire and efforts make the Paralympics as memorable as the Olympic Games, not like ordinary games at all.

Talk About It

Use some of the vocabulary words to tell a friend about your last game or competition.

Wilma Unlimited

by Kathleen Krull / illustrated by David Diaz

No one expected such a tiny girl to have a first birthday. In Clarksville, Tennessee, in 1940, life for a baby who weighed just over four pounds at birth was sure to be limited.

But most babies didn't have nineteen older brothers and sisters to watch over them. Most babies didn't have a mother who knew home remedies and a father who worked several jobs.

Most babies weren't Wilma Rudolph.

Wilma did celebrate her first birthday, and everyone noticed that as soon as this girl could walk, she ran or jumped instead.

She worried people, though—she was always so small and sickly. If a brother or sister had a cold, she got double pneumonia. If one of them had measles, Wilma got measles, too, plus mumps and chicken pox.

Her mother always nursed her at home. Doctors were a luxury for the Rudolph family, and anyway, only one doctor in Clarksville would treat black people.

Just before Wilma turned five, she got sicker than ever. Her sisters and brothers heaped all the family's blankets on her trying to keep her warm.

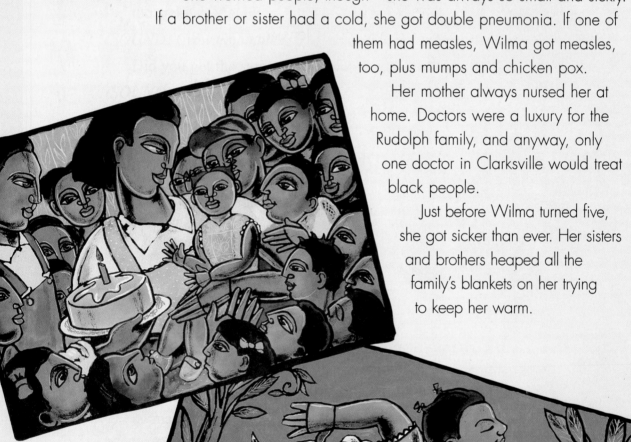

During that sickness, Wilma's left leg
twisted inward and she couldn't move it back. Not even
Wilma's mother knew what was wrong.

The doctor came to see her then. Besides scarlet fever, he said,
Wilma had also been stricken with polio. In those days most children
who got polio either died or were permanently crippled. There was
no cure.

The news spread around Clarksville. Wilma, that lively girl, would
never walk again.

But Wilma kept moving anyway she could. By hopping on one
foot, she could get herself around the house, to the outhouse in the
backyard, and even, on Sundays, to church.

Wilma's mother urged her on. Mrs. Rudolph had plenty to do—
cooking, cleaning, sewing patterned flour sacks into clothes for her
children, now twenty-two in all. Yet twice every week, she and Wilma
took the bus to the nearest hospital that would treat black patients,
some fifty miles away in Nashville. They rode together in the back,
the only place blacks were allowed to sit.

Doctors and nurses at the hospital helped Wilma do exercises to make her paralyzed leg stronger. At home, Wilma practiced them constantly, even when it hurt.

To Wilma, what hurt most was that the local school wouldn't let her attend because she couldn't walk. Tearful and lonely, she watched her brothers and sisters run off to school each day, leaving her behind. Finally, tired of crying all the time, she decided she had to fight back—somehow.

Wilma worked so hard at her exercises that the doctors decided she was ready for a heavy steel brace. With the brace supporting her leg, she didn't have to hop anymore. School was possible at last.

But it wasn't the happy place she had imagined. Her classmates made fun of her brace. During playground games she could only sit on the sidelines, twitchy with impatience. She studied the other kids for hours—memorizing moves, watching the ball zoom through the rim of the bushel basket they used as a hoop.

Wilma fought the sadness by doing more leg exercises. Her family always cheered her on, and Wilma did everything she could to keep them from worrying about her. At times her leg really did seem to be getting stronger. Other times it just hurt.

One Sunday, on her way to church, Wilma felt especially good. She and her family had always found strength in their faith, and church was Wilma's favorite place in the world. Everyone she knew would be there—talking and laughing, praying and singing. It would be just the place to try the bravest thing she had ever done.

She hung back while people filled the old building. Standing alone, the sound of hymns coloring the air, she unbuckled her heavy brace and set it by the church's front door. Taking a deep breath, she moved one foot in front of the other, her knees trembling violently. She took her mind off her knees by concentrating on taking another breath and then another.

Whispers rippled throughout the gathering. Wilma Rudolph was *walking*. Row by row, heads turned toward her as she walked alone down the aisle. Her large family, all her family's friends, everyone from school—each person stared wide-eyed. The singing never stopped; it seemed to burst right through the walls and into the trees. Finally, Wilma reached a seat in the front and began singing too, her smile triumphant.

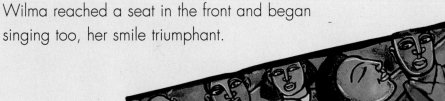

Wilma practiced walking as often as she could after that, and when she was twelve years old, she was able to take off the brace for good. She and her mother realized she could get along without it, so one memorable day they wrapped the hated brace in a box and mailed it back to the hospital.

As soon as Wilma sent that box away, she knew her life was beginning all over again.

After years of sitting on the sidelines, Wilma couldn't wait to throw herself into basketball, the game she had most liked to watch. She was skinny, but no longer tiny. Her long, long legs would propel her across the court and through the air, and she knew all the rules and all the moves.

In high school, she led her basketball team to one victory after another. Eventually, she took the team all the way to the Tennessee state championships. There, to everyone's astonishment, her team lost.

Wilma had become accustomed to winning. Now she slumped on the bench, all the liveliness knocked out of her.

But at the game that day was a college coach. He admired Wilma's basketball playing but was especially impressed by the way she ran. He wanted her for his track-and-field team.

With his help, Wilma won a full athletic scholarship to Tennessee State University. She was the first member of her family to go to college.

Eight years after she mailed her brace away, Wilma's long legs and years of hard work carried her thousands of miles from Clarksville, Tennessee. The summer of 1960 she arrived in Rome, Italy, to represent the United States at the Olympic Games—as a runner.

Just participating in the Olympics was a deeply personal victory for Wilma, but her chances of winning a race were limited. Simply walking in Rome's shimmering heat was a chore, and athletes from other countries had run faster races than Wilma ever had. Women weren't thought to run very well anyway; track-and-field was considered a sport for men. And the pressure from the public was intense—for the first time ever, the Olympics would be shown on television, and all the athletes knew that more than one hundred million people would be watching. Worst of all, Wilma had twisted her ankle just after she arrived in Rome. It was still swollen and painful on the day of her first race.

Yet once it was her turn
to compete, Wilma forgot her ankle and
everything else. She lunged forward, not thinking
about her fear, her pain, or the sweat flying off her face. She ran
better than she ever had before. And she ran better
than anyone else.

Grabbing the attention of the whole world, Wilma Rudolph of
the United States won the 100-meter dash. No one else even came
close. An Olympic gold medal was hers to take home.

So when it was time for the 200-meter dash, Wilma's graceful
long legs were already famous. Her ears buzzed with the sound of
the crowd chanting her name. Such support helped her ignore the rain
that was beginning to fall. At the crack of the starting gun, she surged
into the humid air like a tornado. When she crossed the finish line,
she had done it again. She finished far ahead of everyone else.
She had earned her second gold medal. Wet and breathless, Wilma
was exhilarated by the double triumph. The crowd went wild.

The 400-meter relay race was yet to come.
Wilma's team faced the toughest competition of all. And as the fourth
and final runner on her team, it was Wilma who had to cross the finish
line.

Wilma's teammates ran well, passed the baton smoothly, and kept
the team in first place. Wilma readied herself for the dash to the finish
line as her third teammate ran toward her. She reached back for the
baton—and nearly dropped it. As she tried to recover from the fumble,
two other runners sped past her. Wilma and her team were suddenly
in third place.

Ever since the day she had walked down the aisle at church,
Wilma had known the power of concentration. Now, legs pumping,
she put her mind to work. In a final, electrifying burst of speed, she
pulled ahead. By a fraction of a second, she was the first to blast
across the finish line. The thundering cheers matched the thundering of
her own heart. She had made history. She had won for an astounding
third time.

At her third ceremony that week, as the band played "The Star-
Spangled Banner," Wilma stood tall and still, like a queen, the last
of her three Olympic gold medals hanging around her neck.

Wilma Rudolph, once known as the sickliest child in Clarksville,
had become the fastest woman in the world.

About the Author
Kathleen Krull

Because Kathleen Krull is interested in so many things, she has written books about subjects as varied as music, ecology, nightmares, and World War II. Ms. Krull's writing career began in second grade when she penned her first book, *A Garden Book*. This was followed in fifth grade by *Hairdos and People I Know*. Ever since then, she has been involved in children's literature in some form or other.

Ms. Krull is an accomplished musician as well as an author. Several of her books contain music or tell about the lives of musicians. Her book *Gonna Sing My Head Off!*, a collection of traditional American songs, was named a Best Book by the American Library Association and a Notable Book in the Field of Social Studies. *Lives of the Musicians: Good Times, Bad Times (and What the Neighbors Thought)*, a collection of biographical facts and trivia about musicians, was named an ALA Notable Book and an International Reading Association Teachers' Choice.

About the Illustrator
David Diaz

David Diaz first started to get serious about art in high school. His art teacher encouraged him to enter competitions and introduced him to professional artists. Mr. Diaz worked in advertising before he illustrated his first children's book. He didn't change the way he worked when he began illustrating. "I approach it the same way I do a job for a corporate client or the way in which I work on a design project," he says. "There's no need to 'draw down' to a younger audience." The second book that Mr. Diaz illustrated, *Smoky Night*, about a child who witnesses a night of rioting, won the Caldecott Medal, a great honor.

Reader Response

Open for Discussion

In your opinion, what was Wilma Rudolph's greatest triumph? Explain.

Comprehension Check

1. The setting for Wilma Rudolph's early life was Clarksville, Tennessee, in the 1940s. How did this setting affect her childhood and the kind of medical treatment she received?

2. Make a chart of the people who helped Wilma Rudolph during her life. In the first column, write their names or descriptions. In the second column, write a few words describing how they helped her. Use the text as you need to.

3. Name some of Wilma Rudolph's character traits. In your opinion, which traits enabled her to become an Olympic gold medal winner? Look back at the story for details.

4. In the 1940s, polio usually **caused** one of two **effects** in the children who caught it. What were they? (Cause and effect)

5. Wilma Rudolph was not allowed to attend the local school. What **caused** the school officials to keep her out of school? What was the **effect** on Wilma Rudolph? (Cause and effect)

 Test Prep

Look Back and Write

Look back at pages 316–319. Describe Wilma Rudolph's accomplishments during the 1960 Olympic games in order, from first to last.

Time Almanac

The Olympic Games: Gold Medals

Track and Field—Women

100-Meter Dash

1928	Elizabeth Robinson, United States	12.2s
1932	Stella Walsh, Poland	11.9s
1936	Helen Stephens, United States	11.5s
1948	Fanny Blankers-Koen, Netherlands	11.9s
1952	Marjorie Jackson, Australia	11.5s
1956	Betty Cuthbert, Australia	11.5s
1960	Wilma Rudolph, United States	11.0s
1964	Wyomia Tyrus, United States	11.4s
1968	Wyomia Tyrus, United States	11.0s
1972	Renate Stecher, East Germany	11.07s
1976	Annegret Richter, West Germany	11.08s
1980	Lyudmila Kondratyeva, U.S.S.R.	11.06s
1984	Evelyn Ashford, United States	10.97s
1988	Florence Griffith-Joyner, United States	10.54s
1992	Gail Devers, United States	10.82s
1996	Gail Devers, United States	10.94s

200-Meter Dash

1948	Fanny Blankers-Koen, Netherlands	24.4s
1952	Marjorie Jackson, Australia	23.7s
1956	Betty Cuthbert, Australia	23.4s
1960	Wilma Rudolph, United States	24.0s
1964	Edith McGuire, United States	23.0s
1968	Irena Szewinska, Poland	22.5s
1972	Renate Stecher, East Germany	22.4s
1976	Baerbel Eckert, East Germany	22.37s
1980	Barbara Wockel, East Germany	22.03s
1984	Valerie Brisco-Hooks, United States	21.81s
1988	Florence Griffith-Joyner, United States	21.34s
1992	Gwen Torrence, United States	21.81s
1996	Marie-Jose Perec, France	22.12s

400-Meter Dash

1964	Betty Cuthbert, Australia	52.0s
1968	Colette Besson, France	52.0s
1972	Monika Zehrt, East Germany	51.08s
1976	Irena Szewinska, Poland	49.29s
1980	Marita Koch, East Germany	48.88s
1984	Valerie Brisco-Hooks, United States	48.83s
1988	Olga Bryzguina, U.S.S.R.	48.65s
1992	Marie-Jose Perec, France	48.83s
1996	Marie-Jose Perec, France	48.25s

800-Meter Run

1928	Lina Radke, Germany	2m16.8s
1960	Ljudmila Shevcova, U.S.S.R.	2m4.3s
1964	Ann Packer, Great Britain	2m1.1s
1968	Madeline Manning, United States	2m0.9s
1972	Hildegard Falck, West Germany	1m58.6s
1976	Tatiana Kazankina, U.S.S.R.	1m54.94s
1980	Nadezhda Olizarenko, U.S.S.R	1m53.5s
1984	Doina Melinte, Romania	1m57.60s
1988	Sigrun Wodars, East Germany	1m56.10s
1992	Ellen Van Langen, Netherlands	1m55.54s
1996	Svetlana Masterkova, Russia	1m57.73s

1,500-Meter Run

1972	Ludmila Bragina, U.S.S.R.	4m01.4s
1976	Tatiana Kazankina, U.S.S.R.	4m05.48s
1980	Tatiana Kazankina, U.S.S.R.	3m56.6s
1984	Gabriella Dorio, Italy	4m03.25s
1988	Paula Ivan, Romania	3m53.96s
1992	Hassiba Boulmerka, Algeria	3m55.30s
1996	Svetlana Masterkova, Russia	4m00.83s

80-Meter Hurdles

1932	Mildred Didrikson, United States	11.7s
1936	Trebisonda Valla, Italy	11.7s
1948	Fanny Blankers-Koen, Netherlands	11.2s
1952	Shirley S. de la Hunty, Australia	10.9s
1956	Shirley S. de la Hunty, Australia	10.7s
1960	Irina Press, U.S.S.R.	10.8s
1964	Karin Balzer, Germany	10.5s[1]
1968	Maureen Caird, Australia	10.3s

1. Wind assisted.

100-Meter Hurdles

1972	Annelie Ehrhardt, East Germany	12.59s
1976	Johanna Schaller, East Germany	12.77s
1980	Vera Komisova, U.S.S.R.	12.56s
1984	Benita Fitzgerald-Brown, United States	12.84s
1988	Jordanka Donkova, Bulgaria	12.38s
1992	Paraskevi Patoulidou, Greece	12.64s
1996	Ludmila Engquist, Sweden	12.58s

400-Meter Relay

Year	Country	Time
1928	Canada	48.4s
1932	United States	47.0s
1936	United States	46.9s
1948	Netherlands	47.5s
1952	United States	45.9s
1956	Australia	44.5s
1960	United States	44.5s
1964	Poland	43.6s
1968	United States	42.8s
1972	West Germany	42.81s
1976	East Germany	42.55s
1980	East Germany	41.60s
1984	United States	41.65s
1988	United States	41.98s
1992	United States	42.11s
1996	United States	41.95s

Running High Jump

Year	Athlete	Distance
1928	Ethel Catherwood, Canada	5 ft 3 in.
1932	Jean Shiley, United States	5 ft 5 1/4 in.
1936	Ibolya Csak, Hungary	5 ft 3 in.
1948	Alice Coachman, United States	5 ft 6 1/8 in.
1952	Ester Brank, South Africa	5 ft 5 3/4 in.
1956	Mildred McDaniel, United States	5 ft 9 1/4 in.
1960	Iolanda Balas, Romania	6 ft 3/4 in.
1964	Iolanda Balas, U.S.S.R.	6 ft 2 3/4 in.
1968	Miloslava Rezkova, Czechoslovakia	5 ft 11 3/4 in.
1972	Ulrike Meyfarth, West Germany	6 ft 3 3/8 in.
1976	Rosemarie Ackerman, E. Germany (1.93m)	6 ft 4 in.
1980	Sara Simeoni, Italy	6 ft 5 1/2 in.
1984	Ulrike Meyfarth, West Germany	6 ft 7 1/2 in.
1988	Louise Ritter, United States	6 ft 8 in.
1992	Heike Henkel, Germany	6 ft 7 1/2 in.
1996	Stefka Kostadinova, Bulgaria	6 ft 8 3/4 in.

Long Jump

Year	Athlete	Distance
1948	Olga Gyarmati, Hungary	18 ft 8 1/4 in.
1952	Yvette Williams, New Zealand	20 ft 5 3/4 in.
1956	Elzbieta Krzesinska, Poland	20 ft 9 3/4 in.
1960	Vera Krepkina, U.S.S.R.	20 ft 10 3/4 in.
1964	Mary Rand, Great Britain	22 ft 2 in.
1968	Viorica Ciscopoleanu, Romania	22 ft 4 1/2 in.
1972	Heidemarie Rosendahl, West Germany	22 ft 3 in.
1976	Angela Voigt, East Germany (6.72m)	22 ft 1/2 in.
1980	Tatiana Kolpakova, U.S.S.R.	23 ft 2 in.
1984	Anisoara Stanciu, Romania	22 ft 10 in.
1988	Jackie Joyner-Kersee, United States	24 ft 3 1/2 in.
1992	Heike Drechsler, Germany	23 ft 5 1/4 in.
1996	Chioma Ajunwa, Nigeria	23 ft 4 1/2 in.

Shot-Put

Year	Athlete	Distance
1948	Micheline Ostermeyer, France	45 ft 1 1/2 in.
1952	Galina Zybina, U.S.S.R.	50 ft 1 1/2 in.
1956	Tamara Tishkyevich, U.S.S.R.	54 ft 5 in.
1960	Tamara Press, U.S.S.R.	56 ft 9 7/8 in.
1964	Tamara Press, U.S.S.R.	59 ft 6 in.
1968	Margitta Gummel, East Germany	64 ft 4 in.
1972	Nadezhda Chizhova, U.S.S.R.	69 ft.
1976	Ivanka Christova, Bulgaria (21.16m)	69 ft 5 in.
1980	Ilona Sluplanek, East Germany	73 ft 6 in.
1984	Claudia Losch, West Germany	67 ft 2 1/4 in.
1988	Natalya Lisovskaya, U.S.S.R.	72 ft 11 1/2 in.
1992	Svetlana Kriveleva, Unified Team[1]	69 ft 1 1/4 in.
1996	Astrid Kumbernuss, Germany	67 ft 5 1/2 in.

1. Former Soviet Union team.

Discus Throw

Year	Athlete	Distance
1928	Helena Konopacka, Poland	129 ft 11 7/8 in.
1932	Lillian Copeland, United States	133 ft 2 in.
1936	Gisela Mauermayer, Germany	156 ft 3 3/16 in.
1948	Micheline Ostermeyer, France	137 ft 6 1/2 in.
1956	Olga Fikotova, Czechoslovakia	176 ft 1 1/2 in.
1960	Nina Ponomareva, U.S.S.R.	180 ft 8 1/4 in.
1964	Tamara Press, U.S.S.R.	187 ft 10 3/4 in.
1968	Lia Manoliu, Romania	191 ft 2 1/2 in.
1972	Faina Melnik, U.S.S.R.	218 ft 7 in.
1976	Evelin Schlaak, East Germany (69.0m)	226 ft 4 in.
1980	Evelin Jahl, East Germany	229 ft 6 1/2 in.
1984	Ria Stalman, Netherlands	214 ft 5 in.
1988	Martina Hellmann, East Germany	237 ft 2 1/4 in.
1992	Maritza Marten, Cuba	229 ft 10 1/4 in.
1996	Ilke Wyludda, Germany	228 ft 6 1/2 in.

Javelin Throw

Year	Athlete	Distance
1932	Mildred Didrikson, United States	143 ft 4 in.
1936	Tilly Fleischer, Germany	148 ft 2 3/4 in.
1948	Herma Bauma, Austria	149 ft 6 in.
1952	Dana Zatopek, Czechoslovakia	165 ft 7 in.
1956	Inessa Janzeme, U.S.S.R.	176 ft 8 in.
1960	Elvira Ozolina, U.S.S.R.	183 ft 8 in.
1964	Mihaela Penes, Romania	198 ft 7 1/2 in.
1968	Angela Nemeth, Hungary	198 ft.
1972	Ruth Fuchs, East Germany	209 ft 7 in.
1976	Ruth Fuchs, East Germany (65.94m)	216 ft 4 in.
1980	Maria Colon, Cuba	224 ft 5 in.
1984	Tessa Sanderson, Britain	228 ft 2 in.
1988	Petra Felke, East Germany	245 ft.
1992	Silke Renke, Germany	224 ft 2 1/2 in.
1996	Heli Rantanen, Finland	222 ft 11 in.

Pentathlon

Year	Athlete	Points
1964	Irina Press, U.S.S.R.	5,246 pts.
1968	Ingrid Becker, West Germany	5,098 pts.
1972	Mary Peters, Britain	4,801 pts.
1976	Siegrun Siegl, East Germany	4,745 pts.
1980	Nadyeszhda Tkachenko, U.S.S.R.	5,083 pts.
1984	Daniele Masala, Italy	5,469 pts.
1988	Jackie Joyner-Kersee, United States	7,291 pts.

Skill Lesson

Summarizing

- To **summarize** means to give a brief statement of the main idea of an article or the most important events in a story. A summary can help you remember the important details.

- When you summarize a story, include the actions of the characters and the outcomes of those actions.

- When you summarize an article, include the main idea or ideas and the most important supporting details.

Read "Winners Never Quit" from "How to Win Without Coming in First" by Carol Krucoff from *Jack and Jill* magazine.

Write About It

1. State the main idea of the article in your own words.

2. List some details that support the main idea.

3. Write a summary of the article that includes the main idea and the most important supporting ideas.

Winners Never Quit

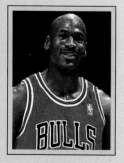

by Carol Krucoff

If Michael Jordan challenged you to a game of one-on-one basketball, what would you do?

Nancy Lieberman-Cline, a teacher at Michael Jordan's Kids Camp in Elmhurst, New York, accepted this challenge.

Nancy knew she was good. She was the first woman to play on a men's professional basketball team. But before she faced off against basketball's top superstar, she admits wondering, *Why is Michael trying to embarrass me?* Then she realized their game would teach the gym full of excited kids a very important lesson.

"Michael ended up winning 10 to 2," Nancy says, "but I was a winner the minute I accepted his challenge."

After the game, Michael and Nancy said to the kids, "How often have you been afraid to play someone who's bigger or better than you? That's a bad attitude. How are you going to get better if you're afraid to lose?"

These pros were sending the kids an important message that leads to success in sports and in life: *You can be a winner even if you don't come in first.* As long as you try your best, improve your skills, and have fun, you've won a victory no matter what the score. For example, Nancy had the courage to play against the greatest basketball player in history, and she even scored two points! That's success.

Unfortunately, some people care only about the score. They get upset if they have fewer points than their opponent. They don't understand that everyone loses sometimes— even the best hitters strike out, and the best goalkeepers miss saves. Top athletes learn from their losses and keep on trying. Remember, quitters never win, and winners never quit.

So instead of letting the final score decide if you've won or lost, create some personal challenges for yourself. Meet them, and you'll be a winner even if you don't wind up on top. For example, before a soccer game, challenge yourself to block five shots or kick the ball ten times during the game. If you meet these goals, you've won. Professional athletes call this "playing the game within the game."

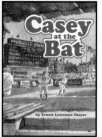

In "Casey at the Bat," the narrative poem that follows, the Mudville nine depend on Casey to meet a challenge. As you read, think about how you would summarize the events of this poem.

Vocabulary

Words to Know

defiance	despair	umpire
grandeur	haughty	scornful

When you read, you may come across a word that you don't know. To figure out the meaning of an unfamiliar word, look for clues in the words and sentences around it. A clue might be found in an explanation given before or after the unknown word.

Read the paragraphs below. Notice how an explanation of *haughty* helps you understand what it means.

The Last Game of the Season

The Sharks hadn't won a game all season, and the Tigers hadn't lost. Now it was the last game, and the Tigers paraded onto the field with the grandeur of kings. They acted so haughty and arrogant that they didn't even seem to notice their opponents. Jake was in despair just looking at them. After all, he had to pitch against them. The Tigers' reputation didn't bother his catcher, though. "They're not so great," Beth said with a scornful laugh. "We can beat them, Jake! They're overconfident."

Jake caught the spirit. "Right! It's time for us to be winners!" he said in defiance.

"Batter up!" called the umpire. The Tigers were about to learn how it feels to lose.

Write About It

Use some of your vocabulary words in a short poem about your favorite sport.

Casey at the Bat

by Ernest Lawrence Thayer

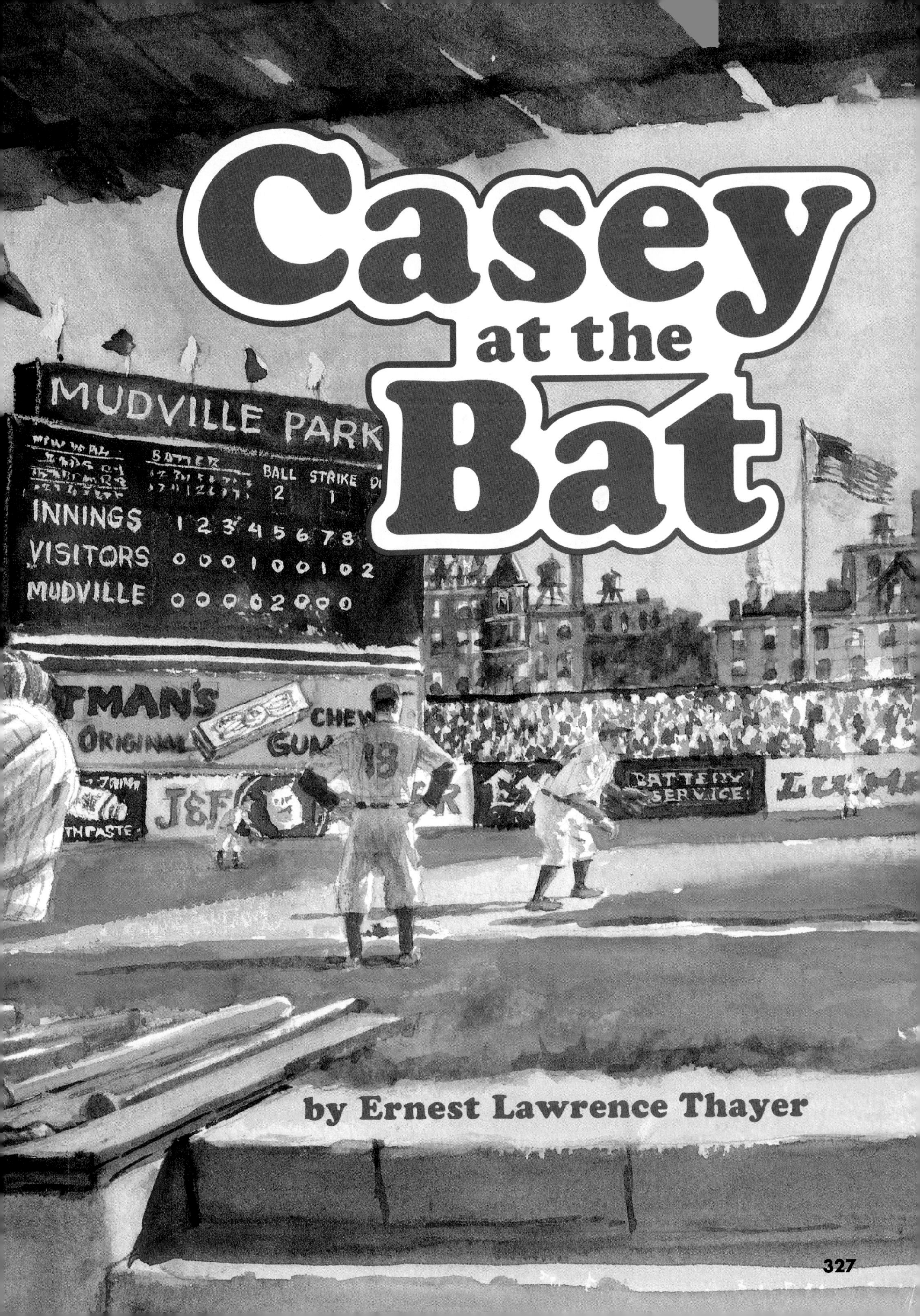

MUDVILLE PARK

| | BATTER | BALL | STRIKE | O |
| | | 2 | 1 | |

INNINGS	1 2 3 4 5 6 7 8
VISITORS	0 0 0 1 0 0 1 0 2
MUDVILLE	0 0 0 0 2 0 0 0

The outlook wasn't brilliant for the Mudville nine that day;
The score stood four to two with but one inning more to play.
And then, when Cooney died at first, and Barrows did the same,
A sickly silence fell upon the patrons of the game.

A straggling few got up to go in deep despair. The rest
Clung to that hope which springs eternal in the human breast;
They thought, If only Casey could but get a whack at that
We'd put up even money now, with Casey at the bat.

But Flynn preceded Casey, as did also Jimmy Blake,
And the former was a lulu and the latter was a cake,
So upon that stricken multitude grim melancholy sat,
For there seemed but little chance of Casey's getting to the bat.

But Flynn let drive a single, to the wonderment of all,
And Blake, the much despised, tore the cover off the ball;
And when the dust had lifted, and men saw what had occurred,
There was Jimmy safe at second, and Flynn a-hugging third.

Then from five thousand throats and more there rose a lusty yell;
It rumbled through the valley, it rattled in the dell;
It knocked upon the mountain and recoiled upon the flat,
For Casey, mighty Casey, was advancing to the bat.

There was ease in Casey's manner as he stepped into his place;
There was pride in Casey's bearing and a smile on Casey's face.
And when, responding to the cheers, he lightly doffed his hat,
No stranger in the crowd could doubt 'twas Casey at the bat.

Ten thousand eyes were on him as he rubbed his hands with dirt,
Five thousand tongues applauded when he wiped them on his shirt;
Then while the writhing pitcher ground the ball into his hip,
Defiance gleamed from Casey's eye, a sneer curled Casey's lip.

And now the leather-covered sphere came hurtling through the air,
And Casey stood a-watching it in haughty grandeur there.
Close by the sturdy batsman the ball unheeded sped;
"That ain't my style," said Casey. "Strike one," the umpire said.

From the benches, black with people, there went up a muffled roar,
Like the beating of the storm waves on a stern and distant shore.
"Kill him! Kill the umpire!" shouted someone on the stand;
And it's likely they'd have killed him had not Casey raised his hand.

With a smile of Christian charity great Casey's visage shone;
He stilled the rising tumult, he bade the game go on;
He signaled to the pitcher, and once more the spheroid flew;
But Casey still ignored it, and the umpire said, "Strike two."

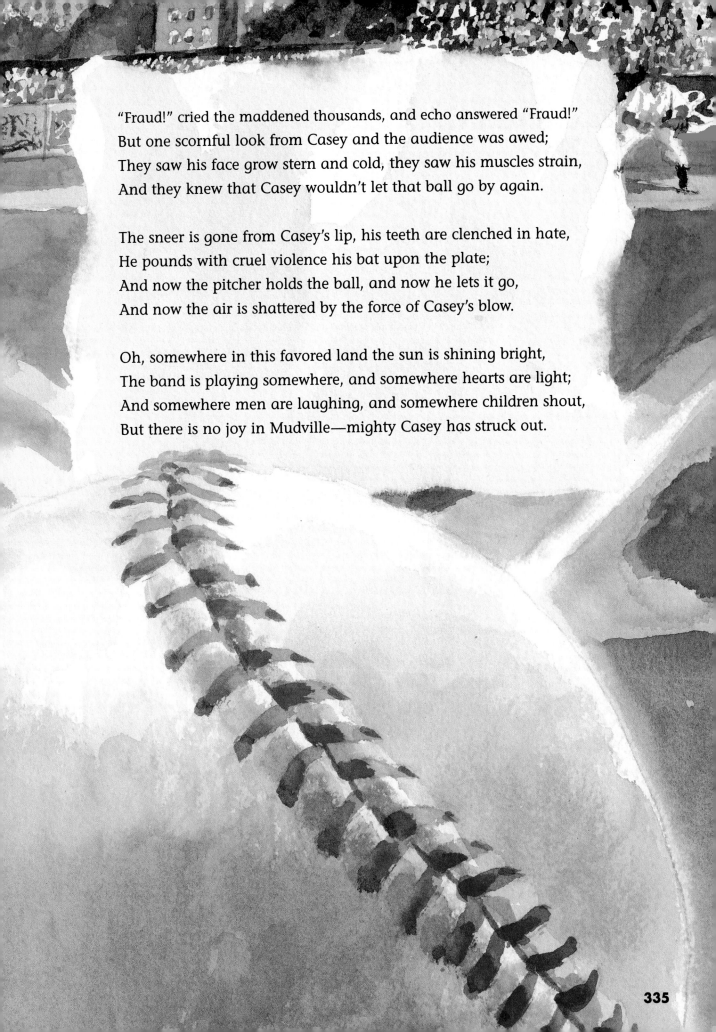

"Fraud!" cried the maddened thousands, and echo answered "Fraud!"
But one scornful look from Casey and the audience was awed;
They saw his face grow stern and cold, they saw his muscles strain,
And they knew that Casey wouldn't let that ball go by again.

The sneer is gone from Casey's lip, his teeth are clenched in hate,
He pounds with cruel violence his bat upon the plate;
And now the pitcher holds the ball, and now he lets it go,
And now the air is shattered by the force of Casey's blow.

Oh, somewhere in this favored land the sun is shining bright,
The band is playing somewhere, and somewhere hearts are light;
And somewhere men are laughing, and somewhere children shout,
But there is no joy in Mudville—mighty Casey has struck out.

Ernest Lawrence Thayer

About the Author

It was Ernest Lawrence Thayer who wrote "Casey at the Bat," but if it weren't for actor De Wolf Hopper, the poem might never have become famous. Mr. Thayer worked for the *San Francisco Examiner* and wrote the poem in 1888 for the newspaper's Sunday supplement. Later that year Mr. Hopper was acting in a musical comedy in New York City. The theater was having a special "baseball night," so there were baseball players and many of their fans in the audience. A friend of Mr. Hopper's gave him a frayed newspaper clipping of "Casey at the Bat," thinking it would be amusing if Hopper recited the poem during the performance. The poem was such a hit with the audience that "Casey at the Bat" became famous that night.

Mr. Thayer had never planned on writing for a newspaper. He went to college with William Randolph Hearst, who, after graduation, went home to San Francisco and took charge of his family's newspaper. When Mr. Thayer finished college, he accepted Mr. Hearst's invitation to write for the newspaper. "Casey at the Bat" was just one of the weekly poems he wrote. None of the others became as well known.

Reader Response

Open for Discussion

Were you surprised by the poem's ending? Would you change the ending if you wrote "Casey at the Bat"? Give reasons for keeping the ending the way it is or for changing it.

Comprehension Check

1. Is the tone of the poem one of comedy or tragedy? Support your answer with examples from the poem.

2. Describe Casey. Look back at the poem for details. Judging from his character, how does the reader expect the poem to end?

3. How does the author keep readers in suspense until the very end? Use examples from the poem to illustrate your answer.

4. Why don't the fans think that they will get to see Casey come to bat again? **Summarize** what happens when Cooney, Barrows, Flynn, and Blake take their turns. (Summarizing)

5. The emotions of the fans are very important to understanding what happens in the poem. **Summarize** how they change from beginning to end. (Summarizing)

 Test Prep

Look Back and Write

How does the author make Casey's turn at bat seem like a battle in a war? Use details from pages 330–335 in your answer.

Cards and Stats

by James Kelley

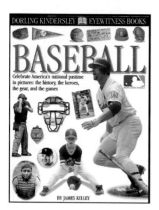

BASEBALL WITHOUT STATISTICS would be like chocolate milk without chocolate. Stats allow fans to compare players of today and yesterday. Baseball has stats for everything from pitching to hitting to baserunning. One of the ways that fans have enjoyed seeing all these stats is on baseball cards. While every sport has cards now, baseball had them first.

EARLY CARDBOARD HEROES

The card on the left features ace pitcher Mordecai "Three-Finger" Brown (1903–1916), who finished his career with a 2.06 career ERA, third-lowest all-time. (A childhood accident cost him parts of two fingers.) On the right is Michael "King" Kelly, who was, until Babe Ruth came along, the most famous baseball player in America.

NO SMOKING

This piece of cardboard is worth more than $100,000. Only a few copies of this 1910 Honus Wagner card exists, and its rarity plus the baseball card-collecting craze has helped drive its value up. This card, sold with packs of tobacco, is rare because Wagner objected to smoking and asked that his image not be used.

Shown in pre game warm-up gear

GETTING FANCY

As printing technologies have evolved, card designs have gotten wilder. Today's cards often include embossing, gold leaf lettering, holograms, day-glo inks, or sparkling paper.

HOW TO CALCULATE TWO IMPORTANT BASEBALL STATISTICS

Batting average: Hits/At-Bats. Example:

$$\frac{125\,\text{H}}{435\,\text{AB}} = .287$$

Earned run average: (Earned Runs $\times$ 9) / Innings Pitched. Example:

$$\frac{(62\,\text{ER} \times 9)}{251\,\text{IP}} = 2.22$$

"FATHER OF BASEBALL"

Henry Chadwick did not invent baseball, or even play it, but no one was more responsible for spreading the word about it. Beginning as a reporter in New York, he then wrote dozens of books on baseball. Chadwick invented the box score (lower right) as well as the system of scoring with symbols still used today.

FIRST THING IN THE MORNING

The first place every baseball fan turns to in the morning paper is the box scores from games played the night before. Each game is summed up in a neat vertical box containing words, symbols, and numbers. Who won, who scored, who got how many hits, who pitched how many innings, even who the umpires were. This box score shows the Padres 10-3 victory over the Cardinals, in which St. Louis's Mark McGwire hit two home runs, the first of which was the 500th of his career.

KEEPING SCORE

Fans can follow the game by keeping score; that is, use a recognized series of symbols and numbers to record the results of each batter throughout the game. This scorecard is from the 1932 World Series game in which Babe Ruth "called his shot."

Some sample symbols: K for strikeout, – for single, 4-3 for a groundout, second to first.

Vital statistics

Name and position, in this case, 1997 NL MVP Larry Walker of the Rockies

Fielding stats

Team logo

Manufacturer's logo

STATS HEAVEN

The back of a player's baseball card usually contains a wealth of statistics. Often included are the player's lifetime batting or pitching statistics, listed year-by-year. Fans can quickly check a player's card for almost anything they might need to know.

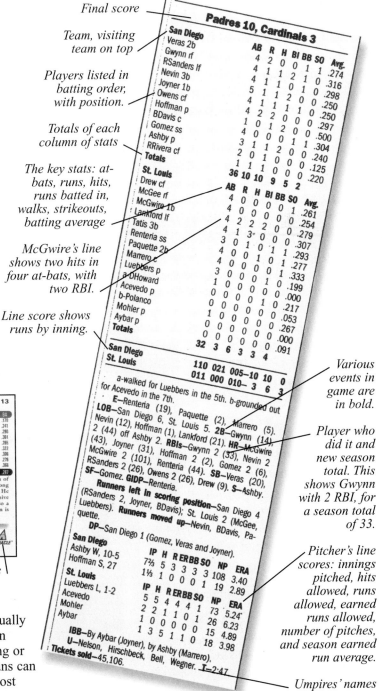

Final score

Team, visiting team on top

Players listed in batting order, with position.

Totals of each column of stats

The key stats: at-bats, runs, hits, runs batted in, walks, strikeouts, batting average

McGwire's line shows two hits in four at-bats, with two RBI.

Line score shows runs by inning.

Various events in game are in bold.

Player who did it and new season total. This shows Gwynn with 2 RBI, for a season total of 33.

Pitcher's line scores: innings pitched, hits allowed, runs allowed, earned runs allowed, number of pitches, and season earned run average.

Umpires' names

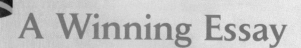

Skill Lesson

Theme

- The **theme** of a story is the underlying meaning or message.

- A theme can be a universal truth, such as *Change is constant,* or a generalization about some aspect of life, such as *Some lessons are learned the hard way.*

- To determine the theme of a story, ask yourself "What does the author want me to learn or know?" Your answer should be a "big idea" that can stand on its own away from the story.

- Many stories have more than one theme. To be valid, a statement of theme should be supported by evidence from the text.

Read "A Winning Essay" from *Circle of Gold* by Candy Dawson Boyd.

Talk About It

1. Why does Mattie enter the essay contest? Explain.

2. What do you think is the author's message about how people express love?

3. Reread Mattie's essay. Is there another theme that occurs to you?

A Winning Essay

by Candy Dawson Boyd

Mattie has tied for first place in the South Side Daily's essay contest, and is being photographed with her mother, brother, and best friend, Toni, in Mr. Phillips's office at the newspaper.

After the photographing session, Mr. Phillips invited everyone to sit down again.

"Mattie, I'd like you to share your essay with us," he said.

Toni took a deep breath.

"All of it?" asked Mattie.

"Well, it isn't very long," he replied.

Mattie got up and took the piece of paper he handed her. She faced her mother, brother, and best friend.

Dear Mr. Phillips,

My name is Mattie Mae Benson. My father is dead. My mother loves my twin brother, Matt, more than me. I love my mother, but I have a hard time telling her. I wanted to win this contest so much that I asked my best friend, Toni, to write an essay. I thought I had a better chance to

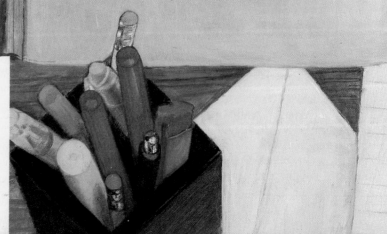

win with her essay. I'm so bad with words. If I could only sing and tell you how I feel about my mother, I could win. I want to win the money so I can buy my mother a beautiful pearl and gold pin at Stern's. It is beautiful and special, just like my mother. This is my essay. I'm sending it to you because I love my mother in good times and bad times. But I love her too much to try to win with a lie.

Sincerely and truthfully,
Mattie Mae Benson

The room was quiet. Mattie looked at her mother.

"But, Mattie, I do love you," said Mrs. Benson with tears in her eyes.

"I just wanted you to know how sad I feel when you cry and miss Daddy and call for Matt and not me," said Mattie.

"But I love you, Mattie. Maybe I don't understand you the way I do Matt, but I love you," she repeated.

"I want to be yours, too, Mama," said Mattie.

Her mother got up and hugged Mattie while the camera clicked away.

"You are mine—my only girl," said her mother.

SOUTH S

25 cents

ESSAY CONTEST WINNER

LOOK AHEAD

The Night of the Pomegranate
by Tim Wynne-Jones

In the next story, "The Night of the Pomegranate," you'll meet Harriet, another girl who creates something. As you read, think about what the author wants you to learn or know. Just what is the theme—the "big idea"?

Dear Mr. Phillips,

My name is Mattie Mae Benson. My father is dead. My mother loves my twin brother, Matt, more than me. I love my mother but I

Vocabulary

Words to Know

constellation	marveled	orbit
relative	solar	universe

Many words have more than one meaning. To decide which meaning of a word is being used, look for clues in the surrounding sentences or the paragraph.

Read the paragraph below. Decide whether *relative* means "a person who belongs to the same family as another" or "compared to each other."

Introduction to the Universe

I never was very interested in outer space until I touched a 1,015 pound meteorite at the local museum. The huge rock was just the beginning. Next, I learned the <u>relative</u> sizes of the planets and the sun from a large model of our <u>solar</u> system. Compared to Jupiter, Earth sure is tiny! The model also showed each planet moving along its <u>orbit</u> around the sun. Later, I looked at charts of the stars. My favorite <u>constellation</u> is Ursa Major, or the "Great Bear." I can't wait to see it for myself in the night sky. Leaving the building, I <u>marveled</u> at what I'd seen and learned. One day at the museum had opened my eyes to the entire <u>universe</u>.

Talk About It

Think about the night sky. Discuss the stars, planets, and constellations with a partner, using as many vocabulary words as you can.

The Night of The Pomegranate

by Tim Wynne-Jones

Harriet's solar system was a mess. She had made it—the sun and its nine planets—out of rolled-up balls of the morning newspaper. It was mounted on a sheet of green bristol board. The bristol board had a project about Austria on the other side. Harriet wished the background were black. Green was all wrong.

Everything about her project was wrong. The crumpled paper was coming undone. Because she had used the last of the Scotch tape on Saturn's rings, the three remaining planets had nothing to keep them scrunched up. Tiny Pluto was already bigger than Jupiter and growing by the minute. She had also run out of glue, so part of her solar system was stuck together with grape chewing gum.

Harriet's big brother, Tom, was annoyed at her because Mom had made him drive her to school early with her stupid project. Dad was annoyed at her for using part of the business section. Mostly she had stuck to the want ads, but then an advertisement printed in red ink in the business section caught her eye, and she just had to have it for Mars. Harriet had a crush on Mars; that's what Tom said. She didn't even mind his saying it.

Mars was near the Earth this month. The nights had been November cold but clear as glass, and Harriet had been out to see Mars every night, which was why she hadn't gotten her solar system finished, why she was so tired, why Mom made Tom drive her to school. It was all Mars's fault.

She was using the tape on Ms. Krensky's desk when Clayton Beemer arrived with his dad. His solar system came from the hobby store. The planets were Styrofoam balls, all different sizes and painted the right colors. Saturn's rings were clear plastic painted over as delicately as insect wings.

Harriet looked at her own Saturn. Her rings were drooping despite all the tape. They looked like a limp skirt on a . . . on a ball of scrunched-up newspaper.

Harriet sighed. The wires that supported Clayton's planets in their black box were almost invisible. The planets seemed to float.

"What d'ya think?" Clayton asked. He beamed. Mr. Beemer beamed. Harriet guessed that he had made the black box with its glittery smears of stars.

She had rolled up her own project protectively when Clayton entered the classroom. Suddenly one of the planets came unstuck and fell on the floor. Clayton and Mr. Beemer looked at it.

"What's that?" asked Clayton.

"Pluto, I think," said Harriet, picking it up. She popped it in her mouth. It tasted of grape gum. "Yes, Pluto," she said. Clayton and Mr. Beemer walked away to find the best place to show off their project.

Darjit arrived next. "Hi, Harriet," she said. The project under her arm had the planets' names done in bold gold lettering. Harriet's heart sank. Pluto tasted stale and cold.

But last night Harriet had tasted pomegranates. Old Mrs. Pond had given her one while she busied herself putting on layer after layer of warm clothing and gathering the things they would need for their Mars watch.

Mrs. Pond lived in the country. She lived on the edge of the woods by a meadow that sloped down to a marsh through rough frost-licked grass and prickly ash and juniper. It was so much darker than town; good for stargazing.

By 11:00 P.M. Mars was directly above the marsh, which was where Harriet and Mrs. Pond set themselves up for their vigil. They found it just where they had left it the night before: in the constellation Taurus between the Pleiades and the Hyades. But you didn't need a map to find Mars these nights. It shone like rust, neither trembling nor twinkling as the fragile stars did.

Mrs. Pond smiled and handed Harriet two folding chairs. "Ready?" she asked.

"Ready, class?" said Ms. Krensky. Everyone took their seats. Harriet placed the green bristol board universe in front of her. It was an even worse mess than it had been when she arrived. Her solar system was ravaged.

It had started off with Pluto and then, as a joke to make Darjit laugh, she had eaten Neptune. Then Karen had come in, and Jodi and Nick and Scott.

"The planet taste test," Harriet had said, ripping off a bit of Mercury. "Umm, very spicy." By the time the bell rang, there wasn't much of her project left.

Kevin started. He stood at the back of the classroom holding a green and blue marble.

"If this was Earth," he said, "then the sun would be this big—" He put the Earth in his pocket and pulled a fat squishy yellow beach ball from a garbage bag. Everybody hooted and clapped. "And it would be at the crosswalk," he added. Everyone looked confused, so Ms. Krensky helped Kevin explain the relative distances between the Earth and the sun. "And Pluto would be fifty miles away from here," said Kevin. But then he wasn't sure about that, so Ms. Krensky worked it out at the board with him.

Meanwhile, using Kevin's example, the class was supposed to figure out where other planets in the solar system would be relative to the green and blue marble in Kevin's pocket. Harriet sighed.

Until last night, Harriet had never seen the inside of a pomegranate before. As she opened the hard rind, she marveled at the bright red seeds in their cream-colored fleshy pouches.

"It's like a little secret universe all folded in on itself," said Mrs. Pond.

Harriet tasted it. With her tongue, she popped a little red bud against the roof of her mouth. The taste startled her, made her laugh.

"Tonight," Mrs. Pond said, "Mars is only forty-five million miles away." They drank a cocoa toast to that. Then she told Harriet about another time when Mars had been even closer on its orbit around the sun. She had been a girl then, and had heard on the radio the famous broadcast of *The War of the Worlds*. An actor named Orson Welles had made a radio drama based on a story about Martians attacking the world, but he had presented it

in a series of news bulletins and reports, and a lot of people had believed it was true.

Harriet listened to Mrs. Pond and sipped her cocoa and stared at the Earth's closest neighbor and felt deliciously chilly and warm at the same time. Mars was wonderfully clear in the telescope, but even with the naked eye she could imagine canals and raging storms. She knew there weren't really Martians, but she allowed herself to imagine them, anyway. She imagined one of them preparing for his invasion of the Earth, packing his laser gun, a thermos of cocoa, and a folding chair.

"What in heaven's name is this?" Ms. Krensky was standing at Harriet's chair, staring down at the green bristol board. There was only one planet left.

"Harriet says it's Mars." Darjit started giggling.

"And how big is Mars?" asked Ms. Krensky. Her eyes said Unsatisfactory.

"Compared to Kevin's marble Earth, Mars would be the size of a pomegranate seed, including the juicy red pulp," said Harriet. Ms. Krensky walked to the front of the class. She turned at her desk. Was there the hint of a smile on her face?

"And where is it?" she asked, raising an eyebrow.

Harriet looked at the calculations she had done on a corner of the green bristol board. "If the sun was at the crosswalk," said Harriet, "then Mars would be much closer. Over there." She pointed out the window at the slide in the kindergarten playground. Some of the class actually looked out the window to see if they could see it.

"You *can* see Mars," said Harriet. "Sometimes." Now she was sure she saw Ms. Krensky smile.

"How many of you have seen Mars?" the teacher asked. Only Harriet and Randy Pilcher put up their hands. But Randy had only seen it on the movie *Total Recall*.

"Last night was a special night, I believe," said Ms. Krensky, crossing her arms and leaning against her desk. Harriet nodded. "Tell us about it, Harriet," said the teacher.

So Harriet did. She told them all about Mrs. Pond and the Mars watch. She started with the pomegranate.

About the Author

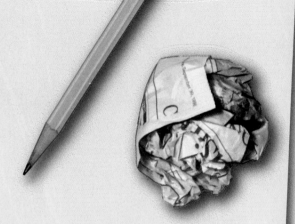

Tim Wynne-Jones

Tim Wynne-Jones believes that fictional stories bring meaning to the world. "I see the world as something which must be identified, over and over again, in words," he says. He feels that the world often presents people with a jumble of events, but fiction can help people make sense of them.

"The Night of the Pomegranate" appears in his book *Some of the Kinder Planets.* In this book, Mr. Wynne-Jones draws an interesting simile: "A crow likes to steal shiny bits of the world and hoard them away in its nest: pull tabs, gum wrappers, bread ties, rings. Writers are like crows. They call their nests 'stories.'" Mr. Wynne-Jones believes that it is the job of writers to bring bits from their life experiences and from the world around them to their writing. *Some of the Kinder Planets* won the Governor General's Award for Children's Literature, an important award given in Canada.

Other books by Mr. Wynne-Jones that you might enjoy include *The Book of Changes,* a collection of humorous short stories, and *The Maestro,* about a boy who meets a musician in the Canadian wilderness. *The Maestro* also won the Governor General's Award for Children's Literature.

Reader Response

Open for Discussion

What grade do you think Harriet deserves on her project? Explain.

Comprehension Check

1. Describe Harriet's model of the solar system. Then compare it to a model created by one of her classmates.

2. What explanation does Harriet provide for the way her project turns out? Look back at the story for details.

3. Who is Mrs. Pond? How does she help Harriet with her project? Use details from the story in your answer.

4. Harriet seems to learn more about the solar system by observing Mars than by making a model. What point do you think the author is trying to make about learning? In your own words, state a **theme** about learning. (Theme)

5. Look back at the story. Think about the characters and events. Is there another "big idea" that occurs to you? State another **theme** of the story. Be prepared to support your theme statement with evidence from the story. (Theme)

Test Prep

Look Back and Write

How are Mars and a pomegranate alike to Harriet? Use details from pages 346–348 in your answer.

What's The Big Idea?

You will learn:
- how Earth moves around the sun.
- how Earth's movements cause the seasons.
- what causes tides, eclipses, and moon phases.

What Is Earth's Place in Space?

Hey! STAND STILL! What do you mean you can't do that? No matter how hard you try to stay in one place, the Earth beneath you is moving. So, let's go for a spin! Spinning is just one way that Earth moves.

Earth's Motion

What do you know about the spheres shown in the diagram below? You may already know that these spheres represent the nine planets that travel around the sun as part of our solar system. Perhaps you know that a band of small, rocky objects called asteroids also moves around the sun. Of course, there's one place in the solar system you know quite a lot about—Earth! The third

Notice the relative distance of each planet from the sun. If this drawing were made to scale, the sun would be the size of a beach ball. Earth and Venus would be about the size of a marble, and Pluto would be only as large as a pin head.

planet from the sun is the only planet scientists know of that supports life. What special features of Earth help it support life?

Earth and all objects in space are constantly rolling, tumbling, or moving in some way. All the planets spin, or **rotate** , on an imaginary line called an axis. On Earth, the axis runs from the North Pole to the South Pole. Each planet rotates on its axis at a different speed. Earth takes 24 hours, or one day, to make one complete turn, or rotation.

As the arrow in the photo shows, Earth rotates in a counter-clockwise direction on its tilted axis. This means Earth rotates from west to east. While Earth rotates, half of the planet faces toward the sun. This half of the planet experiences day. At the same time, the other half of the planet faces away from the sun, creating night. You can't feel Earth's spinning motion, but you can see signs of it. For example, Earth's rotation makes the sun appear to move across the sky from east to west. Most of the other planets also rotate in the same counter-clockwise direction, but at different speeds and at different angles, or tilts.

The planets and asteroids travel, or **revolve** , around the sun in paths called orbits. Earth takes about 365 days, or one year, to complete its orbit around the sun. This trip is one revolution.

The speed of other planets in their orbits may be faster or slower, depending upon the planet's distance from the sun. For example, Mercury, the sun's nearest planet, takes only 88 Earth days to revolve around the sun because it has such a small orbit. The most distant planet, Pluto, has the largest orbit. Pluto takes 90,700 Earth days to complete one revolution.

Other suns in other solar systems probably have planets revolving around them too. It certainly seems that everything in space is on the move! While Earth revolves around the sun, the moon revolves around Earth, and other moons revolve around their planets. In fact, the sun and the entire solar system are moving. So, sit back and enjoy the ride as you learn what all this motion means and where everything is going!

—from *Scott Foresman Science,* Grade 6

Glossary

rotate
(rō′tāt), to spin or make one complete turn on an axis

revolve
(ri volv′), to move in a circular path around another object

Even though you can't really see the North and South Poles of the Earth, it helps to imagine them. Picture the Earth rotating on a pole that is tilted.

Poetry

Nothing More

by María Elena Walsh
translated by Douglas Leiva

With this one coin
I will buy
a bouquet of sky
and a meter of ocean,
the tip of a star,
the true and only sun,
a kilogram of wind,
and nothing more.

Post Early for Space

by Peter J. Henniker-Heaton

Once we were wayfarers, then seafarers, then airfarers;
We shall be spacefarers soon,
Not voyaging from city to city or from coast to coast,
But from planet to planet and from moon to moon.

This is no fanciful flight of imagination,
No strange, incredible, utterly different thing;
It will come by obstinate thought and calculation
And the old resolve to spread an expanding wing.

We shall see homes established on distant planets,
Friends departing to take up a post on Mars;
They will have perils to meet, but they will meet them,
As the early settlers did on American shores.

We shall buy tickets later, as now we buy them
For a foreign vacation, reserve our seat or berth,
Then spending a holiday month on a moon of Saturn,
Look tenderly back to our little shining Earth.

And those who decide they will not make the journey
Will remember a son up there or a favorite niece,
Eagerly awaiting news from the old home-planet,
And will scribble a line to catch the post for space.

by Jacqueline Sweeney

If I were brown I'd be cattail
or turtle deep burrowed
in mud.

If I were orange
I'd be a newt's belly.

If yellow a willow
in Fall.

If pink I'd be a flamingo
or salmon
leaping upstream.

If I were blue
I'd be glacier.

If purple a larkspur
in Spring.

If I were silver
I'm sure I'd be river
   moonshattered
in liquid surprise.

If I were green
I'd be rainforest,

tree canopied.

If green I would help
the world

breathe.

Fiddle-Faddle

by Eve Merriam

Riddle me no,
riddle me yes,
what is the secret
of sweet success?

Said the razor, "Be keen."
"String along," said the bean.
"Push," said the door.
"Be polished," said the floor.
Said the piano, "Stand upright and grand."
"Be on the watch," said the second hand.

"Cool," said the ice cube.
"Bright," said the TV tube.
"Bounce back," said the yo-yo.
"Be well bred," said the dough.
"Plug," said the stopper.
"Shine," said copper.

"Be game," said the quail.
"Make your point," said the nail.
"Have patience," said the M.D.
"Look spruce," said the tree.
"Press on," said the stamp.
"Shed some light," said the lamp.
            "Oh, just have a good head,"
            the cabbage said.

Wrap-Up

How do people accomplish their ambitions?

Talking with Characters

Discuss and Interview

Arnie in "Born Worker," Casey in "Casey at the Bat," and Harriet in "The Night of the Pomegranate" all struggle to accomplish their ambitions.

1. With a partner, **interview** one of them about accomplishing ambitions.

2. **Discuss** the character's struggles. Look back at the selection for details.

3. Decide which of you will be the character and which will be the interviewer. **Do** the interview. Then talk about whether you might face the same struggles someday.

Monumental Accomplishments

Celebrate a Character

Some characters in Unit 3 accomplished their ambitions. How would you celebrate their accomplishments?

1. With a small group, choose a character. **Make notes** on his or her accomplishments and how the character overcame obstacles to those accomplishments.

2. **Plan** a memorial to the character, such as a monument, a museum, a memorial park, or a national holiday. Include drawings, maps, written descriptions, or music.

Their Careers, My Career

Record and Write

Some of the characters in Unit 3 have careers, or jobs. What job skills and traits, such as cleverness or persistence, do they need to succeed?

1. **Make notes** on a character.

Job Skills	Traits

2. Now **make notes** on the skills and traits for a career of your own.

3. **Write** a career description from your notes.

TV Endorsements

Discuss and Videotape

What if the characters in Unit 3 appeared in TV commercials? They might endorse a product, such as athletic shoes, or a business, such as a loan company.

1. **Discuss** these questions in a small group:
   - What are the characters good at?
   - What kinds of modern-day products or services do these characters make you think of?

2. **Plan a commercial** starring one of the characters and **videotape** it.

Test Talk

Answer the Question

Make the Right Choice

Before you can answer a multiple-choice test question, you have to decide on the best answer. A test about "She's the Boss!" pages 282–285, might have this question.

Test Question 1

Why was Kathleen McGrath made commander of the U.S.S. *Jarrett*?

Ⓐ to prove that a woman can do the job

Ⓑ to show that the Navy is changing its ways

Ⓒ to encourage other women to join the Navy

Ⓓ to recognize the best person for the job

Understand the question.
Find the key words. Finish the statement "I need to find out . . ."

Narrow the answer choices.
Read each answer choice carefully. Eliminate any choice that you know is wrong.

Find the answer in the text.
Is the answer *right there* in one place in the text or do you have to *think and search*? Does the answer depend on the *author and you*?

Choose the best answer.
Mark the answer. Check it by comparing it with the text.

See how one student makes the right choice.

Okay, I need to find out why Kathleen McGrath is the commander. It has something to do with her qualifications—like being smart or loving her country. It's not because she's a woman. So it's not **A** or **C**. That leaves **B** or **D**. I'm not sure, so I'll go back and look at the article.

The end talks about why she became a commander. Here it is—"The Best Person for the Job." That's why she's a commander, because she's the best person for the job. The right answer must be **D**.

Try it!

Now decide on the best answer to these test questions about "She's the Boss!" pages 282–285.

Test Question 2

Based on the information in the sidebar on page 285, the participation of women in the U.S. military has

(A) increased since the American Revolution.

(B) expanded to include direct ground combat.

(C) decreased since World War I.

(D) remained the same since the Civil War.

Test Question 3

Why did the author write "She's the Boss!"?

(F) to encourage readers to join the Navy

(G) to inform readers about a woman naval commander

(H) to give readers a close look at life aboard a naval warship

(I) to teach readers about the U.S. military

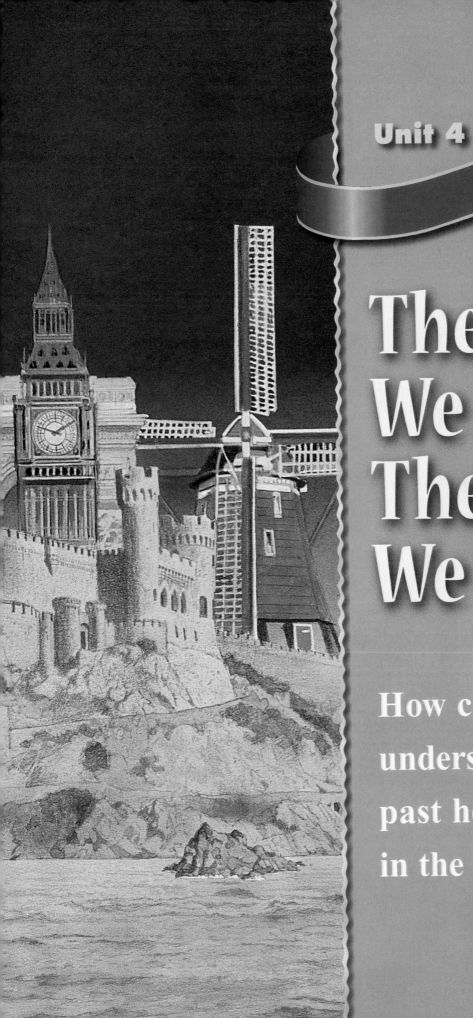

The Way We Were– The Way We Are

How can understanding the past help us live in the present?

Skill Lesson

Drawing Conclusions

- When you **draw a conclusion,** you make a decision or form an opinion about what you read. Drawing conclusions is also known as *making inferences.*

- A conclusion should make sense and be based on facts and details in the writing, as well as your own experience.

- To test a conclusion, ask yourself whether the facts are accurate and whether you are taking anything for granted. Then decide whether there are other possible conclusions you could base on the same information.

Read "Dumbfounded" from *Where the Red Fern Grows* **by Wilson Rawls.**

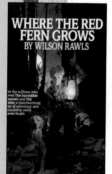

Write About It

1. Describe Grandpa's first reaction to the sight of Billy's money. Why do you think he reacts this way?

2. What is Grandpa like? Base your conclusion on information from the story.

DUMBFOUNDED

by Wilson Rawls

For two years, Billy Colman has secretly saved the fifty dollars he needs to buy two coon hound pups.

Early the next morning, with the can jammed deep in the pocket of my overalls, I flew to the store. As I trotted along, I whistled and sang. I felt as big as the tallest mountain in the Ozarks.

Arriving at my destination, I saw two wagons were tied up at the hitching rack. I knew some farmers had come to the store, so I waited until they left. As I walked in, I saw my grandfather behind the counter. Tugging and pulling, I worked the can out of my pocket and dumped it out in front of him and looked up.

Grandpa was dumbfounded. He tried to say something, but it wouldn't come out. He looked at me, and he looked at the pile of coins. Finally, in a voice much louder than he ordinarily used, he asked, "Where did you get all this?"

"I told you, Grandpa," I said, "I was saving my money so I could buy two hound pups, and I did. You said you would order them for me. I've got the money and now I want you to order them."

Grandpa stared at me over his glasses, and then back at the money.

"How long have you been saving this?" he asked.

"A long time, Grandpa," I said.

"How long?" he asked.

I told him, "Two years."

His mouth flew open and in a loud voice he said, "Two years!"

I nodded my head.

The way my grandfather stared at me made me uneasy. I was on needles and pins. Taking his eyes from me, he glanced back at the money. He saw the faded yellow piece of paper sticking out from the coins. He worked it out, asking as he did, "What's this?"

I told him it was the ad, telling where to order my dogs.

He read it, turned it over, and glanced at the other side.

I saw the astonishment leave his eyes and the friendly-old-grandfather look come back. I felt much better.

He glanced down at my bare feet and asked, "How come your feet are cut and scratched like that?"

I told him it was pretty tough picking blackberries barefoot.

He nodded his head.

It was too much for my grandfather. He turned and walked away. I saw the glasses come off, and the old red handkerchief come out. I heard the good excuse of blowing his nose. He stood for several seconds with his back toward me. When he turned around, I noticed his eyes were moist.

In a quavering voice, he said, "Well, Son, it's your money. You worked for it, and you worked hard. You got it honestly, and you want some dogs. We're going to get those dogs."

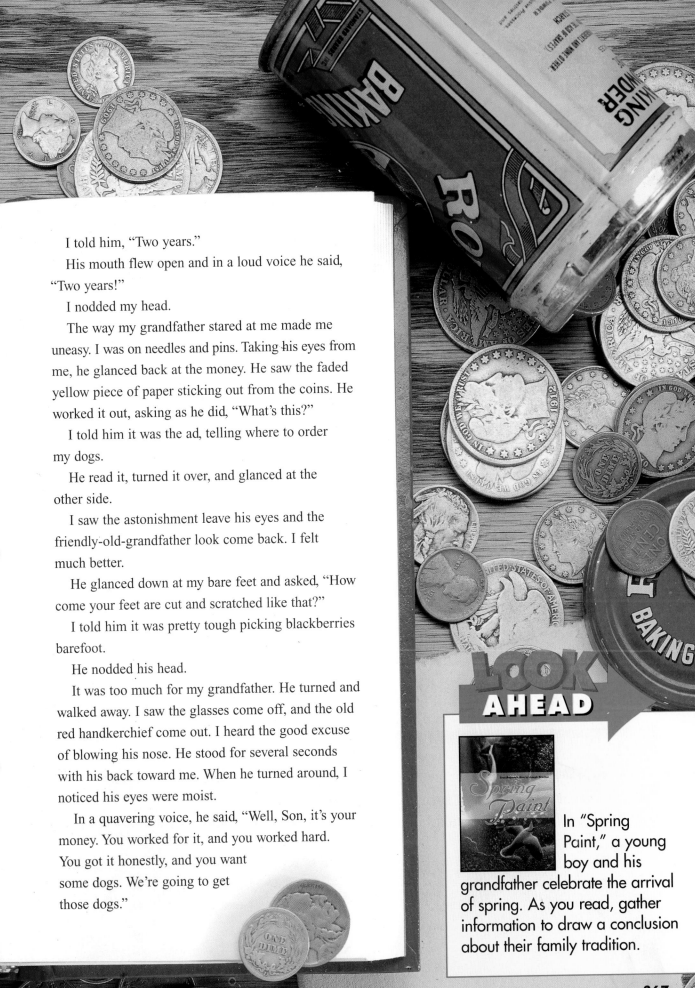

LOOK AHEAD

In "Spring Paint," a young boy and his grandfather celebrate the arrival of spring. As you read, gather information to draw a conclusion about their family tradition.

Vocabulary

Words to Know

ancestor	gnarled	wigwam
boundary	reassuring	

Words with similar meanings are called **synonyms.** You can often figure out the meaning of an unknown word by finding a clue in the words around it. Sometimes this clue is a synonym.

Read this paragraph. Notice how *relative* helps you understand what *ancestor* means.

Our Family Tree

An ancestor of mine planted an oak tree on the far western boundary of our family farm. That relative was my great-grandfather, Alan Burns. Today its branches tower above our cornfields, and its gnarled roots are big enough to sit on. I've always thought of it as my special place. When I was younger, I learned how to climb on its sturdy trunk, and I once built a wigwam with its fallen branches. Whenever I'm upset, I go to the tree. Sitting there I can almost feel the love of my great-grandpa, reassuring me that everything will be OK.

Talk About It

Work with a partner. Try to use each vocabulary word in a conversation.

from *Bowman's Store* by Joseph Bruchac

Spring Paint

There is a story that is told all over the Northeast. I've heard it from the Mohawks and from the Abenakis, from the Algonquin people and the Anishinabe. I don't know who told it first, and so I think it is a story as old as the winter and the spring.

A fierce old man sat in his lodge in the woods. He was alone there, for everyone was afraid of him. His hair was thick and

white and as pale as frost. His nose was as sharp as an icicle. His eyes were as white as sleet. His lodge was a wigwam made of sheets of ice, and whoever came too close would freeze. In the center of his lodge was a cold fire made of white ice that flickered with a chilly light. Whenever he came out of his lodge, the birds and animals would hide because his breath would turn the waters of the streams and lakes into stone; and wherever he stepped, the ground became covered by a thick white blanket. His only friend was the Great White Bear, that storm wind which came down from the Always Winter Land.

One cold day the old man heard someone scratching on the outside of his lodge near the door.

"Go away!" the old man shouted in a harsh voice. "Go away from my lodge."

But now a voice spoke. That voice was as soft as the old man's was hard. It was sweet as the songs of the birds.

"Old Man," the sweet voice said, "you must let me into your lodge."

"Come in, then," said the old man. He smiled a hard smile, knowing that whoever came into his lodge would freeze.

Then a young man entered the wigwam. His face was painted with red lines and circles that looked like the sun. There was a warm smile on his face; and as he sat down on the other side of the fire, the old man felt the young man's warm breath. The old man began to sweat. He felt himself growing weaker.

"Go away," said the old man.

"No," said the young man, his voice as gentle as the sound of a summer breeze. "It is you who must leave now. Your season has ended."

As the young man spoke those words the walls of the old man's lodge fell away. All around the lodge the snow was almost gone, and you could see the dark earth and the green of grass. The old man felt himself shrinking away, smaller and smaller.

"Go with your friend, the Great White Bear," said the young man. "Go back to the Always Winter Land, and do not return until my season has ended."

Then the Great White Bear, who is the North Wind, swept down in one last cold blast. He picked up Old Man Winter and carried him off to the cold land they shared together. Now all the land around the young man came alive with the songs of birds, and the leaves began to appear on the trees. There on the ground before him, where Winter's cold fire had been, was a circle of flowers—the first white flowers of the spring, the bloodroots. They are the sign each year of the victory of that young man, whose Abenaki name, Sigan, means "Spring."

*J*ust below my grandparents' house on Splinterville Hill is a small stretch of woods. Never more than fifty yards deep, it ends at the stone wall that was the boundary, when I was a child, between our property and the property of Mrs. Williams. Mrs. Williams was a retired schoolteacher who lived there in a big old house with her mother. I used to walk through the woods and climb over that stone wall, bags of groceries in my arms, to make deliveries to her from our store.

Following the line of the stone wall, the woods stretch from Route 9N on the east to Mill Road on the west, where they are bordered by Bell Brook. There I first followed the tracks of animals in the snow—the exclamation-mark paw prints of rabbits, the round, delicate tracks of red fox, the tiny marks of field mice that would end at a circle in the snow where their hidden runs dove out of sight. Although it seems small today, that little forest seemed very large to me when I was young. I always called it the Woods; and when I went outside after school or on the weekends or in the long summer days, I only had to say to my grandparents, "I'm going to the Woods," and they'd know where to find me.

It was my grandfather who first walked with me in the Woods, holding my tiny hand and reassuring me that this was a place where I could be safe—as long as I understood what was around me. It was not that I couldn't get hurt there. You could get hurt anywhere, Grampa said—and I surely understood that. But knowing what could hurt you, that could help you keep away from it. He showed me the nettles that would sting my skin, and the thorns on the raspberry bushes.

He pointed out the places where the wire of the old fences that had been buried over the decades stuck up and might trip me. We were always pulling out those old wire-mesh fences, which had once been part of the pens for the wolves that Mr. Otis, who owned the house before Mrs. Williams, bred as pets. An ancestor of his had invented the elevator, and keeping eagles and wolves in his backyard had been his pastime. Knowing the story about those eagles and wolves who had lived here, caged but still wild, always made me feel as if their spirits were watching over me when I was alone in the woods.

For everything in the woods that might harm me, my grandfather pointed out a dozen things that gave me delight.

He showed me the different kinds of trees, from the smooth-limbed maple to the rough-barked elm. He showed me the three big old apples, ancient gnarled trees that were covered with sweet-scented flowers each spring. Although the fruit that came on them each late summer was small and marked by insects, no apples in the world ever tasted as good as theirs, and my grandfather said we'd maybe build a tree house in

the biggest apple tree one day when I was big enough. He showed me how I could swing on the grapevines and how I could make places to hide under the honeysuckle bushes, just like a rabbit does.

He showed me the different rocks, how some of them were soft sandstone that you could break pieces off with your hand, while others were hard and had quartz in them that sparkled brighter than diamonds. He showed me how some rocks were alive once. "Though maybe they still is alive, in a way of saying," he added. They had fossils in them, like the ancient blue cryptozoan stones that made up the stone retaining wall right behind our house, a wall my grandfather had built. More than anything else, though, I remember how he showed me the flowers. And more than any other flower, I remember the first one of them all, the bloodroot.

It was in the Woods that I first saw bloodroot in bloom, that delicate white flower which is the first spring blossom in our Adirondack foothills. Rising up on a smooth stalk, its center is as golden as a tiny sun, surrounded by white rays of light.

"Soon as you see the bloodroot," my grandfather said, "you know winter is goin' fer sure."

When the last mounds of April snow were shrinking down in the huge dirty white piles that the town crews had plowed up below our driveway, Grampa and I would put on our green rubber boots. Mine were exactly the same as his, but so much smaller that I could put on my boots and then pull his on over mine. Then I would go galumphing along next to him, giggling while he said to my grandmother, "Wull, Sonny's got his boots on, but now I can't find mine."

"Grampa!" I would finally say. "Look! I got your boots on."

He was always surprised at how silly he had been, not to be able to see that.

376

Then we would go down into the Woods to look for the bloodroots. There would still be little patches of snow here and there at the bases of trees, and the ground was alternately hard as rock or so soft that our feet would sink in, and we could only pull them out with a sucking sound, as if the earth wanted to swallow us. Soon, though, we'd find the first patch of bloodroot. They would be clustered together in

a circle, the green palmate leaves surrounding the base of the white flowers that thrust up toward the sun. My grandfather would always pick one of those first bloodroot flowers we saw. Then he would take its stem, which dripped orange sap like ink from a broken pen, and made marks on my face as I looked up at him.

"This here's yer spring paint," he said. "Helps keep them bugs away."

The lines and circles he painted on my forehead and cheeks would dry there, and I would forget that I had them—until I looked in the mirror later in the day, or saw how a customer stared at my face as I stood on an empty Coca-Cola box to clean the windshield while Grampa pumped the gas.

Sanguinaria canadensis is the Latin name for the bloodroot. I looked it up when I was eight years old and wrote it down in one of the notebooks I kept then, listing every bird or flower or animal I had seen. I learned, as I read my field guides, that it is a member of the poppy family. Found in the humus-rich woodlands and along streams, its range is across Canada and south from Nova Scotia to New England. Fragile and brief as

the first days of spring when it blooms, its flowers open to the sun and close at night—like small white hands, trying to hold in that first warmth. Its Latin name, *sanguinaria,* means "bleeding." The orange juice that comes from its stems was used by the Abenaki people and the Mohawks as an insect repellent, as a dye for clothing and baskets, and as an ingredient in face paint.

And so, once again, without saying or perhaps even knowing, my grandfather handed down to me a part of my heritage that was as ancient as the story of the coming of spring.

A Personal Essay from Joseph Bruchac

The Oldest Calendar

When I was a kid, the natural world was like a calendar. The oldest and surest one of all! I learned how to tell what time of year it was by the things that were happening around us. My grandparents were always calling my attention to those things. Spring is full of such markers, each one like a step—taking us further into that best time of the year. To this day, every part of the cycle of spring is marked for me by the things that I see or hear, smell or taste—things that belong to part of a season and tell me more than words such as *March* or *April* written on a piece of paper.

I'm afraid that many young people these days don't notice that natural world very much. Oh, they are aware of the fact that it's snowing or that it's a warm and sunny day. And here in the northeast just about every kid is still plenty aware of the way the days grow longer and warmer when it gets closer to the time of summer vacation. Yes! But do you know if there is a

full moon in the sky when you're reading this? If it is one of the warmer months of the year, can you tell exactly what flowers are in bloom, what birds are likely to be singing in the place where you live? Even in cities such as New York, there are lots of little, subtle natural clues. In fact, in Central Park, an alert birdwatcher can see more than 200 different birds throughout the year. But nowadays, most people spend so much time indoors that the natural world is just something they pass through as quickly as possible to get from the bus into school or from the car into the shopping mall.

In the generation of my grandparents, who raised me, such knowledge was not just interesting. Knowing these things affected survival. Much of what we ate in the summer and fall came from our gardens or what we gathered. "Don't plant yer corn," my grandfather might say, "until them leaves on the maple are the size of a squirrel's ear." And his words are true to this day. It is always warm enough to plant corn when the maple leaves get that big.

The world is invisible to us when we don't know these things. I can't imagine what it would be like not to know that hearing the songs of the wood warblers, little birds who sing from the tops of the tallest trees, is a sure sign that winter is over.

In *Bowman's Store,* I talk about one such natural marker, the appearance of the bloodroots. In the Abenaki Indian tradition there is a story connected to just about every bird, animal, and plant. Those stories tell us so much about these things and are a lot easier to remember than a bunch of facts. Although my grandparents didn't tell the traditional stories, in a way they lived the stories. And the things that happened to me with them are as vivid in my memory as a well-told tale.

You know, I can never look at a well-groomed, perfectly green lawn in the spring without feeling sorry for the people who own that lawn. Do you know why? Because there are no dandelions in it. Not long after the bloodroots bloomed, it was time for dandelions.

"Sonny," my grandmother would say, "time to get a mess of dandelion greens."

Then she would hand me the kitchen knife with the wooden handle. I liked the feel of that knife. It had a long blade that had been worn thin by decades of grandfather's honing it razor-sharp, using the whetstone on just one side "so as it would cut right." Even when I was little, they would trust me with that knife. I'd take the colander and go out onto the lawn looking for those first, tender dandelion leaves. If I drove the knife into the ground just right and moved it in a half circle I could pull up the whole dandelion clump, leaves still attached to a neat pale stub of root. A colander full was a "mess," enough to boil up. Boiled and then seasoned with a little vinegar, butter, and salt, those dandelions made a tasty part of early spring that I will never forget.

Reader Response

Open for Discussion

Would you enjoy having Grampa as a neighbor? Why or why not?

Comprehension Check

1. The story about the old man and the young man seems to be meant to explain something about nature. What natural events are explained by this story? How can you tell?

2. Describe the relationship between the boy and his grandfather. What details in the story help you form your description?

3. Joseph Bruchac says that his grandfather "handed down to me a part of my heritage." What did Grampa do, and why does Mr. Bruchac describe it this way?

4. Mr. Bruchac **draws the conclusions** that the Woods is a place full of things that can hurt him and things that can give him delight. Point out evidence that supports each conclusion. (Drawing Conclusions)

5. "Soon as you see the bloodroot," Grampa says, "you know winter is goin' for sure." What evidence do you imagine he might have for **drawing** such a **conclusion?** (Drawing Conclusions)

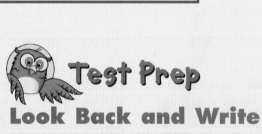

Look Back and Write

How is the Old Man like winter and how is Sigan like spring? Use information from pages 370–372 to support your answer.

Demeter's Daughter

classic myth retold by Judy Freed

Demeter was the goddess of the harvest. She was so happy that wherever she walked, the earth sprang to life at her feet. Grain grew in abundance. The trees blossomed and bore fruit. Throughout Greece, grateful mortals ate the fruits of her bounty and gave thanks.

The source of Demeter's joy was her daughter, Persephone. The two were never apart. When Persephone laughed, Demeter's heart overflowed with love. When Persephone danced, Demeter caused flowers to spring up at her feet. Like all the gods on Mount Olympus, Demeter and Persephone were immortal. Neither one had ever come face to face with death.

But Hades knew death all too well. He was the god of the underworld, the land of the dead. He did not live on Mount Olympus with the other gods. His vast realm lay beneath. His subjects were the tortured souls of men and women who had died. Neither sunshine nor life reached his dark, forbidding land.

Hades was lonely. He longed for company. He yearned for a goddess to rule by his side. One day Hades saw Persephone playing in a field of flowers, and the god of the dead fell hopelessly in love. But he knew that a girl so full of life would never willingly join him in the underworld. So Hades decided to kidnap Demeter's daughter.

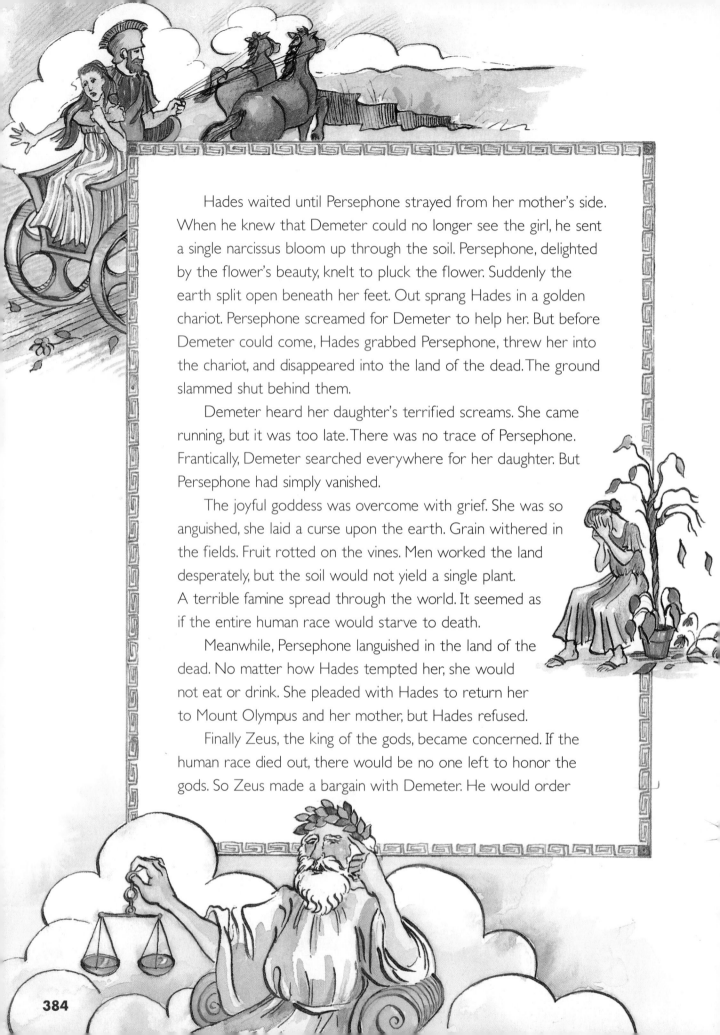

Hades waited until Persephone strayed from her mother's side. When he knew that Demeter could no longer see the girl, he sent a single narcissus bloom up through the soil. Persephone, delighted by the flower's beauty, knelt to pluck the flower. Suddenly the earth split open beneath her feet. Out sprang Hades in a golden chariot. Persephone screamed for Demeter to help her. But before Demeter could come, Hades grabbed Persephone, threw her into the chariot, and disappeared into the land of the dead. The ground slammed shut behind them.

Demeter heard her daughter's terrified screams. She came running, but it was too late. There was no trace of Persephone. Frantically, Demeter searched everywhere for her daughter. But Persephone had simply vanished.

The joyful goddess was overcome with grief. She was so anguished, she laid a curse upon the earth. Grain withered in the fields. Fruit rotted on the vines. Men worked the land desperately, but the soil would not yield a single plant. A terrible famine spread through the world. It seemed as if the entire human race would starve to death.

Meanwhile, Persephone languished in the land of the dead. No matter how Hades tempted her, she would not eat or drink. She pleaded with Hades to return her to Mount Olympus and her mother, but Hades refused.

Finally Zeus, the king of the gods, became concerned. If the human race died out, there would be no one left to honor the gods. So Zeus made a bargain with Demeter. He would order

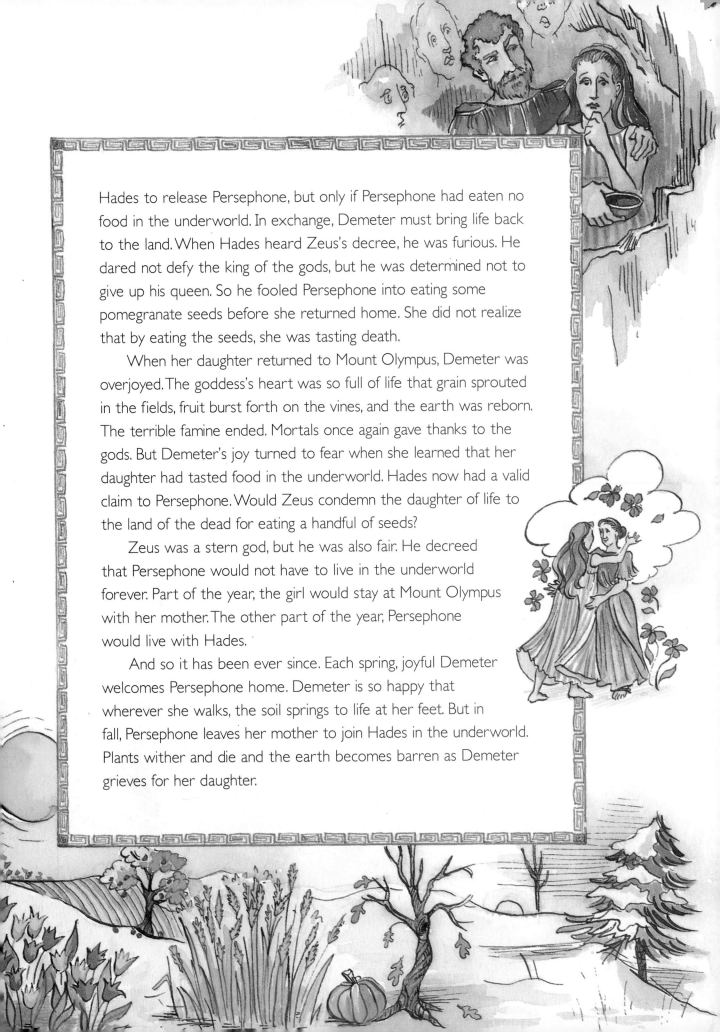

Hades to release Persephone, but only if Persephone had eaten no food in the underworld. In exchange, Demeter must bring life back to the land. When Hades heard Zeus's decree, he was furious. He dared not defy the king of the gods, but he was determined not to give up his queen. So he fooled Persephone into eating some pomegranate seeds before she returned home. She did not realize that by eating the seeds, she was tasting death.

When her daughter returned to Mount Olympus, Demeter was overjoyed. The goddess's heart was so full of life that grain sprouted in the fields, fruit burst forth on the vines, and the earth was reborn. The terrible famine ended. Mortals once again gave thanks to the gods. But Demeter's joy turned to fear when she learned that her daughter had tasted food in the underworld. Hades now had a valid claim to Persephone. Would Zeus condemn the daughter of life to the land of the dead for eating a handful of seeds?

Zeus was a stern god, but he was also fair. He decreed that Persephone would not have to live in the underworld forever. Part of the year, the girl would stay at Mount Olympus with her mother. The other part of the year, Persephone would live with Hades.

And so it has been ever since. Each spring, joyful Demeter welcomes Persephone home. Demeter is so happy that wherever she walks, the soil springs to life at her feet. But in fall, Persephone leaves her mother to join Hades in the underworld. Plants wither and die and the earth becomes barren as Demeter grieves for her daughter.

Skill Lesson

Plot

- The **plot** of a story is the series of important events from the story's beginning, middle, and end. The plot revolves around a central problem, or *conflict*—a struggle between two forces, such as a person against nature or two people against each other.

- In most stories, the conflict is introduced in the beginning. As the story progresses, the conflict leads to other problems. Gradually, the *rising action* builds to a high point, or climax.

- The *climax,* or turning point, is the moment in the story when the struggle between the two forces is greatest.

- Following the climax, there is *resolution* of the conflict. The two forces no longer struggle, and the action winds down.

Read "The Sailor and the Fly" by Alois Mikulka from *Cricket* **magazine.**

Talk About It

1. With what force does the sailor struggle? Describe this conflict.

2. Look back at the story to identify the plot elements of rising action, climax, and resolution.

The Sailor and the Fly

by Alois Mikulka
translated by Ksenija Šoster-Olmer

Somewhere far out on the sea, a sailor was drowning. He was growing weaker and weaker. He was getting ready to part with his life, when he noticed a drowning fly. He smiled at her with great sorrow and said, "Me, a human, and you, a fly, and we'll both meet the same end."

And they both swam with all their might. Suddenly the sailor realized that even though he had no hope, the fly need not die. He put her on his forehead and swam on. Soon the warm sun had dried the fly's wet wings. With a sad smile, the sailor watched her fly away. Then he once again fought with the waves on his own.

The fly flew high up in the sky and spotted a fishing boat in the distance. There were big waves all around, so the sailor couldn't see the boat and the

fisherman couldn't see the sailor. The fly flew to the boat and straight into the fisherman's ear.

She buzzed, "Help, there's someone drowniiiing!"

But the fisherman just swatted at her with his hand and stared into the water for fish.

But the fly didn't give up so easily. She buzzed around his ears. She sat on his hand, his nose, his forehead. She was so persistent that the fisherman got terribly angry and decided to get that fly no matter what it took.

He paddled after her, and the fly led him closer and closer to the drowning sailor. The fisherman nearly crashed into him with his boat. He then forgot all about the fly and quickly pulled the sailor aboard.

The fly flew to shore, and the fisherman paddled there with the sailor.

Once ashore, the grateful sailor said, "Wonder of wonders, me, a human, and her, a fly, and we saved each other's lives."

LOOK AHEAD

A
Brother's
Promise

In "A Brother's Promise," a girl helps the effort to build the Statue of Liberty. As you read, try to identify the plot elements of conflict and climax.

Vocabulary

Words to Know

contribution	fund	gigantic
patriotic	pedestal	spyglass
symbolizes		

When you read, you may come across a word that you don't know. To figure out the meaning of an unfamiliar word, look for clues in the words and sentences around it. A clue might be found in an explanation given before or after the unknown word.

Read the paragraph below. Notice how an explanation of *patriotic* helps you understand what it means.

Red, White, and Blue

Last year my family worked on the organizing committee for our town's gigantic Fourth of July parade. We worked hard to make the event a success. First we created a parade fund and asked every business in town for a cash contribution. We bought little United States flags for everyone and encouraged parents to explain to their children what the flag symbolizes. We hung red, white, and blue streamers from the pedestal of Abraham Lincoln's statue that stands in the town square. We wanted everyone to feel partriotic and proud to be an American. As the parade started, my father let us use his antique spyglass. He wanted us to be able to see everything, even the smallest details.

Write About It

Write about your most memorable Fourth of July. Use some vocabulary words.

A Brother's Promise

by Pam Conrad

Annie watched Geoffrey's every move. Her brother looked very different since he had gone away to art school in Paris. He was almost a stranger, with his new mustache and fancy clothes. She watched him butter his bread while he spoke to their parents, and she imitated the way he smoothed the butter and folded his slice of bread in half.

Her father was speaking in a loud, booming voice. "The *Times* said last week that this Statue of Liberty gift may be a hoax played on the American people by the French. They say it's possible the statue doesn't even exist."

"But, Father," Geoffrey objected, "I've seen it with my own eyes." Annie watched his cheeks flush with excitement. "It towers over the houses on a small Parisian street. It's wonderful! The reason it hasn't arrived here yet has nothing to do with the French people. The problem is with the American people, who haven't collected any money for a pedestal."

"You mean," said Annie, "that when we build the pedestal, they will send over the whole statue?"

"And not until then," Geoffrey answered.

"How long have the statue's hand and torch been here in Madison Square?" she asked. She thought of it rising over the trees just a few blocks away. It had been there nearly all her life, and she was used to it. Until now, until there was talk of sending it back to Paris because there was no pedestal.

"Let's see," her father said, stroking his thick mustache and gazing into the chandelier. "The hand and the torch came over in 1876 for the United States Centennial Exposition in Philadelphia—where, I might add, its presence did little to encourage donations for a pedestal—and in 1877 it was brought here to New York. How old was Annie, dear?" he asked, turning to his wife.

She was pouring Geoffrey more coffee, holding her heavy lace sleeves away from the urn. "Annie was about five, I believe, and now she's twelve, so the statue must have been here for seven years."

"Are you really twelve already, Annie?" Geoffrey asked, suddenly noticing her and smiling across the table. It was that smile that made him so familiar again.

"You missed my birthday as usual, Geoffrey," she teased. "Otherwise you'd know how old I am. Besides, I'm ten years younger than you are, so you should never forget."

"Oh, but I forget how old *I* am," he said, teasing her.

Annie rolled her eyes. "Well, have you forgotten the way to Madison Square?"

"Probably," he replied.

They grinned at each other. Annie was glad he was home, even for just a visit. Now she wanted to go to the Square and up into the torch with him. "Would you like me to lead you there?" she asked.

"Sounds wonderful!" Geoffrey folded his napkin and put it next to his plate. "If you'll excuse us, Mother, Father, we're off to the statue."

"For one last look," Annie added, "before the hand is returned forever to Paris just because the stingy Americans won't make a pedestal for her."

"Don't say that, Annie," Geoffrey objected, pushing his chair quietly under the table. "Nothing is forever."

Geoffrey walked around the table and offered her his arm.

"Well, let's go see her, shall we, mademoiselle?* Get your wrap, and we're off."

It was a cold, blustery morning as Annie and Geoffrey ran down the polished front stoop of their home and started toward Madison Square. Annie kept her cold hands tucked deep inside her furry muff, and she grew sadder and sadder as they walked along.

*Miss (French)

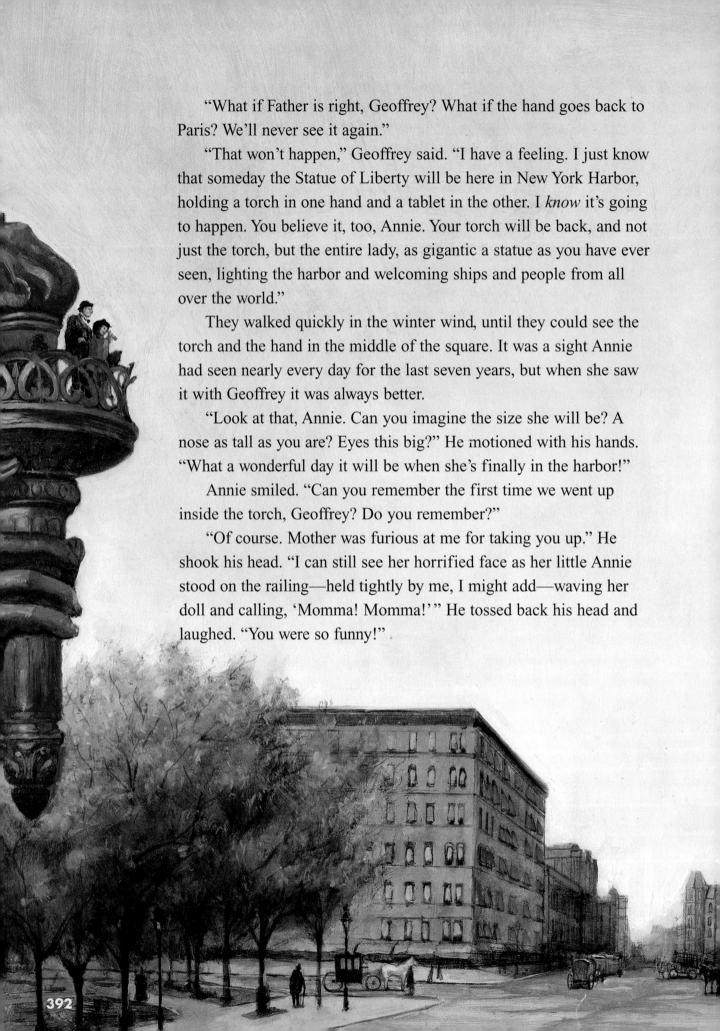

"What if Father is right, Geoffrey? What if the hand goes back to Paris? We'll never see it again."

"That won't happen," Geoffrey said. "I have a feeling. I just know that someday the Statue of Liberty will be here in New York Harbor, holding a torch in one hand and a tablet in the other. I *know* it's going to happen. You believe it, too, Annie. Your torch will be back, and not just the torch, but the entire lady, as gigantic a statue as you have ever seen, lighting the harbor and welcoming ships and people from all over the world."

They walked quickly in the winter wind, until they could see the torch and the hand in the middle of the square. It was a sight Annie had seen nearly every day for the last seven years, but when she saw it with Geoffrey it was always better.

"Look at that, Annie. Can you imagine the size she will be? A nose as tall as you are? Eyes this big?" He motioned with his hands. "What a wonderful day it will be when she's finally in the harbor!"

Annie smiled. "Can you remember the first time we went up inside the torch, Geoffrey? Do you remember?"

"Of course. Mother was furious at me for taking you up." He shook his head. "I can still see her horrified face as her little Annie stood on the railing—held tightly by me, I might add—waving her doll and calling, 'Momma! Momma!'" He tossed back his head and laughed. "You were so funny!"

"Do you know that's the first memory I have in my whole life?" she said. "It's the very first thing I remember—being up in that torch with you holding on to me, and seeing Mother and Father like little people on the ground below us."

"I'm glad," Geoffrey said softly. "That's a wonderful first memory."

Annie felt tears burn her eyes. "Oh, but it's not fair! I don't want it to go back to Paris! I don't want to lose it. We've had so much fun here. What if it never comes back?"

"Nonsense!" said Geoffrey, as they approached the stone base of the statue that loomed three stories above them. They entered the base and started up the narrow staircase that was lit by gas lamps. At the top, they stepped onto a railed, circular walkway. Geoffrey pulled his silver spyglass out of his vest pocket and let her peer through it up and down Fifth Avenue and Broadway. The wind was howling through the metalwork, and the noise of the horse-and-carriage traffic filtered through the park's lining of bare trees.

They shared the spyglass between them, as they had so many times in the past, each quiet in thought. Annie was sure that this was the last time she would stand like this in the great torch overlooking her city. She had an awful feeling that something terrible was going to happen. Something terrible that she couldn't stop. She sighed and leaned on the railing.

"Oh, now, now," Geoffrey said, patting her shoulder. "No sadness today. Try not to think of this as the end, but as the beginning."

"The beginning?" asked Annie.

"The beginning of what this all was originally intended to be, a beautiful statue in the harbor."

"It will never happen," she said.

"Let's make a pact," he said. "I, Geoffrey Gibbon, swear that I will return to this torch someday with you. I promise that one day we'll stand in this very spot, only it will be higher, much higher, nearly a hundred and fifty feet in the sky, overlooking the harbor and all of the city and country of New York, and *that* will be a great day."

"Describe it to me, Geoffrey," she said quietly.

"We'll stand in this very spot," he began, "and when we look over the edge, we'll look down into the statue's huge face. We'll stand right here and see our country spread out before us—the seas, the hills, the people everywhere celebrating and happy."

Annie smiled and looked at him, glad he was home. "You say things so nicely, Geoffrey."

"Now *you* promise," he said.

Annie straightened up and squared her shoulders. "I, Annie Gibbon, promise to come back to this very spot, wherever this spot may be, whenever that may be, with you, Geoffrey. And it will be a great day."

They smiled at each other, and Annie felt all her worry lift from her shoulders, like birds flying away. Then some people came up onto the walkway beside them.

"Do you believe this monstrosity?" one of them said. "Have you ever seen such a ridiculous lighthouse?"

Annie and Geoffrey looked at each other. He winked, and his mustache twitched ever so slightly.

It was almost a year since Geoffrey had returned to Paris, and the American papers were brimming with news of a campaign to bring the statue to America at last. Happily, Annie let the wind sweep her across the cobblestone street, weaving her in and out of the slow-moving carriages, and then let it push her up the polished stone steps of her home. Her one hand was jammed into her fur muff, and the other clutched a copy of the day's *New York World*.

The heavy door opened easily, and as she unwound her scarf from her neck, she began calling, "Mother! Father!" Annie stomped into the parlor, flashing the newspaper at her parents, who sat unusually still on the velvet lounge by the fireplace. "It's really coming! We're really going to get the whole statue, and Geoffrey and I will go up into the torch again, just like he promised, only this time it will be in the harbor, not in the park.

"Imagine!" she cried. "No one thought Americans could raise the money to build the pedestal, but according to the *New York World* pennies and nickels are pouring in from all over."

"Annie," her mother said softly.

Annie rustled the day's newspaper in front of her. "They have a goal of one hundred thousand dollars to raise, and they just might be able to do it."

"Annie," her mother repeated.

"I'm so excited," Annie continued. "I'm going to earn some money and make my contribution. Have you any idea what this means? Geoffrey was right after all.

"Oh, I must write to Geoffrey! He will be so excited! He knew it! He knew it all along!" She looked from her mother to her father for the first time, and then she saw that her mother had been crying and her father was pale.

"Please, Annie," her mother said, her voice shaky and uncertain.

"What is it, Mother?" she asked. "What's wrong?"

"It's Geoffrey, dear," her mother whispered. "Your brother is dead." Annie's mother dropped her head into her hands and began to cry.

"What are you talking about? What do you mean?"

Her father's voice was choked and soft. "He's been killed in an accident, Annie. I can't believe it."

Annie felt frozen to the ground. Her ears were ringing. Her arms grew numb. "What happened?"

"It seems he was visiting with some people in Germany, riding in some kind of motorized vehicle. It went out of control. He was killed instantly."

"How do you know this?" Annie shouted, not wanting to believe she'd never see her brother again.

Her father pointed to the parlor table in front of him, to a letter beside a box. It had been posted in Germany, and like all Geoffrey's letters it had unusual and colorful stamps, but the handwriting was unfamiliar.

Annie read over the letter—the accident, the death—to the closing. "I extend my deepest sympathy. I'm sending a package to Annie, whom Geoffrey spoke of with deepest affection. It's one of his possessions that I feel he would have wanted her to have. Sincerely, Walter Linderbaum."

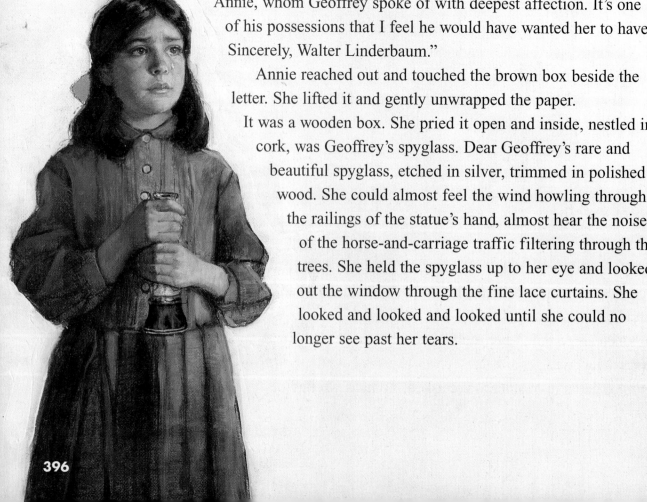

Annie reached out and touched the brown box beside the letter. She lifted it and gently unwrapped the paper.

It was a wooden box. She pried it open and inside, nestled in cork, was Geoffrey's spyglass. Dear Geoffrey's rare and beautiful spyglass, etched in silver, trimmed in polished wood. She could almost feel the wind howling through the railings of the statue's hand, almost hear the noise of the horse-and-carriage traffic filtering through the trees. She held the spyglass up to her eye and looked out the window through the fine lace curtains. She looked and looked and looked until she could no longer see past her tears.

IV

In a few weeks, Annie wrote this letter to the publisher of the *New York World* newspaper.

Dear Mr. Pulitzer,

I am sending this money for the Statue of Liberty Pedestal Fund. I live near Madison Square, and I used to visit the torch with my older brother, Geoffrey. Geoffrey was an art student in Paris, and he told me all about the statue and how the man who built the Eiffel Tower in Paris also built the foundation of the Statue of Liberty. He told me how the statue towers over the buildings in Paris, and how he used to look at it and imagine it in New York Harbor. We even made a solemn promise to meet in the torch when it was finally here again. He was always completely certain that she would be here one day.

I want to make sure of it. You see, my brother died this year, and although he can't keep his promise to me, I can still keep mine. I've been to see a local pawnbroker, and I sold Geoffrey's rare antique spyglass made of silver and wood that we used for looking around New York City, from up inside the torch. I'm sad to sell it, but I'm sure he'd understand. Please take this money in Geoffrey Gibbon's memory. And please build a pedestal.

Respectfully yours,

Annie Gibbon

Annie's letter was published in the *New York World,* and its heartfelt message touched off a series of contributions in memory of beloved relatives. Annie was proud to see the fund grow bigger every week until, finally, Joseph Pulitzer declared the fund to be complete, and the construction of the pedestal on Bedloe's Island was to begin at last.

V

October 28, 1886, was a cold, drizzly day, but it was declared a holiday, and New York was astir with excitement. Even though the city was in a festive mood, Annie felt uneasy. Her parents had promised to take her to Bedloe's Island to see the statue that had finally arrived and had been assembled on its glorious pedestal, but Annie wasn't sure she wanted to see it. It wouldn't be the same without Geoffrey. If he couldn't see it, maybe she shouldn't see it either, she thought. But she got into the carriage with her mother and father and headed for the pier, where they would take a boat over to the island.

Annie was quiet in the carriage as she watched the holiday crowds out the window. Her mother patted her hand reassuringly. "I guess we all miss Geoffrey this day," her mother said. "He would have enjoyed this."

"Oh, yes," sighed Annie, watching the American and French flags on the fronts of buildings. "This should be Geoffrey's day. He saw the statue in Paris, and he should be here today."

They were all quiet and sad and rode in silence until they reached the pier. Her father found the people who would take them across. Annie boarded a boat with her parents, and they started out toward Bedloe's Island. The harbor was afloat with every kind of boat—from ferryboats and freighters to yachts, scows, and battleships. The steam from all the steamships put a cloud over the harbor, but everywhere there was music—"Yankee Doodle Dandy," the "Marseillaise"*—and the laughter of people celebrating.

*the French national anthem

Annie stood shivering by the railing of the boat. Looming ahead, standing majestically in the center of the harbor, was the shape of a gigantic lady holding a torch in one hand and a tablet in the other.

"You believe it, too, Annie," she could almost hear Geoffrey saying. "The Statue of Liberty will be here in New York Harbor—the entire lady, lighting the harbor and welcoming ships and people from all over the world." Tears filled Annie's eyes. She was suddenly glad she had come.

"Look," she whispered. "Look at her, Geoffrey."

Annie had never seen so much excitement and merriment in her life. President Grover Cleveland was there, with bands and dignitaries, and there were speeches and songs and cheers and patriotic excitement. She and her parents joined the crowd and listened to the speeches. She was especially excited when Joseph Pulitzer took the stand and gave his speech. He talked about the American people who had finally come through. He talked about the great crews that had built the pedestal, the wonderful French people who had sent the statue to us. He called it the greatest gift one nation ever gave another. The crowd cheered and laughed, and Joseph Pulitzer beamed with pride as if he had brought the statue over single-handedly.

Then, just when it seemed he was through, he looked over the crowd thoughtfully and shouted out, "By the way, is Annie Gibbon here today?"

"What?" her mother gasped.

Annie froze in disbelief.

"Annie Gibbon?" Joseph Pulitzer called once again.

"Here I am!" Annie cried, waving from her place in the crowd.

"Come up here, Annie!" He laughed, and the crowd parted for her. She made her way to the podium, barely knowing what she was doing, barely believing this was really happening. Mr. Pulitzer reached out his hand and guided her up the steps. He kept her at his side and spoke to the crowd.

"I don't know if you folks remember, but Annie wrote a letter to me that we published in the *World* a while ago. Isn't that right, Annie?" he said, turning to her and smiling.

She nodded numbly.

"Well, I'm so glad you're here. You see," he said, turning back to his audience, "she lost her brother last year, a brother who loved the Statue of Liberty. He'd actually seen it in Paris, and Annie sold his special spyglass and sent the money to the Pedestal Fund in his memory. And that led many others to do the same thing."

A few people clapped, and Annie looked down at their faces.

"Annie, I have a surprise for you." He turned around, and someone handed him a long, thin wooden box. "When I read your letter, I sent

400

my people out to all the pawnshops in your area. I said to myself, 'Joseph, when the statue comes over, that little girl is going to have her spyglass back. Yes, she is.' Now you take this spyglass and climb to the top of that lady and take a good look around, Annie."

People were laughing and clapping, and Joseph Pulitzer was nearly bursting with himself. But all Annie could see was the familiar box in her hand. Carefully she opened it, not believing, but, yes, Geoffrey's spyglass was nestled in the box, waiting for her. The band began to play, and Annie looked up into the face of Joseph Pulitzer. "Thank you," she whispered.

Annie's parents walked her to the base of the statue, where they hugged her and let her go up alone. Holding the spyglass box tightly in her hand, she started up the stairway. The inside of the statue was immense, studded with bolts and held together with girders and supports. She remembered how once Geoffrey had carried her up the stairs in the torch. How huge the torch had seemed then, but it was nothing like this! She climbed and climbed and climbed, 161 steps, never stopping at a rest station, and not even stopping at the observation room in the crown.

Then Annie entered the part of the statue that was so familiar to her. She began to climb up into the raised arm. Her hand touched the cold metal wall; her feet sounded lightly on the stairs. She was alone. Up and up, until at last she stepped out onto the circular walkway around the base of the torch. She felt as if she had arrived home, but only for an instant, and then her breath was whisked away. She had known she would not see Fifth Avenue and Broadway, but there was no way she could have prepared herself for what was before her. She was certain if she reached up she could have touched the gray clouds, yet she clasped the railing tightly with her gloved fingers. The wind whipped around her, whistling through the gratings, and the Earth stretched out in all directions.

"Describe it to me, dear Annie," she thought she heard a voice say.

Her words were blown away by the wind, but she began slowly. "When I look over the edge, I can see down into the statue's beautiful face. Her nose is strong and straight, and I can see her lips, proud and determined. The spikes of her crown are huge and studded with bolts. In her hand is a tablet that reads 'July 4, 1776.' I am standing in the torch that symbolizes the light of freedom, and before me I can see my country spread wide and far, the seas, the hills, and the people everywhere celebrating and happy. I can hear the band, and I can see battleships and steamships, and in the distance I see buildings and steeples. On the ground, I can see people like tiny ants."

She smiled, raised her spyglass to her eye, and scanned the crowds below. "I can't even find Mother and Father." Then she turned the spyglass to the horizon. "It's the haziest of days, Geoffrey. It's difficult to see. I'll have to come back again one day." She smiled. "Yes, I'll come back on a clear day, when I can see the hills and the distant horizon. There will be more days, many more, and I'll come back again and again. I promise. You were right, Geoffrey. This is a great day."

Annie stayed as long as she could, until the wind and the cold seemed to be buffeting her from every direction, and then she started down. On her way home, skimming across the harbor in the boat, Annie turned back to the statue and watched her there in the twilight. A few fireworks had gone up in the foggy night, and everywhere boats were lit with bright lights and lanterns.

And then slowly, very slowly, the torch in the great lady's hand began to glow. It was dim at first, and then brighter, until it glowed with a fierce and proud light. Annie watched, and she was certain that from across the dark waters of the harbor the torch light faintly, but surely, winked at her.

Pam Conrad

When Pam Conrad had her first book published, she started a tradition. "I bought myself a gold necklace and a gold bead," she says. "I told myself I would add a bead for each book that I would have published." She is now up to eighteen beads, with more on the way.

Some of Ms. Conrad's most popular books are historical fiction and are set on the prairie. She believes her love of historical fiction can be traced back to the Laura Ingalls Wilder stories she read when she was young. Ms. Conrad's book *Prairie Songs* tells the story of a young wife who moves from New York City to the prairie with her husband in the 1800s but has trouble adapting to the loneliness of prairie life. A later book, *Prairie Visions,* is a nonfiction account of the life of photographer Solomon Butcher, whose work inspired part of the story in *Prairie Songs.*

Even though Ms. Conrad's books are not autobiographical, she often draws on events in her own life. In her book *Staying Nine,* she writes of a nine-year-old girl about to turn ten. This was written about the time her daughter Sarah turned ten. Ms. Conrad felt her children were growing too quickly and wanted to slow down time just a little.

Ms. Conrad finds great joy in her writing, but she doesn't take all the credit. "I believe that all we write comes *through* us," she says, "not *from* us, that we're channels of sorts for hundreds of stories that are floating around in the universe. And the greatest happiness for me is when all of a sudden little parts of my life begin to take on a strange, new significance. Something slowly opens up inside me like a dam on a Nebraska river, and a story begins to unfold."

Reader Response

Open for Discussion

If you could be on the observation platform of the Statue of Liberty with Annie at the end of the story, what would you say to her?

Comprehension Check

1. Describe the setting, or the time and place in which the story occurs. How does the setting influence the events of the story? Look back at the story for details.

2. Point out examples of what Annie says, thinks, and does. What do these examples tell you about Annie's character?

3. Trace what happens to the spyglass during the course of the story. What do you think the spyglass symbolizes to Annie?

4. What role does a promise have in the events of the **Plot**? Explain, using details from the story. (Plot)

5. The events of a story's **Plot** lead to a high point, or climax. What do you think is the climax of this story? Explain. (Plot)

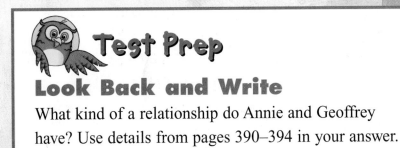

Test Prep

Look Back and Write

What kind of a relationship do Annie and Geoffrey have? Use details from pages 390–394 in your answer.

Test Prep

How to Read a Picture Essay

1. Preview

- A picture essay often brings together several examples of the same topic. The examples help to define the topic.

- Look over the title and pictures. What is the topic of this essay and what are the examples?

2. Read and List Examples

- Read the essay and make a list of the five examples. For each example, note what it symbolizes about the United States.

- Think about other objects that symbolize something about the United States. Add them to your list and note what they symbolize.

3. Think and Connect

Think about Annie and her brother in "A Brother's Promise." Then look over your notes on "Symbols That Make Us Proud."

Why does the Statue of Liberty mean even more to Annie than it would to most Americans?

Symbols That Make Us Proud

All countries have symbols. The ones you see on these pages are symbols of the United States of America. They stand for the things that make our country great. The American flag stands for the land, the people, the government, and the ideals of the United States.

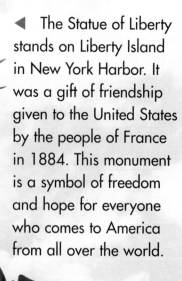

◄ The Statue of Liberty stands on Liberty Island in New York Harbor. It was a gift of friendship given to the United States by the people of France in 1884. This monument is a symbol of freedom and hope for everyone who comes to America from all over the world.

The Liberty Bell is a symbol of America's independence. It was first rung on July 8, 1776, at the first public reading of the Declaration of Independence. The words engraved on the bell, "Proclaim Liberty throughout all the land unto all the inhabitants thereof," are from the Bible.

The Great Seal of the United States is a symbol of America's power. It shows an American eagle with its wings spread. The olive branch in the eagle's right claw and the arrows in its left mean that our country wants to live in peace, but it can wage war. ▼

The bald eagle is the national ▶ bird of the United States. It is a symbol of our country's strength and bravery.

—from *Thorndike Barnhart Children's Dictionary*

Skill Lesson

Main Idea and Supporting Details

- The most important idea about the topic of a paragraph or an article is the **main idea.** Small pieces of information that tell more about the main idea are **supporting details.**

- To find a main idea, first identify the topic. Ask yourself "What is this all about?" Then look for the most important idea about the topic. If it is not stated, put the main idea in your own words.

- To check a main idea, ask yourself "Does this main idea make sense? Does it cover all the important details?"

Read "Quilted Memories" by Allen F. Roberts from *Faces* magazine.

Write About It

1. What is this article all about? Write one or two words that describe the topic of this article.

2. In your own words, state the main idea about this topic.

3. Find at least one detail that supports the main idea.

Quilted Memories

by Allen F. Roberts

In the bitter cold of deep winter, what is nicer than snuggling up in a warm quilt? Nowadays, most of us probably sleep under machine-made blankets and comforters, but some people still make and use handmade quilts. In the old days, many quilts were sewn from a family's old clothing. Some women still enjoy this kind of recycling. The cloth is strong enough for another use, and the women remember whose overalls, velvet dress, or silk necktie each scrap comes from. Such a quilt is made from memories that can keep a body warm in the embrace of family history.

It takes a great deal of effort to save or gather enough cloth, plan a design, cut out the pieces, and then stitch them together to form an attractive top. More work is required to finish the padding and backing of a quilt. Many quilters are justly famous for their tiny stitching, so tight and even that it seems to disappear

into the fabric. A quilt helps us to remember and admire people in our families who possessed these skills and their efforts to produce something so beautiful, useful, and lasting.

Because so much work is required to piece together a quilt, it has often been done collectively. Women have gathered to sew together, perhaps through the afternoons of winter, when it is too cold for outside chores. Quilting bees have been occasions to chat, tell stories, and sing, and memories of such merriment make quilts all the warmer.

Quilt designs offer other ways to remember, for women of different times, places, and cultures make different kinds of quilts. Old Order Amish people of Pennsylvania and the Midwest have made dazzling quilts of such bold design that the colors seem to leap off the bed. Amish quilts are recognized as true works of art and are in such demand by collectors around the world that old quilts are hard to find and new ones cannot be made fast enough.

LOOK AHEAD

In *from Catching the Fire*, Philip Simmons creates another kind of art from metal. As you read, think about what the author is saying about the topic.

409

Vocabulary

Words to Know

anvil	businessman
craftsman	horseshoes
ornamental	workshop

Words with opposite meanings are called **antonyms.** You can often figure out the meaning of an unknown word by finding a clue in the words around it. Sometimes this clue is an antonym.

Read this paragraph. Notice how *plain* helps you understand what *ornamental* means.

A Fiery Tradition

Blacksmithing is an age-old tradition that is still practiced at festivals and fairs throughout the world. During a visit to the blacksmith's booth, fair-goers can watch a blacksmith use a hammer and anvil to make iron into plain objects such as horseshoes. They might also see the craftsman or craftswoman working on ornamental gates and fences. If visitors like what they see in the temporary workshop, they can talk to the blacksmith about objects that are for sale. At the festival, the blacksmith is both an artist who is pleased when his or her work is admired and a businessman or businesswoman who wants to make a living.

Write About It

Write about a craft or hobby that interests you. Use some vocabulary words.

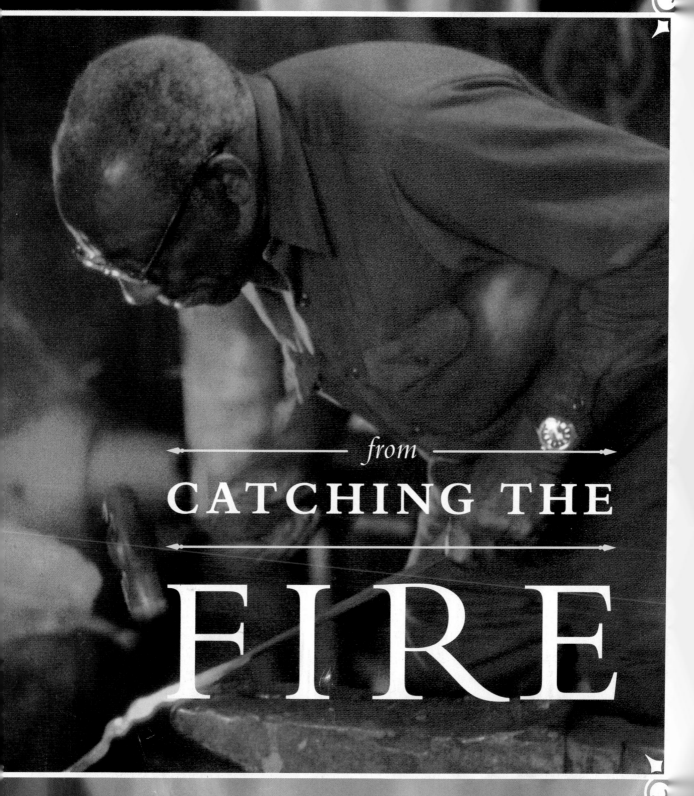

from

CATCHING THE

FIRE

BY MARY E. LYONS

Events in this biography are based on Philip Simmons's memories and described in his own words. He listened to the text after I wrote it. "Let me tell you the real story," he said if I needed to correct a detail. When the scenes were satisfactory, the blacksmith nodded or chuckled. "That's right," he said. "That's a true story!"

Philip Simmons caught the blacksmith fever when he was thirteen years old. Since then the artist has forged more than five hundred pieces of ornamental wrought iron. Most of his gates, fences, and railings decorate the coastal city of Charleston, South Carolina. Several of his finest works are in museums.

To touch a Philip Simmons gate is to touch the past. His craft is over five thousand years old. In 3,500 B.C., Egyptian smiths shaped metal with hammer and fire. In Sierra Leone, West Africa, smiths have worked brass and copper since the thirteenth century.

From 1670 until 1863, thousands of West Africans were enslaved on the coast of South Carolina. Some were blacksmiths who passed the tradition on to their offspring. One descendant, a former slave, showed Philip Simmons how to work iron.

Like his ancestors, Mr. Simmons can hammer life into a dead lump of iron. But he is the first African American smith known to forge

Truck in front of blacksmith shop, about 1918

animal figures. His fish and sly-eyed snakes look as lively as he feels. "I like action!" he declares in his musical Low Country speech.

For over eighty years, action has guided Philip Simmons's life and art. Born on June 9, 1912, he claims he retired in 1987. Yet he remains excited about his craft. After a lifetime of seventeen-hour workdays, he still rises at 6 A.M.

Mr. Simmons often wakes with an idea for a new gate. "I see it finished completely in my mind," he says. Before breakfast, he rolls a squeaky chair up to his office desk and sketches the design.

And he will still play "the old blacksmith tune" on his anvil, especially for young people. Youngsters are drawn to his friendly face and teasing ways.

"You are a role model and a mentor," a young fan wrote to him. "You are showing us we can do anything!" said another.

Philip Simmons's teacher, Peter Simmons, with his nephew and apprentice, Robert Simmons

Although Philip Simmons is always cheerful, he has known trouble in his long life. The great-grandson of slaves, he lived with Jim Crow laws for over fifty years. The hateful rules forced African Americans into separate schools, hospitals, and housing. In the 1930s and 1940s, the blacksmith struggled to feed his family. This was hard to do in Charleston, where often only low-paying jobs were open to black workers.

Mr. Simmons survived the hardships and stayed with work he enjoyed. He tells young people to do the same.

"Number one, you got to love it," he says.

Philip Simmons began his career as an untrained boy. Now he is called the Dean of Blacksmiths by professional smiths across the country. His memories show that skill and patience take years of work. They also prove that everyone can achieve both. An honored artist, teacher, and businessman, Philip Simmons is the working person's hero.

Peter Simmons (no relation to Philip Simmons), was one of the best-known smiths in Charleston. Philip Simmons became his apprentice at age thirteen, but he wasn't allowed to work full-time until he was fifteen. Peter Simmons taught Philip to operate the bellows, a leather lung that forced air into the forge to keep the fire hot, to repair tools, to make horseshoes, and all the other skills needed for this backbreaking but important craft. He also told stories to his workers and the onlookers who crowded around to watch.

Philip Simmons married at age twenty-four. Peter Simmons gave him the workshop on Calhoun Street, where he had learned his trade, as a wedding gift. Years later, after repairing an iron gate, Philip realized that not only could he restore old wrought iron, he could forge new gates using the traditional patterns he had studied as a boy.

"You must be Philip Simmons," the young man said. Sixty-year-old Philip looked up from his pile of scrap iron. The year was 1972, and he was working in his shop yard on Blake Street. Philip shook the visitor's hand. Who was this fellow, anyway? He said he was a graduate student from Indiana, but he had Washington, D.C., plates on his car.

Was he lost? Well, yes, he was. John Michael Vlach had been wandering around the one-way streets near Philip's shop, looking for the man who knew "the old ways of ironwork." John seemed a little nervous, maybe because a scruffy dog named Brownie was barking at him. But the blacksmith liked to talk about old times, so the scholar soon relaxed.

Philip explained the history of his business to John. In the late 1930s, the federal government gave Charleston enough money to build two East Side housing projects: one for black citizens and one for whites. So Philip had to move his shop "for the improvement of the city."

The smith moved four times and landed on Blake Street in 1969. It was here that he replaced the spiteful bellows with an electric forge blower.

Philip Simmons forges a scroll in the early 1970s.

By the time America entered World War II in 1941, most of the city's blacksmiths were gone. When the Charleston Naval Ship Yard wanted parts for ships, they went to Philip Simmons. But after the war was over in 1945, business slowed down.

"I needed to make some money on the side," Philip told John. He drove a taxi, ran a dry-cleaning business, and opened and closed a restaurant. There must be a faster way to "grab a few more pennies," he thought.

Peter Simmons had died in 1953, two days before his ninety-eighth birthday. About this time, Philip decided to modernize his own shop. He bought an electric arc welder that was three times faster than riveting. And he attached an old washing machine motor to his hand drill. Both tools speeded up the work.

When John Vlach wanted to compare the old ways to the new ones, Philip took him on a tour of Charleston. He led John down a

Tools in Philip Simmons's blacksmith shop, Charleston, South Carolina

narrow alley to one of his first "fancy" pieces. Philip was proud of the old-time rivets he had used to join the wiggle tail to the gate.

Next, the two men looked at a bird gate. The customer had given Philip a drawing of an egret. "Can you make it?" the fellow had asked.

Sure he could. Philip knew egrets like the calluses on his hands. He used an acetylene torch to cut the metal talons, and he made a bended knee so the bird was "looking ready to go."

Philip drove John over to East Bay Street to see his Snake Gate. It took him one month to forge that gate. He thought he'd never finish the eye. At first, it stared as if it were dead. Philip "heat and beat, heat and beat, heat and beat," until the snake looked as real as a diamond head rattler. "If it bites you," Philip joked, "you better get to the doctor fast. Blood get up to your heart, you know what happens!"

John Vlach was impressed. These were no ordinary pieces of ornamental ironwork. They were sculpture! Philip Simmons was not just a blacksmith. He was an artist.

Wiggle tail, 2 Stoll's Alley, Charleston, South Carolina. The round bumps are rivets.

Philip Simmons, 1976

John saw Philip often over the next four years. He helped install gates, took photographs, and tape-recorded conversations. And in 1976, John offered Philip the greatest test of his career: an invitation to make a gate at the Festival of American Folklife, a summer-long event in Washington, D.C.

The two men discussed the trip in the dim light of Philip's shop. As they spoke, pinpoints of sun poked through the sheet metal walls. At first the artist didn't want to go.

"No, no, no, no, no," Philip said. He held two scrolls up to the light to see if they matched. "I got business to do."

This wasn't going to be easy. John raked his hands through his dark brown hair. "You'll only be gone fifteen days," he said.

"Any special piece that you want me to make?" Philip asked.

"The choice is yours," John sweet-talked him. "We just want you to come up and demonstrate what you're doing in Charleston."

This offer made sense to the businessman. He could make something small to bring home and "sell for a profit."

"What about the materials? How will I move them?"

"We'll put everything in the trunk of your car."

"Only so much I can do without my 'prentice boys."

"Bring the apprentices with you. We'll pay their expenses, and they can drive the car."

The blacksmith ran out of arguments. "Yes, I'll come," he finally agreed.

There were a few other hurdles. First, Philip needed a portable forge. He always "liked to make the odd thing," so he cut the top off an old hot water heater and packed it with fire clay. He didn't spend more than fifty dollars on his homemade invention.

Second, what kind of gate should he make? Philip "set to the desk," but nothing came to mind. He lay awake at night. Still no ideas. Six weeks passed. Suddenly he realized he was leaving—tomorrow!

Would this be the first test the blacksmith failed? When the airplane left Charleston the next day, Philip peeked out the small oval window next to his seat. He took a long look at the rivers and marshes that hugged Charleston on three sides.

"I'm just crazy about the water," he thought. "Maybe I'll show the stars in the water."

He considered fish. "Fish represents Charleston. It's known for fishing."

Philip imagined the moon over the Cooper River and decided to show a "quarter-moon, just racing along."

But like the old Sea Island tale says, "'sidering and 'cidering won't buy Sal a new shirt." The artist pulled out a scrap of paper and began to draw. By the time the plane landed an hour later, he had solved the puzzle.

He would make a fish in the water and a double star in the sky, one inside the other. "Like watchin' a star," he thought, "it get smaller on you." Two quarter-moons would shine over it all.

Maybe this wouldn't be his prettiest gate, but it would be his most important one. It would be his "sacrificial piece." The one made in front of thousands of people and forged with the ancient tools of ironworking: fire, hammer, and a blacksmith's rugged hands.

"In sixty-two years," Philip says, "I never went in the shop and didn't need a hammer."

Washington, D.C., was almost as hot as Charleston. Especially the last week of July and first week of August, 1976. For these two weeks, Philip and his apprentices, Joseph Pringle and Silas Sessions, worked on the grassy Mall near the Lincoln Memorial. When the sun grew too bright, they moved under a striped tent.

The United States was two hundred years old, and the festival was a birthday party. It celebrated the skills of people from all over the world. Philip was impressed with the other talented folks he saw on the Mall: singers, dancers, cooks, hairdressers, gospel singers, woodcarvers, and seamstresses.

"Doing it the old way." Frances Brewton, a quilter from Des Moines, Iowa, talks with visitors at the 1996 Smithsonian Folklife Festival.

The Star and Fish Gate, 1976

"Everybody on this ground," he noticed, "is doing it the old way."

At first, he and his helpers forged simple chandeliers and plant stands. The rain of sparks and ring of hammers drew a stream of visitors to the demonstration. Philip answered their questions, just as Peter Simmons had done fifty years before.

Then the blacksmiths began the Star and Fish Gate. They cut lengths of iron bars, forged pecan leaves, welded J-curves inside of S-curves. Philip used several pieces of metal to create an open effect in the spot-tailed bass. Finally he made the striking star within a star.

Toward the end of Philip's stay in Washington, John noticed something curious about the outside star.

"The center point is off by twenty degrees," he commented.

"A star can shine all different ways," the artist explained.

That evening Philip started thinking. Nothing is right until it's right. His grandfather had taught him that as a boy on Daniel Island. Peter Simmons had drilled it into him as a young man. And what about his customers? "If it weren't for them," Philip thought, "I wouldn't even be in Washington."

The blacksmith tossed all night in his dormitory bed at George Washington University. The next day, he hurried to the Mall before anyone else was around. It took him fifteen minutes to cut the star out of the gate and weld it back in place.

By the time the demonstrations began at 11 A.M., the star pointed straight up toward the enamel blue sky. Philip Simmons had proved himself once more.

Officials of the Festival of American Folklife invited Philip Simmons back again, and then again. The federal government gave him a Heritage Fellowship, an award for artists who are considered "national treasures." His Star and Fish Gate was bought by the Smithsonian Institution in Washington, D.C., and now travels to museums around the country.

Mr. Simmons continues to win awards, but he also continues to train young blacksmiths, to pass on the knowledge and skill of a master craftsman. "You got to teach kids while the sap is young," he says, "just like you got to beat the iron while it's hot."

About the Author
MARY E. LYONS

Catching the Fire is one of several books Mary E. Lyons has written about African American artists and craftspeople. Her career as a writer started when she was a teacher looking for material on Zora Neale Hurston, a famous African American writer of novels and folklore. Unfortunately, not much had been written about Ms. Hurston at that time. Because her students wanted to learn about Ms. Hurston, Ms. Lyons wrote *Sorrow's Kitchen: The Life and Folklore of Zora Neale Hurston.* It was named a Best Book for Young Adults by the American Library Association.

Other award-winning books followed. *Letters from a Slave Girl* is based on the autobiography of Harriet Jacobs. *Starting Home: The Story of Horace Pippin, Painter,* is about a self-taught artist who created art based on his experiences in World War I.

In much of her writing, Ms. Lyons emphasizes contributions to American culture made by women and African Americans. Because

of her books' subject matter, many readers assume that she is African American. "I'm quite flattered when that happens," Ms. Lyons has said, "because I hope it means I'm an effective writer."

Reader Response

Open for Discussion

What do you find most impressive about Philip Simmons's art? Why?

Comprehension Check

1. How did Mr. Simmons become a blacksmith? Do you think a young person today could become a blacksmith in the same manner? Explain your answer.

2. From what he says and does, describe Mr. Simmons's attitude toward his art.

3. What do you think is the purpose of an event like the Festival of American Folklife? Explain how Mr. Simmons's appearance there fits that purpose.

4. No one sentence expresses the **main idea** of this piece of writing. What is the most important thing the author says about the topic, Mr. Simmons? (Main idea)

5. What are some details that support this **main idea?** (Main idea)

Test Prep
Look Back and Write

Explain what makes Phillip Simmons a blacksmith and what makes him an artist. Use details from pages 416–419 to support your answer.

Fire All Around Us

from *Kids Discover* magazine

Fire must have seemed like a magic power to our cave-dwelling ancestors. Even our technologically sophisticated modern world depends mightily on fire and its power too.

▲

Jet engines are powered by burning liquid petroleum fuel. The great heat causes air inside the engine to expand violently, and as it rushes toward the exhaust outlets, the resulting thrust propels the jetliner forward.

◄ Many trains are powered by diesel engines. In them, diesel fuel, rather than gasoline, explodes in the cylinders.

Look around and you'll see steel everywhere—in your family car, in your bicycle, in the rings of your notebook, in your ball-point pen. The world produces between one million and ten million tons of steel a year. It is made by heating iron ore and coke (from coal) in huge blast furnaces.

Just about all cars use the internal combustion engine. An electric spark (produced by spark plugs) causes a mixture of gasoline and oxygen to explode in the engine's cylinders. The explosion pushes down the pistons, triggering the movement that causes the wheels to go round. ▼

Think Piece!

Try to imagine that fire had never been discovered and what your life would be like. There wouldn't be cars or electricity. What else?

Coal, gas, and oil are burned at power stations, creating high-pressure steam to propel huge generators that produce electricity. ▶

Until the 19th century, fireplaces were equipped with spits to roast meat, hooks to hang hams and other meats so they would be preserved by the smoke, and handles that held pots and kettles over the flame.

▼

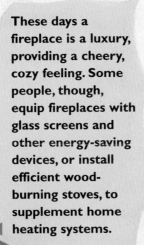

These days a fireplace is a luxury, providing a cheery, cozy feeling. Some people, though, equip fireplaces with glass screens and other energy-saving devices, or install efficient wood-burning stoves, to supplement home heating systems.
◀

In 1769, a Scottish engineer named James Watt perfected the steam engine, ushering in the Industrial Revolution.

In a steam engine a fire in a boiler produces high-pressure steam to drive pistons that create movement.

Steam locomotives led the way to the opening of vast railway systems around the world. Stokers would shovel coal into intense fires to produce the steam that powered the mighty locomotives. Steam engines also replaced sails on ships, opening up the seas to quick travel.

Steam-powered machinery spun cotton, forged iron, milled flour, and performed many other functions that once required hours of arduous hand labor.

The French hit new heights when a steam-powered airship appeared in the skies above Paris in 1852.

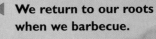

◀ We return to our roots when we barbecue.

Text Structure

- **Text structure** refers to the way a piece of writing is organized.

- Fiction tells of imaginary people and events. It is usually organized in *chronological order,* the order in which the events happen.

- Nonfiction tells of real people and events or tells information about the real world. It may be organized in *chronological order,* or by *topic, cause and effect, problem and solution, comparison and contrast,* or in some other way.

Read "Engineering the Land" from *The Incas* by Tim Wood.

Talk About It

1. Why was the land hard to farm?

2. What two methods did the Incas use to increase the amount of farming land?

3. What clues in the text structure help you find information about these two methods?

Engineering the Land

by Tim Wood

The Incas ruled a large empire in South America from about A.D. 1438 to 1532.

The Incas were very skillful engineers who learned how to manipulate the land to suit their needs. Using only the simplest tools and massive human effort, they created public works that amaze engineers today.

Terracing

Much of the land in the Inca Empire was hard to farm. In places where there was sufficient rainfall, the ground sloped too steeply for farming, and the rain washed the soil away. Where the land was flat enough to work, there was too little rainfall. So the Incas increased the amount of farming land in two main ways. The first, and most spectacular, was by terracing the hillsides. The second was by digging canals to irrigate (water) the land.

All major engineering projects were planned by professional architects sent from the capital, Cuzco. All the work was done by hand. Elaborate terracing transformed steep hillsides into huge flights of stone steps that supported flat fields. These greatly increased the amount of land that could be farmed and also stopped the rain from washing away the soil.

Irrigation

In areas where rain was scarce, engineers built reservoirs and cisterns to store water. Many of these were underground and lined with stone to prevent the water from evaporating. An elaborate network of canals and ditches carried water from wetter areas and mountain streams to irrigate the fields and fill the cisterns. The engineers also built dams and straightened rivers to improve the flow of water and reduce erosion of the fertile banks.

Scientific Knowledge

These works indicate that the Incas had a good knowledge of practical science. Inca engineers were able to introduce water on the top step of a terrace and direct it to run down, watering each of the steps below in turn. They knew that water flowing too fast could erode the banks of a stream and that water flowing too slowly would allow weeds to grow, which in turn could block a channel.

The Seven Wonders of the Ancient World describes seven remarkable accomplishments of ancient civilizations. As you read, notice the text structure, or how the writing is organized.

Vocabulary

Words to Know

archaeologists	classical	excavate
pharaohs	structures	tomb

When you read, you may come across a word that you don't know. To figure out the meaning of an unfamiliar word, look for clues in the words and sentences around it. A clue might be found in an explanation given near the unknown word.

Read the paragraph below. Notice how an explanation of *pharaohs* helps you understand what it means.

Buried History

When I go to college, I want to study archaeology, or the scientific study of ancient history. In my eyes, archaeologists have the best jobs in the whole world. You could say that the whole world is their job. Archaeologists excavate buried cities and discover the structures and treasures of past civilizations. Without archaeology, we wouldn't know about the mysteries of classical Greece and Rome, or that the Great Pyramid at Giza is a tomb built in honor of one of the pharaohs— the kings who ruled ancient Egypt. I can only imagine the wonders that are still undiscovered. One day I hope to find a few of them myself.

Talk About It

Use some of your vocabulary words to tell a story about a real or imaginary discovery.

THE SEVEN WONDERS OF THE ANCIENT WORLD

BY REG COX AND NEIL MORRIS

ILLUSTRATED BY JAMES FIELD

Over 2,000 years ago, writers began to list the amazing buildings and structures they had seen or heard of. In about 120 B.C., a Greek poet called Antipater of Sidon wrote about seven such places. They could all be found in a small region around the eastern Mediterranean—an area the ancient Greek writers knew well. Few had traveled beyond it. Perhaps the list was a kind of tourist guide. The list of wonders has survived to this day, even though only one of the structures still stands. They are known as the Seven Wonders of the Ancient World.

THE GREAT PYRAMID AT GIZA

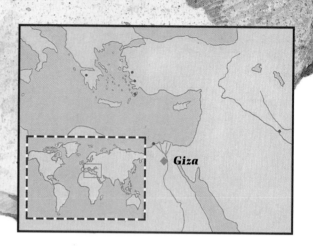

Giza

This vast Egyptian pyramid is the oldest of the Seven Wonders of the Ancient World. It is also the only wonder still standing today. When it was built, the Great Pyramid was the tallest structure in the world. And it probably held that record for almost 4,000 years.

A ROYAL TOMB

The Great Pyramid was built as a tomb for Khufu, known to the Greeks as Cheops. He was one of the pharaohs, or kings of ancient Egypt, and his tomb was finished about 2580 B.C.

Later two more pyramids were built at Giza, for Khufu's son and grandson, as well as smaller pyramids for their queens. Khufu's pyramid is the farthest away in this picture and is the biggest. His son's pyramid is in the middle and looks taller because it stands on higher ground.

Khafre, son of Khufu. In this statue, he is guarded by the god Horus, who has taken the shape of a falcon.

BUILDING THE PYRAMID

The pyramids stand in an ancient cemetery at Giza, on the opposite bank of the Nile River from Cairo, the capital of modern Egypt. Some archaeologists think that it may have taken 100,000 men over 20 years to build the Great Pyramid. It was made from more than 2 million stone blocks, each weighing 2.75 tons or more. The workers hauled these into place using ramps, rollers, and levers and then fit them together without using mortar.

The pyramids were built in layers of stone blocks. Each layer was a bit smaller than the one before. The stones were probably dragged up a huge earth ramp, which was made higher for each layer.

GLEAMING LIMESTONE

When the main structure was complete, it looked like a series of steps. These were then filled in with blocks of white limestone, which were cut to give a smooth, gleaming surface. They fit so closely that a knife blade could not be pushed between the blocks on the outside. When this was finished, the Great Pyramid rose to a height of 482 feet. Its top is now missing, and today only Khufu's son's pyramid has any limestone covering left at the top. The Great Pyramid measures 755 feet along each side of its base. It covers an area larger than 10 football fields.

In contrast to his huge pyramid, a tiny ivory statue is the only known figure of Khufu.

BURYING THE PHARAOH

The ancient Egyptians believed that when a person died, the body had to be looked after, so that the spirit could live on after death. They took out the internal organs, packed the body with salts, and wrapped it in linen bandages. This preserved the body as a mummy. The mummy was then buried with clothes, food, jewelry, and other things that would be useful in the afterlife. Khufu's mummified body was placed in a burial chamber deep inside his pyramid.

THE HANGING GARDENS
OF BABYLON

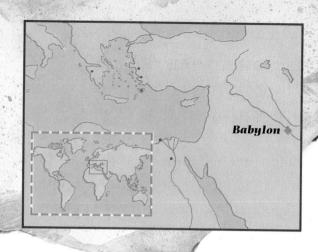

Babylon

The Hanging Gardens were one of the most famous features of the ancient city of Babylon. But although archaeologists have found ruins that may be from the gardens, they cannot be sure. We only know that they existed because people saw them and wrote about them.

NEBUCHADNEZZAR AND AMYTIS

Greek and Roman writers tell us that the gardens were built about 600 B.C. on the orders of Nebuchadnezzar II, King of Babylon. This great city lay on the banks of the Euphrates River, south of present-day Baghdad, the capital of modern Iraq. One story says that the king had the gardens built for his homesick young wife, Amytis, to remind her of her home in the mountains of Persia.

Left: A clay tablet showing an ancient map of the world, as it was known at that time. Babylon was first settled around 3000 B.C. From about 2000 B.C., the Babylonians established a large and powerful empire.

Right: Lions on the Processional Way leading to the area in Babylon where the Hanging Gardens may have been. At the New Year festival, people walked along the Way from the Temple of Marduk, carrying a statue of this main god.

WATERED TERRACES

The Hanging Gardens were probably built near the river, overlooking Babylon's city walls. They were made up of terraces, and the top terrace may have been up to 131 feet above the ground. Nebuchadnezzar had the gardens planted with every kind of tree and plant that can be imagined. These were brought from all over the empire by ox cart and river barge. Figs, almonds, walnut trees, pomegranates, rock roses, water lilies, and incense bushes may all have grown in the garden.

The success of the gardens must have depended on a good watering system, using water drawn from the Euphrates. The water may have been lifted to the top terrace by a chain of buckets driven by slaves on a treadmill. It could then run down into the streams and waterfalls in the gardens and keep the soil wet.

THE TEMPLE OF
ARTEMIS AT EPHESUS

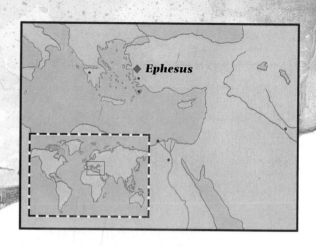

Croesus was the last king of Lydia, a region of ancient Asia Minor that is part of present-day Turkey. He was famous for his great wealth, and in 560 B.C. he had a magnificent temple built at Ephesus. This city had been founded thousands of years before. According to legend, the founders were Amazons, a race of women warriors.

This coin was produced in Ephesus in the third century A.D. It shows how the temple looked.

THE BIGGEST MARBLE TEMPLE

Croesus decided to build the temple in honor of the goddess of the moon and protector of animals and young girls. The Greeks called her Artemis; the Romans called her Diana. The temple was made of limestone and marble, which workmen quarried in the nearby hills.

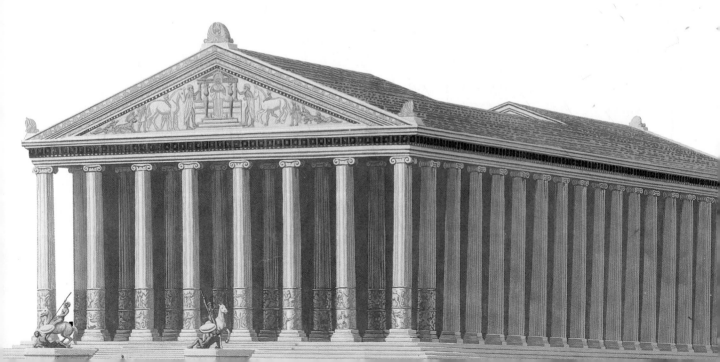

The main structure of the temple was supported by about 120 marble columns. Each vast column was 66 feet high. The huge blocks that made up the columns had to be hauled into place by pulleys and were held together by metal pegs. Once the roof had been put on, artists completed the building with beautiful sculptures and decorations. A statue of Artemis stood in the middle of the temple.

This was one of the largest temples of the classical world, much bigger than the Parthenon, which was built later at Athens. The platform on which it was built was 430 feet long and 259 feet wide.

HEROSTRATUS AND ALEXANDER

Two hundred years later, in 356 B.C., the temple was burned to the ground. The fire was started by a man called Herostratus, who simply wanted to make himself famous. Strangely, the temple was destroyed on the very day that Alexander the Great was born. Some years later Alexander visited Ephesus and gave orders for the temple to be rebuilt on the same site.

FINAL DESTRUCTION

Alexander's temple survived until the third century A.D. Gradually the harbor at Ephesus silted up, and the town became less important. The temple was plundered by Goths and later swamped by floods. All that is left of the temple at Ephesus today are a few foundation blocks and a single rebuilt column.

Only a single column of the temple stands today. This was rebuilt from the ruins in recent years. But there are many other remains of the once great city—a ruined theater, a library, baths, and many other buildings.

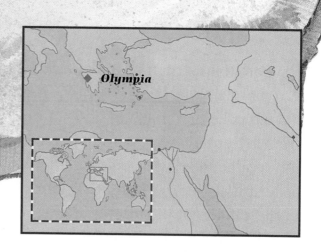

Olympia

Almost 3,000 years ago, Olympia was an important religious center in southwest Greece. The ancient Greeks worshiped Zeus, king of the gods, and held regular festivals there in his honor. These included athletic competitions. The first Olympic Games, as they came to be known, were probably held in 776 B.C. For over 1,100 years the games then took place every four years. They were very important, and all wars had to stop to allow competitors and spectators to attend the games.

THE TEMPLE OF ZEUS

In the fifth century B.C., the citizens of Olympia decided to build a temple to Zeus. A magnificent structure was put up between the years 466 and 456 B.C. It was built with huge stone blocks surrounded by massive columns. For some years after it was finished, the temple had no proper statue of Zeus, and it was soon decided that this was needed. A famous sculptor from Athens was chosen to make the statue.

BUILDING THE STATUE

The sculptor's name was Phidias, and in Athens he had already made two magnificent statues of the goddess Athena. At Olympia, Phidias and his workmen first put up a wooden framework, to act as a skeleton for Zeus. They then covered this with plates of ivory for the god's skin and sheets of gold for his clothing. The workers covered up where they joined so that the finished statue looked like a solid figure.

HIGH ABOVE THE GROUND

Zeus was seated on a throne inlaid with ebony and precious stones. The finished statue was 43 feet high and reached almost to the ceiling of the temple. It gave the impression that if Zeus stood up, he would lift off the roof. Viewing platforms were built along the walls so that people could climb up and see the god's face. When it was completed around 435 B.C., the statue stood as one of the world's greatest wonders for the next 800 years.

MOVING THE STATUE

About A.D. 40, the Roman emperor Caligula wanted to have the statue moved to Rome. Workers were sent to collect it, but according to legend the statue let out such a bellow of laughter that the workers fled. Then in A.D. 391, with the rise of Christianity, the Romans banned the Olympic Games and closed the Greek temples. Some years later the statue of Zeus was shipped to Constantinople. In A.D. 462 the palace containing the statue was destroyed by fire, leaving nothing behind.

The whole area of Olympia was shaken by earthquakes in the sixth century. The temple and stadium were destroyed by landslides and floods, and the remains were covered by mud. This helped to preserve certain parts of Olympia for over a thousand years. In recent times archaeologists have uncovered the site. Now people can walk around the ruins of the temple and see where the magnificent statue of Zeus once stood. The statue itself is gone forever.

A plaque from a sculptured frieze that ran around the walls of the temple. The frieze shows the 12 labors of Hercules. Athena looks on, as Atlas offers golden apples. Hercules, in the middle, is holding up the world on his shoulders. Hercules and Athena were both children of Zeus.

THE MAUSOLEUM AT HALICARNASSUS

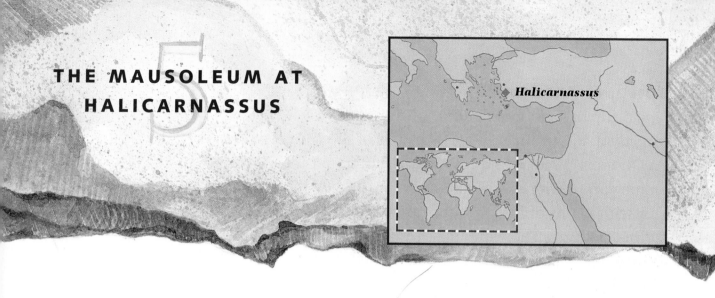

Halicarnassus

Mausolus was ruler of Caria, part of the Persian Empire, from 377 to 353 B.C. The region's capital was Halicarnassus, which is now a tourist center in modern Turkey, called Bodrum. Mausolus had followed his father as ruler and as provincial governor to the King of Persia. But he broke free of the Persians and acted as an independent king.

THE ORIGINAL MAUSOLEUM

As Mausolus grew more powerful, he planned a tomb for himself and his queen, Artemisia. But this was to be no ordinary tomb. Mausolus wanted a magnificent monument that would remind the world of his wealth and power long after he had died.

Mausolus died before his tomb was finished, but his widow supervised the building until it was complete, in about 350 B.C. It was called the Mausoleum, after the king, and this word is still used for any large, stately tomb.

A chariot horse that stood at the top of the building. Its bridle is made of bronze.

LIONS GUARD THE CHAMBER

The royal couple's ashes were put in golden caskets in a burial chamber at the base of the building. A row of stone lions guarded the chamber. Above the solid stone base was a structure that looked like a Greek temple, surrounded by columns and statues. At the top of the building was a stepped pyramid. This was crowned, 141 feet above the ground, by the statue of a horse-drawn chariot. Statues of the king and queen probably rode in it.

DESTROYED BY EARTHQUAKE

Eighteen hundred years later an earthquake shook the Mausoleum to the ground. In 1489 the Christian Knights of St. John began using its stones to build a castle nearby. They built some of their castle walls from blocks of green stone that had formed the main part of the Mausoleum. Some years later the knights discovered the burial chamber of Mausolus and Artemisia. But when they left the chamber unguarded overnight, it was raided by pirates for its gold and other precious contents.

STATUES EXCAVATED

Another 300 years passed before archaeologists began to excavate the site. They dug up parts of the base of the Mausoleum, as well as the statues and sculptures that had not been broken up or stolen. Among these were the huge statues that archaeologists believe show the king and queen. In 1857 these were taken to the British Museum in London, where they can still be seen. There have been further excavations in recent years, and today there are just a few stones left at the site in Bodrum.

A marble head from a statue of Apollo, Greek god of music, archery, and healing, and twin brother of Artemis. This statue stood at the tomb.

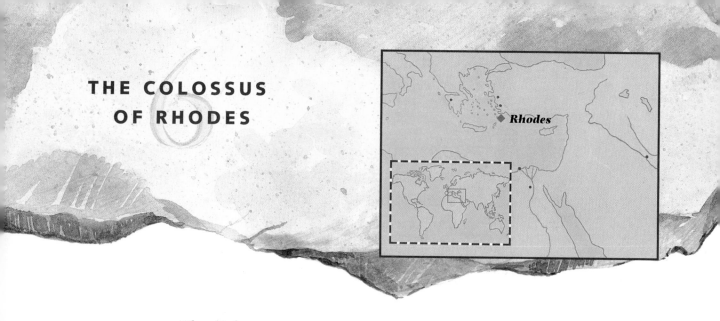

THE COLOSSUS OF RHODES

The Colossus was a giant statue that stood at the city-port of Rhodes, in the Aegean Sea off present-day Turkey. In ancient times the people of Rhodes wanted to be independent traders. They tried to stay out of other people's wars, but they were conquered many times.

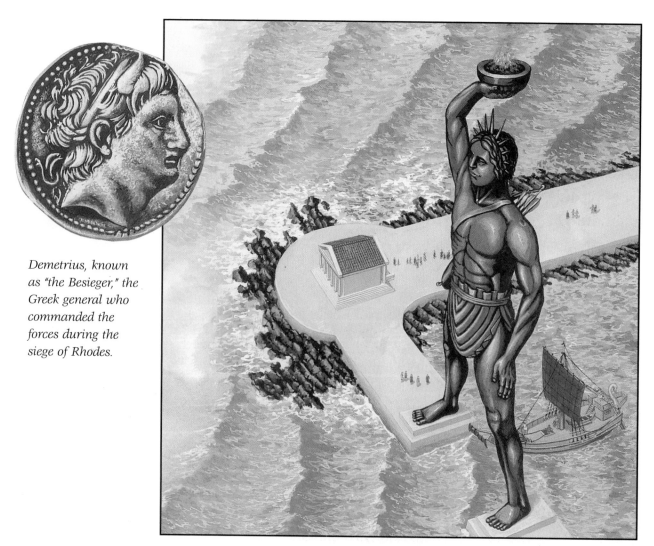

Demetrius, known as "the Besieger," the Greek general who commanded the forces during the siege of Rhodes.

HELIOS, THE SUN GOD

At the end of the fourth century B.C., the people of Rhodes wanted to celebrate a victory. They had just successfully defended their city, on the island of Rhodes, against a year-long siege by Greek soldiers. The Greeks, realizing they could not win, had even left some of their battle equipment behind. The people of Rhodes decided to sell this equipment and build a statue of Helios, their sun god, to thank him for protecting them.

Demetrius attacked Rhodes with 200 warships and 40,000 soldiers. The most famous type of Greek warship was the trireme, with three banks of rowers on each side. This modern reconstruction was built to show how the oars were arranged. Soldiers fought on the flat deck of the boat.

A BRONZE COLOSSUS

We do not know exactly what the statue looked like, or even where it stood. But we do know that it was made of bronze and was about 108 feet high. It was designed by an architect named Chares and took 12 years to build.

ACROSS THE HARBOR

The outer bronze shell was attached to an iron framework. The hollow statue was built from the ground up, and as it grew, it was filled with stones to help it stand firmly. The Colossus was finished around 280 B.C. For many centuries people believed that the Colossus towered across the entrance to Rhodes Harbor. This would have been impossible. The harbor mouth was about 1,312 feet across, and the statue was not quite so colossal. Writings suggest that it may have stood in the heart of the city, overlooking the sea and the harbor.

A COLOSSAL CRASH

In about 226 B.C., little more than 50 years after it was completed, the Colossus fell. It was toppled by an earthquake and snapped off at the knees. The people of Rhodes were told by an oracle not to rebuild the statue, and so they left it lying where it had fallen. It stayed like this for nearly 900 years, and people would travel to Rhodes just to gaze at the ruins of the fallen sun god.

In A.D. 654 a Syrian prince captured Rhodes and stripped the statue of its bronze plates. People said that he took them back to Syria on the backs of 900 camels. The bronze was sold by merchants and probably turned into coins.

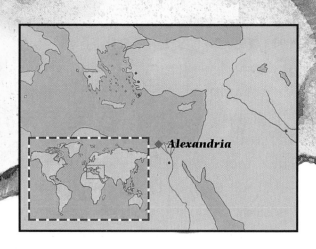

Alexandria

In the third century B.C., a lighthouse was built to guide ships safely past the reefs into the harbor of Alexandria. It did this by reflecting the flames of a fire at night, and with a column of smoke by day. This was the world's first lighthouse, and it stood for 1,500 years.

ISLAND AND LIGHTHOUSE

The lighthouse was built on the small island of Pharos, in the Mediterranean Sea, off the city of Alexandria. This busy port was founded by Alexander the Great during his visit to Egypt. The building was named after the island. It must have taken about 20 years to build and was completed about 280 B.C., during the reign of the Egyptian king Ptolemy II.

THREE TOWERS

The Pharos lighthouse was made up of three marble towers, built on a base of massive stone blocks. The first tower was rectangular and filled with rooms where workers and soldiers lived. On top of that was a smaller, eight-sided tower, with a spiral ramp leading up to the top tower.

A GUIDING LIGHT

The top tower was shaped like a cylinder, and in it burned the fire that guided boats safely into the harbor. Standing on the top tower was a statue of the sun god, Helios. The overall height of the Pharos was about 384 feet.

POLISHED BRONZE MIRROR

Huge amounts of fuel were needed to keep the fire alight. Wood was carried up the spiral ramp on carts pulled by horses or mules. Sheets of bronze stood behind the fire and reflected its light out to sea. Ships up to 31 miles away could see this beacon. By the twelfth century A.D., the harbor at Alexandria had become so clogged with mud that it could no longer be used by ships. The lighthouse fell into disrepair. The sheets of bronze that had acted as mirrors were probably melted down for coins.

In the fourteenth century the Pharos was destroyed by an earthquake. Some years later Muslims used the ruins to build a military fort. The fort has been rebuilt since that time and still stands on the site of the world's first lighthouse.

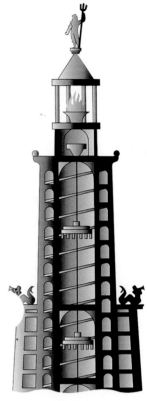

This drawing suggests how the Pharos may have looked inside. It shows the fire in the top section and the ramp winding its way upward.

Alexandria was a very important city in Roman times. This pillar, called Pompey's Pillar, and a sphinx are nearly all that remain from that period.

Roman coins give us an idea of what the Pharos looked like. Here a ship sails past the lighthouse. Today the word pharos *means "lighthouse" in many languages.*

MORE WONDERS

Reg Cox and Neil Morris have written other books about the wonders of the world, including The Seven Wonders of the Modern World *and* The Seven Wonders of the Natural World. *The places described below are from* The Seven Wonders of the Historic World. *Which of these wonders do you know something about? Which would you like to learn about?*

(1) CAVE OF TEN THOUSAND BUDDHAS • Around A.D. 600, thousands of tiny statues of the Buddha were carved into the walls of this cave temple, one of a series of cave temples located along the Yishui River in eastern China.

Great Zimbabwe

(2) GREAT ZIMBABWE • Huge stone ruins in the modern African country of Zimbabwe mark what was once the center of a great African empire that lasted for hundreds of years, until the 1600s.

(3) ANGKOR WAT • This huge temple—almost one square mile—was the capital of the once-great Khmer empire in what is now Cambodia. It was attacked and left in ruins in 1431.

Angkor Wat

(4) KRAK DES CHEVALIERS • This medieval castle, whose name means "Castle of the Knights," was built on a mountaintop in Syria by Christian crusaders after they captured a Muslim stronghold on this spot.

(5) SALISBURY CATHEDRAL • Built between 1220 and 1315, this cathedral in Salisbury, England, has the tallest spire in England.

Alhambra

(6) ALHAMBRA • Built in the 700s by invading Arab and Berber Muslims from North Africa, this citadel, or stronghold, in Granada, Spain, was later captured and rebuilt by Christians.

(7) TENOCHTITLÁN • The ruins of this once-great city, center of the powerful Aztec empire for almost 200 years, now lie beneath modern Mexico City.

Reader Response

Open for Discussion

Which of these Seven Wonders of the Ancient World would you have liked to visit? Why?

Comprehension Check

1. What makes each of these ancient structures a "wonder"? Use details from the selection in your answer.

2. Describe the most unusual or striking feature of each of the Seven Wonders.

3. Think about each structure's purpose or function. What does that purpose or function tell you about the beliefs and practices of these ancient peoples? Use specific details in your answer.

4. Look back at the selection. Notice how the information is organized and the order in which it is presented. Describe the **text structure** of this selection. (Text Structure)

5. Suppose you had come across the same information in several different books and Internet sites. How might you have organized it differently? Describe a different **text structure** that might be used to present this information. (Text Structure)

Test Prep

Look Back and Write

How is the drawing of the Colossus of Rhodes on page 440 different from what people today know about the statue's actual size and location? Use details from pages 440–441 in your answer.

The Great Pyramids

by George Hart

THE FIRST PYRAMID was built as the burial place of King Djoser c. 2630 B.C. by his gifted architect Imhotep. It rose in six stages, and is called the Step Pyramid. It was supposed to represent a gigantic stairway for the king to climb to join the sun god in the sky. The idea of this pyramid was to re-create the mound that had emerged out of the watery ground at the beginning of time, on which the sun god stood and brought the other gods and goddesses into being.

CLIMBERS
Today there is a law in Egypt forbidding visitors from climbing the Great Pyramid. But in the 19th century many people felt the urge to climb the pyramid and admire the view below.

GRAND GALLERY
This gallery, 154 ft (47 m) long and 28 ft (8.5 m) high, rises toward the burial chamber. It has an elaborate stone roof. After the burial, great blocks of granite were slid down the gallery to seal off the burial chamber.

Small pyramids, the burial places of the three chief wives of Khufu

Mortuary temple where offerings could be made

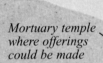

Causeway connecting pyramid to temple in Nile valley

THE GREAT PYRAMID
Built for King Khufu about 4,500 years ago, the Great Pyramid was one of the Seven Wonders of the Ancient World. It contains over 2.3 million limestone blocks ranging from 2.5 to 15 tons. The builders may have had levers to help get the stones into place, but they had no pulleys or other machinery. The whole pyramid probably took about 20 years to build. There was a standing work force of craftsmen and laborers, which swelled every year for three months when the Nile flooded and the field workers were sent on national service to help with the construction work. The pyramids were just one part of the funerary complex devoted to the pharaoh's afterlife. There was also a mortuary temple for cult offerings and a causeway leading to the valley temple—the place where the king's body was received after its last journey along the Nile River.

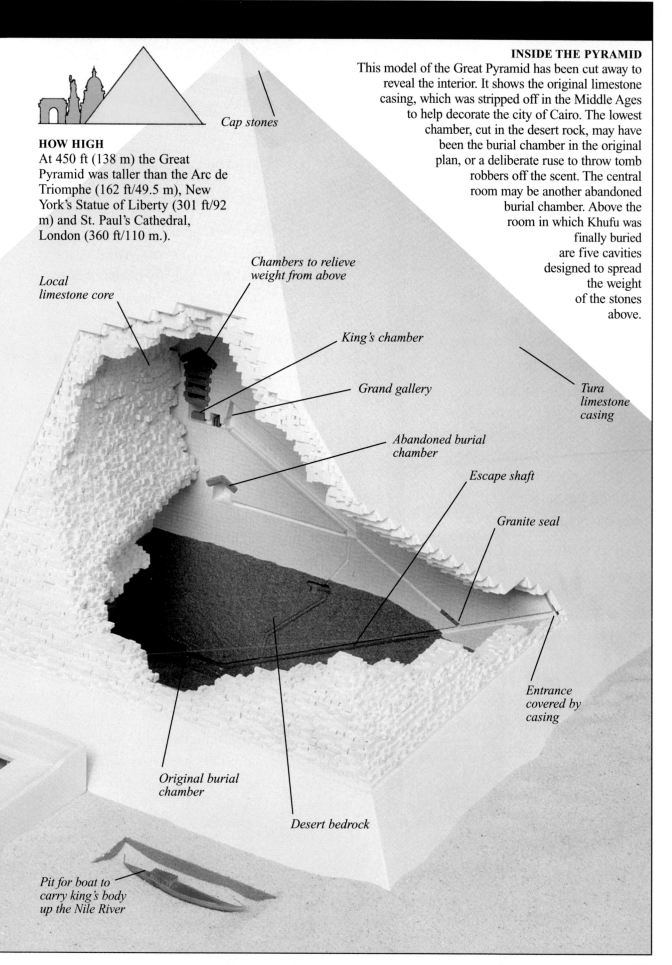

Cap stones

HOW HIGH
At 450 ft (138 m) the Great Pyramid was taller than the Arc de Triomphe (162 ft/49.5 m), New York's Statue of Liberty (301 ft/92 m) and St. Paul's Cathedral, London (360 ft/110 m.).

Local limestone core

Chambers to relieve weight from above

King's chamber

Grand gallery

Abandoned burial chamber

Escape shaft

Granite seal

Entrance covered by casing

Original burial chamber

Desert bedrock

Pit for boat to carry king's body up the Nile River

INSIDE THE PYRAMID
This model of the Great Pyramid has been cut away to reveal the interior. It shows the original limestone casing, which was stripped off in the Middle Ages to help decorate the city of Cairo. The lowest chamber, cut in the desert rock, may have been the burial chamber in the original plan, or a deliberate ruse to throw tomb robbers off the scent. The central room may be another abandoned burial chamber. Above the room in which Khufu was finally buried are five cavities designed to spread the weight of the stones above.

Tura limestone casing

Skill Lesson

Author's Purpose

- **Author's purpose** refers to an author's reason or reasons for writing.

- Four common purposes for writing are to inform, to persuade, to entertain, and to express. Often an author has more than one purpose for writing.

- Understanding an author's purpose helps you know how slowly or quickly to read and how closely to examine the author's ideas. It also helps explain the author's choice of words and writing style.

Read "The Tortoise in the Tree" from *The Mean Hyena: A Folktale from Malawi* retold by Judy Sierra.

Talk About It

1. Do you think the author's purpose in this story is to persuade, to entertain, or both? Explain.

2. In your opinion, does the author succeed in meeting her purpose? Tell why or why not.

The Tortoise in the Tree
retold by Judy Sierra

Fisi, the trouble-making hyena, has stuck Kamba, the tortoise, in a tree. Unable to free himself, Kamba offers to paint beautiful new coats for the animals of the jungle.

"Coats! New coats! Beautiful new coats! Come and get your beauty!" Animals lined up beneath the tree to receive new colors and designs from the tortoise.

Finally, night-skulking Fisi heard about Kamba's wonderful coat painting. The hyena was quite proud of his smooth, brown coat, but it seemed dull compared to Mbanda's [the zebra's] and Nyalugwe's [the leopard's]. So he went to see the tortoise in the tree.

"Eh! Give me my beauty!" he demanded.

"First, help me get down from here," said the tortoise.

The hyena took the tortoise in his mouth and gently lowered him to the ground.

"Now, bring sticky tree gum," said the tortoise. "The more the better."

Fisi soon returned with a bowl of tree gum. The tortoise cheerfully dabbed globs and splots of gum onto the hyena's coat.

"Am I beautiful?" asked the hyena when the tortoise had finished.

"You have the coat you deserve," the tortoise answered, nodding with satisfaction.

"Look at me! Look at me!" the hyena yipped as he ran through the tall, dry grass. The grass stuck to his coat, but the hyena didn't notice. Then the gum began to itch. The hyena rolled in the dirt. Twigs and burrs and pebbles stuck to him. "Look at me! Look at me!" he yelped.

When he was tired of running, the hyena pranced into the village to show off his new coat. But instead of admiring him, people began to laugh.

"Eh? Am I not beautiful? Like Mbanda? Like Nyalugwe?" he asked. Then he turned his head, and for the first time, he saw his new coat. He looked as beautiful as the garbage heap.

"Ha, ha, ha!" laughed the hyena. "I look really funny, don't I? Eh? Eh? I was trying to make you laugh. Now, I'll go wash this off. Ha, ha, ha!"

But Fisi couldn't wash the gum off his fur. He chewed and chewed at it until the sticky gum filled his teeth. It was months before all the gum was gone. The hyena's fur, which had once been so smooth and shiny, stood up in rough patches on his back.

So, you see, don't play a trick on someone unless you want an even bigger trick played on you.

LOOK AHEAD

The GOLD COIN

As you read *The Gold Coin*, think about the author's purpose for writing and whether or not that purpose is met.

Vocabulary

Words to Know

distressed	insistent	stunned
impatience	recovery	

Many words have more than one meaning. To decide which meaning of a word is being used, look for clues in the surrounding sentences or the paragraph.

Read this paragraph. Decide whether *stunned* means "knocked unconscious" or "overwhelmed and shocked."

Tender Love and Care

Sara was distressed. Missing school was bad enough, but missing rehearsals for the class play was worse. She told her father that she didn't have time to be sick, but he was insistent. "You have a fever, and you have to rest," he said. "If I take care of you, you'll be acting soon." Sara was stunned. What if she lost the role? Would the play go on without her? She was too weak to argue. One day passed, then another. Sara lost hope for a quick recovery. Her impatience grew with every passing hour. Then on the third day, the fever broke, and she felt full of energy. Her father had been right, Sara thought. When the play went on, she would be in it.

Talk About It

Tell a friend about the last time you were sick. Who helped you recover? Use some vocabulary words.

The
GOLD COIN

by Alma Flor Ada · illustrated by Neil Waldman

Juan had been a thief for many years. Because he did his stealing by night, his skin had become pale and sickly. Because he spent his time either hiding or sneaking about, his body had become shriveled and bent. And because he had neither friend nor relative to make him smile, his face was always twisted into an angry frown.

One night, drawn by a light shining through the trees, Juan came upon a hut. He crept up to the door and through a crack saw an old woman sitting at a plain, wooden table.

What was that shining in her hand? Juan wondered. He could not believe his eyes: It was a gold coin. Then he heard the woman say to herself, "I must be the richest person in the world."

Juan decided instantly that all the woman's gold must be his. He thought that the easiest thing to do was to watch until the woman left. Juan hid in the bushes and huddled under his poncho, waiting for the right moment to enter the hut.

Juan was half asleep when he heard knocking at the door and the sound of insistent voices. A few minutes later, he saw the woman, wrapped in a black cloak, leave the hut with two men at her side.

Here's my chance! Juan thought. And, forcing open a window, he climbed into the empty hut.

He looked about eagerly for the gold. He looked under the bed. It wasn't there. He looked in the cupboard. It wasn't there, either. Where could it be? Close to despair, Juan tore away some beams supporting the thatch roof.

Finally, he gave up. There was simply no gold in the hut.

All I can do, he thought, is to find the old woman and make her tell me where she's hidden it.

So he set out along the path that she and her two companions had taken.

It was daylight by the time Juan reached the river. The countryside had been deserted, but here, along the riverbank, were two huts. Nearby, a man and his son were hard at work, hoeing potatoes.

It had been a long, long time since Juan had spoken to another human being. Yet his desire to find the woman was so strong that he went up to the farmers and asked, in a hoarse, raspy voice, "Have you seen a short, gray-haired woman, wearing a black cloak?"

"Oh, you must be looking for Doña Josefa," the young boy said. "Yes, we've seen her. We went to fetch her this morning, because my grandfather had another attack of—"

"Where is she now?" Juan broke in.

"She is long gone," said the father with a smile. "Some people from across the river came looking for her, because someone in their family is sick."

"How can I get across the river?" Juan asked anxiously.

"Only by boat," the boy answered. "We'll row you across later, if you'd like." Then turning back to his work, he added, "But first we must finish digging up the potatoes."

The thief muttered, "Thanks." But he quickly grew impatient. He grabbed a hoe and began to help the pair of farmers. The sooner we finish, the sooner we'll get across the river, he thought. And the sooner I'll get to my gold!

It was dusk when they finally laid down their hoes. The soil had been turned, and the wicker baskets were brimming with potatoes.

"Now can you row me across?" Juan asked the father anxiously.

"Certainly," the man said. "But let's eat supper first."

Juan had forgotten the taste of a home-cooked meal and the pleasure that comes from sharing it with others. As he sopped up the last of the stew with a chunk of dark bread, memories of other meals came back to him from far away and long ago.

By the light of the moon, father and son guided their boat across the river.

"What a wonderful healer Doña Josefa is!" the boy told Juan. "All she had to do to make Abuelo better was give him a cup of her special tea."

"Yes, and not only that," his father added, "she brought him a gold coin."

Juan was stunned. It was one thing for Doña Josefa to go around helping people. But how could she go around handing out gold coins—*his gold coins?*

When the threesome finally reached the other side of the river, they saw a young man sitting outside his hut.

"This fellow is looking for Doña Josefa," the father said, pointing to Juan.

"Oh, she left some time ago," the young man said.

"Where to?" Juan asked tensely.

"Over to the other side of the mountain," the young man replied, pointing to the vague outline of mountains in the night sky.

"How did she get there?" Juan asked, trying to hide his impatience.

"By horse," the young man answered. "They came on horseback to get her because someone had broken his leg."

"Well, then, I need a horse too," Juan said urgently.

"Tomorrow," the young man replied softly. "Perhaps I can take you tomorrow, maybe the next day. First I must finish harvesting the corn."

So Juan spent the next day in the fields, bathed in sweat from sunup to sundown.

Yet each ear of corn that he picked seemed to bring him closer to his treasure. And later that evening, when he helped the young man husk several ears so they could boil them for supper, the yellow kernels glittered like gold coins.

While they were eating, Juan thought about Doña Josefa. Why, he wondered, would someone who said she was the world's richest woman spend her time taking care of every sick person for miles around?

The following day, the two set off at dawn. Juan could not recall when he last had noticed the beauty of the sunrise. He felt strangely moved by the sight of the mountains, barely lit by the faint rays of the morning sun.

As they neared the foothills, the young man said, "I'm not surprised you're looking for Doña Josefa. The whole countryside needs her. I went for her because my wife had been running a high fever. In no time at all, Doña Josefa had her on the road to recovery. And what's more, my friend, she brought her a gold coin!"

Juan groaned inwardly. To think that someone could hand out gold so freely! What a strange woman Doña Josefa is, Juan thought. Not only is she willing to help one person after another, but she doesn't mind traveling all over the countryside to do it!

"Well, my friend," said the young man finally, "this is where I must leave you. But you don't have far to walk. See that house over there? It belongs to the man who broke his leg."

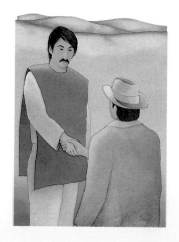

The young man stretched out his hand to say good-bye. Juan stared at it for a moment. It had been a long, long time since the thief had shaken hands with anyone. Slowly, he pulled out a hand from under his poncho. When his companion grasped it firmly in his own, Juan felt suddenly warmed, as if by the rays of the sun.

But after he thanked the young man, Juan ran down the road. He was still eager to catch up with Doña Josefa. When he reached the house, a woman and a child were stepping down from a wagon.

"Have you seen Doña Josefa?" Juan asked.

"We've just taken her to Don Teodosio's," the woman said. "His wife is sick, you know—"

"How do I get there?" Juan broke in. "I've got to see her."

"It's too far to walk," the woman said amiably. "If you'd like, I'll take you there tomorrow. But first I must gather my squash and beans."

So Juan spent yet another long day in the fields. Working beneath the summer sun, Juan noticed that his skin had begun to tan. And although he had to stoop down to pick the squash, he found that he could now stretch his body. His back had begun to straighten too.

Later, when the little girl took him by the hand to show him a family of rabbits burrowed under a fallen tree, Juan's face broke into a smile. It had been a long, long time since Juan had smiled.

Yet his thoughts kept coming back to the gold.

The following day, the wagon carrying Juan and the woman lumbered along a road lined with coffee fields.

The woman said, "I don't know what we would have done without Doña Josefa. I sent my daughter to our neighbor's house, who then brought Doña Josefa on horseback. She set my husband's leg and then showed me how to brew a special tea to lessen the pain."

Getting no reply, she went on. "And, as if that weren't enough, she brought him a gold coin. Can you imagine such a thing?"

Juan could only sigh. No doubt about it, he thought, Doña Josefa is someone special. But Juan didn't know whether to be happy that Doña Josefa had so much gold she could freely hand it out, or angry for her having already given so much of it away.

When they finally reached Don Teodosio's house, Doña Josefa was already gone. But here, too, there was work that needed to be done . . .

Juan stayed to help with the coffee harvest. As he picked the red berries, he gazed up from time to time at the trees that grew, row upon row, along the hillsides. What a calm, peaceful place this is! he thought.

The next morning, Juan was up at daybreak. Bathed in the soft, dawn light, the mountains seemed to smile at him. When Don Teodosio offered him a lift on horseback, Juan found it difficult to have to say good-bye.

"What a good woman Doña Josefa is!" Don Teodosio said, as they rode down the hill toward the sugarcane fields. "The minute she heard about my wife being sick, she came with her special herbs. And as if that weren't enough, she brought my wife a gold coin!"

In the stifling heat, the kind that often signals the approach of a storm, Juan simply sighed and mopped his brow. The pair continued riding for several hours in silence.

Juan then realized he was back in familiar territory, for they were now on the stretch of road he had traveled only a week ago— though how much longer it now seemed to him. He jumped off Don Teodosio's horse and broke into a run.

This time the gold would not escape him! But he had to move quickly, so he could find shelter before the storm broke.

Out of breath, Juan finally reached Doña Josefa's hut. She was standing by the door, shaking her head slowly as she surveyed the ransacked house.

"So I've caught up with you at last!" Juan shouted, startling the old woman. "Where's the gold?"

"The gold coin?" Doña Josefa said, surprised and looking at Juan intently. "Have you come for the gold coin? I've been trying hard to give it to someone who might need it," Doña Josefa said. "First to an old man who had just gotten over a bad attack. Then to a young woman who had been running a fever. Then to a man with a broken leg. And finally to Don Teodosio's wife. But none of them would take it. They all said, 'Keep it. There must be someone who needs it more.'"

Juan did not say a word.

"You must be the one who needs it," Doña Josefa said.

She took the coin out of her pocket and handed it to him. Juan stared at the coin, speechless.

At that moment a young girl appeared, her long braid bouncing as she ran. "Hurry, Doña Josefa, please!" she said breathlessly. "My mother is all alone, and the baby is due any minute."

"Of course, dear," Doña Josefa replied. But as she glanced up at the sky, she saw nothing but black clouds. The storm was nearly upon them. Dona Josefa sighed deeply.

"But how can I leave now? Look at my house! I don't know what has happened to the roof. The storm will wash the whole place away!"

And there was a deep sadness in her voice.

Juan took in the child's frightened eyes, Doña Josefa's sad, distressed face, and the ransacked hut.

"Go ahead, Doña Josefa," he said. "Don't worry about your house. I'll see that the roof is back in shape, good as new."

The woman nodded gratefully, drew her cloak about her shoulders, and took the child by the hand. As she turned to leave, Juan held out his hand.

"Here, take this," he said, giving her the gold coin. "I'm sure the newborn will need it more than I."

About the Author
ALMA FLOR ADA

As a schoolgirl, Alma Flor Ada made a pact with herself. "I made a firm commitment while in the fourth grade," she says, "to devote my life to producing schoolbooks that would be fun—and since then I am having a lot of fun doing just that." Ms. Ada was born in Cuba and came to the United States after studying in Peru. In this country, she has worked to promote bilingualism, the ability to speak and understand more than one language. Often her books are published in both English and Spanish. Her daughter helps with many of the translations. Ms. Ada's story *The Gold Coin* was awarded the Christopher Award and was named a Notable Children's Trade Book. Other books by Ms. Ada that you might enjoy include *Where the Flame Trees Bloom* and *The Rooster Who Went to His Uncle's Wedding*.

About the Illustrator
NEIL WALDMAN

"I was raised in a house where all the arts were encouraged," Neil Waldman says. "I sensed as a child that finger paints and coloring books were more than just fun. They were important tools that led to a road of joy, discovery, and fulfillment." Mr. Waldman started working as an illustrator on various projects not related to books. He designed postage stamps and record covers (which won him a Grammy nomination) and won a competition for designing a United Nations poster. It took some convincing by an editor to persuade Mr. Waldman to illustrate his first children's book. Once he finished the art, however, he knew that he had found his life's work. He was awarded the Washington Irving Award for illustration for that book, *Bring Back the Deer,* and for *The Highwayman*.

Reader Response

Open for Discussion

What do you think the gold coin represents?

Comprehension Check

1. Why does Juan follow Doña Josefa across the river, over the mountains, and finally back home again? Point out details from the story to support your answer.

2. Everyone has something to say about Doña Josefa. Describe her character, based on what others say about her.

3. At the end of the story, Juan gives back the gold he has tried so hard to get. Why do you think he does this? Use story details to support your answer.

4. Do you think the **author's purpose** in writing *The Gold Coin* was to inform, to persuade, to entertain, to express, or a combination of these? Explain your answer with story details. (Author's Purpose)

5. As Juan searches for Doña Josefa, he just misses her not once, but four times. What do you think was the **author's purpose** for including so many similar episodes? (Author's Purpose)

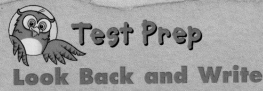

Test Prep

Look Back and Write

What are some good things that Juan does before returning the gold coin and why does he do them? Use details from pages 453–455 in your answer.

Literature Connection

Test Prep

How to Read a Tall Tale

1. Preview

- Most tall tales tell about characters who can perform amazing feats that other characters could never do. They use exaggeration to create characters who are bigger than life.

- Look over the pictures and read the first paragraph. What is exaggerated about this character?

2. Read and Make Sketches

- Read the tall tale and draw quick sketches of different scenes from the story.

- Label your sketches to explain details.

3. Think and Connect

Think about Juan in "The Gold Coin." Then look over your sketches on "Pecos Bill and the Cyclone."

Look carefully at the drawings of Juan on page 453 and Pecos Bill on page 463. How do these drawings and the sketches you made help show the differences between the two characters?

PECOS BILL
AND THE CYCLONE

from *American Tall Tales* by Mary Pope Osborne

Once Bill settled down with the gang, his true genius revealed itself. With his gang's help, he put together the biggest ranch in the Southwest. He used New Mexico as a corral and Arizona as a pasture. He invented tarantulas and scorpions as practical jokes. He also invented roping. Some say his rope was exactly as long as the equator; others argue it was two feet shorter.

Things were going fine for Bill until Texas began to suffer the worst drought in its history. It was so dry that all the rivers turned as powdery as biscuit flour. The parched grass was catching fire everywhere. For a while Bill and his gang managed to lasso water from the Rio Grande. When that river dried up, they lassoed water from the Gulf of Mexico.

No matter what he did, though, Bill couldn't get enough water to stay ahead of the drought. All his horses and cows were starting to dry up and blow away like balls of tumbleweed. It was horrible.

Just when the end seemed near, the sky turned to a deep shade of purple. From the distant mountains came a terrible roar. The cattle began to stampede, and a huge black funnel of a cyclone appeared, heading straight for Bill's ranch.

The rest of the gang shouted, "Help!" and ran.

But Pecos Bill wasn't scared in the least. "Yahoo!" he hollered, and he swung his lariat and lassoed that cyclone around its neck.

Bill held on tight as he got sucked up into the middle of the swirling cloud. He grabbed the cyclone by the ears and pulled himself onto her back. Then he let out a whoop and headed that twister across Texas.

The mighty cyclone bucked, arched, and screamed like a wild bronco. But Pecos Bill just held on with his legs and used his strong hands to wring the rain out of her wind. He wrung out rain that flooded Texas, New Mexico, and Arizona, until finally he slid off the shriveled-up funnel and fell into California. The earth sank about two hundred feet below sea level in the spot where Bill landed, creating the area known today as Death Valley.

"There. That little waterin' should hold things for a while," he said, brushing himself off.

After his cyclone ride, no horse was too wild for Pecos Bill. He soon found a young colt that was as tough as a tiger and as crazy as a streak of lightning. He named the colt Widow Maker and raised him on barbed wire and dynamite. Whenever the two rode together, they back-flipped and somersaulted all over Texas, loving every minute of it.

Ode to
Family Photographs

by Gary Soto

This is the pond, and these are my feet.
This is the rooster, and this is more of my feet.

Mamá was never good at pictures.

This is a statue of a famous general who lost an arm,
And this is me with my head cut off.

This is a trash can chained to a gate,
This is my father with his eyes half-closed.

This is a photograph of my sister
And a giraffe looking over her shoulder.

This is our car's front bumper.
This is a bird with a pretzel in its beak.
This is my brother Pedro standing on one leg on a rock,
With a smear of chocolate on his face.

Mamá sneezed when she looked
Behind the camera: the snapshots are blurry,
The angles dizzy as a spin on a merry-go-round.

But we had fun when Mamá picked up the camera.
How can I tell?
Each of us laughing hard.
Can you see? I have candy in my mouth.

"The Keystone State"

I've Got a Home IN THAT ROCK...

by Ray Patterson

I had an uncle, once, who kept a rock in his pocket—
Always did, up to the day he died.
And as far as I know, that rock is still with him,
Holding down some dust of his thighbone.

From Mississippi he'd got that rock, he'd say—
Or, sometimes, from Tennessee: a different place
    each year
He told it, how he'd snatched it up when he first
    left home—
Running, he'd say—to remind him, when times
    got hard
Enough to make him homesick, what home was
    really like.

My Moccasins Have Not Walked

by Duke Redbird

My moccasins have not walked
Among the giant forest trees

My leggings have not brushed
Against the fern and berry bush

My medicine pouch has not been filled
with roots and herbs and sweetgrass

My hands have not fondled the spotted fawn
My eyes have not beheld
The golden rainbow of the north

My hair has not been adorned
With the eagle feather

Yet
My dreams are dreams of these
My heart is one with them
The scent of them caresses my soul

Seeds

by Javaka Steptoe

You drew pictures of life
with your words.
I listened and ate those words you said
to grow up strong.
Like the trees, I grew,
branches, leaves, flowers, and then the fruit.

I became the words I ate in you.
For better or worse
the apple doesn't fall far from the tree.

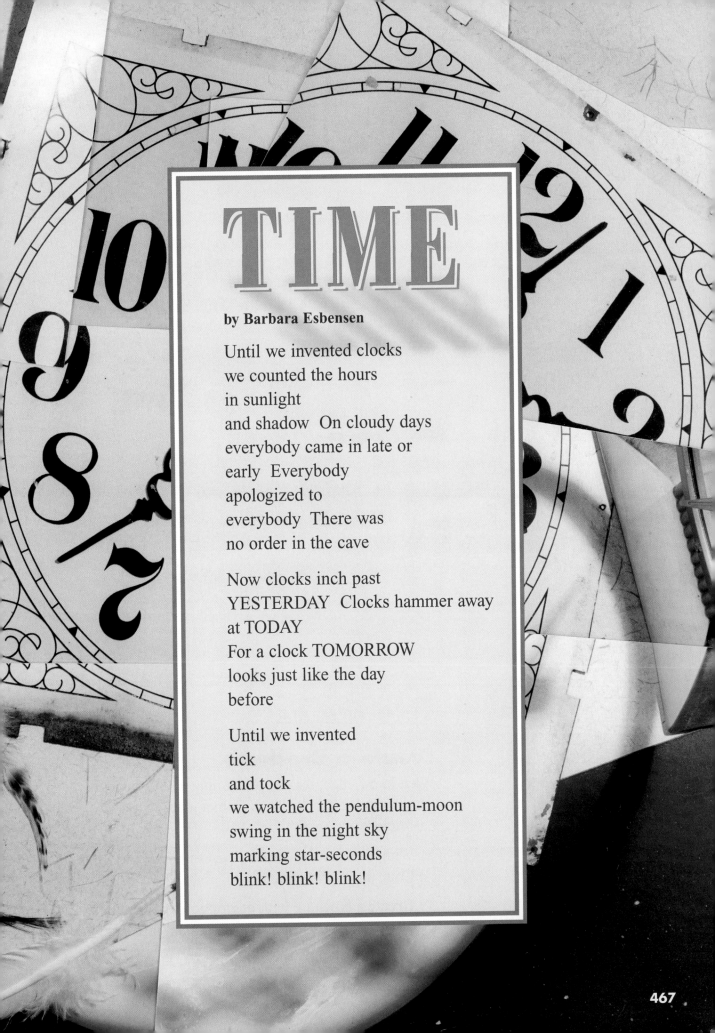

TIME

by Barbara Esbensen

Until we invented clocks
we counted the hours
in sunlight
and shadow On cloudy days
everybody came in late or
early Everybody
apologized to
everybody There was
no order in the cave

Now clocks inch past
YESTERDAY Clocks hammer away
at TODAY
For a clock TOMORROW
looks just like the day
before

Until we invented
tick
and tock
we watched the pendulum-moon
swing in the night sky
marking star-seconds
blink! blink! blink!

Wrap-Up

How can understanding the past help us live in the present?

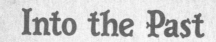

Into the Past

Create a Brochure

What knowledge, lesson, or warning would someone from the present bring back from a journey to a past time?

1. With a partner, **choose** the past time in "The Gold Coin" or "Spring Paint."

2. **Create** a brochure with descriptions and pictures that persuade others to travel back to that time. Add the knowledge, lesson, or warning they will bring back.

A Display of Ancestors

Design a Quilt

Joseph Bruchac in "Spring Paint" and Philip Simmons in *Catching the Fire* both learned about their ancestors. What did they learn?

1. With a small group, **find details** about what Joseph Bruchac or Philip Simmons learned about his ancestors.

2. **Design** a quilt. Divide a paper into squares, and draw or write in each square. Include what you feel are important about the character's ancestors.

What This Symbol Means to Me

Explain a Symbol

The Statue of Liberty symbolizes freedom. What do other symbols mean to people?

1. **Choose** one of the following. Decide what it symbolizes for the main character in the selection.

   - the coin in *The Gold Coin*
   - the spyglass in "A Brother's Promise"
   - the bloodroot flower in "Spring Paint"

2. **Explain** to others what the object symbolizes and why the character feels it has this meaning.

I Am a Wonder

Write a Poem

"A Brother's Promise" and *The Seven Wonders of the Ancient World* are about huge structures from the past. If these structures could speak, what would they say?

1. **Choose** one of these structures. **Brainstorm** what it might say.

2. **Write** a poem in the first person, as if you were the structure itself. Tell about how you were made and events that happened in or near you. Illustrate your poem and **present** it to the class.

Test Talk

Answer the Question

Use Information from the Text

Some test questions tell you to support your answer with details from the text. To answer such questions correctly, you must include information from the text.

A test about "Demeter's Daughter," pages 383–385, might have this question.

Test Question 1

How does Demeter change during the story? Use details from the story to support your answer.

Understand the question.
Read the question carefully to find the key words. Finish the statement "I need to find out . . ."

Decide where you will look for the answer.
The answer may be *right there* in one place, or you may have to *think and search* for it. The answer may depend on the *author and you*. Make notes about details that answer the question.

Check your notes.
Reread the question and your notes. Ask yourself "Do I have enough information?" If details are missing, go back to the text.

See how one student uses information from the text to answer the question.

Okay, I need to find out how Demeter changes in the story. I think she is both happy and sad. At the beginning, it says she is happy—happy because of her daughter. I'll note that. Then I'll go on to the next part.

If my notes are right, she's happy when she has her daughter. Then she's full of grief when Hades kidnaps her daughter. Then she's happy again when her daughter comes back. I'll look back at the question to check my information.

Try it!

Now use what you have learned to answer these test questions about "Demeter's Daughter," pages 383–385.

Test Question 2

How are Demeter and Hades alike and how are they different? Use details from the story to support your answer.

Test Question 3

How does Zeus help Demeter solve her problem? Use details from the story to support your answer.

Into the Unknown

What can we learn from visiting real and imaginary times and places?

Fact and Opinion

- A **statement of fact** can be proven true or false. You can prove it true or false by reading, observing, asking an expert, or checking it in some way.

- A **statement of opinion** tells someone's belief, judgment, or way of thinking about something. It cannot be proven true or false, but it can be supported or explained. Some statements of opinion begin with clue words, such as *I believe* or *In my opinion*.

- Some sentences contain both facts and opinions.

Read "Mount Everest: The Ultimate Challenge" from *Junior Scholastic* magazine.

Talk About It

1. Sir Edmund Hillary states, "I have a feeling that people have been getting just a little bit too casual with Mount Everest." Is this a statement of fact or a statement of opinion? How can you tell?

2. Look back at the article to find a statement of fact. Explain how you would prove it true or false.

Mount Everest:
THE ULTIMATE CHALLENGE
from *Junior Scholastic* magazine

The peak of Mount Everest, the highest spot on Earth, used to be a tough place to get to. The mountain is set deep in the Himalayas, on the border of Nepal and China. For centuries, only the heartiest of souls could even reach the mountain, let alone climb it.

In 1953, Sir Edmund Hillary and his guide, Tenzing Norgay, became the first people to scale all 29,028 feet of Everest. Since then, more than 4,000 people have tried to reach its peak. Many climbers have come away with an incredible experience. They also have contributed $90 million to Nepal's struggling economy. But some people say that Everest is too dangerous—and its environment is too fragile—for this kind of heavy traffic.

Modern technology, such as e-mail and cellular phones, now makes it easier for climbers to communicate with faraway people—including rescue squads. The number of businesses that take amateur climbers to the summit of Everest has grown too. Critics say that these advantages allow too many inexperienced climbers to attempt Everest's treacherous terrain. About one in every 30 Everest climbers dies in the attempt.

The perils of Everest became especially clear in May, 1996. Thirty-one people were on the summit when a sudden storm blew up. The wind chill was minus 140° Fahrenheit and hurricane-force winds blew sheets of snow. The climbers struggled back to their camp, but their oxygen supply dwindled. Eight of them died.

The increasing number of climbers is harming the mountain's fragile environment. Climbers use up valuable resources, such as wood, at a faster rate than the local people. Exhausted, air-starved climbers also leave behind oxygen cylinders, food remains, and other garbage. At that high altitude, land is delicate. Everest has been called the world's highest dump.

Despite these problems, Everest remains the ultimate challenge to climbers. Some people hope, though, that the 1996 disaster will make some climbers rethink their attitudes. "I have a feeling that people have been getting just a little bit too casual with Mount Everest," says Sir Edmund Hillary. Incidents like these "will bring them to regard it rather more seriously."

Tenzing Norgay and Sir Edmund Hillary

LOOK AHEAD

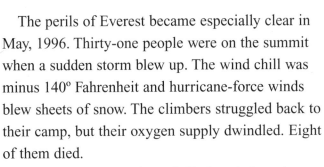

To the Pole!

In "To the Pole!" a group of explorers journey across the Arctic to the North

Vocabulary

Words to Know

Arctic	collide	expeditions
latitude	longitude	satellite
strenuous	terrain	

When you read, you may come across a word that you don't know. To figure out the meaning of an unfamiliar word, look for clues in the words and sentences around it.

Read the paragraph below. Notice how a description of *strenuous* helps you understand what it means.

Tracking Polar Bears

Polar bears are fascinating animals. To learn more about them, scientists go on expeditions to the icy terrain of the Arctic. Finding a bear may be a hard task under these strenuous conditions: snowdrifts are deep, and the ice is often unstable. Sometimes research teams are stopped by pressure ridges, walls of ice formed when sections of ice collide. Once they locate a bear, researchers tag it with a collar equipped with special sensors. The precise latitude and longitude of the bear at any given moment can be transmitted to research computers by satellite. Then scientists can continue to track this particular bear without going back out in the cold.

Write About It

Write a brief article about a cold land. Use as many vocabulary words as you can.

To the Pole!

from *Over the Top of the World*
by **Will Steger and Jon Bowermaster**

In 1994, six people, led by veteran explorer Will Steger, headed for the North Pole. They traveled from the Siberian coast of Russia by dogsled, crossing frozen snow and sometimes floating ice. After camping at the Pole, they started south again by canoe, this time headed for northern Canada. Their purpose, said Will Steger, was "to combine a great adventure with a new way of teaching, to bring the Arctic into the classroom and people's homes." To do this, they communicated every day by computer and satellite technology with students around the world. Through their trip, they hoped to call attention to the signs of pollution in the Arctic.

April 3

Finally, we are on the move again. Yesterday we were dropped off by Russian helicopter, after flying across 300 miles of open water and unstable ice. We waited nearly three weeks for the water between Siberia and the hard pack to refreeze, but it never did.

Out on the ice the weather is much better—clear and cold, and the winds have died down. As I write in my journal, the sun is pouring through my yellow tent, a comforting sight. It is light now 24 hours— as bright as it is at 10:00 in the morning back home—which makes for good traveling.

A lead that the team had to cross.

After the second helicopter flight dropped off the last of the dogs and our gear, Victor and I went for a walk to check out the conditions, which look good. The ice is very old, which means it is thick—and safe. Big mounds of ice are covered by snowdrifts, which make them like ramps, easy for the dogs to pull up and over. Our biggest challenge is open water, what we call "leads"—rivers or lakes of water created when the ice pack splits apart. They can be as narrow as three feet or as wide as 400 feet—longer than a football field. Getting across them can be as simple as jumping over or as complicated as putting an entire sled on a raft of ice and pulling it across by ropes or by paddling. Another method is to dump big chunks of ice into the water and use the floating blocks as steppingstones. I am sure we will try all of those methods and more in the coming months.

As we walked, Victor and I talked about his job as point person. It is a very important job. He will ski out ahead of the dog teams, sometimes ahead of us by half a mile. "I am the guinea pig," he said with a laugh. Victor enjoys the responsibility, even though it means he skis almost twice as much as the rest of us as he searches out the best

route. Takako will ski between him and the lead sled, signaling his instructions—telling us to come straight ahead, stop and wait, go left, or go right.

The 22 dogs are now divided into three teams. Martin's lead dog is Mooch. The others on his team are Palmer, McKenzie, Dylan, Dakota, Charlie, Royster, and South. On Julie's team are just seven—Tex, her lead dog, and Bear, Shaklee, Assute, Woody, Rocky, and Cochise. My guess is she will have a tough time with her dogs in the early days, because they have not trained together as a team. My team is also just seven and will be led by Patches, who has traveled with me since 1991. She will be joined by Vinson, Rex, Totem, Miles, Balzer, and Canyon. While it is unusual to have a female dog on the team, it is not unusual for them to be in the lead, as often they are very bright.

We are carrying enough food and extra gear for 30 days, just in case. By that time we should have reached the North Pole, where a plane carrying supplies will meet us.

Will, with his dog team hitched to the sled, ready to go.

April 6

Yesterday we covered 21 miles, even though the morning was slow-going as we crossed a zone of fractured and shattered ice. The only disaster was Martin's sled tipping over in a half-frozen lead. With quick teamwork we were able to right it. We are getting very good at such "emergencies." The hard part of the day was the cold—it got only as warm as −30°. The windchill is a bitter −60°, the sky is slightly overcast, and my face is sore and puffed from frostbite. On days like this it is best just to keep moving, to try to stay warm, so we had a very short lunch of hot soup, Shaklee energy bars, nuts, and chocolate. As we hurriedly ate, we talked about which parts of our bodies were coldest. For me, it was my fingers. Takako agreed. Martin, who rarely complains, said it was his face. We all keep our faces almost completely covered during the day. "My nose gets the coldest," admitted Julie. "The one thing that helps me warm up, though, is eating."

We spent much of the day chopping through small, six-foot-tall pressure ridges—walls of ice formed when two icepacks collide, creating piles of jumbled ice several miles long and up to 40 feet high.

Left: Takako chopping a trail through a pressure ridge with a pick.

Right: An example of the many pressure ridges the team crossed. Some were as high as forty feet.

One of the sleds makes it across a large lead.

Our challenge was to hack our way through, using pickaxes, creating paths smooth enough for our dog teams to travel over.

Since we sat in camp for the last several weeks, we are all a little out of shape, and exhaustion during the day is a problem. We have to be very careful how we run beside the dogsled, careful not to trip and fall. Being a dog musher is like being in a rodeo. You fall often on the uneven ice and must pay close attention every minute. Because of the cold and all the exercise, we also have to be careful about our diet. I carry a small thermos of hot drink with me, and a bar of chocolate, from which I take bites throughout the day. At lunch I eat a large cup of potato leek soup, which I've prepared in the morning in a thermos. I drop in big chunks of cheese and nuts. This usually keeps me strong until late in the afternoon, just before making camp, when I start to get tired.

As I pushed my sled up and over pressure ridges today, my mind was filled with plans of how we are going to keep our schedule, how we are going to arrive at the North Pole by Earth Day, April 22, as we promised.

April 8

Today we got into a good rhythm. The ice is drifting three to four miles a day to the northeast—perfect for us. I call it the "drift dividend"—even while we sleep we continue to travel north, sometimes making five miles a night. Victor calls them "sleepy miles."

Victor and I are sharing a tent. In our travels across Antarctica and Greenland we have tented together many nights before. He is good company—we know each other's habits well, and his optimism is always a boost to me.

We're like a little family of two, living inside a space the size of a car. Our arrangement is that I prepare dinner and he makes breakfast. In the morning, while I'm still in my sleeping bag, I know exactly what time it is by the breakfast sounds Victor is making. When I hear him stirring dried fruit and hot chocolate powder into a steaming bowl of leftover rice—my favorite on-the-ice breakfast—I know it is 6:40. Ten minutes later he will pour hot water for our tea. Julie and Takako—who have known each other for years and have traveled together in many cold places—are sharing a tent. For now, Martin is tenting by himself. We will trade off as the weeks go by—no one wants to spend that many nights alone.

Despite below zero temperatures outside, we were snug and comfortable in our tents.

April 10

Here are the conditions we face most days: The ice is more than three years old and thick, so leads are usually less than three feet wide. Each time we come to one we have to decide whether to try to cross over it or find a way around. There's roughly two feet of snow covering the ice, and we're traveling through an area filled with 10-to-15-foot-tall pressure ridges.

All the jumbled ice makes traveling difficult for the dogs, so we quit early, before noon. The dogs are still in good spirits but are having a tough time pulling the sleds over the bumpy terrain. Today even Bear, who never wants to stop, had a hard time!

April 16

The temperatures continue to drop, and today was a very cold, difficult day. We were lucky to hit a fairly good stretch of smooth ice with no open leads. But the smooth ice made for a boring day for the dogs. Cochise, always looking for mischief, tried to pick a few fights, but without success. By day's end, we and the dogs were all very tired.

Our goal now is to reach land in Canada some time in July. That will mean another 100 days living in tents, eating the same frozen food, rarely bathing or changing clothes. I see why some people can't understand why we do these expeditions!

Left: Will chose to keep his face clean shaven during the trip because a beard collects frost and snow. However, this meant his face had to be covered during the day to prevent frostbite.

Right: Will maneuvering his sled over very thin ice.

The dogs wait patiently as Will takes a reading with the Global Positioning System computer.

April 17

We passed 89 degrees north latitude, which means we are less than 60 miles from the Pole! Unlike explorers who traveled to the North Pole at the turn of the century, we are able to find out exactly where we are at any moment using a handheld computer called a Global Positioning System, or GPS. By communicating with a satellite orbiting the Earth, in just minutes it can tell us our exact latitude and longitude. We use it every night to see how far we've traveled—and every morning to see how far we've drifted.

April 20

Today was the first whole day of smooth sledding—it was nice not to have to chop a path through rough ice and pressure ridges. It snowed all day though, which made navigating difficult.

A growing problem is that Julie's dog team is having a hard time keeping up. In part, it is because it is a new team, not the one she trained with. Tex is doing a good job as her lead dog, but it's hard for a dog to have so much new responsibility put on his shoulders in such strenuous conditions.

April 22

We have reached the North Pole exactly as planned, on Earth Day. It's been nine years since I first dogsledded here, and I've seen and learned a lot since then. I've now traveled to both poles, North and South, and find something calm and peaceful about being at the top, or the bottom, of the world.

For Martin and Julie, this is the first time they've been to the North Pole. Victor is the first Russian to reach both the North and

South poles by skis. Takako had been here before, but still feels that it "looks like where God should live."

"It has been hard travel to get to the Pole," she said to me. "But then, just before we got here, it began to look like heaven. The sky was deep blue, and pink and orange. It was so pretty it filled me with hope."

We were greeted by a small group of friends who had flown up for the occasion with our resupply. We spent the morning having our pictures taken while our fingers and toes nearly froze. As we posed, the Arctic Ocean showed off for our guests. There was lots of creaking and groaning of ice as new pressure ridges developed in front of our eyes and cracks emerged where minutes before the ice had appeared solid.

Our friends have brought supplies with them—including letters and small gifts from our families, whom we haven't seen for two months. In addition they carried with them 15 more days of food and fuel, a half-dozen waterproof bags, and some boards and plastic necessary for repairing our sleds, which have been quite punished by the rough ice. We also received extra rope and first-aid supplies, a new compass for Martin, and some blank videotapes for Julie and Takako, who are making a film about their experience. But I got the best present—an apple pie baked by my mother back in Minneapolis.

Left: Julie, Takako, Will, Martin, and Victor pose proudly with the International Arctic Project flag in front of their camp at the North Pole.

Right: Inside his tent, Will opens the apple pie his mother sent him.

The team's camp at the North Pole.

April 24

We are camped at the North Pole, resting ourselves and the dogs. Our guests have departed. Unfortunately, the weather conditions are getting worse. There is more open water, more snow, strong winds, deep snowdrifts, and bitter cold.

So far, the most surprising aspect of the whole trip is all the snow. Most years the Arctic is like a desert, with very little precipitation. This year is different—it snows almost every day! Even when the skies are clear there is a light sprinkling. Some storms dump five or six inches overnight. On top of that, the winds have been incredible. Temperatures have gone as low as −40°, but the average is −20°. Since we left Siberia, the warmest temperature was zero.

April 27

When we left the North Pole, it seemed like a perfect day—sunny and −4°. We took our time packing the sleds, enjoying the relative warmth. We sledded along until 11:00 this morning, when I stopped the sled as the others in front bunched up. I could see Victor ahead poking the ice with a harpoonlike pole that he uses to check its thickness. Martin's sled was just behind; Julie's was next.

I began to notice that the ice beneath our skis was dark, almost black. I could make out in the ice what I call "snow flowers," a flowerlike frost formation that forms on thin ice. I was just about to walk ahead to warn Martin, when his dogs bolted. Almost immediately his sled broke through the ice and tipped onto its side, half in the water, half on thin ice. I left my dogs with Julie, then raced to help, signaling for the help of Takako.

We quickly surveyed the scene. The sled runner in the water was stuck under the lip of the ice. Martin proposed breaking the ice that was already freezing around the runner, and then trying to right the sled. I was afraid this would cause the whole sled to tip and fall into the water. Instead, I suggested knocking the ice out from underneath the other runner, the one on firm ice, and then, as soon as it was level, using the dogs to pull the sled forward.

It was dangerous work. As he chopped at the ice, Martin went into the water a couple of times, up to his waist. After 30 minutes we finally got the sled level, but now it was almost totally submerged underwater.

Takako, Victor, and I stood back as Martin called out commands for the dogs to pull forward, fast and hard. "Hup, hup, dogs. C'mon, Mooch, PULLL!!! PULLL!!!"

As the dogs strained, the front of the sled came out of the water. But our plan wasn't working. While the sled was moving forward, the ice kept breaking beneath it.

Finally, with one last giant pull, the dogs managed to get the sled onto firm ice. We were lucky that the dogs were fresh and excited. They saved the day.

Top: The team tries to right Martin's sled, which has tipped over into the broken ice.

Bottom: At last, the dogs are able to pull Martin's sled from the water.

Pollution in the Arctic by Barbara Horlbeck

Atmospheric (air), river, and marine (ocean) currents all move in major patterns from the midlatitudes of our planet up to the Arctic region and then back down. Recently, scientists have noticed that in these circulation pathways, pollutant pesticides from cities and farms are found. In a process known as "transboundary pollution," these contaminants enter the atmosphere as a river system and are carried to the Arctic. Once in the Arctic they are not easily burned off by the sun nor do they evaporate as they do in warmer climates. In the Arctic it is as though they are being preserved in a freezer. One contaminant in particular lasts 8 months in warmer climates, but when it gets to the Arctic it lasts 40 years!

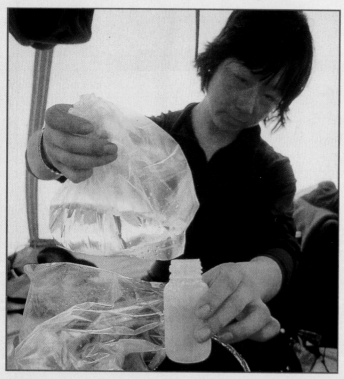

In the Arctic, these contaminants enter the food web. They are found in the fish, which are eaten by the seal. They are found in the seal, which are eaten by the polar bear and the Inuit people. Unfortunately, they are now found at very high levels in mammals and humans. And the closest known source of these contaminants is thousands of miles away from the Arctic, in areas such as India, Europe, and the United States.

Takako took a number of snow samples for the Japan Polar Institute to study for pollution. Here she's melting snow in plastic bags, which would later be transferred to sterile vials.

The Peoples of the Arctic by Barbara Horlbeck

In the harsh conditions of the Arctic, where temperatures are well below freezing and the sun doesn't rise for months at a time, human beings have dwelled for thousands of years. The peoples of the Arctic have learned to understand and adapt to this harsh environment. Each community has found unique ways to survive on the borders of the Arctic Ocean, just 500 miles from the North Pole.

In the Russian and Scandinavian Arctic, where there are vast regions of sparsely populated tundra, forest, and coastline, the people are sustained by reindeer and reindeer breeding. Reindeer herdsmen travel on foot and on the reindeer from one region to another, seeking fertile pastures for their stock.

Along the coastlines of Alaska, Canada, and Greenland, the Inuit live off the sea. Hunting seal, whale, and fish, the Inuit have adapted to the bounty the ocean offers. Inland, from the treeline to points further south, tribes of Indians have long-established roots. The Gwich'in Athabascan Indians, for example, have lived for thousands of years with the migrating caribou populations.

Animals of the Arctic by Barbara Horlbeck

Polar Bears

Long the symbol of the Arctic world, the mighty polar bear roams among many Arctic nations. Well-adapted to live on the Arctic Ocean sea ice, the polar bear is one of the largest carnivores in the world. A male polar bear can average 8 to 11 feet in length and weigh more than 1,000 pounds!

The polar bear is covered with a dense coat of white fur. This helps the animal survive in a climate where temperatures can reach −60°. The hairs on the bear's coat are actually hollow and allow ultraviolet light to reach the dark skin of the bear. This lets the body absorb the warmth of the sun. The polar bear is also protected from the cold by a thick layer of fat under its skin.

Although polar bears are basically land animals, they are very powerful swimmers. Their bodies are well-adapted to a life in and near the water. Their thick fur coat is water-repellent to keep out the damp cold. And their huge feet are partly webbed, making them more effective paddlers when they swim.

The diet of the polar bear is largely seal. For several months of the year they live in a world of total darkness, and they have very good eyesight. Their hearing is also excellent, as is their sense of smell. The bears use their noses to catch scents in the wind that might be carried from as far as several miles away. This is how they find and track seals.

Home

Security

Stop

Search

Seals

Several kinds of seals make their homes in the Arctic. One of the largest is the bearded seal, named for its distinctive set of whiskers. Hooded seals are another kind of large seal. They are also known as bladdernose

seals, because the males have an inflatable pouch that usually hangs limp and wrinkled over their noses. For display, the pouch may be blown up to twice the size of a soccer ball! The hooded seals also have an inflatable membrane that can be thrust out of one nostril like a bright red balloon.

Ringed seals are the most common and the smallest type of northern seal. They are found throughout the Arctic and subarctic waters. They are the main source of food for polar bears, which stalk the basking seals in the summer or catch them when they surface at breathing holes in the sea ice in the winter.

Arctic Wolves

Arctic wolves tend to be smaller than their cousins, the timber or tundra wolves, because the conditions are harsher and food is sparser farther north. Their white or cream-colored coats are thick, made of long, coarse outer hair and shorter, softer fur underneath.

The females give birth to a litter of four to seven pups in late May or early June. Pups remain with their pack for the first year of their lives. While many wolves leave the pack during their second year—

usually because of some rivalry with the other wolves in their pack—some remain in the pack for several years.

Wolves closely follow the migrating caribou and also hunt musk oxen. Because they hunt animals larger than themselves, they have developed organized hunting methods. They tend to hunt as a pack and rely on surprise, strategy, and group hunting to catch their prey.

Facts from the Trip

The team has made it to the end of the journey.
From left: Will, Victor, Takako, Paul, Martin, and Julie.

Time spent melting ice for tea, milk, and soups: **37.5** days

Average dog weight: **90** pounds

Amount of dog food consumed by dog team: **10,000** pounds

Weight of five-layer clothing system, per person: **10** pounds

Weight of sleeping bag: **6** pounds

Calories burned, per team member each day: **5,000**

Total calories burned, per team member: **1,200,000**

Average weight change, per team member: **9** pounds lost

Victor and Takako exchange jokes with children around the world through the computer. Early explorers would never have dreamed of this kind of communication from the Arctic.

About the Authors

Will Steger has always been the adventurous type. When he was 15, he and his brother traveled by boat down the Mississippi River from their home in St. Paul, Minnesota, to New Orleans, Louisiana. As an adult, Mr. Steger has made several expeditions to places like Alaska and Greenland and even Antarctica. "At the outset of any expedition, I look for the longest and most challenging route," Mr. Steger says. "I've never been one to follow in anybody's footsteps." He has traveled farther by dogsled in the Arctic and Antarctic than any other living person.

Will Steger

Although he seems to thrive on cold weather, it can cause problems. There was the time he unzipped his coat, and—because the zipper froze—he couldn't get it zipped again. Normally, that situation wouldn't be life-threatening, but when the temperature is 40 degrees below zero, a body needs to keep its warmth with the help of a closed coat. Fortunately, he managed to warm the zipper up enough to work, and he survived.

Jon Bowermaster calls himself "a writer who travels." His travels to Africa resulted in the book *The Adventures and Misadventures of Peter Beard in Africa,* and his trip to the North Pole gave him material for *Over the Top of the World.* In addition to writing books, he has worked as a newspaper reporter, a magazine editor, and an author who has contributed articles to many magazines, including the *New York Times Magazine, National Geographic,* and *Rolling Stone.*

Jon Bowermaster

Reader Response

Open for Discussion

Imagine that you can communicate by computer with these explorers. What questions would you ask the team?

Comprehension Check

1. What were some of the reasons that Will Steger and his team journeyed to the North Pole? Look back at the selection for details.

2. Think about the modern technology that this team was able to use. How did it make their expedition different from earlier ones? Use information from the selection in your answer.

3. In your opinion, what was the most difficult challenge faced by the team? Why do you think so?

4. Mr. Steger's entry for April 22 contains both **statements of fact** and **opinion**. Make a chart, listing the facts in the first column and the opinions in the second column. Find at least one statement in which both fact and opinion appear. (Fact and Opinion)

5. Skim the selection to find at least one **statement of opinion** that is supported or explained. Does the support or explanation convince you to share the opinion? (Fact and Opinion)

Test Prep
Look Back and Write

Explain why it is important for the people on the expedition to get along well with each other. Use information from pages 480–483 to support your answer.

Science Connection

Test Prep

How to Read an Informational Article

1. Preview

- Some informational articles deal with places in the world. This science article deals with a place that is changing.

- Read the title and subtitle. Look over the photos, map, and diagrams. Where is this place and what seems to be happening there?

2. Read and Note Main Ideas and Details

- The article has many pieces (supporting details), but the pieces are all about a single place and what is happening to it (main idea).

- As you read, jot down notes on the article's main idea and on supporting details for each piece of the article.

3. Think and Connect

Look back at "To the Pole!" Then look over your notes for "Antarctica Melts."

Both "To the Pole!" and "Antarctica Melts" deal with how human activities affect a remote place on Earth. How are human activities changing each of these places?

Scientists want to know why Earth's frozen continent is vanishing.

Imagine sailing through dark, frigid Antarctic waters. In the distance you spot an *iceberg,* a floating chunk of ice, creeping toward you. Only this monster is the size of Rhode Island—24 miles long by 48 miles wide and 200 feet high, with a total area of 3,000 square kilometers (1,150 square miles). It's a chiller that makes the *Titanic*-sinker seem like an ice cube.

One such mammoth ice island, which trackers call B-10A, broke or calved off Antarctica, Earth's most southerly continent, in 1986. But by August 1999, B-10A spelled imminent danger as it drifted into busy shipping lanes between Antarctica and South America. For every

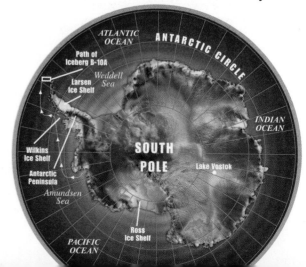

Antarctica Melts

by Miguel Vilar

foot of B-10A above sea level, three to five feet of ice jut below sea level—and "icebergs cut through a steel ship like a knife into a stick of butter," says Jeff Andrews, an analyst at the National Ice Center in Washington, D.C.

What's more, last year *glaciologists,* scientists who study *glaciers* (moving bodies of ice), made an alarming discovery. Nearly 3,000 sq km of the Antarctic Peninsula's Larsen and Wilkins *ice shelves,* continental ice masses that extend over the sea, vanished into the oceans in one year (*see map on opposite page*). The massive thaw only fuels scientists' worst fear: Antarctica may be headed for a gradual meltdown.

Antarctica Heat-up

In the past 50 years, average daily Antarctic temperatures have risen 3° C (5.4° F), a rate of heating that is faster than anywhere else on Earth—and faster than any time in recorded history. Since 99 percent of Antarctica is blanketed in ice, scientists worry that even partial melting could swell the world's oceans by 5 m (17 ft) and submerge many coastal cities!

A substantial Antarctic meltdown isn't probable in the foreseeable future. Yet, "if this trend continues, there'll certainly be reason for great concern," says Richard Moritz, a *climatologist* (climate scientist) at the University of Washington in Seattle.

Now researchers are scrambling to get a handle on the potential crisis. Last September, NASA and the Canadian Space Agency (CSA) launched Radarsat, an Earth-sensing satellite that uses radar (radio waves) to create the most detailed map ever made of Antarctica. Over the next year, mapmakers will stitch together more than 8,000 images collected by Radarsat—images so detailed they can detect buried snow-tractor tracks made 40 years ago! Researchers will use the new map to study how quickly Antarctica is shrinking.

Bottom of the World

Antarctica, the coldest, windiest continent on Earth, boasts summer temperatures of −30° C (−22° F); frigid winds rage at 400 km (250 mi) per hour. Antarctica is also the planet's largest *desert,* or dry region (either hot or cold) that supports little vegetation. It gets less than 5 cm (2 in.) of snow or rain a year.

But Antarctica wasn't always a frozen wasteland. Scientists first found clues to a far warmer continent in 1982, when *paleontologists* (scientists who study fossils) unearthed the world's oldest *marsupial* (mammals that carry babies in pouches) fossils in the Antarctic Peninsula.

How Glaciers Melt

A glacier (moving body of ice) drains into the oceans like a river. Due to the pressure of its own weight, ice underneath its surface becomes water and carries the glacier downhill. As the glacier flows, it collects debris, anything from particles to boulders. Once the river of ice reaches the snout (point where it meets the sea), it breaks apart into icebergs. Like ice cubes in a glass of water, icebergs melt. Larger icebergs often take years before they completely thaw.

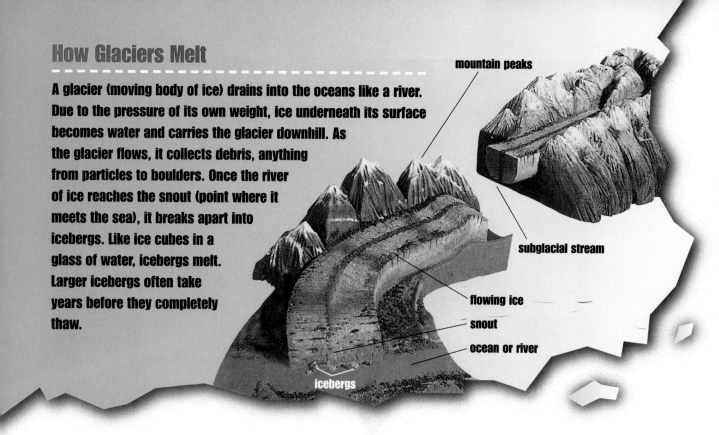

mountain peaks

subglacial stream

flowing ice

snout

ocean or river

icebergs

The mammal never could have survived today's frigid Antarctic temperatures. How did the marsupial get there? Another clue: Antarctic *sedimentary* (formed by erosion) rocks' age, structure, and composition closely match those of rocks in South America and Australia—two far warmer continents.

Two hundred million years ago, scientists now deduce, the continents of South America, Africa, Australia, and Antarctica formed a single "super-continent," *Gondwana;* fossil evidence suggests it was once a tropical, dino-roamed landmass.

Over the course of 100 million years, *plate tectonics*— the movement of *continental plates* (chunks of Earth's crust)—split Antarctica from the vast continent and caused it to drift to the South Pole. There, hardly any direct sunlight reached the new continent and months elapsed without a sunrise. Earth's tilt keeps the South Pole away from the sun during the northern summer. Even during Antarctic summers, most sunlight reflects off snow instead of melting it.

During the next 100 million years, the continent froze and melted several times, until ice eventually amassed to a thickness of 5 km (3 mi) in some regions. As Antarctica iced up, it became unlivable for most animals and plants. Today only insects and tiny organisms called *microbes (see sidebar, right)* inhabit the continent's interior year-round. Whales *migrate* or travel to Antarctica during its warmer months from November to March. So, if Antarctica was warmer millions of years ago, is the present thaw part of Earth's natural periodic warming/cooling cycle?

Searching for Answers

Many scientists think a warming Antarctic climate is induced by human activity. Factories, cars, and *deforestation* (destruction of forests) are among factors that increase atmospheric levels of *greenhouse gases*—heat-trapping gases like carbon monoxide and methane. Scientists link increasing greenhouse gases in the atmosphere to Antarctica's rising temperatures.

Life Grows On!

Talk about extremes. In Antarctica's underground Lake Vostock, scientists just discovered microbes, or tiny organisms, living in total darkness under 5 km (3 mi) of ice. The critters thrive in average temperatures of −89° C (−128° F)— some of the coldest temperatures on Earth. Brrrr!

In 1996, using ice-piercing radar, scientists first discovered the nearly frozen lake—about the size of Lake Ontario—buried directly underneath the Russian research station at Vostock in East Antarctica. The hidden lake is home to microbes that have survived in apparent isolation from all other forms of life for more than one million years.

Like an igloo, ice protects the lake's microbes from frigid Antarctic air temperature, while the planet's hot core warms the lake bottom. The weight of the protective ice also increases the lake's surface pressure, speeding up water molecules, causing the lake to remain liquid in sub-zero temperatures.

Scientists hope the critters will answer questions about climate patterns and evolution on Earth and other planets. They're also mapping the microbes' genetic code, or hereditary material, to see if the microbes have relatives anywhere else on Earth.

A different type of gas, *chlorofluorocarbons* (CFCs), produced by spray cans and refrigeration systems, for example, may also trigger Antarctica's shrinking *ozone layer,* or layer of heat-blocking gas in the atmosphere.

Already, satellite data from Radarsat are yielding vital clues. "Radar images of the Antarctic taken in 1997 show a different picture from satellite pictures snapped in the 1980s," says Kenneth Jezek, a *geophysicist* (scientist who studies Earth's physical aspects) at the Byrd Polar Research Center in Columbus, Ohio. "In some cases, ice shelves seem to be advancing into the oceans—in others they aren't."

Radarsat maps also reveal how ice shelves, moving through river-like *ice streams,* reach the ocean and splinter into icebergs. And when icebergs the size of Rhode Island break off and float away, scientists take quick notice.

ice surface

Vostok Station

ice

subglacial land

Lake Vostok

499

Skill Lesson

Context Clues

- **Context clues** are words that come before or after an unfamiliar word and help you figure out what it means.

- A context clue may be a synonym, a word with nearly the same meaning as the unknown word, or it may be an antonym, a word with an opposite meaning.

- A context clue may also be a definition or explanation of the unknown word, or a series of examples. *Such as* and *for example* are phrases that often begin examples.

- If a context clue doesn't give you a complete or accurate meaning of an unknown word, use a dictionary to check the word's meaning.

Read "For the First Time" from . . . *And Now Miguel* by Joseph Krumgold.

Write About It

1. Write the words that explain the meaning of *chili colorado con carne.* Where do they appear in the sentence?

2. Use context clues to define *tortilla.* Then check your definition in a dictionary.

For the First Time

by Joseph Krumgold

Twelve-year-old Miguel Chavez has spent the day helping the Chavez men shear sheep. Now, for the first time, he joins the men at the table for supper.

In the middle of the table there was a big plate with *gallina rellena,* turkey stuffed with meat and *piñon* nuts and a little taste of cinnamon, then there was this big bowl of *chili colorado con carne,* a stew that was made to taste good with red chili. Then, on one side of this, was a pot of *frijoles machacados,* mashed up *bolita* beans, and on the other side a potato loaf made with eggs and garlic

and bacon. Then there were a lot of little dishes, one with sweet chili sauce, and another with *guacamole* salad which is made out of avocadoes and tomatoes and things, and another with peach preserves and then a bowl with cole slaw. There were two kinds of bread, the *bollitos* my mother bakes which is a roll that is fat and round and *tortillas* which is flat but also round. There were two kinds of angel food cake, one chocolate and the other vanilla but only one kind of pie, just apple.

I had a good time. I was hungry, and there were so many good things to eat I hardly had time to listen. But there was so many good stories to hear, about all the sheepherders up and down the Rio Grande Valley, I didn't hardly want to waste time eating. I got along as best I could doing both, eating and listening, and feeling good.

LOOK AHEAD

The next story, from *El Güero, A True Adventure Story,* is also about a boy in the Southwest. As you read, use context clues to help you figure out the meaning of unfamiliar words.

Vocabulary

Words to Know

bandits	caravans	conserve
embark	exiled	merciful

Words with opposite meanings are called **antonyms.** You can often figure out the meaning of an unknown word by finding a clue in the words around it. Sometimes this clue is an antonym.

Read the paragraph below. Notice how *waste* helps you understand what *conserve* means.

Heading West

The pioneers of the American West chose to embark on courageous journeys into unknown territories. Severe weather, rugged mountains, and even bandits threatened their survival. They lived with few comforts, having left most of their belongings behind in order to conserve room in the wagons for food. They couldn't afford to waste cargo space on unnecessary items. These travelers must have felt exiled from civilization until they settled and built new communities. Yet, despite the dangers and discomforts, their caravans of wagons rolled on. They held to their beliefs that the weather would cooperate, the mountains would be passable, and any bandits would prove to be merciful. In short, they believed in their dream that a better life awaited them out west.

Talk About It

Tell a story about the Old West to a classmate. Use some vocabulary words.

from El Güero:
A True Adventure Story

by Elizabeth Borton de Treviño
illustrated by Leslie W. Bowman

For Mexico, 1876 was a year of revolutionary change. A new president seized control of the country and forced Judge Treviño to take a new assignment. The Judge and his family were told to leave Mexico City immediately for a town in far-off Baja California.

My name is Porfirio, but nobody ever calls me by my name. It is because most people in this country have dark eyes and dark hair, while my eyes are green and my hair is yellow. It is for this reason that everyone calls me El Güero, or the Blond One. My little sister, María, is called Maruca. I call my Aunt Victoria Tía Vicky, and my mother Mamacita. Everyone in Mexico has a nickname, or a short, affectionate form of his name. Only my father, the Judge, who is so dignified and taciturn, is called by his name, Cayetano, and then only by Mamacita and Tía Vicky. I have been told to call him Papá, though the other children I know call their fathers Papacito, dear little father.

On the day our great adventure began, I was at school, as usual. We were studying geography and drawing on a map the boundaries of Mexico. I had no idea that in a few days my whole family would be traveling toward the northern border.

I was called out of class and taken hurriedly home by our caballerango, our stable boy, Epifanío. I sat up front in the carriage with him.

"What is the matter? What has happened?" I asked, and I was worried because my Mamacita was delicate, and often had terrible nervous headaches.

"Your father the Judge has come home and has told us to pack up your family to leave," replied Epifanío, as he gave the horses a flick with his whip.

"To leave? To leave the city?"

"To leave the region," he answered.

At that I was silent, as we clop-clopped along, until we had come to our own big *zaguán*, our carriage gate, and Epifanío turned into the driveway.

I found Mamacita in tears, and Tía Vicky with her. My father was home. He told me quickly that we must choose a few things we loved— only three—and pack two sets of clothes. We were going away, to a strange part of Mexico, and we could not carry much baggage with us. He had been exiled by the president, and we must leave within two days.

At first I enjoyed the excitement. Everyone was running about. Mamacita and Tía Vicky were packing up bedding and kitchen things, and crying all the time, and old friends of my father came visiting. But then I learned that I had to leave my pony and my dog behind, and Maruca had to leave her cat Michi-Fu, who was going to have kittens. So she was crying too. Finally our cook, who was also in tears, said she would take my dog and Michi-Fu, and Papá sold our horses and my pony to a friend who would take good care of them. I hated to say goodbye to my pets; they were like people to me, and I loved them. I hated to leave the servants too.

Papá explained that we were to be taken over the highway to Acapulco by Don Leandro, an experienced leader of caravans, who supplied his own horses and mules. This journey would take many days, and then we were to embark on a steamer to carry us miles to the north, to Ensenada in Baja California.

We set out while it was still dark. Maruca was asleep, in the little riding chair they had made for her, slung across a mule's back. There was one for me too. Mamacita and Tía Vicky rode mules, and Papá was mounted on a horse. He rode up in front with Don Leandro, a tall, thin man with a long mustache. Then came the baggage mules, and Don Leandro's men, who rode alongside us and in the rear, to keep watch that all was well, and to defend us.

I was wide-awake. I didn't want to miss anything, for this was the first Big Adventure of my life.

Everything that happened was unusual and strange. For example, when we stopped for breakfast, it was one I had never tasted before. The men had made coffee over a fire, and they gave us *tlacoyos*, thick cakes of blue corn stuffed with beans. They tasted wonderful to me, and I loved the coffee, black and strong and sweetened with dark sugar.

At home, I had always breakfasted on sweet buns and hot chocolate. But this was only the beginning. Sometimes the men rode ahead and shot quail and broiled them over the fire, and once Don Leandro even shot a deer and we feasted on venison.

Along the way were travelers' huts here and there, small stone shelters in which the family slept on blankets on the floor, all five of us, while the men slept by a fire outside, one always keeping watch. In the morning we washed in streams, and started out early on the road again.

About three days into our journey, when we had halted under the shade of some trees to rest the animals, we saw a cloud of dust on the road ahead. It was early in the afternoon. Instantly Don Leandro ordered the men to form the beasts into a circle and he told us, Papá and Mamacita and Tía Vicky and Maruca and me, to get inside the circle and stay there.

"There are many bandits on this road, Judge Treviño," explained Don Leandro. "Very few caravans get through without being robbed."

My father saw that the men had taken out their rifles, and that Don Leandro had a pistol.

"No shooting," ordered my father. "If we are accosted and they are hostile, we will parley."

We waited. A group of masked men came toward us, pulling up their great horses a little way from us. There was a silence; I could hear the creaking of the leather saddles, and the breathing of the horses. Then Tía Vicky let out a terrified sob.

The leader dismounted, dropped his mask, and cried, "Judge Treviño!"

My father made no answer, and the bandit leader went on, "I know you, Judge. You sent me to prison five years ago. I was tried for murder in your court. I am Victor Cobián."

"I remember you now," said my father. "And today you assault innocent travelers on the highway!"

"They call me El Chato now," the man went on. "Yes, we ride the highway. We have to eat. And nobody would give us work, knowing we had been in prison."

"What are you going to do with us?" I asked El Chato. I was afraid that he was very angry at my father for having sent him to prison.

"Why, nothing, *joven,* young man. We are going to protect you. How far are you traveling, Judge?"

"To Acapulco."

"We, my men and I, will watch over you all the way. I am grateful to you, for you believed me when I told you that I had killed in defense of my home. No one else believed me. They would have had me shot at once. But you were merciful. You gave me a short prison sentence."

"Señor Cobián," said my father with dignity, "I cannot accept favors from a bandit. I am a man of the law."

"Well, in this case, you can't help yourself" was the answer. "We will protect you whether you like it or not! I am known on these roads and the other bands respect me. You will be safe."

"Cayetano," whispered my mother, "thank him."

At her words, my father smiled and bowed slightly. "Since we are fellow travelers," he said, "you must accept our hospitality. Please have some coffee."

At first the road rose slowly upward into the mountains. It grew colder and we were glad of the little travelers' shelters. Later, when we dropped down into a lower and warmer country, we often slept in hammocks that the men slung between the trees, first tying bunches of thorns into the ropes. The thorns were to keep scorpions from walking down from the trees and onto us while we slept. The hot country was famous for these small reddish insects, whose sting could be mortal. Once we even found a large dark blue scorpion, almost four times as large as the others. When Don Leandro squashed it, it gave off a smell like vinegar.

As soon as we got to the hot plains, Don Leandro stopped at a village and bought white cotton cloth, which he cut up and fashioned into a sort of cape for each of us, with a hole for the head. We were to wear these over our clothes so that we could see leeches as they fell down on us from the trees. We were also given a strong flexible branch with which to brush them off. There were snakes too; we had to be vigilant all the time.

There were so many things to learn! So much that was new and strange. Once in a while, we would come to a village where we could bathe and sleep in beds. When we did, Tía Vicky, who had never done any housework in her life, begged soap from the villagers and set to washing everybody's clothes. She had stopped crying about a week into the journey, and seemed to be enjoying herself. She became very bossy with everybody. I heard my mother complain softly to my father about her, but he answered, "Good, Juanita. Let her be. A weeping woman is no help on a dangerous journey, but a bossy one can be useful." Later on, I was to see the reason for his words.

Maruca fell sick with a fever. Tía Vicky demanded that we stop in the next town and find a place where she could take care of her. But Don Leandro said, "No, señorita. We must go on. In Acapulco we can buy the white powder, quinine, to cure her; if we stay here, without the medicine, she will die. We are not so far from the port now. In two days' march, we will see the ocean."

Tía Vicky was angry, but she obeyed. She rode beside Maruca, who slept and whimpered in a kind of daze. Tía Vicky had a gourd of water with her and she kept sponging Maruca's forehead with a wet cloth, to cool the fever. And at night she slept close to Maruca to keep her warm, because at night she trembled with cold. We were all silent and worried, and Mamacita clamped her lips shut and tried not to cry.

"My little angel is so delicate," I heard her say. "I will lose her on this horrible journey."

"Have faith. Be strong, my love," Papá whispered, putting his arms around her.

I was very sad for Maruca and also for Mamacita. They were suffering, but most of all, I felt sorry for my father, who had brought us on this adventure. I knew that he felt guilty and unhappy to be the cause of so much trouble.

My father was almost a stranger to me, because he had always gone to his office before I had awakened and had breakfast, and at night he had been tired, and we children had been ordered to be quiet, and not noisy and troublesome. We had our supper an hour before Mamacita and Papá had theirs; we kissed his hand and said good night, and he placed his hand on our heads and blessed us, but we never stayed to talk and tell him about our days. On Sundays he and Mamacita often went to dine in the homes of other judges and lawyers, or sometimes Papá sat in his library in our house, studying his cases.

But now, on the journey, we were close to him all day, and often, when we stopped to rest the animals, he dropped his arm across my shoulders and told me about when he was a boy and how later he studied in Monterrey. There he had written poetry and had declaimed it before large audiences.

"I have it written down somewhere," he told me, "but I have forgotten it all."

We even laughed together, as he remembered some anecdotes of the time when he was a young man learning the law.

It was wonderful now to hear him shout, first thing every morning, "Where is El Güero? Where is my son?"

Don Leandro hurried us along, and as he had promised, by evening of the second day he halted us on a high part of the road and told us to look. Acapulco! And there, below it, was the ocean. I had never seen the ocean, and I did not expect it to be so large. It was like a piece of blue silk, stretched out as far as the eye could see. We came down from the hill and went closer and at last we could take in the sharp salty smell and hear the ocean breathing.

There was a splendid white ship riding on the waters of the bay and it was due to sail the next day for the north. I asked if we would travel on it, but Papá said no, we must wait and get Maruca well before we ventured any farther.

We took rooms in a simple hotel and Papá found a pharmacist who sold him the quinine powder, made from a tree in Peru.

Chato and his men had left us two days before, and Don Leandro was busy arranging to accompany other travelers back to Mexico City. My father had given each of the men in both bands, Don Leandro's and Chato's, a present of money. He had gold pieces hidden in a *víbora*, a flexible woven belt, inside his clothes.

While Maruca got better, I was free to roam the beach and play in the waves that came hurling in, dashing themselves into foam on the sand.

After about a week, Maruca could walk around again, and she began to eat. Papá bought more of the quinine to take with us, and told us that now he would go and buy passage for us all on the first ship going north to San Diego in California. We needed to go there to get our supplies.

The ship turned out to be a Portuguese freighter called *Esperança*. My father met with the captain, a man named Silva—who didn't look much like a captain to me. I thought he should have been in uniform, with a cap and perhaps a sword. He was a short, dark, fat man wearing greasy trousers and shirt, and with a red bandana on his head. He demanded the passage money in gold and said he was sailing the next day. We all went aboard with our baggage and fitted ourselves into the small rooms, with their narrow bunk beds built into the wall.

We slid out of the bay and into the great ocean just at sunset. The ship had a strange smell and it moved along easily, so silently, we thought, after our many days riding to the sound of horses' and mules' hooves beating against the road. But once out at sea, there came the steady sound of an engine, and the ship began to sway in the water, up and down, and also from side to side.

At this unaccustomed motion, Mamacita and Tía Vicky and Maruca all became very sick and had to lie on their wooden bunks, and couldn't eat. But Papá and I did not mind and we walked the decks and explored the ship. We went down into the lower part of the ship and watched almost naked men throwing shovelfuls of coal into a great furnace, which made the steam to carry us forward. When there was a good stiff breeze, the captain hoisted sails, stilled the engines, and then we skimmed over the water without a sound.

Watching from the rail of the deck, we saw a school of flying fish one day, almost like birds, with the sun shining on them, so that they seemed to be silver, and another day we saw dolphins leaping and playing in the sea around us. We were never so far out at sea that we could not see the distant shore, a smudge of blue and tan against the sky.

What we did not like was the food, very heavy and salty, but Papá said to eat it up, as we were not carrying any food of our own, and we had to keep up our strength.

"We will need all our strength, Güero," he told me, "to take care of the women. They are all seasick, and will be weak and wobbly when we get off the ship in San Diego."

"When will that be?"

"Captain Silva says in about ten days."

But we did not disembark in San Diego.

A few days later, when we saw land rather close, the ship came in slowly and carefully until we could make out rocks and a beach and, in the distance, a little white building.

"Are we stopping here for supplies?" my father asked Captain Silva.

"For water. And to put you and your family off" was the reply.

"But you can't! I have paid in gold for our passage all the way to San Diego."

"I am obliged to change course," answered the captain. "You can order me arrested next time I dock at Acapulco," he continued, disrespectfully. "You and your luggage are being put off here. I will carry you no farther. We are making for some islands, and I have just enough food for my crew and me. None for you. So get ready. The men will take you ashore in rowboats."

I could see that Papá was furiously angry. He turned quite white and a little pulse beat in his cheek as he clamped his jaws together. But even I could tell that there was nothing we could do.

Mamacita and Tía Vicky and Maruca could hardly walk the few steps on the deck, and the crewmen were kind and carried them into the rowboats. As we got to the beach, the boats grated against the sand, and we jumped out, my father and I getting wet to the knees. The crewmen carried the women up a little way. Then they made several journeys carrying buckets to a small spring where fresh water bubbled up, and went back to the ship. One more trip and they brought our luggage and threw it down.

I went with Papá up a long, sloping hillside to the white building we had seen perched on the top. It looked clean and inviting in the sunshine. I pushed open the door; it was empty.

Mamacita and Tía Vicky had come toiling up the slope, and when Mamacita saw that we were alone in the empty place, she sank down on the porch and began to cry.

"Cayetano, what are we going to do?" she asked my father, her eyes streaming.

"We will make the best of it. Somehow," answered Papá. "Anyhow," he went on, "be grateful that we are all alive. That pirate could have murdered us all and thrown us into the ocean. Who would have known?"

He was silent then, and went looking about, and seemed to be calculating.

"We will sleep in here," he said. "Güero and I will bring the baggage up, and we can make beds with blankets and coats. Fortunately, it isn't cold. No doubt this is a mission, used occasionally. It has been well cared for, though it is empty. Perhaps the missionaries will arrive in a few days. And there is fresh water near. That is a mercy."

"But what will we eat?" asked Tía Vicky, sobbing.

"The sea is full of fish," I said to her. "We will eat fish, and Papá and I will catch them!"

That first night was eerie, because we were so alone and there were sounds in this strange land that we had never heard before. Some animal howled far away, and then came nearer, and then went away again. The wind rose and made a sad sound and the waves crashed louder and louder on the beach until it seemed to me that they would come and drown us. I got up and went out on the porch to look, but the waves were still a good distance away.

In the morning, in bright sunshine, Papá and I explored.

The place was desert country, very dry and barren. There were a few trees in clumps around another small spring, but many thorny bushes everywhere.

"The thornbushes will do for our firewood," said Papá. "I have a strong, broad-bladed knife with me, to cut them, and matches. But matches can be used up. I think we must keep a fire going day and night, and never let it go out. And we can use it to signal passing ships."

"Papá, I can take branches from the trees to make fishing poles, and the ropes that bound the luggage can be our lines. I will fish!"

"Excellent, Güero. We will manage. Somehow."

I noticed that he had said "Somehow" several times. Perhaps it was wise. Because everything we did, we did "somehow."

Mamacita unpacked her household things, and we went every morning to the spring to fill her pots and pans and pitchers, and bring the water back to the house.

"However, we must conserve this," said Papá. "Springs sometimes retreat back into the earth. We will not use the water for washing. We will wash in the sea."

"But I can't wash clothes in salt water," cried Tía Vicky. "The soap won't make suds."

"Then we will wear our clothes dirty," said Papá. And I thought he hid a little smile, for Tía Vicky was always so concerned about her appearance; she took great care of her hair and her complexion, and even on our long journey on muleback, she had been careful of her skirts and her shoes, and had worn a shade hat.

It was a hard time.

Even fishing wasn't easy. There was no rock or promontory over the water so that we could drop our line into deep water. We had to fish in the surf, standing in the second line of waves, with trousers rolled up above the knees, our feet bare. Sometimes the waves were rough and tumbled me, but my clothes dried quickly enough, for the sun was hot. After a while we got the hang of casting and were able to catch plenty of small flat fish, which Papá gutted and scaled with his knife. Tía Vicky had to tend the fire, and she learned to fry the little fish just right, and for a few days they tasted delicious. But soon we got awfully tired of them.

Papá's feet and legs were sunburned and painful; in fact, we both were sunburned and peeling. Tía Vicky had scissors and thread and cloth in her baggage and she made sunbonnets for Mamacita, Maruca, and herself, which protected them.

One day there was a sudden storm, with heavy rain which did not soak into the dry ground but ran off it. We put out every vessel Mamacita had and caught all the rainwater we could, and it was quite a lot.

Papá told Tía Vicky she could have some to wash with, but she shook her head. She went and burrowed in her boxes and came back with a package, which she handed to him.

"I am tired of fish," she said. "Everybody is. Here is my rice, which I was saving to grind up for face powder. Let us cook it in the rainwater."

Papá thanked her gravely and said, "We will use a little seawater with it, for salty flavor, and save all the rainwater we can."

That simple rice, boiled over the fire, tasted like heaven to us. I looked around at us all as we sat eating it. Mamacita was thin and her hair was all tumbled down, as she had lost most of her hairpins, one by one. But it was curly and didn't look bad. Tía Vicky looked dreamy as she ate. All her ideas for beautification had given way; her clothes were soiled and she had gathered her hair into braids. She was even eating her face-powder rice! Papá looked much older, for in his effort to conserve water, he did not shave, and his beard had silver in it. He had always worn a mustache, but a stylish one, with the ends turned up and stiffened with wax. Now his mustache was bushy, and his hair was growing long and hung over his collar.

But Maruca looked better than ever. She had gained some weight, and from running in the sun and bathing in the sea, she seemed to have recovered her lost health. I saw Mamacita watching her, with satisfaction and joy in her face. Maruca was always a worry.

For some reason I seemed to be growing taller fast; my shirts were all tight and the sleeves too short, and my trousers were also too short. Even my shoes seemed small. But I didn't care, because I went mostly barefoot, anyhow.

Papá and I took turns tending the fire at night. It was getting harder and harder to find enough bushes to burn, and we had to range farther for them. Several times we saw ships go by, and we frantically signaled with the smoke from our fire, but they never stopped or paid any attention to us.

Then one day, when we had lost the spirit of adventure and were just enduring and trying to keep alive, a boat came nearer and nearer. It seemed to be heading for us, and my father ran out and waved his shirt and shouted, and to our joy, the boat came in, and a man stood up on the deck and shouted back at us. It was not a large vessel and did not carry many men. They put down an anchor and lowered a rowboat, and two men began bringing it to shore. As they grated on the sand and beached, an agile little man in a long black robe tied with a piece of rope around his waist jumped out. After him the second man got out, and they pulled the rowboat up out of reach of the waves. The second man was short and brawny and he had thick red whiskers. He came smiling toward us.

"Welcome, welcome!" cried my father. "You can't know how welcome you are!"

Tía Vicky and Mamacita came running down from the house. They took the hand of the man in black and kissed it, so I knew he must be a priest.

"I am Padre José, of this mission," he explained. "And this is Captain Forker, who brought me and my supplies. How long have you been here at Cabo San Lucas?"

"I reckon it to be about a month," my father told him. "We were forcibly put off here, after having bought passage to San Diego."

"Well, I can take you to San Diego," said Captain Forker, "though you may not be very comfortable in my small boat."

"We are five," explained Papá, as Maruca came rushing toward us from the little mission cottage, where she had been asleep.

"We could manage. We could manage," cried Captain Forker, and I could see that Tía Vicky and Mamacita were of a mind to kiss his hand too, they were so relieved and happy to be rescued at last.

Elizabeth Borton de Treviño

About the Author

"When I was a child," Elizabeth Borton de Treviño says, "I really suffered when I had to lay down my book in order to set the table or dust the parlor for my mother. My greatest reward for tasks well done was to be allowed to go to the library and browse among the shelves so laden with treasure." Ms. Borton de Treviño was raised by a family that loved literature, from parents who quoted Shakespeare to a grandmother who could recite pages and pages of poetry.

Her love of music and her musical talent helped her get her first job as an assistant music reviewer. Later, her ability to speak Spanish enabled her to go to Mexico as a reporter. In Mexico, she met her future husband and stayed with him there. Since then she has written many books, both fiction and nonfiction, for children and adults.

Ms. Borton de Treviño was awarded the Newbery Medal for writing *I, Juan de Pareja.* This book was based on a true story about the friendship between the famous Spanish painter Diego Velázquez and Juan de Pareja, a slave who lived in Velázquez's household.

When asked where her ideas come from, Ms. Borton de Treviño says, "I generally get story ideas from some true event or moment in history that fires my imagination. All of my books contain a little kernel of truth, something that really happened."

Reader Response

Open for Discussion

Describe the effects of the journey on the family. Do you think it has made the family stronger?

Comprehension Check

1. The story has several different settings. Pick the one you like the best and describe it. Look back in the story for details.

2. Describe El Güero's new relationship with his father. Why doesn't El Güero think he really knew his father before the journey? Use specific details from the story in your answer.

3. Find two examples in the story to support the statement "everything we did, we did 'somehow.'"

4. What **context clues** help you identify and understand the Spanish words used in the story? (Context Clues)

5. How do **context clues** help you understand the meaning of the word *range* in the sentence, "It was getting harder and harder to find enough bushes to burn, and we had to *range* farther for them"? (Context Clues)

  **Test Prep**

Look Back and Write

How does Tía Vicky change after she gets off Captain Silva's ship? Use details from pages 511–515 in your answer.

The CALIFORNIA Rancheros

by Carlos Cumpián

Spain ruled
and mapped California
into little kingdoms since the 1770s,
with mission churches like adobe palaces,
until 1822, when a new sun rose
over upper and lower California,
becoming a province of the Republic of Mexico.

With Spain no longer setting aside
chunks of land to be used by Catholic friars,
the Mexicans tried to meet their people's needs
and turned mission lands into family farms
for native-born Californios.

Those first *ranchos* and *haciendas*
had their boundaries marked
by free men on horseback
using strong rope,
with piles of stone, desert brush,
or a notched tree trunk for markers.

The families Pacheco, Carillo, Pico,
and Vallejo became rich
selling sun-dried cattle hides
tied in bales for cargo ships
that sailed off to places that made
saddles, harnesses, coats, and shoes.

California's coast connected
money with cheap labor.
People from everywhere wanted to live there,
where weather laid a fertile carpet
for rich harvests.

After tasks were done,
in every rancho and village
there was time for fun—
piñatas, and songs at
birthdays, wedding dances,
and feasts on Catholic saints' days—
and you could expect a rodeo fiesta
even when it was time for cattle branding.

Yes, once the Californios strummed their guitars
and sang under a starlit sky,
their music rising from the ranchos
as the American pioneers,
eager for gold and land,
headed westward.

rancho—farm with mostly cattle ranching
ranchero—person who owns or works on a ranch
hacienda—a large farm; an estate; property
piñata—a container filled with fruit, candies,
money, used in a children's game

Steps in a Process

- The actions you perform in order to make something or to reach a goal are the **steps in a process.**

- Sometimes the steps in a process will have numbers. Other clues to the order of the steps are words like *first, begin, next, then,* and *last.*

- If there are no clue words or numbers to help you keep the steps in order, use your common sense. Think about what you already know about the process and how it is done.

- Sometimes the steps in a process refer to a process in nature, such as the growth of a plant.

Read "Living in Space" from *Universe* by David Glover.

Talk About It

1. You should read all the directions before you begin. What else do you need to do next before you follow the directions in Step 1?

2. Can you do Step 3 before Step 2? Can you do Step 4 before Step 3? Explain.

3. With a partner, take turns reading the steps. Instead of reading the numbers, use clue words like *first, next,* and *then.*

Living in Space

by David Glover

The space pioneers who eventually set off to colonize Mars and the asteroids will have to create their own sealed environment in which to live. Growing plants for food and providing enough oxygen will be the main priorities. The pioneers will use solar energy and will have to recycle all their water and waste materials.

A space colony could work in a similar way to a bottle garden. Plants sealed inside the bottle need only the energy of sunlight to grow.

During the day, the plants' green leaves collect energy from sunlight, which they use to convert water from the soil and carbon dioxide from the air into a simple sugar called glucose. This process is called **photosynthesis** (fo′tō sin′thə sis). As the leaves make glucose, they also make oxygen.

Plants and the tiny animals (worms or insects) in the bottle use the food (glucose) and oxygen to grow. When they do this they release water and carbon dioxide. This is called respiration.

In a bottle garden, the sun's energy constantly recycles oxygen, water, and carbon dioxide between the soil, the living things, and the air.

To make a bottle garden you will need

- water
- a trowel
- potting soil
- four plants
- large glass jar with a lid

(Small, well-established plants that like a warm, damp atmosphere, such as ferns, miniature ivy, African violets, mosses, begonias, and small spider plants, are the best.)

1. Fill the bottom of the jar with a layer of potting soil, about 4–6 inches deep. Level it off and then pat the soil firm.

2. Gently remove your plants from their pots. Using the trowel, make holes in the soil large enough to accommodate the roots of the plants. Put the plants in the holes and replace the soil, pressing it down firmly.

3. Water the garden carefully. The potting soil should be moist but not too wet.

4. If you want to make your garden look more like a space colony, place some model people, animals, and space vehicles among the plants.

5. Put the lid on the bottle and seal it tightly.

6. Stand your bottle garden by a window where it will receive plenty of sunlight. The plants should grow happily without extra water. If the inside of the bottle steams up, take off the lid for an hour or so to let it clear.

LOOK AHEAD

"Destination Mars" is about space travel to another planet. As you read, you'll learn the steps in this process.

523

Vocabulary

Words to Know

commander   concepts   detected
organism   radiation

When you read, you may come across a word that you don't know. To figure out the meaning of an unfamiliar word, look for clues in the words and sentences around it.

Read the paragraph below. Notice how an explanation of *organism* helps you understand what it means.

Moonwalk

On July 20, 1969, the *Apollo 11* lunar module landed on the moon. Neil Armstrong, commander of the mission, and Edwin "Buzz" Aldrin, pilot of the lunar module, became the first humans to explore the surface of the moon on foot. Spacesuits supplied oxygen and shielded them from the sun's harmful radiation. Over the next few hours, the astronauts conducted experiments testing scientific concepts about the moon. As expected, they couldn't find evidence of even a single lunar organism. That is, no signs of life were detected. Their mission accomplished, Armstrong and Aldrin rejoined the third crew member, Michael Collins, in the command module orbiting the moon. The *Apollo 11* crew returned to Earth as heroes.

Write About It

Write a paragraph about space travel. Use as many vocabulary words as you can.

Destination: Mars

from Life on Mars

by DAVID GETZ

Blast-off

Your commander turns down the lights in the cabin to cut the glare. It is night and you are flying southeast, across the United States. You are in your last orbit, a few hundred miles up. You can identify all of the major cities by their lights. You pass over the Gulf of Mexico and down across South America. And then, as the lights of Buenos Aires fade from view, you see a shooting star slash a white stripe through the atmosphere beneath you.

You are looking down at shooting stars. How wonderful.

"Get ready to say good-bye," your commander says.

Within minutes your ship will leave its Earth orbit. You are going to Mars. You will be the first humans to visit another planet.

The sun begins to rise over Earth's horizon. You glance back down at your home. You will not see your family again for almost three years.

You are high enough to see the curvature of Earth. You stare at the fluorescent blue band on the horizon. It is the Earth's atmosphere, the layer of air that surrounds the planet. You are struck by how thin the atmosphere looks on the horizon. How strange it is to be looking down on the air that fills the lungs of 6 billion people.

Where you are going, there will be no air to fill your lungs. Mars's atmosphere is one hundred times thinner than Earth's. It is too thin to breathe. It lacks oxygen. It is almost entirely carbon dioxide, the same stuff that makes up the bubbles in your soft drink.

You steal another glance at Earth. It is mostly white and blue. White from drifting clouds, blue from the oceans.

Clouds will be a rare sight on Mars. You will never see an ocean. There are no oceans on Mars, no rivers, streams, lakes, or ponds. No puddles. Mars is bone-dry. There is no flowing water anywhere on its surface.

No air to breathe, no water to drink.

"Ready to fire rockets," your commander announces.

Your commander's timing must be perfect. The Earth races around the sun at about 70,000 miles per hour! As you orbit 250 miles above the ground, gravity keeps you connected to this speeding Earth, as if by a long string. When your commander fires the rockets, that "string" will be severed, and your ship will be flung away from Earth at 70,000 miles per hour, plus the speed your rockets have given you. The sun's gravity will slow you down a little and set you on a curving path that will eventually intersect the path Mars takes as it orbits the sun.

This slide from one racing planet to another is called the *Hohmann transfer*. The trip from the Earth to Mars is a long one, over 250 million miles, and it takes 6 months.

And then there's the stay.

Since the planets orbit the sun at different speeds and at different distances, you cannot "leap" from Earth to Mars at any time. Leaving too soon or too late will cause you to miss Mars altogether. Make a mistake, and you will wind up just another dark object forever orbiting the sun. Your *launch window*, the moment when it is possible to be flung from the Earth to Mars, occurs about once every two years and lasts only a few weeks. Similarly, you will have to wait eighteen months on Mars before it is safe to be flung back home.

Six months to get there; a year-and-a-half stay; six months to get back.

"Firing the rockets," your commander announces.

You hope your five crewmates are good company.

You watch your home planet recede.

You remove from your pocket one of the funny postcards your parents brought you from the Planetary Society.

"Vacationing on Mars," it says. "Wish you were here."

The card shows a photo of Mars taken from the unmanned *Viking* spacecraft that landed on the planet in 1976. It reveals a dramatic desert landscape complete with sand dunes and huge boulders. Though the ground is pink, it does not appear much different from the deserts of southern Colorado or Nevada. The scientist Carl Sagan once said he would not have been too surprised to see a prospector and a mule appear in one of these photos.

Except this mule and the prospector would have to be wearing spacesuits.

You turn the card over. You will not see your family again for almost three years.

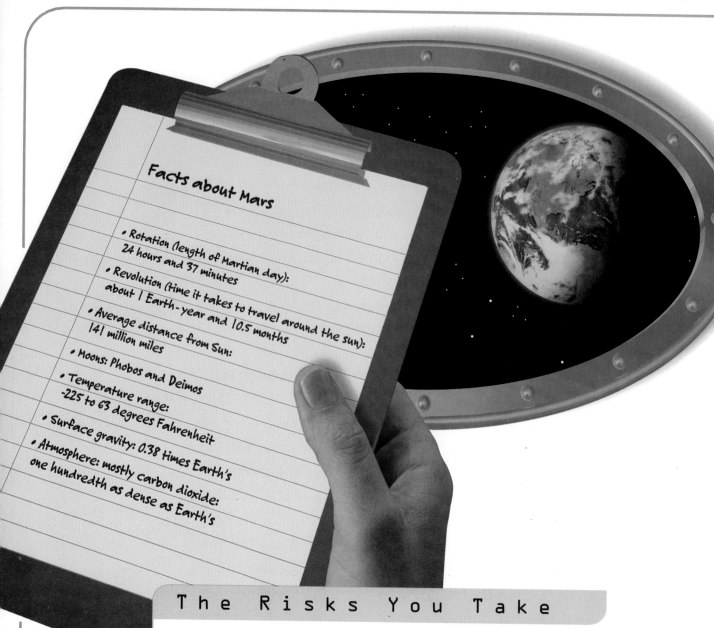

Facts about Mars

- Rotation (length of Martian day): 24 hours and 37 minutes
- Revolution (time it takes to travel around the sun): about 1 Earth-year and 10.5 months
- Average distance from Sun: 141 million miles
- Moons: Phobos and Deimos
- Temperature range: -225 to 63 degrees Fahrenheit
- Surface gravity: 0.38 times Earth's
- Atmosphere: mostly carbon dioxide: one hundredth as dense as Earth's

The Risks You Take

There is no turning back. You have been driven, like a tennis ball from a racket. You must land on Mars before you can be sent back home. Day after day, Earth becomes smaller and smaller. Your radioed voice takes longer to reach mission control. Halfway to Mars, you radio home, "Ma, how are you?"

It takes 10 minutes to hear your mother's answer.

The view outside your window stays the same day after day. You can see so many stars, they look like fog.

As gravity is pretty much meaningless to you now, so are the concepts of up and down. On Earth, "down" is the direction gravity pulls things. "Down" is where things fall. Well, nothing falls in your craft. Your clipboard tied by a string to your wrist, you slowly drift in your cabin as you discuss the geology of Mars with another floating crewmate.

At this point, you do not talk about the risks. But you are an explorer. And like all great explorers, potentially deadly obstacles stalk your mission.

The first lurks within your own mind.

"All the conditions needed to drive a man to murder," the Russian cosmonaut Valery Ryumin wrote in his diary in 1980, "exist when you lock two people together in a small cabin in space for 2 months."

And what about six people in two small cabins for nearly three years? Your "habitat" is 15 feet in diameter and 16 feet tall. It has two decks, each with 8 feet of headroom. Will that be too confining? There are no screen doors opening onto porches and backyards. You are stuck. You will have no other people to confide in, to discuss your interests with, to listen to your jokes. You will be forced to listen to the same voices, day after day for three years. What will it be like listening to their worries, their stories, their jokes?

You will have your books on computer, movies and music to entertain and distract you, and your own small private space where you can be by yourself. There will be plenty of work for you to do to occupy your mind. But the questions remain. You are going to be with the same five people for almost three years. There will be arguments. There will be tension. How well will you manage the conflicts that arise? How well will you get along after spending months on the hostile, lonely surface of Mars? How close will you or your crewmates come to contemplating a violent crime?

Not too close. NASA spent years searching for the six best candidates. They knew what they were looking for, and you and your crewmates had it.

What was NASA looking for? Colonel Steve Nagel, an astronaut and space shuttle commander, explains that the ideal explorer needs to be a team player.

"There's no room, on a trip to Mars, for a person who has to have his own way. You will need people who can get along under good, reasonable leadership. The crew will want their views heard, but when a decision is made they may not be in favor of, they will still salute and say, 'Yes, I'll do this.'"

That is you. Thousands of people applied to join the first Mars mission, but only you and your five crewmates were chosen. You passed the psychological testing, went through countless interviews, participated in role playing and crisis-intervention training. As a finalist, you were sent with a crew to train in Antarctica, the closest thing on Earth to Mars. You lived in a small habitat. Anytime you went out, you wore your spacesuit. You explored the terrain, looked for rocks and fossils. You took weather readings. You returned to your cabin and conducted experiments in your laboratory. You held meetings with your teammates. You worked out your differences. You helped keep everybody in high spirits. You performed beautifully.

Will the six of you continue to succeed as a team?

You have no choice.

Just for fun, you take out a postcard of your own, a diagram of our solar system with a tiny white arrow pointing to the black space between Earth and Mars.

"Here we are," the card says. "Enjoying the view!"

You write a note on the back to your family. When you hand-deliver it, you will be almost three years older.

You write that as you look at all those unblinking stars, you find it hard to believe there is not life somewhere else in the universe. Why should life exist only on Earth? What makes Earth so special?

You cannot wait to get to Mars. Perhaps you will find some answers, something new to write home about.

You hope you are alive in three years to deliver your letters.

Weightless Dangers and Invisible Bullets

You were not meant to live without gravity.

"The force of gravity has shaped the way our bodies are built," says Dr. Arnauld Nicogossian, chief medical officer for NASA. Just as fighting gravity on Earth made your bones, your heart, and your muscles strong, removing that gravity will make you weak.

On Earth, your heart pumped hard and blood vessels squeezed powerfully to pump your blood up against the downward pull of gravity. Now that you are weightless, your heart does not need to work as hard. It gets weaker. Your blood vessels slacken.

Along with your heart, the other muscles of your body weaken as well. Since they no longer have to push you up, keep you standing, or raise your weight, they lose their tone.

You exercise in your cabin to make your muscles work harder to prevent this decay. You ride your stationary bike. You walk on your treadmill. You think of the Russian cosmonaut Yuri Romanenko, who became something of a human hamster. Up in space for a year, he became so afraid of his body falling apart that he pedaled his stationary bike four hours a day, leaving him few hours to actually work.

You are not that afraid. You will be weightless for only six months at a time. When you land on Mars, where gravity is a little more than one third of Earth's, it will be easier to make your heart and muscles work hard again. You weighed 80 pounds back home. You will weigh 30 pounds on Mars.

What you cannot avoid is bone loss. Since your bones do not need to be as sturdy in space, they begin to shed the calcium that makes them strong. Most of this loss occurs in your spine and hips. The loss is not rapid, but if it is allowed to continue for over a year, your bones could become brittle and easily fracture. What makes this bone loss doubly unpleasant is that calcium leaves your body through your kidneys. This could lead to kidney stones. Kidney stones are terribly painful.

There are other effects of living in weightlessness that are still not well understood. It is possible that your immune system, which helps you fight disease, also breaks down.

"As a matter of fact," Dr. Nicogossian explains, "space flight produces the symptoms of aging."

This was not a big deal for the astronauts who went into space before you. Most of those symptoms, with the exception of calcium loss, were reversible. All the astronaut had to do to get better was return to Earth.

But you will not be doing that for a long time.

"Can we protect astronauts one hundred percent against the risk of microgravity?" Dr. Nicogossian says. "The answer is no. There are no magic pills for gravity yet."

Still, you will not let gravity get you down. You have other bullets to dodge.

Galactic rays, which originate in the explosions of stars, will constantly bombard your craft. Though you are not expected to receive high doses of this radiation, you cannot dismiss the possible dangers. Some scientists fear that the rays, which can penetrate anything, act like microscopic bullets. The damage they cause depends on what part of the body they strike and at what angle. Galactic rays could cause you or one of your crew members to experience loss of judgment, memory, and coordination.

More threatening are *solar flares*, which are intense bursts of radiation from the sun. Exposure to this radiation could cause anemia, infections, bleeding, and damage to your bone marrow. Long-term effects could lead to cancer.

Fortunately, solar flares are preceded by a warning: radio waves. Your crew could detect the flares an hour before they reach your ship. Given notice, you can retreat into a room in the craft that is insulated by your supply of food and water. This will protect you, and your food and water will not be damaged by the radiation from the flares.

The only problem would be if you are outside your craft, doing repair work, when the radio waves are detected. In that case, you might get hit by the flares before you made it back inside.

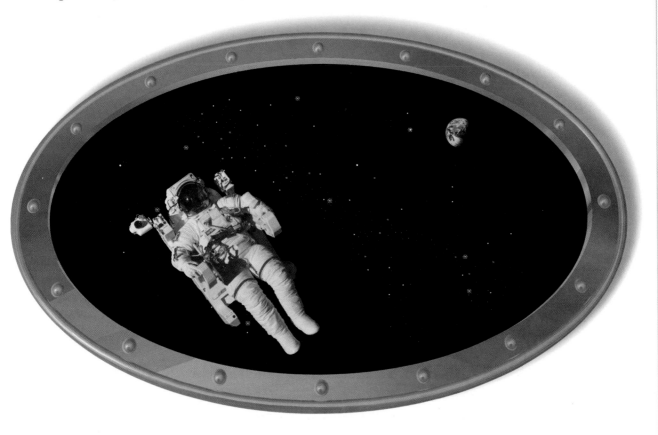

Then there are accidents, serious illness, and any other medical emergency that might arise. One member of your crew might get sick enough in the next three years to require a hospital stay or surgery. That could be a problem.

"You can't build a flying hospital," Colonel Nagel says. "You can minimize the chances of something happening by physical screening." A physician can examine you and declare you healthy. But no physician can look into the future and declare you healthy for the next three years. Your crew can include a doctor. Your ship can carry certain medicines and equipment, but you cannot prepare for every possible emergency. As Colonel Nagel puts it, "You are going to have to assume some risk."

You wonder if what you are doing is the right thing. The risks really do not bother you. You have faith in the scientists and engineers who put your program together. But you think of the cost of sending your crew to Mars: 50 billion dollars. What does that mean? How much is 50 billion dollars?

It is 200 dollars for every man, woman, and child in the United States. How many homes could be built with that money? How many medical bills could be paid? What rivers could be cleaned?

You doubt many other explorers cared about the money that was spent on their adventures. Sending you to Mars has employed tens of thousands of people. It has brought Russia, much of Europe, and the United States together in the pursuit of a common goal. Millions of people pray for your success.

You open a snack of sandwich cookies. The average adult requires about 3 pounds of food, 5 pounds of water, and 2 pounds of oxygen a day. You can get by with a little less. For your long trip your crew of six will need to pack about 54,000 pounds of food, water, and oxygen. To save on space and weight, and to last a long time without spoiling, most of your food was *dehydrated*—its water removed. To prepare a meal, you just open a packet, add water, and put your rehydrated beef goulash into the microwave. In the next three years you will eat about 2,700 meals in this way.

You did not become an explorer for the food.

If you get bored, or hungry between meals, you can open a bag of peanuts or cookies.

"Sleeping is kind of weird," Colonel Nagel says. Your bed is actually a sleeping bag you climb into, then slip your arms through. "You zip it up, and you just kind of float there. It's very strange because you're not lying on anything. You're just floating." Your pillow is strapped to your head with a piece of Velcro.

Your toilet looks just like the one you have at home, only it works on a vacuum system, and it has a seat belt so you don't float away.

You remind yourself you are a colonist, not a tourist. But unlike the Pilgrims, you will not be accommodated by a native civilization that has already mastered the art of living off the land. There will be nobody to greet you, and there will be no land to farm, streams to fish, or animals to hunt. Still, you cannot bring everything you will need with you.

Most significantly, you do not bring the rocket fuel for the return trip. Bringing that fuel would have made your ship impossibly heavy, too heavy to launch from Earth.

Two years before your lift-off, an unmanned rocket was sent to Mars, carrying a 40-ton payload. That cargo contained life-support systems, nearly a year's supply of food for your crew, the Earth Return Vehicle, and surface rovers. It also carried a robotic factory that instantly began sucking in the Martian air. This carbon dioxide was combined with hydrogen brought from Earth to make the methane rocket fuel needed for your return trip.

How convenient! A gas station awaits you on Mars! You think of the car trips you took on Earth. Next rest stop 50 million miles!

Life on Mars

You will look for evidence of life on Mars. You will look for fossils. You will have a rover, equipped with a pressurized cabin, to get you where you want to go. You will explore the dry rivers and lake beds. The hunting will not be easy. Fossils on Earth are tough to find, and the Earth has been teeming with life for billions of years. For an organism on Earth to become a fossil, it has to be buried shortly after it dies. Otherwise, other organisms will make a meal of it, and the wind and rain will sweep away its memory. If it is buried, it has to leave some hard clue. It could create an impression in soft mud. That sculpted mud could harden into rock. Or its bones can become *mineralized*. Or it could be frozen. Or trapped in amber, or preserved in peat. Then it has to have been exposed to the surface only recently. If it showed up on the surface long ago, it would have been destroyed by the effects of wind and water.

Nobody is really sure how, if there was life on Mars, that life formed fossils. How hard then will your work be to find fossils on Mars?

"I live near Morrison, Colorado," says Robert Zubrin, a scientist and expert on Martian explorations. "It is one of the richest areas for finding dinosaur fossils in the world. I've never found one. Professional paleontologists come out here and it takes years before they make a serious find."

So, if you cannot find a dinosaur in Colorado, how easy will it be to find traces of life on Mars? If anything ever lived on Mars, most likely it was a lot smaller than an apatosaurus. It may not have had any hard parts to leave impressions in the Martian mud. Or its traces may have been erased by the geological forces of Mars, or by the effects of the ultraviolet radiation on the soil. You will be looking for the footprints of something that may never have walked, the remains of something that may never have lived.

But *you* will be proof that life can exist on Mars. Soon after landing, your crew will cover your habitat with sandbags to protect it against ultraviolet radiation and solar flares. You will set up experimental greenhouses, to see what plants can be grown without soil, *hydroponically.* You will determine what needs to be done to the Martian soil so that it can support plant life. Perhaps you will set up pools for fish, as a future source of protein. You will study the Martian weather and geology. You will investigate the possibilities of terraforming.

In your rovers, you will hunt for areas where you could dig for frozen water. You will begin preparing Mars for the next crew to follow you in two years. Already, another unmanned payload is on its way, sent up two weeks after your launch. Along with your pioneering work, this unmanned moving van will help prepare Mars for the people who follow you. They in turn will prepare the planet for the next group of colonists.

Slowly, a string of frontier towns will arise on the pink Martian surface. Perhaps new laws will be written to govern these settlers, new governments established. With Earth over 35 million miles away, with the spoken word taking nearly 10 minutes to reach Earth, and a response taking another 10 minutes, the New Martians will grow more independent of their mother planet.

One day, a baby will be born on Mars, the first Martian. If the human body grows strong in order to fight against gravity on Earth, how will that child's body develop on Mars? What if that child's heart muscles and bones grow only strong enough to survive the weak gravity on Mars? Will that first Martian ever be able to visit the Earth?

Imagine an adult female Martian who wishes to visit the green, oxygen-rich planet of her parents. She wishes to see trees, oceans, dolphins, and blue skies. She weighs 45 Martian pounds, roughly the same as 110 Earth pounds.

She will travel six months through the zero gravity of space weighing next to nothing. Slowly her heart, muscles, and skeleton will grow weaker. Then, on landing on the Earth, she will suddenly weigh 110 pounds.

Will her heart survive?

Your ship travels silently through space. Are you an explorer, or are you simply a seed, carried across great distances to land on new, strange soil?

Why are you going?

How will you change the history of life on Mars?

Update

The story of life on Mars continues. On August 6, 1996, scientists at NASA, led by David Stewart McKay, announced that they may have discovered fossil evidence of life on Mars. They found their evidence inside a meteorite recovered from Antarctica. After studying pockets of trapped gases within the meteorite, researchers determined that it could only have come from Mars. The meteorite was probably knocked into space after a comet collided with the planet. It landed on Earth 13,000 years ago.

Dr. McKay claimed that microscopic circular- and tubular-shaped marks inside the meteorite were probably fossils of simple organisms. Scientists also found chemicals linked to amino acids, the building blocks of life. In addition, they discovered minerals that are produced by simple organisms. Researchers determined that the meteorite was around 4 billion years old. The fossils—or what might be fossils—were probably from 3.6 to 4 billion years ago, a time when Mars was warmer and wetter, with a thick carbon-dioxide atmosphere.

Some scientists, however, dispute Dr. McKay's findings. They are now doing further tests on this meteorite to determine whether the marks found were made by life-forms or caused by something else.

The story continues. . . .

About the Author

David Getz has come full circle since the beginning of his writing career. "I started writing as a nine-year-old with the goal of making my fellow fourth graders laugh." When he grew up, Mr. Getz became a fourth-grade teacher. "Without missing a beat, I was back to making nine-year-olds laugh," he relates.

The first two books that Mr. Getz wrote were humorous. *Thin Air* is a funny book about a serious topic. It features a sixth grader who has severe asthma, but who wants to be treated just like everybody else. Mr. Getz's second book, *Almost Famous,* is about a child inventor with two goals. She wants to appear on a famous television show, and she wants to help her brother, who has a heart murmur. The book describes her attempts to come up with a new invention to accomplish both goals.

After his two novels, Mr. Getz began writing nonfiction books. By this time, he had discovered his interest in science. "I set out to write stories that would place my readers next to scientists as they did their work," he says. In addition to *Life on Mars,* Mr. Getz wrote the nonfiction book *Frozen Man.* This book tells about the discovery of the "Ice Man," the frozen body of a man from about 5,000 years ago, who was found in the mountains in Italy in 1991.

David Getz

Reader Response

Open for Discussion

Based on the information given in "Destination: Mars," what would be appealing about a career in space travel? What would not be appealing?

Comprehension Check

1. The author states that Antarctica is "the closest thing on Earth to Mars." How are the two places similar? Use details from the selection in your answer.

2. What are some of the dangers of living in an environment without gravity? Look back at the selection for details.

3. How are the atmospheres of Earth and Mars different? Use information from the selection in your answer.

4. Scientists hope to find fossil evidence of life on Mars, but fossils are difficult to find even here on Earth. For a fossil to form, conditions must be perfect. List the main **steps in the process** of fossil formation. (Steps in a Process)

5. On a mission to Mars, there is little room for error. What are some of the key **steps in the process** of reaching Mars, and more importantly, returning to Earth? (Steps in a Process)

Test Prep

Look Back and Write

What does the author means when he writes, "... you are a colonist, not a tourist"? Use specific details from pages 534–535 to support your answer.

Vacationing on Mars

Wish You Were Here

Exploring Mars
by Peter Bond

ASTRONOMERS HAVE LONG DREAMED of sending people to Mars, but so far only robotic probes have landed there. The first mission to the planet's surface took place in 1976, when the two Viking landers made a successful touchdown. More recently, the Pathfinder probe made a dramatic landing in a bouncing air bag.

LOOKING FOR LIFE
The two Viking landers looked for signs of life on Mars. Each lander had a robotic arm to scoop up soil. An on-board laboratory then analyzed the soil for the telltale organic chemicals that living organisms produce. The results were disappointing—neither lander found any evidence that life has ever existed on Mars.

Rotating camera
Satellite dish
Weather monitor
Robotic arm and scoop

Viking Lander being tested on Earth

Viking Lander's view of a Martian landscape

VIKING INVADERS
After their year-long flights from Earth, the Viking landers parachuted onto two carefully selected locations on Mars. They beamed back the first-ever pictures of the surface, revealing a dusty, rock-strewn landscape and an orange sky.

MARTIAN PANORAMA
The Pathfinder probe used a rotating camera to take the picture below. This is the view you would see if you stood on Mars and turned around in a full circle.

Martian sand dunes
Antennae
Solar panels
Hills called Twin Peaks
Ramp for Sojourner

These hills may have been shaped by floods millions of years ago.

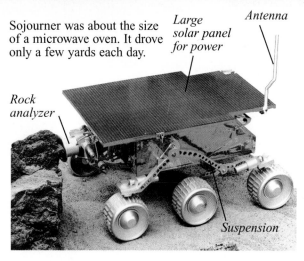

Sojourner was about the size of a microwave oven. It drove only a few yards each day.

Large solar panel for power

Antenna

Rock analyzer

Suspension

TWIN PEAKS
Pathfinder landed in 1997, tantalizingly close to two hills, nicknamed the Twin Peaks. The hills were only 0.6 miles (1 km) away, yet they were too far for Pathfinder's rover vehicle to reach.

MARS BUGGY
The Pathfinder probe carried a remote-controlled buggy called the Sojourner rover. Sojourner explored the area around the landing site, using onboard instruments to analyze chemicals in Martian rocks.

Ramp for Sojourner

Camera

Satellite dish

Solar panels

Protective shield

Weather monitor

Deflated air bags

BLUE SUNSET
Because there is so much dust high into the atmosphere, the sky glows for more than an hour after sunset.

BOUNCING TO A STOP
The Pathfinder probe parachuted onto Mars inside a giant "beach ball"—a set of air bags designed to cushion the probe's landing.

Sojourner rover

Rover tracks

Deflated air bag

Deflated air bag

Skill Lesson

Summarizing

- To **summarize** means to give a brief statement of the main idea of an article or the most important events in a story.

- When you summarize a story, include only the main actions and their outcomes.

- If a character performs several related actions, try to think of one action that includes them all. For example, instead of saying "He got an envelope, he licked a stamp, and he put the letter in the mailbox," say "He mailed a letter."

- If a list of items is given, try to think of a word or phrase that names the whole list. For "hammer, saw, and wrench," you might just say "tools."

Read "To Surprise the Children" by Alois Mikulka from *Cricket* magazine.

Write About It

1. The first paragraph describes what the brick is and isn't doing. Write the phrase that best describes it.

2. Summarize the story. Remember to include only the main actions of the characters. If a character performs several related actions, combine them into one action.

To Surprise the Children

by Alois Mikulka

translated by Ksenija Šoster-Olmer

Once I went somewhere, and I don't know why, I suddenly looked up and what did I see? There was a brick in the air. I looked at it—it wasn't falling down, it wasn't floating, it wasn't supported by anything, it wasn't hanging on anything. It was quite happy just sitting in the air as if it were a moon or a star.

I thought, "That is not safe. It can fall down on somebody's head."

Just then a bricklayer strolled by. I cried out to him, "Look up there!"

He took a look and said, "There's a brick." Then he turned to walk away. I quickly added, "What if it falls on somebody?"

Only then did the bricklayer stop in his tracks and say, "You're right." He called for the other bricklayers to come. Soon

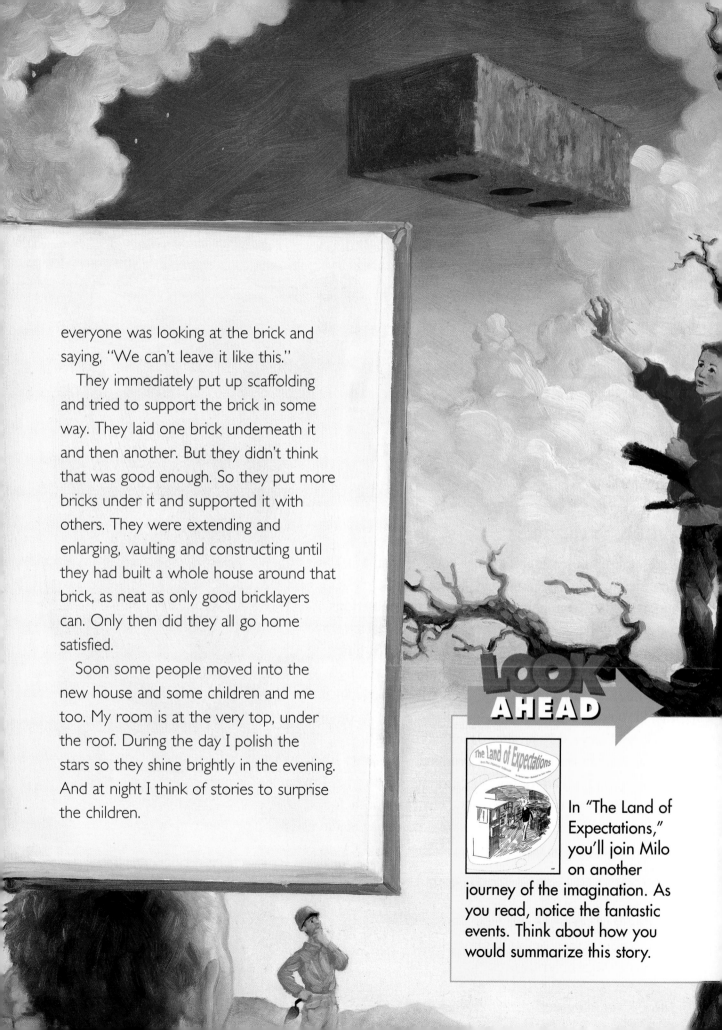

everyone was looking at the brick and saying, "We can't leave it like this."

They immediately put up scaffolding and tried to support the brick in some way. They laid one brick underneath it and then another. But they didn't think that was good enough. So they put more bricks under it and supported it with others. They were extending and enlarging, vaulting and constructing until they had built a whole house around that brick, as neat as only good bricklayers can. Only then did they all go home satisfied.

Soon some people moved into the new house and some children and me too. My room is at the very top, under the roof. During the day I polish the stars so they shine brightly in the evening. And at night I think of stories to surprise the children.

LOOK AHEAD

In "The Land of Expectations," you'll join Milo on another journey of the imagination. As you read, notice the fantastic events. Think about how you would summarize this story.

Vocabulary

Words to Know

assembled	destination
encounter	expectations
regulations	tollbooth

Words with similar meanings are called synonyms. You can often figure out the meaning of an unknown word by finding a clue in the words around it. Sometimes this clue is a synonym.

Read the paragraph below. Notice how *rules* helps you understand what *regulations* means.

Family Vacation

Here we are in the van, on a cross-country road trip. Our final destination is Yellowstone National Park, eight hundred miles from home. Dad has high expectations that this will be our best vacation ever. Just to make sure, he assembled a "Bailey Family Travel Kit" that holds information about every important place that we might encounter. Its contents include tapes, maps, magazines, travel brochures, and rules and regulations for camping in national parks. My brother, Jason, is reading a brochure about river rafting in Wyoming. My sister, Ellen, is looking over an ad for horseback riding. As for me, I'm just holding onto the change for the next tollbooth for Dad. It doesn't matter to me what we do on this vacation. I'm just happy to be on our way.

Write About It

Write about a memorable family trip. Use some vocabulary words.

The Land of Expectations

from *The Phantom Tollbooth*

by Norton Juster • illustrated by Jules Feiffer

There was once a boy named Milo who didn't know what to do with himself—not just sometimes, but always.

When he was in school he longed to be out, and when he was out he longed to be in. On the way he thought about coming home, and coming home he thought about going. Wherever he was he wished he were somewhere else, and when he got there he wondered why he'd bothered. Nothing really interested him—least of all the things that should have.

"It seems to me that almost everything is a waste of time," he remarked one day as he walked dejectedly home from school. "I can't see the point in learning to solve useless problems, or subtracting turnips from turnips, or knowing

where Ethiopia is or how to spell February." And, since no one bothered to explain otherwise, he regarded the process of seeking knowledge as the greatest waste of time of all.

As he and his unhappy thoughts hurried along (for while he was never anxious to be where he was going, he liked to get there as quickly as possible) it seemed a great wonder that the world, which was so large, could sometimes feel so small and empty.

"And worst of all," he continued sadly, "there's nothing for me to do, nowhere I'd care to go, and hardly anything worth seeing." He punctuated his last thought with such a deep sigh that a house sparrow singing nearby stopped and rushed home to be with his family.

Without stopping or looking up, Milo dashed past the buildings and busy shops that lined the street and in a few minutes reached home—dashed through the lobby—hopped onto the elevator—two, three, four, five, six, seven, eight, and off again—opened the apartment door—rushed into his room— flopped dejectedly into a chair, and grumbled softly, "Another long afternoon."

He looked glumly at all the things he owned. The books that were too much trouble to read, the tools he'd never learned to use, the small electric automobile he hadn't driven in months— or was it years?—and the hundreds of other games and toys, and bats and balls, and bits and pieces scattered around him. And then, to one side of the room, just next to the phonograph, he noticed something he had certainly never seen before.

Who could possibly have left such an enormous package and such a strange one? For, while it was not quite square, it was definitely not round, and for its size it was larger than almost any other big package of smaller dimension that he'd ever seen.

Attached to one side was a bright-blue envelope which said simply: "FOR MILO, WHO HAS PLENTY OF TIME."

Of course, if you've ever gotten a surprise package, you can imagine how puzzled and excited Milo was; and if you've never gotten one, pay close attention, because someday you might.

"I don't think it's my birthday," he puzzled, "and Christmas must be months away, and I haven't been outstandingly good, or even good at all." (He had to admit this even to himself.) "Most probably I won't like it anyway, but since I don't know where it came from, I can't possibly send it back." He thought about it for quite a while and then opened the envelope, but just to be polite.

"ONE GENUINE TURNPIKE TOLLBOOTH," it stated—and then it went on:

"EASILY ASSEMBLED AT HOME, AND FOR USE BY THOSE WHO HAVE NEVER TRAVELED IN LANDS BEYOND."

"Beyond what?" thought Milo as he continued to read.

"THIS PACKAGE CONTAINS THE FOLLOWING ITEMS:

"One (1) genuine turnpike tollbooth to be erected according to directions.

"Three (3) precautionary signs to be used in a precautionary fashion.

"Assorted coins for use in paying tolls.

"One (1) map, up to date and carefully drawn by master cartographers, depicting natural and man-made features.

"One (1) book of rules and traffic regulations, which may not be bent or broken."

And in smaller letters at the bottom it concluded:

"RESULTS ARE NOT GUARANTEED, BUT IF NOT PERFECTLY SATISFIED, YOUR WASTED TIME WILL BE REFUNDED."

Following the instructions, which told him to cut here, lift there, and fold back all around, he soon had the tollbooth unpacked and set up on its stand. He fitted the windows in place and attached the roof, which extended out on both sides, and fastened on the coin box. It was very much like the tollbooths he'd seen many times on family trips, except of course it was much smaller and purple.

"What a strange present," he thought to himself. "The least they could have done was to send a highway with it, for it's terribly impractical without one." But since, at the time, there was nothing else he wanted to play with, he set up the three signs,

SLOW DOWN APPROACHING TOLLBOOTH
PLEASE HAVE YOUR FARE READY
HAVE YOUR DESTINATION IN MIND

and slowly unfolded the map.

As the announcement stated, it was a beautiful map, in many colors, showing principal roads, rivers and seas, towns and cities, mountains and valleys, intersections and detours, and sites of outstanding interest, both beautiful and historic.

The only trouble was that Milo had never heard of any of the places it indicated, and even the names sounded most peculiar.

"I don't think there really is such a country," he concluded after studying it carefully. "Well, it doesn't matter anyway." And he closed his eyes and poked a finger at the map.

"Dictionopolis," read Milo slowly when he saw what his finger had chosen. "Oh, well, I might as well go there as anywhere."

He walked across the room and dusted the car off carefully. Then, taking the map and rule book with him, he hopped in and, for lack of anything better to do, drove slowly up to the tollbooth. As he deposited his coin and rolled past he remarked wistfully, "I do hope this is an interesting game, otherwise the afternoon will be so terribly dull."

Suddenly he found himself speeding along an unfamiliar country highway, and as he looked back over his shoulder neither the tollbooth nor his room nor even the house was anywhere in sight. What had started as make-believe was now very real.

"What a strange thing to have happen," he thought (just as you must be thinking right now). "This game is much more serious than I thought, for here I am riding on a road I've never seen, going to a place I've never heard of, and all because of a tollbooth which came from nowhere. I'm certainly glad that it's a nice day for a trip," he concluded hopefully, for, at the moment, this was the one thing he definitely knew.

The sun sparkled, the sky was clear, and all the colors he saw seemed to be richer and brighter than he could ever remember. The flowers shone as if they'd been cleaned and polished, and the tall trees that lined the road shimmered in silvery green.

"WELCOME TO EXPECTATIONS," said a carefully lettered sign on a small house at the side of the road.

"INFORMATION, PREDICTIONS, AND ADVICE CHEERFULLY OFFERED. PARK HERE AND BLOW HORN."

With the first sound from the horn a little man in a long coat came rushing from the house, speaking as fast as he could and repeating everything several times:

"My, my, my, my, my, welcome, welcome, welcome, welcome to the land of Expectations, to the land of Expectations, to the land of Expectations. We don't get many travelers these days; we certainly don't get many travelers these days. Now what can I do for you? I'm the Whether Man."

"Is this the right road for Dictionopolis?" asked Milo, a little bowled over by the effusive greeting.

"Well now, well now, well now," he began again, "I don't know of any wrong road to Dictionopolis, so if this road goes to Dictionopolis at all it must be the right road, and if it doesn't it must be the right road to somewhere else, because there are no wrong roads to anywhere. Do you think it will rain?"

"I thought you were the Weather Man," said Milo, very confused.

"Oh no," said the little man, "I'm the Whether Man, not the Weather Man, for after all it's more important to know whether there will be weather than what the weather will be." And with that he released a dozen balloons that sailed off into the sky. "Must see which way the wind is blowing," he said, chuckling over his little joke and watching them disappear in all directions.

"What kind of a place is Expectations?" inquired Milo, unable to see the humor and feeling very doubtful of the little man's sanity.

"Good question, good question," he exclaimed. "Expectations is the place you must always go to before you get to where you're going. Of course, some people never go beyond Expectations, but my job is to hurry them along whether they like it or not. Now what else can I do for you?" And before Milo could reply he rushed into the house and reappeared a moment later with a new coat and an umbrella.

"I think I can find my own way," said Milo, not at all sure that he could. But, since he didn't understand the little man at all, he decided that he might as well move on—at least until he met someone whose sentences didn't always sound as if they would make as much sense backwards as forwards.

"Splendid, splendid, splendid," exclaimed the Whether Man. "Whether or not you find your own way, you're bound to find some way. If you happen to find my way, please return it, as it was lost years ago. I imagine by now it's quite rusty. You did say it was going to rain, didn't you?" And with that he opened the umbrella and looked up nervously.

"I'm glad you made your own decision. I do so hate to make up my mind about anything, whether it's good or bad, up or down, in or out, rain or shine. Expect everything, I always say, and the unexpected never happens. Now please drive carefully; good-by, good-by, good-by, good. . ." His last good-by was drowned out by an enormous clap of thunder, and as Milo drove down the road in the bright sunshine he could see the Whether Man standing in the middle of a fierce cloudburst that seemed to be raining only on him.

The road dipped now into a broad green valley and stretched toward the horizon. The little car bounced along with very little effort, and Milo had hardly to touch the accelerator to go as fast as he wanted. He was glad to be on his way again.

"It's all very well to spend time in Expectations," he thought, "but talking to that strange man all day would certainly get me nowhere. He's the most peculiar person I've ever met," continued Milo—unaware of how many peculiar people he would shortly encounter.

As he drove along the peaceful highway he soon fell to daydreaming and paid less and less attention to where he was going. In short time he wasn't paying any attention at all, and that is why, at a fork in the road, when a sign pointed to the left, Milo went to the right, along a route that looked suspiciously like the wrong way.

Things began to change as soon as he left the main highway. The sky became quite gray and, along with it, the whole countryside seemed to lose its color and assume the

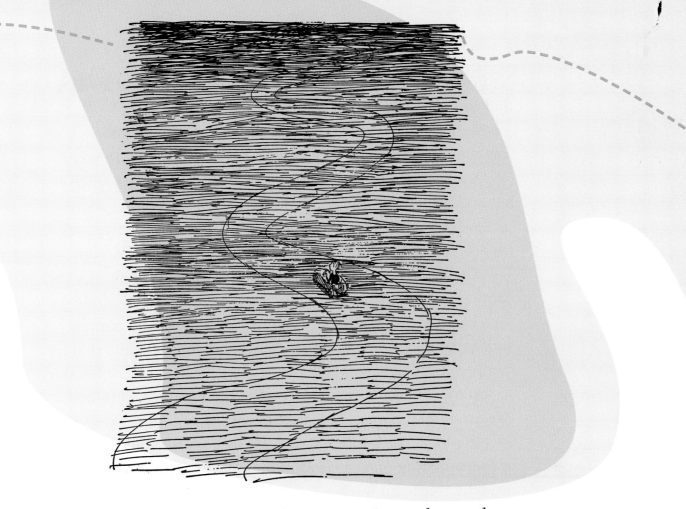

same monotonous tone. Everything was quiet, and even the air hung heavily. The birds sang only gray songs and the road wound back and forth in an endless series of climbing curves.

Mile after

mile after

mile after

mile he drove, and now, gradually, the car went slower and slower, until it was hardly moving at all.

"It looks as though I'm getting nowhere," yawned Milo, becoming very drowsy and dull. "I hope I haven't taken a wrong turn."

Mile after

mile after

mile after

mile, and everything became grayer and more monotonous. Finally the car just stopped altogether, and, hard as he tried, it wouldn't budge another inch.

"I wonder where I am," said Milo in a very worried tone.

"You're . . . in . . . the . . . Dol . . . drums," wailed a voice that sounded far away.

He looked around quickly to see who had spoken. No one was there, and it was as quiet and still as one could imagine.

"Yes . . . the . . . Dol . . . drums," yawned another voice, but still he saw no one.

"WHAT ARE THE DOLDRUMS?" he cried loudly, and tried very hard to see who would answer this time.

"The Doldrums, my young friend, are where nothing ever happens and nothing ever changes."

This time the voice came from so close that Milo jumped with surprise, for, sitting on his right shoulder, so lightly that he hardly noticed, was a small creature exactly the color of his shirt.

"Allow me to introduce all of us," the creature went on. "We are the Lethargarians, at your service."

Milo looked around and, for the first time, noticed dozens of them—sitting on the car, standing in the road, and lying all over the trees and bushes. They were very difficult to see, because whatever they happened to be sitting on or near was exactly the color they happened to be. Each one looked very much like the other (except for the color, of course) and some looked even more like each other than they did like themselves.

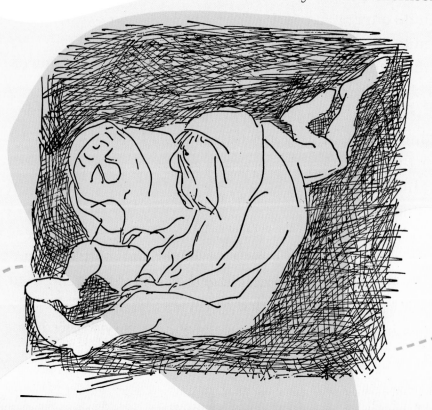

"I'm very pleased to meet you," said Milo, not sure whether or not he was pleased at all. "I think I'm lost. Can you help me please?"

"Don't say 'think,'" said one sitting on his shoe, for the one on his shoulder had fallen asleep. "It's against the law." And he yawned and fell off to sleep too.

"No one's allowed to think in the Doldrums," continued a third, beginning to doze off. And as each one spoke, he fell off to sleep and another picked up the conversation with hardly any interruption.

"Don't you have a rule book? It's local ordinance 175389-J."

Milo quickly pulled the rule book from his pocket, opened to the page, and read, "Ordinance 175389-J: It shall be unlawful, illegal, and unethical to think, think of thinking, surmise, presume, reason, meditate, or speculate while in the Doldrums. Anyone breaking this law shall be severely punished!"

"That's a ridiculous law," said Milo, quite indignantly. "Everybody thinks."

"We don't," shouted the Lethargarians all at once.

"And most of the time *you* don't," said a yellow one sitting in a daffodil. "That's why you're here. You weren't thinking, and you weren't paying attention either. People who don't pay attention often get stuck in the Doldrums." And with that he toppled out of the flower and fell snoring into the grass.

Milo couldn't help laughing at the little creature's strange behavior, even though he knew it might be rude.

"Stop that at once," ordered the plaid one clinging to his stocking. "Laughing is against the law. Don't you have a rule book? It's local ordinance 574381-W."

Opening the book again, Milo found Ordinance 574381-W: "In the Doldrums, laughter is frowned upon and smiling is permitted only on alternate Thursdays. Violators shall be dealt with most harshly."

"Well, if you can't laugh or think, what can you do?" asked Milo.

"Anything as long as it's nothing, and everything as long as it isn't anything," explained another. "There's lots to do; we have a very busy schedule—

"At 8 o'clock we get up and then we spend

"From 8:00 to 9:00 daydreaming.

"From 9:00 to 9:30 we take our early midmorning nap.

"From 9:30 to 10:30 we dawdle and delay.

"From 10:30 to 11:30 we take our late early morning nap.

"From 11:30 to 12:00 we bide our time and then eat lunch.

"From 1:00 to 2:00 we linger and loiter.

"From 2:00 to 2:30 we take our early afternoon nap.

"From 2:30 to 3:30 we put off for tomorrow what we could have done today.

"From 3:30 to 4:00 we take our early late afternoon nap.

"From 4:00 to 5:00 we loaf and lounge until dinner.

"From 6:00 to 7:00 we dillydally.

"From 7:00 to 8:00 we take our early evening nap, and then for an hour before we go to bed at 9:00 we waste time.

"As you can see, that leaves almost no time for brooding, lagging, plodding, or procrastinating, and if we stopped to think or laugh, we'd never get nothing done."

"You mean you'd never get anything done," corrected Milo.

"We don't want to get anything done," snapped another angrily; "we want to get nothing done, and we can do that without your help."

"You see," continued another in a more conciliatory tone, "it's really quite strenuous doing nothing all day, so once a week we take a holiday and go nowhere, which was just where we were going when you came along. Would you care to join us?"

"I might as well," thought Milo; "that's where I seem to be going anyway."

"Tell me," he yawned, for he felt ready for a nap now himself, "does everyone here do nothing?"

"Everyone but the terrible watchdog," said two of them, shuddering in chorus. "He's always sniffing around to see that nobody wastes time. A most unpleasant character."

"The watchdog?" said Milo quizzically.

"THE WATCHDOG," shouted another, fainting from fright, for racing down the road barking furiously and kicking up a great cloud of dust was the very dog of whom they had been speaking.

"RUN!"

"WAKE UP!"

"RUN!"

"HERE HE COMES!"

"THE WATCHDOG!"

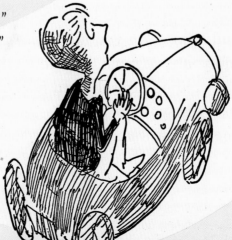

Great shouts filled the air as the Lethargarians scattered in all directions and soon disappeared entirely.

"R-R-R-G-H-R-O-R-R-H-F-F," exclaimed the watchdog as he dashed up to the car, loudly puffing and panting.

Milo's eyes opened wide, for there in front of him was a large dog with a perfectly normal head, four feet, and a tail—and the body of a loudly ticking alarm clock.

"What are you doing here?" growled the watchdog.

"Just killing time," replied Milo apologetically. "You see—"

"KILLING TIME!" roared the dog—so furiously that his alarm went off. "It's bad enough wasting time without killing it." And he shuddered at the thought. "Why are you in the Doldrums anyway—don't you have anywhere to go?"

"I was on my way to Dictionopolis when I got stuck here," explained Milo. "Can you help me?"

"Help you! You must help yourself," the dog replied, carefully winding himself with his left hind leg. "I suppose you know why you got stuck."

"I guess I just wasn't thinking," said Milo.

"PRECISELY," shouted the dog as his alarm went off again.

"Now you know what you must do."

"I'm afraid I don't," admitted Milo, feeling quite stupid.

"Well," continued the watchdog impatiently, "since you got here by not thinking, it seems reasonable to expect that, in order to get out, you must start thinking." And with that he hopped into the car.

"Do you mind if I get in? I love automobile rides."

Milo began to think as hard as he could (which was very difficult, since he wasn't used to it). He thought of birds that swim and fish that fly. He thought of yesterday's lunch and tomorrow's dinner. He thought of words that began with J and numbers that end in 3. And, as he thought, the wheels began to turn.

"We're moving, we're moving," he shouted happily.

"Keep thinking," scolded the watchdog.

The little car started to go faster and faster as Milo's brain whirled with activity, and down the road they went. In a few moments they were out of the Doldrums and back on the main highway. All the colors had returned to their original brightness, and as they raced along the road Milo continued to think of all sorts of things; of the many detours and wrong turns that were so easy to take, of how fine it was to be moving along, and, most of all, of how much could be accomplished with just a little thought. And the dog, his nose in the wind, just sat back, watchfully ticking.

"You must excuse my gruff conduct," the watchdog said, after they'd been driving for some time, "but you see it's traditional for watchdogs to be ferocious. . ."

Milo was so relieved at having escaped the Doldrums that he assured the dog that he bore him no ill will and, in fact, was very grateful for the assistance.

"Splendid," shouted the watchdog. "I'm very pleased—I'm sure we'll be great friends for the rest of the trip. You may call me Tock."

"That is a strange name for a dog who goes tickticktickticktick all day," said Milo. "Why didn't they call you—"

"Don't say it," gasped the dog, and Milo could see a tear well up in his eye.

"I didn't mean to hurt your feelings," said Milo, not meaning to hurt his feelings.

"That's all right," said the dog, getting hold of himself. "It's an old story and a sad one, but I can tell it to you now.

"When my brother was born, the first pup in the family, my parents were overjoyed and immediately named him Tick in expectation of the sound they were sure he'd make. On first winding him, they discovered to their horror that, instead of going tickticktickticktick, he went tocktocktocktocktocktock. They rushed to the Hall of Records to change the name, but too late. It had already been officially inscribed, and nothing could be done. When I arrived they were determined not to make the same mistake twice and, since it seemed logical that all their children would make the same sound, they named me Tock. Of course, you know the rest—my brother is called Tick because he goes tocktocktocktocktocktocktock and I am called Tock because I go tickticktickticktickticktick and both of us are forever burdened with the wrong names. My parents were so overwrought that they gave up having any more children and devoted their lives to doing good work among the poor and hungry."

"But how did you become a watchdog?" interjected Milo, hoping to change the subject, as Tock was sobbing quite loudly now.

"That," he said, rubbing a paw in his eye, "is also traditional. My family have always been watchdogs—from father to son, almost since time began.

"You see," he continued, beginning to feel better, "once there was no time at all, and people found it very inconvenient. They never knew whether they were eating lunch or dinner, and they were always missing trains. So time was invented to help them keep track of the day and get places when they should. When they began to count all the time that was available, what with 60 seconds in a minute and 60 minutes in an hour and 24 hours in a day and 365 days in a year, it seemed as if there was much more than could ever be used. 'If there's so much of it, it couldn't be very valuable,' was the general opinion, and it soon fell into disrepute. People wasted it and even gave it away. Then we were given the job of seeing that no one wasted time again," he said, sitting up proudly. "It's hard work but a noble calling. For you see"—and now he was standing on the seat, one foot on the windshield, shouting with his arms outstretched—"it is our most valuable possession, more precious than diamonds. It marches on, it and tide wait for no man, and—"

At that point in the speech the car hit a bump in the road and the watchdog collapsed in a heap on the front seat with his alarm again ringing furiously.

"Are you all right?" shouted Milo.

"Umphh," grunted Tock. "Sorry to get carried away, but I think you get the point."

As they drove along, Tock continued to explain the importance of time, quoting the old philosophers and poets and illustrating each point with gestures that brought him perilously close to tumbling headlong from the speeding automobile.

Norton Juster

About the Author

When *The Phantom Tollbooth*—the novel from which "The Land of Expectations" is taken—first came out in 1961, many librarians didn't quite know what to do with it. It was unlike any children's book before it, and many thought it was too sophisticated for young readers to understand. Today it is regarded as a modern classic. Its author, Norton Juster, is an architect and professor of design, who occasionally writes books.

Another book by Mr. Juster, *As: A Surfeit of Similes,* is somewhat similar in style to *The Phantom Tollbooth.* In this book, two gentlemen are on a journey to collect similes—comparisons—in any way possible. When Mr. Juster is not writing or designing buildings, he enjoys cooking, gardening, bicycling, and reading.

About the Illustrator

Jules Feiffer is well-known for his whimsical line drawings. Besides creating cartoons and the illustrations for *The Phantom Tollbooth,* he has written plays and screenplays for adults as well as writing and illustrating several books for young people. Mr. Feiffer's first book for young people, *The Man in the Ceiling,* was named one of the best books of the year by *Booklist* and *Publishers Weekly.* Other books he has written for young people include *Meanwhile . . .* and *A Barrel of Laughs, a Vale of Tears.* Mr. Feiffer has received a Pulitzer Prize for his editorial cartoons.

Jules Feiffer

Reader Response

Open for Discussion

If you had Milo's tollbooth, where would it take you? What would the journey do for you?

Comprehension Check

1. Describe Milo's attitude at the opening of the story. How does the appearance of the tollbooth begin to change that attitude? Use details from the story in your answer.

2. Why does Milo get stuck in the Doldrums? How does he escape? Look back at the story for details.

3. What is "our most valuable possession, more precious than diamonds," according to Tock, the watchdog? Why?

4. One of the Lethargarians describes a typical day in the Doldrums. **Summarize** their "very busy schedule" in one sentence. (Summarizing)

5. **Summarize** Milo's eventful day in a few sentences. (Summarizing)

 Test Prep

Look Back and Write

Look at the words and lines of text on pages 555 and 556. The size and position of some of the words and lines look unusual. Why did the author write this way?

On the Move

by Miguel Vilar

Mini Wheels

It's small enough to weave between lanes and park in a motorcycle space. Smart Cabrio may be your best bet for beating traffic gridlock. Smart, a division of Daimler-Chrysler, launched the 2.5 m (8 ft) long, 1.5 m (5 ft) wide, and 1.5 m high Cabrio in 1998. The Cabrio convertible version debuted in March 2000. Made in Germany and now sold in Europe, the two-seater Cabrio gets 21km per liter (50 mi per gallon), making gas station visits—like the Cabrio itself—well, minimal.

Driverless Taxi

Want to visit a friend on the far side of town? Imagine walking down the block to a PRT (Personal Rapid Transit) station. You buy a ticket, and a central computer miles away dispatches a driverless subway to pick you up and whisk you nonstop to your destination. No way? Researchers at Raytheon, an engineering company in Lexington, Massachusetts, are perfecting the PRT2000—an automated public transport system—at their test site. There, three rubber-tired vehicles glide along a 610 m (2,000 ft) circuit of elevated rail tracks at 130 km (80 mi) per hour.

Raytheon's scheme for the next century: vehicles similar to "Peoplemovers" (already used in downtown Miami and Detroit) that speed on 6-foot wide railways 16 feet above city streets. Passengers will head to hundreds of PRT stations one-third of a mile apart. But unlike Peoplemovers, central computers calculate the most direct route specified on each passenger ticket, then guide you to the car going your way. Engineers plan to construct a working prototype of PRT2000 in Rosemont, Illinois, within three years. Get ready to glide!

Personal Flying Machine

You step into a machine and secure yourself in a standing position. Then, using regular gas, you crank up the engine—and blast off! In the next decade you may hit the skyways instead of highways in your own air scooter. With funding from NASA, flight engineer Michael Moshier is testing a *prototype,* or preliminary model, of his personal flying vehicle. SoloTrek stands 2.4 m (8 ft) high and 2.7 m (9 ft) wide. It takes off like a helicopter, climbs to 3 km (10,000 ft) and breezes along at 128 km (80 mi) per hour. SoloTrek gets 32 km (20 mi) to the gallon and can fly for 90 minutes, or about 193 km (120 mi), before needing a refuel. "We've dreamed of such a vehicle for many years," says Moshier. "Now the dream is becoming a reality."

How does it work? You stand on footrests and use your hands to grip levers that control two circular *air ducts,* or fans, above your head. When you ignite the engine, the spinning fans generate enough *thrust,* or force of downward air, to render the craft airborne. (The principle behind takeoff: Newton's Third Law of Motion—for each action there's an equal and opposite reaction.)

You use hand levers to steer the vehicle through the air. To go forward, you tilt the fans backward. Rushing air pushes downward and backward, propelling the machine forward and maintaining what Moshier calls *hover,* or float. In the same way, by tilting SoloTrek's fans right or left, you navigate your turns. To land, you slow the speeding fans to reduce the downward air thrust, allowing gravity (Earth's downward pull) to gently pull SoloTrek to the ground. The vehicle weighs 245 kg (540 lb), and can land on "any level surface larger than a dining room table," says Moshier.

Skill Lesson

Character

- **Characters** are the people or animals who take part in the events of a short story, novel, play, or other form of fiction.

- You can learn about characters by noticing what they think, say, and do. You can also learn about characters by paying attention to how other characters treat them and what others say about them.

- The lasting qualities of a character's personality are called character traits. *Brave, stubborn,* and *honest* are examples of character traits. Character traits can help you predict how a character will act in a new situation.

Read "The Pleasantest Days" from *The Trumpet of the Swan* by E. B. White.

Talk About It

1. What do you learn about Sam from the way his father treats him?

2. Why doesn't Sam tell his father about seeing the swans? What name would you give to this character trait?

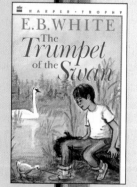

The Pleasantest Days

by E. B. White

Sam returns to camp after discovering the nest of a trumpeter swan. His father is frying fish for lunch.

"Did you see anything over there?" asked his father.

"Well," said Sam, "it's a swampy pond with a lot of reeds and cattails. I don't think it would be any good for fishing. And it's hard to get to—you have to cross a swamp."

"See anything?" repeated Mr. Beaver.

"I saw a muskrat," said Sam, "and a few red-winged blackbirds."

Mr. Beaver looked up from the wood stove, where the fish were sizzling in a pan.

"Sam," he said, "I know you like to go exploring. But don't forget—these woods and marshes are not like the country around home in Montana. If you ever go over to that pond again, be careful you don't get lost. I don't like you crossing swamps. They're treacherous. You could step into a soggy place and get bogged down, and there wouldn't be anybody to pull you out."

"I'll be careful," said Sam. He knew perfectly well he would be going back to the pond where the swans were. And he had no intention of getting lost in the woods. He felt relieved that he had not told his father about seeing the swans, but he felt queer about it too. Sam was not a sly boy, but he was odd in one respect: he liked to keep things to himself. And he liked being alone, particularly when he was in the woods. He enjoyed the life on his father's cattle ranch in the Sweet Grass country in Montana. He loved his mother. He loved Duke, his cow pony. He loved riding the range.

But the thing he enjoyed most in life was these camping trips in Canada with his father. Mrs. Beaver didn't care for the woods, so she seldom went along—it was usually just Sam and Mr. Beaver. They would motor to the border and cross into Canada. There Mr. Beaver would hire a bush pilot to fly them to the lake where his camp was, for a few days of fishing and loafing and exploring. Mr. Beaver did most of the fishing and loafing. Sam did the exploring. These were the pleasantest days of Sam's life, these days in the woods, far, far from everywhere—no automobiles, no roads, no people, no noise, no school, no homework, no problems, except the problem of getting lost.

LOOK AHEAD

In "The Trail Drive," you'll meet another young man who goes on an adventure. As you read, try to identify his character traits.

Vocabulary

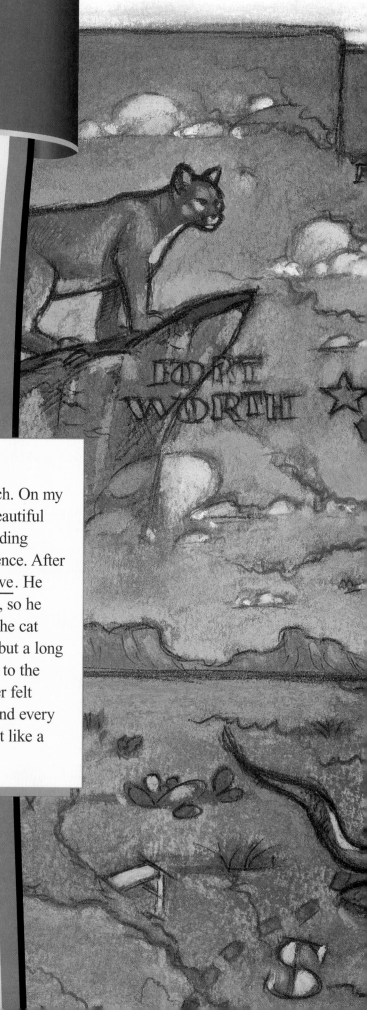

Words to Know

drive	mustang	pounce
scorching	weariness	

Many words have more than one meaning. To decide which meaning of a word is being used, look for clues in the surrounding sentences or the paragraph.

Read the paragraph below. Decide whether *drive* means "a trip in a motor vehicle" or "the act of moving cattle."

Cowboy for a Summer

Last summer I worked on my uncle's cattle ranch. On my very first day Uncle Chris let me saddle up a beautiful mustang. I was a little scared at first, but the riding lessons I had taken back home gave me confidence. After a few weeks he let me participate in a cattle drive. He had recently spotted a mountain lion in the area, so he thought he should sell his young calves before the cat could pounce upon them. It was a short drive, but a long day. After covering twelve miles from the ranch to the train yard in town, I felt a weariness I had never felt before. I was burned from the scorching sun, and every muscle in my body ached, but I was proud. I felt like a real cowhand.

Talk About It

Pretend you're sitting around a campfire. Tell a story about ranching in the West. Use as many vocabulary words as you can.

The Trail Drive

from *The Adventures of Midnight Son*   by Denise Lewis Patrick

The year is 1863. With the help of his parents, thirteen-year-old Midnight escapes from slavery. He hides during the day and travels on his horse, Dahomey, at night. Finally he arrives in Mexico, where there is no slavery. He takes the last name of Son and finds work on a ranch. Mississippi Slim, an African American cowboy, becomes his friend and helps him find a job caring for the remuda, or spare horses, on a cattle drive.

When Joe B. halted the herd for the day, Midnight had already spotted a grassy flat spot northeast of the camp. *The horses hafta be tied good and tight through the night. I've gotta drive these pickets down solid into the ground. That's a good place, not too many rocks. Firm ground to hold the stakes when I get 'em in.*

He tied Dahomey to the chow wagon, took out his tools, and set to work. He pounded his first picket into the hard ground, working up a sweat. He used the toe of his boot to nudge the picket. It didn't move. He marked off twenty paces from the picket and drove another one down. Next, he knotted and double-knotted one end of his coiled rope around the first picket. He stretched the rope and pulled it, checking again to make sure the picket was secure in the ground. Finally he looped and tied the end of the rope to the second picket, knotting it carefully.

Then he went over to Rusty, who was nibbling some sweet grass. She seemed to be the leader, and when she moved, the others moved too. One by one Midnight tethered six ponies to the picket line.

He worked on, not paying attention to anyone or anything else. Sweat rolled down his temples. He licked the salty taste off his lips

and kept going. Six more. At last he tied Dahomey to the line and stood to wipe his forehead. Midnight looked back at the work he'd done. The horses hadn't really given him any trouble. His first day on the drive was over, and he was satisfied.

"Good job for your first time." Joe B. strolled up and tugged on the last rope line Midnight had stretched. It was so tight that the rope bounced against Joe's hand. He nodded and looked at Midnight.

"Looks like you need a cooldown, son."

"Sure could use it," Midnight said, still wiping sweat from his neck.

"Well, now that you're out of the saddle for the day, you can take it easier. Pablo and Big Lou are on duty tonight, patrolling the edges of the herd for trouble. We call it night herding. They'll get fresh mounts right after chow. If Slim don't need you for anything, you're a free man till wake-up. But remember, you stand guard over these ponies." Joe B. walked off just like he had come, with his thumbs hung in his pants pockets and his hat pushed back on his head. Midnight realized that he'd never seen the big man move suddenly, or fast.

Bet that don't mean he couldn't beat a deer in a footrace. Midnight chuckled to himself and walked down a low ridge to the pond. He gulped a handful of water, threw some of it up onto his face, and sat back on his haunches.

Midnight looked all around. Texas land was mostly flat with a few ridges. This part of the country had more wild grass and ground cover than the West. Some low hills rose up here and there. Beyond them, the sky was stripes of pink and yellow and orange behind the dull blaze of the setting sun.

I'm a free man till wake-up call, Joe B. says. Well, well. A man who could be my master has told me I'm free. Ain't that like a fox passin' up a chicken house. This new life is somethin' else.

Midnight stretched his legs, then his arms. Sniffing the air, he caught the smell of sowbelly and beans. He scrambled up and made his way to the chow wagon.

"Well, here's the horse man!" Mississippi Slim was standing over a steaming kettle, his ladle dripping onto Lou Boy's already full plate. Lou Boy snatched a handful of fried bread and hungrily slopped it into the creamy mound of white beans.

"Better hurry up, Midnight! Slim's beans and bacon go faster'n a mad bull chasin' a tenderfoot cowhand!"

"I sure hope that tenderfoot cowhand ain't me!" Midnight felt easy around Slim and Lou Boy. He got his plate filled too. Slim gave him a quick, private look with his eyebrows raised, like he was asking if everything was really all right. Midnight just raised his chin a little, with a smile. Slim moved his eyes on to the next cowpoke in line, telling Pablo he'd better watch how much he was eating, or his horse would end up bowlegged.

"First day go all right?" Lou Boy mumbled through his food.

"Mmmm." Midnight swallowed. "Didn't see hide or hair of you."

"Man, them cattle spread out so far that I was miles behind. All the dust they kick up, it's a wonder I could see myself!" They both laughed. Midnight watched the others get food and gather around the fire where the coffeepot was bubbling.

There was a pattern to it all. The days were long. Riding for so many hours was hard. Grit and dirt lay on the men's clothes, skin, and hair. They traveled under the scorching sun. They sloshed through rain. Only the weather changed. Otherwise, each day was like another.

Midnight liked it because even though he thought he knew what to expect, something unexpected could happen at any time. A cow might decide to have a calf. Slim might spot wild quail and go off on a hunt. A swollen creek might cause them to go miles out of the way to find an easier crossing.

Soon enough they had skirted Fort Worth. Within days they were nearing the border between Texas and Indian territory. This was their first big river crossing.

The mighty Red River seemed to sneak up on them; one day there was only land before them and the next day the ground turned to red clay hills sloping down to all that water. Midnight had never seen so much water in his life.

Joe B. decided to cross the river right then and bed down for the night once the whole herd cleared the other side. Unlike before, he now rode with the men and the herd. Midnight sat tall in Dahomey's saddle and listened hard.

"Midnight, I want you to follow tight behind Slim. This is an easy crossing place, but we can't afford to have any ponies taking a bad step on the riverbed and breaking a leg. Once you're over, you're gonna ride about five miles north. Picket the remuda there and help Slim set up. Got it?"

"Right." Midnight set his lips and took one last turn around his horses, first moving silently like he had that very first day. Then he leaned into them and spoke in a low voice. "Stay with me, now, ponies. Stay with me." Slowly he headed Dahomey up to lead them splashing into the river.

The water rushed beneath them. Crossing against the strong current was like pushing a solid tree trunk. Dahomey nosed forward. Midnight looked from side to side, keeping count. Water was up to the top of his boots. Water rose up to his knees. Midnight felt his fear rising too. He'd never been in a river, never in any water this deep. *Gotta keep my mind on these horses. I know I can't control no river. Gotta beat this fear down.* Midnight dug his heels into Dahomey's sides.

"Come on, ponies! Get along! Get!" His voice rang out. The horses plunged ahead, staying body to body and straining against the water.

"Stay on 'em, Midnight Son!" Slim's voice cheered him on. "Almost to the riverbank! Almost there!"

Midnight dared to look up from the animals. Slim was right.

"All right, ponies! Up we go!"

Dahomey splashed up onto the riverbank and the others scrambled behind. Midnight patted Dahomey's neck.

"We did it, Dahomey," he said quietly. "We did it."

Slim turned his wagon and led Midnight, Dahomey, and the sputtering remuda to the campsite.

That night, weariness was in Midnight's bones. He felt as if he'd carried every horse over that river on his own back. He was so tired that he didn't even remember what Slim's dinner meal was or tasted like. When he fell into sleep, it was on the bare ground. His still-tied-up bedroll was under his head.

Midnight dreamed. His dream was one of noises: the plantation noises, his family's voices, Spanish talking, water gurgling, and horses splashing. He tossed and turned. But then there was another noise.

"AAAAAAaaaaaaaaaaahhhheeeeee!" Midnight's eyes flew open. Sounded like a woman's scream, but Midnight knew that wasn't it. He sat up, and in the darkness he could see Joe B. doing the same, only with his rifle in hand. Without turning his head, Joe B. hissed, "Shhhhh!"

"AAAAAAAaaaaaaaahhheeeeee!" Where was it? The sound wasn't loud. Still, it was clear and too close to let any man sleep easy. Other heads popped up.

"Slim!" Joe B. called out in a hoarse whisper. "Check out the rear. I'll handle up here." Midnight quickly loosened a mottled gray horse from the picket. Slim didn't wait for a saddle.

"Think it's a bobcat?" Midnight asked.

"Doggone right," Slim muttered. "Sure don't need no cougars 'round here," he said as he sped off. Joe B. mounted his own horse and followed. He'd said he would pay extra if the entire herd got to Wyandotte. But a cougar could pick them off, one by one, just for sport, if he was evil enough.

The crew sat restless in the dark for two hours, listening to the night. The cougar's call didn't come again. No rifle shot came either. When Slim and Joe B. rode in together, their faces were tight, their jaws clenched. Midnight guessed that the bobcat was still out there somewhere. He checked the horses once more before spreading out his bedroll and lying on it. The sleeping he did after that was so light that he could hear the horses' heavy breathing. A cat stalking a herd was big trouble, and they all knew it.

For nearly a week the cat made itself known by wailing off somewhere in the night, but nobody could spot it. They moved the few calves away from the outer edges of the herd. Joe put two more men on night duty. Nobody slept. On the sixth night, Joe B. stationed Midnight between the remuda and the left flank of the herd. Midnight took his spot an hour or so after chow. He didn't bother to lie down. He propped his back against a smooth rock. The air was cool and still. Midnight huddled in his blanket. He dozed. . . . Suddenly, trouble called.

"Grrrrrr . . ." The growl was low, close. Every man froze. Midnight remembered his nights on the run. That fear of every sound, every movement in the dark except his own came back to him fast. But with the fear came a strength. Darkness was also Midnight's old friend. His sight was as sharp now as it was at midday.

Midnight relaxed his shoulders and stretched his neck upward, looking toward the cattle. *Nothin' there. Wait! Somethin's close to me.* He felt the heat of another living creature. Only a few feet away, the cougar passed him. It passed right by the herd.

Sly animal. It's after the horses. Midnight watched the cougar leap silently upon another rock nearer the remuda. The animals sensed him. They began to sputter and shuffle. Midnight rolled out of his blanket. *I ain't got a weapon in sight,* he thought, crawling backward behind another rock. *If I was smart, I'd double-back to camp. But I'm gettin' paid to keep these horses safe. Anything could happen if I leave it like this. 'Sides, I ain't never called myself smart.*

The cougar was young, maybe on one of its first hunts. Clearly, it had its eyes on a particular horse, and it was stalking the animal. The cougar paced along the picket rope, moving around in a circle. Midnight tried to follow with his own eyes in the direction the cat's eyes were fixed. *It was Rusty!* Now Midnight couldn't turn away.

I been in this position too many times. When Nile died, I couldn't do nothin'. Lady got pulled outta my own arms, and I couldn't do nothin'. How can I leave poor Rusty at the mercy of this wild thing? She's the first horse in this whole remuda that took a likin' to me.

Midnight felt his muscles tighten. *Gotta have a weapon.* He scrambled around on the ground, looking for a stick, a rock, anything that he could use. His foot went down on something hard, and he reached for it. A square-shaped brown stone glinted in the moonlight. Midnight picked it up, weighing it with his hand. It was heavy, maybe as large as his palm.

If I can throw it right at his temple, I can bring him down.
Midnight nodded to himself. He had a plan. He crawled closer, ready
to spring up and throw in one movement. The cat flattened its whole
body against the rock, even laying back its ears. Ready to pounce at
any minute.

Midnight drew back his arm and jumped up. The cat suddenly
turned its head and saw him. Midnight flung the rock. The cat sprang
at him. Midnight twisted his body away as he fell down, feeling the cat
dig its claws into his shoulder.

"Yow!" Midnight yelled. Pain shot through his arm and neck, but
he managed to force his elbow back into the animal's ribs.

"AAAAaaaaahhhhheeeee!" the cat screamed. Midnight could feel
the warm blood running down his chest from his shoulder. *Awww,
bobcat. You're not gonna kill ME tonight!* The cat spun around and
jumped back toward Midnight's face. This time, Midnight grabbed at
the cat's throat. The animal snarled, batting its paws out to strike
Midnight wherever he could. They tussled and wrestled and rolled.
First Midnight was on top, then they flipped around. The cat was on
top, but he'd gotten turned belly up. With his good arm, Midnight
managed to grab hold of the scruff of the cat's neck, yanking its head
back with all his strength.

"Midnight! Get clear!" He heard Joe B., but he couldn't let go.
The cat twisted, digging its back claws into Midnight's stomach. The
new pain made Midnight's anger come up. It was all back. The anger
got bigger and hotter. Like a wave passing over him, Midnight's arms,
legs, and shoulders began to tremble with anger that was bubbling up.

Midnight shot out his bleeding arm and locked his hand around
one of the cat's hind legs.

"YEEEE!" The cat squealed and wriggled, but Midnight couldn't,
wouldn't let go. He still clutched the animal's neck, feeling its hot
breath as it jerked its head from side to side. He could hear the men
shouting at him, but they sounded far, far away.

*This is like some kind of dream . . . or nightmare. If I let go now,
this madness might take over me and I'll die. I gotta get rid of it.*

The pain in his shoulder and stomach burned like fire, but the boiling anger gave Midnight a power he'd never known before. With a strength he didn't know he had, he raised the cat over his head and flung him like a rag into the night.

"AWWWWWWWWWW!" the cat howled, and three men took off after it. Midnight slumped to the ground, breathing hard. *The pain is somethin' terrible, but the anger is all gone.* He smiled, and that was how they found him.

Midnight heard voices in the distance.

"He's hurt!"

"Boy, that cat knows he's been in a fight!"

"Why didn't you wait for a gun?"

"I ain't never seen nothin' like that before!"

Midnight tried to sit up but sprawled backward. "I'm all right. I—I just did it for the remuda, that's all. Wasn't smart, but I did it." Midnight was bloody and still panting, but all he felt was calm.

Slim appeared with a handful of thick green leaves and a small bottle.

"Boy, I believe your heart was bigger than your brain this time. What possessed you to jump that cat like that?" He tore open Midnight's shirt. The bobcat's claws had already ripped it pretty badly.

"The red mustang . . ." Midnight was suddenly very tired. "I had to do somethin' this time . . ."

"What? Whatcha mean, this time?" Slim was tearing the shirt up to make a bandage.

Midnight lowered his voice. The other cowboys were still stomping through the brush a distance away. "When my sister got sold, she was snatched right outta my hands, and I . . . I couldn't do nothin'. I figured I could *do* somethin' this time." Slim looked at him thoughtfully.

"So you got mad, huh? Cats and horses ain't people, Midnight. You can't go 'round, savin' up madness till it blows up on you. You lucked out this time. People like us can't always let our bad memories rule us. Hmmm. You got cut up pretty bad, all right. This shoulder's clawed kinda deep."

He broke one of the leaves in half, and a thick juice oozed out over Midnight's skin. It was cool. "This here's aloe. It's a healing plant. I'll rub it in and bandage you up. The pain is gonna be rough before it gets better, but I'll put some more aloe on in the morning. Rest easy, now." Midnight had already closed his eyes.

He heard Joe B.'s voice. "The cat's long gone. Won't trouble this herd no more. And I hope this kid won't take no more crazy chances, either. You told me he was ready, Slim."

Slim grunted. "Midnight wasn't fighting no bobcat, Joe B. He was fighting somethin' none of us could see."

About the Author
Denise Lewis Patrick

Denise Lewis Patrick has been telling stories since she was eight years old. She remembers, as a child, sewing her handwritten manuscripts together to create her own books. Before writing full-time, she worked for a publisher as a staff writer and editor. She has written more than twenty books for children.

One of these is *The Car Washing Street.* It tells a story about a boy and his father who watch their neighbors wash their cars every Saturday morning. Even though the boy and his dad do not have a car, they join in when a water fight breaks out among the neighbors. *The Adventures of Midnight Son*—from which "The Trail Drive" is taken—is Ms. Patrick's first book for middle-grade readers. Through her story, readers meet cowboys of different ages and races. They also see what cowboy life was really like.

Reader Response

Open for Discussion

Is Midnight's job one that you would enjoy doing? Why or why not?

Comprehension Check

1. Why does his job of caring for the spare horses in the *remuda* give Midnight satisfaction? Use details from the story in your answer.

2. Name some of the problems or challenges the cowboys face on the trail drive. How do they meet each of these challenges? Use details from the story to support your answer.

3. What are some of the reasons that cause Midnight to fight the cougar the way he does? Which do you think is most important?

4. Midnight's thoughts are presented in *italics,* or slanted type. What do these thoughts tell you about his **character?** (Character)

5. What do you learn about Midnight's **character** from the way other characters treat him? from what these other characters say about him? (Character)

 Test Prep

Look Back and Write

How does Midnight feel about his work on his first day of the trail drive? Use details from pages 572–574 in your answer.

How to Read Historical Nonfiction

1. Preview

- Historical nonfiction deals with real-life people, places, and events from the past. Some historical nonfiction describes a way of life that no longer exists.

- Read the title and subheads. Look over the illustrations and the labels that go with them. What kind of job does the title refer to?

2. Read and Note Terms

- Terms are words or phrases about a special subject, such as a job.

- As you read, make a list of terms about a cowboy's job. Add notes about what these terms mean.

3. Think and Connect

Look back at "The Trail Drive." Then look over your notes for "A Cowboy's Job."

How does Midnight Son's job fit in with the other jobs in the trail drive? What job would he probably move up to next?

A COWBOY'S JOB
BY LINDA GRANFIELD

The Birth of the Cowboy

Cowboy is actually a very old word. It has been traced to Ireland, where horsemen were called *cow-boys* almost two thousand years ago. During the American Revolution (1775–1783), the word *cowboy* became ugly. Some say it referred to thieves who stole cattle from the American colonists and sold them to the British army. Others claim it was used to describe people who were loyal to England and lured their enemies into ambush by jingling cowbells and pretending to be lost cattle.

By the mid-1800s the word had returned to its original meaning—a hired man who works with cattle and performs many of his duties on horseback. Mexican cowboys were called *vaqueros*; later, American cowboys used the term *buckaroo*, which is how *vaquero* sounded to their ears.

The era of the cowboy lasted only about twenty years, from about 1866 to 1886. During this time the demand for beef grew in the eastern United States, and men were needed to watch over the cattle as they grazed on the open range. More important, cowboys had to round up the cattle twice a year and herd them over the countryside to the railroad to be shipped east.

Ex-soldiers and runaway boys alike moved west looking for adventure and danger. For a while Eastern college men were also fascinated by the free, open life they had heard about. They flocked to the West, too, only to find they weren't up to the hard grind. A cowboy's job wasn't an easy one. He was often sinewy and strong, able to ride and rope well, able to withstand danger, heavy workloads, long days, and paltry pay. It's not surprising to learn that fewer than fifty thousand men rode the cattle trails during the cowboy's boom years.

The Boss, the Cook, and the Cowboy

The most important member of the cattle drive crew was the trail boss. He rode ahead of the herd, and scouted for water, pasture,

and campsites along the trail. He checked the provisions, kept records, assigned duties to the men, and settled any problems, for his word was law. For all this work, the trail boss received the grand sum of about $125 a month—more than anyone else on the drive crew.

The cook was paid about $50 a month to keep the men full and happy; cowboys received about $30 and their grub.

During the drive, the herding cowboys followed the trail boss in pairs, traveling on either side of the herd. Point riders led the way, swing riders helped turn the herd, and flank riders moved alongside, watching for strays and keeping the cattle moving at a slow pace. The men often took turns at the various positions. But the drag riders, usually inexperienced cowboys, had the dustiest and most unpopular positions of all. They traveled at the back of the herd, along with the wrangler and the *remuda*.

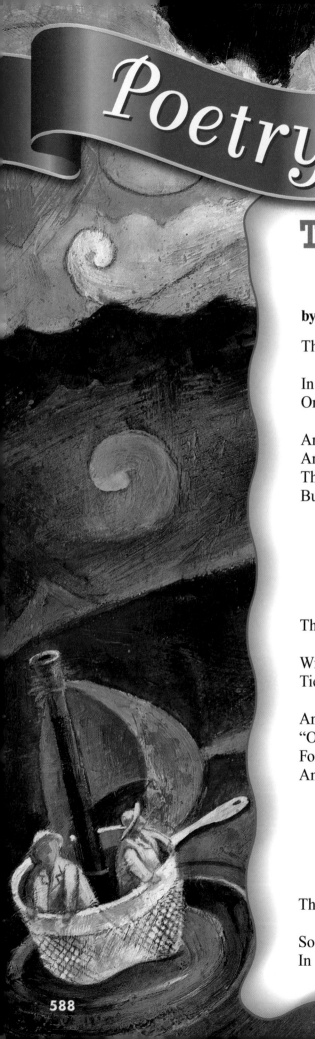

The Jumblies

by Edward Lear

They went to sea in a Sieve, they did,
  In a Sieve they went to sea:
In spite of all their friends could say,
On a winter's morn, on a stormy day,
  In a Sieve they went to sea!
And when the Sieve turned round and round,
And every one cried, "You'll all be drowned!"
They called aloud, "Our Sieve ain't big,
But we don't care a button! We don't care a fig!
  In a Sieve we'll go to sea!"
      Far and few, far and few,
        Are the lands where the Jumblies live;
        Their heads are green, and their hands are blue,
          And they went to sea in a Sieve.

They sailed away in a Sieve, they did,
  In a Sieve they sailed so fast,
With only a beautiful pea-green veil
Tied with a ribbon by way of a sail,
  To a small tobacco-pipe mast;
And every one said, who saw them go,
"O won't they be soon upset, you know!
For the sky is dark, and the voyage is long,
And happen what may, it's extremely wrong
  In a Sieve to sail so fast!"
      Far and few, far and few,
        Are the lands where the Jumblies live;
        Their heads are green, and their hands are blue,
          And they went to sea in a Sieve.

The water it soon came in, it did,
  The water it soon came in;
So to keep them dry, they wrapped their feet
In a pinky paper all folded neat,

And they fastened it down with a pin.
And they passed the night in a crockery-jar,
And each of them said, "How wise we are!
Though the sky be dark, and the voyage be long,
Yet we never can think we were rash or wrong,
    While round in our Sieve we spin!"
        Far and few, far and few,
            Are the lands where the Jumblies live;
        Their heads are green, and their hands are blue,
            And they went to sea in a Sieve.

And all night long they sailed away;
    And when the sun went down,
They whistled and warbled a moony song
To the echoing sound of a coppery gong,
    In the shade of the mountains brown.
"O Timballo! How happy we are,
When we live in a sieve and a crockery-jar,
And all night long in the moonlight pale,
We sail away with a pea-green sail,
    In the shade of the mountains brown!"
        Far and few, far and few,
            Are the lands where the Jumblies live;
        Their heads are green, and their hands are blue,
            And they went to sea in a Sieve.

And in twenty years they all came back,
    In twenty years or more,
And every one said, "How tall they've grown!
For they've been to the Lakes, and the Torrible Zone,
    And the hills of the Chankly Bore."
And they drank their health, and gave them a feast
Of dumplings made of beautiful yeast;
And every one said, "If we only live,
We too will go to sea in a Sieve, —
    To the hills of the Chankly Bore!"
        Far and few, far and few,
            Are the lands where the Jumblies live;
        Their heads are green, and their hands are blue,
            And they went to sea in a Sieve.

Riding the Wind

by Doris Bircham

I am going to ride the wind
when it's blowing hard and strong.
I'll jump on its back
and we'll follow a track
where clouds go loping along.

I am going to ride the wind
when it chases behind the rain,
and whenever it snows
I'll be saddled to go
I'll mount up and grab hold of the reins.

I am going to ride the wind
when it turns to a warm chinook.
We'll spur to the moon,
whistle springtime tunes
and melt icicles in every nook.

I am going to ride the wind
when it whispers to waving grass.
We'll call out to the creek,
sing flowers to sleep
and whinny "Good Night" as we pass.

I Will Never Be Able to Know the Sea

by Erika Ramírez Diez
translated by Joan Darby Norris

I will never be able to know the sea
Every time it arrives
    it leaves

Long Trip

by Langston Hughes

The sea is a wilderness of waves,
A desert of water.
We dip and dive,
Rise and roll,
Hide and are hidden
On the sea.
    Day, night,
    Night, day,
The sea is a desert of waves,
A wilderness of water.

Night Train

by Robert Francis

Across the dim frozen fields of night
Where is it going, where is it going?
No throb of wheels, no rush of light,
Only a whistle blowing, blowing.
Only a whistle blowing.

Something echoing through my brain,
Something timed between sleep and waking,
Murmurs, murmurs this may be the train
I must be sometime, somewhere taking,
I must be sometime taking.

Wrap-up

What can we learn from visiting real and imaginary times and places?

Strange Places

Visualize and Describe

The characters in *El Güero* and "The Land of Expectations" travel to strange places. What strange places have you visited?

1. **Make notes** on what these characters learned from their visits to these strange places.

2. Now **describe** a strange place you have visited and tell what you learned. Save your description and use it as the setting for a story.

A Journey in Sound

Create Sound Effects

If you made a movie of one of the Unit 5 selections, what kinds of sounds would you use?

1. With a small group, look back at a selection and **list** sounds you might use in a movie version of the selection.

2. Invent ways to produce these sounds and **tape-record** them. Have classmates listen and guess where each sound would come in the story and how you produced it.

Tense Moments

Create a Storyboard

A storyboard is a series of drawings of key scenes in a story. How would a scene from a Unit 5 selection look in storyboard form?

1. **Choose** a tense scene in a selection and break it down into five moments, from start to finish.

2. **Draw** the five moments on posterboard and write an explanation for each drawing. Compare your storyboards with classmates' versions.

World Travelers

Plan a Trip

There are many ways to get from place to place. The people in the Unit 5 selections use many forms of transportation, from a horse to a spaceship.

1. With a partner, look back at the selections and **list** the different forms of transportation that were used.

2. **Plan** a trip around the world, using different forms of transportation. Make a map showing your route. Compare your plan with classmates' plans.

Test Talk

Answer the Question

Write the Answer

Tests often tell you to write the answer. A test about "The Trail Drive," pages 570–583, might have this question.

Test Question 1

What is the setting of "The Trail Drive"? Describe it using details from pages 571–573.

Get ready to answer.

- Read the question to find key words.

- Finish the statement "I need to find out . . ."

- Decide where to look for the answer.

- Make notes on details for your answer and check them.

Write your answer.

- Begin your answer with words from the question. Include details from your notes.

- Check your answer. Ask yourself:

  ✓ **Is my answer correct?** Are some details incorrect?

  ✓ **Is my answer complete?** Do I need to add more details?

  ✓ **Is my answer focused?** Do all my details come from the text? Do they all help answer the question?

See how one student writes a correct, complete, and focused response.

I'll start my answer with words from the question. The setting of "The Trail Drive" is. . . I remember that the time is in the past, when there was still slavery, but I need to find out exactly when and where. I'll look back at the story and make more notes.

The setting of "The Trail Drive" is Texas in 1863, a time when there was still slavery. The land is mostly flat, except for a few ridges and low hills. The ground is covered with wild sweet grass and ground cover, but there is plenty of dust for the cattle to stir up when they move around . . .

Try it!

Now write correct, complete, and focused answers to these test questions about "The Trail Drive," pages 570–583.

Test Question 2

How are days on the trail alike and how are they different? Use details from pages 574–575 to explain your answer.

Test Question 3

Why does Midnight get angry as he fights the bobcat? Use details from pages 580–583 to support your answer.

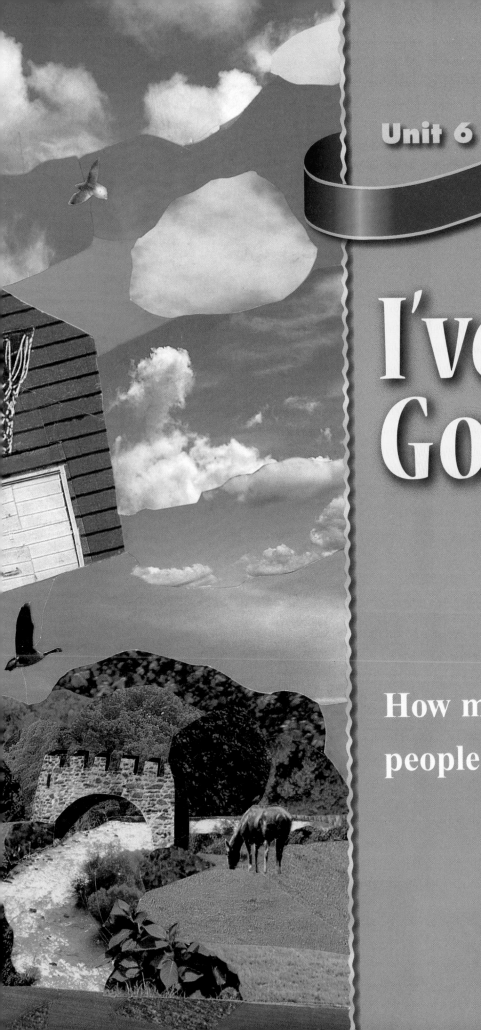

Unit 6

I've
Got It!

How many ways can
people be creative?

597

Generalizing

- A broad statement about what several people or things have in common is a **generalization.** *Most doctors work in a hospital* is an example of a generalization.

- Some generalizations contain clue words, such as *most, many, all, sometimes, generally, always,* or *never.* If a statement does not contain a clue word, but you can add one without changing the statement's meaning, the statement may be a generalization.

- A valid generalization is supported by facts and agrees with what you already know. A faulty generalization is not supported by facts.

Read "Almost Ready for School" from *The Agony of Alice* by Phyllis Reynolds Naylor.

Talk About It

1. Find the generalization Alice makes about sixth-graders. Tell whether you think it is valid or faulty.

2. Explain how you could determine whether the following statement about dentists is a generalization: "They ask you questions when your mouth's open and then they answer for you."

Almost Ready for School

by Phyllis Reynolds Naylor

I had been looking forward to sixth grade all my life. It would be the very first time I was an "upper classman." There wouldn't be any older boys on the playground to trap me on the slide. Sixth graders were always chosen to help out in the office or in the halls, and the only ambition I had in life that summer was to be a safety patrol when school started.

There were a few things that had to be done before September, however. Dad made an appointment for me with a new dentist.

It's weird about dentists. They always slip into the room so quietly you don't even know they're there until you hear them washing their hands at the sink. I'd been looking at a poster taped on the wall just in front of me. It had a big mince pie on it and the words, "Before you finish eating your dinner, your dinner starts eating your teeth."

The dentist came around from behind and sat down on a stool with his little mirror and his silver pick. I immediately opened my mouth. I always feel like a baby bird in a dentist's office. As soon as he comes near me, my mouth opens automatically. His fingers smelled like Novocain and all the while he was examining my teeth he was asking me questions. That's another thing about dentists. They ask you questions when your mouth's open and then they answer for you.

"Almost ready for school?" he said.

"Gaaauuu," I answered.

He told me that I didn't have any cavities, but that I must be grinding my teeth because the enamel was worn. People do that, he said, when they're tense. Then he recited a little poem that he hoped I would always remember:

"From this rule I won't depart,
Lips together, teeth apart."

I figured I'd forget it in a day or two, but it stuck in my head like library paste.

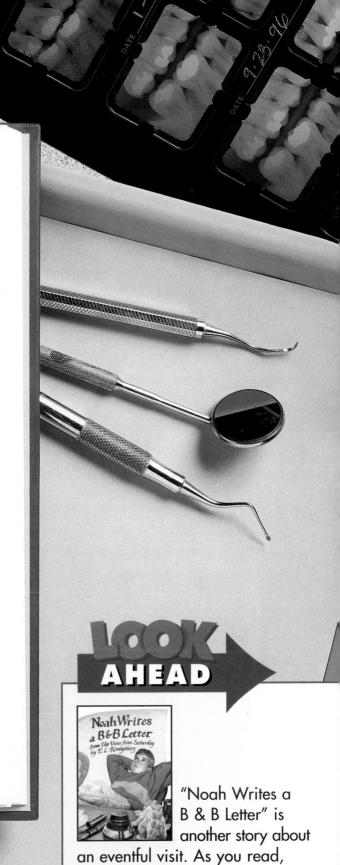

LOOK AHEAD

"Noah Writes a B & B Letter" is another story about an eventful visit. As you read, watch for faulty generalizations.

Vocabulary

Words to Know

calligraphy	circumstances
committee	generation
handwriting	stationery

Words that are pronounced the same but spelled differently are called **homophones.** They also have different meanings. To understand the difference between homophones, such as *stationery* and *stationary,* look for clues in the surrounding words and sentences.

Read the paragraph below. Why is *stationery* used and not *stationary?*

Making the Best of It

Last summer my parents hosted a family reunion. We all worked hard to make it a success. My dad, who knows calligraphy, wrote the invitations on fancy stationery. I used my finest handwriting to address the envelopes. My mom was in charge of the refreshments committee. She even made her famous lemonade! My sisters decorated our backyard for the big day. Everything was perfect, except for one thing—the weather. It rained all day. Yet, even under those circumstances, we managed to have a great time. The party simply moved indoors. Grandma Lily taught us how to play chess, and in return, the younger generation introduced our elders to video games. Rain or shine, it was a blast!

Write About It

Write about a party you helped plan.
Use as many vocabulary words as you can.

Noah Writes a B&B Letter

from The View from Saturday
by E. L. Konigsburg

My mother insisted that I write a B & B letter to my grandparents. I told her that I could not write a B & B letter, and she asked me why, and I told her that I did not know what a B & B letter was. She explained—not too patiently—that a B & B letter is a *bread and butter* letter you write to people to thank them for having you as their houseguest. I told her that I was taught never to use the word you are defining in its definition and that she ought to think of a substitute word for *letter* if she is defining it. Mother then made a remark about how Western Civilization was in a decline because people of my generation knew how to nitpick but not how to write a B & B letter.

I told her that, with all due respect, I did not think I owed Grandma and Grandpa a B & B. And then I stated my case. Fact: I was not just a houseguest, I was family; and fact: I had not been their houseguest by choice because fact: She had sent me to them because she had won a cruise for selling more houses in Epiphany than anyone else in the world and if she had shared her cruise with Joey and me instead of with her husband, my father, I would not have been sent to Florida in the first place and fact: She, not me, owed them thanks; and further fact: I had been such a wonderful help while I was there that Grandma and Grandpa would probably want to write me a B & B.

My brother Joey had been sent to my other set of grandparents, who live in a normal suburb in Connecticut. "Is Joey writing a B & B to Grandma and Grandpa Eberle?"

"Even as we speak," Mother replied.

"Well, maybe he has something to be thankful for," I said.

Mother drew in her breath as if she were about to say something else about what children of my generation were doing to Western Civilization, but instead, she said, "Write," and closed my bedroom door behind her. I opened the door and called out to her, "Can I use the computer?"

She said, "I know you can use the computer, Noah, but you *may* not." I was about to make a remark about who was nitpicking now, but Mother gave me such a negative look that I knew any thoughts I had had better be about bread and butter and not nitpicking.

I gazed at my closed bedroom door and then out the window. Door. Window. Door. Window. There was no escape.

I took a box of notepaper out of my desk drawer. The notes were bigger than postage stamps, but not by much. I took out a ballpoint pen and started pressing it against a piece of scrap paper, making dents in the paper but not making a mark. Ballpoint pens sometimes take a while to get started. When I was down in Florida, Tillie Nachman had said, "The ballpoint pen has been the biggest single factor in the decline, of Western Civilization. It makes the written word cheap, fast, and totally without character." My mother and Tillie should get together. Between them, they have come up with the two major reasons why Western Civilization is about to collapse.

Not because I was trying to save Western Civilization but because I wanted to actually get my B & B letter written, I put the ballpoint pen back into the drawer and took out my calligraphy pen, the one that uses wet ink. I didn't fill it. I would fill it when I was ready to write. I also took out a sharpened pencil and a pad of Post-it notes to jot down any ideas that might come to mind.

I wrote *red wagon*. The red wagon had definitely been a gift—even though, under the circumstances, I didn't bring it back to Epiphany with me. I thought a while longer and wrote *tuxedo T-shirt*. It, too, had been a gift, but I didn't have that either. I wrote *calligraphy pen and bottle of ink*. A wet ink pen and a bottle of ink had been given to me, but the ones I took out of my desk drawer were ones I had bought myself. The calligraphy pen made me remember about the Post-it notes I had bought to correct the problem that had developed with the ink. Even though I had bought the Post-it notes myself, I added *Post-it notes* to my list. I peeled off the Post-it note containing my list and stuck it on the wall in front of my desk, and then, as my mother had commanded, I thought again.

Century Village where my Gershom grandparents live is not like any place I had ever been to. It is in Florida, but it is not exactly Disney World or Sea World or other regular destinations. It is like a theme park for old people. Almost everyone who lives there is retired. Grandma Sadie and Grandpa Nate fit in nicely.

It all started when Margaret Draper and Izzy Diamondstein decided to get married, and the citizens of Century Village called a meeting in the clubhouse to organize the wedding.

In their former lives, Grandma Sadie and Grandpa Nate had owned a small bakery right here in Epiphany, New York, so Grandma volunteered to do the wedding cake, and Grandpa Nate, whose chief hobby had always been violin playing, promised to arrange for the music.

Mr. Cantor, a retired postman from Pennsylvania, who was devoted to growing orchids, said that he would have enough blossoms for the corsages. And Mrs. Kerchmer said that she would lend her African violets for the centerpieces.

Tillie Nachman volunteered to do the invitations, and Rabbi Friedman, who was a rabbi in his former life, said he would perform the ceremony even though Margaret Draper was not Jewish and Izzy Diamondstein was. This was a late second marriage, and there wouldn't be any concern about what religion they should choose for their children since all their children were already grown up and chosen. Grandpa Nate later explained to me that unlike the average citizen of Century Village, rabbis don't have former lives. They are what they were; once a rabbi, always a rabbi.

Many citizens of Century Village were widows who had once been great family cooks, so they formed a committee to plan the wedding dinner. Everyone agreed to share the cost, and they made up a menu and a master shopping list.

After that first meeting, Grandpa Nate and I took Tillie Nachman, a former New York City person who had never learned to drive, to the stationery store so that she could buy the invitations. While she shopped for the invitations, Grandpa and I went to Wal-Mart to pick up Grandma's prescription, and that is when we saw the red wagon special. Grandpa bought it for me, and it's a good thing he did. It came in handy until Allen came along.

I checked my list. *Post-it notes.* I had bought them when we ran out of invitations. Of course, we didn't run out of invitations until Tillie's cat got its paws into the ink.

Tillie was filling in the *who-what-when-and-where* on the invitations when I noticed that she had the prettiest handwriting I had ever seen. "Calligraphy," she said. "It means beautiful writing," and she asked me if I would like to learn how to write like her. I said yes. She said she would give me lessons if I would help her address the envelopes. So Grandpa drove us to an art supply store where she bought me a calligraphy pen and a bottle of ink. It was while Tillie was trying out various pen points (called *nibs*) that she made the remark about the ballpoint pen being the biggest single factor in the decline of Western Civilization.

After choosing a nib Tillie said, "I hope in the future, Noah, that you will use a ballpoint pen only when you have to press hard to make multiple carbons."

I couldn't promise that. There were times in school when a person had to do things fast, cheap, and without character.

Tillie said, "There are pens that come with ink in a cartridge, Noah, but I will have nothing to do with them." So when we were back at her condo, Tillie taught me how to fill a pen, or, as she said, "How to *properly* fill a pen."

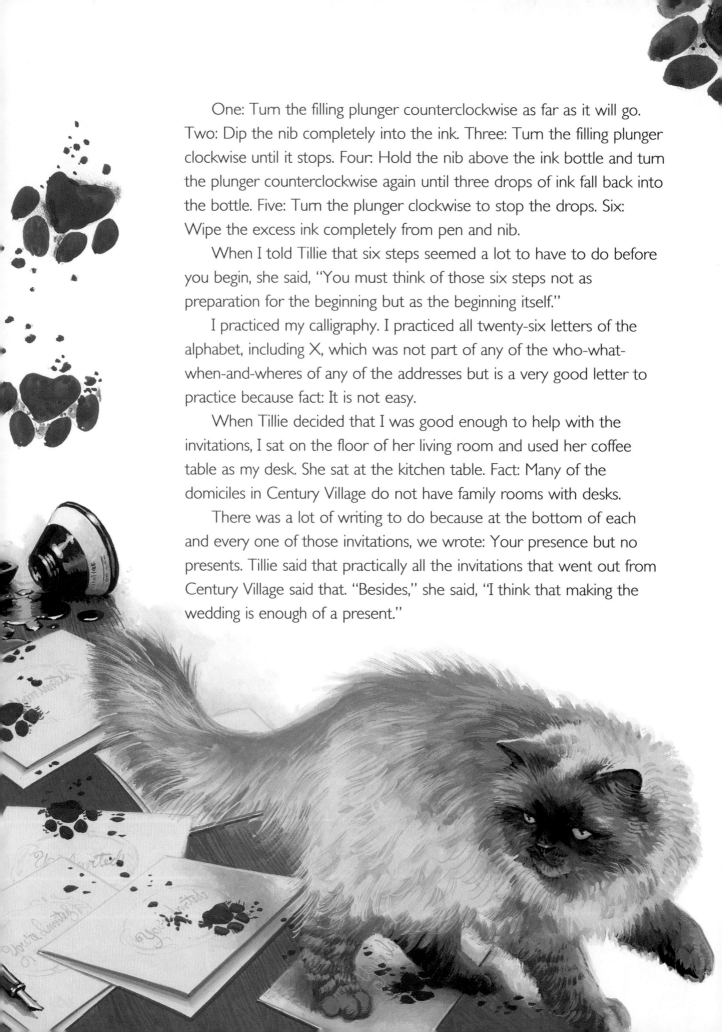

One: Turn the filling plunger counterclockwise as far as it will go. Two: Dip the nib completely into the ink. Three: Turn the filling plunger clockwise until it stops. Four: Hold the nib above the ink bottle and turn the plunger counterclockwise again until three drops of ink fall back into the bottle. Five: Turn the plunger clockwise to stop the drops. Six: Wipe the excess ink completely from pen and nib.

When I told Tillie that six steps seemed a lot to have to do before you begin, she said, "You must think of those six steps not as preparation for the beginning but as the beginning itself."

I practiced my calligraphy. I practiced all twenty-six letters of the alphabet, including X, which was not part of any of the who-what-when-and-wheres of any of the addresses but is a very good letter to practice because fact: It is not easy.

When Tillie decided that I was good enough to help with the invitations, I sat on the floor of her living room and used her coffee table as my desk. She sat at the kitchen table. Fact: Many of the domiciles in Century Village do not have family rooms with desks.

There was a lot of writing to do because at the bottom of each and every one of those invitations, we wrote: Your presence but no presents. Tillie said that practically all the invitations that went out from Century Village said that. "Besides," she said, "I think that making the wedding is enough of a present."

I was doing a wonderful job until Thomas Stearns, called T. S., Tillie's cat, pounced into my lap, and I jumped up and spilled the ink, and the cat walked through the spilled ink and onto a couple of the invitations I was addressing. A few—five altogether—now had cat's paws.

Tillie was pretty upset because she had not bought extras because she said, "I don't make mistakes." In her former life Tillie had been a bookkeeper. I heard her say, "I can add up a column of figures with the best of them." I didn't know if she meant the best of the computers or the best of the bookkeepers, and I didn't ask because I was afraid I already knew.

I told Tillie not to worry. I told her that I would think of something. And I did. That's when I bought the Post-it notes. I put a Post-it note into each of the invitations that had a cat's paw mark. On the Post-it I wrote (in faultless calligraphy): Bring this specially marked invitation to the wedding and receive a surprise gift. When Tillie asked me what the surprise would be, I told her not to worry, that I would think of something. And I did. But fact: It wasn't easy.

On the day the groceries were to be purchased, the citizens of Century Village formed their version of the Home Shopping Network. They met in the clubhouse again. Everyone sat in rows, holding coupons they'd clipped since printing began. They asked me to be master of ceremonies.

I sat at a table in front of the clubhouse room and called out items from the master grocery list. It was a lot like a game of Go Fish. I said, "I need one Crisco, four margarines, *pareve,** and let's have all your paper towels." Everyone searched through their fistfuls of coupons and gave me the ones that were needed. Tillie circled the items we had coupons for.

Then we checked the newspaper for supermarket specials and made out lists for each of the stores, depending on which one had the best buy in a particular item. I wrote the Gershom list in calligraphy. It didn't slow things down too much, and the citizens of Century Village are accustomed to waiting.

*Made without milk, so that it can be eaten with meat, according to Jewish dietary law (Yiddish)

Later that day, everyone returned to the clubhouse with the groceries and the store receipts. Tillie added, divided, and straightened out who owed and who was owed, and no one bothered to check because everyone knew that Tillie Nachman did not make mistakes. Then we had to check the grocery list against the menu and who was cooking what. I helped distribute the groceries to the proper households, using the new red wagon.

Fact: I did a wonderful job.

On the day of the wedding I was in great demand to take things over to the clubhouse in my wagon. The African violets alone took three trips, and the briskets took two. Next, Mr. Cantor and I delivered the orchid corsages to the bride and her maid of honor. In the real world, I had never met anyone who spent as much time with flowers as Mr. Cantor. Mrs. Draper's maid of honor was to be her daughter, Mrs. Potter. Mrs. Draper used to live in my hometown, which is Epiphany, New York, and her daughter, Mrs. Potter, still does. Mrs. Potter bought a new dress and flew down for the wedding, but we didn't fly down together. I had come weeks before—my first trip as an unaccompanied minor.

Mr. Cantor and I took flowers over to the groom and his best man to put in their buttonholes. Allen, who was Izzy Diamondstein's son, was to be best man. They both live in Florida and have the same last name.

Allen Diamondstein still lived in the real world because even though he was Izzy's child and even though he was full-grown, he was too young to live in Century Village. Fact: Allen Diamondstein was the most nervous human being I have ever seen in my entire life. Fact: His wife had left him. She had moved to Epiphany and taken a job with my father, who is the best dentist in town (fact).

Allen Diamondstein kept saying, "Isn't it ironic? My father is getting married just as I am getting divorced." This was not the greatest conversation starter in the world. No one knew what to say after he said it. Some cleared their throats and said nothing. Others cleared their throats and changed the subject.

I must have heard him say it a dozen times, and I never knew what to say either. At first I wondered if that was because I didn't know the meaning of *ironic*. So I looked it up.

The meaning that best fits (and does not use the same word in its definition) is "the contrast between what you expect to happen and what really happens." But after I looked it up, I couldn't figure out what was ironic about Allen Diamondstein's getting divorced and Izzy Diamondstein's getting married. The way Allen Diamondstein acted, I can tell you that divorce would be the only possible thing you could expect from marriage to him. And the way Izzy acted around Margaret, marriage would not only be expected, it would be necessary. *Sha! A shanda far die kinder.** They were embarrassing to watch, but not so embarrassing that I didn't.

Wedding cakes are not baked as much as they are built. In the real world, people don't build wedding cakes. They order in. If you are going to build it yourself, it is not done in a day. It takes three. On the first day, Grandma Sadie baked the layers. On the second, she constructed the cake, using cardboard bases and straws for supports, and made the basic icing to cover the layers. On the third day, she made the designer icing for the rosebuds and put the little bride and groom on top. Fact: The cake was beautiful.

Fortunately, Grandpa Nate took its picture right after she finished it, so Grandma Sadie can remember how it looked for a little while.

Allen Diamondstein would tell you that the red wagon was the problem, but I would say that it's ironic that he should say so. It definitely wasn't. He was. How else were we supposed to deliver the cake to the clubhouse? It was too tall to fit in the trunk of the car, and since on an average day the outside temperature in Century Village is body temperature, there would be a major meltdown before the cake got to the clubhouse where the wedding was to take place. That's when I got the idea to load up the wagon with ice, put a sheet of plastic over the ice, put the cake on top of that, and slowly wheel it over there, with me pulling and Grandpa checking the rear.

Grandpa Nate went to the Jiffy store and bought three bags of ice, and we loaded them into the wagon. Too much. Since we didn't want the bed of the wagon filled right up to the edge, we emptied some, dumping it out on the cement of the patio. That's where we were going to load the wagon so we wouldn't have to wheel the wagon down any steps to get it to the meeting room.

*Hush up! It's a shame for the children.
(Yiddish)

609

Just after we loaded the cake onto the wagon, Allen Diamondstein came over to Grandma's. He said his father wanted him to pick up a prayer book, but I think his father sent him because he was making the groom nervous.

No one answered when he rang the front doorbell because we were all in the back loading the cake into the red wagon, so he walked around back to the patio. Unfortunately, he didn't see the wagon handle, so he tripped on it, slid on the wet concrete, fell in the puddle of melted ice and, unfortunately, toppled the wedding cake.

The little top layer was totally smashed; it fell in the same puddle as Allen, and the little bride and groom were seriously maimed.

So was Allen's ankle. Which fact I detected when he grabbed his foot and started to moan while still sitting in the puddle on the patio. Grandpa Nate called 911. Grandma Sadie returned to the kitchen to whip up a repair batch of icing. Grandpa Nate took the remains of the cake to the clubhouse, and I sat with Allen until the ambulance came. He was not good company.

The groom called to see what was taking Allen so long. I answered the phone, and I thought I would have to call 911 for him too. "Don't panic," I said. "I'll be your best man."

I did not tell Izzy what had happened to the couple on top of the wedding cake because people get very superstitious at weddings, and no one wants a wounded bride and groom sitting on top of the cake with which they are to start a happy marriage. I had seen that sort of thing often enough in the movies: A close-up of the shattered little bride and groom floating in a puddle of melted ice signifying the fate of the real bride and groom. So although I had to tell Izzy Diamondstein what had happened to Allen, I didn't say a word about the top of the wedding cake. I didn't think I could convince him that having the little bride and groom fall into a puddle was ironic.

He seemed to calm down when I volunteered to be best man, which was about the same time that we found out from the ambulance driver that Allen would be back at Century Village in time for the wedding even if he probably wouldn't be able to walk down the aisle.

As soon as the ambulance took Allen away, I ran over to Mr. Cantor's place and asked him to please, please find another orchid for the top of the cake although it would be better if he could find two since the second layer was now the top layer and was bigger. Mr. Cantor found two beautiful sprays of orchids, which Grandma Sadie artistically arranged around the new top layer.

Since I had promised to be best man, not having a tux was a problem. I couldn't fit in Allen's, not that I would have wanted to if I could. That's when Grandpa Nate called Bella Dubinsky.

In her former life, Bella had been an artist. She painted the pictures that went into the pattern books for people who sew their own clothes. In the real world I had never met anyone who sewed her own clothes, but in Century Village, I had met three. Bella had a supply of fabric paints, and within two hours, we had painted a T-shirt that looked like a tuxedo with a red bow tie. I say we because I helped color in the

lines she drew. It's not easy filling in the lines on T-shirt material; it scrunches up under the weight of the brush, leaving skip marks. You have to go over it again and again. Fortunately, the paints dry fast, and by four o'clock, it was ready to wear.

Repaired, the wedding cake looked beautiful. If Allen had not told, no one would have guessed that those orchids didn't belong on top. But Allen told. He told everyone. He also apologized for my being best man. I didn't think that I was someone he had to apologize for. I had helped a lot, and I looked totally presentable in my tuxedo T-shirt, which was a real work of art.

Fact: Being best man is not hard. You walk down the aisle with the maid of honor. Who, in this case, was a matron of honor because she is married. I admit that having the son of the groom, Allen, as best man would have been a better match, size-wise, for the daughter of the bride even though one is married and the other divorced, but the essential fact is that I did a very good job. I stood beside the groom. Mrs. Potter stood beside the bride, and the four of us stood in front of the rabbi, and all five of us stood under the bridal canopy, which

I know is called a *chupah* and which I think is spelled the way I spelled it. I didn't yawn, sneeze, or scratch any visible thing. I held the wedding ring until the rabbi nodded, and I handed it over.

I did an excellent job of being best man even though when I was under the chupah, I was under a lot of pressure trying to think of surprises for the cat's paw invitations. The idea came to me at the very moment Izzy smashed the glass and everyone yelled *mazel tov.** Even before Izzy stopped kissing the bride, I knew what I could do. (Fact: It was a very long and thorough kiss.)

It wouldn't be easy. It would mean giving up things I loved, but I had to do it.

When everyone except Allen was dancing the *hora,* I slipped out of the clubhouse and ran back to Grandma Sadie's. I took off my tuxedo T-shirt, folded it nicely, and put it in my red wagon. I found the package of Post-it notes, my calligraphy pen, and bottle of ink, and after making sure that the ink was tightly closed, I put those in the wagon too. When I returned to the wedding party, the dance was over, and everyone was sitting around looking exhausted. My moment had arrived.

I tapped a glass with a spoon as I had seen grown-ups do, and I said, "Ladies and gentlemen, will those lucky few who have the specially marked invitations, please come forward. It is time to choose your surprise gift." I saw them pick up their cat's-paw invitations and walk over to the band where I was standing beside my red wagon. "First," I said, "we have one hand-painted T-shirt, which is an original work of art done by Mrs. Bella Dubinsky. In addition, we have a calligraphy pen, almost new, and a bottle of ink, almost full. These are the perfect instruments for beautiful handwriting. We have one packet of Post-it notes, complete except for five." I swallowed hard and added, "And we have one red wagon."

Tillie Nachman, who could count precisely, said, "But that's only four gifts, and there were five cat's-paw invitations."

"Oh, yes," I said, "the fifth gift is the best gift of all."

Everyone asked at once, *Whatisit? Whatisit? Whatisit?*

I sucked in my breath until my lungs felt like twin dirigibles inside my ribs. "The best gift of all is . . . the very best . . . the very best gift of all is . . . to give up your gift."

*Good luck; congratulations (Hebrew)

A thick silence fell over the room. Then Tillie Nachman started clapping. Soon the others joined in, and I noticed Grandma Sadie and Grandpa Nate looking proud.

At first everyone who held a cat's-paw invitation wanted to be the one to give up his gift, but I did not want that. If they didn't take my presents, I would feel as if they didn't matter. Mr. Cantor stepped forward and took the Post-it notes. He said he could use them for labeling his plants. He said that he was donating an orchid plant as the fifth gift. Then Tillie promised calligraphy lessons to the person who took the pen and ink, and Bella promised fabric painting lessons to the person who took the tuxedo T-shirt. In that way each of my gifts kept on giving.

Four cat's-paw gifts were now taken.

Only the red wagon remained. Guess who had the fifth cat's-paw invitation?

Allen, the son of.

Allen said he didn't want the little red wagon. He said that he had no use for a wagon in the real world where he was an accountant.

When Izzy, the groom, rose from the table to make a toast, he lifted his glass of wine and said, "Margy and I want to thank all our friends in Century Village. We don't know if we can ever thank you enough for giving our life together this wonderful start. As you know, Margy and I have pooled our resources and bought a little condo on the ocean. Not exactly *on* the ocean. It is, after all, a high-rise. We will miss the community life here, but we don't want to miss our friends. We'll visit. We want you to visit us. Our welcome mat is out. Always. We leave many memories behind. And we are also leaving this little red wagon. Every time you use it, please think of this happy occasion."

Izzy started to sit down, but halfway he got up again and added, "Consider it a gift to everyone from the best man." He never said which best man he meant, but I'm pretty sure he meant me.

Now back in the real world, I sat at my desk and crossed every single item off the list. I didn't have the wagon, the Post-it notes, the T-shirt that Bella Dubinsky had designed, or the pen and ink that Tillie Nachman had bought me. I did have a new pad of Post-it notes and a new calligraphy pen—both of which I had bought with my own money when I got back to Epiphany.

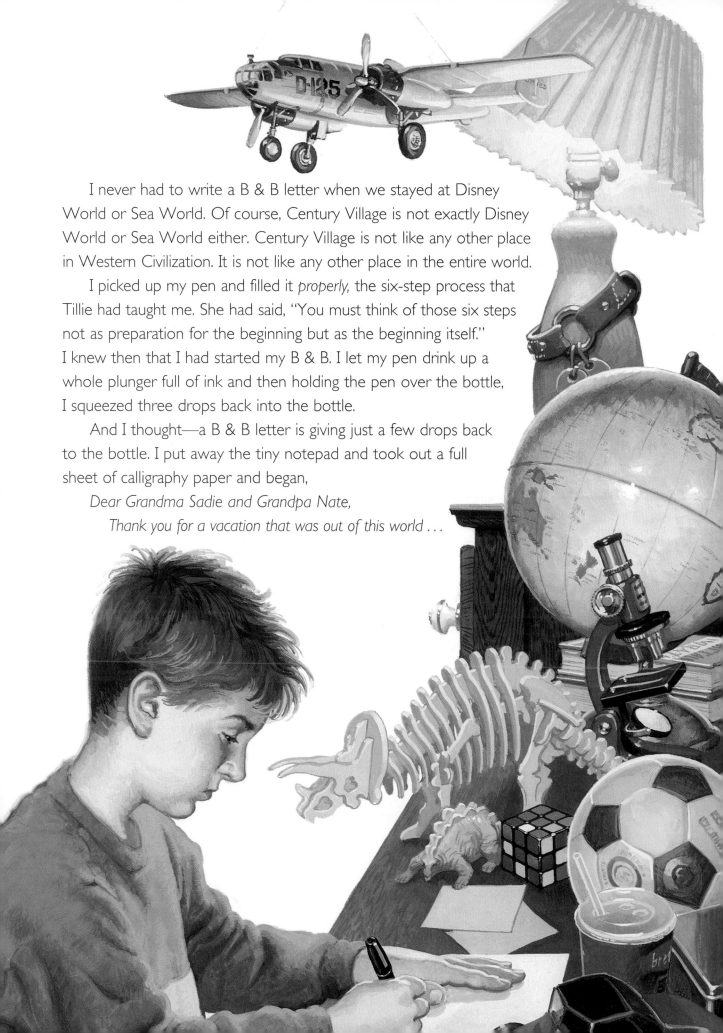

I never had to write a B & B letter when we stayed at Disney World or Sea World. Of course, Century Village is not exactly Disney World or Sea World either. Century Village is not like any other place in Western Civilization. It is not like any other place in the entire world.

I picked up my pen and filled it *properly,* the six-step process that Tillie had taught me. She had said, "You must think of those six steps not as preparation for the beginning but as the beginning itself." I knew then that I had started my B & B. I let my pen drink up a whole plunger full of ink and then holding the pen over the bottle, I squeezed three drops back into the bottle.

And I thought—a B & B letter is giving just a few drops back to the bottle. I put away the tiny notepad and took out a full sheet of calligraphy paper and began,

Dear Grandma Sadie and Grandpa Nate,

Thank you for a vacation that was out of this world . . .

About the Author

E. L. Konigsburg

"Who am I? What makes me the same as everyone else? What makes me different?" These are the kinds of basic problems E. L. Konigsburg writes about. She started writing for her own children's sake. She explains, "I recognized that I wanted to write something that reflected their kind of growing up, something that addressed the problems that come about even though you don't have to worry, if you wear out your shoes, whether your parents can buy you a new pair. . . ."

Ms. Konigsburg draws on her children's and her own life experiences in many of her books. And she keeps lots of files. Whenever she reads an article about a subject that interests her, she adds it to her files. Items from the files often show up in her stories.

Ms. Konigsburg's first two books, *From the Mixed-up Files of Mrs. Basil E. Frankweiler* and *Jennifer, Hecate, Macbeth, William McKinley, and Me, Elizabeth,* won the Newbery Medal and the Newbery Honor Award, respectively. Ms. Konigsburg won the Newbery Medal again for *The View from Saturday,* the novel from which "Noah Writes a B & B Letter" is taken. Other books by Ms. Konigsburg include *The Second Mrs. Giaconda,* about the artist Leonardo da Vinci and his painting the *Mona Lisa,* and *Altogether, One at a Time,* a book of short stories.

Reader Response

Open for Discussion

If you were Noah, what would you say in your B & B letter to Grandma Sadie and Grandpa Nate? Explain.

Comprehension Check

1. Why does Noah object to writing a B & B letter to his grandparents? Look back at the story for details.

2. How does Noah react under pressure? Describe three occasions when things go badly and tell how Noah reacts.

3. Something that is ironic is different from what you might expect. Is it ironic that Allen Diamondstein holds the last cat's-paw invitation? Explain your answer.

4. What **generalizations** do Noah's mother and Tillie Nachman make about the reasons for the decline of Western Civilization? (Generalizing)

5. Find a **generalization** that Noah makes about Century Village. Do you agree with it? Explain. (Generalizing)

Test Prep

Look Back and Write

What goes wrong with the wedding and how are the problems solved? Use information from pages 610–613 to support your answer.

Learn Calligraphy

adapted from *Teach Yourself Calligraphy* by Ellen Korn

You will need the following supplies to learn calligraphy:

- a calligraphy pen and a bottle of ink or a chisel-tip felt marker
- lined paper

Take your pen or marker in your hand, at about a 45-degree angle, and hold it and your paper as shown:

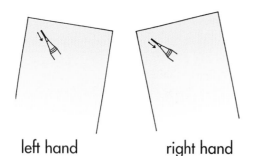

left hand   right hand

Holding your pen or marker as shown, make an X, starting at the top of the line and going down. The position of your marker should look like this as you are making the **X**:

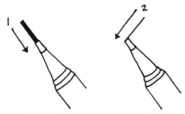

Practice writing an X on your paper. It should look like this: **not** **or**

If you are holding the marker correctly, the X will be thick in one direction and thin in the other, as shown:

You should be holding your marker at a 45-degree angle to the guidelines. Do not twist the marker as you change from one stroke to the other. Then the thicks and thins will come naturally.

Follow these patterns of strokes. Begin at the dot numbered 1, and make that stroke in the direction of the arrow. Do the same for strokes 2, 3, and so on.

With some practice, you can create an alphabet that looks as distinctive as this one. You, too, can create "beautiful writing."

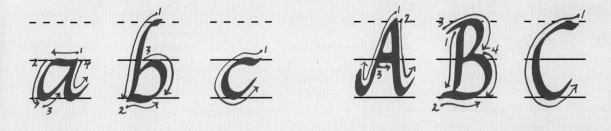

abcdefghijklm
nopqrstuvwxyz
1234567890&
ABCDEFGHI
JKLMNOPQ
RSTUVWXYZ

Skill Lesson

Author's Viewpoint/Bias

- **Author's viewpoint** is the way an author thinks about the subject of his or her writing.

- You can identify an author's viewpoint by looking at the words an author uses. Some authors use loaded words, such as *terrible* or *wonderful*, to express a strong preference, or **bias.**

- *Balanced writing* presents both sides of an issue. *Biased writing* shows strong feeling for or against someone or something and presents only one side of an issue. You should read biased writing critically.

Read "Normal" by Karin-Leigh Spicer from *Skipping Stones* magazine.

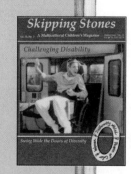

Talk About It

1. What is the author's viewpoint about the meaning of *normal?*

2. Does the author show strong feeling for or against something? Explain.

NORMAL

by Karin-Leigh Spicer

The word *normal* is commonly defined as "an accepted standard" or average. I always assumed I was pretty normal, did normal things, ate normal food, went to normal places. Until one night I was in a car accident that damaged my spinal cord, leaving me paralyzed from the waist down. I still remember what the doctor said before I was taken into surgery: "Karin, you'll never walk again, but we'll try to make your life as normal as possible."

I remember thinking to myself, "What does he mean by *normal?* Could I finish college? Play sports? Find a job? Drive? Take care of myself?" Since that night, this twenty-year adventure has taught me my own definition of *normal.*

I've learned that *normal* is what you make it to be, not someone else's perception of what someone in a wheelchair should be or do. I finished college and then went on to earn my Master's and Ph.D. degrees. I can't play softball or ride a bike, but I do play catch and croquet and swim. I drive a car and take care of myself. None of these

things were easy at first, but I've learned, and now they are as second nature to me as walking once was.

I love working with my students, teaching and writing, advising and research. Through working with and observing me, my students have come to better understand what it is to be a person in a wheelchair. A student once said that she was leery about a wheelchair-bound teacher. What could I teach her? What could she possibly learn? By the end of the class she had forgotten about the wheelchair. Her definition of *normal* had changed.

Still, sometimes, I become frustrated when I can't reach something, or I encounter a set of stairs instead of a ramp. But each one of us faces problems that we must resolve. Conflicts are a normal part of everyday life.

I write stories about adventures my family and friends have encountered. I've written about fishing trips, my aunt growing up in a coal-mining town, a ninety-four-year-old lady's stories of her grandpa's farm. Someone once asked why I haven't written about wheelchairs. I honestly had to say I'd never thought about it . . . Too normal, I guess.

LOOK AHEAD →

LOUIS BRAILLE
BY STEPHEN KEELER ILLUSTRATED BY TROY HOWELL

Louis Braille also had to make adjustments in order to lead a "normal" life. As you read, try to identify the author's viewpoint.

Vocabulary

Words to Know

advantages	ambitions	merit
blindness	complicated	
recognition	visual	

Words with opposite meanings are called **antonyms.** You can often figure out the meaning of an unknown word by finding a clue in the words around it. Sometimes this clue is an antonym.

Read the paragraph below. Notice how *simple* helps you understand the meaning of *complicated.*

Looking Ahead

For many years, eyeglasses were the only solution to many visual problems, such as nearsightedness. Later, contact lenses became popular. Eye surgery was often too risky and complicated. Now laser eye surgery has won recognition as a safe and simple alternative to glasses and lenses. Many doctors say that laser procedures have merit. One of the advantages of laser surgery is that patients usually recover quickly from the operation. With the success of this new technology, researchers have ambitions of correcting many vision problems, including some forms of blindness.

Write About It

Work with a classmate. Write a paragraph that uses the vocabulary words.

LOUIS
BRAILLE

BY STEPHEN KEELER   ILLUSTRATED BY TROY HOWELL

LOUIS'S FAMILY

On January 4, 1809, Monique Baron-Braille gave birth to her fourth child. Three days later he was baptized and named Louis.

Fifteen years earlier, Louis's grandfather, a master saddler and harnessmaker, had settled with his wife in the small town of Coupvray, a few miles southeast of Paris. By 1782, when Louis's father, Simon-René, took over the business, the Brailles had established a reputation for excellent craftsmanship.

The family was not rich. Their stone house, with its huge, moss-covered roof, was dark and gloomy inside. The windows were small and unglazed, so the heavy oak shutters were kept closed except in very hot weather. There was no running water and lighting was by candles. Their furniture was simple and practical.

But the house was surrounded by cornfields and vineyards. The Brailles kept chickens and a cow and they lived well on wholesome country food.

Like most people at the time, the Brailles had no need for reading or writing.

A HISTORIC ACCIDENT

Louis Braille was a bright, blue-eyed child with blonde curls. He was the baby of the family and his brother and sisters loved to play with him. As soon as Louis could talk he began asking questions and by the age of three he was taking part in the daily routine of the family.

Louis's father was very proud of his youngest son and had great plans for him. He would go to school, learn to read and write and perhaps one day enter the university in Paris and become a doctor, an engineer, or a scientist.

As Louis's father worked in his saddlemaker's workshop, he enjoyed his little son's company and would give him scraps of leather to play with. Louis would sit on the bench, watching his father working with his razor-sharp knives.

In spite of his father's warning that "Louis must never touch Papa's knives," one day, while Simon-René was in the yard, fitting a new harness to a customer's horse, Louis found himself alone in the workshop. He knew which tools were for punching, which for

stitching and which for cutting, and picking up one of
the sharpest knives, he started to copy what he'd seen his father
do so easily. The leather was too tough for the child and the knife
slipped, the blade slicing through his left eye.

As little Louis screamed in agony, his family tried to soothe
him and stop the bleeding. There were no antiseptic ointments
or antibiotics in those days. The nearest doctor was more than
32 kilometers (20 miles) away, and in any case, Simon-René was
suspicious and afraid of medical men. Instead, a local woman,
skilled with herbal medicines, bathed the damaged eye until the
bleeding stopped.

But the real damage had already been done. The eye was badly
infected and soon became useless. The infection spread to Louis's
undamaged right eye and within two years the child was
completely blind.

THE WAR YEARS

Louis Braille's world changed completely. The five-year-old child had to learn his way around the house by touch and sound. He was soon back in the workshop, but would never again be able to watch his father at work. His sister, Monique, used to entertain him by telling him stories. But everything was about to change in Louis's life again.

First, Monique married and went to live with her husband in another part of Coupvray—too far from the family home for Louis to find his own way there.

Then there was bad news for the whole of France. The French emperor, Napoleon, was fighting a war in Bavaria and Russia, but in the winter of 1812 his armies had to retreat. The towns and villages around Paris had to provide food and equipment for the battered returning French army.

The village of Coupvray supplied many tons of oats and thousands of bales of hay for Napoleon's army, and cows and horses were also taken. But soon Russian armies invaded France, and on April 14, 1814, troops occupied Coupvray and seized most of the remaining food, goods, and money. Almost every family in the village, including the Brailles, had to house and feed Russian soldiers.

Louis couldn't see these unknown and unwelcome visitors, who spoke a different language. And to them the child was just a blind idiot. They didn't care about him or help him in the way the people of Coupvray did. Louis was constantly pushed aside or ignored. He had by now lost all his visual memory. He was confused, lonely, and unhappy. He became silent and solemn and withdrew into his lonely world of private darkness.

AT SCHOOL

The future was not promising. As an adult, Louis would have been lucky to make a living as a street beggar. Now, certainly, he would never be a doctor, an engineer, or a scientist. But to keep his active mind occupied, his father made small leather figures for

Louis to distinguish by touch, and there is a story that he made a nameboard by hammering nails, in the shapes of the letters of Louis's name, into a piece of wood, for Louis to feel with his fingertips.

In 1815, a new priest, Jacques Palluy, moved to Coupvray. He heard about Louis and visited the Brailles to see whether he could help. Although Louis was still reluctant to talk with strangers, Father Palluy could see that the boy was intelligent and he offered to teach him.

At first Father Palluy came to the Brailles' house, but soon Louis had memorized the route from his home to the church, in his eagerness to spend more time with the priest. Using a simple cane his father had whittled out of a twig, the boy tapped his way up the cobbled streets of Coupvray.

Louis was a quick learner. He had no difficulty distinguishing between different birds by their song. He remembered every detail of the Bible stories which the priest told him, and he loved to listen to music.

The following year, a schoolmaster, Antoine Becheret, opened a school in Coupvray and Father Palluy arranged for Louis to become a pupil there with the other children of the town. Sending a blind child to a normal school was unheard of in those days, but Becheret was a kind young man and the other pupils at school all knew and liked Louis. Of course, Louis had to rely entirely on listening to others, but he developed a marvelous memory and was usually at the top of his class by the end of each term.

BEING BLIND IN THE NINETEENTH CENTURY

Life for the blind is never easy, but in Louis Braille's time it was especially miserable. There were no trained teachers for the blind so they couldn't go to school. There was no way to teach them to read or write, and there were no jobs for them.

Blind people were often mocked and teased in the streets. They were thought of as stupid and treated as outcasts.

Louis was very lucky to have Jacques Palluy and Antoine Becheret as his teachers and also as his friends. Their kindness and concern helped him to begin the work that would eventually change forever not only life for the blind, but also people's attitudes toward blindness all around the world.

OFF TO PARIS

At the school in Coupvray, Louis Braille had already demonstrated his remarkable memory and his tremendous powers of concentration. He had excellent general knowledge and had learned to discuss and work out problems. He liked to listen to Bible stories and had become deeply religious.

Toward the end of 1818, Jacques Palluy and Antoine Becheret suggested to Louis's father that the boy should be sent to the only school for the blind in the whole of France. This was the National Institute for Blind Youth, in Paris. There, they thought, he would be given the kind of help and encouragement that they were unable to give him in Coupvray.

So, early on a bright and frosty morning in February, 1819, Louis Braille, who was just ten years old, set off with his father by stagecoach for Paris.

THE NATIONAL INSTITUTE FOR BLIND YOUTH

The Institute had been founded in 1748 by Valentin Haüy, who had also invented a system of raised wooden letters to help the blind read and write.

When Louis first arrived at the Institute he was very homesick. He had never been away from Coupvray or his family before. He enjoyed wearing the uniform of gray trousers, cashmere vest and dark blue jacket with light blue collar and cuffs, and brass buttons, but the stone floors and walls of the cold, damp building had a chilling echo. However, he soon made friends, and Gabriel Gauthier, who had the next bunk in the dormitory, became his best friend.

Louis was an intelligent boy and he realized that the world of learning, which was open to sighted people, would remain forever closed to him as long as he was unable to read or write. He was disappointed to find that there were very few books at the Institute, and that these were almost unusable because they were printed in Haüy's system of large embossed letters. Reading like this—feeling each letter individually—took a long time, and pupils had usually forgotten the beginning of a sentence before they reached its end.

So, even at the National Institute for Blind Youth, most of the teaching was carried out orally. Louis was an outstanding pupil and learned mathematics, grammar, and composition with ease. He also learned to play several musical instruments by ear. He won many prizes for his work and was even made foreman of the workshop, where the pupils at the Institute made slippers. He grew to enjoy living at the Institute, although he could never quite rid his bones of the cold dampness of the place.

READING AND WRITING SYSTEMS

Braille is not the only reading and writing system for the blind, and it certainly wasn't the first. Six hundred years ago, a blind professor in Persia invented a system to help him read books and make notes from them.

In the two hundred years before Louis Braille was born, many systems were developed, using carved wooden letters or wax-coated sheets into which words were cut with a stylus. One system, developed in Scotland, used string! Different types of knots, representing letters of the alphabet, were tied in the string at regular intervals. Readers simply pulled the string from a reel and "read" the knot. They could also "write" by tying knots in the string.

In 1819, Charles Barbier, a French army officer, invented a system using dots and dashes punched into paper tape. He had developed his invention, called "Night Writing," to help his soldiers communicate with each other silently on the battlefield at night. In 1821, Barbier was invited to the National Institute for Blind Youth to demonstrate "Night Writing."

Although it was complicated, pupils at the Institute found they could read Barbier's system much more quickly than Haüy's embossed books. By using a stylus and a small metal frame to position the dots and dashes correctly, they could also write quite easily.

One of the pupils present at Barbier's demonstration was the twelve-year-old Louis Braille. He realized immediately that "Night Writing" offered the chance he had been looking for—the opportunity to open up to the blind people the world of literature and knowledge.

"Night Writing," in its original form, was not the perfect system. It was complicated and difficult to distinguish the dots and dashes accurately with the fingertips. From now on, Louis Braille was to spend every spare minute trying to improve Barbier's system.

FROM PUNCHED HOLES TO RAISED DOTS

Louis Braille's great advantage was his blindness. He understood the problems of the blind from the inside. He knew what blind people could do and what was too difficult for them.

"Night Writing" used as many as fourteen dots and dashes for each letter or sound. This was too many to feel with the fingertips at one time.

Braille knew from his own experience that dots were easier to feel than dashes. So he got rid of the dashes and produced a remarkably simple system of dots based on the domino, using only six dots.

He also knew from experience that embossed letters were easier for blind people to feel than punched holes. He therefore took the best ideas from several systems. But the real genius was in the six-dot combinations.

Braille arranged his dots in two columns, numbered like this:

1 • •4

2 • •5

3 • •6

He divided the alphabet into three groups. Group 1, the first ten letters (A–J), uses only the top four dots (1, 2, 4, and 5).

Group 2, the second ten letters (K–T), is the same as Group 1 except that dot 3 is added each time (so A becomes K with the addition of dot 3).

The third group finishes the alphabet and includes some simple words. This group just adds dot 6.

W is not used in the French alphabet, but it was added to Braille later. It was made up from dots 2, 4, 5, and 6.

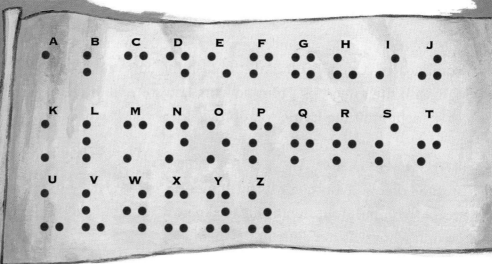

OPPOSITION

Although Braille's system was brilliant, and although it was supported by all the pupils and many of the teachers at the National Institute for Blind Youth, it was disliked by the Institute's governors. They supported other systems of reading and writing, such as Haüy's raised wooden letters, which they knew how to read themselves but which was far too cumbersome to be efficient when used by the blind.

Because the governors of the Institute were not blind themselves, they couldn't understand the tremendous advantages of Braille. They did not realize its simplicity and the fact that it allowed blind people to write as well as read. They distrusted a new system that they were unable to use without first having to learn Braille's language of dots. They weren't prepared to study and learn this new language.

Some of the governors also believed that since Braille was the invention of one of the Institute's own pupils, and not of some great inventor, it couldn't possibly be very good!

And so the governors of the National Institute banned the use of Braille for its pupils. Later in 1840, they fired the principal, Dr. Pignier, when they discovered that he had had several textbooks produced in the new "dot" system.

Louis Braille must have been very disappointed to know that all his long hours of effort to perfect his brilliant new system of reading and writing appeared to be wasted and that Braille was being ignored.

For many more years, pupils at the National Institute for Blind Youth would learn their lessons through the old accepted system of embossed lettering, which was so awkward and hard to learn.

BRAILLE THE TEACHER

When it came time for Louis Braille to think about leaving the Institute to seek work, Dr. Pignier, the principal at the time, offered him a job as a teacher. And so Louis Braille became a junior teaching assistant at the Paris Institute where he had been for so long a pupil himself.

Braille had always been an excellent pupil and now he was to show that he was also a very good teacher. He taught history, geography, mathematics, grammar, and music, using the Haüy method of reading and writing, with raised wooden letters of the alphabet. Sometimes he and his pupils would secretly use his new six-dot system. The way he taught his pupils was very different from the way that was usual at the time. In most schools, including the Institute, teachers were very strict. They used to beat the boys regularly, believing that this treatment was the only way to get their pupils to learn.

Louis Braille, perhaps remembering his own gentle teachers, Jacques Palluy and Antoine Becheret in Coupvray, knew that students respond to kindness and patience and that they learn much more easily when their teachers do not beat them. He prepared his lessons carefully and was always patient, gentle, and thorough in his teaching.

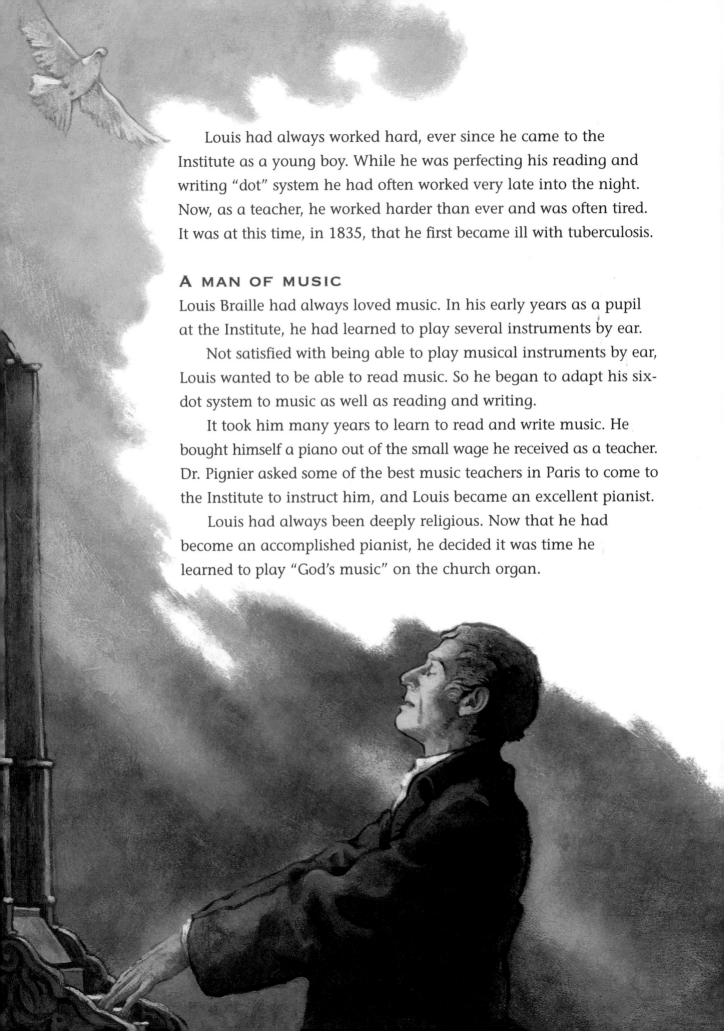

Louis had always worked hard, ever since he came to the
Institute as a young boy. While he was perfecting his reading and
writing "dot" system he had often worked very late into the night.
Now, as a teacher, he worked harder than ever and was often tired.
It was at this time, in 1835, that he first became ill with tuberculosis.

A MAN OF MUSIC

Louis Braille had always loved music. In his early years as a pupil
at the Institute, he had learned to play several instruments by ear.

Not satisfied with being able to play musical instruments by ear,
Louis wanted to be able to read music. So he began to adapt his six-
dot system to music as well as reading and writing.

It took him many years to learn to read and write music. He
bought himself a piano out of the small wage he received as a teacher.
Dr. Pignier asked some of the best music teachers in Paris to come to
the Institute to instruct him, and Louis became an excellent pianist.

Louis had always been deeply religious. Now that he had
become an accomplished pianist, he decided it was time he
learned to play "God's music" on the church organ.

Dr. Pignier was convinced that the church organ, with its massive foot pedals, double keyboard, and rows of stops, would be beyond the abilities of even Louis Braille. But, as always, Louis was determined to master the instrument. He talked to music teachers about his ambitions at every opportunity, and eventually he persuaded them to make arrangements for him to learn. Soon Louis was playing the organ every Sunday in a small church near the Institute, and sometimes he played at three different churches on the same day.

THE FINAL YEARS

Louis Braille had spent most of his life within the cold, damp stone walls of the National Institute for Blind Youth. He worked very hard for many years on his six-dot system and struggled to get it recognized and used officially. As a teacher he spent hours preparing his lessons and, in what little free time he had, he was usually to be found in some cold and drafty church, practicing on the organ.

At the age of twenty-six he became ill and gradually he grew weaker. Sometimes he would have to stop teaching in the middle of a lesson because he was completely out of breath.

At the time there was no cure for Louis Braille's illness— tuberculosis. Despite frequent visits to his family home in Coupvray for rest and country air, Louis knew that he was dying.

In 1851, when Louis was very seriously ill, a group of his friends signed a petition and presented it to the French Government. The petition asked for the official recognition of Braille as a system of reading and writing for blind people. The petition also requested that Louis Braille should be awarded the Legion of Honor (the highest award for merit in France) for his services to the blind.

But the French Government ignored the petition and on January 6, 1852, just two days after his forty-third birthday, Louis Braille died.

Sad to say, Braille died unknown, except for the small group of family and friends who had loved him and who were deeply grateful for his lifelong commitment to the blind. Only later did he become famous as the man who invented a brilliant, simple system of reading and writing for the blind, universally used and recognized around the world.

About the Illustrator
TROY HOWELL

For anyone who dreams of becoming an artist, Troy Howell has some advice. "If you want to be an artist," he says, "open your eyes to the world around you, open your mind to the imagination within you, and draw, draw, draw, and then draw some more."

When Mr. Howell was young, he knew that he wanted to be an artist, but he enjoyed another hobby as well. "When I was a sixth grader, I had two major interests," he says, "a live snail collection— 100 snails in jars!—and drawing. I soon learned not to show my drawings at school. My teacher liked them so much, she kept them, but she wouldn't touch the snails."

Mr. Howell went on to study art at the Art Center School in Los Angeles, and by the time he was nineteen, he was submitting art to *Cricket* magazine. He has illustrated over thirty books, including *The Night Swimmers*, an American Book Award winner by Betsy Byars, and his own retelling of *The Ugly Duckling*.

To create the illustrations for *The Maiden on the Moor* by Marilyn Singer, Mr. Howell traveled to the Scottish wastelands, called moors, for inspiration. This book is based on a medieval ballad about a beautiful maiden found by two brothers, one rich and one poor, on a cold wintry night.

Reader Response

Open for Discussion

There is much to admire in the life of Louis Braille. What do you admire most?

Comprehension Check

1. Jacques Palluy, Antoine Becheret, and Valentin Haüy each played an important role in the life of Louis Braille. Why was each person important?

2. Explain the author's statement that Louis Braille "took the best ideas from several systems." Which ideas? Which systems?

3. Why was the Braille system ignored for so many years by education and government officials? Use details from the selection to support your answer.

4. List three words that the author uses to describe Louis Braille and his invention. How do they reflect the **author's viewpoint?** (Author's Viewpoint/Bias)

5. The author states that "Louis Braille's great advantage was his blindness." What information does he give to support this **viewpoint?** (Author's Viewpoint/Bias)

 Test Prep

Look Back and Write

What advantages does Braille's system have over "Night Writing"? Use details from pages 631–632 in your answer.

Test Prep

How to Read Expository Nonfiction

1. Preview

- The job of expository nonfiction is to explain things. Some expository nonfiction explains what things are made of and how they work.

- Read the title and the words in dark type. Look over the illustrations and the diagram of the eye.

2. Read and Locate Information

- Much of the text refers to things that are pictured and labeled in the eye diagram.

- As you read, look at the diagram to locate parts of the eye that are mentioned in the text.

3. Think and Connect

Look back at "Louis Braille." Then look over your notes for "How Do We Know We See What We See?"

Both selections would be valuable for an eye doctor to read, but for different reasons. What are different reasons why an eye doctor would find each selection valuable?

How Do We Know We See What We See?

by Anita Ganeri

Aristotle was the first person to make a formal list of the five senses as sight, touch, hearing, smell, and taste. Of the five, our eyesight provides us with most of the information we use to build up a picture of our surroundings. So important are our eyes that things we have seen account for about three-quarters of all the knowledge entering our brains. And yet scientists are only just beginning to understand exactly how the eyes and brain work together to make us see.

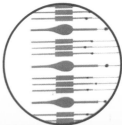

Rods and cones

There are two types of light-sensitive cells on your retina: rods and cones. Rods work well in dim light, but cannot detect color. Cones are sensitive to color and bright light. The cells get their names because of their shapes.

Moving eyes

Your eyes are constantly moving, even when they appear to be quite still. Six muscles around each eye coordinate eye movement, so you do not look in two directions at once. Scientists have monitored eye movement by fitting people with mirrored contact lenses and recording the reflections on film. Two types of movement have been seen: involuntary flicks and drifts of the eye and voluntary movements, such as those you make when you are reading this page.

Sclera and cornea

The sclera is the outermost layer of the wall of the eyeball. In front of the eye it covers the cornea, a clear layer that allows light into the eye.

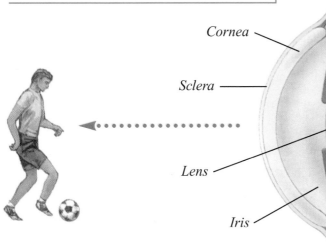

Cornea

Sclera

Lens

Iris

How we see

You see an object when light rays travel from the object into your eyes. Light enters your eye through a small hole, called the pupil. It is focused by the lens at the front of the eye and falls onto a screen at the back of the eye, called the retina. Light-sensitive cells on the retina send information about the image to your brain. At this stage, the image is upside down. Your brain processes the information it receives and turns the image right-side up again.

Pupil

Your pupil looks like a black dot in the center of your eye but is in fact a small hole through which light enters. Muscles in the colored part of your eye, the iris, can alter the size of the pupil. It gets bigger in dim light to let in as much light as possible and smaller in bright light, so you do not lose clear vision.

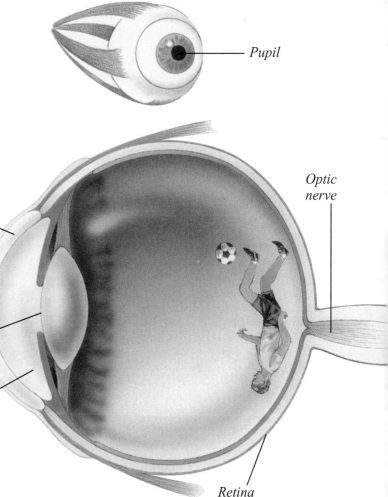

Pupil

Optic nerve

Retina

Optic nerve

The optic nerve carries information about the image on the retina to your brain. The point at which it leaves your eye is called your blind spot. There are no rods or cones in this spot.

Skill Lesson

Graphic Sources

- A **graphic** or **graphic source of information** is something that shows information visually.

- Some common graphic sources of information are pictures, charts, maps, graphs, and diagrams.

- A graphic source may present the information in the text differently, or it may show more information.

- Before you read, preview a story or article to see if there are graphic sources that give you an idea of what the text will be about. As you read, compare information in the graphic sources to information in the text.

Read "Ptolemy—An Early Mapmaker" from *Explorers and Mapmakers* **by Peter Ryan.**

Write About It

1. What various graphic sources appear on these two pages? How do they relate to the text?

2. Do these graphic sources repeat the information in the text or present different information? Explain.

Ptolemy—
AN EARLY MAPMAKER
by Peter Ryan

The ancient Greeks were very good at measuring distances and using scale. One of them, a geographer from Alexandria called Ptolemy (tol′ə mē), began drawing a map of the world about 1,800 years ago.

It was a difficult task. Traders often kept the routes of their journeys secret. Ptolemy had to persuade them to show him their maps and charts.

He succeeded. But no one could tell him that he had missed two huge, inhabited continents—America and Australia—and the vast Pacific Ocean that lies between them.

Unknown to Ptolemy, hunting and gathering tribes had long before reached America from the eastern end of Asia. Nor did he know of the

Aborigines of Australia, or of the seafaring islanders of the Pacific.

Yet his map shows an extensive area of Europe, Asia, and the northern part of Africa. Much of Ptolemy's knowledge was later lost, and had to be rediscovered.

Modern map showing Ptolemy's world

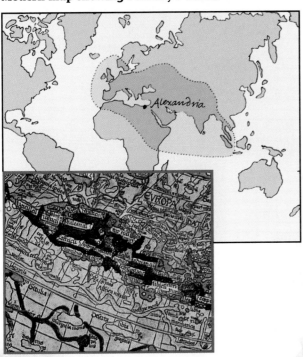

Alexandria

Detail of Ptolemaic map showing the Mediterranean Sea

LOOK AHEAD

The Librarian Who Measured the Earth is a biography about another man who looked at the world in a new way. Use graphics in the text to help you understand how he did it.

Vocabulary

Words to Know

accurate	angle	arc
calculate	estimate	formula
scholar	sphere	

Words that are spelled and pronounced the same but have different origins and meanings are called **homonyms.** For example, *bark* can mean "the covering of a tree" or "the sound a dog makes."

Read the paragraph below. Decide whether *angle* means "the space between two lines that meet" or "to fish with a hook and line."

Circling the Globe

Nearly two thousand years before Christopher Columbus set sail in 1492, a Greek scholar named Eratosthenes used a simple mathematical formula to calculate the distance around the Earth. First, he found the angle between the center of the Earth and two points on its surface. Then he measured the length of the arc between those two points. Lastly, he figured out how many of these arcs would be needed to make up the 360 degrees of a circle or sphere. His calculations were very accurate. Unfortunately, the same cannot be said for the information that Columbus used to estimate the distance between Europe and India. In fact, the actual distance was over three times what Columbus thought it was.

Talk About It

Tell a classmate about a difficult math problem that you once solved. Use as many vocabulary words as you can.

THE LIBRARIAN
WHO MEASURED THE EARTH

BY KATHRYN LASKY · ILLUSTRATED BY KEVIN HAWKES

More than two thousand years ago, a very smart baby was born. His name was Eratosthenes (AIR-uh-TOS-thuh-neez). His parents were Greek, and they lived in Cyrene (SI-ree-nee), a Greek city on the coast of Africa in the country that is now called Libya.

Even as a baby, Eratosthenes was curious and full of wonder.

He would crawl across the kitchen floor to follow the path of ants.

He wondered why there were beads of water on the cistern in the morning.

And in the evening, when he looked out the window of his bedroom, he wondered why the stars stayed in the sky.

When he could speak, he began asking hundreds and even thousands of questions:

How far away is the sun?

What is it made of?

Where do the winds come from?

What makes the stars move?

Many of these questions his parents couldn't answer.

When he was six years old, he went to school. It was called the gymnasium. Although the original meaning of the word was exercise ground, a gymnasium was also a school. Every morning, Eratosthenes, like other Greek boys, would be taken there by a family slave.

At the gymnasium there were no desks, no paper, and no pencils. And there were no girls. The girls stayed home and learned to cook and weave. Not many learned to read or write.

Students sat on the floor, and instead of pens they had styluses, sticks with one sharp end that were used for writing on tablets made of wax.

Eratosthenes loved the gymnasium. It was a chance to ask more questions.

In between asking questions, he and the other students learned reading, writing, arithmetic, music, and poetry. They even learned how to play the lyre and recite poetry at the same time. Eratosthenes was good at all these subjects, and he was a real whiz in math. But his absolute favorite subject was geography. He bombarded his teachers with questions:

How much of the Earth is land?

How high is the highest mountain?

Is there a map of the Earth?

When Eratosthenes had learned all he could at the gymnasium, he, like many Greek boys, was sent to the famous Greek capital city to learn more. He said good-bye to his parents and his teachers and sailed to Athens.

In Athens he studied mathematics, philosophy, and science. There wasn't much time for the lyre or marbles, but there was always time for questions.

In addition to being a great questioner, Eratosthenes was a terrific list maker. He liked making lists. It was a good way to organize information so it could be shared with other people. He made a list of all the important dates in the history of Greece. This kind of list is called a chronology. He also made a list of all the winners of the Olympic Games. And he began to write books. He wrote one on comedy, one on history, and one on the constellations.

Eratosthenes' name started to get around.

When Eratosthenes was thirty years old, a king called Ptolemy III, the ruler of Egypt, asked him to serve as tutor for his son Philopator in Alexandria. Eratosthenes was ecstatic. For a scholar like himself, Alexandria was the most exciting place to be. It was the center of all learning. It boasted a library and a museum that were the best in the world. All the great questions about science, literature, and history could be asked and researched here.

For indeed this museum was not just a collection of things on exhibit. The word *museum* literally means place of the Muses. In Greek mythology, the Muses are the nine daughters of Zeus, who help inspire artists and scientists.

At the museum there were laboratories and libraries, dining halls and private studios. There were special promenades that wound through quiet gardens for thoughtful strolls. Great minds were supposed to come to this place to read, study, and be inspired. And if the stomachs of these great minds started to growl with hunger, there were meals—porridge, fruit, nuts, and cheese.

It was here that the first dictionaries and encyclopedias were written. It was in the dissecting laboratories of the museum that a scientist named Herophilus first recognized the connection between a person's heartbeat and pulse and discovered the differences between arteries and veins.

A man named Ctesibius invented the first water-driven clock as well as the first keyboard musical instrument.

It was at the Alexandria Museum that punctuation and grammar were invented by Aristophanes. Before this, one word ran into the next with no spaces between them. There were no question marks, periods, or exclamation points either. Reading was hard!

And two thousand years ago, books were handwritten on scrolls of animal skins or papyrus, paper made from a tall grass that grows along the Nile. In the library at Alexandria, there were seven hundred thousand papyrus scrolls and forty librarians who, just like modern-day librarians, helped readers find what they were looking for and kept the materials in order. Each scroll was rolled up on a painted stick and tied with a colored string with a name tag attached. Often the scrolls were tucked into clay jars or simply placed on wooden shelves. There was a lot of rolling and tagging and tying that had to be done to keep a library as large as the one at Alexandria in order.

Eratosthenes fit right in with all his questions and ideas. In fact he got a new nickname, Pentathlos. The word refers to an athlete who competes in five different events. It had also come to mean all-rounder in Greek. They called him that because he was good at so many different things.

It was not long after he arrived that the head librarian died and Eratosthenes was appointed in his place. For a question asker and a list maker like Eratosthenes, being the head librarian was a dream come true. Now he could start to find answers to all of his questions. And the questions that were beginning to interest him the most were the ones right under his own two feet: questions about the Earth—geography.

As chief librarian, Eratosthenes was kept busy helping other scholars find information. He also had to keep in the good graces of his employer, King Ptolemy, who had a touchy and nervous temperament. In fact, a royal flatterer was employed just to keep the king's spirits up. But Eratosthenes himself had to be ready with compliments and praise for the king at all times.

So on one occasion, when he had solved a particularly difficult geometry problem, Eratosthenes dedicated the solution to the king. He then wrote a little poem about it and had it carved into a column that he had erected in the king's honor.

Eratosthenes' main interest, however, was not writing poetry to flatter the king. It was geography.

Once upon a time it had been thought that the Earth was flat. Then for a while people thought that it was the shape of a cylinder. But by the time Eratosthenes was born, they knew for sure that the Earth was round, a sphere. They had known this for at least one hundred years. But Eratosthenes had a lot of other questions about the Earth. How far does the Earth tilt on its axis? Does the ocean go all the way around the Earth? One of the most interesting questions of all was how big around *was* the Earth? It seemed impossible to figure out, for one could not walk around the Earth without running into an ocean, and at that time the Greeks did not have ships that they would dare sail as far as these oceans might reach. Could one, however, stand in one spot and figure it out?

Eratosthenes began his research, unrolling scroll upon scroll, looking for bits and pieces of information that would help him answer his questions. He soon realized that the information he was looking for was scattered all over the place—in math scrolls, scrolls about people, and scrolls about history. In the richest library on Earth, there was no single scroll that combined even a few of the answers. For someone

like Eratosthenes, who liked to organize information, it was clear that before he could find any answers, the facts must be brought together and rolled up in one single scroll.

Eratosthenes knew what he must do. He had to write the first complete geography book.

It would take Eratosthenes many years. Much of the information about the Earth that Eratosthenes wanted to include was mathematical and could never be found in scrolls or by talking to people from other lands. Eratosthenes had to figure out methods of knowing, of measuring, of describing. And, more than anything, he wanted to measure the circumference of the Earth. He knew his book would be incomplete without it.

Nobody had ever thought of measuring the size of such a large circle as the circumference of the Earth—nobody except for Eratosthenes. Perhaps he imagined the Earth as a grapefruit. If it is sliced in half, you can see its sections. In order to measure the distance all the way around the edge of the grapefruit (the circumference), you would need to know only the distance along the edge of one section (the arc) and how many of these same-size sections it would take to make up the whole grapefruit.

How could Eratosthenes find out how many sections were needed? He knew that every circle, whether it is as small as a grapefruit or as big as the Earth, is made up of 360 degrees. So if he could measure the inside angle of one section of his imaginary grapefruit in degrees, he could divide 360 by that number and know how many sections of that size would make up the whole.

Eratosthenes pictured a section of the Earth whose outside edge ran from Alexandria to Syene (SI-ee-nee), a city in southern Egypt. If he could figure out the distance between Alexandria and Syene, and if he could measure the inside angle of the section they created, he would be able to calculate the Earth's circumference. But how would he ever be able to measure that angle? It lay far below the ground, at the center of the Earth.

Eratosthenes realized that the sun could help him with his angle problem, and he picked Syene for a reason. He had heard from a caravan passing through Alexandria that on the twenty-first day of June at precisely midday, the sun would shine directly down a certain well in Syene, lighting up the well but casting no shadows on its walls. But at the exact same time in Alexandria, shadows would be cast.

Eratosthenes knew why. It was because the Earth was round. If the Earth were flat, the sun would strike every place at the same angle and the shadows would all be exactly the same.

Eratosthenes knew a thing or two about shadows and angles. He knew you could measure the angle of the sun by the shadow it cast. And he knew, from the mathematical texts he had read, that the angle of the sun in Alexandria at noon on June 21 would be the same as the angle that lay at the center of the Earth making the inside of his Alexandria-to-Syene "grapefruit" section.

So Eratosthenes walked out of the library a few minutes before noon on the twenty-first day of June to measure a midday shadow at Alexandria, just as the sun was falling straight down the well at Syene. He measured an angle of about 7.2 degrees. Then he divided 360 by 7.2, which equals 50. Now he knew that it would take 50 Alexandria-to-Syene sections to make up the circumference of the Earth.

But knowing that was still not enough. Eratosthenes had to know the length of his section's arc—the distance between the two cities.

Then he could multiply this distance by 50 to find that distance around the whole Earth. It would be so simple!

But it wasn't. There was a problem. The problem was camels! Camels were the main manner of transport in the desert, and Eratosthenes had planned to measure the distance between the two cities by calculating how long it took camels to get from one city to another. He thought camels would be perfect. But he forgot that they are ornery, stubborn, and have minds of their own.

Some camel caravans went slow and some went fast and some camels ran off in the wrong direction. No matter how hard Eratosthenes tried, he could not record travel times for camels that were accurate enough for his mathematical equations.

Finally he threw up his hands in despair. "Enough with these camels. I'm going to see the king!"

He asked the king if he could borrow the services of his best bematists—surveyors trained to walk with equal steps. In this way linear distances could be measured with some accuracy.

The king agreed. And the bematists he supplied walked with equal steps just as they had been trained to do. It was then easy to estimate that

the distance between Alexandria and Syene was five thousand stades. A stade was supposed to equal the length of a Greek stadium. The stade that Eratosthenes used was 515 feet, or just under one-tenth of a mile.

Eratosthenes now had all the numbers he needed for the formula. He calculated the circumference of the Earth to be 252,000 stades, or 24,662 miles. When the Earth was remeasured in this century, there was only a two-hundred-mile difference between the modern-day figure and the one that Eratosthenes had calculated over two thousand years ago!

Eratosthenes' measurements provided the first accurate, mathematically based map of the world. His *Geographica,* the first geography book of the world, was now complete.

Eratosthenes lived to be a very old man. He continued to work on math problems and to study and measure the Earth. But most important of all, he kept asking questions.

No question was ever too big or small for Eratosthenes to think about.

About the Author
KATHRYN LASKY

Kathryn Lasky remembers how boring nonfiction books seemed to her when she was a child in school. "I didn't like nonfiction as a kid—the nonfiction books were really dry back then," she says. "But then I realized that you can make the characters in nonfiction as fascinating as those in fiction." As a writer of nonfiction, she has tried to do just that. Her biography of Eratosthenes, *The Librarian Who Measured the Earth,* was named a *School Library Journal* Best Book of the Year and a Notable Book by the American Library Association. *Sugaring Time,* a book about collecting maple tree sap and making maple syrup in Vermont, was a Newbery Honor Book.

About the Illustrator
KEVIN HAWKES

Because his father was in the U.S. Air Force, Kevin Hawkes spent his childhood traveling the world. He remembers attending kindergarten in France, exploring castles, and swinging on vines with his sister and brothers elsewhere in the world. His drawings in *The Librarian Who Measured the Earth* are inspired by the landscape of Greece. In this book, he enjoyed the challenge of bringing ancient history to life through his artwork. Mr. Hawkes has written and illustrated other books, including *Then the Troll Heard the Squeak* and *His Royal Buckliness.*

Reader Response

Open for Discussion

Eratosthenes was a "great questioner." If he were alive today, what questions might he ask?

Comprehension Check

1. What made the Alexandria Museum a great center of learning? Use details from the selection in your answer.

2. Why was Eratosthenes' position as the head librarian in Alexandria "a dream come true"? Look back at the selection for details.

3. What did Eratosthenes need to complete his book? Why did he believe that his book would be "incomplete without it"?

4. **Graphic sources** can help you visualize complex ideas. Use the illustrations on page 649 to explain, in your own words, how Eratosthenes measured the distance around the Earth. (Graphic Sources)

5. Eratosthenes made good use of graphic sources. The chronology, or time line, that Eratosthenes once made of important dates in the history of Greece is a **graphic source.** Compile a chronology of important events in Eratosthenes' life. Include his age whenever possible. (Graphic Sources)

Test Prep

Look Back and Write

How was the library at Alexandria like and different from libraries today? Use specific details from pages 646–648 to support your answer.

A Revolution!

from *Kids Discover* magazine

Early mapmakers would be astounded—and a bit befuddled—by the tools available to cartographers today. But so would anyone who had retired from the profession even just 20 years ago. In the past two decades, the art and science of mapmaking has been revolutionized by technology.

AERIAL PHOTOGRAPHY began in 1858 when French photographer Gaspard Tournachon photographed the village of Petit Bicêtre from the basket of a hot-air balloon. However, it wasn't until after World War II that aerial photography was used widely to map many countries. This aerial photo is of the Ile de la Cité in France. ▼

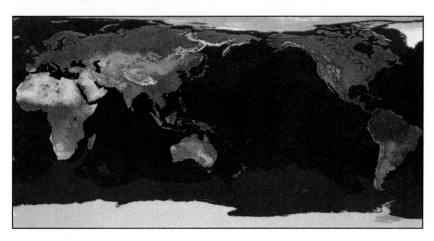

▲ **IF AN AIRPLANE CAN GET A** broad view of the land, imagine the view from a satellite. A satellite can photograph the entire surface of the Earth in 18 days. Some photographs are taken with conventional cameras, using the sun as a source of light. Others use remote-sensing methods that allow them, for example, to record the amount of infrared radiation coming from different areas. With such methods, satellite photography has, among other things, revealed how much of the world's rain forests have been burned.

▲ **THE BIGGEST REVOLUTION IN** mapmaking has been the use of computers to store information. With computers, cartographers can update maps and combine information from many sources without having to redraw a map every time it is changed.

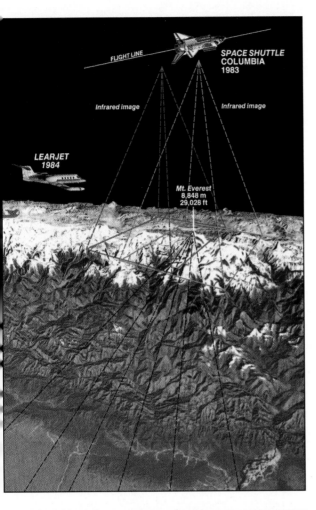

FLIGHT LINE

SPACE SHUTTLE
COLUMBIA
1983

Infrared image   Infrared image

LEARJET
1984

Mt. Everest
8,848 m
29,028 ft

◀ **IN 1984 THE NATIONAL** Geographic Society and the Boston Museum of Science launched a joint project to map the Himalayas from the air. A jet plane flying at 40,000 feet took mapping photos of 380 square miles of the region. The project also used British, Austrian, and Chinese topographic maps made between 1921 and 1975 by ground surveyors and low-altitude flights. Another key element in the project was using infrared images taken from the space shuttle Columbia when it passed over Mount Everest 156 miles above the Earth on December 2, 1983.

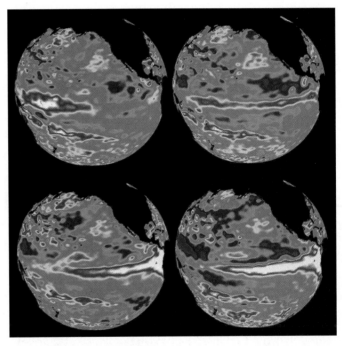

▲ **UNTIL THE LATE 20TH** century, maps were made by people who had no way of seeing the world in its entirety. Space photography and satellite imagery have created a revolutionary new look at the planet. Still, maps can never be totally objective. Because of the technology, images must be manipulated and interpreted to make sense of what is being seen. These 1997 satellite images show the pattern of El Niño events in the Pacific Ocean.

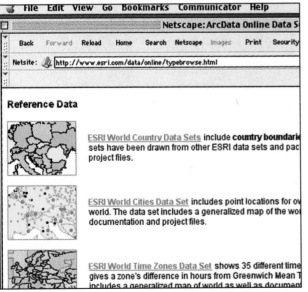

File Edit View Go Bookmarks Communicator Help

Netscape: ArcData Online Data S

Back Forward Reload Home Search Netscape Images Print Security

Netsite: http://www.esri.com/data/online/typebrowse.html

Reference Data

ESRI World Country Data Sets include country boundarie sets have been drawn from other ESRI data sets and pac project files.

ESRI World Cities Data Set includes point locations for ov world. The data set includes a generalized map of the wor documentation and project files.

ESRI World Time Zones Data Set shows 35 different time gives a zone's difference in hours from Greenwich Mean T includes a generalized map of world as well as document

▲ **WITH A COMPUTER** and a Geographic Information System (GIS), almost anyone can make a map today. The GIS works with computer software that contains information about many different features of the Earth, including physical features, climate, political boundaries, and population.

Paraphrasing

- To **paraphrase** is to explain something in your own words.

- To paraphrase a piece of writing, first ask yourself what the author is trying to say. Then restate the ideas or description in your own words, without changing the meaning or adding opinions of your own.

- To check your paraphrase, ask yourself "Did I use my own words? Did I keep the author's meaning?"

- Paraphrasing can be a useful research and study tool. It can be used to prepare for a test or to gather information from reference sources.

Read "A Lesson from the Master" from *Boy of the Painted Cave* by Justin Denzel.

Write About It

1. Reread the third paragraph. Make a list of what happens in that paragraph. Then paraphrase the paragraph, using the list as help.

2. "Tao outlines another reindeer before Graybeard rudely interrupts him." Is this a good paraphrase of the last paragraph on this page? Why or why not?

A Lesson from the Master

by Justin Denzel

Tao is a boy in prehistoric times who befriends Graybeard, a master cave painter. Here, Graybeard teaches him painting.

Graybeard got to his feet. He lifted his thin arms over his head and stretched. Then he looked down at the boy. "Now it is time to begin," he said.

He took a slate stone from his deerskin pouch. "When we were together before, I showed you how to rough out your image, how to draw a bison. Now you must try something harder." He handed Tao the stone.

Tao took it and studied the carved engraving. It was the figure of a reindeer with branching antlers and long, thin legs. He knew it would not be easy. He picked up one of the chalks and stepped to the wall. It was clean and unmarked and he ran the palm of his hand over the surface, feeling the smoothness of it. Then he lifted his other hand and made the first bold strokes, starting with the shoulder and back.

The old man stopped him immediately, shaking his head briskly. "That is wrong. I have told you, always make your first sketch in charcoal. Black is better. And start with an outline of the body and the head."

Tao groaned inwardly. In his excitement he had already forgotten the first lesson the old man had taught him. He picked up a stick of charcoal and began again.

The old master watched for a while, then reached out and stopped the boy's hand again. "No," he said sharply. "You draw with short, choppy strokes. Let your hand go free. Let it glide over the wall. There is plenty of room, reach out as far as you can."

As he followed Graybeard's instructions Tao found he was drawing easier, faster. He smiled with a quick feeling of satisfaction. Just a few words from the master made a big difference.

Graybeard nodded. "You are learning, my friend. It takes time, but you are learning."

Tao drew the outline of two more reindeer before the old man stopped him again. "Now I will show you something else," said Graybeard. He took another graven stone from his leather pouch and handed it to Tao. On it was the sketch of a rhino. Then he brushed his long fingers across the wall. "Look, here," he said. "When you draw the rhino, use this bulge as the high part of the back. The hollow place below it then becomes the dark area where the head meets the shoulder."

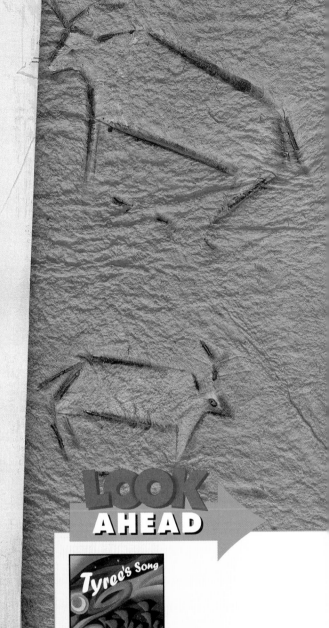

LOOK AHEAD

In "Tyree's Song," a human boy becomes the student of an alien musician on the planet Harmony. Try paraphrasing parts of the story to check your understanding.

Vocabulary

Words to Know

abandoned	alien	anxiety
improvise	themes	variations

Many words have more than one meaning. To decide which meaning of a word is being used, look for clues in the surrounding sentences or the paragraph.

Read the paragraph below. Decide whether *alien* means "a person who is not a citizen of the country in which he or she lives" or "an imaginary creature from outer space."

A Strange Duet

There are five minutes until my piano recital, and I'm getting nervous. It's so scary up on stage. I feel as though I've been abandoned, even when my family is in the audience. I worry that I'll forget parts of my piece, and I'll have to improvise. To calm my anxiety, I imagine that a friendly alien from a music-loving planet is sitting next to me on the piano bench. The alien helps me through the most difficult variations on the themes, or melodies. I know it sounds funny, but it really works. Well, the five minutes are up. We're ready to perform.

Write About It

Write about a situation that made you nervous. Use as many vocabulary words as you can.

660

Tyree's Song

from *Sweetwater*

by Laurence Yep

On the planet Harmony, most of the earth colonists abandoned the city of Old Sion when it was flooded by rising tides. Those who remain speak the Intergal language and call themselves Silkies. Young Tyree's father is the leader of the Silkies. After discovering music through his friend Jubal, Tyree began practicing on a homemade flute. Now Tyree is upset because his father, who thinks it is undignified to be a musician, does not want anyone to hear his son play again.

I figured that Pa's order could be taken two ways, his way and my way. I could play the flute as long as no Silkie heard me, and I knew there was one place at night in Old Sion where no Silkie would hear me, because no Silkie would dare go there. I was willing to go there that very night to find a place where I could practice. I planned to go to Sheol. I was that desperate.

We still called the area by its old name, given when Sheol was the most elegant and expensive area in Old Sion, but now after the floods the mansions were occupied by the Argans, the only intelligent race native to Harmony. The Argans were a strange race, and they liked to keep their secrets. No human ever knew how they reproduced, though their words for family relations translated loosely into "uncle" and "nephew."

There were some humans who had never forgiven the aliens because they didn't warn the colonists about the tides, but then we weren't asked to come to their world. And anyway, the colonists weren't exactly kind to the aliens.

Later when the city, Old Sion, was abandoned, the Argans drifted back from the wastelands, claiming that the land was still theirs, and by that time it did not matter who Old Sion belonged to legally, because the sea had already filled most of the city. There was a silent agreement between the humans and the Argans—though both would have been the first to deny it—not to go into certain sectors, or at least never to be seen there. No man ever saw an Argan in Old Sion unless that Argan wanted him to, not even if it was in that human's own home. So when I went into the Argans' area, I was the one in the wrong. I was the invader.

At night Sheol didn't look like it belonged to man anymore. The half-submerged elegant houses looked like ancient monsters surfacing. Their great stone faces were covered with delicate beards of green seaweed or soft mustachios of barnacles. The seaworn doors opened like the mouths of Seadragons through which the water twisted and untwisted, and the windows were like eyes, hollow and black and waiting—with ripples fanning outward as though from some creature sleeping inside.

It was really scary, but I thought like a human in those days and I figured that whether the Argans and the animals and the houses liked it or not, I was going to practice there. On purpose I picked out the finest and biggest mansion, which had been built on a hill. It had belonged to Nimrod Senaar, the Governor who had cheated my ancestors. The statue of our old enemy rose from the water lonely and proud, frowning at the change in his old city. I thumbed my nose at him as I passed.

I moored my skiff to one of the pillars of the portico and splashed up the steps. My bare feet made wet slapping sounds as I walked across the portico and through the entrance hall with its huge rotunda. I checked the rooms on both floors for the acoustics until I found one that satisfied me. Then for about an hour I practiced my scales until I heard something strange.

At first I thought it was the wind but then I realized it was music, and the more I listened, the more I felt that I had never heard anything more lovely. The song was at once sad and yet beautiful, moving like the veiled ghosts of bold knights or unfulfilled maidens. The echoes floated up the street over the hissing water, past the empty, slime-covered apartment houses, bounced and danced past walls whose rotting mortar slowly spilled stone after stone into the sea. It was a song for Old Sion.

I had to find the musician and I searched the entire mansion until I found him sitting on the portico by my skiff. It was an Argan, an old one, sitting there calmly. The bristly fur on his back and arm-legs was a peppery gray, the flesh on his belly was all wrinkled, and he stooped slightly from old age. He looked very much like a four-foot-high Earth spider, though you would never suggest that to an Argan. They hate to be reminded of their resemblance to their Earth cousins the way humans hate to be reminded that they look like apes.

He put down his reed pipes when he saw me and with six of his arm-legs slowly pushed himself off the portico. He seemed surprised and walked around me. He walked delicately on two arm-legs like a ballet dancer imitating an old man, with his six other arm-legs stretched out to balance his overpuffed body. He stepped back in front of me and examined me boldly, even though Argans usually kept their eyelids down low because they knew how their eyes bothered humans. Argans have myriads of tiny eyes on their orbs. They shine like clouds of stars in dim light and it takes some getting used to—it's like being watched by a one-man crowd.

"What can I do for you, Manchild?" he asked in Intergal.

I shifted uncomfortably from one foot to the other. I told myself that it was silly to feel like I had invaded this Argan's home. In those days I believed I had as much right to this place as the Argans did. "I heard you playing," I said finally.

"And my nephews and my neighbors heard your free concert," the old Argan said. "They found me and told me so I could come home and hear my competition."

"There's no competition," I mumbled. It was easy enough to get embarrassed about my playing in those days. I could even be shamed by aliens. "Well," I added, "I guess I'll be moving on. I don't want to drive folk away from their homes."

The old Argan grabbed hold of me and I knew I couldn't get away. The Argans had small but very strong disc-shaped suction pads at the base of their finger-toes. They could retract the suction pads into their skin or extend them so that the bottoms of their hand-feet appeared to be rimmed with tiny white circles. When he used his suction pads, his grip was unbreakable.

"What do they know? It's the song that counts, not the singer." He pointed at the flute. "And that's a mighty nice flute. Did you carve it?"

I turned my ornate flute over in my hands self-consciously. "I'm afraid I spent more time carving pictures into it than I did playing it."

"Do you like music?"

"More than anything," I said. "But there's no one to teach me."

"Of course." The old Argan was thoughtful for a moment. "What did you think of my song? It was just a little night music."

"I thought it was beautiful," I said and added truthfully, "it was the most beautiful thing I've ever heard."

I don't know what he was looking for, but he studied me for a long time. His myriad eyes reflected my image so I saw a hundred Tyrees—each a perfect miniature.

"Would you like me to teach you?" the old Argan said.

"But what about your nephews and your neighbors?"

"I told you to forget them. Music's the only important thing."

I felt a warm rush of gratitude inside me. "I'd like it an awful lot if you would teach me, Mister . . ." I realized that I had almost made a bad mistake, because Argans, like some people on Earth, don't believe in giving their true names because that gives the listener power over the person named. Argans have what they call use-names, which they change every so often.

"My use-name is Amadeus." The old Argan let go of my wrist with a slight popping noise.

I rubbed the small circles on my wrist where the suction pads had gripped me. A new question had occurred to me but it took me a while before I worked up enough nerve to ask him. "Since you're an Argan, how can you teach me to play a human musical instrument?"

"It's enough that I know," Amadeus snapped. "Now no more questions if you want me to teach you."

It was a puzzle how an alien could teach me about human music, but I was willing to try anything. "All right," I said.

"Come back tomorrow night and I'll see if I can teach you that you have only two thumbs and not ten."

I knew that I had met one of the aliens' songsmiths, and all the way home I felt warm and good inside, knowing what a privilege I was being given. If there is one thing the Argans love, it's their music—you could hear one or more of them playing on their reed pipes whenever you passed near Sheol. The Argans think that the gods directly choose someone to be a songsmith. Important councils have been moved to decisions by an inspired songsmith suddenly getting up and playing a particular song in a particular way.

The Argans don't think of music as we humans do. An Argan song seems skimpy by human standards. It just has a basic story line—like how the three moons were created—and a theme of music which represents the song. It's up to the musician to improvise and create variations on the theme and to combine these with certain other established themes which the audience recognizes as representing a castle, or a feast, or a heroic battle, or anything like that.

In Argan music, songs keep on evolving and changing as they are played. The Argans think that the human style is the mark of a mediocre musician. Only mediocre musicians play a song in the same way all the time. In human music, since you usually have a song sheet, the musician is limited to an already-fixed pattern of themes and variations and his performance is judged by his skill in playing the

song. But in Argan music, the best musicians have to be not only skilled craftsmen but also geniuses at finding new and original patterns.

Of course, Argan music isn't really that loose. When I first started to play it, I wondered how a musician knew what to play next, since you had to choose while performing at the same time; but there's a kind of logic to it—like knowing the ending to a story halfway through the telling. For example, if two Argan heroes meet, you have to describe both of them, and their battle, and the funeral for the loser.

Amadeus was very patient about explaining things like that about music. He really earned his title, the Ultimate Uncle—which was his social position among the Argans, though Amadeus would never tell me any more. He hated to talk about himself and Argan affairs, but about music there was almost no stopping him. I took to visiting Sheol three times a week, and Amadeus would listen patiently as I butchered his people's music. Whenever I tried to apologize for a particularly clumsy performance, he would encourage me by telling me that my song and I had not found one another yet. According to Argan belief, it's the song that finds the singer and not the other way around.

After a while, though, not even that belief could satisfy me. I was tired from having to do my chores during the daytime, keep my secret from my parents, and still have nothing to show for all my sacrifices but some bad playing.

"It's no use, Amadeus. I'm never going to be a musician."

Amadeus sighed and shook his head. "Manchild, you have everything that a person needs to make music: you have the talent, you have the skills now, but you still hold your soul back from the music—like you can't forget you're a human playing Argan music. You just have to remember that it's the music that counts—not the one who plays it."

And with that he put the reed pipes to his mouth and began to play the human song, "Moonspring." I sat in astonishment as he slipped next into "Shall We Gather by the Stars" and "These Happy Golden Years."

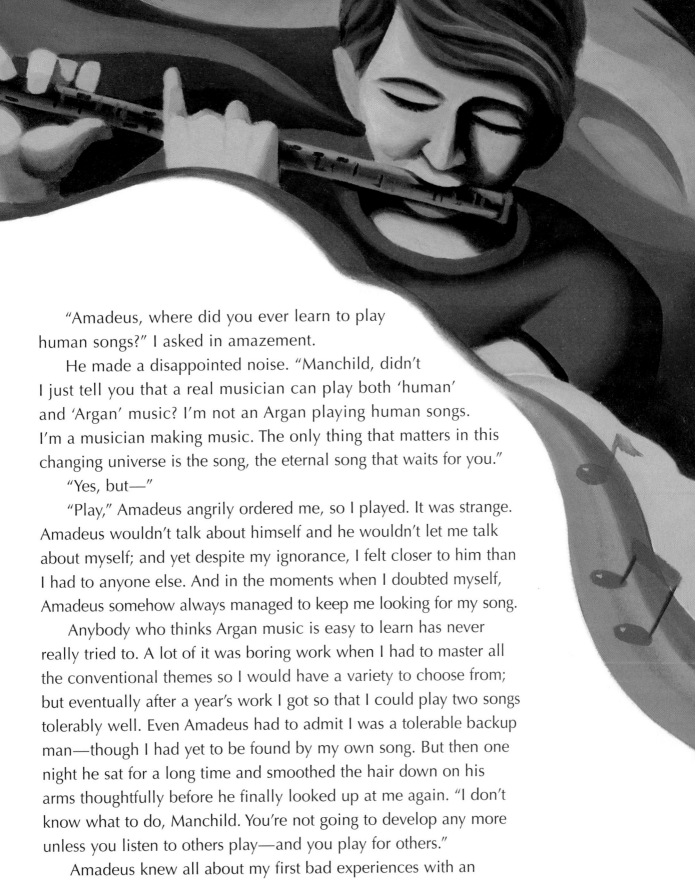

"Amadeus, where did you ever learn to play human songs?" I asked in amazement.

He made a disappointed noise. "Manchild, didn't I just tell you that a real musician can play both 'human' and 'Argan' music? I'm not an Argan playing human songs. I'm a musician making music. The only thing that matters in this changing universe is the song, the eternal song that waits for you."

"Yes, but—"

"Play," Amadeus angrily ordered me, so I played. It was strange. Amadeus wouldn't talk about himself and he wouldn't let me talk about myself; and yet despite my ignorance, I felt closer to him than I had to anyone else. And in the moments when I doubted myself, Amadeus somehow always managed to keep me looking for my song.

Anybody who thinks Argan music is easy to learn has never really tried to. A lot of it was boring work when I had to master all the conventional themes so I would have a variety to choose from; but eventually after a year's work I got so that I could play two songs tolerably well. Even Amadeus had to admit I was a tolerable backup man—though I had yet to be found by my own song. But then one night he sat for a long time and smoothed the hair down on his arms thoughtfully before he finally looked up at me again. "I don't know what to do, Manchild. You're not going to develop any more unless you listen to others play—and you play for others."

Amadeus knew all about my first bad experiences with an audience, so he knew how shy I was of those situations. "Amadeus," I finally said, "have they been staying away because of me or have you been keeping them away so I wouldn't be nervous?"

"A little of both," Amadeus said reluctantly.

"The Argans don't like the idea of your giving me lessons, do they?"

"Who told you?" he asked angrily. "You pay those fools no mind. They've heard you play but they just won't believe."

"Believe what?" I asked.

"That an Argan song will ever find a human," Amadeus was forced to admit.

"Have they been giving you trouble?" I asked.

"It doesn't matter," Amadeus said.

I had noticed that the rooms were a lot dustier of late, as if most of the house was no longer occupied. A brilliant songsmith like Amadeus should have had quite a few Argans around him—not only to hear him play but also to serve him as befitted his status. Yet whenever I went over there, Amadeus was alone.

"Do your family come back after I leave, or do they stay away all the time now?"

"Mind your own business," Amadeus snapped.

"But, Amadeus—"

Amadeus held up one hand-foot as a warning. "Let's get something straight, Manchild. We're here to play music, not to talk."

I gave up asking any more questions and just thought for a while. After all he had done for my sake I could hardly do less. "If you can get some of them together, I'll play for them," I said. "We'll show them."

Amadeus made sure I wanted to go through with it before he named the next night for my test. I had to trade twenty feet of my best nylon fishing line to Red Genteel, but he agreed to do my chores in the garden for that day while I napped. I wanted to be at my best for the Argans.

That night there must have been some twenty Argans sitting on the porch; six of them were my "classmates" while the others were nephews, skeptics, critics, and creatures who liked to see minor disasters. The moment I sat down to warm up they began to crack jokes in the clicking language of the Argans. I did not know the words but their jokes were obviously about me. They might not be able to make fun of Amadeus, but I was fair game.

One of them, Sebastian, had painfully learned some Intergal, so I could understand. "My cousin, he say, are your fingers broke? But I say, no, you just sitting on your hands."

I started to blush but Amadeus, he gave me a wink—which for an Argan is a considerable maneuver. It was a mannerism that I thought he had picked up from me. "You just start whenever you like, Manchild. Don't you mind the noise. 'Pears to be an undue number of insects out tonight." Amadeus stopped their jokes for maybe a minute and then they started in again. If I had been Amadeus, I would have been jumping up

and down with anxiety, but Amadeus had a quiet kind of strength. He was like a calm pool of water that you could have dropped anything into and it wouldn't have disturbed the pool besides a momentary ripple. Just having Amadeus there gave me confidence.

"I'd like to play now, Amadeus," I said.

"Well," and Amadeus nodded to me approvingly, "well, go on."

I shut my eyes against all the furry faces and the star-clustered eyes and I tilted my head up toward the night sky, toward the real stars. Suddenly my song had found me. It was "Sweetwater," the song Jubal had played at that winter fête—but now I made it my own. I took the melody and I played it like an Argan, modeling my song after an Argan song about a lost child looking for its mother. All the months of frustration and loneliness poured out of me and I played like *I* was the lost, lonely child calling across the empty light-years of space to Mother Earth.

The notes blended into a song that floated majestically over the rooftops, wheeling like a bird fighting through the wind and the rain, striving to break into the open, free sky, where the sun would dry his wings so he could turn toward home: to ride the winter winds to his home. I felt as lonely as when I used to lie on the roof watching the flocks of birds overhead and imagining what it was like to fly. Gliding with long, strong wings—floating along through the light, so far above the world that land and sea blurred into one. The wind raced through their pinions, bore them up on an invisible hand, and then, passing through their bodies, there came the smell of sweetwater.

When I felt the song was finished, I put the flute down to see Amadeus chuckling to himself. The other Argans looked a little stunned. Amadeus started to play a theme, this time an Argan song, "The Enchanted Reed Pipes." I played backup man but he was the master, sending his song ringing and echoing up the abandoned streets, the two of us gone mad with music.

About the Author
Laurence Yep

As a young boy, Laurence Yep often felt like an outsider. He grew up a Chinese American boy in an African American neighborhood in San Francisco. When he went to school in Chinatown, his feeling of not fitting-in continued. Mr. Yep spoke English while many of his classmates spoke Chinese. In his books, these early feelings of alienation often come through in his characters. "Probably the reason that much of my writing has found its way to a teenage audience," he explains, "is that I'm always pursuing the theme of being an outsider— an alien—and many teenagers feel they're aliens."

Mr. Yep started writing when he was still in high school. He had his first story published when he was only eighteen years old. The book *Sweetwater* was published five years later, to many favorable reviews.

His next work, and perhaps his best known, *Dragonwings,* takes place in the early 1900s. During this time many Chinese men came to America to earn money to send to their families in China. This book follows a boy who travels to San Francisco to be with his father. Together the boy and his father fulfill the father's dream of inventing and flying an airplane. To be able to write about this period in history, Mr. Yep did much research. He also had to imagine his childhood as if it were set in a different time. This book was named a Newbery Honor book in addition to winning several other awards.

Reader Response

Open for Discussion

What song do you know that you'd like to hear Tyree improvise upon? Why?

Comprehension Check

1. Why do you think Tyree is so determined to play music? What does he do to achieve this goal? Look back at the story for details.

2. In your opinion, why does Amadeus offer to teach Tyree to play Argan music? Use details from the story in your answer.

3. Why do the other Argans seem stunned when they hear Tyree play "Sweetwater"? Look for story details to use in your answer.

4. Look back at Tyree's description of the city of Sheol on pages 662–663. **Paraphrase** it. (Paraphrasing)

5. **Paraphrase** Tyree's description of Argan music on pages 666–668. Does any part of this description remind you of Earth music? Explain your answer. (Paraphrasing)

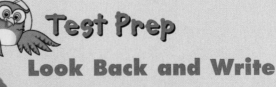

Test Prep

Look Back and Write

Why does Tyree feel such a deep sense of friendship with Amadeus? Use details from pages 665–669 to support your answer.

Pipes and Flutes

by Neil Ardley

The Pied Piper lured children from Hamelin.

THE BREATHY, INTIMATE SOUND of pipes and flutes gives them a haunting quality. Sound is made simply by blowing across the end of an open pipe or a hole in the pipe. This sets the air inside the pipe vibrating to give a lovely, mellow tone. Blowing harder into the pipe produces higher notes.

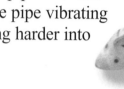

Notch

WHISTLING FISH
This pottery fish makes music like a recorder. Both have ducts—short air channels that lead air from the mouth to a blowhole in the side.

Blowholes

Notch

Finger holes

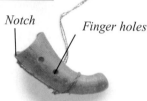

STONE ANIMALS
The frogs and eagle are unusual and attractive decorations on this 19th century flageolet, a wind instrument something like a flute. It was carved in soapstone by the Haida Indians, a tribe who live on islands off Canada.

EARLY MUSIC
Whistles made of reindeer toe bones date from 40,000 B.C. These French bones may have been used for signaling rather than to make music.

MUSIC FROM FRUIT
This whistle from the Sudan (North Africa) is made from a piece of gourd. It is played by blowing into a notch in the open end and closing the holes with fingers.

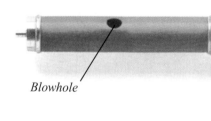

Blowhole

Lip plate around blowhole

MUSIC OF THE GODS
Panpipes get their name from the Greek god Pan. When the nymph that Pan loved was turned into a reed, he cut the reed into a set of different length pipes, which he played to console himself.

ORIENTAL DESIGN
The notch cut in the end of the Japanese *shakuhachi* might make it easier to play than simple end-blown flutes such as panpipes.

Elaborately carved wood in the shape of a dragon's head

Transverse Flutes

Any pipe with finger holes and a blown end or hole can be called a flute, but the name is usually given only to instruments that sound by being blown across a hole. These are classified as transverse, or side-blown, flutes and are held horizontally.

Opening covered by the hand to change the note

HANDY DEVICE
Although blown like a transverse flute, this bamboo instrument from Guyana (South America) is unusual in that the player changes the note by blocking and changing the shape of the large opening in the side with one hand.

THE BOEHM SYSTEM
The flute was greatly improved by the German instrument-maker Theobald Boehm (1794–1881), who invented a key system in which pads, operated by keys or the fingers, covered all the holes. This gave a better sound and made the flute easier to play.

Blowhole

Blowhole

NOSE NOISE
Nose flutes are very common in the Pacific area. This beautifully decorated bamboo example comes from Fiji. It has a blowhole at each end and three finger holes in the center. The player blows with one nostril, blocking the other with his hand.

Finger holes

Keys

Early wooden flute, c. 1830

Keys for little fingers

Modern concert flute

Thumb keys

Pad closed by finger

Pad closed by key

FROM SIMPLICITY TO SOPHISTICATION
The concert flute, with its superior sound, passed the recorder and flageolet in popularity during the 1800s. The simple keywork of the early wooden instrument contrasts with the complex keywork of the modern metal flute, but the modern instrument is easier to play and has a brighter sound.

DRAGON FLUTE
The *lung ti,* or dragon flute, is an elegant and unusual Chinese transverse flute used in religious ceremonies. It is made of lacquered bamboo and has a thin sheet of paper covering the blowhole. This gives it a penetrating, buzzing sound.

Ornate lacquer decoration

Fact and Opinion

- A **statement of fact** can be proven true or false by reading, observing, asking an expert, or checking it in some way.

- A **statement of opinion** tells someone's belief, judgment, or way of thinking about something. It cannot be proven true or false, but it can be supported or explained. Some statements of opinion begin with clue words, such as *I believe* or *In my opinion*.

- A valid statement of opinion can be supported by facts or by the authority of an expert. A faulty statement of opinion cannot.

Read "Three Wondrous Buildings" from *Round Buildings, Square Buildings, & Buildings That Wiggle Like a Fish* **by Philip M. Isaacson.**

Write About It

1. Look back at the article to find a statement of fact. Explain how you would prove it true or false.

2. Skim the article to find a statement of opinion. Tell whether it is valid or faulty.

3. Which of the three buildings is the most beautiful? Write your own statement of opinion.

THREE WONDROUS BUILDINGS

by Philip M. Isaacson

This is a building (1) in a small city in northern India. People come from all over the world to see it. Many of them come because they feel that it is the most beautiful building in the world. It is called the Taj Mahal, and it is a valentine from a great emperor to a wife who died when she was very young. It is made of marble the color of cream. Each afternoon the sun changes the color of the Taj Mahal. First it turns it pink, then yellow, then the color of apricots. In the evening it becomes brown, and when the moon shines on it, it is blue and gray. In the moonlight it becomes the old emperor, asleep and dreaming.

The Taj Mahal is about three hundred years old. This building (2) is much older. It was built about 2,500 years ago and stands on a white marble hill in Greece. Because it too is made of white marble, it seems to grow out of that hill as though it were a group of great trees standing in a small forest. It is called the Parthenon in honor of an ancient Greek goddess. Though it is made only of marble

2

posts—called columns—and a very simple roof, it is just as famous as the Taj Mahal and has just as many admirers. Many people feel that it is the most beautiful building in the world.

This building (3) is also very famous. It is in a French city near Paris called Chartres. Its name is Our Lady of Chartres. One part of it is almost nine hundred years old, and so it is older than the Taj Mahal but not nearly as old as the Parthenon. It is made of a hard stone that is not very friendly and has many moods. On a sunny day, with fast-moving clouds behind

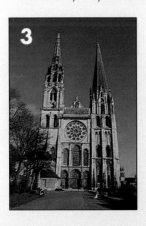

3

it, Chartres looks like a great ship sailing along against the sky, but on a dark day it can be cold and gray and a little frightening. Chartres is another building that many people feel is the most beautiful of all.

LOOK AHEAD

Cutters, Carvers, and the Cathedral is about another wondrous building. As you read, look for statements of fact and opinion.

Vocabulary

apprentices	carver	cathedral
architecture	intricate	
masons	quarry	

Words with similar meanings are called **synonyms.** You can often figure out the meaning of an unknown word by finding a clue in the words around it. Sometimes this clue is a synonym.

Read the paragraph below. Notice how *detailed* helps you understand what *intricate* means.

A Man of Many Trades

Many great artists started out as apprentices to older craftsmen. Michelangelo Buonarroti began this way. He spent his youth working with a painter and sculptor in Florence, Italy. Michelangelo learned that both sculptors and masons must search one quarry after another to find the perfect stone. Although he created many famous paintings, Michelangelo was, above all, a master carver. Many of his sculptures are so intricate and detailed that the marble seems to come alive. His famous sculpture *David* was originally created for a cathedral in Florence, but it was considered too beautiful to be kept indoors. It was placed in Florence's public square instead. During his final years, Michelangelo concentrated on architecture, in particular the dome of Saint Peter's Basilica in Rome.

Talk About It

Discuss what you know about types of art. Use as many vocabulary words as you can.

Cutters, Carvers, *and the* Cathedral

by George Ancona

Perched on the scaffolding in front of the giant bronze doors of the Cathedral of Saint John the Divine, Simon Verity works at carving the limestone columns with a chisel and mallet. So intent is this master carver on his work that he barely hears the noise of the New York City traffic below. For more than one hundred years, since long before Simon was born, the cathedral has been rising, stone upon stone . . . and it is still not finished.

It takes many people to build a cathedral: architects, engineers, carpenters, glass makers, electricians, masons, quarriers. And it takes a tremendous amount of stone. Most of the limestone for Saint John comes from faraway Indiana.

Bruce Poole works as a machinist in an Indiana quarry mill. During the summer, his son Josh likes to join him for lunch. They sit together on a limestone block to eat and watch the crew at work. Many of the workers trace their family roots to quarriers who sailed from England to America in the early nineteenth century. Sons work alongside their fathers and grandfathers, cutting giant blocks of limestone from the earth. Someday Josh may work in the quarry too.

A warning whistle sounds, and everyone leaves the area. After a moment of silence, the earth rumbles. Dynamite charges explode on the far side of the quarry, uncovering a new section of the limestone seam.

When the rain of stone and dirt stops, a giant power shovel moves in to scoop up the overburden of earth and load it into the hauler trucks that take it away. It may take weeks to expose the high-quality limestone. Someday, this stone will be part of a skyscraper, a museum . . . or the Cathedral of Saint John the Divine.

Once the seam is cleared, the saw runners take over. These are the men who operate the fifteen-foot diamond-tipped saw, cutting blocks called ledges into the stone. Each block is as long as two school buses.

The quarry bursts with the roar of pneumatic drills as drill runners drive holes into the base of the ledge where it is still attached to the seam.

The drill runners are followed by the breakers, who set steel wedges into the holes. Then, swinging their sledge hammers, they pound the wedges into the stone, separating the ledge from the seam.

Mike Edwards has worked in the quarry as a laborer, drill runner, and breaker. "Each has its own skill," says Mike. "The breaker has to have a good 'lick' to hit those wedges just right, so the stone breaks in a straight line. We take the stone from the ground with drills, wedges, hammers, and sweat. It's a painful job, and by the end of the day your hands are pretty numb."

Once the ledge is free, the crewmen slip flat rubber bags into the cuts that the saw runners made. As the bags are inflated by high-pressure hoses, they gradually push the ledge out, tipping it farther and farther. Finally it topples over and crashes to the ground in a cloud of dust.

As the air clears, David Prince, the quarry foreman, scrambles onto the ledge to mark out smaller blocks for the crew to cut. Often, they find fossils in the limestone and chip them out to save. Three million years ago, oceans covered the land we know as Indiana. As the waters receded, the prehistoric creatures that swam there were left on the ocean floor, and their skeletons became solid limestone. "It's all those bones," says Dave. "That's why the limestone is so rich in calcium."

A loader picks up the smaller blocks and puts them onto flatbed trucks. Each truck can carry two of the 11$\frac{1}{2}$-ton blocks across Indiana, Ohio, Pennsylvania, and New Jersey to New York City, where they will become part of the cathedral.

At the cathedral, where Edgar Reyes takes the blocks off the truck, scaffolds stand where towers will someday be. Still, even in its unfinished form, the cathedral soars above the surrounding neighborhood.

The cornerstone, the first stone of the building, was laid in 1892. It took fifty years—until November 30, 1941—to complete the main body of the church. The following Monday, the United States entered the Second World War. No construction was done for thirty years, until the Very Reverend James Parks Morton became dean of the cathedral. Under the Dean's leadership, a covered stone yard was built next to the cathedral and master stone carvers were invited from Europe to train neighborhood youths to become masons and carvers.

Edgar, one of the first neighborhood apprentices, also works in the machine shop, cutting up the huge blocks with the 11-foot circular saw. Computers control the saws that cut and shape the limestone into the precise forms called for by the architect's plans. These smaller blocks need very little hand finishing by the masons.

After years of learning his craft, Edgar's pride is obvious: "When I stand back and look at the cathedral, I can say, 'I did that!'"

Deep below the cathedral floor, "Jeep" Kincannon, the chief masonry draftsman, works in the architecture office. "To be a good mason, you must have a good sense of geometry," he says. "With the computer, I can produce the templates for the blocks that go into the cathedral. The masons use these templates, or patterns, to shape each block of stone." All the blocks are cut to fit into their specific places, and they rise one above the other into columns, arches, walls, and steeples.

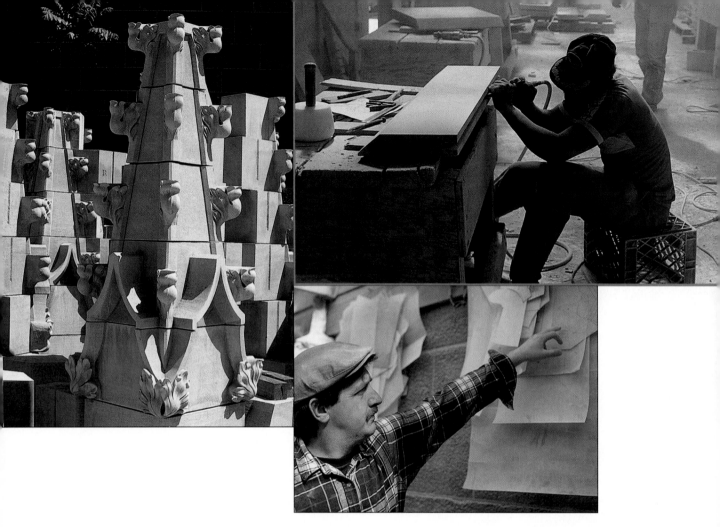

     Through the haze of limestone dust, the early-morning sun sends shafts of light into the stone shed. Masons and carvers are busy working on blocks and sculptures. Their tools range from modern pneumatic drills and grinders to the traditional chisel and mallet.

     Stephen Boyle, the stone-yard foreman, picks out a template for one of the masons. Stephen worked on the restorations of the twelfth-century Yorkminster and Salisbury cathedrals in England before coming to the United States. "Masons shape and finish the blocks," he explains, "while carvers cut intricate decorations for cornices, capitals, and pinnacles. On a pinnacle, the highest point on the cathedral, for example, it is the mason who cuts and assembles the blocks and the carver who cuts the crockets that go up the sides."

     The men and women who work on the cathedral come from the neighborhood and from other countries as well, and they form their own small international community.

Wearing safety glasses, a hearing protector, and dust mask, Lisa Young finishes a block with sandpaper. When asked why she joined the apprenticeship program, she says, "I wanted a job that would give me the discipline to stay in school."

"When I first came to this country, I looked around for work," says Rafael Taverna, who grew up in Guatemala. "I saw the cathedral, came in, and there was an opening. I enjoy the work, to cut stone, to sculpt."

Michael Orekunrin left his native Nigeria after studying sculpture and carves blocks as an apprentice at Saint John.

When he was sixteen, John Sutton worked in a quarry in England. He decided he liked working with stone and went to school to earn his mason's certificate. He uses an angle grinder to smooth out a stone he has cut.

"How did I fall in love with stone?" asks Amy Breyer, who has worked at the cathedral for five years. "I went to Italy and got my hands on a piece of marble and that was it."

Jin Sheng Wong was a stone carver in China. For him, carving is a communication with the stone. "When I look at the stone, I can feel its power," he says while chiseling out a relief. "You cannot fight the stone. If you do, hitting it hard, your hand will get bloody. You've got to be gentle. To be a stone carver, you've got to love this kind of work. It's noisy, dusty, and hard."

Simon Verity comes down from the scaffolding to get a better view of his work and to talk of his career. "My family are French architects who have built cathedrals since the fourteenth century. As a boy I collected fossils, and I knew I'd be either a geologist or a sculptor. I'm mostly self-taught.

"To be a carver, you have to have a passion for it, to love it with all your heart. It's a desire to create order out of chaos, to seek harmonies. My figures are designed in relationship to the architecture and floor plan of the cathedral, and my tools are simply a hammer and chisel.

"My work as master carver is considered glamorous," he says. "But it is less important than the masons', who carve the blocks that hold the cathedral together."

Construction on the cathedral has stopped for lack of funding. Pinnacles, blocks, and gargoyles stand in the stone yard, awaiting the day when they will become part of the façade. Some of the figures portray leaders in the struggle for social justice, such as Nelson Mandela. Others represent some of the men and women who have worked on the cathedral.

Yet, services are held, concerts are performed, and festivals are celebrated. The helpless and homeless are fed, clothed, and befriended within its walls. Messages of peace and goodwill are sent out to the world.

It takes years of dedication and work, by people from near and far, to build the cathedral. But if the limestone took three million years to form, a hundred years to build a monument to faith doesn't seem so very long.

George Ancona

George Ancona was born in New York, New York, of parents who had emigrated from the Yucatán region of Mexico. When he was a child, his father used to take him to the docks in Brooklyn to show him the big ships anchored there. "When I do a book I try to bring to it the same feeling I had when my father would show me the big ships," he says. "It's like seeing something awe-inspiring and you just have to say, 'Wow.'"

Mr. Ancona's first children's book was *Faces,* by Bobbie Brenner, for which he supplied the photographs. Since then he has worked on books with subjects as varied as turtles, cities, special-needs children, and dancers; several of these have won awards. Some years after his photographs appeared in *Faces,* he also started writing the text for many of his books.

If you're interested in photography, you may enjoy Mr. Ancona's book *My Camera.* In it, he demonstrates how to use a 35-millimeter camera and explains other aspects of photography. Though it is important for a photographer to have technical skills, it is not the only thing that matters. "Curiosity is the biggest element in my work," Mr. Ancona relates. "I think people are fascinating, and I love to find myself in strange places, meeting people, getting to know them, and learning about them. This helps me to learn about myself."

Reader Response

Open for Discussion

If you could spend the day working on the cathedral alongside one of these cutters or carvers, whom would you choose? Why?

Comprehension Check

1. What steps are needed in the process of removing the limestone from the ground and getting it to the cathedral? Describe them in a list or diagram. Look back in the text for help.

2. Why did construction on the cathedral stop in 1941? What happened to make it begin again?

3. Think about the people who have worked on the cathedral. How are they different? How are they alike? Look back at the text for details.

4. Rafael Taverna says, "I saw the cathedral, came in, and there was an opening. I enjoy the work, to cut stone, to sculpt." What part of the quotation is a **statement of fact?** What part is a **statement of opinion?** (Fact and Opinion)

5. The author states that "It takes years of dedication and work, by people from near and far, to build the cathedral." Do you think that this is a **statement of fact** or **opinion?** Support your answer with examples. (Fact and Opinion)

Test Prep
Look Back and Write

Look at the five pictures on pages 682 and 683. Who or what does each picture show? Begin with the first picture on page 682 and work from left to right. Use details from the text on these pages in your description.

Test Prep

How to Read Expository Nonfiction

1. Preview

- The job of expository nonfiction is to explain things. Some expository nonfiction is made of several small pieces that are united by one main idea.

- Read the title and the words in dark type. Look over the illustrations and headings. What is the main idea that unites all these small pieces?

2. Read and Locate Reasons

Each building looks the way it looks for certain reasons. As you read, make notes on the reasons why the buildings look the way they look.

3. Think and Connect

Look back at *Cutters, Carvers, and the Cathedral*. Then look over your notes for "Why Do Buildings Look Like They Do?"

Both selections deal with the look of buildings. Why does the Cathedral of Saint John the Divine look the way it looks?

Sometimes it is hard to believe buildings are actually buildings—they look so strange!

Norman House, Oklahoma, 1961
This extraordinary prairie house, designed by the architect Herb Greene, looks like a cross between a slide and a garbage dump. It is based on the ramshackle buildings found in a shantytown.

Some buildings give you strong clues as to what they are used for. Their design helps them carry out certain functions.

Large glass top sends out a narrow beam of light which can sweep around in a circle.

Cylindrical, tall structure allows good views of the coast and the sea.

A Lighthouse

Buildings Look the Way They Do?

by Caroline Grimshaw

How does the use of a building affect what it ends up looking like?

Homes in the Netherlands The Dutch architect Piet Blom drew inspiration from treehouses when he designed these topsy-turvy homes. These odd-looking buildings are only made possible by the power of reinforced concrete.

U.S. Pavilion, Montreal Expo, Canada, 1967 This enormous dome, designed by Richard Buckminster Fuller, is made from lightweight steel and acrylic panels. The architect had a vision of covering whole cities with such domes.

Mystery Building

➤ It is not always easy to guess a building's function. What do you think this building is used for?

The mystery building is a cathedral in Tokyo, Japan.

Large vanes or sails turn as the wind blows. These are attached to a shaft, which in turn moves a stone for grinding corn, or a water pump.

Some mills rotate on a vertical post, so that they can change direction as the wind does.

A Windmill

Battlements and narrow windows allowed archers to aim outward, while offering protection.

Massive walls and towers are too thick and tall to be destroyed by enemy attack.

A Castle

Poetry

The Thinker
by John Ciardi

There was a young fellow who thought
Very little, but thought it a lot.
    Then at long last he knew
    What he wanted to do,
But before he could start, he forgot.

There Was a Young Maid . . .

There was a young maid who said, "Why
Can't I look in my ear with my eye?
    If I give my mind to it,
    I'm sure I can do it.
You never can tell till you try."

My Sister
by Margaret Mahy

My sister's remarkably light,
She can float to a fabulous height.
    It's a troublesome thing,
    But we tie her with string,
And we use her instead of a kite.

A Farmer in Knox . . .

A farmer in Knox, Ind.,
Had a daughter he called Mar.
    But the neighbors said, "O,
    We really must go,"
Whenever she played the p.

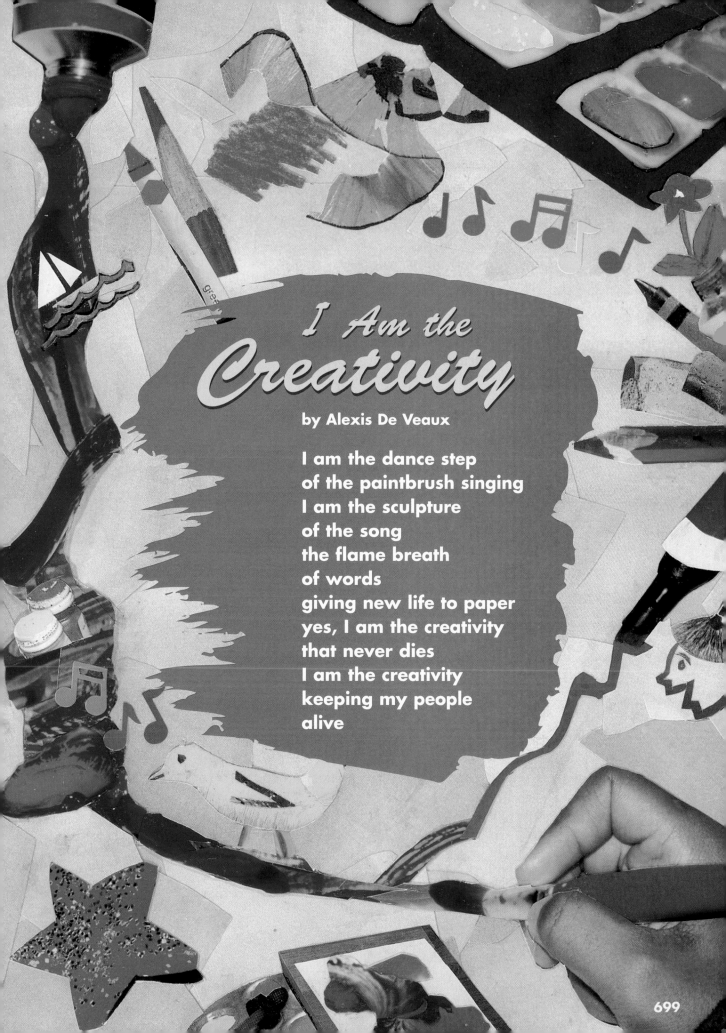

I Am the
Creativity

by Alexis De Veaux

I am the dance step
of the paintbrush singing
I am the sculpture
of the song
the flame breath
of words
giving new life to paper
yes, I am the creativity
that never dies
I am the creativity
keeping my people
alive

A Short Story

by David Escobar Galindo
translated by Jorge D. Piche

The ant climbs up a trunk
carrying a petal on its back;
and if you look closely
that petal is as big as a house
especially compared to the ant that
carries it so olympically.

You ask me: Why couldn't I carry
a petal twice as big as my body and my head?

Ah, but you can, little girl,
but not petals from a dahlia,
rather boxes full of thoughts
and loads of magic hours, and
a wagon of clear dreams, and
a big castle with its fairies:
all the petals that form the soul of
a little girl who speaks and speaks . . . !

Sing Me a Song of Teapots and Trumpets

by N. M. Bodecker

Sing me a song
of teapots and trumpets:
Trumpots and teapets
and tippets and taps,
trippers and trappers
and jelly bean wrappers
and pigs in pajamas
with zippers and snaps.

Sing me a song
of sneakers and snoopers:
Snookers and sneapers
and snappers and snacks,
snorkels and snarkles,
a seagull that gargles,
and gargoyles and gryphons
and other knickknacks.

Sing me a song
of parsnips and pickles:
Picsnips and parkles
and pumpkins and pears,
plumbers and mummers
and kettle drum drummers
and plum jam (yum-yum jam)
all over their chairs.

Sing me a song—
but never you mind it!
I've had enough
of this nonsense. Don't cry.
Criers and fliers
and onion ring fryers—
It's more than I want to put up with!
Good-by!

Unit 6 *Wrap-Up*

How many ways can people be creative?

How Are We Creative?

Share Ideas

The main characters in the first four selections in this unit were all creative in their own ways. How are you creative?

1. **List** each main character. Then **make notes** on how he was creative. What skills did he use? How did he use them?

2. Add your name to the list and make notes on the ways you are creative. With classmates, **create** an interesting way to share this information so that others are inspired to be more creative.

Web site Sights

Design a Home Page

Design a home page for the Cathedral of St. John the Divine or for a museum dedicated to Eratosthenes.

1. **Choose** one of these ideas and plan. What will your home page look like? What departments will it feature to click on? What links to other Web sites will it feature? Look back at the selection for ideas.

2. **Design** your home page. Describe it in words and draw a picture of what it will look like.

Celebrate!

Create an Invitation

Imagine that you are in charge of a celebration of Tyree's music or the achievements of Louis Braille. With a partner, plan one of these celebrations.

1. Make a **list** of guests, real and imaginary, from both past and present.

2. **Create** the invitation. Include what will be celebrated and how.

Puppets Tell the Story

Write and Produce

Imagine that you will retell one of the selections to an audience of young children, using puppets. What would your production be like?

1. With a partner, **choose** a selection and **talk** about the characters together. Give them names and personalities.

2. **Write** a script for a puppet show that retells the story. You might create your puppets and puppet stage and **produce** your play for young children.

Test Talk

Answer the Question

Score High!

A scoring checklist shows you what makes up a good answer to a test question. You can learn how to write answers that score high by using a scoring checklist.

Read the scoring checklist at the right.

A test about "A Revolution!" pages 656–657, might have this question.

Test Question 1

What tools do today's cartographers use to make maps? Use details from the article to support your answer.

Look at the First Try answer on top of page 705. Then see how the student used the scoring checklist to improve the answer.

Scoring Checklist

✓ **The answer is correct.** It has only correct details from the text.

✓ **The answer is complete.** It has all the necessary details from the text.

✓ **The answer is focused.** It has only details from the text that answer the question.

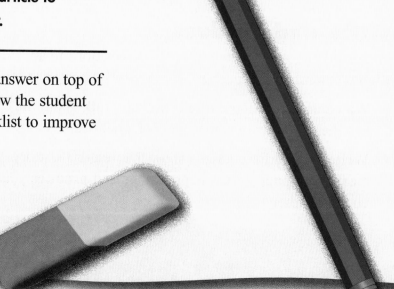

First Try

It's not complete. It needs more details about tools.

Today's cartographers use many tools to make maps. Some of these tools are computers, photographs, and satellites. Aerial photography began in France in 1858. GYS is a system you can use with a computer to make maps.

It's not focused. The detail about 1858 doesn't belong.

It's not correct. It's GIS, not GYS.

Improved Answer

Tell why this is a better answer. Look back at the scoring checklist for help.

Today's cartographers use many tools to make maps. Some of these tools are computers, aerial photographs, and satellite images. Other tools are topographic maps, space photographs, and infrared images from space. GIS is a system cartographers can use with a computer to make maps.

Try it!

Now look at the First Try answer below. Then rewrite the answer and improve it. Look back at the scoring checklist for help.

Test Question 2

How has the use of computers revolutionized mapmaking? Use details from pages 656–657 to support your answer.

First Try

The use of computers has revolutionized mapmaking because computers can store information. Some computers, like the new handheld models, are so compact and portable that mapmakers can take them anywhere and map places that have never been mapped before.

Glossary

How to Use This Glossary

This glossary can help you understand and pronounce some of the words in this book. The entries in this glossary are in alphabetical order. There are guide words at the top of each page to show you the first and last words on the page. A pronunciation key is at the bottom of every other page. Remember, if you can't find the word you are looking for, ask for help or check a dictionary.

The entry word is in dark type. It shows how the word is spelled and how the word is divided into syllables.

The pronunciation is in parentheses. It also shows which syllables are stressed.

Abbreviated part-of-speech labels show the function or functions of an entry word and any listed form of that word.

grit·ty (grit′ē), ADJ. covered by or containing small bits of sand, dust, and so on: *The swirling dust made my skin feel gritty.* ❏ ADJ. **grit·ti·er, grit·ti·est. –grit′ti·ness,** N.

Sometimes, irregular and other special forms will be shown to help you use the word correctly.

The definition and example sentence show you what the word means and how it is used.

Aa

a·ban·don (ə ban′dən), V. to leave someone or something without intending to return; desert.

Ab·e·na·ki (ab nä′kē), N. a Native American tribe of Maine and southern Quebec. ❏ N., PL. **Ab·e·na·ki** or **Ab·e·na·kis.**

a·buse (ə byüs′), N. rough or cruel treatment.

ac·com·pa·ny (ə kum′pə nē), V. to go along with.

ac·cost (ə kȯst′), V. to approach and speak to someone in an unpleasant way: *The building guard accosted the trespasser.*

ac·cur·ate (ak′yər it), ADJ. without errors or mistakes; precisely correct; exact.

ace (ās), ADJ. very skilled; expert.

a·do·be (ə dō′bē), **1** N. a building material made of clay baked in the sun. **2** ADJ. built or made of this material. **3** N. brick made of this material.

adobe

ad·van·tage (ad van′tij), N. anything that is in your favor, or is a benefit; help in getting something desired.

aer·a·tion (âr ā′shən), N. the process of exposing something to chemical action with oxygen.

af·flict (ə flikt′), *v.* to cause pain to; trouble greatly; distress: *The trees were afflicted by parasites and disease.*

ag·gres·sive (ə gres′iv), *ADJ.* ready to attack others or to take something by force.

al·ien (ā′lyən), *N.* **1** person who is not a citizen of the country in which he or she lives. **2** an imaginary creature from outer space.

al·ma·nac (ȯl′mə nak), *N.* a reference book published yearly, with tables of facts and information on many subjects.

al·ti·tude (al′tə tüd), *N.* height above sea level.

am·a·teur (am′ə chər), *N.* someone who does something for pleasure, not for money.

am·bi·tion (am bish′ən), *N.* something for which you have a strong desire.

an·a·lyst (an′l ist), *N.* person who examines carefully and in detail.

an·a·lyze (an′l īz), *v.* to separate anything into its parts to find out what it is made of.

an·ces·tor (an′ses′tər), *N.* person from whom you are descended, such as your great-grandparents; relative: *Their ancestors came to the United States in 1812.*

an·gle (ang′gəl), *v.* to fish with a hook and line.

an·guish (ang′gwish), *N.* very great pain, grief, or distress.

an·vil (an′vəl), *N.* an iron or steel block on which metals are hammered and shaped.

anx·i·e·ty (ang zī′ə tē), *N.* uneasy thoughts or fears about what may happen; troubled, worried, or uneasy feelings.

ap·pli·ca·tion (ap′lə kā′shən), *N.* a formal request for something, such as employment, admission into a college, and so on.

ap·pren·tice (ə pren′tis), *N.* person learning a trade or art. In return for instruction the apprentice agrees to work for the employer a certain length of time with little or no pay.

arc (ärk), *N.* any section of the boundary line of a circle or the distance around a sphere.

ar·chae·ol·o·gist (är′kē ol′ə jist), *N.* scientist who studies the people, customs, and life of ancient times.

ar·chi·tec·ture (är′kə tek′chər), *N.* science or art of planning and designing buildings.

Arc·tic (ärk′tik *or* är′tik), *N.* Usually, **the Arctic,** the north polar region.

ar·roz (ä rōs′), *N.* (Spanish) rice.

as·sem·ble (ə sem′bəl), *v.* to put together; fit together.

as·tound·ing (ə stound′ing), *ADJ.* amazing: *The view of the Grand Canyon was astounding.*

ath·let·ic (ath let′ik), *ADJ.* of or for someone trained in sports or athletics.

at·ti·tude (at′ə tüd), *N.* way of thinking, acting, or feeling.

at·trib·ute (at′rə byüt), *N.* a quality thought to belong to a person or thing; characteristic.

au·then·tic (ȯ then′tik), *ADJ.* genuine; real.

ax·is (ak′sis), *N.* a straight line around which an object turns or seems to turn. The axis of the Earth is an imaginary line through the North Pole and the South Pole. ❑ *N., PL.* **axes.**

B b

bac·ter·i·a (bak tir′ē ə), *N. PL.* very tiny and simple living things, so small that they can usually be seen only through a microscope.

a	hat	ė	term	ô	order	ch	child		a in about
ā	age	i	it	oi	oil	ng	long		e in taken
ä	far	ī	ice	ou	out	sh	she	ə<	i in pencil
â	care	o	hot	u	cup	th	thin		o in lemon
e	let	ō	open	ů	put	ŦH	then		u in circus
ē	equal	ȯ	saw	ü	rule	zh	measure		

ban·dit (ban′dit), N. robber or thief, especially one of a gang of outlaws.

ba·ton (ba ton′), N. a stick passed from runner to runner in a relay race: *Sasha passed the baton to me, and I ran the last lap.*

bel·lows (bel′ōz), N., SING. or PL. device for producing a strong current of air, used for making fires burn hotter or sounding an organ, accordion, etc.

be·wil·der·ment (bi wil′dər mənt), N. a completely puzzled or confused condition; great confusion.

bi·o·me·chan·ics (bī′ō mə kan′iks), N. the science dealing with the action of forces on living bodies.

blind·ness (blīnd′nis), N. inability to see.

blood·root (blud′rüt), N. a North American wildflower. Bloodroots have red roots, red sap, and white flowers.

blow·er (blō′ər), N. fan or other machine for forcing air into a building, furnace, mine, or other enclosed area: *The blower caused cool air to circulate in the large office building.*

boom (büm), N. a long pole or beam, used to extend the bottom of a sail: *We ducked our heads as the boom swung across the boat.*

bound·ar·y (boun′dər ē), N. a limiting line or thing; limit; border.

bridge (brij), N. platform above the deck of a ship for the officer in command.

busi·ness·man (biz′nis man′), N. person who is in business or who runs a store, factory, or other place that makes or sells goods and services.

Cc

cal·cu·late (kal′kyə lāt), V. to find out by adding, subtracting, multiplying, or dividing; compute.

cal·lig·ra·phy (kə lig′rə fē), N. art or practice of beautiful handwriting.

cam·paign (kam pān′), N. series of connected activities to do or get something: *Our town had a campaign to raise money for a new hospital.*

camp·site (kamp′sīt′), N. place where people camp: *Our campsite was surrounded by trees.*

cap·size (kap sīz′ or kap′ sīz), V. to turn bottom side up; upset; overturn: *The sailboat capsized in the squall.* ❑ V. **cap·sized, cap·siz·ing.**

car·a·van (kar′ə van), N. (earlier) group of merchants or pilgrims traveling together for safety through difficult or dangerous country. Desert caravans often used camels for transportation.

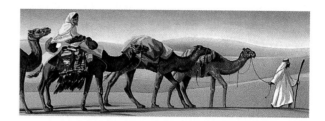

caravan

car·go (kär′gō), N. load of goods carried by a ship, plane, or truck.

car·tog·ra·pher (kär tog′rə fər), N. maker of maps or charts.

car·ver (kär′vər), N. someone who makes works of art by carving blocks of stone or wood; sculptor.

ca·the·dral (kə thē′drəl), N. a large or important church.

chan·nel (chan′l), N. passage for liquids; groove or canal; duct: *He dug a channel so water could get to his crops.*

chop·sticks (chop′stiks′), N., PL. pair of small, slender sticks used to raise food to the mouth.

cir·cuit (sėr′kit), N. circular or roundabout route.

cir·cum·fer·ence (sər kum′fər əns), N. the distance around: *The circumference of the Earth at the equator is almost 25,000 miles.*

cir·cum·stance (sėr′kəm stans), N. condition that accompanies an act or event.

clas·si·cal (klas′ə kəl), ADJ. of or about the literature, art, and life of ancient Greece and Rome.

clean·up (klēn′up′), N. act of cleaning up.

cli·mate (klī′mit), N. the kind of weather a place has year after year. Climate includes heat and cold, moisture and dryness, clearness and cloudiness, wind and calm.

clin·ic (klin′ik), N. place connected with a hospital or medical school where people can receive medical treatment, sometimes at a reduced cost.

cloud·burst (kloud′bėrst′), N. a sudden, heavy rain: *We got wet in the sudden cloudburst.*

col·lapse (kə laps′), V. to fall down suddenly.

col·lide (kə līd′), V. to hit or strike together; crash.

co·los·sal (kə los′ əl), ADJ. of huge size; gigantic; vast: *Skyscrapers are colossal structures.* **–co·los′sal·ly,** ADV.

com·mand·er (kə man′dər), N. person who has control of something; leader.

com·mit·tee (kə mit′ē), N. group of people appointed or elected to do some special thing.

com·pen·sate (kom′pən sāt), V. to pay: *They compensate her for much of her work.* ❏ V. **com·pen·sat·ed, com·pen·sat·ing.**

com·pe·ti·tion (kom′pə tish′ən), N. contest.

com·pli·cat·ed (kom′plə kā′tid), ADJ. hard to understand; not simple.

con·cept (kon′sept), N. a thought; idea; general notion.

con·crete (kon′krēt′ *or* kon krēt′), **1** N. mixture of crushed stone or gravel, sand, cement, and water that hardens as it dries. Concrete is used for foundations, buildings, sidewalks, roads, dams, and bridges. **2** ADJ. existing as an actual object, not merely as an idea or as a quality; real: *A painting is concrete; its beauty is abstract.*

con·serve (kən sėrv′), V. to keep from loss or from being used up; preserve.

con·stel·la·tion (kon′stə lā′shən), N. any of 88 groups of stars having recognized shapes. Orion is a constellation of the winter sky.

con·sume (kən süm′), V. to destroy, burn up: *I read about a huge fire consuming a forest.* ❏ V. **con·sumed, con·sum·ing.**

con·tam·i·nate (kən tam′ə nāt), V. to make something impure by mixing it with something else; pollute.

con·tri·bu·tion (kon′trə byü′shən), N. donated money or help; gift.

con·trol (kən trōl′), N. the power to guide the flight of a baseball while throwing it.

con·ven·tion·al (kən ven′shə nəl), ADJ. (in the arts) following custom and traditional models; formal: *The ode and the sonnet are conventional forms of English poetry.*

con·vert·ed (kən vėrt′id), ADJ. changed into a different form or used in a different way.

cope (kōp), V. to struggle or deal with something successfully.

co·pi·lot (kō′pī′ət), N. the assistant or second pilot in an aircraft: *The captain asked his copilot for information about flight patterns.*

a hat	ė term	ô order	ch child	⎧ a in about
ā age	i it	oi oil	ng long	⎪ e in taken
ä far	ī ice	ou out	sh she	ə ⎨ i in pencil
â care	o hot	u cup	th thin	⎪ o in lemon
e let	ō open	u̇ put	ᵀH then	⎩ u in circus
ē equal	ò saw	ü rule	zh measure	

cor·ner·stone (kôr′nər stōn′), N. a stone built into the corner of a building as its formal beginning. Cornerstones are often marked with important information, such as the name of the builder and the date of completion.

cor·re·spond·ence (kôr′ə spon′dəns), N. exchange of letters.

cou·gar (kü′gər), N. mountain lion: *The cougar crept between the rocks as it stalked its prey.*

coun·ter·clock·wise or **coun·ter–clock·wise** (koun′tər klok′wīz′), ADV., ADJ. in the direction opposite to that in which the hands of a clock go.

cove (kōv), N. a small, sheltered bay; inlet on the shore.

crafts·man (krafts′mən), N. person skilled in a craft or trade. ❏ N., PL. **crafts·men.**

cross·ing (krò′sing), N. act of going across, especially a voyage across water: *The ocean liner made a crossing to New York.*

cul·ture (kul′chər), N. beliefs, customs, arts, and tools of a nation or people at a certain time: *Our textbook includes a chapter on the culture of the ancient Romans.*

cus·tom (kus′təm), N. an old or popular way of doing something: *Shaking hands is a social custom.*

cyl·in·der (sil′ən dər), N. a long, round chamber containing a piston in an engine.

Dd

daw·dle (dò′dl), V. to waste time, idle, loiter: *Don't dawdle so long over your work.* ❏ V. **daw·dled, daw·dling. –daw′dler,** N.

ded·i·ca·tion (ded′ə kā′shən), N. devotion to a purpose: *Our teacher shows great dedication to her job.*

de·fi·ance (di fī′əns), N. bold disregard of authority or opposition; open resistance to power: *The colonists' defiance of the king led to war.*

de·hy·drate (dē hī′drāt), V. to take water or moisture from; dry: *We dehydrated the vegetables.* ❏ V. **de·hy·drat·ed, de·hy·drat·ing. –de′hy·drat′tion.** N.

de·pres·sion (di presh′ən), N. a low place; hollow: *Rain made puddles in the depressions.*

de·spair (di spâr′), N. loss of hope; hopeless feeling; dreadful feeling that nothing good can happen: *Despair overcame the losing team in the final moments of the game.*

des·ti·na·tion (des′tə nā′shən), N. place to which someone or something is going or is being sent.

de·tect (di tekt′), V. to find; discover: *We detected my little brother's hiding place.*

di·plo·ma (də plō′mə), N. a written or printed paper given by a school or college, which states that someone has completed certain courses, or has received a degree. ❏ N., PL. **di·plo·mas.**

dis·as·ter (də zas′tər), N. a sudden event that causes great suffering or loss.

dis·re·pair (dis′ri pâr′), N. bad condition; need of being fixed: *The house was in disrepair.*

dis·tinct·ly (dis tingkt′lē), ADV. in a way or manner that is unmistakable, definite, or decided: *He distinctly heard a baby crying.* **–dis·tinct,** ADJ. **–dis·tinct′ness,** N.

dis·tressed (dis trest′), ADJ. feeling great pain or sorrow; unhappy: *I was sad and distressed when we moved away.*

dol·drums (dol′drəmz or dōl′drəmz), N., PL. gloomy feeling; low spirits: *Ed has been in the doldrums since he failed his math test.*

drag (drag), N. the force acting on an object in motion through a fluid, in a direction opposite to the object's motion.

drift·wood (drift′wùd′), N. wood carried along by water or washed ashore from the water.

drive (drīv), N. **1** trip in a motor vehicle: *On Sunday we took a drive in the country.* **2** act of moving cattle overland to a shipping point.

E e

e·clipse (i klips′), N. process of complete or partial blocking of light passing from one astronomical object to another. **Solar eclipses** occur when the moon passes between the sun and the Earth. **Lunar eclipses** occur when the Earth passes between the sun and the moon.

solar eclipse

ec·o·log·i·cal ((ē′kə loj′ə kəl *or* ek′ə loj′ə kəl), ADJ. of or about living things and their environment: *He wanted to be a zookeeper so he took many classes in ecological studies.*

eer·ie (ir′ē), ADJ. causing fear because of strangeness or weirdness: *a dark and eerie old house.* ❑ ADJ. **eer·i·er, eer·i·est.**

e·lude (i lüd′), V. to avoid or escape by cleverness or quickness; slip away from: *I saw the fox elude the dogs.* ❑ V. **e·lud·ed, e·lud·ing.**

em·bark (em bärk′), V. to set out; start: *After leaving college, the young woman embarked upon a business career.* **–em·bar·ka′tion,** N.

em·boss (em bòs′), V. to cause to stand out from the surface: *The letters on the book's cover had been embossed.* **–em·boss′er,** N.

em·pa·thy (em′pə thē), N. ability to imagine yourself in someone else's situation and to understand that person's feelings.

en·coun·ter (en koun′tər), V. to find by chance; meet with; come upon: *What if we should encounter a bear on our hike?*

en·thu·si·asm (en thü′zē az′əm), N. eager interest; zeal: *The pep talk filled the team with enthusiasm.*

en·vi·ron·ment (en vī′rən mənt), N. all the surrounding things, conditions, and influences affecting the growth of living things, especially air, water, and soil: *We're working for a pollution-free environment.* **–en·vi′ron·men′·tal,** ADJ. **–en·vi′ron·men′tal·ly,** ADV.

er·a (ir′ə), N. a period of time or history: *We live in the era of space exploration.* ❑ N., PL. **er·as.**

es·ti·mate (es′tə māt), V. to form a judgment or careful guess about amount, size, value, and so on: *Can you estimate how long it will take you to finish your chores?* ❑ V. **es·ti·mat·ed, es·ti·mat·ing.**

e·ter·nal (i tėr′nl), ADJ. without beginning or ending; lasting throughout all time: *It felt like the test was eternal and would never end.* **–e·ter′nal·ly,** ADV. **–e·ter′nal·ness,** N.

e·vap·o·rate (i vap′ə rāt′), V. to vanish; disappear: *My good resolutions evaporated soon after January first.* ❑ V. **e·vap·o·rat·ed, e·vap·o·rat·ing. –e·vap′o·ra′tion,** N.

e·vap·o·ra·tion (i vap′ə rā′shən), N. the process of changing from a liquid into a gas.

ex·as·pe·ra·tion (eg zas′pə rā′shən), N. extreme annoyance; irritation; anger: *Jill was filled with exasperation when her younger brother sang the song for the twelfth time.*

a	hat	ė	term	ô	order	ch child
ā	age	i	it	oi	oil	ng long
ä	far	ī	ice	ou	out	sh she
â	care	o	hot	u	cup	th thin
e	let	ō	open	ü	put	₮H then
ē	equal	ò	saw	ü	rule	zh measure

ə { a in about / e in taken / i in pencil / o in lemon / u in circus

ex·ca·vate (ek′skə vāt), v. to uncover by digging: *They excavated an ancient buried city.* ❏ v. **ex·ca·vat·ed, ex·ca·vat·ing.**

ex·ile (eg′zīl *or* ek′sīl), v. to force someone to leave his or her country or home, often by law, as a punishment; banish: *Napoleon was exiled from France.* ❏ v. **ex·iled, ex·il·ing.**

ex·ot·ic (eg zot′ik), *ADJ.* strange and unusual, often coming from a different country: *exotic plants.*

ex·pec·ta·tion (ek′spek tā′shən), *N.* a good reason for thinking that something will happen: *They have expectations of money from a rich aunt.*

ex·pe·di·tion (ek′spə dish′ən), *N.* journey for some special purpose, such as exploration or scientific study: *There have been several expeditions into outer space.*

ex·traor·di·nar·y (ek strôr′də ner′ē), *ADJ.* beyond what is ordinary; very remarkable.

Ff

fa·çade (fə säd′), *N.* the front part of a building, especially the part that faces a street or an open space: *The façade of the old house was made of stone.* ❏ *N.,* *PL.* **fa·çades.**

fer·tile (fèr′tl), *ADJ.* able to produce crops easily.

fi·es·ta (fē es′tə), *N.* holiday or festivity.

flau·tist (flô′tist), *N.* person who plays a flute; flutist.

fo·cus (fō′kəs), v. to bring rays of light or heat to a point.

foot·hill (fùt′hil′), *N.* a low hill at the base of a mountain or mountain range.

for·ci·bly (fôr′sə blē), *ADV.* in a way or manner made or done against someone else's will: *The boy was forcibly pushed against the fence by a bully.* ❏ v. **–for′ci·ble,** *ADJ.*

fo·reign·er (fôr′ə nər), *N.* person from another country.

form (fôrm), *N.* mold; pattern: *Ice cream is often made in forms.*

for·mu·la (fôr′myə lə), *N.* combination of symbols used in mathematics to state a rule or principle. EXAMPLE: $(a + b)^2 = a^2 + 2ab + b^2$ is an algebraic formula. ❏ *N.,* *PL.* **for·mu·las.**

frac·ture (frak′chər), v. to break; crack: *I fractured a bone in my arm.* ❏ v. **frac·tures, frac·tured, frac·tur·ing.**

frag·ile (fraj′əl), *ADJ.* easily broken, damaged, or destroyed; delicate; frail: *Be careful; that thin glass is fragile.* **–fra·gil·i·ty** (frə jil′ə tē), *N.*

fran·tic (fran′tik), *ADJ.* very much excited; wild with rage, fear, pain, or grief: *The trapped animal made frantic efforts to escape.* **–fran′ti·cal·ly,** *ADV.* **–fran′tic·ness,** *N.*

freight·er (frā′tər), *N.* ship that carries goods.

fri·jo·les (frē hō′ lēz), *N.,* *PL.* beans often used for food in Mexico and in the southwestern United States.

fruit·less·ly (früt′lis lē), *ADV.* in a way or manner having no results; uselessly; unsuccessfully: *We searched fruitlessly; we could not find the lost book.* **–fruit′less,** *ADJ.*

fund (fund), *N.* sum of money set aside for a special purpose: *The school has a fund of two thousand dollars to buy books with.*

Gg

gas (gas), *N.* substance that is not a solid or a liquid.

ga·lac·tic (gə lak′tik), *ADJ.* of or about the Milky Way or other galaxies: *A meteor shower delayed their galactic mission.*

gen·e·ra·tion (jen′ə rā′shən), N. all the people born at about the same time. Your parents and their friends belong to one generation; you and your friends belong to the next generation.

gig (gig), N. a long, light ship's boat moved by oars or sails: *We rowed the gig from the ship to the shore.*

gi·gan·tic (jī gan′tik), ADJ. like a giant; huge: *An elephant is a gigantic animal.*

gnarled (närld), ADJ. rough and twisted; having knots: *the gnarled roots of a tree.*

Goth·ic (goth′ ik), ADJ. a style of architecture using pointed arches and high, steep roofs, developed in western Europe during the Middle Ages.

gran·deur (gran′jər), N. greatness; majesty; dignity; splendor.

gran·ite (gran′it), N. a very hard gray or pink rock that is formed when lava cools slowly underground. Granite is used for buildings and monuments. **–gran′ite·like′,** ADJ.

grass·land (gras′land′), N. land with grass on it: *the grasslands of Kansas.*

grat·i·tude (grat′ə tüd), N. feeling of being thankful because someone has done something for you; thankfulness: *I can't fully express my gratitude for your help with my homework.*

grime (grīm), N. dirt rubbed deeply and firmly into a surface.

grit·ty (grit′ē), ADJ. covered by or containing small bits of sand, dust, and so on: *The swirling dust made my skin feel gritty.* ❑ ADJ. **grit·ti·er, grit·ti·est. –grit′ti·ness,** N.

guide·line (gīd′līn′), N. Usually, **guidelines,** PL., lightly marked lines on a sheet of paper, used to guide your penmanship.

H h

hand·writ·ing (hand′rī′ting), N. writing done by hand, with a pen or pencil.

hatch·et (hach′it), N. a small ax with a short handle, for use with one hand. **–hatch′et·like′,** ADJ.

hate·ful (hāt′fəl), ADJ. showing strong dislike; not loving: *hateful behavior.* **–hate′ful·ly,** ADV. **–hate′ful·ness,** N.

haugh·ty (hò′tē), ADJ. too proud; arrogant: *A haughty person is often unpopular.* ❑ ADJ. **haugh·ti·er, haugh·ti·est.**

ha·zy (hā′zē), ADJ. containing a small amount of dust, mist, smoke, and so on; not clear; murky: *a hazy sky.* ❑ ADJ. **ha·zi·er, ha·zi·est.**

hearth (härth), N. the stone or brick floor of an oven or fireplace.

her·it·age (her′ə tij), N. traditions, skills, and so on, handed down from one generation to the next: *Freedom is our most precious heritage.*

home·land (hōm′land′), N. your original or native land: *I live here now, but Ireland is my homeland.*

horse·shoe (hôrs′shü′ or hôrsh′shü′), N. a flat piece of metal shaped like a **U.** Horseshoes are nailed to a horse's hoofs to protect them.

hos·til·i·ty (ho stil′ə tē), N. extreme unfriendliness or dislike: *He showed signs of hostility toward our plan.*

I i

i·de·al (ī dē′əl), N. goal; principle: *a person with high ideals.*

a	hat	ė	term	ô	order	ch	child		a in about
ā	age	i	it	oi	oil	ng	long		e in taken
ä	far	ī	ice	ou	out	sh	she	ə	i in pencil
â	care	o	hot	u	cup	th	thin		o in lemon
e	let	ō	open	ù	put	ᴛʜ	then		u in circus
ē	equal	ò	saw	ü	rule	zh	measure		

ig·nite (ig nīt′), *v.* to set on fire: *We needed a campfire, but we couldn't ignite the damp wood.* ❑ *v.* **ig·nit·ed, ig·nit·ing.**

im·pa·tience (im pā′shəns), *N.* inability to wait quietly for something you want or to put up with something difficult or annoying; condition of being impatient.

im·pro·vise (im′prə vīz), *v.* to make up music, poetry, or the like, on the spur of the moment; sing, recite, speak, and so on, without preparation: *She likes to improvise songs on the piano.* ❑ *v.* **im·pro·vised, im·pro·vis·ing.**

in·de·pend·ent (in′di pen′dənt), *ADJ.* not depending on others for support: *Now that I am older, I am independent enough to go to the movies without my parents.* **–in′·de·pend′ent·ly,** *ADV.*

Industrial Revolution the change from an agricultural to an industrial society in England and other lands from about 1750 to about 1850.

in·fec·tion (in fek′shən), *N.* disease caused by contact with germs, viruses, fungi, and so on.

in·fra·red (in′ frə red′), *ADJ.* of or about the invisible rays with wavelengths longer than those of red light.

in·laid (in′lād′ *or* in lād′), *ADJ.* decorated with a design or material set in the surface: *The desk had an inlaid top of silver.*

in·sist·ent (in sis′tənt), *ADJ.* continuing to make a strong, firm demand or statement; insisting: *In spite of the rain, she was insistent on going out.*

in·sti·tute (in′stə tüt), *N.* organization or society for some special purpose. An art institute teaches or displays art. A technical school or college is often called an institute.

in·tense (in tens′), *ADJ.* very great; very strong; extreme: *Intense heat melts iron. A bad burn causes intense pain.* **–in·tense′ly,** *ADV.*

in·tent·ly (in tent′ lē), *ADV.* in way or manner that is very attentive, with the eyes or thoughts earnestly fixed on something: *He stared at the painting intently.* **–in·tent′ness,** *N.*

in·tim·i·date (in tim′ə dāt), *v.* to make afraid; frighten; influence by fear: *intimidate a witness.* ❑ *v.* **in·tim·i·dat·ed, in·tim·i·dat·ing. –in·tim′i·da′tion,** *N.*

in·tri·cate (in′trə kit), *ADJ.* detailed or complicated: *intricate designs, an intricate plot.*

in·vol·un·tar·y (in vol′ən ter′ ē), *ADJ.* not controlled by the will.

i·ron·ic (ī ron′ik), *ADJ.* contrary to what would naturally be expected: *It was ironic that the man was struck by his own car.*

i·ron·work·ing (ī′ərn wėr′king), *N.* act or process of ironwork; making things out of iron; working in iron: *The artist, skilled in ironworking, made an elaborate gate.*

ir·ri·ga·tion (ir′ə gā′shən), *N.* the act or process of supplying land with water by using ditches, by sprinkling, etc.: *The irrigation system must have been broken because water wasn't getting through.* ❑ *v.* **ir·ri·gat·ed, ir·ri·gat·ing.**

J j

jel·ly·fish (jel′ē fish′), *N.* any of numerous related sea animals without backbones, with bodies formed of a mass of almost transparent jellylike tissue. Most jellyfish have long, trailing tentacles that may bear stinging cells. ❑ *N.,* *PL.* **jel·ly·fish** or **jel·ly·fish·es.**

jolt (jōlt), *N.* a sudden jerk, shock, or jar: *I put the brakes on suddenly, and the car stopped with a jolt.*

Kk

key (kē), N. the middle stone, brick, block, or wedge at the top of an arch or other structure that holds the other parts together; keystone. ❑ N., PL. **keys.**

Ll

la·bor·er (lā′bər ər), N. person who does work that requires strength rather than skill or training.

lat·i·tude (lat′ə tüd), N. distance north or south of the equator, measured in degrees. A degree of latitude is about 69 miles (111 kilometers).

lin·e·ar (lin′ē ər), ADJ. made of lines; making use of lines: *The wallpaper had a linear pattern.*

long·ing (lông′ing), N. earnest desire: *a longing for home.* **–long′ing·ly,** ADV.

lon·gi·tude (lon′jə tüd), N. distance east or west on the Earth's surface, measured in degrees from a line (the prime meridian) that runs north and south through Greenwich (gren′ich), England. A degree of longitude is about 69 miles (111 kilometers) at the equator.

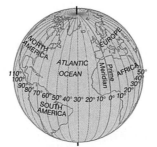

latitude　　　　**longitude**

loom (lüm), V. to appear dimly or vaguely as a large, threatening shape: *A large iceberg loomed through the thick fog.*

lu·nar (lü′nər), ADJ. of or like the moon or its movement around the Earth.

Mm

mag·nif·i·cent (mag nif′ə sənt), ADJ. splendid; richly handsome; grand; stately: *a magnificent palace, a magnificent view of the mountains.*

ma·jes·ti·cal·ly (mə jes′tik lē), ADV. in a way or manner that is impressive, grand, noble, dignified, or stately: *The mountains towered majestically above us.* **–ma·jes′tic,** ADJ.

marsh (märsh), N. low, soft land covered at times by water, where grasses and reeds but not trees grow. ❑ N., PL. **marsh·es. –marsh′like′,** ADJ.

mar·vel (mär′vəl), V. to be filled with wonder; be astonished: *She marveled at the beautiful sunset.* ❑ V. **mar·veled, mar·vel·ing** or **mar·velled, mar·vel·ling.**

ma·son (mā′sn), N. someone whose work is building with stone, brick, or similar materials: *The school hired masons to build a new brick wall.*

mast (mast), N. a long pole of wood or metal set upright on a ship to support the sails and rigging: *We raised the sail on the mast.*

mel·an·chol·y (mel′ən kol′ē), N. depression; sadness: *The family felt a heavy sense of melancholy when their dog died.*

mel·low (mel′ō), ADJ. soft and rich.

mem·or·a·ble (mem′ər ə bəl), ADJ. worth remembering; not to be forgotten; not ordinary: *Graduation is a memorable occasion.*

mer·ci·ful (mėr′si fəl), ADJ. showing or feeling kindness beyond what normally can be expected: *The judge handed down a merciful decision.* **–mer′ci·ful·ly,** ADV. **–mer′ci·ful·ness,** N.

mer·it (mer′it), N. worth or value; goodness: *Students will be graded according to the merit of their work.*

a	hat	ė	term	ô	order	ch	child		a in about
ā	age	i	it	oi	oil	ng	long		e in taken
ä	far	ī	ice	ou	out	sh	she	ə	i in pencil
â	care	o	hot	u	cup	th	thin		o in lemon
e	let	ō	open	u̇	put	ŦH	then		u in circus
ē	equal	ȯ	saw	ü	rule	zh	measure		

mer·ri·ment (mer′ē mənt), N. laughter; fun; mirth; merry enjoyment: *The gathering of friends was full of merriment.*

mo·not·o·nous (mə not′n əs), ADJ. tiring or boring because of its sameness: *monotonous work.* **–mo·not′o·nous·ly,** ADV.

mon·u·ment (mon′yə mənt), N. something set up to honor a person or an event. A monument may be a building, pillar, arch, statue, and so on.

mor·tar (môr′ tər), N. mixture of lime, cement, sand, and water. Mortar is used for holding brick or stones together.

mor·tu·ar·y (môr′chü er′ ē), N. building where the dead are kept until burial or cremation.

muck (muk), N. dirt, filth, or slime.

mul·ti·tude (mul′tə tüd), N. a great many; crowd: *a multitude of difficulties, a multitude of friends.*

mus·tang (mus′tang), N. a small wild or stray horse of the North American plains.

N n

Ni·sei (nē′sā′), N. person born in the United States or Canada whose parents were Japanese immigrants. ❑ N., PL. **Nisei**

no·mad·ic (nō mad′ik), ADJ. of or about a group of people that moves from place to place to find food; wandering: *Nomadic people often live in tents.*

norm (nôrm), N. standard for a certain group; type, model, or pattern: *Her reading level and vocabulary are above the norms for her age.*

nor·mal (nôr′məl), ADJ. usual; regular.

northern lights, streamers or bands of light appearing in the sky at night in the northern regions of the Northern Hemisphere; aurora borealis.

O o

ob·jec·tive (əb jek′tiv), ADJ. not influenced by personal thoughts or feelings: *The witness gave an objective report of the accident.* **–ob·jec′tive·ly,** ADV. **–ob·jec′tive·ness,** N.

Olympics, Olympic Games. international athletic contests, held once every four years in a different country. Separate summer and winter games are held, alternating every two years.

or·bit (ôr′bit), N. the curved path of any astronomical object around another object in space. **–or′bit·al,** ADJ.

or·gan·ic (ôr gan′ik), ADJ. containing carbon.

or·gan·ism (ôr′gə niz′əm), N. a living thing formed of separate parts, such as cells, tissues, and organs, which work together to carry on the various processes of life; an individual animal, plant, fungus, and so on.

or·na·men·tal (ôr′nə men′tl), ADJ. decorative; not plain: *ornamental designs on wallpaper.* **–or′na·men′tal·ly,** ADV.

or·phan (ôr′fən), N. child whose parents are dead.

out·look (out′lùk′), N. way of thinking about things; attitude of mind; point of view: *a cheerful outlook on life.*

out·wit (out wit′), V. to get the better of by being more intelligent; outsmart: *She usually outwits me and wins at checkers.* ❑ V. **out·wit·ted, out·wit·ting.**

o·zone (ō′zōn), N. a form of oxygen that shields the Earth from some ultraviolet rays.

P p

pains·tak·ing (pānz′tā′king), ADJ. requiring careful effort or attention: *Building model cars is a painstaking hobby.* **–pains′tak′ing·ly,** ADV.

pan·o·ram·a (pan′ə ram′ə), N. a wide, unbroken view of a surrounding region.

pa·pas (pä′pəs), N., PL. (Spanish) potatoes.

par·a·lyzed (par′ə līzd), ADJ. unable to feel or move: *The accident left his arm paralyzed.*

pas·sage (pas′ij), N. the right to have transportation, especially by boat: *obtain passage for Europe.*

pa·tri·ot·ic (pā′trē ot′ik), ADJ. showing love and loyal support for your own country.

patriotic

pa·tron (pā′trən), N. person who gives approval and support to some person, art, cause, or undertaking: *Patrons of art help artists.*

pawn·shop (pȯn′shop′), N. store that lends money at an interest on items that are left as a pledge that the money will be paid back.

pe·cul·iar (pi kyü′lyər), ADJ. strange; odd; unusual: *It was peculiar that the fish market had no fish last Friday.* **–pe·cul′iar·ly,** ADV.

ped·es·tal (ped′i stəl), N. base on which a column or a statue stands.

pe·nin·su·la (pə nin′sə lə), N. piece of land almost completely surrounded by water, or extending far out into the water. Florida is a peninsula. ❑ N., PL. **pe·nin·su·las.**

pen·nant (pen′ənt), N. a flag that indicates a championship.

per·form·ance (pər fôr′ məns), N. the giving of a play, concert, circus, or other show: *The performance is at eight o'clock.*

per·pen·dic·u·lar (pėr′pən dik′yə lər), ADJ. at right angles to another line or direction.

per·sist (pər sist′), V. to continue or carry on, despite opposition or resistance: *We asked the children to quiet down, but the noise persisted.*

phar·aoh (fâr′ō), N. any of the kings of ancient Egypt. Some of the pharaohs were buried in pyramids.

pharaoh

phase (fāz), N. the shape of the lighted part of the moon or a planet at a particular time. A full moon is one of the lunar phases.

pick·ax or **pick·axe** (pik′aks′), N. tool with a heavy metal bar, pointed at one or both ends, attached through the center to a wooden handle; pick. Pickaxes are used for breaking up dirt, rocks, etc. ❑ N., PL. **pick·ax·es.**

pick·et (pik′it), N. a pointed stake or peg placed upright to make a fence, to tie a horse to, etc.: *He tied his horse to the picket.*

a	hat	ė	term	ô	order	ch	child		a in about
ā	age	i	it	oi	oil	ng	long		e in taken
ä	far	ī	ice	ou	out	sh	she	ə	i in pencil
â	care	o	hot	u	cup	th	thin		o in lemon
e	let	ō	open	u̇	put	ᴛʜ	then		u in circus
ē	equal	ȯ	saw	ü	rule	zh	measure		

pi·o·neer (pī′ə nir′), N. person who goes first, or does something first, and so prepares the way for others: *a pioneer in medical science.*

pneu·mat·ic (nü mat′ik), ADJ. worked or powered by air: *a pneumatic drill.*

po·li·o (pō′lē ō), N. **poliomyelitis,** a severe, infectious, viral disease that destroys nervous tissue in the spinal cord, causing fever, paralysis and wasting away of various muscles, and sometimes death.

pom·e·gran·ate (pom′ə gran′it), N. the reddish gold fruit of a small tropical tree. The pomegranate has a thick skin and many seeds in a red pulp with a pleasant, slightly sour taste.

pon·cho (pon′chō), N. a large piece of cloth, often waterproof, with a slit in the middle for the head to go through.

port (pôrt), N. the side of a ship, boat, or aircraft to the left of someone facing forward.

pounce (pouns), V. to come down with a rush and seize something: *The cat pounced upon the mouse.* ❑ V. **pounced, pounc·ing.**

pred·a·tor (pred′ə tər), N. animal that lives by killing and eating other animals.

prej·u·dice (prej′ə dis), N. an unreasonable dislike of an idea, group of people, and so on.

pres·sur·ize (presh′ə rīz′), V. to keep the atmospheric pressure inside the cabin of an aircaft at a normal level in spite of the altitude: *a pressurized cabin.* ❑ V. **pres·sur·ized, pres·sur·iz·ing. –pres′sur·i·za′tion,** N.

prey (prā), N. animal or animals hunted and killed for food by another animal.

prin·ci·ple (prin′sə pəl), N. a rule of science explaining how things act.

pro·claim (prə klām′), V. to make known publicly and officially; declare publicly: *The congresswoman proclaimed that she would run for reelection.*

prop·er·ly (prop′ər lē), ADV. in a proper, correct, or fitting manner: *Eat properly.*

pro·vi·sions (prə vizh′ənz), N. PL. supply of food and drinks: *After a long winter the settlers were low on provisions.*

pueb·lo (pweb′lō), N. a Native American village of homes grouped together to form a large building which is several stories high. A pueblo is built of adobe and stone and usually has a flat roof.

pul·ley (pu̇l′ē), N. wheel with a grooved rim in which a rope can run to change the direction of a pull.

pur·pose·ful·ly (pėr′pəs fəl lē), ADV. in a determined, intentional manner: *She hurried about the house purposefully, getting her work done quickly.* **–pur′·pose·ful,** ADJ.

Q q

qual·i·fied (kwäl′ə fīd), ADJ. having desirable or required characteristics, skills, or abilities; competent: *A qualified airplane pilot must have good eyesight and hold a license to fly.*

quar·ry (kwôr′ē or kwär′ē), N. place where stone is dug, cut, or blasted out for use in building. ❑ N., PL. **quar·ries.**

quill (kwil), N. a stiff, sharp hair or spine like the pointed end of a feather. A porcupine has quills on its back. **–quill′·like′,** ADJ.

R r

ra·cial (rā′shəl), *ADJ.* of or involving groups of people with similar ancestry: *racial harmony.*

ra·di·a·tion (rā′dē ā′shən), *N.* particles or electromagnetic waves produced by the atoms of a radioactive substance as a result of nuclear decay; radioactivity. Radiation can be harmful to living tissue.

ram·shack·le (ram′shak′əl), *ADJ.* loose and shaky; likely to come apart.

ran·sack (ran′sak), *v.* 1 to search thoroughly through: *A thief ransacked the house for jewelry.* 2 to rob; plunder: *The invading army ransacked the city and carried off its treasure.*

rar·i·ty (râr′ə tē), *N.* the quality of being rare, or scarce.

ra·tion (rash′ən *or* rā′shən), *v.* to distribute in limited amounts: *Food was rationed to the public during the war.*

re·as·sure (rē′ə shùr′), *v.* to make someone feel more calm or confident about something: *I'm always reassuring my little brother that monsters don't exist.* ❑ *v.* **re·as·sured, re·as·sur·ing.** **–re′as·sur′ing·ly,** *ADV.*

rec·og·ni·tion (rek′əg nish′ən), *N.* favorable notice; acceptance: *The author soon won recognition from the public.*

re·cov·er·y (ri kuv′ər ē), *N.* act or process of coming back to health or normal condition: *She had a rapid recovery from surgery.* ❑ *N., PL.* **re·cov·er·ies.**

reg·u·la·tion (reg′yə lā′shən), *N.* a rule; law: *traffic regulations.*

re·jec·tion (ri jek′shən), *N.* condition of not being accepted or act of turning someone or something down: *Most of my ideas met with rejection, but I didn't give up.*

rel·a·tive (rel′ə tiv), **1** *N.* person who belongs to the same family as another, such as a father, brother, aunt, nephew, or cousin. **2** *ADJ.* related or compared to each other: *We discussed the relative advantages of city and country life.*

rem·e·dy (rem′ə dē), *N.* a means of removing or relieving diseases or any bad condition; cure: *Aspirin is used as a remedy for headaches.* ❑ *N., PL.* **rem·e·dies.** *v.* **rem·e·died, rem·e·dy·ing.**

remuda (ri′mü′də), *N.* a group of spare horses used on a cattle drive: *When the cowboy's horse got hurt, he chose another one from the remuda.*

re·pel·lent (ri pel′ənt), *N.* anything that forces or drives something away: *insect repellent.*

re·search (ri sėrch′ *or* rē′sėrch′), *v.* to hunt for facts or truth; inquire; investigate: *My father researched the history of our family.*

re·tain·ing wall (ri tān′ing wȯl), *v.* a wall used to hold back earth, especially at the edge of a terrace or excavation: *They built a retaining wall for safety at the building site.*

re·tired (ri tīrd′), *ADJ.* withdrawn from your occupation or office; no longer working: *a retired accountant.*

re·volve (ri volv′), *v.* to move in a curve around a point.

riv·et (riv′it), *N.* a metal bolt with a head at one end, the other end being hammered into a head after insertion. Rivets fasten heavy steel plates together. **–riv′et·er,** *N.*

ruse (rüz), *N.* a scheme to mislead others; a trick.

a	hat	ė	term	ô	order	ch	child	⎧a in about
ā	age	i	it	oi	oil	ng	long	e in taken
ä	far	ī	ice	ou	out	sh	she	ə ⎨i in pencil
â	care	o	hot	u	cup	th	thin	o in lemon
e	let	ō	open	ù	put	⊤H	then	⎩u in circus
ē	equal	ȯ	saw	ü	rule	zh	measure	

S s

sat·el·lite (sat′l īt), N. an artificial object launched by a rocket into an orbit around Earth or some other astronomical object.

scan·dal·ous (skan′dl əs), ADJ. bringing disgrace; shameful; shocking: *scandalous behavior.* **–scan′dal·ous·ly,** ADV.

schol·ar (skol′ər), N. someone whose regular work is study or research: *The professor is a famous scholar.* **–schol′ar·ly,** ADJ.

scorch·ing (skôrch′ing), ADJ. very hot; burning: *scorching temperatures, the scorching sun.*

scorn·ful (skôrn′fəl), ADJ. showing disrespect or contempt; mocking: *a scornful glance.* **–scorn′ful·ly,** ADV. **–scorn′ful·ness,** N.

scout (skout), V. to observe or examine to get information: *Campers scouted the valley to see if there was any drinking water.*

se·cre·tive (sē′krə tiv), ADJ. known to keep things from the knowledge or sight of others; crafty; sneaky. **–se′cre·tive·ly,** ADV.

seg·re·ga·tion (seg′rə gā′shən), N. separation of people of different races, especially in schools, housing, etc.

self-con·trol (self′kən trōl′), N. control of your actions, feelings, etc.

sim·plic·i·ty (sim plis′ə tē), N. freedom from difficulty; clearness: *The simplicity of that book makes it suitable for children.*

skep·tic (skep′tik), N. person who questions the truth of theories or apparent facts; doubter: *The skeptics argued that the Earth is flat.*

smol·der (smōl′dər), V. to burn and smoke without flame: *The campfire smoldered for hours after the blaze died down.*

smug·gling (smug′ ling), V. bringing something into or taking something out of a country secretly and against the law.

so·lar (sō′lər), ADJ. of or from the sun: *a solar eclipse, solar rays.*

so·lu·tion (sə lü′shən), N. **1** answer to a problem, mystery, riddle, and so on. **2** mixture formed by dissolving a substance in a liquid: *When you put sugar in tea, you form a solution.*

song·smith (sông′smith), N. a composer of songs; songwriter.

spar (spär), N. a stout pole used to support or extend the sails of a ship; mast, yard, gaff, boom, and so on, of a ship.

spec·u·late (spek′yə lāt), V. to think carefully; reflect; meditate; consider: *The students speculated about the poem.* ❏ V. **spec·u·lates, spec·u·lat·ed, spec·u·lat·ing.**

sphere (sfir), N. a round object; globe. Every point on the surface of a sphere is the same distance from the center. The sun, moon, Earth, and stars are spheres.

spin·dly (spind′lē), ADJ. very long and slender; too tall and thin: *a spindly plant.* ❏ ADJ. **spin·dli·er, spin·dli·est.**

spi·ral (spī′rəl), ADJ. winding; coiled: *a spiral staircase.* ❏ V. **spi·raled, spi·ral·ing** or **spi·ralled, spi·ral·ling.** **–spi′ral·ly,** ADV.

spy·glass (spī′glas′), N. a small telescope. ❏ N., PL. **spy·glass·es.**

stag·nant (stag′nənt), ADJ. foul from standing still: *a stagnant pool of water.* **–stag′nant·ly,** ADV.

star·board (stär′bərd), ADJ. on the right side of a boat or aircraft: *Look over the starboard side and you will see a dolphin.*

star·gazing (stär′gāz′ing), N. act or hobby of looking at the stars: *When I was little, Grandpa and I enjoyed stargazing each night.*

sta·tion·ar·y (stā′shə ner′ē), ADJ. not movable: *A furnace is stationary.* ■Another word that sounds like this is **stationery.**

sta·tion·er·y (stā′shə ner′ē), N. writing materials such as paper, cards, and envelopes. ■ Another word that sounds like this is **stationary.**

sta·tis·tics (stə tis′tiks), N., PL. numerical facts about people, sports, etc.

sti·fling (stī′fling), ADJ. producing suffocation or restraint; oppressive; hampering: *He worked in the fields all summer in the stifling heat.* ❏ V. **sti·fled, sti·fling. –sti′fling·ly,** ADV.

stren·u·ous (stren′yü əs), ADJ. requiring much energy; difficult: *Running is strenuous exercise.* **–stren′u·ous·ness,** N.

stroke (strōk), N. movement or mark made by a pen, pencil, brush, or the like: *I paint with heavy brush strokes.*

struc·ture (struk′chər), N. something built; a building or construction. Dams, bridges, tunnels, and skyscrapers are structures.

structure

stunned (stund), ADJ. **1** overwhelmed; shocked; dazed; bewildered: *The witnesses to the accident wore stunned expressions.* **2** knocked unconscious; senseless: *The fall left the rock climber stunned for a few minutes.*

sty·lus (stī′ləs), N. 1 a pointed tool for writing on wax. 2 a hard pointed instrument for punching the dots in writing Braille with a Braille slate: *He used a stylus to compose a story in Braille.* ❏ N., PL. **sty·lus·es, sty·li** (stī′lī).

sub·merged (səb mėrjd′), ADJ. underwater; covered by water: *The boat crashed upon a group of submerged rocks.*

su·per·vise (sü′pər vīz), V. to look after and direct work or workers, a process, and so on; oversee; manage: *Study halls are supervised by teachers.* ❏ V. **su·per·vised, su·per·vis·ing.**

sur·geon (sėr′jən), N. doctor who performs operations: *A surgeon removed my tonsils.*

sur·vey·or (sər vā′ər), N. person who surveys land, measuring for size, shape, position, boundaries, etc.

sur·viv·al (sər vī′vəl), N. act or fact of staying alive: *The survival of the avalanche victims depended on a quick rescue.*

sym·bol·ize (sim′bə līz), V. to be a symbol of; stand for; represent: *A dove symbolizes peace.* ❏ V. **sym·bol·ized, sym·bol·iz·ing.**

sy·ringe (sə rinj′), N. a narrow tube fitted with a plunger or rubber bulb for drawing in a quantity of fluid and then forcing it out in a stream. A syringe can be used for cleaning wounds, injecting fluids into the body, etc.

Tt

tact·ful (takt′fəl), ADJ. having or showing an ability to do and say the right things; skilled or showing skill in dealing with people or handling difficult situations: *a tactful person, a tactful reply.* **–tact′ful·ly,** ADV. **–tact′ful·ness,** N.

a hat	ė term	ô order	ch child	⎰a in about
ā age	i it	oi oil	ng long	⎱e in taken
ä far	ī ice	ou out	sh she	ə⎰i in pencil
â care	o hot	u cup	th thin	⎱o in lemon
e let	ō open	ù put	ᴛʜ then	⎱u in circus
ē equal	ò saw	ü rule	zh measure	

tank·er (tang′kər), N. a ship, airplane, or truck with tanks for carrying oil or other liquid freight.

tarp (tärp), N. tarpaulin, a sheet of canvas or other waterproof material, used as a protective covering.

teem·ing (tē′ming), ADJ. full of; alive with: *ponds teeming with fish.* **–teem′ing·ly,** ADV.

tem·per·a·ment (tem′pər ə mənt), N. someone's nature or disposition: *a shy temperament.*

tem·plate (tem′plit), N. any model or pattern on which something is formed: *Use these templates when you create your own charts.*

ten·ta·cle (ten′tə kəl), N. a long, slender, flexible growth on the head or around the mouth of an animal, used to touch, hold, or move.

ter·rain (tə rān′), N. region of land that is thought to have particular natural features: *The hilly, rocky terrain of the island made farming difficult.*

thatch (thach), N. straw, palm leaves, etc., used as a roof or covering: *After we built the sod house, we covered the roof with thatch.*

theme (thēm), N. **1** the main subject or idea of a book, play, or the like. **2** the principal melody of a piece of music. Themes are often repeated in different forms, or variations.

thrust (thrust), N. the force driving a rocket or a jet engine forward.

tol·e·rate (tol′ə rāt′), V. to bear; endure; put up with: *The dog tolerated the puppy's playfulness.* ❏ V. **tol·e·rat·ed, tol·e·rat·ing.**

toll[1] (tōl), N. sound of a bell being struck.

toll[2] (tōl), N. **1** tax or fee paid for some right or privilege: *We pay a toll when we cross the bridge.* **2** something suffered or lost: *Traffic accidents take a heavy toll of human lives.*

toll·booth (tōl′büth′), N. booth or gate at which tolls are collected before or after going over a bridge, along a highway, and so on.

tomb (tüm), N. grave, vault, mausoleum, or the like, for a dead body, often above ground.

top·o·graph·i·cal (top′ə graf′ə kəl), ADJ. of or about the surface features of a place, such as mountains, rivers, and roads.

top·soil (top′soil′), N. soil at or near the surface: *Rich topsoil helps produce good crops.*

tox·ic (tok′sik), ADJ. of or caused by poison: *toxic plants.* **–tox′i·cal·ly,** ADV.

tra·di·tion·al (trə dish′ə nəl), ADJ. handed down from one generation to the next; made or done according to tradition: *traditional crafts.*

tran·sit (tran′sit), N. transportaion by trains, buses, etc.

trans·verse (trans vėrs′), ADJ. having a mouth-hole across which a player's breath is directed.

treat (trēt), V. to add a chemical substance to food or water in order to purify it: *The city treated our drinking water to remove impurities.*

tre·men·dous (tri men′dəs), ADJ. incredible; extraordinary: *The firefighters showed tremendous bravery.* **–tre·men′dous·ly,** ADV.

trow·el (trou′əl), N. tool with a broad, flat blade, used for spreading or smoothing plaster or mortar.

tu·ber·cu·lo·sis (tü bėr′kyə lō′sis), N. an infectious disease affecting various tissues of the body, but most often the lungs. Half of all untreated cases of tuberculosis are fatal.

tum·ble·down (tum′bəl doun′), ADJ. ready to fall down; not in good condition; dilapidated: *a tumbledown shack in the mountains.*

tux·e·do (tuk sē′dō), N. a man's suit including a coat for evening wear, made without tails, usually black with satin lapels: *My brother rented a tuxedo to wear to his senior prom.* ❏ N., PL. **tux·e·dos** or **tux·e·does**

U u

ul·tra·vi·o·let (ul′ trə vī′ə lit), *ADJ.* of or about the invisible rays with wavelengths shorter than those of violet light.

um·pire (um′pīr), *N.* person who rules on the plays in a game: *The umpire called strike three.*

u·ni·verse (yü′nə vėrs′), *N.* everything there is, including all space and matter; the cosmos. Our planet is a very tiny part of the universe.

un·lim·it·ed (un lim′ə tid), *ADJ.* not restrained; not restricted: *unlimited power, unlimited potential.*

un·sta·ble (un stā′bəl), *ADJ.* not firm or steady; shaky; unsteady.

up·root·ed (up rüt′id), *ADJ.* torn away or removed from your home, country, and so on; displaced: *The war left many uprooted families in its wake.*

V v

var·i·a·tion (vâr′ē ā′shən), *N.* (in music) a tune or theme repeated with changes in rhythm, harmony, and so on: *The symphony consisted of a theme and four variations.*

veg·e·ta·tion (vej′ə tā′shən), *N.* plant life; growing plants.

venge·ance (ven′jəns), *N.* punishment in return for a wrong; revenge: *The queen swore vengeance against her hateful enemies.*

ver·te·brae (vėr′tə brā), *N., PL.* bones that form the backbone.

vig·il (vij′əl), *N.* act of staying awake for some purpose; act of watching; watch: *All night the parents kept vigil over the sick child.*

vin·dic·tive (vin dik′tiv), *ADJ.* bearing a grudge; wanting revenge: *A vindictive person is unforgiving.* **–vin·dic′tive·ly,** *ADV.*

voy·age (voi′ij), *N.* a journey by water.

vul·ner·a·ble (vul′nər ə bəl), *ADJ.* capable of being wounded or injured; open to attack: *The army's retreat left the city vulnerable.* **–vul′ner·a·bil′i·ty, –vul′ner·a·bly,** *ADV.*

W w

war·y (wâr′ē), *ADJ.* cautious or careful: *The bird in the tree kept a wary stare on the cat below.* ❑ *ADJ.* **war·i·er, war·i·est. –war′i·ly,** *ADV.* **–war′i·ness,** *N.*

wear·i·ness (wir′ē nis), *N.* condition of being worn out or tired; exhaustion: *We felt complete weariness after climbing the mountain.*

weight·less·ness (wāt′lis nis), *N.* condition of being free from the pull of gravity: *Astronauts experience weightlessness in outer space.*

wide·spread (wīd′spred′), *ADJ.* occurring in many places; spread over a large area: *widespread pollution.*

wig·wam (wig′wäm), *N.* a small shelter made of bark, mats, or skins laid over a dome-shaped frame of poles, used by certain North American Indians.

wiz·ened (wiz′nd), *ADJ.* dried up; withered; shriveled: *a wizened apple, a wizened face.*

won·der·ful·ly (wun′dər fəl ē), *ADV.* marvelously; remarkably: *He performed wonderfully in his first play.* **–won′der·ful,** *ADV.* **–won′der·ful·ness,** *N.*

work·shop (wėrk′shop′), *N.* shop or building where work is done.

a	hat	ė	term	ô	order	ch	child		ə	a in about
ā	age	i	it	oi	oil	ng	long			e in taken
ä	far	ī	ice	ou	out	sh	she			i in pencil
â	care	o	hot	u	cup	th	thin			o in lemon
e	let	ō	open	ù	put	ᴛʜ	then			u in circus
ē	equal	ò	saw	ü	rule	zh	measure			

Handbook of Reading Skills

How to Use This Handbook

The following reading skills and definitions are found throughout this book. Understanding these skills can help you as you read. In this section, the skills are arranged in alphabetical order. Use these pages to help you review the terms and definitions. When reading, refer back to these pages as often as needed.

Author's Purpose

- **Author's purpose** refers to an author's reason or reasons for writing.

- Four common reasons for writing are to inform, to persuade, to entertain, and to express. Often an author has more than one purpose for writing.

- Understanding the author's purpose helps you know how slowly or quickly to read and how closely to examine the author's ideas. It also helps explain the author's choice of words and writing style.

Author's Viewpoint/Bias

- **Author's viewpoint** is the way an author thinks about the subject of his or her writing.

- An author's viewpoint may be one of fear, admiration, pity, amusement, or some other feeling.

- You can identify an author's viewpoint by looking at the words an author uses. Some authors use loaded words, such as *terrible* or *wonderful*, to express a strong preference, or **bias.**

- *Balanced writing* presents both sides of an issue. *Biased writing* shows strong feeling for or against someone or something and presents only one side of an issue. You should read biased writing critically.

Cause and Effect

- An **effect** is something that happens. A **cause** is why something happens.

- To find an effect, ask yourself "What happened?" To find a cause, ask yourself "Why did this happen?"

- An effect may have more than one cause, and a cause may have more than one effect.

- Clue words, such as *cause, because,* and *reason,* can help you find a cause. Clue words, such as *so, consequently, therefore,* and *thus,* can help you find an effect.

Character

- **Characters** are the people or animals who take part in the events of a short story, novel, play, or other form of fiction.

- You can learn about characters by noticing what they think, say, and do. You can also learn about characters by thinking about how other characters treat them and what others say about them.

- The lasting qualities of a character's personality are called character traits. *Brave, stubborn,* and *honest* are examples of character traits. Character traits can help you predict how a character will react in a new situation.

Compare and Contrast

- To **compare** means to tell how two or more things are alike. To **contrast** means to tell how two or more things are different.

- Sometimes authors use clue words to help you notice likenesses *(like, similarly, in addition,* and *likewise)* and differences *(but, however, although,* and *in spite of).*

- Compare and contrast what you read with your own knowledge and experience.

Context Clues

- **Context clues** are words that come before or after an unfamiliar word and help you figure out what it means.

- A context clue may be a *synonym,* a word with nearly the same meaning as the unknown word, or it may be an *antonym,* a word with an opposite meaning.

- A context clue may also be a definition or explanation of the unknown word, or a series of examples. *Such as* and *for example* are phrases that often begin examples.

- If a context clue doesn't give you a complete meaning of an unknown word, use a dictionary to check the word's meaning.

Drawing Conclusions

- When you draw a conclusion, you make a decision or form an opinion about what you read. **Drawing conclusions** is also known as *making inferences.*

- A conclusion should make sense and be based on facts and details in the writing, as well as your own experience.

- To test a conclusion, ask yourself whether the facts are accurate and whether you are taking anything for granted. Then decide whether there are other possible conclusions you could base on the same information.

Fact and Opinion

- A statement of **fact** can be proved true or false by reading, observing, asking an expert, or checking in some way.

- A statement of **opinion** tells someone's belief, judgment, or way of thinking about something. It cannot be proved true or false, but it can be supported or explained. Some statements of opinion begin with clue words, such as *I believe* or *in my opinion.*

- A valid statement of opinion can be supported by facts or by the authority of an expert. A faulty statement of opinion cannot.

Generalizing

- A broad statement about what several people or things have in common is a **generalization.** *Most doctors work in a hospital* is an example of a generalization.

- Some generalizations contain clue words, such as *most, many, all, sometimes, generally, always,* or *never.* If a statement does not contain a clue word, but you can add one without changing the statement's meaning, the statement is a generalization.

- A **valid generalization** is supported by facts and agrees with what you already know. A **faulty generalization** is not supported by facts.

Handbook of Reading Skills

Graphic Sources

- A **graphic source** is something that shows information visually.

- Some common graphic sources are pictures, charts, maps, graphs, and diagrams.

- A graphic source may present the information in the text differently, or it may show more information.

- Before you read, preview a story or article to see if there are graphic sources that give you an idea of what the text will be about. As you read, compare information in the graphic sources to information in the text.

Main Idea and Supporting Details

- The most important idea about the topic of a paragraph or an article is the **main idea.** Small pieces of information that tell more about the main idea are **supporting details.**

- To find a main idea, first identify the topic. Ask yourself, "What is this all about?" Then look for the most important idea about the topic. If it is not stated, put the main idea in your own words.

- To check a main idea, ask yourself, "Does this main idea make sense? Does it cover all the important details?"

Making Judgments

- **Making judgments** means forming opinions about someone or something.

- When you make a judgment, you think about information the author provides as well as your own experiences and beliefs.

- As you read, look for evidence to support your judgments. You may need to change your judgment based on new information.

- When an author expresses a judgment about someone or something, test the author's judgment by looking for evidence to support it.

Paraphrasing

- To **paraphrase** is to explain something in your own words.

- To paraphrase a piece of writing, first ask yourself what the author is trying to say. Then restate the ideas or description in your own words, without changing the meaning or adding opinions of your own.

- Paraphrasing can be a useful tool to check your understanding. As a research and study tool, it can be used to prepare for a test or to gather information from reference sources.

Persuasive Devices

- **Persuasive devices** are the special techniques an author uses to influence the way you think or feel.

- One type of persuasive device is the use of *loaded words.* Authors use loaded words to bring out an emotional response in readers and to convince readers of their ideas and views.

- As you read persuasive writing, think about whether the author is appealing to your reason through facts and ideas or to your emotions through loaded words.

Plot

- The **plot** of a story is the series of important events from the story's beginning, middle, and end. The plot revolves around a central problem, or *conflict*—a struggle between two forces, such as a person against nature or two people against each other.

- In most stories, the conflict is introduced in the beginning. As the story progresses, the conflict leads to other problems. Gradually, the *rising action* builds to a high point, or climax.

- The *climax,* or turning point, is the moment in the story when the struggle between the two forces is the greatest.

- Following the climax, there is *resolution* of the conflict. The two forces no longer struggle and the action winds down.

Predicting

- To **predict** means to state what might happen next in a story or article.

- To make a prediction, think about what you already know and what has already happened. Look for clues in the photographs and illustrations.

- After you make a prediction, continue reading to check its accuracy. Revise your prediction if it does not agree with new information.

Sequence

- **Sequence** is the order in which things happen or characters perform actions.

- Some clue words that can help you follow the order of events are *when, first, then,* and *next.* Dates and times of day are other clues to sequence.

- Steps in a process occur in a sequence. Events in fiction and nonfiction may also occur in a sequence.

Setting

- The **setting** of a story is the time and place in which the story occurs.

- In some stories, the author describes exactly when and where the story takes place. In other stories, the author reveals the setting through details.

- The setting of a story can influence what happens to a character and how a character behaves. The setting can also contribute to an overall feeling or mood.

Steps in a Process

- The actions you perform in order to make something or to reach a goal are the **steps in a process.**

- Steps in a process may be numbered or shown by clues words, such as *first, begin, next, then,* and *last.*

- If there are no clues words or numbers to help you keep the steps in order, think about what you already know about the process and how it is done.

Summarizing

- To **summarize** means to give a brief statement of the main idea of an article or the most important events in a story.

- When you summarize a story, include only the main actions and their outcomes.

- When you summarize an article, include the main idea and the most important details.

Text Structure

- **Text structure** refers to the way a piece of writing is organized.

- Fiction is usually organized in *chronological order,* the order in which the events happen.

- Nonfiction may be organized in *chronological order,* by *topic, cause and effect, problem and solution,* or *comparison and contrast.*

Theme

- The **theme** of a story is the underlying message.

- A theme can be a universal truth or a generalization about some aspect of life.

- To determine the theme of a story, ask yourself, "What does the author want me to learn or know?" Your answer should be a "big idea" that can stand on its own away from the story.

- Many stories have more than one theme. To be valid, a statement of theme should be supported by evidence from the text.

Visualizing

- To **visualize** is to create a mental image.

- One way an author can help you visualize is by using imagery, words that produce strong images.

- Another way an author can help you visualize is by using sensory details, words that describe how something looks, sounds, smells, tastes, or feels.

Spelling Lists

Tony and the Snark

admire	canyon	magnify	cannon	lemonade
method	decorate	distance	swimming	strict
injury	tissue	modern	comedy	honesty
property	husband	clumsy	hundredth	dungeon

Teammates

ceiling	receipt	deceive	neither	leisure
protein	receiver	seize	conceited	field
achieve	belief	brief	relief	apiece
shield	niece	diesel	grief	yield

April's Mud

reduce	attitude	costume	absolutely	assume
sewer	New York	renew	review	viewpoint
interview	preview	value	continue	rescue
humid	universe	uniform	reunion	United States

Hot Dogs and Bamboo Shoots

report	order	sword	forty	enormous
explore	ignore	therefore	expert	service
determine	permanent	research	earning	worth
worst	thorough	attorney	disturb	purchase

The Telephone Call

poetry	beautiful	thirteen	tongue	pieces
thousand	through	unusual	building	license
remodel	grateful	enemy	instrument	perform
prefer	judged	adjusted	soldier	neighborhood

Unit 2

A Trouble-Making Crow

moose	cobra	alligator	vanilla	banana
tomato	mustard	hula	picnic	barbecue
crocodile	coyote	koala	macaroni	catsup
polka	ballet	waltz	banquet	buffet

From a Spark

doubt	fascinate	science	scenic	autumn
column	guilty	league	guardian	disguise
subtle	debt	reminiscent	descent	condemn
solemn	guidance	vague	fatigue	intrigue

Storm-a-Dust

myself	themselves	hallway	homeroom	everything
teenage	teammate	skateboard	everybody	doughnut
ice cream	locker room	tape recorder	root beer	dead end
air conditioner	polka dot	roller coaster	ice pack	solar system

The Day of the Turtle

basketball	everywhere	outside	summertime	something
afterthought	cheerleader	quarterback	bookstore	courthouse
baby-sit	roller-skating	drive-in	self-control	part-time
ice-skated	ninety-five	brother-in-law	water-skied	old-fashioned

Saving the Sound

interested	usually	American	toward	business
vegetable	really	opposite	difficult	Christmas
magazine	apologize	multiply	jealousy	elementary
oxygen	Maryland	sensitive	laughter	disease

Spelling Lists

Unit 3

Elizabeth Blackwell: Medical Pioneer

entrance	performance	appearance	clearance	insurance
independence	difference	excellence	confidence	coincidence
brilliant	important	pollutant	ignorant	hesitant
intelligent	apparent	persistent	convenient	consistent

Born Worker

scarfs	staffs	sheriffs	reefs	chiefs
shelves	wolves	ourselves	knives	thieves
solos	stereos	studios	volcanoes	dominoes
buffaloes	quizzes	pants	scissors	measles

Wilma Unlimited

different	register	carnival	variety	atmosphere
favorite	pattern	understand	sentence	instance
elegant	aquarium	communicate	gasoline	factory
definite	Chicago	heavily	garage	illustrate

Casey at the Bat

slogan	citizen	urban	orphan	forgotten
kindergarten	propeller	encounter	conquer	appetizer
collector	dishonor	tractor	level	tunnel
easel	double	single	example	recycle

The Night of the Pomegranate

their	there	they're	wring	ring
chili	chilly	scent	sent	cent
oversees	overseas	patients	patience	cereal
serial	coarse	course	counsel	council

Unit 4

Spring Paint

similar	doesn't	experience	forward	exactly
partner	drawer	expensive	develop	familiar
pigeon	tickling	penalty	frustrated	athletic
celebration	circling	helicopter	trembling	sparkling

A Brother's Promise

probably	cabinet	separate	wondering	clothes
average	beginning	restaurant	promise	aspirin
desperate	twelfth	skiing	unwritten	roughly
schedule	overrule	awfully	fishhook	temperature

from Catching the Fire

answered	answering	decided	deciding	included
including	omitted	omitting	satisfied	satisfying
delayed	delaying	remembered	remembering	exercise
exercising	interfered	interfering	occurred	occurring

The Seven Wonders of the Ancient World

connect	command	mirror	accomplish	according
allowance	college	address	Mississippi	recess
committee	immediate	barricade	interrupt	broccoli
collect	afford	possess	Tennessee	announce

The Gold Coin

human	humane	clean	cleanse	nature
natural	major	majority	poem	poetic
equal	equation	unite	unity	bomb
bombard	muscle	muscular	resign	resignation

Spelling Lists

Unit 5

To the Pole!

illegal	illogical	illegible	inexpensive	inaccurate
indirect	informal	incapable	incredible	impolite
improper	imperfect	impatient	imbalance	immature
irresponsible	irregular	irrational	irresistible	irreplaceable

from El Güero: A True Adventure Story

relaxation	exploration	occupation	destination	orientation
recommendation	determination	infection	collection	reaction
situation	television	generation	reflection	destruction
attention	deduction	reception	solution	convention

Destination Mars

pretrial	prearrange	premeditated	prehistoric	precaution
postdate	postwar	postponement	postgraduate	overcook
overlook	overflow	overpopulated	undercover	undernourished
underweight	include	inhale	exclude	exhale

The Land of Expectations

originate	fortunate	activate	affectionate	considerate
obligate	productive	defective	constructive	attractive
inventive	negative	creative	ownership	membership
hardship	relationship	friendship	championship	leadership

The Trail Drive

it's	let's	that's	we'd	don't
there's	coach's	coaches'	man's	men's
you're	she'd	mustn't	o'clock	guide's
guides'	director's	directors'	city's	cities'

Unit 6

Noah Writes a B & B Letter

since	sense	choose	chose	finally
finely	except	accept	beside	besides
recent	resent	access	excess	later
latter	metal	medal	personal	personnel

Louis Braille

outlast	account	astound	boundary	southeast
counter	sunflower	somehow	chowder	coward
disappointed	voices	tabloid	employee	joyful
applaud	faucet	caution	author	trauma

The Librarian Who Measured the Earth

automobile	autograph	automatic	autobiography	autopilot
telescope	telecast	telegram	telegraph	telephone
portable	import	export	transport	passport
microphone	headphones	symphony	saxophone	megaphone

Tyree's Song

social	precious	commercial	especially	artificial
financial	gracious	glacier	national	dictionary
motion	position	population	cautious	question
suggestion	mention	fraction	exhaustion	digestion

Cutters, Carvers, and the Cathedral

direct	direction	history	historical	fact
factual	critic	criticize	produce	production
magic	magician	electric	electrician	distract
distraction	remedy	remedial	origin	original

Acknowledgments

Text

Dorling Kindersley (DK) is an international publishing company specializing in the creation of high quality reference content for books, CD-ROMs, online, and video. The hallmark of DK content is its unique combination of educational value and strong visual style—this combination allows DK to deliver appealing, accessible, and engaging educational content that delights children, parents, and teachers around the world. Scott Foresman is delighted to have been able to use selected extracts of DK content within the Scott Foresman Reading program. **62–63:** "Baseball Legends" from "The Negro Leagues" by James Kelley from *Baseball.* Copyright © 2000 by Dorling Kindersley Limited; **222–223:** "Tortoises and Turtles" from *Nature Encyclopedia.* Copyright © 2000 by Dorling Kindersley Limited; **338–339:** "Cards and Stats" by James Kelley from *Baseball.* Copyright © 2000 by Dorling Kindersley Limited; **446–447:** "The Great Pyramids" by George Hart from *Ancient Egypt.* Copyright © 1990 by Dorling Kindersley Limited; **542–543:** "Exploring Mars" by Peter Bond from *Guide to Space.* Copyright 1999 by Dorling Kindersley Limited; **676–677:** "Pipes and Flutes" by Neil Ardley from *Music.* Copyright © 1989 by Dorling Kindersley Limited.

20: "Jerry Takes Off" from *The Winning Stroke* by Matt Christopher. Copyright © 1994 by Matt Christopher (text), illustrations © 1994 by Karin Lidbeck. By permission of Little, Brown and Company; **22:** Reprinted with the permission of Simon & Schuster Books for Young Readers, an imprint of Simon & Schuster Children's Publishing Division, "Tony and the Shark" from *Windcatcher* by Avi. Copyright © 1991 by Avi Wortis; **41:** "Swimming for the Gold" from *Science World*, May 8, 2000. Copyright © 2000 Scholastic Inc. Reprinted by permission of Scholastic Inc.; **44:** From *Batboy* by Joan Anderson, photographs by Matthew Cavanaugh. Copyright © 1996 by Joan Anderson, text. Copyright © 1996 by Matthew Cavanaugh, photographs. Used by permission of Lodestar Books, an affiliate of Dutton Children's Books, a division of Penguin Putnam Inc.; **46:** *Teammates* by Peter Golenbock, copyright © 1990 by Golenbock Communications, illustrations copyright © 1990 by Paul Lee, reprinted by permission of Harcourt, Inc.; **64:** "Leaving Home" from "A Packet of Seeds" by Deborah Hopkinson in *Cricket.* Copyright © 1998 by Deborah Hopkinson. Reprinted by permission of the author; **66:** "April's Mud" from *Rio Grande Stories,* copyright © 1994 by Carolyn Meyer, reprinted by permission of Harcourt, Inc.; **82:** "El Horno" by Michael Miller, adapted from *Cobblestone's* May 1998 issue: *New Mexico: Celebrating 400 Years of History.* Copyright © 1998 by Cobblestone Publishing Company, 30 Grove St., Suite C, Peterborough, NH 03458. Reprinted by permission of the publisher; **84:** "The Mystery Key" is from *Even a Little is Something: Stories of Nong,* copyright © 1997 by Tom Glass. Reprinted by permission of Linnet Books/The Shoe String Press, Inc., North Haven, Connecticut; **86:** Reprinted with the permission of Simon & Schuster Books for Young Readers, an imprint of Simon & Schuster Children's Publishing Division from *The Invisible Thread* by Yoshiko Uchida. Copyright © 1991 Yoshiko Uchida; **102:** "Society and Culture" from *Our World: Yesterday and Today* by Dorothy Drummond and Bruce Kraig. Copyright © 1991 by Scott, Foresman and Company; **104:** "Granny's Chair" from "Apple Butter Time" by Joann Mazzio. Copyright © 1997 by Joann Mazzio. Reprinted by permission of the author; **106:** Excerpt from *Meet the Austins* by Madeleine L'Engle. Copyright © 1997 by Crosswicks, Ltd. Reprinted by permission of Farrar, Straus & Giroux, LLC; **128:** "Going Through the Phases" from *Eye on the Universe: The Moon* by Bobbie Kalman. Copyright © 1998 by Crabtree Publishing Company. All rights reserved. Reprinted by permission of Crabtree Publishing; **130:** "Andre" from *Bronzeville Boys and Girls* by Gwendolyn Brooks. Copyright © 1956 by Gwendolyn Brooks Blakely. Used by permission of HarperCollins Publishers; **130:** "Who Will Teach Me?" from *Many Winters* by Nancy Wood. Copyright © 1974 by Nancy Wood. Reprinted by permission of Doubleday & Company, Inc. and the author; **131:** "Goodness" by Benny Andersen, translated by Alexander Taylor. Reprinted by permission of Benny Andersen; **132:** "The New Suit" by Nidia Sanabria de Romero, translated by Arnoldo D. Larrosa Morán with Naomi Shihab Nye, is reprinted with the permission of Simon & Schuster Books for Young Readers, an imprint of Simon & Schuster Children's Publishing Division from *This Same Sky* selected by Naomi Shihab Nye. Copyright © 1992 by Naomi Shihab Nye; **133:** "Almost Ready" from *Slow Dance Heart Break Blues* by Arnold Adoff. Text copyright © 1995 by Arnold Adoff. Used by permission of HarperCollins Publishers; **140:** "The Truth About Wolves" from *Wolves* by Seymour Simon. Copyright © 1993 by Seymour Simon. Used by permission of HarperCollins Publishers; **142:** From *The Tarantula in My Purse and 172 Other Wild Pets* by Jean Craighead George. Used by permission of Curtis Brown Ltd. Copyright © 1994 by Jean Craighead George. All rights reserved; **161:** "The Crow and the Pitcher" from *Aesop's Fables.* Copyright 1947 by Grosset & Dunlap, Inc.; **162:** "At the Water's Edge" from *The Black Stallion* by Walter Farley, copyright © 1941 by Walter Farley. Copyright renewed 1969 by Walter Farley. Used by permission of Random House Children's Books, a division of Random House, Inc.; **164:** Reprinted with the permission of Simon & Schuster Books for Young Readers, an imprint of Simon & Schuster Children's Publishing Division from *Hatchet* by Gary Paulsen. Copyright © 1987 by Gary Paulsen; **178:** "Wilderness Challenge" by Suzanne Wilson from *National Geographic World*, May 2000. Copyright © 2000 National Geographic Society. Used by permission of NGS Image Collection; **180:** "The Glittering Cloud" from *On the Banks of Plum Creek* by Laura Ingalls Wilder. Text copyright 1937 by Laura Ingalls Wilder. Copyright © renewed 1963 by Roger L. MacBride. Used by permission of HarperCollins Publishers, Inc.; **182:** Excerpt from *Drylongso,* text copyright © 1992 by Virginia Hamilton, illustrations copyright © 1992 by Jerry Pinkney, reprinted by permission of Harcourt Inc.; **204:** "What is a Drought?" from *Drought* by Christopher Lampton. Copyright © 1992 by Christopher Lampton. Used by permission of The Millbrook Press; **206:** "The Wexford Doe" from *Hold Fast to Dreams* by Andrea Davis Pinkney. Text copyright © 1995 by Andrea Davis Pinkney. Used by permission of HarperCollins Publishers; **208:** "The Day of the Turtle" from *The Wreck of the Zanzibar* by Michael Morpurgo. Text copyright © 1995 by Michael Morpurgo. Illustrations copyright © 1994 by Françios Place. Reprinted by permission of Penguin Putnam Inc. and David Higham Associates Limited; **224:** "Why Care?" from *Life on Land Our Endangered Planet:* by Mary Hoff and Mary M. Rodgers. Copyright © 1992 by Lerner Publications. Used by permission of the publisher. All rights reserved; **226:** From *Spill! The Story of the* Exxon Valdez by Terry Carr. Copyright © 1991 by Terry Carr. Reprinted by permission of Franklin Watts Publishing; **242:** "How Do People Help Provide a Clean Environment?" from *Health for Life.* Copyright © 1992 by Scott, Foresman and Company; **244:** "Earth Song" from *One at a Time* by David McCord. Copyright © 1974 by David McCord. By permission of Little, Brown and Company; **245:** "The Birth of a Stone" by Kwang-Kyu Kim from *Faint Shadows of Love,* translated by Brother Anthony. Copyright © 1991 by Kwang-Kyu Kim. Reprinted by permission of Kwang-Kyu Kim; **246:** From *This Big Sky* by Pat Mora, published by Scholastic Press, a division of Scholastic, Inc. Copyright © 1998 by Pat Mora. Reprinted by permission of Scholastic, Inc.; **247:** "This Land is Your Land," words and music by Woody Guthrie. TRO - Copyright 1956, (Renewed) 1958, (Renewed) 1970 by Ludlow Music, Inc., New York, New York. Used by permission; **254:** From "Clara Barton: 'Angel of the Battlefield'" by Mike Weinstein. Excerpted from *Cobblestone's* October, 1997 issue: *The Battle of Antietam: September 17, 1862.* Copyright © 1997, Cobblestone Publishing Company, 30 Grove Street, Suite C, Peterborough, NH 03458. All rights reserved. Reprinted by permission of the publisher; **256:** From *Ms. Courageous: Women of Science* by Joanna Halpert Kraus. Copyright © 1997 by Joanna Halpert Kraus. Used by permission of New Plays Inc.; **282:** "She's the Boss!" by Mark Thompson. Used with permission from *TIME for Kids* magazine, © 2000, 2001; **286:** "One for All" from *Class President* by Johanna Hurwitz. Text copyright © 1990 by Johanna Hurwitz. Used by permission of HarperCollins Publishers; **288:** "Born Worker" from *Petty Crimes,* copyright © 1998 by Gary Soto. Reprinted and recorded by permission of Harcourt, Inc.; **304:** "Doing Dishes" from *Canto Familiar* by Gary Soto. Copyright © 1995 by Gary Soto. Reprinted by permission; **306:** "Sunday Visitors" from *Small Steps: The Year I Got Polio* by Peg Kehret. Text copyright © 1996 by Peg Kehret. Excerpt reprinted by permission of Albert Whitman & Company; **308:** *Wilma Unlimited: How Wilma Rudolph Became the World's Fastest Woman* by Kathleen Krull. Text copyright © 1996 by Kathleen Krull, illustrations copyright © 1996 by David Diaz. Reprinted by permission of Harcourt, Inc.; **322:** "Olympic Track and Field Winners—Women" from *1998 Information Please ® Almanac.* Copyright © 1997 by Information Please LLC. All rights reserved. Reprinted by permission; **324:** "Winners Never Quit" from "How to Win Without Coming in First" by Carol Krucoff in *Jack and Jill,* September 1995. Copyright © 1995 by Children's Better Health Institute, Benjamin Franklin Literary & Medical Society, Inc., Indianapolis, Indiana. Used by permission; **340:** From *Circle of Gold* by Candy Dawson Boyd. Copyright © 1984 by Candy Dawson Boyd. Reprinted by permission of Scholastic, Inc.; **342:** "The Night of the Pomegranate" from *Some of the Kinder Planets* by Tim Wynne-Jones. Published by Orchard Books, an imprint of Scholastic Inc. Copyright © 1993 by Tim Wynne-Jones. Reprinted by permission of Scholastic Inc.; **356:** "Nothing More" by María Elena Walsh; **357:** "Post Early for Space" by Peter J. Henniker-Heaton. Copyright 1952 by the Christian Science Publishing Society. Reproduced with permission. All rights reserved; **358:** "Choose a Color" by Jacqueline Sweeney. Copyright © 1993, 1994 by Jacqueline Sweeney. Used by permission of Marian Reiner for the author; **359:** "Fiddle-Faddle" from *A Word Or Two with You* by Eve Merriam. Copyright © 1981 by Eve Merriam. Used by permission of Marian Reiner; **366:** From *Where the Red Fern Grows* by Wilson Rawls. Copyright © 1961 by Sophie S. Rawls, Trustee, or successor Trustee(s) of the Rawls Trust, dated July 31, 1991. Copyright © 1961 by The Curtis Publishing Company. Used by permission of Dell Books, a division of Bantam Doubleday Dell Publishing Group, Inc.; **368:** "Spring Paint" from *Bowman's Store* by Joseph Bruchac. Copyright © 1997 by Joseph Bruchac. Used by permission of Dial Books for Young Readers, a division of Penguin Putnam Inc.; **386:** "The Sailor and the Fly" by Alois Mikulka, translated by Ksenija Sŏster-Olmer, in *Cricket,* October 1994. Reprinted by permission of Ksenija Sŏster-Olmer; **388:** "A Brother's Promise" by Pam Conrad from *Within Reach: Ten Stories,* edited by Donald Gallo. Copyright © 1993 by Pam Conrad. Used by permission of HarperCollins Publishers; **408:** "Quilted Memories" by Allen F. Roberts. Excerpted from *Faces'* February 1996 issue: *Memory.* Copyright © 1996 by Cobblestone Publishing Company, 30 Grove Street, Suite C, Peterborough, NH 03458. All rights reserved. Reprinted by permission of the publisher; **410:** Excerpts from *Catching the Fire: Philip Simmons, Blacksmith,* by Mary E. Lyons. Text Copyright © 1997 by Mary E. Lyons. Reprinted by permission of Houghton Mifflin Company. All rights reserved; **424:** "Fire All Around Us" from *Kids Discover: Fire*, Vol. 4, Issue 1, January 1994. Copyright © 1994 KIDS DISCOVER. All rights reserved. Reprinted by permission;

426: "Engineering the Land" from *The Incas* by Tim Wood. Copyright © 1996 by Tim Wood. Used by permission of Viking Penguin, a division of Penguin Putnam Inc.; **428:** Reprinted with the permission of Macmillan Library Reference USA, a division of Ahsuog, Inc., from *The Seven Wonders of the Ancient World* by Reg Cox and Neil Morris. Copyright © 1996 by Silver Burdett Press, an imprint of Macmillan Library Reference; **448:** "The Tortoise in the Tree" from *The Mean Hyena* by Judy Sierra. Copyright © 1997 by Judy Sierra. Used by permission of Lodestar Books, an affiliate of Dutton Childrens Books, a division of Penguin Putnam Inc.; **450:** From *The Gold Coin,* text by Alma Flor Ada and illustrated by Neil Waldman. Text copyright © 1991, by Alma Flor Ada. Illustrations copyright © 1991, by Neil Waldman. Reprinted with permission of Atheneum Books for Young Readers, Simon & Schuster Children's Publishing Division; **462:** "Pecos Bill and the Cyclone" from *American Tall Tales* by Mary Pope Osborne. Copyright © 1991 by Mary Pope Osborne. Used by permission of Alfred A. Knopf Children's Books, a division of Random House, Inc.; **464:** "Ode to Family Photographs" from *Neighborhood Odes* by Gary Soto. Copyright © 1992 by Gary Soto. Reprinted by permission of Harcourt, Inc.; **465:** "I've Got a Home in That Rock" from *26 Ways of Looking at a Black Man* by Raymond R. Patterson. Reprinted by permission of the author; **466:** "My Moccasins Have Not Walked" by Duke Redbird from *Red on White: The Biography of Duke Redbird* by Marty Dunn. Reprinted by permission of Stoddart Publishing Company Limited; **466:** "Seeds" from *In Daddy's Arms I Am Tall* by Javaka Steptoe. Text copyright © 1997 by Javaka Steptoe. Reprinted by permission from Lee & Low Books Inc., 95 Madison Ave., New York, NY 10016; **467:** "Time" from *Who Shrank My Grandmother's House? Poems of Discovery* by Barbara Juster Esbensen. Copyright © 1992 by Barbara Juster Esbensen. Used by permission of HarperCollins Publishers; **474:** "Mount Everest: The Ultimate Challenge" from *Junior Scholastic,* November 15, 1996 issue. Copyright © 1996 by Scholastic, Inc. Reprinted by permission of Scholastic, Inc.; **476:** From *Over the Top of the World* by Will Steger and Jon Bowermaster. Copyright © 1997 by Expeditions Unlimited Inc. Published by Scholastic Press, a division of Scholastic Inc. Reprinted by permission; **496:** "Antarctica Melts" from *Science World*, February 7, 2000. Copyright © 2000 Scholastic Inc. Reprinted by permission of Scholastic Inc.; **500:** "For the First Time" from . . . *And Now Miguel* by Joseph Krumgold. Copyright © 1953 by Joseph Krumgold. Used by permission of HarperCollins Publishers; **502:** Excerpt from *El Güero* by Elizabeth Borton de Treviño, pictures by Leslie W. Bowman. Text copyright © 1989 by Elizabeth Borton de Treviño. Illustrations copyright © 1989 by Leslie W. Bowman. Reprinted by permission Farrar, Straus & Giroux, LLC; **520:** "The California Rancheros" from *Latino Rainbow: Poems about Latino Americans* by Carlos Cumpián. Copyright © 1994. Reprinted by permission; **522:** From "Living in Space" from *Make It Work! Universe* by Andrew Haslam. Design © 1995 by Andrew Haslam. Reprinted by permission of Two Can Publishing Ltd. and Ediciones SM; **524:** "Destination: Mars" from *Life on Mars* by David Getz. Copyright © 1997 by David Getz. Reprinted by permission of Henry Holt & Co., LLC; **544:** "To Surprise the Children" by Alois Mikulka, translated by Ksenija Sŏster-Olmer, in *Cricket,* November 1996. Used by permission of Kesenija Sŏster-Olmer; **546:** From *The Phantom Tollbooth* by Norton Juster, illustrated by Jules Feiffer. Text copyright © 1961 and renewed 1989 by Norton Juster. Illustrations copyright © 1961 and renewed 1989 by Jules Feiffer. Reprinted by permission of Random House, Inc.; **566:** "On the Move" from *Science World*, January 17, 2000. Copyright © 2000 Scholastic Inc. Reprinted by permission of Scholastic Inc.; **568:** "The Pleasantest Days" from *The Trumpet of the Swan* by E. B. White. Text copyright © 1970 by E. B. White. Used by permission of HarperCollins Publishers; **570:** From *The Adventures of Midnight Son* by Denise Lewis Patrick. Copyright © 1997 by Denise Lewis Patrick. Reprinted by permission of Henry Holt & Co., LLC.; **586:** "The Birth of the Cowboy" and "The Boss, the Cook and the Cowboy" from *Cowboy: An Album* by Linda Granfield. Text copyright © 1993 by Linda Granfield. Reprinted by permission of Houghton Mifflin Company. All rights reserved; **590:** "Riding the Wind" from *Pastures, Ponies and Pals: Cowboy Poetry and Songs for Children* by Anne Slade. Copyright © 1993 by Anne Slade and Doris Bircham. Reprinted by permission; **590:** "I Will Never Be Able to Know the Sea" by Erika Ramírez Diez; **591:** "Long Trip" from *Collected Poems* by Langston Hughes. Copyright © 1994 by the Estate of Langston Hughes. Reprinted by permission of Alfred A. Knopf Inc.; **591:** "Night Train" reprinted from Robert Francis' *Robert Francis: Collected Poems 1936–1976.* (Amherst: University of Massachusetts Press, 1976.) Copyright © 1936 by Robert Francis; **598:** "Almost Ready for School." Reprinted with the permission of Atheneum Books for Young Readers, an imprint of Simon & Schuster Children's Publishing Division from *The Agony of Alice* by Phyllis Reynolds Naylor. Copyright © 1985 by Phyllis Reynolds Naylor; **600:** "Noah Writes a B & B Letter." Reprinted with the permission of Atheneum Books for Young Readers, an imprint of Simon & Schuster Children's Publishing Division from *The View from Saturday* by E. L. Konigsburg. Copyright © 1996 by E. L. Konigsburg; **618:** From *Teach Yourself Calligraphy* by Ellen Korn, illustrated by Boche Kaplan. Text copyright © 1982 by Ellen Korn; illustrations copyright © 1982 by Boche Kaplan. Reprinted by permission of William Morrow and Company; **620:** "Normal" by Karin-Leigh Spicer in *Skipping Stones,* January–February 1998. Copyright © 1998 by Skipping Stones. Reprinted by permission; **622:** From *Louis Braille* by Stephen Keeler. Copyright © 1986 by Stephen Keeler. First published in 1986 in Great Britain by Wayland Publishers Ltd. Reprinted by permission; **638:** "How Do We Know We See What We See?" *from How Do We Know What's Inside Us?* by Anita Ganeri. Copyright © 1995, text, Steck-Vaughn Company. All rights reserved. Reprinted by permission.; **640:** From "Ptolemy—An Early Mapmaker" in *Explorers & Mapmakers* by Peter Ryan. Text copyright © 1989 by Peter Ryan. Illustrations copyright © 1989 by Chris Molan. Used by permission of Lodestar Books, an affiliate of Dutton Children's Books, a division of Penguin Putnam Inc.; **642:** *The Librarian Who Measured The Earth* by Kathryn Lasky. Text copyright © 1994 by Kathryn Lasky; illustrations copyright © 1994 by Kevin Hawkes. By permission of Little, Brown and Company; **656:** "A Revolution!" from *Kids Discover: Maps*, Vol 10, Issue 10, Issue 9, October 2000. Copyright © 2000 KIDS DISCOVER. All rights reserved. Reprinted by permission.; **658:** From *Boy of the Painted Cave* by Justin Denzel. Copyright © 1988 by Justin Denzel. Used by permission of Philomel Books, a division of Penguin Putnam Inc.; **660:** From *Sweetwater* by Laurence Yep. Text copyright © 1973 by Laurence Yep. Used by permission of HarperCollins Publishers; **678:** "Three Wondrous Buildings" from *Round Buildings, Square Buildings & Buildings That Wiggle Like a Fish* by Philip M. Isaacson. Copyright © 1988 by Philip M. Isaacson. Reprinted by permission of Alfred A. Knopf, Inc.; **680:** *Cutters, Carvers and the Cathedral* by George Ancona. Photos and text © by George Ancona. Used with the permission of the author; **696:** "Why Do Buildings Look the Way They Do?" from *Round Buildings, Square Buildings, and Buildings that Wiggle Like a Fish* by Phillip M. Isaacson. Copyright © 1998 by Phillip M. Isaacson. Used by permission of Alfred A. Knopf Children's Books, a division of Random House, Inc.; **698:** "The Thinker" from *The Hopeful Trout and Other Limericks* by John Ciardi. Text copyright © 1989 by Myra J. Ciardi. Reprinted by permission of Houghton Mifflin Company. All rights reserved; **698:** "My Sister," reprinted with the permission of Margaret K. McElderry Books, an imprint of Simon & Schuster Children's Publishing Division from *Nonstop Nonsense* by Margaret Mahy. Copyright © 1977 by Margaret Mahy; **699:** "I Am the Creativity" by Alexis De Veaux; **700:** "A Short Story" by David Escobar Galindo; **701:** "Sing Me a Song of Teapots and Trumpets." Reprinted with the permission of Margaret K. McElderry Books, an imprint of Simon & Schuster Children's Publishing Division from *Hurry, Hurry, Mary Dear! and Other Nonsense Poems* by N. M. Bodecker. Copyright © 1976 by N. M. Bodecker. Selected text and images in this book are copyrighted © 2002.

Artists

22, 39, 40, 308, 464–467: Sharon Hoogstraten; **22–40:** Joel Spector; **42:** Seattle Times/Liason Agency; **12, 43, 128, 136–137, 178, 226, 250–251, 308, 362–363, 379–382, 470–471, (Web art) 476–494, 496, 524–541, 594–595, 704–705, 732:** Tony Klassen; **46–61:** Paul Bacon; **64–65:** Stephanie Garcia; **4, 66–79, 728:** Gail Piazza; **89–101:** Dom Lee; **104–105:** Burgandy Beam; **106–127, 620–621:** Todd Leonardo; **130–133, 426–427:** Roberta Ludlow; **134–135:** Eric Larsen; **46:** Kelly Hume; **142–160:** Gary Phillips; **159 (CR):** Courtesy Jean Craighead George; **161:** Kathy Lengyel; **162–163, 208–221, 383–385, 518, 618–619:** Tracy L. Taylor; **164–177:** Barbara Emmons; **180–181:** Catherine Davinier; **182–201:** Jerry Pinkney; **6, 206–207, 729:** Patrick Gnan; **224–225, 248–249, 386–387, 588–591:** Antonio Cangemi; **236–237, 520:** Lee Christiansen; **254–255:** Jeff Berlin; **256–279:** Clint Hansen; **288–301:** Maria Jimenez; **304:** Ilene Richard; **304–305, 590, 592–593:** Dave Jonason; **8, 308–319, 730:** David Diaz; **326–337:** Larry Day; **10, 340–341, 388–405, 731:** Gabriela Dellosso; **342–353:** Don Stewart; **360–361:** Mark Zahnd; **368–378:** Tim Spransey; **408–409, 570–585:** Jeff Meyer; **424–425:** Claudia Hammer; **428–445:** James Field; **448–449:** Francesco Santalucia; **450–461:** Neil Waldman; **462–463:** Laura Ovresat; **466:** Alexi Natchev; **468–469, 472–473:** Tom Foty; **500–501:** Gerardo Suzan; **502–519:** Leslie W. Bowman; **520–521:** Teresa Flavin; **544–545:** Andy Newsom; **547–562:** Jules Feiffer; **568–569:** Joseph Daniel Fiedler; **596–597, 698–701:** Wendy Wax; **14, 600–617, 733:** Tom Newsom; **622–637:** Troy Howell; **642–655:** Kevin Hawkes; **658–659:** Susan Leopold; **660–675, 678–679:** Chris Gall; **702–703:** Mario Noche

Photographs

Every effort has been made to secure permission and provide appropriate credit for photographic material. The publisher deeply regrets any omission and pledges to correct, in subsequent editions, errors called to its attention.

Unless otherwise acknowledged, all photographs are the property of Scott Foresman, a division of Pearson Education. Page abbreviations are as follows: (T) top, (B) bottom, (L) left, (R) right, (C) center, (INS) inset, (S) spot, (BK) background.

17, 20–21(BK), 84–85, 202–203, 286–287, 306–307, 320–321, 356–359, 366–367, 464–467, 522–523, 598–599, Sharon Hoogstraten; **18–19:** David Young-Wolff/PhotoEdit; **39(TL):** Photograph by Lorie K. Stover/McIntosh and Otis, Inc.; **41(B):** Simon Bruty/Allsport; **42(TL):** Al Bello/Allsport; **44(BR), 45:** From *Bat Boy* by Joan Anderson, photographs by Matthew Cavanaugh. Copyright ©1996 by Joan Anderson, text. Copyright ©1996 by Matthew Cavanaugh, photographs. Used by permission of Lodestar Books, an affiliate of Dutton Children's Books, a division of Penguin Putnam, Inc.; **46–47(BK):** Private Collection of Herb Ross; **49(BR), 52(TL), 55(T), 339(TL):** National Baseball Hall of Fame Library, Cooperstown, NY; **53(R), 54(TL), 62(BL), 62(BC), 63(L), 63(CR), 564(B):** AP/Wide World; **56:** Courtesy of the Cincinnati Reds; **60(T):** Herb Snitzer for Scott Foresman/Addison Wesley; **62(TR)**: © Michael Burr/© Dorling Kindersley; **62(BL), 62(BR), 338(CL), 339(CL):** David Spindel; 63**(BR):** Library of Congress; **76, 176:** Gary Paulsen Courtesy Gary Paulsen; **80–81(BK):** David

Glossary

The contents of the glossary have been adapted from *Thorndike Barnhart Intermediate Dictionary.* © 1999 Addison Wesley Educational Publishers, Inc., Glenview, Illinois.